Programming with Motif™

Keith D. Gregory

Programming with Motif™

With 112 Illustrations

Springer-Verlag

New York Berlin Heidelberg London Paris
Tokyo Hong Kong Barcelona Budapest

Keith D. Gregory
Wakefield, MA 01880
U.S.A.

Library of Congress Cataloging-in-Publication Data
Gregory, Keith D.
    Programming with motif / Keith D. Gregory
        p.   cm.
    Includes bibliographical references and index.
    ISBN 0-387-97877-1. — ISBN 3-540-97877-1
    1. X Window System (Computer System) 2. Motif (Computer program)
    I. Title.
    QA76.76.W56G84   1992
    005.4'3—dc20   92-17576

Printed on acid-free paper.

Production supervised by Ken Dreyhaupt; manufacturing coordinated by Vincent Scelta.
Camera-ready copy prepared from the author's Microsoft Word files.
Printed and bound by Edwards Brothers, Inc., Ann Arbor, Michigan.
Printed in the United States of America.

9 8 7 6 5 4 3 2 1

ISBN 0-387-97877-1 Springer-Verlag New York Berlin Heidelberg
ISBN 3-540-97877-1 Springer-Verlag Berlin Heidelberg New York

For Jennifer

Preface

About this Book

This book is a detailed introduction to programming with the OSF/Motif™ graphical user interface. It is an introduction in that it does not require the reader to have experience programming in the X Window environment. It is detailed in that it teaches you how to use the interface components provided by Motif in a complex application. Although it contains a great deal of reference material, it is not meant as an authoritative reference — that is the job of the *OSF/Motif Programmer's Reference*, which uses over 900 pages in the process. Instead, this book provides its reference material in a practical, "how to" manner and allows the reader to use the *Programmer's Reference* effectively.

The target reader is an experienced C programmer and user of the X Window System under the UNIX operating system. The reader should be familiar with the tools provided by UNIX for the compilation and testing of programs; while this book does examine the process by which a Motif program is compiled, it does not explain that process. It also assumes that the reader is familiar with "X" terms such as 'pointer' and 'display'.

How this Book Came to Exist

As a programmer learning Motif, I found that Motif books assumed that the reader knew the X toolkit, needed to know a bit about the capabilities of Motif, but really wanted to write widgets. Books that covered the X toolkit only quickly went in a direction away from Motif and ended with the reader writing widgets. I was a programmer who had used Xlib for some small projects and wanted to make the leap to Motif; I didn't know what a widget was, and I certainly didn't want to write one.

I have written this book for people in a similar situation, which I believe is the one facing most programmers learning Motif. At one time, a programmer would enter the world of X through Xlib or Xt and eventually move on to writing a new widget set. At the present time, however, I believe that most programmers enter the world of X seeking solutions to business problems and find themselves directly at the door of Motif or Open Look.

With this in mind, I start the book with the basics of toolkit programming and end before widget implementation. Throughout, I try to present information that is needed for an actual application, without the details used to get "the last 10%" from the environment.

As source material, I use documentation and code from the X11 distribution, with Motif documentation published by the Open Software Foundation. In addition, I have received information from the large group of programmers represented by the *comp.windows.x* and *comp.windows.x.motif* newsgroups.

Suggested Reading Plan

Looking at this book, you may be intimidated by its length — and become more intimidated when I suggest that you start at the front cover and end at the back cover. I say this because Motif is a complex environment, and I have attempted to structure the book such that each chapter builds upon the ones before it. The chapter descriptions below will give you an idea of this structure.

If, however, you are one of those people who likes to see something work right away, there is an abbreviated introduction that gives you "Hello World" in one hour or less. This abbreviated process is also described in the chapter listings.

Chapters

Chapter 1 describes Motif: what it is, why it exists, and what benefit it provides to users and programmers. If you are unfamiliar with the purpose and organization of X and Motif — from Xlib to toolkits to the Motif library — I recommend reading this chapter. For those on the "quick start" plan, it may be safely skipped.

Chapter 2 describes the widget, the abstract graphical object that is the core of Motif programming. This description is from both the abstract perspective of object-oriented programming and the programming perspective of "what does a widget do." Along the way, it presents the key ideas of derivation (the creation of a new type of widget by building on an existing widget) and parentage (the hierarchical organization of widgets in a program). This chapter provides the foundation for the rest of the book and should be read by everyone.

Chapter 3 describes resources, which are used to customize the appearance and interaction of a widget. It presents a large amount of material, covering various attributes of resources. This material is invaluable and should be read in detail, but is best read in the context of an actual program — which has not yet been presented. For this reason, I recommend reading the introductory sections (through *Sample Resource File*) at first and then rereading the whole chapter once you've written your first program.

Chapter 4 describes the format of a Motif program and provides you with an understanding of what happens when you press the *Return* key. It too is invaluable and should be read in detail, but this reading may be postponed until after Chapter 5. I do, however, recommend at least skimming this chapter and reading *Compiling A Motif Program* in detail.

Chapter 5 introduces the first widget: *XmLabel*, which is used to display static text. It also presents the first program — like most books, this is "Hello, World."

This program completes the "quick start" plan, and I recommend that skimmed chapters should be reread.

Chapter 6 describes manager widgets, which are used to position other widgets and thus control the appearance of a program's interface. The four most common Motif managers: *XmBulletinBoard*, *XmRowColumn*, *XmPanedWindow*, and *XmForm* are described, with examples showing the uses of each.

Chapter 7 describes the standard Motif button widgets: *XmPushButton*, *XmArrowButton*, and *XmToggleButton*. In this chapter, they are presented as user-interface objects; their link to the program is postponed to Chapter 8.

Chapter 8 describes the X event mechanism by which programs receive input. It starts at the lowest level, that of actual events, and describes what events are and how the program uses them. After this, it describes the callback mechanism, which is a high-level link between programs and events. Next are actions and translations, a yet higher level of event processing.

Chapter 9 describes methods of keyboard input. It starts with a low-level description of keyboard events and then presents the *XmText* widget, which is Motif's primary means of keyboard input. This chapter contains three progressively complex examples of *XmText* usage: as an entry field, as a single-screen memo pad, and as a replacement for the *more* utility.

Chapter 10 describes scrollbars, a user-interface object used to control the position and scope of a program's displayed data. This chapter starts at a low level, with the *XmScrollBar* widget and its interface. Next is a description of *XmScrolledWindow*, a manager widget that transparently handles the scrolling of its contents. The chapter finishes with a description of the *XmScale* widget, a related widget that is used to input and display data values.

Chapter 11 describes the program as a whole. This description is from two perspectives: the appearance of a program, as defined by the *OSF/Motif Style Guide*, and those widgets that exist to assist the programmer in implementing a program with the desired appearance. This chapter also presents the beginnings of a text editor implemented with Motif widgets.

Chapter 12 describes menus, the primary means by which a user controls the operation of a Motif program. It starts with a description of the menu bar and its pull-down menus and adds these items to the text editor. It also presents pop-up and option menus, which are used to provide context-sensitive input.

Chapter 13 describes dialogs, which provide the program with auxiliary windows for user interaction. Examples include a custom dialog that implements a search facility for the text editor, as well as the use of Motif's "canned" message dialogs.

Chapter 14 describes lists and the way that the user interacts with them. It starts with the basic list, as implemented by *XmList*, and follows with widgets built around a list: *XmSelectionBox*, *XmFileSelectionBox*, and *XmCommand*. It also presents examples of uses of lists, ranging from an e-mail address-selection dialog to a file-selection module for the text editor.

Chapter 15 is an introduction to the use of Xlib — the low-level X drawing functions — with Motif. It describes the general form of an Xlib call and presents the *XmDrawingArea* widget, which acts as a "canvas" for such calls. The scope of this chapter is necessarily limited — Xlib could easily occupy an entire book by itself.

Chapter 16 presents advanced resource topics. These range from the way that Motif associates resource specifications with a program's invocation name, to the use and creation of functions that convert resource data from one type to another. Along the way, it describes the X approach to command-line program options and a method by which the resource file may be used to change program variables.

Chapter 17, the final chapter, describes interclient communication. This topic involves both the X-specific methods of interclient communications, along with the traditional communication methods such as pipes. This chapter is quite long and presents a variety of communications methods — a subject that I feel other books have omitted.

The appendices exist for reference only. Appendix A is simply a character chart, showing the ISO Latin 1 character set — an extension of ASCII used by X and many other modern systems. Appendix B presents a summary of widget information — a "mini Programmer's Reference." Appendix C provides a complete reference for X events — seemingly a requirement for X-related books. Appendix D contains a summary of changes in X and Motif, while Appendix E lists other sources of information, from the official OSF/Motif documentation to various X user groups.

The book finishes with a glossary of X and Motif terms.

Source Code Conventions

Like most books on programming, this book contains a lot of source code. I believe that the keys to understanding any program are its naming conventions. Mine generally follow those of the MIT X consortium and are as below:

- Function names consist of one or more words, run together, with the first letter of each word capitalized (*eg*, `MyFunction`).

- Variables consist of one or more words, with all characters in lowercase. Where a variable name consists of several words, underscores separate the words; in cases where the name is a contraction of multiple words (*eg*, `appshell` for 'application shell'), no underscores are used.

  My conventions do not follow those of the X consortium in the naming of variables used for widgets: I do not differentiate between such variables and other program variables. The X standard specifies that widget names consist of one or more words, run together, with the first letter of every word but the first capitalized.

- Macro names and symbolic constants consist of one or more words, separated by underscores, with all characters in uppercase (*eg*, `A_CONSTANT`). This follows the X Consortium specification; mixed case is reserved for X "action" macros such as `XtSetArg`.

- Names beginning with a capital 'X' are reserved for use by the X libraries and are not used as program variables or functions. Specific prefixes are: "X" for low-level names (those associated with Xlib), "Xt" for names associated with the X Toolkit (also known as the Intrinsics), and "Xm" for Motif.

- I do not use naming techniques to differentiate between global and local variables. All global variables are declared in one location and typically carry the same names from program to program. As my tendency is to use global variables to hold utility data only (and, for Motif programs, some widgets of general interest), I feel that no naming conventions are needed.

My source-code structuring rules are as follows:

- Indentation is four characters per level.

- Braces are aligned with the level they enclose, except for function bodies (where they are aligned at column 1). Braces always occupy their own line: I do not follow the "K&R" style of putting an opening brace at the end of the line above the block it encloses.

- Function parameter declarations are indented four characters and appear between function definition and function body; as described below, the ANSI format is not used. Function variables are similarly indented four characters. I do not use block-level variables.

- Function parameters are declared using the "old style": parameter names are specified in the header line, with declarations between the header line and the function body. I do this primarily because ANSI C compilers have been slow to arrive in the UNIX world.

- When a new function is introduced, it is "prototyped" out of context. In this case only, I align the function's parameters with its name — I believe this approach is less cluttered than standard indentation.

Text Conventions

The text of this book is set in a proportional typeface. Italics are used to highlight the initial use of glossary terms, for names of Motif widget classes, names of standard programs (*eg, a.out*), common parenthetical abbreviations (*eg, eg*), and *occasionally*, to emphasize a point in the text. Italics are also used for computer names in captions. Boldface is used in the text to highlight user-interface items in a specific program (*eg*, the **File** menu).

Computer text is set in a monospaced font (`Letter Gothic`) that resembles lineprinter output. Such usage includes source listings (which are separate from the text), as well as variable and function names that appear in the text. This typeface is italicized to indicate that the italicized word(s) are replaced in actual usage (*eg*, the name of a prototype function would be italicized).

This book uses two types of quotation marks: text and literal. Text quotation marks are used to highlight idiomatic phrases and actual quotations; single quotes (' and ') for "jargon" words, double quotes (" and ") for all else. Literal quotation marks (") are used in the text to delimit literal strings (*eg*, "MyString"). Single quotes (') are used in the C manner to delimit single-character strings (*eg*, '\n'); such strings may contain C "escape" characters. Double quotes (") do not connote C semantics (*ie*, such strings are not NUL-terminated) unless otherwise indicated.

A final note about notes. I footnote heavily and use footnotes to provide information tangential to the topic under consideration. I consider such notes important — they often clarify obscure points of a topic — but understand that some people find them distracting. They may be safely skipped, or their reading may be postponed until a more convenient time.

Caveats

The first and foremost caveat is that this book is written from the perspective of Motif 1.0 and X11 Release 3 (X11R3) — versions that are essentially obsolete. I made this decision after an informal poll indicated that many sites are limited to this configuration; I did not want to give such sites a book that they couldn't use.

For Motif, this decision was easy to make: Motif 1.1 was released during the writing of this book and did not come into widespread usage until just before it went to press. Where I feel that 1.1 provides a better technique than 1.0, I note this possibility, either in the text or as a footnote. The only place where this rule does not hold is in Chapter 18: the clipboard mechanism did not work properly under 1.0 and thus must be discussed from the perspective of 1.1.

For X, this was a more difficult decision: X11 Release 4 (X11R4) was commonly available while I was writing this book, and R5 was released before the final draft. However, my poll indicated that many people were still using R3. Moreover, the differences between R3 and R4 have a minimal effect on this book: the biggest impact is on type conversion, as described in Chapter 17.

The second caveat is that this book is written from a UNIX perspective, while X and Motif are available on other platforms. In answer to this, I must answer "I go with what I know" — I use a UNIX system and am not able to test on other platforms. There is also the question of how much information to include — adding information specific to VMS and other systems would cause the book to grow in size. I believe that the information contained in this book is of use to such people; the examples, however, are most likely not.

A third (and final) caveat is that every vendor's system is slightly different. The placement of files, even the names of some files, may differ between your site and this book. I have attempted, in all cases, to use standard names. In some cases, where I know of differences, I present alternatives.

Acknowledgments

I've been working on this book for approximately one and a half years, and I've tried to keep track of all the people that had an influence on it; at one time, that list even included the Boston Red Sox. The first influence occurred in 1987, when Art Shane gave me the opportunity to branch out from programming into writing. The idea for this particular book came from my brother, David, who impressed upon me the fact that the Motif market was wide open.

For help and support during the writing, I thank my editors at Springer-Verlag, Mark, David, and Andrea. For their comments, I thank both the reviewers that I know — Andy, Ed, Luke, Rob, and Ted — and those that I don't; although not all of their comments resulted in change, each added to what is here. I would also like to thank Apple Computer for providing me with A/UX, and Integrated Computer Solutions for providing me with Motif.

Finally, I wish to thank everyone at Symmetrix for adapting to my schedule of "sometimes here, more often not" while this book was being written. And, oh yes, the Boston Red Sox, for reasons that only one person knows.

Contents

8   Events and Callbacks   125

9   Keyboard Input   165

10   Scrollbars   205

11 The Motif "Look"   233

12 Menus   261

13 Dialogs   305

17 Interclient Communication   467

Appendix A:
ISO Latin 1 Character Set   533

Appendix B:
Widget Class Summary   535

Appendix C:
X Event Reference   **563**

Appendix D:
Changes In X And Motif   **615**

1
An Introduction To Motif

"Mechanism, not Policy"

This phrase is one of the design goals of the X window system. It means that X provides a mechanism for graphical user interfaces, but does not dictate the appearance of programs using such interfaces. "Mechanism, not policy" could be applied equally to PostScript: it provides a mechanism for formatting a printed page, but does not specify the content of that page.

By eliminating questions of policy, the X Consortium was able to simplify the design of X and avoid a system "designed by committee." There are two important results of this simplification. The first is that an X program is portable; an X program running on one vendor's system may display output and receive input from a user on another vendor's system. The second result is that each vendor is free to implement its own "look and feel"; X does not prevent creativity.

The drawback to such an approach is that it can lead to chaos. An example of such chaos is seen in software for the IBM PC. Until recently, every program had a unique user interface, and a typical user had to remember five different ways to exit five different programs.

In the case of X, this chaos did not occur. One reason was that graphical user interfaces were well understood by the time X appeared. Another and perhaps more important reason was that writing an X program was not a trivial task. Every program interacted with the server at a very low level, essentially using an "assembly language" for the X protocol.

As a result, few production programs were written using the early releases of X — and many of those that were came from the X Consortium. It wasn't until the release of the *X Intrinsics* (*Xt*) that the writing of an X program became simple. This was because the intrinsics introduced the *widget*: a self-contained object that provides user-interface functionality.

Along with the intrinsics — which provided the structure for widgets — the X Consortium released the *Athena* widget set. Although Athena was meant as sample code only, it provided most of the elements of a user interface: menus, text boxes, and so on. As a result, an X program could be written easily, and the number of X programs (and programmers) proliferated.

Enter Motif

With the intrinsics in place, vendors could produce their own widget sets. Unfortunately, these sets were vendor-specific — one vendor had little reason to support another vendor's product. Again, this was a situation that could have led to chaos, but did not.

The reason was that the late-1980s saw the formation of two industry consortiums, UNIX International (UI) and the Open Software Foundation (OSF), both of which had the goal of producing a standardized operating system.[1] As part of this collaboration, each produced an X-based user interface: Open Look for UI and Motif for OSF.

Figure 1.1 presents a sample Motif program. One of the most striking features of such a program is its three-dimensional appearance, which came from the HP widget set. Other Motif features, shared with MS-Windows and OS/2 Presentation Manager, are the use of mnemonics (highlighted characters) to select menu choices and the presence of a **Help** menu on the right-hand side of the menu bar. In other respects, a Motif program has the features that one expects from a modern graphical user interface, such as pull-down menus and other controls that enable the user to interact with the program in a simple and straightforward manner.

Figure 1.1. Sample Motif program

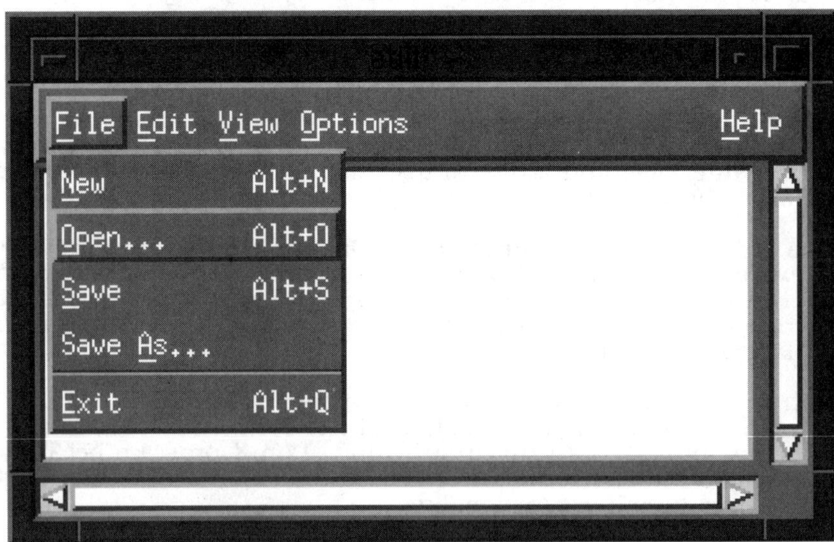

---

[1] For UI, this system is UNIX System V; for OSF, it is OSF/1.

The Layers of X

One result of the development of X is that an X program is built in layers, as shown by Figure 1.2. At the top level is the application code, which processes data and defines the context for user interaction. User-interface functionality — menus, controls, and such — is provided by Motif, which in turn makes use of the intrinsics and Xlib. Application-level code makes some use of the intrinsics, such as when it opens a display connection. Some applications may even call Xlib directly — a CAD program, for example, may need to perform low-level graphics operations. At the bottom is the X protocol, which is hidden behind the functions in Xlib.

Figure 1.2. Layers of an X program

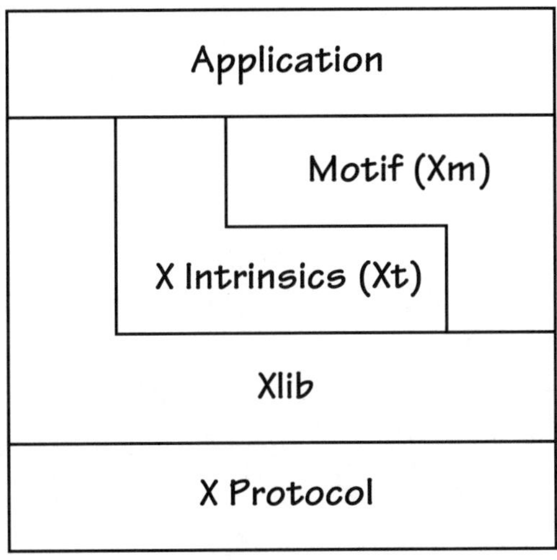

The benefit of this layering is that it minimizes the amount of implementation that must go into providing each layer. Since Xlib provides an interface to the X protocol, the intrinsics need not replicate that functionality. Instead, they provide window-management functionality. Since the intrinsics handle window management, the implementers of a widget set can concentrate on specific user-interface features. Finally, since the user interface is handled by the widget set, an application programmer can concentrate on the goals of the application.

2
The Widget

What Is a Widget?

Traditionally, the word "widget" is used for an object that doesn't need a better name. For example, in economics, you can speak of firms and the widgets that they produce using principles that work without knowledge of what the widgets are.

When applied to the X Window System, however, "widget" has a very specific meaning. It is an *object* that controls the interaction between an application program and an X *window*. Since this definition needs further explanation, read on.

An Introduction to Object-Oriented Programming

What Is Object-Oriented Programming?

The traditional, "procedural," programming paradigm regards a program as a set of procedures that manipulates data. Program flow is dependent on the order that the programmer links the procedures. As an example, an array is sorted using a "sort" procedure, then printed using a "print" procedure.

Object-Oriented Programming (*OOP*) is a paradigm in which data drives the program. An *object* contains both data and the procedures (*methods*) that manipulate that data. These methods are invoked by program requests (*messages*). In terms of the array, the program first requests the array to sort itself, then requests it to print itself.

Although the distinction may seem minor, it has great implications. For example, an `int` array is handled differently from a `float` array. If a procedural program is written to use an `int` array, it must be rewritten to use a `float` array — while similar, the procedures are slightly different. More importantly, if a procedural program uses both types of arrays, it must choose the appropriate procedure for each array.

Under the object-oriented paradigm, however, the program simply requests the array to sort or print itself. Although each data type still requires its own sort and print procedures, these procedures are part of the data type itself. High-level program code is not dependent on the array's data type and does not select the procedure used.

This is one of the often-stressed benefits of OOP: data is "hidden" and may be changed almost at will without affecting program logic. This leads to programs that are both flexible and maintainable, with both to a greater degree than programs written under the procedural paradigm.

Separation of Class and Instance

In addition to combining data and methods to form an object, OOP has two other tenets: separation of class and instance, and inheritance. The first of these, separation of class and instance, may be explained with a noncomputer example.

In cars, the Ford Crown Victoria may be viewed as a class. The definition of this class is a body-on-frame automobile, 212.5 inches long, 77.8 inches wide, 56.7 inches high, and so on. Instances of this class belong to Aunt Sally and the Massachusetts State Police. While these instances are essentially the same car, their data — paint, upholstery, engine, etc. — differ.

It is important to remember that methods are part of an object's class definition, whereas data is part of an object's instance. A method from one class may not be invoked for an instance of another class — that would be like moving the Crown Victoria's power-steering components to a Volkswagen Beetle.

Inheritance

The final tenet is *inheritance*, or the *derivation* of a new object class (the *subclass*) from an existing class (the *superclass*). Although on the surface derivation may appear identical to the standard C technique of building complex data structures from simpler ones, it is radically different: instead of the superclass(es) being fields of the subclass, they are components of the subclass. Depending on the needs of the program, an object may be treated as if it were identical to its superclass.[1]

Inheritance provides for reusability of object classes. Consider linked lists. Such lists are used in many programs to hold many different types of data. However, the form of all such lists is similar: a series of discrete link entries, each of which contains a data item and a pointer to the next entry in the list. This is a perfect place for object-oriented code: create standard "linked list" and "list item" classes and derive program-specific classes from them.

From here on, this book will often use the terms instance, class, superclass, subclass, inheritance, and derivation. To minimize wordiness, the term "widget" always refers to a widget instance; references to a widget's class are explicit.

---

[1] Continuing the automobile metaphor, inheritance is similar to creating a dune buggy from a Volkswagen — to a mechanic, they're the same car, while to the user they're very different.

Widgets as Objects

Widget sets, including Motif, follow the object-oriented paradigm. The widget is an object: its data is a window, its methods are the internal functions that maintain the appearance of that window, and its *resources* (described in the next chapter) are the messages that control the operation of its methods.

One benefit of the object-oriented approach is that an application programmer can build a program in a very modular fashion. Once the program's general functionality and layout are determined, a "scaffold" of widgets may be built. Then, each widget's function may be expanded in isolation, allowing the programmer to concentrate on program functionality instead of implementation details.

The Motif Class Tree

Inheritance is central to the implementation of a widget set and is represented by that set's *class tree*. Each widget class is represented by a node in the tree; it inherits the functionality implemented by widgets in a direct line between it and the root of the tree.

Some of the classes in a widget class tree are *supporting*: they exist only to provide specific functions to their subclasses. Other classes are used directly by the program and are known as *instantiated* classes — they are classes for which a program has instances.

An abbreviated class tree for Motif is shown in Figure 2.1. This tree contains the major supporting classes in the Motif class tree, some of which come from Xt. Each widget description in this book contains an excerpt from this tree, expanded to show the widget(s) being described.[2]

---

[2] This book's class tree diagrams use heavy boxes to indicate supporting classes, and regular boxes to indicate instantiated classes.

Figure 2.1. Motif class tree

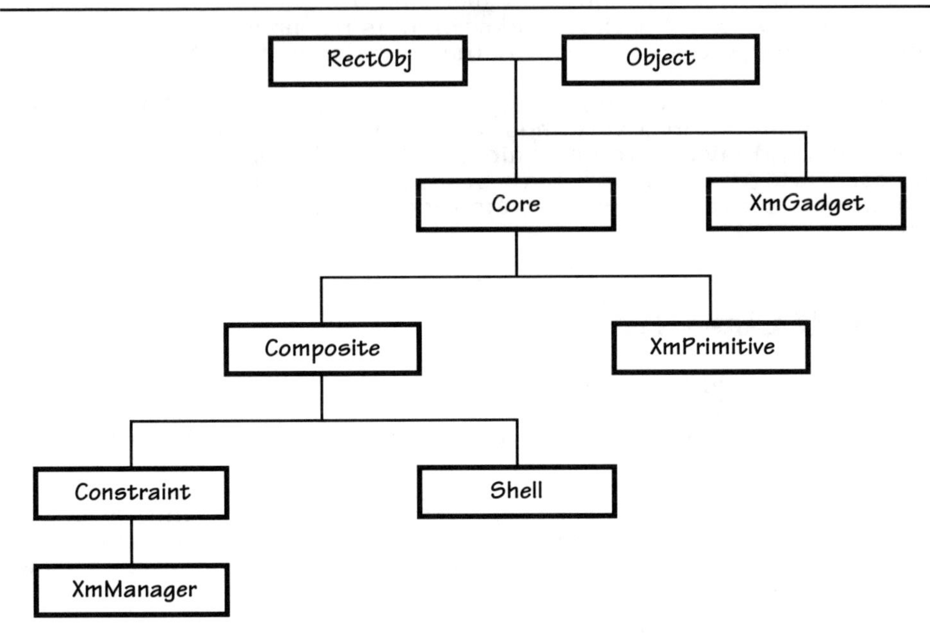

RectObj, Object, Core

These three classes are the root of all widget sets and are defined by the intrinsics. *Core* is the root of the widget class tree and combines the functionality of *RectObj*, *Object*, and *WindowObj* (not shown here). Together these classes provide the functions of instantiation and basic window maintenance.

Figure 2.1 presents *RectObj* and *Object* to show the derivation of *XmGadget*. As this book does not present gadgets, *Core* is shown as the root of all subsequent class trees.

XmPrimitive

The *XmPrimitive* class is used as the supporting superclass of the "primitive" widgets. Primitive widgets, such as pushbuttons, are a program's controls. The name "primitive" is used because these widgets perform single-purpose functions — they are unable to be the parents of other widgets.

The *XmPrimitive* class provides appearance details, such as top and bottom shadow color, and functional details, such as traversal and focus.

XmGadget

"Gadgets" are one of DEC-Windows' contributions to Motif. In essence, a gadget is a windowless widget. As such, it is not derived from *Core*, but from *RectObj* and *Object*. In other respects, *XmGadget* is identical to *XmPrimitive*, and most primitive widgets (such as pushbuttons) have corresponding gadgets.

Being windowless means that the appearance of a gadget is completely controlled by its parent. As an example, consider a dialog box that has a foreground color of green and a background color of red. The components of this dialog box may be either widgets or gadgets. If they are gadgets, then they must use the same colors as the dialog; if widgets, their appearance may differ.

The benefit of a gadget vs. a widget is efficiency. A widget has a window, which must be maintained by the display server, whereas a gadget is simply a region of its parent's window. This means that both the display server and the application use less memory. In addition, the display server can perform its operations (such as event reporting and screen update) more efficiently because its internal tables are not as large.

Although a gadget may be used wherever a primitive widget is, they are used primarily in places where their windowless nature does not present an obstacle. A prime example is a pull-down menu system, which by its nature should have a uniform appearance.

This book does not cover gadgets. My belief is that the efficiency gains from appropriate use of gadgets do not offset the increased code complexity and executable size resulting from their use.[3] As this book does not cover gadgets, it considers *Core* to be the root of the Motif class tree.

Composite

Composite widgets are those widgets that can be the parents of other widgets. The *Composite* widget class is the supporting superclass of all composite widgets and provides support for maintaining a list of children. It is defined by Xt and is present in all widget sets.

Shell

Shells are widgets that provide a link between the program and the root window. Any widget that appears in a window manager frame has a shell that exchanges information with the window manager; widgets that "pop up" over other widgets also use shells. Different shells serve different purposes: an *Application Shell* is the top level shell around a program, whereas a *Dialog Shell* is the shell around a movable dialog box.

The *Shell* widget class is the supporting superclass for all shells. It handles the basic functions of resizing and moving its child widget (a shell may only have a

---

[3] The increased code complexity and size result from the fact that few programs can use gadgets alone. Since widget code must therefore be present, adding the equivalent gadgets simply means that more code is used.

single child; that child is responsible for any of its own children). *Shell*, like *Composite*, is part of Xt and is therefore provided by all widget sets.

Constraint, XmManager

Both *Constraint* and *XmManager* are supporting superclasses for *manager* widgets, such as *XmForm*. *Constraint* comes from Xt; it provides basic functionality for maintaining the position of child widgets. *XmManager* is defined by Motif and provides the Motif appearance resources.

Widget Instance Tree

When a widget is created, it is created as the *child* of another widget (its *parent*). The parent-child relationships produced by this process form a tree structure, known as the *instance tree* or *management tree*. The leaves of this tree are primitive widgets, and its branches are composite widgets.

It is important to remember that the class tree and instance tree are two different trees. The class tree is part of Motif; it specifies the way that the widget set is implemented. The instance tree is unique to a particular program; it specifies how widgets within the program interact.

The instance tree specifies the "chain of command" applicable to a particular widget. A parent controls its children's position and size and may control as well their color scheme and contents. Such controls (*constraints*) are applied down each branch of the tree: an *XmForm* widget near the root of the tree applies constraints to its children, one of which might be another *XmForm*. This form then applies constraints to its children based on the constraints applied to it, and so on down the tree.

The instance tree is closely related to the *window tree* of X, in which each window is the child of another window, with the *root window* as the topmost ancestor. In fact, the instance tree contains the window tree within it: a widget's window is the child of its parent's window.

Instance trees are described in depth in the next chapter as they are a key to understanding the assignment of resources and the naming of widgets.

3
Widget Resources

What Are Resources?

Resources are the interfaces between the programmer and the internal code of a widget. They are used to specify everything from the widget's background color to the functions it calls in response to user input. The use of resources reflects the OOP principle of *encapsulation*, or shielding the programmer from the internals of an object.

All resources have an associated value, which is of a specific data type. Resource values are associated with a widget instance. As a result, two widgets of the same class can have drastically different appearances, as shown by Figure 3.1, where six resource values differ between the two widgets.

Figure 3.1. Two instances of a single widget, using different resources

A typical widget class has dozens of resources. Some of these resources are specific to the widget class, but many are inherited from the widget's

superclasses. In addition to resources that are defined for a widget class, *Constraint* widgets define resources that are imposed on the widget's children and appear to belong to the child's class.

Resources are identified by name, such as `topShadowColor`. You must know a resource's name to set or examine its value. By convention, these names start with a lowercase letter, and any imbedded words start with an uppercase letter.

Resource Tables

This book describes the resources of a widget class in a tabular form, as exampled by Table 3.1. Such tables are excerpted from the *OSF/Motif Programmer's Reference* and combine resources specific to the widget class with those of its superclass(es). You should note that the resource tables in this book are targeted at the novice or intermediate Motif programmer. They contain only those resources that are commonly used.[1]

Table 3.1. Excerpts from *XmLabel* resource list

Name	Inheritance	Type	Default Value
background	Core	Pixel	*dynamic*
height	Core	Dimension	0
width	Core	Dimension	0
labelString	XmLabel	XmString	NULL

Name is used to identify the resource. As described below, this name is prefixed by `XmN` when used in program code, and it is not prefixed when used in a resource file.

Inheritance specifies where in the class tree the resource is defined. In this example, one resource is defined by the *XmLabel* class and the others are defined by the *Core* class. This column is labeled *Inheritance* (and not *Class*) so that it will not be confused with *resource class*, which you will see later in this chapter.

Type is the resource's data type. In some cases, this is a C type such as `unsigned`. More often, because of the portability goal, it is an X- or Motif-specific type.

Default Value is the value used for the resource if you do not explicitly set it. This value is typically a constant, such as `0`, or `TRUE`, or `XmALIGNMENT_CENTER`. Occasionally, it is `NULL`, indicating that there is no default value (although this may result in a default behavior). Another possibility is `dynamic`, which indicates that the resource defaults to the value of the identically named resource of the widget's parent.

---

[1] Based on my usage. Your usage may differ, which is why the *Programmer's Reference* remains useful.

A Short Note on Resource Naming Conventions

As you will see in this chapter, resources and the values that apply to them may be referenced both from within program code and from a resource file. Each resource, and many resource values, are assigned symbolic constants in the header file `Xm/Xm.h`.

Constants representing resource names are identical to those names, but are prefixed by `XmN` (*eg*, `background` is `XmNbackground`). As the resource names themselves do not contain a prefix, this book presents those names without prefix. If you access such resources from within program code, you must remember to add the prefix; it is omitted when used in a resource file.

Constants representing resource values are prefixed with `Xm` and are composed entirely of capital letters. This book follows the convention of leaving the prefix intact: this will help to separate value names from resource names and will also reinforce the fact that the value name is a symbolic constant representing the actual value. When used in a resource file, the prefix is omitted; when used in program code, it is retained (*eg*, in a file, use `ALIGNMENT_CENTER`; in a program, use `XmALIGNMENT_CENTER`).

Resource Files

Resource files, also known as *defaults files*, are text files that specify initial resource values for a program's widgets. These specifications override the widgets' default resource values and are themselves overridden by any "command line" or "hard-wired" resource specifications. Several layers of resource files exist, from system-wide specifications for all programs to specifications for a single program when run by a single user.

All resource files associated with a program are read when the program starts, and the specifications in them are stored in a *resource database*. When a widget is created, the database is queried for all resources associated with the widget's name or class.

The primary benefit of resource files is that they increase the flexibility of a program. If one user wants his word processor to use white text on a black background, while another wants hers to use black text on a white background, both can be satisfied by changing two resource specifications. From a programmer's viewpoint, resource files make layout easy: decide which widgets to use, write a program that builds the instance tree, then adjust resource settings until the display looks right.

The Naming of Widgets

Since resource files specify resources by name, it's important to know how resources are named. And if T.S. Eliot was a Motif programmer, I'm sure he would have written the following as a memory aid.

> *The Naming of Widgets is a difficult matter,*
> *It isn't just one of your holiday games;*
> *You may think at first I'm as mad as a hatter,*
> *When I tell you, a widget has a MULTIPLICITY OF NAMES.*

> *First there's the name that the program uses always,*
> *Such as* Label_1, TextWin, *or* Quit;
> *Such as* MenuBar *or* TheButton *or* Save,
> *Reasonable names, if you think about it.*
>
> *In addition, a widget has a name that's specific,*
> *Based on its parents, and their parents too;*
> *This name is needed, in the case that is common,*
> *When there's not one* Label_1, *but two.*
>
> *But for most widgets, this is too much,*
> *It over-specifies, and takes time to say;*
> *For these, a wildcard is enough to suffice,*
> *And* TheShell.TextWin *can be* *TextWin *any day.*

This poem contains three important facts about widgets. First, each widget has a "given name," assigned to the widget at the time of its creation. Second, to uniquely identify a specific widget in a specific program, you must specify all of that widget's ancestors, including the *program class name*; if you don't, widgets on different branches of the instance tree may be considered equal.[2] Finally, since many widgets may be uniquely identified by their given names, you can often use wildcards in a name specification.

Figure 3.2 is a widget instance tree that will put this information into practice. The root of the tree is the program's class name. This name is specified by the programmer and is used to uniquely identify the program.[3]

In this example, the program class name is `TheProg`, and the program contains six widgets. The topmost is `Form_1`, which has children `Form_2`, `Label_1`, and `Label_2`. `Form_2` also has children named `Label_1` and `Label_2`.

---

[2] As you will see in Chapter 6, in some cases specifying a widget's full name does not uniquely identify the widget. It is possible to have two (or more) widgets that are siblings but have the same given name — meaning that they have the same full name. In this case, the only way to tell the widgets apart is by their IDs — the resource manager is unable to do this, so it applies the same specifications to both widgets. This situation is unusual, however, and will only occur due to programmer choice (or mistake). In almost all cases, a widget may be uniquely identified by its given name and ancestors.

[3] The relationship between the program's executable name and its class name is fixed by convention. The class name is built from the executable name, with the first letter of each embedded word capitalized. For example, the *xterm* program has the class name *XTerm*.

Figure 3.2. Instance tree for a sample program

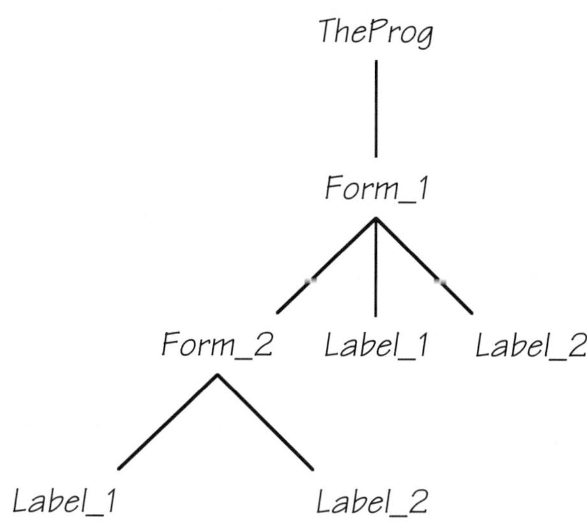

Listing 3.1 contains the full names of all of the widgets in this instance tree. The full name of a widget is specified by listing all of its ancestors in order from the program class name, using a dot (.) to separate each given name. The technical name of this dot is a *tight binding*, which indicates that the relationship between the widgets is explicitly known and is parent to child.

Listing 3.1. Full names of widgets from Figure 3.2

```
TheProg
TheProg.Form_1
TheProg.Form_1.Label_1
TheProg.Form_1.Label_2
TheProg.Form_1.Form_2
TheProg.Form_1.Form_2.Label_1
TheProg.Form_1.Form_2.Label_2
```

In many cases, there is no need to specify the widget's complete name, and for these cases, a star (*) may be used to "wildcard" unneeded portions. The technical term for this technique is *loose binding*, indicating that the relationship between the two widgets is ambiguous. The most common use of this technique is to wildcard the program class name in a program-specific resource file (or to specify generic settings in a multiprogram resource file). Listing 3.2 shows wildcarding in action.

Listing 3.2. Examples of wildcarded widget names for Figure
3.2

```
*Form_1
*Label_1
*.Label_1
TheProg.*.Label_1
*Form_2.Label_1
```

The first example specifies "all widgets with a given name of `Form_1`." Since Figure 3.2 only has one `Form_1`, this specification is unique. However, the program name is wildcarded, which could cause ambiguity in a file used by several programs.

The second and third specifications do not result in unique widget names, but specify "all widgets named `Label_1`, wherever they are." This could apply to `Form_1.Label_1`, or it could apply to `Form_1.Form_2.Label_1`. Such specifications are often used to group widgets by name.

The fourth specification is similar to the two previous, but specifies the program class name. This approach would be used in a multiple-program resource file, where many programs could contain a widget named `Label_1`.

The final example specifies the `Label_1` that is a child of `Form_2`. Applied to Figure 3.2, this specification names a single widget.

Two things to note: First, a wildcard will substitute for any number of names. This could be zero (`TheProg.*.Form_1` is the same as `TheProg.Form_1`), or there could be many names (as in the description of `*Label_1`). Second, dots are not needed on either side of the wildcard. I use them to improve readability.[4]

Format of a Resource Specification

How are these names used in resource files? As stated above, a resource file is simply a text file that contains resource specifications — usually lots of specifications. Each specification uses the format shown in Listing 3.3.

Listing 3.3. Resource file specification format

```
widget_name.resource_name:        resource_value
```

---

[4] This brings up another of my conventions: when a wildcarded specification identifies a single widget, I do not use a dot-separator. Where it can affect multiple widgets, I note that possibility by use of the separator.

The first part of this specification, *widget_name*, specifies a widget named according to the conventions described above. The second part, *resource_name*, specifies a resource name from the resource table for that widget. A dot (tight binding) separates the widget name from the resource name.[5]

The final part of the resource specification is the resource value, separated from the widget-name/resource-name combination by a colon. This value is always expressed in ASCII; the resource manager handles conversion to the data type of the resource.

Any amount of whitespace (spaces and tabs) may appear between the widget/resource name and its value. Whitespace is not permitted in the widget/resource name; it is treated as a literal part of a value. In some cases, such as strings, whitespace makes sense as part of the resource value; in others, such as numbers, it doesn't.

Sample Resource File

Figure 3.3 is an example of how the widgets of Figure 3.2 might appear in real life. The boundaries of the various widgets are identified by shading.

Figure 3.3. Instantiation of Figure 3.2

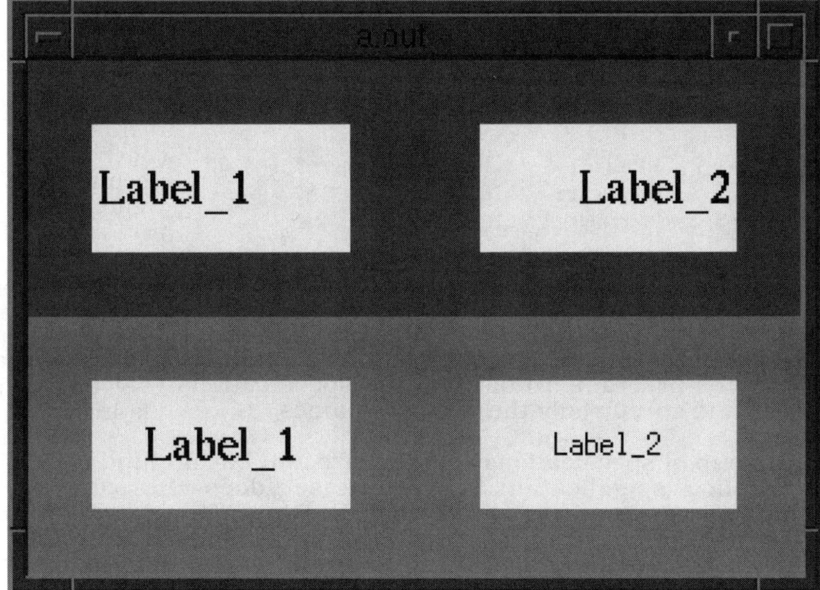

---

⁵ The widget name may be wildcarded, in which case the specification applies to all widgets with the named resource.

Listing 3.4 contains an excerpt of the resource file used to produce this output. For brevity, most of the "constraint resources" (those that determine size and position) are omitted. Other resources have been purposefully omitted to illustrate default values.

Listing 3.4. Resource file responsible for Figure 3.3

```
!-----------------------------------------------------------------
!
! Sample resource file to produce output of Figure 3.3
!
!-----------------------------------------------------------------

*.foreground:              Black
*.background:              White

TheProg.Form_1.height:     200
TheProg.Form_1.width:      300
TheProg.Form_1.background: Gray25

*Form_2.height:            100
*Form_2.width:             300
*Form_2.background:        Gray50

*XmLabel.height:           50
*XmLabel.width:            100

*.Label_1.fontList:        -*-times-medium-r-*--*-180-*

*Form_1.Label_2.fontList:  -*-times-medium-r-*--*-180-*
*Form_1.Label_1.alignment: ALIGNMENT_BEGINNING
*Form_1.Label_2.alignment: ALIGNMENT_END
```

The first pair of specifications sets default foreground and background colors for all widgets in the program. To do this, the specifications wildcard all possible widget names and specify only the resource names.

The second group of specifications sets the size and background color of `Form_1`, using an explicit specification. The third set does the same for `Form_2`, wildcarding the excess parts of the specification. These background color specifications take precedence over the general specification in the first group because they more precisely specify the affected widget. Precedence rules are described in more detail below.

The fourth group of specifications sets the height and width of all labels in the program by specifying the *XmLabel* class. This technique is described in detail below.

The next specification sets the font used for all labels with a given name of Label_1. As explained above, since more than one widget fits a name specification, both are changed.

The next three specifications set various resources of the labels that are children of Form_1. Each specification identifies a unique label by specifying all ancestors of that label save the program class name.

Setting Resources by Class

Each widget class has a name, such as *XmLabel* or *XmForm*. You can use this class name in a resource specification to refer to all instances of the class. This was used in Listing 3.4 to set the height and width of all of the program's labels.

Resources are also assigned to named classes. Unlike widget classes, a resource class has nothing to do with inheritance; it is simply a method for grouping resources. For example, the *XmCPosition* class includes the x and y resources. Appendix B identifies the class for each resource; for brevity, it is omitted from resource tables in the rest of the book.[6]

Resolution of Wildcarded Widget Names

Consider Listing 3.5 when applied to the instance tree of Figure 3.2. What will the widgets look like? The answer is that Form_1.Label_1 will have a white background, and Form_2.Label_1 will have a black background.

Listing 3.5. Seemingly overlapped wildcarded resource
specifications

```
*.Label_1.background:          Black
*.Form_1.Label_1.background:   White
```

Although both name specifications can apply to Form_1.Label_1, the second is more precise in its identification. Whenever two name specifications resolve to the same widget, the more precise version takes precedence. As an example, Listing 3.6 refers to the same widget in two ways. The second, however, completely specifies the widget (whereas the first omits the application shell name), so it takes precedence.

---

[6] In my opinion, setting resources by resource class has limited application. In many cases, such as when the resource class contains many members, using a class name may have unexpected side effects.

Listing 3.6. Definitely overlapped wildcarded resource specifications

```
*.Form_1.Label_1.background:          Black
TheProg.Form_1.Label_1.background:    White
```

In the event that two or more specifications are identical in precision, precedence is given to the one read last. This is important to remember, as specifications may appear in many resource files.

The Resource not Set

By now you may be thinking "each widget has a dozen or more resources, and some programs use hundreds of widgets ... that means a lot of specifications!"

Fortunately, you don't need to specify values for all of a widget's resources; most default to reasonable values. For example, a widget's color resources will default to those of its parent. An *XmLabel*'s label text will default to the widget's name. Listing 3.4 made use of this fact to avoid specifying the `XmNlabelString` resource for the label widgets.

On the other hand, a widget's height, width, and position default to zero. This means that, unless you specify values for these resources, all widgets will be too small to see (or use) and will be positioned at the top left corner of their parents.

Specifications that affect all the children of a manager widget go a long way toward preventing problems, as do class-wide specifications. However, you will probably end up writing more resource specifications than you thought possible.

Commenting the Resource File

Comments are used in a resource file for two purposes. The first is for explanation and grouping of the resource specifications. Resource files can become large and unwieldy very easily, unless comments are used to break things up.

The second purpose is to temporarily "turn off" a resource specification. This is done quite often during program development in order to test certain combinations of resources.

Comments take two forms: blank lines and lines beginning with an exclamation point (!). Comments always occupy the complete line; there is no way to specify an "end-of-line" comment.

It is important to remember that an exclamation point is the *only* proper way to identify a comment line. Many people use a pound sign (#), and many resource managers will properly handle this case. However, this technique is not specified by the resource file format specification and is not guaranteed to work.

How Many Resource Files Could One Program Use?

In the beginning of this chapter, it was mentioned that resource files could be "system wide" or "application- and user-specific." Moreover, it was implied that there are many steps between these two extremes. Understanding these steps is the key to customizing a program's appearance and interaction.

As you will see in the next chapter, the function `XtInitialize` is the first X-specific function called by a Motif program. This function is responsible for making a connection to the server and creating the program's application shell widget (the root of the widget instance tree). It is also responsible for building the program's resource database.[7]

The resource database is built from several sources, ranging from resource files to command-line resource specifications. These sources are accessed in the following order, with specifications from higher-numbered sources overriding those from lower-numbered sources (subject to the precedence rules described above).

1) System application-defaults file on the local host.[8]

   This is a file in the directory `/usr/lib/X11/app-defaults`, with the same name as the program's class name.[9] If such a file does not exist, this step is ignored.

   This directory typically contains the "standard settings" for finished clients. Due to administrative protections, it is usually not available for general use, and the files it contains may not be writable by users.

2) User application-defaults file on the local host, from `XAPPLRESDIR`.

   This is a file with the same name as the program's class name, found in the directory specified by the environment variable `XAPPLRESDIR`. If `XAPPLRESDIR` is not defined, this step is ignored.

   `XAPPLRESDIR` has two primary uses. The first is for user "personalization" of standard clients. Each user can create a directory identified by `XAPPLRESDIR`, copy the standard defaults files from `/usr/lib/X11/app-defaults`, then edit these files. Since `XAPPLRESDIR` is specific to a host system, users with many hosts could make a client appear differently when run from each host.

---

[7] The `appres` program allows you to preview all of the resource specifications that apply to a particular program.

[8] *Local Host* refers to the host from which the client application was run. This host may or may not be the same host that is running the display server.

[9] Although this file (and the file accessed via `XAPPLRESDIR`) are application-specific, the resources they specify are not implicitly associated with the program. In other words, a specification of `*.background` in a program-specific resource file will be overridden by an identical specification from the server's resource property (step 3 above).

The secondary benefit of `XAPPLRESDIR` is for programmers: it provides an easy way to specify where the development defaults files exist. I specify the current directory (".") in order to keep the program's source and defaults file together.

3) Server's resource property/generic user defaults file on local host.

An X display server can store a resource database that is available for all clients using that server, regardless of their local host. This database is loaded by running the *xrdb* program, which typically happens as part of server startup (it depends on the way that you start the server).

If the server does not hold a resource database, then `XtInitialize` looks for the file `.Xdefaults` in the user's home directory on the local host. If neither is found, this step is ignored.

This step is used for generic specifications, such as `*background`. Although client-specific specifications could be stored in either location, it is not recommended because server memory may be limited (and therefore shouldn't be filled with resource specifications), and a generic resource file will get unwieldy if filled with program-specific resources.

It is important to remember that the server's resource database is applied to all clients, regardless of the host from which they are run. It can thus be a convenient way to specify a common appearance for all of a user's client's. Furthermore, it can be initialized or updated at any point using the *xrdb* program.

4) Alternate user defaults file, from `XENVIRONMENT`.

If defined, the environment variable `XENVIRONMENT` specifies a defaults file residing on the local host (in any directory). This file, like `.Xdefaults`, is primarily used for general resource specifications — it describes the user's preferred environment.

5) Command-line specifications

The final changes to a client's resource database occur when the user specifies values on the command line. This process is described in greater detail below.

Setting Resources from the Command Line

There are two ways to change the resource database from the command line. The first way is to use a "standard option," such as `-fg`. Such options provide for generic resource specifications, such as `*foreground`. They are not used to control specific resources.

To set a specific resource value, you must use the `-xrm` command-line option. This option takes a complete resource specification, as it would appear in a resource file, and passes it to the program. Listing 3.7 shows this technique in use with one of the specifications from Listing 3.4.

Listing 3.7. Example of *-xrm* command-line option

```
theprog -xrm 'TheProg.Form_1.height: 250'
```

You should note that such a specification is subject to the precedence rules above (*ie*, it will be overridden by a more precise specification). However, since command-line options are loaded last, they will take precedence over equivalent specifications from resource files, providing a simple way to handle "one-time" changes.

Setting Resources Programmatically

While resource files provide a very flexible and effective way to set a client's resources, there are times when they are unusable. Consider, for example, the text editor shown in Chapter 1. To be useful, such an editor must be able to read a file in order to edit it. However, the *XmText* widget treats its text as a resource. This means that either (1) you must store the text to be edited in a resource file, which is patently absurd, or (2) you must be able to set the text resource while the program is running.

To programmatically set resources, you first use the `XtSetArg` macro to load an *argument array* with resource name/value pairs, then use the function `XtSetValues` to install the new values into the widget instance.

Listing 3.8 contains the relevant definitions. First is the `Arg` data type, used for the resource name/value array. This data type simply associates a NUL-terminated character string containing the resource name (such as `background`) with a value for the resource. The `XtArgVal` data type is a type sufficient to hold either a pointer (used to programmatically retrieve resource values) or a 32-bit signed integer (`long`).

`XtSetArg` is a simple macro that stores its arguments in a variable of the `Arg` data type. The `XtSetValues` function performs the actual work. It takes a widget ID, a pointer to an array of `Arg` values, and a count of arguments, and stores the resource values in the widget.

The header file `Xm/Xm.h` is filled with definitions that associate resource names (such as `background`) with constants (such as `XmNbackground`). Although you could pass the resource name to `XtSetArg`, the convention is to use the associated constant.

Listing 3.8. Definitions for setting resources programmatically

```
typedef struct
            {
            String      name;
            XtArgVal    value;
            }
        Arg, *ArgList;


#define XtSetArg( arg, name, value ) \
        ( (arg).name = name, (arg).value=(XtArgVal)(value) )


void    XtSetValues( w, args, num_args )
        Widget      w;
        ArgList     args;
        Cardinal    num_args;
```

Listing 3.9 contains a program fragment wherein XtSetValues is used to set the height and width of a form widget. The three lines in this fragment perform the same function as two lines in a resource file. In all cases, programmatic resource setting takes more lines of code than a resource file. In some cases, it requires many more because the resource manager handles data conversion automatically, while the program must perform it explicitly.

Listing 3.9. Example of programmatic resource setting

```
Widget  form_1;
Arg     arglist[16];
    .
    .
    .
XtSetArg( arglist[0], XmNheight, 200 );
XtSetArg( arglist[1], XmNwidth,  300 );
XtSetValues( form_1, arglist, 2 );
```

A note on my coding technique: I explicitly reference the arguments passed to XtSetArg. This makes changes more difficult (as they may require renumbering the arguments), but I believe that it improves readability. An alternative approach, which you will find used in much X code, is to use an index variable to number the arguments automatically.

"Hard-Wiring" Resource Values

The practice of "hard-wiring" a resource value is used in cases where the programmer believes that a resource's value is too important to be changed. For example, the job of a customer-support person is made easier if certain options (such as a menu choice) cannot be changed — especially if the person with problems did not perform the customization.

In practice, hard-wiring is similar to setting resource values during runtime. Both use an array of `Arg` data, and both use the `XtSetArg` macro to store values into that array. The difference is that run-time resource setting passes that array to the `XtSetValues` function, whereas hard-wiring passes the array to the widget creation function. Listing 3.10 shows this in action.

Listing 3.10. Setting widget resources at creation

```
Widget   form_1;
Arg      arglist[16];
.
.
.
XtSetArg( arglist[0], XmNheight, 200 );
XtSetArg( arglist[1], XmNwidth,  300 );
form_1 = XmCreateForm( theShell, "Form_1", arglist, 2 );
```

At this point, I must caution you not to overuse hard-wired resources. The flexibility of resource files is a major benefit to both program development and maintenance, in addition to allowing user customization. Plus, setting resource values at compile time can "bury" the actual creation statements, leading to code that is more difficult to read and maintain. Finally, as mentioned above, many resources require special conversion routines, which in themselves add complexity.

Getting Resources Programmatically

The companion to setting resource values under program control is getting resource values under program control. In nontrivial programs, you will probably do this quite often — as an example, the aforementioned text editor needs to retrieve the *XmText* widget's contents every time the user saves the file.

The process of getting resource values is similar to that for setting them. The difference is that you store pointers to destination variables in the `Arg` array, and you call the function `XtGetValues`, prototyped in Listing 3.11, to retrieve the values.[10]

Listing 3.11. Function prototype: *XtGetValues*

```
void    XtGetValues( w, args, num_args )
        Widget      w;
        ArgList     args;
        Cardinal    num_args;
```

Listing 3.12 shows this process, which is used to retrieve the height and width of an already-created form widget. Note the use of pointers to destination variables, which leads to the requirement that the `XtArgVal` data type be able to hold a pointer.

Listing 3.12. Example use of *XtGetValues*

```
Widget      form_1;
Arg         arglist[16];
Dimension   height;
Dimension   width;
.

.

.
XtSetArg( arglist[0], XmNheight, &height );
XtSetArg( arglist[1], XmNwidth,  &width );
XtGetValues( form_1, arglist, 2 );
```

---

[10] I remember the "pointer or value" difference by equating `XtSetValues` with `printf`, and `XtGetValues` with `scanf`.

4
Writing A Motif Program

The *Widget* Data Type

To this point, widgets have been treated in an abstract manner; the working definition has been "an object that provides user-interface functionality in a Motif program." While this is a very good description of a widget's function, it says nothing about how a widget is actually used by a program.

The `Widget` data type provides the interface between a program's high-level code and the internals of a widget. A variable of this data type is capable of holding a *widget ID*, which is an integer value that uniquely identifies a widget. Most Motif and Xt functions take widget IDs as arguments and return widget IDs as results.

Although program code treats widget IDs as integer values, at the level of widget internals a widget ID is a pointer to the widget's instance data. This dichotomy is a result of the "data hiding" ethos of object-oriented programming, and is enforced by the design of the C language — a standard Motif program has no way of accessing the widget's internal data. However, by knowing that a widget ID is in fact a pointer, you can do such things as comparison with `NULL` to detect a failed creation or comparison of one ID with another.

Stages in the Life of a Motif Program

The life of a typical Motif program has four stages: Initialization, Widget Creation and Management, Realization, and The Event Loop. Except in rare cases, these stages occur in the order given and do not overlap.

Initialization

Initialization consists of making a connection to the display server and building the internal resource tables from the appropriate resource files. There is a single function that does this, `XtInitialize`, prototyped in Listing 4.1.[1]

Listing 4.1. Function prototype: *XtInitialize*

```
Widget  XtInitialize( name, class, options, num_opts, argc, argv )
        char                *name;
        char                *class;
        XrmOptionDescRec    options[];
        Cardinal            num_opts;
        Cardinal            *argc;
        char                *argv[];
```

The `name` parameter is used to pass the program's executable name, which, as you will see in Chapter 16, is used to access the program's resources. You should always pass `argv[0]` in this parameter.

The `class` parameter points at the program's class name. This is the name that is used to identify resources belonging to the program, as described in Chapter 3. By convention, this name is the program's executable name, with the first letter of each imbedded word (or abbreviated word) capitalized. For example, the *xterm* program has the class name *XTerm*.

The `options` and `opt_count` parameters are used to specify additional command-line options for the resource manager. This technique is described fully in Chapter 16; programs that don't make use of it pass `NULL` and `0`, respectively.

The last two parameters, `argc` and `argv`, are the program's command-line arguments. `XtInitialize` recognizes options (such as `-fg` or `-xrm`) by examining the arguments specified by these parameters. When it finds a recognized option, it physically removes that argument from the `argv` array (and decrements `argc`, which is why it is passed as a pointer). If you wish to perform additional parsing of the command line, this should occur after `XtInitialize` has performed its work.

Widget Creation

`XtInitialize` returns a widget, the *application shell*, which is the program's link to the display server and window manager.[2] This widget is the first widget

---

[1] `XtInitialize` is used only by programs using Motif 1.0 and X11R3. If you are using Motif 1.1 or above, you must use `XtAppInitialize`, described in Appendix D.

[2] My convention is to name this widget `appshell` and make it a global variable for ease in access. This book follows that convention.

created by a program, and all of the program's other widgets are in some way descended from it — resulting in the program's instance tree.[3]

Widget creation is performed by a creation function, as prototyped in Listing 4.2. Motif provides approximately 60 of these functions, one for each class of widget.[4] All such functions are named similarly, all take the same four parameters, and all return a widget ID.

Listing 4.2. Function prototype: Generic widget creation function

```
Widget   funcname( parent, name, arg_list, arg_cnt )
         Widget      parent;
         String      name;
         ArgList     arg_list;
         Cardinal    arg_cnt;
```

The actual function name — such as `XmCreateForm` or `XmCreateLabel` — replaces *funcname*. This name always begins with `XmCreate`, followed by the name of the widget class being instantiated. Some widget classes, such as *XmMessageBox*, have multiple creation functions; in such cases, each function sets different resource values at time of creation.

The `parent` parameter specifies the widget's parent. This parameter establishes the parent-child relationships that form the program's instance tree.

The `name` parameter specifies the widget's given name. As stated previously, any number of widgets may share the same given name; the widget is identified not only by its given name, but by its position in the instance tree.

The `arg_list` and `arg_count` parameters are used to programmatically set a widget's resources at creation time, as described in Chapter 3. If you are not doing this, pass `NULL` and `0`, respectively.

Widget Management

Once a widget is created, it must be *managed*. When a widget is managed, its parent allocates space for it and makes it visible. This process is described in detail in Chapter 6. For now, you need only know that widget management is initiated by the program, by passing the child's ID to either `XtManageChild` or `XtManageChildren`.

---

[3] One point to note is that the application shell is permitted to have only one child. The purpose of the shell is to provide an interface between that child and the window manager — in essence, it acts as the child's guardian.

[4] The toolkit provides a generic widget creation function, `XtCreateWidget`. In addition to the parameters shown in Listing 4.2, this function includes a parameter that specifies the widget class. This book uses Motif's class-specific functions only, but you may find a use for the generic function (for example, to localize widget creation).

Both of these functions are prototyped in Listing 4.3. `XtManageChild` is used to manage a single widget and takes that widget's ID as its sole parameter. `XtManageChildren` manages a group of widgets, all of which must be children of the same parent. Its first parameter, `children`, is an array of widget IDs. Its second parameter, `num_children`, contains the number of children referenced by that array.

Listing 4.3. Function prototypes: *XtManageChild* and *XtManageChildren*.

```
void    XtManageChild( w )
        Widget      w;


void    XtManageChildren( children, num_children )
        Widget         children[];
        Cardinal       num_children;
```

Widget management is not strictly a part of creation. However, convention is to manage the widget immediately after creation in order to guarantee that the widget actually does get managed.[5] Neglecting to manage a widget is a surprisingly common occurrence, with the result that the widget (and its children, if any) simply do not appear as part of the program's window.

Realization

Widget creation is the process whereby the program allocates space for the widget's internal data structures. Widget *realization* is the process whereby the display server allocates a widget's window. Realization is performed by the `XtRealizeWidget` function, prototyped in Listing 4.4.

Listing 4.4. Function prototype: *XtRealizeWidget*

```
void    XtRealizeWidget( w )
        Widget  w;
```

`XtRealizeWidget` is usually called after all of a program's widgets have been created. It takes the application shell widget (`appshell`) as an argument and recursively realizes each widget in the instance tree.

This sequence — create all widgets then realize them in one step — is done for efficiency, not necessity. A widget will be realized at the time of management if

---

[5] The toolkit provides the function `XtCreateManagedWidget`, which combines the creation and management operations into a single function.

its parent is realized. This means that you could realize `appshell` immediately after creating it, and all of its descendents would be realized as they are managed.[6] The drawback to this approach is lower efficiency: realizing all widgets in one step results in less client-server communication than realizing each widget as it is managed.

The Event Loop

This is the stage where a program spends most of its time. The function `XtMainLoop`, prototyped in Listing 4.5, is typically the last statement in a program's `main` function. It waits for events to occur, then passes them off to either a programmer-defined event handler or the widget class's default event handler.

Listing 4.5. Function prototype: XtMainLoop

```
void    XtMainLoop()
```

Notice that `XtMainLoop` does not have any parameters. When you call this function, you are putting your program into an event-driven state — essentially, you are giving control of your program to `XtMainLoop`. At that point, it is assumed that the program is ready for event-driven operation, and no more information is needed.

Widget Destruction

A normal Motif program creates some widgets, does some work, and then terminates. At the time of program termination, all widgets created by the program are destroyed, and their memory is returned to the free pool.

Some programs, however, have a need to destroy widgets while the program is running. An example would be a multiwindow text editor: when the user is finished with a window, then the widgets for that window should be destroyed and the memory they used recovered.[7]

The function `XtDestroyWidget`, prototyped in Listing 4.6, is used to destroy a widget before program termination. It takes a single parameter, the widget's ID. Note that, if the passed widget is a manager, all of its children are destroyed at the same time.

---

[6] Why is this important? It means that you can create widgets while your program is running (after the realization step), and they will be realized automatically. I made use of this in a scheduling program: each step in the schedule was assigned to a pushbutton, which could be pressed to provide more information about that step. Step information was stored in a data file, which was read while the program was running and used to create the widgets.

[7] In the real world, this desire is blunted by widget implementation — many widgets do not release all of the memory or other resources that they have allocated. As Motif (and Xt) become more mature, these "memory leak" bugs will be eliminated.

Listing 4.6. Function prototype: XtDestroyWidget

```
void    XtDestroyWidget( w )
        Widget      w;
```

A Program Template

Listing 4.7 contains a template for Motif programs, containing the steps described above. Although this template can be compiled (see *A Short Note About Program Size*, below), it is not runnable.[8]

Listing 4.7. Motif program template

```
/*******************************************************************
**                                                               **
**   listing_4_7.c                                               **
**                                                               **
**   This program is a generic template, containing the layout of a   **
**   normal Motif program.                                       **
**                                                               **
*******************************************************************/


#include <Xm/Xm.h>                  /* Standard Motif definitions */


Widget  appshell;                   /* Application Shell          */


void main( argc, argv )
```

---

[8] If you do try to run this program, you will get the error message "X Toolkit Error: Shell widget a.out has zero width and/or height". This message does not occur because the application shell needs to have its width and height specified in a resource file. Instead, it occurs because a shell widget determines its height and width from its child — in other words, a shell must have a child.

Listing 4.7. Continued.

```
    int     argc;
    char    *argv[];
{

    appshell = XtInitialize( argv[0], "Listing_4_7", NULL, 0,
                                              &argc, argv );


    /*** Creation/Management of instance tree goes here ***/


    XtRealizeWidget( appshell );
    XtMainLoop();
}
```

Note that this program makes use of the header file `Xm/Xm.h`. This file contains common Motif definitions, ranging from data types to symbolic constants. More importantly to the sample program, it loads the file `X11/Intrinsic.h`, which contains the function prototype for `XtInitialize`. A typical Motif program does not access `Xm/Xm.h` directly, but accesses it indirectly via widget-specific header files (described below).

The main function is the same as for any C program. The `argc` parameter contains a count of the number of command-line arguments, and the `argv` parameter is an array containing pointers to these arguments.

As stated above, `XtInitialize` is the first function called by the program. Note that "Listing_4_7" is the program name, transformed by the class name conventions. Note also that `argc` is passed as a pointer — again, this is required so that recognized command-line options may be physically removed from the argument list in `argv`.

A normal program would create its widgets after the call to `XtInitialize`. Once its widgets were created, it would call `XtRealizeWidget` to assign windows and then call `XtMainLoop`. At that point, user/program interaction would be handled by the widgets.

Header Files

In order to have access to the symbolic constants, data types, and functions provided by Motif, a program must make use of one or more header files. Each widget class has its own header file, listed in Table 4.1. In addition to class-specific definitions, these files provide access to the common Motif and Xt definitions.[9]

---

[9] Class-specific files `#include` the common file `Xm/Xm.h`, which in turn `#include`'s the common toolkit file `X11/Intrinsic.h`.

The header files from Table 4.1 are found in the directory `/usr/include/Xm`. Header files for Xlib and the toolkit (Xt) are found in `/usr/include/X11`.

If you look in the Motif header directory, you will see many files in addition to those listed in Table 4.1. Most have names similar to those listed, but which end with "P", or "G", or "GP". Filenames ending with "P" are the "private" header files for the widget class; they contain data definitions internal to the widget class. Those files ending with "G" are for gadgets; most primitive widgets (those derived from *XmPrimitive*) have an equivalent gadget. Those files ending in "GP" are the private header files for the gadgets.

Table 4.1. Motif header files

Widget Class / Contents	Header File
Common definitions	Xm.h
XmArrowButton	ArrowB.h
XmBulletinBoard	BulletinB.h
XmCascadeButton	CascadeB.h
XmCommand	Command.h
Clipboard interface	CutPaste.h
XmDialogShell	DialogS.h
XmDrawingArea	DrawingA.h
XmDrawnButton	DrawnB.h
XmFileSelectionBox	FileSB.h
XmForm	Form.h
XmFrame	Frame.h
XmLabel	Label.h
XmList	List.h
XmMainWindow	MainW.h
XmMenuShell	MenuShell.h
XmMessageBox	MessageB.h
XmPanedWindow	PanedW.h
XmPushButton	PushB.h
XmRowColumn	RowColumn.h
XmScale	Scale.h

Table 4.1. Continued.

XmScrollBar	ScrollBar.h
XmScrolledWindow	ScrolledW.h
XmSelectionBox	SelectioB.h
XmSeparator	Separator.h
XmText	Text.h
XmToggleButton	ToggleB.h

Compilation of a Motif Program

Compilation of a Motif program differs from compilation of a non-Motif program in that you must specify Motif- and X-specific libraries for linking. Depending on your system, the specific libraries may vary; Listing 4.8 shows three sample compilation lines. If none of these command lines work for you, you will need to contact your system administrator or vendor to learn the proper compiler invocation.

Listing 4.8. Sample compiler invocations for Motif programs

```
cc sourcename.c -lXm -lXt -lX11 -o progname

cc sourcename.c -lXm -lXtm -lX11 -o progname

cc sourcename.c -lXm -lXt -lX11 -lPW -o progname
```

The first example is for a "perfect system." It specifies the Motif library (Xm), the toolkit library (Xt), and the Xlib library (X11). For most systems, this command is sufficient to compile and link a Motif program.

The second variant is specific to Motif as supplied by Integrated Computer Solutions (ICS) for systems that do not come with Motif. Because Motif requires changes to the intrinsics, ICS provides Xtm ("Xt for Motif"), which is installed alongside the standard Xt.[10] This allows non-Motif programs to compile and link normally (using the standard Xt library).[11]

---

[10] Sites that use ICS Motif for all program development (to the exclusion of other widget sets such as Athena) might replace the distributed Xt with Xtm. In this case, the "perfect system" command will work. Ask your system administrator for details.

[11] The primary changes are to the *Core* widget class. The R3 toolkit does not derive *Core* from *Object* and *RectObj*; that derivation is specific to Motif. The Xtm library contains this derivation, as well as the *WindowObj* class, and some other Motif-specific changes. Vendors (such as Hewlett Packard) that supply Motif as an integral part of their X distribution will make these changes to the distributed Xt.

The third variant includes the Programmer's Workbench library (PW). This library contains regular expression code; it is only needed for System-V-based systems and then only when you are using *XmFileSelectionBox*, which is described in Chapter 13. If you are using a BSD-derived system (such as Ultrix), the contents of this library are part of the standard C library.

The order of library specifications is important because the C compiler will search libraries in the order specified. As shown in Figure 2.2, Motif relies upon the X toolkit, which in turn relies upon Xlib. Failure to specify these libraries in the proper order will result in compilation errors.

A Short Note About Program Size

It is an axiom of programming that program efficiency and programming ease do not mix. This is often seen when using a "fourth-generation language" to access a database and finding that it executes more slowly than an equivalent C program. In the world of Motif, execution speed is rarely a factor (after all, your programs are simply reacting to events). On the other hand, program size is a concern.

Listing 4.9 contains a directory listing showing the source file from Listing 4.7, along with the executable file produced from it. All numbers are in bytes, the fifth column contains the file size, and the number associated with a.out is not a typographical error — this source file, which contains three executable lines, generated an executable file of over 300 kilobytes.

Listing 4.9. Directory listing showing sample program of
Listing 4.7, specifically, source and executable sizes.

```
total 686
-rwxr-xr-x    1 kdg        users      347050 Mar 24 18:57 a.out
-rw-r--r--    1 kdg        users         951 Mar 24 18:56 listing.4.7.c
```

To understand the size of this executable, you must gain an intuitive feel for Figures 2.1 and 2.2. The application shell (class *ApplicationShell*) is derived from the *Shell* class, which Figure 2.1 shows to be derived from four other classes. Not coincidentally, these five classes provide much of the functionality implied by Figure 2.2.

The result is that the program in Listing 4.7 is perhaps the worst example of program size vs. complexity to be found in the Motif environment (the "Hello World" program in the next chapter isn't much better). Fortunately, program complexity grows at a much greater rate than executable size. Each widget class adds to program size, but the process of derivation means that this added size is less than what would be produced by adding the functionality "from scratch."

The benefit of Motif comes from reduced programmer time since most of the "hard work" is already done. For example, the text editor shown in Figure 1.1 (and developed in Chapters 11–14) represents hundreds of hours of programmer time. However, only a few of those hours were mine; the rest were from the Open

Software Foundation. This implementation time represents a single fixed cost —
the price of a Motif license. Programmers can build complex applications using
widgets without incurring the costs of writing low-level widget code.

What About Standard I/O?

A typical C program uses the standard I/O facility — *standard input, standard
output*, and *standard error* — for user interaction. Standard input is used with
the `scanf` and `gets` functions; standard output is used with `printf` and `puts`
functions; standard error is accessed via `fprintf` or special-purpose functions
such as `perror`. These three "files" nominally access the user's terminal.
However, they can be "redirected" to any openable character-stream source or
destination — be it a terminal, a file, a TCP socket, or `/dev/null`.

Although an X client uses its window as the primary means of user interaction,
the standard I/O facility is still available. In fact, the X (and Motif) libraries use
standard error for reporting runtime errors. However, exactly what the standard
files are connected to may be a mystery.

If the client is run from a terminal session (such as *xterm*), then the standard
files access that session. This can be quite useful during debugging — as `printf`
always has been. Be aware, however, that if you run the client in the
background (as most clients are), the program will stop if you attempt to use
standard input, and wait for the user to bring it to the foreground.

The mystery comes when you run a program from somewhere other than a
terminal session, such as the Motif system menu. In this case, standard output
and standard error go to the "console" terminal session — an *xterm* started with
the `-C` argument. Standard input in this case is redirected to `/dev/null`, which
means that you lose the use of it.

5
XmLabel

Overview

The *XmLabel* class provides a basic mechanism for display of static text and pictures. This mechanism consists of a window and resources that specify the contents of that window. *XmLabel* is also used as the superclass of the various button widgets, which are described in future chapters.

XmLabel Inheritance

XmLabel has a relatively short class tree, shown in Figure 5.1. *Core* provides the basic window functionality, *XmPrimitive* provides appearance details, and *XmLabel* provides facilities for text or pixmap display.

Figure 5.1. *XmLabel* class tree

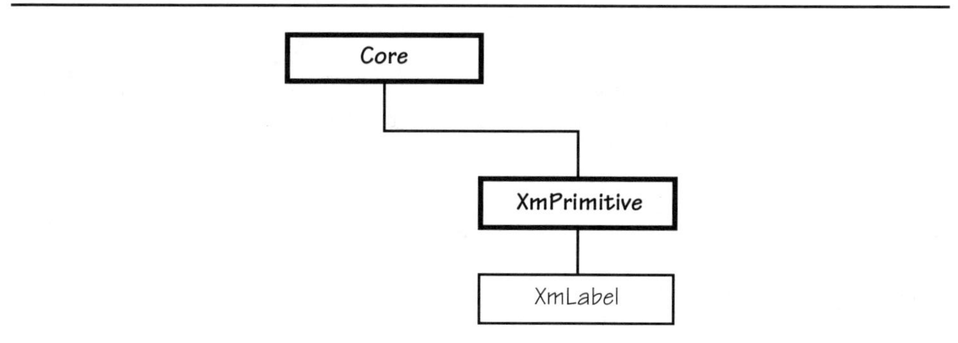

XmLabel Resources

Of the more than 50 resources provided by *Core*, *XmPrimitive*, and *XmLabel*, I have found those listed in Table 5.1 to be most often used.

Table 5.1. Frequently used resources: *XmLabel*

Name	Inheritance	Type	Default Value
alignment	XmLabel	unsigned char	XmALIGNMENT_CENTER
fontList	XmLabel	XmFontList	"Fixed"
labelPixmap	XmLabel	Pixmap	XmUNSPECIFIED_PIXMAP
labelString	XmLabel	XmString	*dynamic*
labelType	XmLabel	unsigned char	XmSTRING
recomputeSize	XmLabel	Boolean	TRUE
string Direction	XmLabel	XmString Direction	XmSTRING_DIRECTION_L_ TO_R
foreground	XmPrimitive	Pixel	*dynamic*
unitType	XmPrimitive	unsigned char	XmPIXELS
background	Core	Pixel	*dynamic*
height	Core	Dimension	0
width	Core	Dimension	0
x	Core	Position	0
y	Core	Position	0

Usage: labelType

The *XmLabel* class is capable of displaying two types of labels: text and picture. The labelType resource is used to identify which type of data a specific label instance handles. The two legal values for this resource are XmSTRING and XmPIXMAP, and the default is XmSTRING.

Size and Position: height, width, x, y

The size and position of the widget are specified by the resources height, width, x, and y, which are part of the *Core* class. The values associated with these resources are typically set by the widget's parent, based on the widget's constraints and the value of its recomputeSize resource.[1]

---

[1] Constraints are described in Chapter 6.

The `Dimension` and `Position` data types are unit-independent and hold integer values (`Dimension` is equivalent to `unsigned`, `Position` is equivalent to `int`). These types are unit-independent in that the internal representation of a widget's size and position may differ from the external representation, depending on the contents of the `unitType` resource.

Measurement Control: unitType

Internally, a widget's size and position are stored in terms of screen pixels. This means that a widget with a `width` value of 100 will be 1 inch wide on a 100 dpi screen, but only ¾ inches wide on a 75 dpi screen. The `unitType` resource allows a program to avoid size discrepancies by providing an external representation of this data that is not tied to the characteristics of the display.

A complete description of `unitType` will be deferred until Chapter 6, as it is a topic that is closely related to management. For the present, the default unit of screen pixels is sufficient.

Geometry Control: recomputeSize

This resource controls whether or not the widget will change its size to guarantee that its contents are fully exposed. If the value of `recomputeSize` is `TRUE`, the widget will calculate the minimum size sufficient to fully display its contents and will not permit its actual size to drop below that minimum. If its value is `FALSE`, the actual size of the widget may drop below the minimum, with the result that part of the widget's label may be obscured.

Although this resource may seem innocuous, its effects are anything but. If a program attempts to change the size of a label, and that new size is less than the minimum, the change will be ignored — or half-executed (*eg*, `height` changes but `width` doesn't). Since `recomputeSize` defaults to `TRUE`, many people run into problems from this effect.[2]

Color Specification: foreground, background

The background color, specified by `background`, is the color of the widget's window. The foreground color, specified by `foreground`, is the color of the widget's text. If you do not specify values for these resources, the widget will default to the colors used by its parent.

Contents: labelPixmap, labelString, fontList

Pixmap labels use the `labelPixmap` resource to specify the pixmap displayed by the label. This resource is described in detail in *Using XmLabel with Pictures*, below.

---

[2] I first learned about this effect when writing the scheduling program mentioned in Chapter 4. Several hours were lost while I tried to determine why certain labels did not conform to the sizes dictated by the schedule data. Subsequently, I have heard similar questions from numerous Motif programmers.

Text labels use the `labelString` resource to specify the text displayed by the label. This resource is a compound string, as described in *Compound Strings*, below. The default value for this resource is the widget's given name (*eg*, "Label_1").

The font used to display this text is described by the `fontList` resource, the use of which is described in *Setting a Label's Font*, below. The default value for this resource is the "fixed" font, which is an installation-dependent monospaced font.

Text Format: alignment, stringDirection

The `alignment` and `stringDirection` resources determine the way that the label text is justified within the label's window. Possible values are `XmALIGNMENT_BEGINNING`, `XmALIGNMENT_CENTER`, and `XmALIGNMENT_END`. The actual appearance of the label depends on its string direction: for left-to-right labels, `XmALIGNMENT_BEGINNING` results in left-alignment, while `XmALIGNMENT_END` results in right-alignment.

The `stringDirection` resource specifies whether the label string is drawn left-to-right or right-to-left. Its value may be `XmSTRING_DIRECTION_L_TO_R` for a left-to-right string or `XmSTRING_DIRECTION_R_TO_L` for a right-to-left string. The default orientation is left-to-right.

You should note that the compound string used for a textual label also contains information about the direction in which it should be drawn. This imbedded information takes precedence over that specified by the `stringDirection` resource. As a result, `stringDirection` becomes useless when a label's string is set from the resource file: the resource manager defaults to strings that are explicitly left-to-right.

Using *XmLabel*: "Hello, World!"

"Hello, World!" is traditionally the first program one writes when one is confronted by a new environment. It provides the programmer with a "quick and dirty" way to see something work. It happens to be the perfect use for an *XmLabel* widget, and the output of such a program is shown in Figure 5.2.

Figure 5.2. "Hello, World!" using *XmLabel*

The program that produced this output and its resource file are shown in Listing 5.1. This program is simply an adaptation of the template from Listing 4.6, with the sole addition being the creation of a label widget. Note that the resource file specifies the label's height, width, and contents; all other resources take on default values.[3]

Listing 5.1. Program and resource file: "Hello, World"

```
/**********************************************************************
**                                                                  **
**    listing_5_1.c                                                 **
**                                                                  **
**    "Hello World" for Motif.  This program demonstrates use of the **
**    XmLabel class for displaying text.                            **
**                                                                  **
**********************************************************************/


#include <Xm/Label.h>                /* Definitions for XmLabel
                                        (includes Xm.h)             */
Widget  appshell,                    /* Application Shell           */
        the_label;                   /* The one and only label      */


void main( argc, argv )
    int     argc;
    char    *argv[];
{
    appshell = XtInitialize( argv[0], "Listing_5_1", NULL, 0,
                                            &argc, argv );

    the_label = XmCreateLabel( appshell, "TheLabel", NULL, 0 );
    XtManageChild( the_label );

    XtRealizeWidget( appshell );
    XtMainLoop();
}
```

---

[3] In particular, foreground and background take on default values. As the label does not have a parent from which to acquire these values, they come from defaults compiled into the toolkit — on my system, black for foreground and light blue for background.

Listing 5.1. Continued.

```
!
! Resource file to produce Figure 5.2
!

*TheLabel.height:      50
*TheLabel.width:       100
*TheLabel.labelString: Hello, World!
```

Setting a Label's Font

Figure 5.2 contained a label using the default "fixed" font. Compare it with Figure 5.3, which uses 14pt Times Roman. This change was effected via the label's `fontList` resource.

Figure 5.3. "Hello, World" using a different font

Fonts Then and Now

One of the advances of X11 Release 3 was the addition of *font families*. In Release 2 and before, fonts had simple names like *vg-25* or *sans12*. The fonts you had depended on the server you were using: some simply used the MIT fonts, some used a subset, and some used a superset (due to programmers stepping into font design).

For Release 3, several font vendors, including Adobe and Bitstream, provided the X Consortium with families of fonts, such as *Courier*, *Times*, and *Helvetica*. These families contain sizes ranging from 8 to 24 point, along with various styles such as boldface and italic (in addition to the roman, or upright, style).

The old fonts are still supported by many servers, and you can continue to use them.[4] The new fonts, however, are significantly more portable. Moreover, this portability is not limited to the X world: the new fonts are well-known designs from the world of printing.

Name That Font

Under the old method, fonts were individual entities, not members of families. To use a larger size or different style of a particular font, you specified a different name (*eg, fg-40* is a larger version of *fg-30*). If the larger size or different style did not exist, you either did without or implemented it yourself.

For Release 3, the *X Logical Font Description Conventions* manual presented a new method of identifying fonts. Under this method, a font is specified by its family, size, and characteristics, as shown in Listing 5.2.[5]

Listing 5.2. X11 Release 3 font specification format

```
-foundry-family-weight-slant-set_width--pixels-points-
hres-vres-spacing-avg_width-char_set
```

Although this specification appears intimidating, most of it can be wildcarded away, using a star (*) to replace unneeded fields. The specification is extensive in order to minimize the possibility of yet another standard at some point in the future.

It is important to note the use of dashes in the specification. Each field is delimited by a dash, meaning that no field may have an imbedded dash except *char_set*, which is the last field. The *set_width* and *pixels* field are separated by two dashes.

The *foundry* field specifies the creator of the font. Examples are `adobe`, `bitstream`, `dec`, and `misc` (which is used for the old-style fonts). This field is only needed in the case where two foundries produce the same font; it is usually wildcarded.

The *family* field specifies the font family; it is one field that is never wildcarded. As of Release 3, supported families were `charter`, `courier`, `helvetica`, `new century schoolbook`, `symbol`, and `times`. Release 4 added `lucida`, `lucida bright`, and `lucida typewriter`, but the list is subject to change, depending on your vendor. Your server may include families not shown here, or it may not contain all of those shown (although the list given is fairly representative).

The *weight* field specifies whether the font should be boldfaced or not. Boldfaced fonts are specified with a weight of `bold`, otherwise `medium` is used. At some point in the future, other weights may be provided (such as light or semibold). You should always specify a value for this field.

---

[4] To see the fonts supported by your server, run the program `xlsfonts`.
[5] This specification is shown on two lines, due to the space available. It is actually a single line.

The *slant* field determines another stylistic modification to the font. To use the normal, upright version of the font, use the value r (for Roman). For a true italic font, use the value i. For an oblique style (simply slanting the Roman characters), use the value o. Fonts tend to have either an oblique or an italic form, but not both; as a result, you should know which style is supported by your desired font and use it (*ie*, you should not wildcard this field).

The *set_width* field describes the track kerning of the font: whether the characters are set closely together, normally, or widely. Although the font specification supports the values condensed, narrow, normal, and double width, all current fonts use normal. As a result, this field may be wildcarded.

The *pixels* field contains the height of the font in terms of the pixel size of your display. The older fonts used this method to specify size (*ie*, *fg-40* meant that font height was 40 pixels). Since the actual size of the font will depend on your display, this field is nonportable and should be wildcarded.

The *points* field also specifies the height of the font. It does so in terms of *point size*, commonly used in the world of printing. One point is equal to 1/72 inch, so a 12-point font has a 1/6-inch character box. In the font specification, you multiply the point size by 10, so that a 12-point font would have a *points* value of 120. Commonly supported *points* values are 80, 100, 120, 140, 180, and 240 (corresponding to point sizes of 8, 10, 12, 14, 18, and 24). If your server is unable to find the specified size, it simply ignores the font specification (and you get the default "fixed" font).[6]

You should use either the *pixels* field or the *points* field, not both. Since point size is inherently more portable (as the design of your display does not influence it), it is the preferred approach. On the other hand, if you specify all sizes in terms of pixels (a bad practice), you will want to use the *pixels* field.

At this point, all of the "important" fields have been discussed. The fields below are usually wildcarded, as they provide more information than the server really needs. For completeness, however, here they are.

The *hres* and *vres* fields specify the characteristics of the display in pixels per inch. The horizontal resolution is specified by *hres*, the vertical by *vres*. Since your display server should know its own resolution, specifying values for these fields is more than a bit redundant.

The *spacing* field contains m to specify a monospaced font or p to specify a proportional (variable width) font. Font spacing is an inherent part of the font design (*eg*, Courier is monospaced, Times is proportional), so this field is also redundant.

The *avg_width* field contains the average width, in tenths of a pixel, of all characters in the font. It is possible that you will have a reason to use this field: consider the case of a fixed-size entry field, where you want to pick a font that will "fit" in that field. You could specify the font by wildcarding the point size (or all other fields, if you don't care what you get), and specifying a predetermined *avg_width* value (*eg*, a 100 pixel field should be able to hold 10 characters with an average width of 10 pixels).

---

[6] X11 Release 5 includes scalable fonts, courtesy of Bitstream. A server that supports these fonts will be able to produce a font of any point size from data describing the shapes of that font's characters.

Finally, the *char_set* field describes the method used to translate numeric character values into actual characters. The International Standards Organization (ISO) has specified several such translation tables: for English-speaking countries, the set is *ISO Latin 1*, a superset of ASCII . This character set is specified by the value `iso8859-1`. Wildcarding this field indicates the default character set, which fits well with strings created using `XmSTRING_DEFAULT_CHARSET`.

Putting Font Specifications to Work

To specify the 14pt Times font used in Figure 5.3, add the contents of Listing 5.3 to the resource file. Notice that the only non-wildcarded fields are *family, weight, slant,* and *point size.* In most cases, these are the only fields that you will need to specify. Notice also that all fields to the right of *points* are wildcarded with a single wildcard character.

Listing 5.3. Resource specification used to change font for Figure 5.3

```
*TheLabel.fontList:      -*-times-medium-r-*--*-140-*
```

Giving fontList *a List of Fonts*

In many applications, `fontList` is specified as above: a single font specification, which may or may not be associated with a single widget. However, there may come a time when you will want a single widget to use multiple fonts, as in Figure 5.4. This ability is present because the `fontList` resource, as its name implies, can specify a *list* of fonts, associating each font with a program-usable name.

Figure 5.4. Multiple fonts in one widget

To produce this output, you must do two things. The first is to specify multiple fonts for `fontList`, using the format of Listing 5.4. The second thing is to set the label's `labelString` resource programmatically, as described below.

Listing 5.4. Specifying multiple fonts in a single *fontList*

```
widget_name.fontList:     font1=charset1, font2=charset2, ...
```

In this specification, the fonts — *font1*, *font2*, and so on — are standard font specifications, as described above. The character sets — *charset1* and *charset2* in the listing — are programmer-defined names, which are used by program code when the label's string is created. These names may consist of any number of characters, but may not contain embedded whitespace.

Fonts are assigned to character sets with an equals sign (=); the font-specification, equals sign, and character set name must be run together, without whitespace. Individual specifications are separated by commas; any amount of whitespace may appear between such specifications. If a font specification is presented without an associated character-set name (and equals sign), it is associated with the default character set; only one such specification may be present.

Due to the line-length limitations of a resource file, it may be necessary to break specifications into multiple lines. This is done by placing a backslash (\) at the end of all nonterminal lines. The resource manager, when it reads such lines, concatenates them until a terminal line is read.

The *XmString* Data Type

Motif is meant to be a universal user interface and, as a result, has several features that make internationalization simpler. The *compound string*, represented by the `XmString` data type, is one of these features. A compound string contains textual data, along with information about the character set used for that text and the direction (left-to-right or right-to-left) in which the text should be displayed. A compound string may contain a single text segment, or it may contain many different segments, each with different instructions.[7]

The primary usage of the `XmString` data type is as the label string for widgets of the *XmLabel* class and its subclasses. Its capabilities are largely underutilized in this role, but it provides the flexibility needed for easy internationalization, especially where fonts are concerned.

---

[7] Do not confuse `compound string' with `compound text'.The former is a creation of OSF and is used for most output-bound strings in Motif. The latter is a creation of the X consortium and was designed for data interchange between applications. In actuality, they are almost identical in content.

It is important to remember that the `XmString` data type is distinct from the `String` data type and the `XmSTRING` constant. The former, which is simply a redefinition of `char *`, is used by the *XmText* widget and is one of the data definitions supplied by the X toolkit. The `XmSTRING` constant is specific to the `labelType` resource of the *XmLabel* class; it specifies that the label is textual in nature.

Internal Structure of a Compound String

A compound string is made up of individual data segments, as shown by Figure 5.5. Some segments provide contextual information, such as the current character set, while others contain data — the string to be displayed. The number of segments in a string is limited only by the computer's addressing ability. The simplest string has two segments (character set and text), while an irrationally complex string could have hundreds.

Note that character set and directional information is not associated with a single text segment, but represents state information. The string is processed from start to finish, regardless of the direction of its text, and directional and character-set specifications remain in effect until explicitly changed.

Figure 5.5. Compound string

Direction	CharSet	Text
LtoR	iso8859-1	Hello, World

Common XmString Functions

The *Programmer's Reference* specifies over 30 functions for `XmString` manipulation, but a typical program uses only the five prototyped in Listing 5.5. These five are declared in `Xm/Xm.h` along with declarations for the other `XmString` functions.

Listing 5.5. Prototypes of five commonly used *XmString*
functions

```
XmString      XmStringCreate( text, charset )
              char            *text;
              XmStringCharSet charset;


XmString      XmStringCreateLtoR( text, charset )
              char            *text;
              XmStringCharSet charset;

void          XmStringFree( string )
              XmString        string;


XmString      XmStringConcat( string1, string2 )
              XmString        string1;
              XmString        string2;


Boolean       XmStringGetLtoR( string, charset, text )
              XmString        string;
              XmStringCharSet charset;
              char            **text;
```

The functions `XmStringCreate` and `XmStringCreateLtoR` both create an `XmString`
from a normal C string.[8] The first creates a string that contains segments for
character set and text, whereas the second creates segments for character set,
text, and direction (which defaults to left-to-right). In addition,
`XmStringCreateLtoR` can accept strings with imbedded newlines ('\n'); it properly
converts them to multiple-segment strings.

The `charset` parameter specifies the character set to use for the created string.
You can specify the default character set for your installation (ISO Latin 1 for the
United States) by passing the constant `XmSTRING_DEFAULT_CHARSET`.[9] Other
character sets are identified by NUL-terminated strings defined by the
programmer and associated with fonts via the `fontList` resource.

The `XmString` creation functions allocate memory (using `malloc`) for the created
string. This memory should be freed when it is no longer needed, which is why
the function `XmStringFree` exists. It takes a string pointer as an argument and
simply calls `free` on the memory represented by that pointer.

---

[8] Motif Release 1.1 contains an additional function, `XmStringCreateSimple`, which
converts a C string to an `XmString`, using the default character set. If you are working
on a Release 1.1 system, I recommend that you use this function in preference to
`XmStringCreate`.

[9] Appendix A contains a chart of ISO Latin 1 characters.

The `XmStringConcat` function concatenates two strings, allocates space for the result, and returns a pointer to that result. This function is useful if you need to use two character sets in a string: you can create each component with the appropriate character set, then concatenate them for output. If you use this technique, remember to call `XmStringFree` on the source strings.

`XmStringGetLtoR` retrieves a text segment from an `XmString`. The first two parameters specify the string and the desired character set. If the function can find a text segment using that character set, it will allocate memory for the segment (using `malloc`), store the segment's text in the allocated memory as a C string, and return a pointer to that string via the `text` parameter. Its return value will be `TRUE` if able to do all that, `FALSE` otherwise. You should remember to use `free` if you wish to discard the returned C string.

One obvious limitation of `XmStringGetLtoR` is that it can only retrieve the first segment of a multiple-segment string. For multiple-segment strings, you must use the function `XmStringGetNextSegment`, not shown here. Most applications, however, use strings with a single text segment.

Setting *labelString* Programmatically

To demonstrate use of the `XmString` data type, Listing 5.6 contains a modification of the "Hello World" program that sets the label's string programmatically.[10] While this program is quite simple — it creates a widget, creates a string, and stores the string into the widget — it uses several of the functions described above.

Listing 5.6. "Hello, World" that sets label string programmatically

```
/*****************************************************************
**                                                             **
**                                                             **
**   listing_5_6.c                                            **
**                                                             **
**   This program demonstrates programmatic setting of an XmLabel's   **
**   labelString resource. Along the way, it demonstrates use of the  **
**   XmString data type.                                       **
**                                                             **
*****************************************************************/
```

---

[10] Installing the new label string could also be done at the time it's created, as described under *Hard Wiring Resource Values* in Chapter 3. I chose the two-step process for illustrative purposes.

Listing 5.6. Continued.

```c
#include <Xm/Label.h>          /* Definitions for XmLabel
                                  (includes Xm.h)          */

Widget      appshell,          /* Application Shell        */
            the_label;         /* The one and only label   */
Arg         arglist[16];       /* Used to store label      */
XmString    str1,              /* Strings for the label    */
            str2,
            the_string;


void main( argc, argv )
    int     argc;
    char    *argv[];
{
    appshell = XtInitialize( argv[0], "Listing_5_6", NULL, 0,
                                        &argc, argv );

    the_label = XmCreateLabel( appshell, "TheLabel", NULL, 0 );
    XtManageChild( the_label );

    str1 = XmStringCreateLtoR( "Hello\n", XmSTRING_DEFAULT_CHARSET );
    str2 = XmStringCreate( "World!", "CharSet1" );
    the_string = XmStringConcat( str1, str2 );
    XmStringFree( str1 );
    XmStringFree( str2 );
    XtSetArg( arglist[0], XmNlabelString, the_string );
    XtSetValues( the_label, arglist, 1 );
    XmStringFree( the_string );

    XtRealizeWidget( appshell );
    XtMainLoop();
}
!
! Resource file for "Hello, World" with programmatic label setting
!
```

Listing 5.6. Continued.

```
*TheLabel.height:        50
*TheLabel.width:         100
*TheLabel.recomputeSize:  FALSE
*TheLabel.fontList:       -*-times-medium-r-*--*-240-*,              \
                          -*-helvetica-medium-r-*--*-240-*=CharSet1
```

Instead of creating the string in one step, I decided to do a two-step creation and use different fonts for the two segments. The first segment was created with `XmStringCreateLtoR`, because it contains an embedded newline. As the second did not, it was created with `XmStringCreate`. To join the two halves, I called `XmStringConcat` and then called `XmStringFree` to deallocate the component strings.

One reason for creating the label string in two pieces was the use of two character sets. The first piece uses the default character set, represented by the `XmSTRING_DEFAULT_CHARSET` constant; the second string uses a named character set. Both the default character set and the named character set are associated with fonts in the resource file; the details are described below, under *Setting a Label's Font*.

One noteworthy feature of this program is that it illustrates the `recomputeSize` "problem": although the label's size is specified in the resource file, this specification is only valid until the new string is loaded.[11] At that time, the label recomputes its size to accommodate its new string — and the new size happens to be smaller than the desired size. To avoid this problem, you must explicitly set `recomputeSize` to `FALSE`.

Using *XmLabel* with Pictures

In addition to displaying textual labels, an *XmLabel* widget is capable of displaying graphical labels. This capability is useful for icons, especially in the case of buttons. As an example, Figure 5.6 shows a pixmap label displaying the X logo.

---

[11] Remember, if a label is created without an explicit value for `labelString`, it defaults to its given name.

Figure 5.6. Sample pixmap label

This example was produced using the program of Listing 5.1, along with the resource file of Listing 5.7. The label's height and width were changed to accommodate the logo (which is a 64 x 64 bitmap), but the only real changes were the addition of `labelType` and `labelPixmap` specifications and the removal of the `labelString` specification.

Listing 5.7. Resource file used to produce Figure 5.6

```
!
! Resource file to produce Figure 5.6
!

*TheLabel.height:        100
*TheLabel.width:         100

*TheLabel.labelType:     PIXMAP
*TheLabel.labelPixmap:   xlogo64
```

The `labelPixmap` resource requires some explanation. This resource is specified in a resource file as a filename. If the file is fully identified (*ie*, with path information), then it is loaded. If, however, just the filename is specified, then the resource manager looks for a file in one of the following directories, in the order given:[12]

1) `/usr/lib/X11/`*lang*`/bitmaps/`*image_name*`/`*class_name*

2) `/usr/lib/X11/`*lang*`/bitmaps/`*image_name*

---

[12] In the *Programmer's Reference*, this sequence is documented under `XmGetPixmap`(3X).

3)   `/usr/lib/X11/bitmaps/`*image_name*

4)   `/usr/include/X11/bitmaps/`*image_name*

In the above list, *lang* represents the contents of the `LANG` environment variable, *image_name* is the filename specified for the resource, and *class_name* is the class name of the program. In Listing 5.7, `/usr/include/X11/bitmaps/xlogo64,` was the expanded name of the bitmap file.[13]

One caveat about this resource: its name is misleading. Although the name indicates that the resource is a *pixmap*, under Motif 1.0 the image must be a *bitmap*.[14] If you attempt to specify a multicolor pixmap, you will get nothing (the label's contents will be blank).

---

[13] This file is one of the bitmaps released with the standard X distribution. Your system should have it.

[14] A *pixmap* is an image that uses multiple bits per pixel; it can therefore hold a color image. A *bitmap* is an image that uses a single bit per pixel; it can only hold a two-color (foreground and background) image. Bitmaps may be created using the `bitmap` program, which is part of the standard X distribution.

6
Managers

Overview

Management in the Motif world is similar to management in the business world. In both, managers exist in hierarchical organizations: the corporation and instance tree. A business manager is responsible for representing his or her department to the rest of the corporation and for delegating work to subordinates. In Motif, a manager widget is responsible for acquiring window space for its children and then distributing that space among them.

Inheritance

In Motif, manager widgets are subclasses of the *XmManager* widget class. Figure 6.1 shows the managers covered in this chapter in the context of the Motif class tree.

As their names indicate, *Composite* and *Constraint* are defined by the X toolkit, whereas *XmManager* and its subclasses are specific to Motif. *Composite* provides the capability for a widget to have children, and *Constraint* supports management of child geometry. *XmManager* provides support for Motif-specific appearance and action resources, similar to those that *XmPrimitive* provides for primitive widgets.

XmBulletinBoard is the simplest of the manager widgets. It simply provides a window in which children may be placed; in most cases, no geometry management is performed on these children. *XmForm* provides extensive geometry management; it can resize and reposition its children as needed to suit its allotted space.

XmRowColumn is a manager that packs its children together in rows and columns, forming a grid. One of the primary uses for an *XmRowColumn* widget is menu support: the menu bar is a row of widgets, while pull-down and pop-up menus are columns of widgets. This chapter describes *XmRowColumn*'s use in simple tabular displays; its use for menus is postponed to Chapter 12.

Figure 6.1. Motif manager class tree

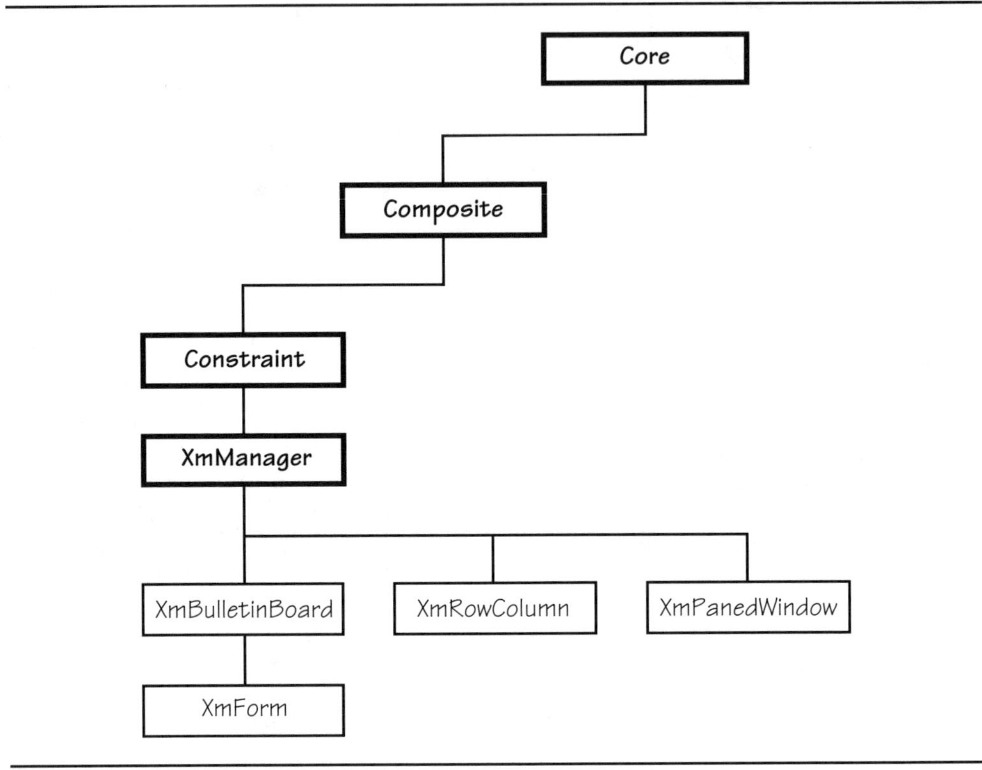

XmPanedWindow arranges its children in a single row, oriented vertically. An *XmPanedWindow* forces the same width on all of its children and divides its total height among them, assigning each a "window pane." While the program is running, the user may change the space allotted to each pane by dragging the pane's "sash" with the pointer.

Constraints: An Overview

Constraints are, as their name suggests, rules that a manager widget imposes on its children. Traditionally, the word "constraint" refers to per-child geometry controls, supported by the *Constraint* superclass. This book expands that definition: the word 'constraint' applies to any rule that a parent uses to modify its children's resources.

Explicit geometry constraints are resources that are provided by the manager widget, but that appear to be provided by the child.[1] Such resources are

---

[1] How is this done? The *Core* class contains a constraints pointer in its instance record. A child of a manager that supports explicit geometry constraints will use this field to point to additional instance data — the explicit constraint resources.

identified by the child's name and are stored in the child's instance data. However, the child does not use these resources. They are used by the manager to control the child's geometry resources (`x`, `y`, `width`, and `height`).

Implicit geometry constraints are resources that are associated with the manager widget and affect the geometry of its children. An example is the margin provided by all Motif managers: this margin essentially reduces the area available to the manager's children. If any child overlaps this margin due to its preferred geometry settings, its geometry is changed such that it no longer overlaps (*ie*, it will be moved into the area bordered by the margin).

Finally, *non-geometry constraints* are resources associated with the manager that contain values to be stored in the child's instance data. An example is *XmRowColumn*'s ability to set the `alignment` resource of any of its children that are derived from *XmLabel*. This book does not consider 'dynamic' resources, such as `background`, to be non-geometry constraints, because the child retrieves such values from the parent; constraints are values imposed on the child by the parent.

Management Revisited

What happens when a child is managed? Chapter 4 stated that management is where a widget's parent applies constraints to the widget's geometry and makes it visible. At this point, you understand what these constraints are, and the process of management may be examined in greater detail.

What Happens when a Widget Is Created, Managed, and Realized

As stated at the beginning of this chapter, only widget classes derived from *Composite* may have children, because the *Composite* class supplies the mechanisms by which a list of children is maintained. When a widget is created, the creation function allocates and initializes the structures associated with the widget instance, then stores a pointer to the instance in its parent's list of children.

Management is the process by which the parent allocates its window space among its children, and this allocation can only happen once the parent is realized and has a window on the server.[2] However, you call `XtManageChild` immediately upon widget creation, which occurs (usually) before realization — what happens then?

Widgets are created unmanaged; a flag in the widget instance data indicates its state. If, at the time of the call to `XtManageChild`, the parent is not realized, this flag is set to `TRUE`, but nothing else happens. When the parent is realized — or if it is already realized when the child is managed — then the parent

---

[2] This point has important ramifications for debugging. If, for example, you place a breakpoint before the call to `XtRealizeWidget`, you will not be able to learn any useful information about actual widget geometry. You must place the breakpoint after the widget geometry is determined, which happens after the call to `XtRealizeWidget`. As a practical matter, communication between the client and server must have taken place also; `XtRealizeWidget` does not do this automatically, so you must either call `XSync` or place the breakpoint in the event loop.

adjusts the geometry of *all* children. This is done because each child may affect the geometry of its siblings; the parent is responsible for resolving such disputes.

This in part explains why it is better to perform widget creation and management before realization. If management was performed after realization, each call to `XtManageChild` would result in geometry recalculation for all existing children, which could result in a huge amount of client-server interaction.

Geometry Negotiation

The simple term 'geometry management' covers a complex process of negotiation for window space. Each manager in the instance tree must put in a space request to its parent, based on the space requests passed to it by its children. It may or may not receive the requested space, but must distribute what it gets to its children. To understand the process, keep the following rules in mind:

1) The window manager makes the ultimate decision on how much space is granted to the program. When the program first starts, the window manager grants space on the root window, based on the size requested by the application shell.[3] If the shell asks for too much space (*eg*, a window larger than the screen), its request will be denied — but it will be given what space is available. In addition, the user can physically change a client's size while it is running.

   As a result, the shell must be prepared to accept whatever space it is granted, as well as any changes made by the user. It passes the allotted (or changed) size to its child, which makes suballotments and passes them to its children, and so on.

2) X maintains a tree of windows, with the root window as the root of the tree. No window in this tree may be larger than its parent. This has the obvious effect in Motif: because a widget's window is the child of its parent's window, no widget may have a window larger than that of its parent. Since the application shell is the root of a program's window tree, and since the shell's window may change under user control, it follows that each manager in the tree must be prepared to have its window size changed while the program is running.

3) If able, a manager widget will initially size its window such that all of its children may be arranged according to their preferred geometry. In other words, a manager grows to fit its children, unless prevented from doing so. It may be prevented by its parent or by an explicit size specification (*ie*, a manager that has an explicit size specification of 100x100 cannot display five 50x50 labels).

4) Each widget in the instance tree has a preferred geometry, reflected by its `x`, `y`, `width`, and `height` resources. These resources may be set

---

[3] The specific algorithm depends on the design goals of the window manager. The Motif window manager (*mwm*) will almost always give the application shell all the space that it desires, even if that allotment means that part of the shell's window extends off the screen.

explicitly by the programmer, implicitly due to widget design (*eg*, the `recomputeSize` resource of *XmLabel*) or as a result of constraints applied by the widget's manager.

Looking at these rules, you can see that, in general, a manager's children determine the size of the manager. Taking this idea one step further, you can see that the size of a program's window is determined by the leaves of the instance tree — provided the result is acceptable to the window manager and is not changed by the user. This means that a programmer must design a program's interface in such a way as to remain consistent, no matter what the user does.

Unmanagement

Unmanagement is the process by which a widget is removed from its parent's list of managed children. In the process, the widget is made invisible, and the geometry of its siblings is recomputed by the parent.[4] Note that unmanagement *does not* remove the widget from its parent's list of children — once the parent-child relationship is established, it cannot be broken without destroying the child.

Unmanagement is initiated in one of two ways: either explicitly by the programmer or implicitly at the time of widget destruction. Explicit unmanagement is performed with the functions `XtUnmanageChild` and `XtUnmanageChildren`, prototyped in Listing 6.1. These functions have the same parameters as their counterparts for management.

Listing 6.1. Function prototypes: *XtUnmanageChild* and *XtUnmanageChildren*

```
void     XtUnmanageChild( w );
         Widget      w;


void     XtUnmanageChildren( children, num_children )
         Widget       children[];
         Cardinal     num_children;
```

Explicit unmanagement is often used when changing the contents of a manager widget while the program is running. If the widget remains managed while these changes take place, program efficiency is impaired because each change requires geometry recalculation, and the user is often able to see the changes as they are performed.

---

[4] Again, geometry calculations only take place when the parent is realized.

Management vs. *Mapping*

A widget must be managed to be visible, but management does not automatically make a widget visible. To be visible, a widget must be both managed and *mapped*. Normally, mapping occurs during management, based on the value of the `mappedWhenManaged` resource.[5] The default value of this resource is `TRUE`, which means that the widget will always be mapped when it is managed.

Mapping is separate from management for both efficiency and aesthetic reasons. The efficiency concerns are easy to understand: managing and unmanaging a widget means that the geometry of all of the widget's siblings must be recalculated. The aesthetic reason is also due to geometry computation: in many cases, a widget's siblings will "fill in" the space left by an unmanaged widget, changing the appearance of the program.

As a general rule, if you simply want to make widgets visible or invisible while the program is running, use mapping instead of management. If you need to recompute geometry each time, or if you are making extensive changes to a manager widget, use management. Listing 6.2 contains prototypes for the functions that map and unmap a widget; the widget's ID is the sole argument to both.

Listing 6.2. Function prototypes: *XtMapWidget* and *XtUnmapWidget*

```
void    XtMapWidget( w )
        Widget     w;


void    XtUnmapWidget( w );
        Widget     w;
```

Measurement: The *unitType* Resource

As stated in Chapter 5, the default form of measurement in a Motif program is in terms of screen pixels. This means that program appearance differs depending on the resolution of the screen: using constant pixel measurements, objects on a 75 dpi screen are 25% larger than on a 100 dpi screen. At that time, however, it was mentioned that the `unitType` resource allows other terms for measurement. Specifically, it allows measurements in terms of screen pixels (the default), millimeters, inches, points, or an abstract unit based on font size.

The `unitType` resource is defined by both the *XmPrimitive* and the *XmManager* classes (as well as the *XmGadget* class), so it is present in all Motif classes. Moreover, each child defaults its `unitType` value to that of its parent; setting `unitType` at the top of the instance tree will cause it to be set throughout.

---

[5] This resource is defined by the *Core* class and is present in all widgets.

It is important to note, however, that the resources holding a widget's size and position are defined by the *Core* class, which is *not* part of Motif. This means that, internally, size and position are held in terms of screen pixels — they are converted between this representation and the user-specified representation on an as-needed basis. In some cases, conversion will result in a loss of accuracy — on a 75 dpi screen, 10 points become 10.4 pixels, which is rounded to 10.[6]

Unit Types

The valid values for the `unitType` resource are as follows:

- `XmPIXELS`. The default unit of measure, representing counts of screen pixels. As described above, this form of measurement is display dependent — an effect especially noticeable when text is specified by point size but widgets are specified by pixel size.

- `Xm100TH_MILLIMETERS`. All measurements are in terms of $\frac{1}{100}$th of a millimeter, meaning that a measurement of one inch is represented by the value 2540.

- `Xm1000TH_INCH`. All measurements are in terms of $\frac{1}{1000}$th of an inch, meaning that a measurement of one inch is represented by the value 1000.

- `Xm100TH_POINTS`. All measurements are in terms of $\frac{1}{100}$th of a point, meaning that a measurement of one inch is represented by the value 7200. This value is especially convenient when working with text, since text is traditionally identified by point size.

- `Xm100TH_FONT_UNITS`. All measurements are in terms of $\frac{1}{100}$th of the 'quad width' of a specified font. The quad width is the width of the character 'M,' which is the widest character in any font.[7]

The XmConvertUnits *Function*

The function `XmConvertUnits`, prototyped in Listing 6.3, allows a program to convert values between unit types. It takes information about the context for conversion (the screen resolution and units from- and to-), along with the value, and returns the converted value.

---

[6] This effect is rarely a problem as far as widget layout is concerned because all measurements will be changed in the same way. However, if you read-change-write a widget's size and/or position resources while the program is running, the widget could "creep."

[7] Although this value would appear to be very useful in text-based applications, its usefulness is limited by its implementation. First, a single font unit is applied to all measurements in the program (*ie,* the font used by an individual widget does not affect measurements for that widget). Second, the font must be explicitly set using either the `XmSetFontUnit` function call or the font resource (which is separate from `fontList`; font is used solely to set the conversion size).

Listing 6.3. Function prototype: *XmConvertUnits*

```
int      XmConvertUnits( w, orientation, from_units, value, to_units )
         Widget      w;
         int         orientation;
         int         from_units;
         int         value;
         int         to_units;
```

The `w` and `orientation` parameters provide information about the screen resolution. Any widget will suffice for `w`; the application shell is a good choice. `Orientation` must contain one of the constants `XmHORIZONTAL` or `XmVERTICAL` — if the screen's horizontal resolution is different from its vertical resolution, the choice is important, otherwise either will do.

The `from_units` and `to_units` parameters must be from the list of unit types above. Since this function is called from program code, you must remember the `Xm` prefix. Finally, the `value` argument is the value that you wish to convert.

If any of the arguments are invalid, `XmConvertUnits` returns zero. Otherwise, it returns the converted value.

How to Use unitType

Unfortunately for the programmer, the Motif design team decided not to provide direct resource-file support for unit types. As a result, if you try to specify a `unitType` value in a resource file, you will get an error message.[8] To make use of the `unitType` resource, you must either set it programmatically or install a *resource converter*.

The `unitType` resource may be set programmatically using the technique described in Chapter 3. You can set it in the application shell, and this setting will be propagated to all widgets in the program.[9]

If you plan to use different `unitType` settings in different parts of the instance tree, or if you want to keep all resource specifications in the resource file, installing a resource converter is the best approach. Resource converters are functions that translate values specified by a resource file into their internal representations; they are described in detail in Chapter 16.

---

[8] The specific message is "X Toolkit Warning: No type converter registered for 'String' to 'unitType' conversion", indicating that the toolkit does not know how to convert the name of the value (which is an ASCII string in the resource file) to its actual value.

[9] You may wonder how this can happen, since the *ApplicationShell* class is defined by the intrinsics and not Motif. In actuality, *ApplicationShell* is a Motif widget class — its purpose is defined by the intrinsics, but its implementation depends on the toolkit in use.

Motif provides a resource converter for the `unitType` resource, `XmCvtStringToUnitType`. To use it in your program, include the contents of Listing 6.4 *after* the call to `XtInitialize` but *before* any other widgets are created.

Listing 6.4. Installing *XmCvtStringToUnitType* as a resource converter

```
XtAddConverter( XmRString, XmRUnitType,
                XmCvtStringToUnitType, NULL, 0 );
```

XmBulletinBoard

The *XmBulletinBoard* class is the simplest of the Motif managers. It is very similar to a real-world bulletin board: it is a location where things can be placed, without concern for how they are placed. *XmBulletinBoard* has few geometry constraints; it will move children that are placed in its "margin," and it can prevent a child from moving and overlapping another child, but usually it allows children to have their preferred geometry.

Because of its simplicity, *XmBulletinBoard* is rarely used in a "stand-alone" manner as a program's main window. Instead, it is used as the superclass for other widget classes, such as *XmForm*, and in dialogs. This chapter examines *XmBulletinBoard* as a stand-alone widget; Chapter 13 describes its use in dialogs.

Resource Table

Table 6.1 contains resources useful with a "stand alone" instance of *XmBulletinBoard*. Additional resources are used when the bulletin board is part of a dialog; they are described in Chapter 13.

Table 6.1. Frequently used resources: *XmBulletinBoard*

Name	Inheritance	Type	Default Value
allowOverlap	XmBulletinBoard	Boolean	TRUE
marginHeight	XmBulletinBoard	short	10
marginWidth	XmBulletinBoard	short	10
resizePolicy	XmBulletinBoard	unsigned char	XmRESIZE_ANY
shadowType	XmBulletinBoard	unsigned char	XmSHADOW_OUT
bottomShadow Color	XmManager	Pixel	*dynamic*
foreground	XmManager	Pixel	*dynamic*
shadowThickness	XmManager	short	0
topShadowColor	XmManager	Pixel	*dynamic*
unitType	XmManager	unsigned char	XmPIXELS
background	Core	Pixel	*dynamic*
height	Core	Dimension	0
width	Core	Dimension	0
x	Core	Position	0
y	Core	Position	0

Geometry Resources: height, width, x, y

As with *XmLabel*, the size of a bulletin board is specified by its geometry
resources, defined by *Core*. These resources may be set explicitly or by
parental constraint. As with any widget, constraints take precedence over
explicit settings.

Shadow Border: shadowThickness, topShadowColor, bottomShadowColor, shadowType

Part of the distinctive appearance of a Motif program comes from its shadow
border, inherited from the HP widget set. This shadow border is drawn inside
the widget using a color scheme that is by default based on the widget's
background color. In all cases, the shadow's "light source" appears to be
coming from the top-left corner of the screen; depending on the shadow type,

the widget may appear to be protruding from the screen, inset into the screen, or set off from the rest of the screen by a "groove" or "ridge" meant to simulate the joints in panels.

The thickness of this shadow border is determined by the `shadowThickness` resource. This resource holds a count of pixels, which is converted according to the current unit type. The thickness of the border influences the three-dimensional effect: a thin border may be almost unnoticeable, while a too-thick border is distracting.

The shadow's color scheme is specified by the `topShadowColor` and `bottomShadowColor` resources. By default, the values of these resources are dynamically assigned, based on the background color: `topShadowColor` is lighter than the background, while `bottomShadowColor` is darker. If you do not like the dynamic values, you are free to change them; specifications in a resource file override the default settings.

The names `topShadowColor` and `bottomShadowColor` are actually misnomers. For a protruding shadow, they are accurate: `topShadowColor` is used for the top and left sides of the shadow, while `bottomShadowColor` is used for the bottom and right sides. However, for an inset shadow, they are reversed, and `topShadowColor` is actually used for the bottom shadow. While this may be confusing, if their names were truly consistent with their usage, you would have to change shadow colors depending on the widget; with the current design, three resource specifications can set a color scheme for an entire program.

The `shadowType` resource controls the appearance of the shadow border. As described above, the border can make the widget appear to be inset or protruding, or it can simply be a line around the widget that separates it from the rest of the screen. The constants producing each type of shadow are as follows:

- `XmSHADOW_IN`. The bulletin board appears to be inset from the rest of the screen.

- `XmSHADOW_OUT`. The bulletin board appears to be protruding from the rest of the screen. This is the default value.

- `XmSHADOW_ETCHED_IN`. The bulletin board appears to be flush with the rest of the screen, but is separated from the rest of the screen by an inset border.

- `XmSHADOW_ETCHED_OUT`. The bulletin board appears to be flush with the rest of the screen, but is separated from the rest of the screen by a protruding border.

You should note that shadow borders are not specific to the bulletin-board class: the shadow resources are defined by *XmManager*, which means that all manager widgets can use them. In addition, *XmPrimitive* defines a shadow border, although it is more limited than that defined by *XmManager*, and its implementation depends on the specific widget: *XmLabel* does not allow any shadow border, while *XmPushButton* uses its border to provide feedback on "presses."

Implicit Geometry Constraints: allowOverlap, marginHeight, marginWidth

The `allowOverlap` resource controls whether a child of the bulletin board is permitted to request a size or position that overlaps that of another widget. This only affects widgets that attempt to move or resize after realization; initial placement is not affected. If this resource contains `TRUE`, the geometry request is ignored, and the widget keeps its former geometry.

The resources `marginHeight` and `marginWidth` specify a border between the edge of the bulletin board and its contents. If a child's geometry would make it overlap the margin, then that child's geometry is changed so that it won't overlap.[10] The default size of the margin is ten pixels, converted according to the unit type in effect.

Bulletin Board Geometry Control: resizePolicy

The `resizePolicy` resource controls whether or not the bulletin board will grow or shrink as children are added and removed. Valid values for this resource are as follows:

- `XmRESIZE_NONE`. The bulletin board will not grow or shrink as children are added or removed. Its initial size is set either explicitly or by parental constraint, and it will grow or shrink as commanded by its parent.

- `XmRESIZE_ANY`. The bulletin board determines its initial size from the preferred geometry of its children and will grow or shrink depending on the number of managed children — provided that it is permitted by parental constraint. This is the default value.

- `XmRESIZE_GROW`. The bulletin board will attempt to grow as children are added, but will not shrink if they are removed. Again, size-changes are subject to parental constraint.

XmBulletinBoard Examples

Three Labels and a Bulletin Board

Figure 6.2 contains a single bulletin board and its three label children. These children are the same size, but differ in color. The bulletin-board's margin has been set to zero to permit the children to be arranged as shown.

---

[10] This constraint is applied from the time of realization, unlike allowOverlap.

Figure 6.2. Three labels and a bulletin-board

The program and resource file responsible for Figure 6.2 are shown in Listing 6.5. Note that all labels are managed at the same time, using `XtManageChildren`. They could be managed individually, with little decrease in program efficiency, but I chose the all-at-once method to minimize the number of lines of code.

Listing 6.5. Program and resource file: Three labels and a bulletin board

```
/************************************************************************
**                                                                    **
**   listing_6_5.c                                                    **
**                                                                    **
**   Three labels and a Bulletin Board. This program demonstrates the **
**   use of XmBulletinBoard.                                          **
**                                                                    **
************************************************************************/
```

Listing 6.5. Continued.

```c
#include <Xm/BulletinB.h>
#include <Xm/Label.h>


Widget  appshell,                          /* Application Shell      */
        the_bb,                            /* The Bulletin Board     */
        labels[3];                         /* The children           */


void main( argc, argv )
    int     argc;
    char    *argv[];
{
    appshell = XtInitialize( argv[0], "Listing_6_5", NULL, 0,
                                            &argc, argv );

    the_bb = XmCreateBulletinBoard( appshell, "TheBB", NULL, 0 );
    XtManageChild( the_bb );

    labels[0] = XmCreateLabel( the_bb, "Label_0", NULL, 0 );
    labels[1] = XmCreateLabel( the_bb, "Label_1", NULL, 0 );
    labels[2] = XmCreateLabel( the_bb, "Label_2", NULL, 0 );
    XtManageChildren( labels, 3 );

    XtRealizeWidget( appshell );
    XtMainLoop();
}
```

```
!
! Resource file used to produce Figure 6.2
!

*TheBB.marginWidth:     0
*TheBB.marginHeight:    0
*XmLabel.height:        50*XmLabel.width: 100

*Label_0.x:             0
*Label_0.y:             0
*Label_0.background:    red

*Label_1.x:             100
*Label_1.y:             50
```

Listing 6.5. Continued.

```
*Label_1.background:     white

*Label_2.x:              200
*Label_2.y:              100
*Label_2.background:     blue
```

Chinese Bulletin Boards

Figure 6.3 contains an example of each shadow border supported by
XmBulletinBoard. This program uses five bulletin boards, each containing a
single child, much like a set of Chinese boxes. The outermost bulletin board
doesn't have a shadow border; each of the others has a unique border. These
borders are exaggerated by the thickness of the shadows and the width of the
bulletin-boards' margins.

Figure 6.3. Chinese bulletin boards

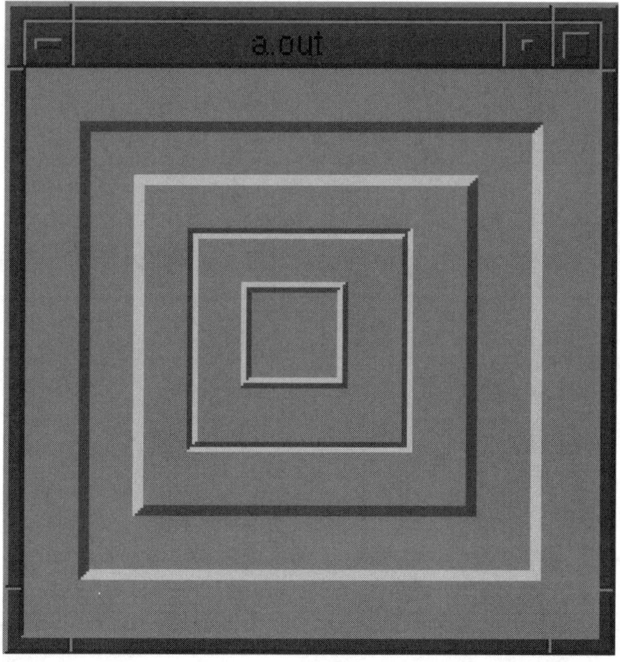

The program and resource file are shown in Listing 6.6. Note the class-wide resource specifications: this program is a perfect example of when to use them. Note also that the shadow was removed from the topmost bulletin board by setting its thickness to zero — there is no shadowType value to do this.

Listing 6.6. Program and resource file: Chinese bulletin boards

```
/**********************************************************************
**                                                                  **
**   listing_6_6.c                                                  **
**                                                                  **
**   "Chinese Bulletin Boards". This program demonstrates the shadow **
**   borders provided by XmBulletinBoard (and other managers), using **
**   a series of "stacked" bulletin boards                          **
**                                                                  **
***********************************************************************/


#include <Xm/BulletinB.h>


Widget  appshell,                        /* Application Shell       */
        bb0, bb1, bb2, bb3, bb4;         /* The Bulletin Boards     */


void main( argc, argv )
    int     argc;
    char    *argv[];
{
    appshell = XtInitialize( argv[0], "Listing_6_6", NULL, 0,
                                            &argc, argv );

    bb0 = XmCreateBulletinBoard( appshell, "BB0", NULL, 0 );
    XtManageChild( bb0 );

    bb1 = XmCreateBulletinBoard( bb0, "BB1", NULL, 0 );
    XtManageChild( bb1 );
    bb2 = XmCreateBulletinBoard( bb1, "BB2", NULL, 0 );
    XtManageChild( bb2 );

    bb3 = XmCreateBulletinBoard( bb2, "BB3", NULL, 0 );
    XtManageChild( bb3 );
```

Listing 6.6. Continued.

```
    bb4 = XmCreateBulletinBoard( bb3, "BB4", NULL, 0 );
    XtManageChild( bb4 );

    XtRealizeWidget( appshell );
    XtMainLoop();
}
```

```
!
! Resource file used to produce Figure 6.3
!

*XmBulletinBoard.marginWidth:          20
*XmBulletinBoard.marginHeight:         20
*XmBulletinBoard.background:           Gray50
*XmBulletinBoard.topShadowColor:       Gray75
*XmBulletinBoard.bottomShadowColor:    Gray25
*XmBulletinBoard.shadowThickness:      4

*BB0.shadowThickness:    0
*BB1.shadowType:         SHADOW_IN
*BB2.shadowType:         SHADOW_OUT
*BB3.shadowType:         SHADOW_ETCHED_IN
*BB4.shadowType:         SHADOW_ETCHED_OUT
```

XmRowColumn

XmRowColumn is a manager that arranges its children into linear or rectangular arrays, as shown in Figure 6.4. The primary use of *XmRowColumn* is in program menus: a horizontally oriented row-column holds the buttons comprising the menu bar, and vertically oriented row-columns hold the individual "pull-down" menus. Chapter 12 describes the use of *XmRowColumn* with menus; this chapter describes its generic use as a means of organizing children in a tabular layout.

Figure 6.4. Examples of *XmRowColumn* widgets

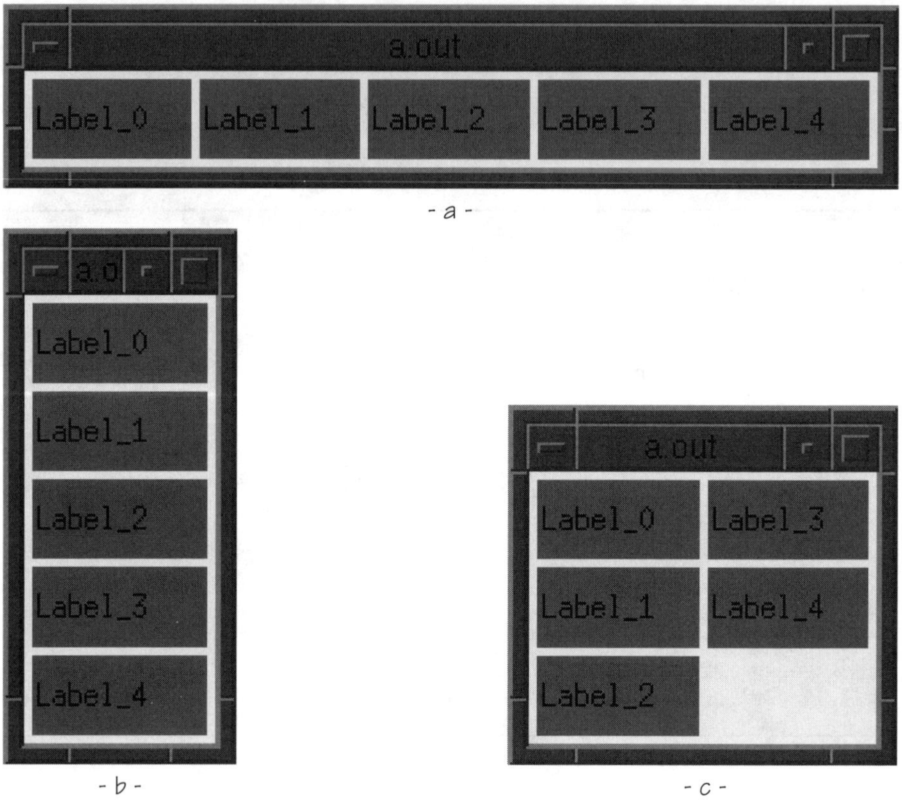

Resource Table

Table 6.2 contains resources useful with a "stand-alone" instance of *XmRowColumn*. For brevity, those from *Core* and *XmManager* are not listed here. Additionally, description of resources specific to use of *XmRowColumn* as a menu is postponed until Chapter 12.

Table 6.2. Frequently used resources: *XmRowColumn*

Name	Inheritance	Type	Default Value
`adjustLast`	**XmRowColumn**	`Boolean`	`TRUE`
`entryAlignment`	**XmRowColumn**	`unsigned char`	*dynamic*
`isAligned`	**XmRowColumn**	`Boolean`	`TRUE`
`marginHeight`	**XmRowColumn**	`Dimension`	`3`
`marginWidth`	**XmRowColumn**	`Dimension`	`3`
`numColumns`	**XmRowColumn**	`short`	`1`
`orientation`	**XmRowColumn**	`unsigned char`	*per* `rowColumnType`
`packing`	**XmRowColumn**	`unsigned char`	`XmPACK_TIGHT`
`radioAlwaysOne`	**XmRowColumn**	`Boolean`	`TRUE`
`radioBehavior`	**XmRowColumn**	`Boolean`	`FALSE`
`resizeHeight`	**XmRowColumn**	`Boolean`	`TRUE`
`resizeWidth`	**XmRowColumn**	`Boolean`	`TRUE`
`rowColumnType`	**XmRowColumn**	`unsigned char`	`XmWORK_AREA`
`spacing`	**XmRowColumn**	`short`	`1`

Usage: rowColumnType

This resource specifies the way that the widget is used. The default value is `XmWORK_AREA`, indicating that it is used as a generic table. The complete set of values and their meanings is as follows:

- `XmWORK_AREA`. The row-column widget is used as a generic table and may contain children from any widget class. Its layout is dictated by the resources numColumns, orientation, and packing.

- `XmMENU_BAR`. The row-column widget is used to hold "pull-down" menu choices. It is oriented horizontally, is of fixed width (determined by the programmer), and contains one or more rows, depending on the number of children. Children must be of class *XmCascadeButton.*

- `XmMENU_PULLDOWN`. The row-column widget is used to hold a "pull-down" menu. It is oriented vertically, its width is dependent on the size of the longest child, and its height depends on the number of children. Children may be from any widget class.

- XmMENU_POPUP. The row-column widget is used to hold a menu formatted as a table, which will "pop up" under program control. It is oriented vertically (although this can be changed), and its width and height are determined by the programmer. Children may be from any widget class.

- XmMENU_OPTION. The row-column widget is used as an option menu: a combination of a label identifying the menu, a button that both displays the current choice and enables a submenu of choices, and the submenu itself. The geometry of the row-column that holds these children is determined by the width and height of the label and button children; the submenu appears when invoked and overlaps the option menu.

Layout: numColumns, orientation, packing

An *XmRowColumn* widget arranges its children by order of creation. The first child is positioned at the top left of the row-column, and the last child is positioned at the bottom right. The arrangement of intermediate children depends on the resources orientation, packing, and numColumns.

A row-column's orientation resource specifies whether children are sequenced in *column-major* or *row-major* order. Figure 6.5 diagrams the difference: column-major ordering places each widget below the preceding one, starting a new column as needed, whereas row-major places each child to the right of the previous, starting a new row as needed. Figure 6.4 shows examples of both types of ordering: 6.4(a) is an example of row-major ordering, while (b) and (c) are column-major.

Figure 6.5. Diagram of column-major and row-major ordering

Column-Major		Row-Major	
First	Fourth	First	Second
Second	Fifth	Third	Fourth
Third	Sixth	Fifth	Sixth

An orientation value of XmVERTICAL specifies column-major ordering, while XmHORIZONTAL specifies row-major ordering.[11] The direction specified by orientation is known as the row-column's *major dimension* — the direction in

---

[11] A row-column is normally identified by its orientation, rather than the ordering of its children. The ordering is a result of the orientation.

which it prefers to grow. The *minor dimension* is the other direction — width for a vertical row-column, height for a horizontal row-column.

Given an ordering method specified by `orientation`, the `packing` resource specifies how the row-column's available space is divided among its children. Permissible values are as follows:

- `XmPACK_TIGHT`. This is the default value and specifies that the row-column attempts to pack its children as tightly as possible. If space is available, the children will be ordered in a single row or column, as exampled by Figures 6.4(a) and (b).

  In most cases, however, the row-column will not be able to produce such an ordering — either its parent will not provide it with enough linear space, or its size will have been set by the programmer. In this situation, the row-column arranges its children by starting in the top left corner and adding children as dictated by its orientation. When lack of space makes it unable to add another child in its major dimension, it starts a new row or column — a vertical row-column starts a new column to the right of the first child, a horizontal row-column starts a new row below the first child. Arrangement of children proceeds in this fashion, with new rows/columns added as needed. If the row-column runs out of space in its minor dimension, it continues to place children, but they are not visible unless the row-column is permitted to grow.

  Under tight packing, children are allowed to specify their own dimension in the major direction, but the row-column sizes each child identically in the minor direction. Taking the example of a column-major ordering [as in Figure 6.4(b)], each child may specify its own height, but the row-column widget sets its width. The width used is that of the widest child; the rest of the children are expanded as necessary.

- `XmPACK_COLUMN`. This value specifies that the row-column divides its available space into identically sized boxes. Each child is placed into one of these boxes, starting at the top left and proceeding according to orientation. As the row-column must divide its space into a whole number of rows and columns, boxes may be left empty, as shown by Figure 6.4(c).

  Each child is expanded or contracted to fit the size of its box. If the row-column's size has been set explicitly, the size of each box is calculated from this total size. If, on the other hand, the row-column sizes itself to fit its children, the size of each box is the size of the largest child.

- `XmPACK_NONE`. This value specifies that the row-column will not attempt to perform any ordering of its children. In such a case, orientation is ignored, and the row-column essentially becomes a bulletin board.

The `numColumns` resource is only applicable to row-columns with `packing` of `XmPACK_COLUMN`; for `XmPACK_TIGHT` and `XmPACK_NONE` it is ignored. Its purpose is to specify how the row-column divides its space between rows and columns.

Its name is somewhat misleading: in actuality, its meaning depends on orientation. If the row-column is vertically oriented (column-major), `numColumns` specifies the number of columns. For horizontally oriented (row-major) row-columns, it specifies the number of rows. Given the division of the major dimension, the division of the minor dimension may be determined.[12]

Row-Column Geometry Controls: resizeHeight, resizeWidth

Under normal circumstances, a row-column widget resizes itself as needed to display all of its children at their desired sizes, unless prevented from doing so by its parent. The resources `resizeHeight` and `resizeWidth` are responsible for this behavior: when they contain `TRUE` (the default), the specified dimension will resize as children are added or removed. When they contain `FALSE`, the specified dimension remains at its initial size (or the size set by its parent). If this means that the row-column is unable display all of its children in the allotted space, they are simply not displayed.[13]

Implicit Geometry Constraints: adjustLast, marginHeight, marginWidth, spacing

As described above, a row-column modifies its children's geometry as needed to produce an orderly arrangement. If its packing is `XmPACK_TIGHT`, a child's minor dimension is changed, but its major dimension is left alone. If packing is `XmPACK_COLUMN`, both the major and minor dimensions of a child may be changed. In addition to these constraints, the row-column applies implicit constraints specified by the resources `adjustLast`, `marginHeight`, `marginWidth`, and `spacing`.

Like *XmBulletinBoard*, *XmRowColumn* supports a margin between its outside edge and its children. Also like *XmBulletinBoard*, this margin is specified by the resources `marginHeight` and `marginWidth`. Unlike *XmBulletinBoard*, the default size of this margin is three pixels. Another difference is that, while *XmBulletinBoard* merely moves children that would infringe on its border — and leaves others alone — *XmRowColumn* explicitly uses its border for child placement.

The `spacing` resource specifies the number of pixels of "dead space" on each side of a child. The default value is one pixel, resulting in a two-pixel gap between children.[14] This spacing may be seen quite clearly in Figure 6.4.

The final child constraint resource, `adjustLast`, is used to eliminate dead space between the last row or column of children and the side of the row-column. When this resource contains `TRUE` (the default value), the minor dimension of the children comprising this row-column is expanded until the right (or bottom) edge of each child touches the inside of the row-column's margin.

---

[12] Using Figure 6.4(c) as an example: The number of children is five, the orientation is vertical, and the number of columns is specified as two. The number of rows is determined to be three, providing enough space for all children with a minimal amount of wasted space.

[13] But they are placed and will be displayed if the row-column is allowed to grow.

[14] Unless the row-column is being used as a menu bar (`rowColumnType` contains `XmMENU_BAR`), in which case the default spacing is 0 pixels (resulting in an uninterrupted list of menu titles).

Figure 6.6 shows `adjustLast` in use. In both cases, the row-column was initially sized based on its children and then expanded. In 6.6(a), `adjustLast` was `TRUE`, and children in the second row were expanded. In 6.6(b), `adjustLast` was `FALSE`, so the children were left alone — and the new space was filled with the row-column's background color.

Figure 6.6. Different settings for *adjustLast* resource

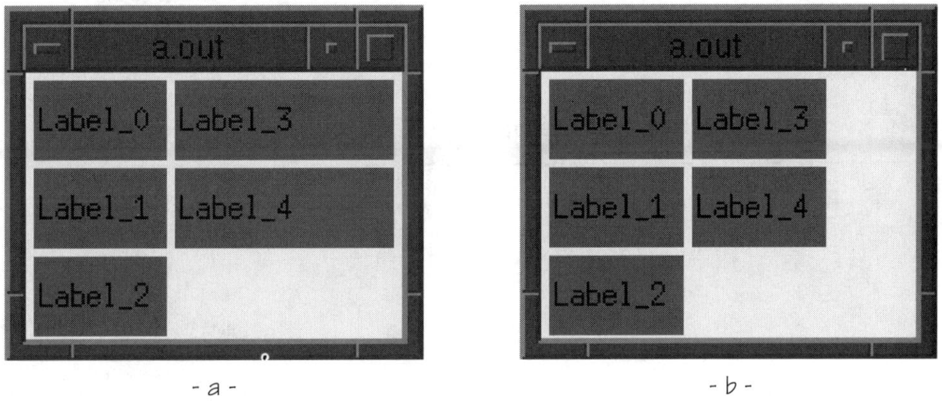

Imposed Child Label Appearance: entryAlignment, isAligned

To maintain a consistent appearance, *XmRowColumn* can modify the `alignment` resource of any children derived from class *XmLabel*. The `isAligned` resource controls whether this modification takes place: if it contains TRUE (the default), modification will take place; if it contains FALSE, the label is able to specify its own alignment.

If `isAligned` contains `TRUE`, `entryAlignment` specifies the value imposed on the alignment resource of the row-column's children. Like the `alignment` resource itself, the legal values for `entryAlignment` are `XmALIGNMENT_BEGINNING`, `XmALIGNMENT_END`, and `XmALIGNMENT_CENTER`. The default entryAlignment value is `XmALIGNMENT_BEGINNING`, unlike the default label alignment of `XmALIGNMENT_CENTER`.

It is important to note that the `entryAlignment` resource is a non-geometry constraint. It will take precedence over the children's alignment resource, even if that resource is set explicitly. While this behavior is reasonable for menus, it may not be reasonable for a tabular array of labels.

Radio-Button Resources: radioBehavior, radioAlwaysOne

As you will see in the next chapter, a row-column can impart special behavior to its children that are toggle buttons (class *XmToggleButton*). These resources are used to control that behavior. Since they only make sense in the context of toggle buttons, their description is postponed to Chapter 7.

XmRowColumn **Examples**

The three examples of Figure 6.4 were produced from a single program, shown in Listing 6.7. The dramatic differences between the samples are a result of resource specifications applied to the row-column widget. These resource files are described below, with suggested experiments. The section finishes with a useful application, modeled after *xfd*.

Listing 6.7. Sample *XmRowColumn* program.

```c
/*****************************************************************
**                                                             **
**   listing_6_7.c                                             **
**                                                             **
**   Lots of labels and a RowColumn widget. This program is the base  **
**   for all of the figures in the section of XmRowColumn.     **
**                                                             **
*****************************************************************/


#include <Xm/RowColumn.h>
#include <Xm/Label.h>


Widget  appshell,                       /* Application Shell      */
        rowcol,                         /* The RowColumn widget   */
        labels[5];                      /* The children           */


void main( argc, argv )
    int     argc;
    char    *argv[];
{
    appshell = XtInitialize( argv[0], "Listing_6_7", NULL, 0,
                                                &argc, argv );

    rowcol = XmCreateRowColumn( appshell, "RowCol", NULL, 0 );
    XtManageChild( rowcol );

    labels[0] = XmCreateLabel( rowcol, "Label_0", NULL, 0 );
    labels[1] = XmCreateLabel( rowcol, "Label_1", NULL, 0 );
    labels[2] = XmCreateLabel( rowcol, "Label_2", NULL, 0 );
```

Listing 6.7. Continued.

```
    labels[3] = XmCreateLabel( rowcol, "Label_3", NULL, 0 );
    labels[4] = XmCreateLabel( rowcol, "Label_4", NULL, 0 );
    XtManageChildren( labels, 5 );

    XtRealizeWidget( appshell );
    XtMainLoop();
}
```

A Single Column

The resource file of Listing 6.8 produced the single column of labels of Figure 6.4(b). As you can see, no resource specifications were applied to the *XmRowColumn*: a vertical orientation with tight packing is the default appearance of an `XmWORK_AREA` row-column. Note that the labels' alignment is `XmALIGNMENT_BEGINNING`, imposed by the row-column.

Note also the explicit value for `recomputeSize`. If you remove this specification, the geometry negotiation between parent and child will result in minimally sized labels, ignoring the explicit size specification.

Listing 6.8. Resource file to produce a single column of labels

```
!
! Resource file used to produce Figure 6.4(b)
!

*XmLabel.height:        30
*XmLabel.width:         60
*XmLabel.background:    Red
*XmLabel.foreground:    Black
*XmLabel.recomputeSize: FALSE
```

As an experiment, try changing the row-column's size using the window frame. Notice how the labels are expanded, due to the `adjustLast` resource. Notice also that, if you shrink the window vertically, the labels are arranged into two columns (parts of which may not be visible). Finally, try expanding the window horizontally to expand the labels. Then shrink it vertically while expanding it horizontally. You will see the labels form into two columns, but they will not contract: when `adjustLast` contains `TRUE`, a row-column will expand its children but not shrink them.

A Single Row

To produce the row of labels from Figure 6.4(a), use the resource file in Listing 6.9. The sole difference is a change to the row-column's `orientation` resource, but the appearance is dramatically different.

Listing 6.9. Resource file to produce single row of labels

```
!
! Resource file used to produce Figure 6.4(a)
!

*XmLabel.height:        30
*XmLabel.width:         60
*XmLabel.background:    Red
*XmLabel.foreground:    Black
*XmLabel.recomputeSize: FALSE


*RowCol.orientation:    HORIZONTAL
```

For further experimentation, try changing some of the other row-column defaults. For example, changing `isAligned` to `FALSE` will permit the labels' default alignment to appear. The row-column's overall appearance may be modified with `marginWidth`, `marginHeight`, **and** `spacing`.

Three Rows, Two Columns

Figure 6.4(c) may be generated with the resource file from Listing 6.10. The big change is the packing method: using `XmPACK_COLUMN` means that the row-column will divide its space equally among its children. Specifying a value for `numColumns` resulted in the tabular array.[15] Note also that the row-column grows to contain its children, since the only absolute size specifications are for the labels — and since the row-column does not have a parent imposing size constraints upon it.

---

[15] `numColumns` defaults to a value of 1, which would produce an output identical to Figure 6.4(b).

Listing 6.10. Resource file to produce tabular arrangement of labels

```
!
! Resource file used to produce Figure 6.4(c)
!

*XmLabel.height:        30
*XmLabel.width:         60
*XmLabel.background:    Red
*XmLabel.foreground:    Black
*XmLabel.recomputeSize: FALSE

*RowCol.packing:        PACK_COLUMN
*RowCol.numColumns:     2
```

As an experiment, change `adjustLast` to `FALSE` and increase the size of the window. Note that the labels remain the same size; `PACK_COLUMN` guarantees that the children are identically sized, and that guarantee takes precedence over `adjustLast`.

Font-Display Program

One of the clients contained in the standard X distribution is *xfd*, a font-display program. When invoked with the name of a font, it displays a table containing the 256 characters that comprise that font. This client may be duplicated in Motif, using an *XmRowColumn* widget and 256 *XmLabel* widgets, as shown in Figure 6.7.

Figure 6.7. A font-display program

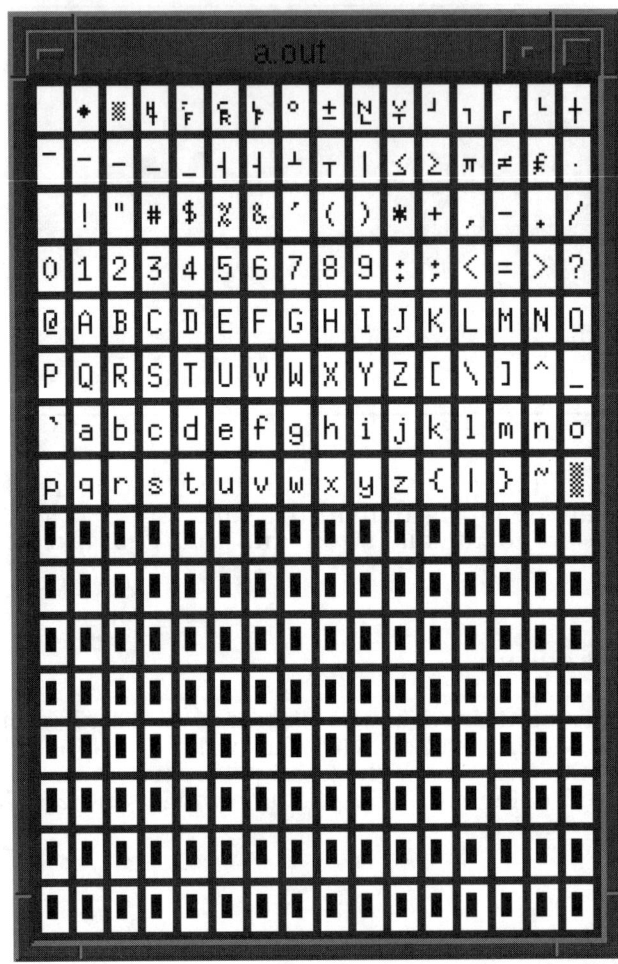

The implementation of this program, shown in Listing 6.11, is relatively straightforward but points out techniques often used by nontrivial Motif programs. In particular, the creation of the labels bears examination.

Listing 6.11. A font-display program

```c
/*******************************************************************
**                                                               **
**   listing_6_11.c                                              **
**                                                               **
**   A replacement for the xfd(1X) program, using an XmRowColumn and **
**   lots of labels.                                             **
**                                                               **
*******************************************************************/


#include <Xm/RowColumn.h>
#include <Xm/Label.h>


Widget       appshell,              /* Application Shell        */
             rowcol,                /* The RowColumn widget     */
             labels[256];           /* The children             */

Arg          arglist[16];           /* Used to set resources    */

int          lbl_num;               /* Used to index labels[]   */
char         c_str[2];              /* Used to build labelString */
XmString     lbl_str;               /* Ditto                    */


void main( argc, argv )
    int     argc;
    char    *argv[];
{
    appshell = XtInitialize( argv[0], "Listing_6_11", NULL, 0,
                                          &argc, argv );
    rowcol = XmCreateRowColumn( appshell, "RowCol", arglist, 1 );
    XtManageChild( rowcol );

    c_str[1] = '\0';
    for (lbl_num = 0 ;  lbl_num < 256 ;  lbl_num++)
        {
        c_str[0] = lbl_num;
```

Listing 6.11. Continued.

```
        lbl_str = XmStringCreate( c_str, XmSTRING_DEFAULT_CHARSET );
        XtSetArg( arglist[0], XmNlabelString, lbl_str );
        labels[lbl_num] = XmCreateLabel( rowcol, "Lbl", arglist, 1 );
        XmStringFree( lbl_str );
        }
    XtManageChildren( labels, 256 );

    XtRealizeWidget( appshell );
    XtMainLoop();
}
```

```
!
! Resource file used to produce Figure 6.7
!

*RowCol.orientation:     HORIZONTAL
*RowCol.packing:         PACK_COLUMN
*RowCol.numColumns:      16
*RowCol.background:      blue
*RowCol.isAligned:       FALSE

*Lbl.foreground:         black
*Lbl.background:         white
```

The first thing to note about the labels is that they all have the same given name. This means that they also all have the same full name (because they are siblings). Looking at the resource file listing, you can see the result of this — a single resource specification is applied to each label. The effect is similar to a class-wide specification, but is limited to only those labels with the same name.

The second thing to note is that the `labelString` resource is set programmatically, at the time of the label's creation. As you can see, this is a complex process: first a C string must be loaded with the character code, then that C string must be converted to an `XmString`, then the label must be created, then the `XmString` must be freed.[16] However, this process — complex though it may be — is certainly less complex than individually setting each label's string in the resource file.

Looking at the resource file, there are four things to note. First, the row-column's packing resource is set to `PACK_COLUMN`. Along with the `numColumns`

---

[16] The value of the `XmString` has been copied into the label's instance data, so the program's copy is no longer needed. Forgetting to free `XmStrings` when they are no longer needed is a common bug, and one that causes a program's memory requirements to grow quickly.

setting of 16, this guarantees that the display will form a 16x16 grid. Second, note that the orientation resource is set to `HORIZONTAL` (`XmHORIZONTAL`). Most ASCII tables are organized by hexadecimal value: the row value is the leftmost nibble of the byte, the column number is the rightmost nibble. Row-major ordering accomplishes this. The third thing to note is that `isAligned` is set to `FALSE`. For this program, I wanted the labels to be centered; leaving `isAligned` as `TRUE` wouldn't allow that.[17]

The third and most subtle thing to note is the fact that the labels aren't sized. Instead, the `recomputeSize` resource is relied upon to set an appropriate size for the specified font. Unfortunately, as may be seen in Figure 6.7, sometimes this does not give the label enough space (note especially the top row, fifth box from the left, where "FF" is only partially displayed). A much more appropriate technique would be to explicitly set the labels' size, based on the font used — say, to 150% of the font's quad width. Unfortunately, there is no simple way to do this under Motif — as stated above, a `unitType` setting of `Xm100TH_FONT_UNITS` will not work.

This brings up the question of how to set the font for display. Figure 6.7 shows the default label font ("Fixed"), which will be displayed if no font is explicitly set. To explicitly set a font, you could either edit the resource file or use a command line like that shown in Listing 6.12, which specifies a 14pt Times Roman font using the *-xrm* command-line option.

Listing 6.12. Sample invocation for font-display program

```
a.out -xrm '*fontList: -*-times-medium-r-*--*-140-*'
```

If you experiment with the fonts supplied by your server, you may be surprised by the following fact: X11 Release 4 fonts do not contain a complete character set! Instead, they contain just the printable ASCII characters — codes 32 to 126.

XmPanedWindow

XmPanedWindow is a manager that arranges its children in a vertical order, as shown in Figure 6.8. Children are ordered from top to bottom by creation order. The initial height of each child may be specified in a resource file or may be determined by dividing the height of the paned window by the number of children. The width of each child is expanded to match that of the widest child.

The user can change a child's height allotment by dragging a window 'sash' — the small box between windows — up or down with a mouse. Each sash controls the border between two children: moving the sash up decreases the size of the upper child, while it increases the size of the lower child.

---

[17] Unless, of course, I also set the `entryAlignment` resource. Allowing the labels to use their default alignment was the easier approach.

Figure 6.8. Example of *XmPanedWindow*

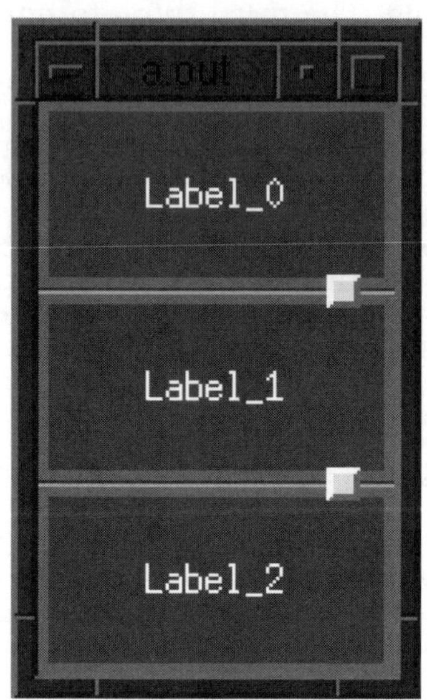

Resource Table

Table 6.3(a) contains those resources defined by *XmPanedWindow*. For brevity, resources inherited from *XmManager* and its superclasses are not shown; they are identical to those shown for *XmBulletinBoard*. Table 6.3(b) describes the explicit constraint resources — those resources associated with the child but defined by *XmPanedWindow*.

Table 6.3a. Frequently used resources: *XmPanedWindow*

Name	Inheritance	Type	Default Value
marginHeight	XmPanedWindow	short	3
marginWidth	XmPanedWindow	short	3
refigureMode	XmPanedWindow	Boolean	TRUE
sashHeight	XmPanedWindow	Dimension	10
sashIndent	XmPanedWindow	Position	-10
sashShadowThickness	XmPanedWindow	int	2
sashWidth	XmPanedWindow	Dimension	10
separatorOn	XmPanedWindow	Boolean	TRUE
spacing	XmPanedWindow	int	8

Table 6.3b. Explicit constraint resources: *XmPanedWindow*

Name	Inheritance	Type	Default Value
`allowResize`	XmPanedWindow	`Boolean`	`TRUE`
`maximum`	XmPanedWindow	`int`	`1000`
`minimum`	XmPanedWindow	`int`	`1`
`skipAdjust`	XmPanedWindow	`Boolean`	`FALSE`

Implicit Geometry Constraints: marginHeight, marginWidth, refigureMode, spacing

XmPanedWindow's `marginHeight`, `marginWidth`, and `spacing` resources are similar to those of *XmRowColumn*. Like *XmRowColumn*, margin width is three pixels. Unlike *XmRowColumn*, the default spacing refers to the total space between two children, not the space on each side of a child. Note that the default value is 8, which gives one pixel of overlap to the default sash height of 10.

The `refigureMode` resource specifies whether the paned window will maintain the relative size of its children when its size is changed programmatically. When `TRUE` (the default), children will be resized appropriately. When `FALSE`, programmatic resizing is performed in the same way as physical resizing: only those children immediately affected are changed.[18]

Sash Appearance: sashIndent, sashHeight, sashWidth, sashShadowThickness, separatorOn

The window sash is the box appearing at the right side of the window. The default size of this box is 10 pixels by 10 pixels, it has a 2-pixel-wide shadow border, and it is positioned 10 pixels in from the right side of the paned window. The sash's color scheme (foreground and shadow, background isn't used) is identical to that of the paned window.

The `sashHeight` and `sashWidth` resources are used to set the sash size — all sashes are the same size. The sash is placed "above" the paned-window's children, so if the sash height is greater than the interwindow space defined

---

[18] This is easier to show than to explain and will become apparent when you compile and run the sample program. While it is running, shrink the window vertically by "pulling up" on the bottom of the window frame. You will see that only the bottom-most child shrinks at first. At some point, it will become only 1 pixel high, at which point the middle child will begin to shrink. When the middle child becomes 1 pixel high, the topmost child will shrink.

by `spacing`, part of the child's window will be obscured.[19] The paned window will correct any "strange" values — if you try to put a 200-pixel-wide sash on a 100-pixel-wide window, the width of the sash will be decreased to fit the window.

The `sashIndent` resource specifies where the sash is to be placed. Positive values specify the distance between the left edge of the paned window and the left edge of the sash. Negative values specify the distance between the right edge of the pane and the right edge of the sash. If the specified value is too large (magnitude greater than the width of the window), then it is replaced by zero.

The `sashShadowThickness` resource specifies the width of the sash's shadow border. This resource is distinct from the `shadowThickness` resource of the paned window (which comes from the *XmManager* superclass). However, the sash shadow and the paned-window shadow both use the same color scheme — there is no way to change the sash's shadow colors other than changing those of the window.

The final sash-related resource is `separatorOn`, which specifies whether a horizontal "groove" is present in the middle of the interchild space. The default value is `TRUE`, with a result as shown in Figure 6.8.

Explicit Geometry Constraints: allowResize, maximum, minimum, skipAdjust

The first explicit geometry constraint, `allowResize`, specifies whether or not the associated child is permitted to resize itself as the program runs. Like the `allowOverlap` resource of *XmBulletinBoard*, `allowResize` is applied only to programmatic size changes (via `XtSetValues`) initiated by the child after realization. If the size change is initiated by the user (via the sash), or if the size change is required by the paned window (as when it is shrunk), the child will be resized regardless of the contents of `allowResize`. The default value of this resource is `FALSE`, meaning that the user and parent are the only ways that a child's size may be changed.

The `maximum` and `minimum` resources set limits on the child's height. Again, these resources only affect programmatic size changes; user- or parent-initiated size changes ignore these limits.[20] The default values are 1000 and 1 pixels, respectively; if these values are changed, `maximum` must remain greater than `minimum` (any requests that violate this rule are ignored).

The final explicit constraint is `skipAdjust`, which controls whether or not a child's size is adjusted automatically when the paned window is resized. If it contains `FALSE` (the default), the child's size is adjusted as described

---

[19] This happens with the default settings: the sash is 10 pixels high, but the interchild spacing is only 8 pixels, so the sash obscures a 1-pixel-high portion of the children above and below it.

[20] Note, however, that the absolute minimum height of a child is 1 pixel. Neither the user nor the paned window can shrink the child below this height.

previously. If it contains TRUE, the child's size is not adjusted until all children with `skipAdjust` of FALSE are adjusted.[21]

XmPanedWindow Example: Three Labels and a Paned Window

Figure 6.8 was produced with the program and resource file shown in Listing 6.13. By now the program should look familiar: it is essentially the same as that in Listings 6.5 and 6.7; only the manager has changed. The resource file leaves most of the paned-window's resources with their default values; it does, however, show the use of explicit geometry constraints, applied to `Label_1`.

Listing 6.13. Program and resource file: *XmPanedWindow* example

```
/*********************************************************************
**                                                                 **
**   listing_6_13.c                                                **
**                                                                 **
**   Three labels and a paned-window. This program demonstrates the **
**   use of XmPanedWindow.                                         **
**                                                                 **
*********************************************************************/


#include <Xm/PanedW.h>
#include <Xm/Label.h>
Widget  appshell,                  /* Application Shell       */
        the_win,                   /* The Paned-Window        */
        labels[3];                 /* The children            */


void main( argc, argv )
    int     argc;
    char    *argv[];
{
    appshell = XtInitialize( argv[0], "Listing_6_13", NULL, 0,
                                                &argc, argv );

    the_win = XmCreatePanedWindow( appshell, "PanedWin", NULL, 0 );
    XtManageChild( the_win );
```

---

[21] Again, this is easier to show than describe. Considering the former example, but with `skipAdjust` set to TRUE for the middle widget: first the bottom child is shrunk, then the top child, then the middle child. The sample program shows this in action.

Listing 6.13. Continued.

```
    labels[0] = XmCreateLabel( the_win, "Label_0", NULL, 0 );
    labels[1] = XmCreateLabel( the_win, "Label_1", NULL, 0 );
    labels[2] = XmCreateLabel( the_win, "Label_2", NULL, 0 );
    XtManageChildren( labels, 3 );

    XtRealizeWidget( appshell );
    XtMainLoop();
}
```

```
!
! Resource file used to produce Figure 6.8
!

*XmLabel.height:        50
*XmLabel.width:         100
*XmLabel.background:    red
*XmLabel.foreground:    white

*PanedWin.background:   Gray50

*Label_1.skipAdjust:    TRUE
```

Since the middle label has `skipAdjust` set to `TRUE`, you can see how it is the last to be shrunk when you shrink the window. However, if you also set `skipAdjust` to `TRUE` for the topmost label (Label_0), the adjustment order will be the same as if all were `FALSE` (or `TRUE`): first Label_2 is shrunk, then Label_1, then Label_0.

For further experimentation, try adjusting the size and position of the sashes. Notice especially the positioning differences between positive and negative values. Also, set `separatorOn` to `FALSE` to see how the "feel" of the window changes.

XmForm

XmForm is the most complex — and one of the most used — of Motif managers. Derived from *XmBulletinBoard*, it adds the ability to specify "attachment" constraints — the ability to specify a child's position in terms of the sides of the form or other children. As the size of the form changes, it adjusts the size of its children to maintain the relationships defined by those constraints.

Resource Table

Table 6.4(a) contains those resources defined by *XmForm* that are associated with the form itself. For brevity, resources inherited from *XmManager* and its superclasses are not shown; they are identical to those shown for *XmBulletinBoard*. Resources defined by *XmBulletinBoard* are listed in Table 6.4(a) as a memory aid, but they are not described.

Table 6.4(b) contains the explicit constraint resources defined by *XmForm*. The descriptions for both types of resources are mixed together; many of the resources associated with the form modify the explicit constraints applied to the form's children.

Table 6.4a. Frequently used resources: *XmForm*

Name	Inheritance	Type	Default Value
fractionBase	XmForm	int	100
horizontalSpacing	XmForm	int	0
rubberPositioning	XmForm	Boolean	FALSE
verticalSpacing	XmForm	int	0
allowOverlap	XmBulletinBoard	Boolean	TRUE
buttonFontList	XmBulletinBoard	XmFontList	NULL
labelFontList	XmBulletinBoard	XmFontList	NULL
marginHeight	XmBulletinBoard	short	0
marginWidth	XmBulletinBoard	short	0
resizePolicy	XmBulletinBoard	unsigned char	XmRESIZE_ANY
shadowType	XmBulletinBoard	unsigned char	XmSHADOW_OUT
textFontList	XmBulletinBoard	XmFontList	NULL

Table 6.4b. Explicit geometry constraints: *XmForm*

Name	Inheritance	Type	Default Value
`bottomAttachment`	XmForm	`unsigned char`	`XmATTACH_NONE`
`bottomOffset`	XmForm	`int`	`0`
`bottomPosition`	XmForm	`int`	`0`
`bottomWidget`	XmForm	`Widget`	`NULL`
`leftAttachment`	XmForm	`unsigned char`	`XmATTACH_NONE`
`leftOffset`	XmForm	`int`	`0`
`leftPosition`	XmForm	`int`	`0`
`leftWidget`	XmForm	`Widget`	`NULL`
`rightAttachment`	XmForm	`unsigned char`	`XmATTACH_NONE`
`rightOffset`	XmForm	`int`	`0`
`rightPosition`	XmForm	`int`	`0`
`rightWidget`	XmForm	`Widget`	`NULL`
`topAttachment`	XmForm	`unsigned char`	`XmATTACH_NONE`
`topOffset`	XmForm	`int`	`0`
`topPosition`	XmForm	`int`	`0`
`topWidget`	XmForm	`Widget`	`NULL`

Types of Attachment

Attachment is the method used to specify a child's position in terms of the form. The form uses this information to determine how to position and size the child as the form's size is changed. For example, if a child's position and size are specified as a certain percentage of the size of the form, then that child will be resized each time the form is — but will maintain a constant position and size relative to the form's window.

Each side of the child has an attachment resource associated with it, which describes how that side of the child is attached. These attachment resources are named `topAttachment`, `bottomAttachment`, `leftAttachment`, and `rightAttachment`. Legal values are from the list below:

- `XmATTACH_NONE`. The associated side of the child is not attached. This value is often used to maintain a constant size for the child:

`topAttachment` and `leftAttachment` are used to set position, `width` and `height` specify size, and `bottomAttachment` and `rightAttachment` contain `XmATTACH_NONE` — allowing the bottom and right sides to "float."

All four attachment resources have a default value of `XmATTACH_NONE`. However, the form will not permit this situation in practice. As described below, it forces the child to be attached both vertically and horizontally.

- `XmATTACH_SELF`. The associated side of the child is permanently attached to its initial position. This position may be calculated based on the attachment of another side of the same child or explicitly specified by the child's `x`, `y`, `width`, and `height` resources.

  If one side of the child is permanently attached (via `XmATTACH_SELF`), and the opposite side is attached in a relative manner (via `XmATTACH_FORM`, `XmATTACH_POSITION`, etc), then the child will grow and shrink with the form, but will not maintain a constant relative size. If all four sides are specified as `XmATTACH_SELF`, then the form acts as a bulletin board in respect to that child — the child will maintain a constant physical size and position.

- `XmATTACH_FORM`. The associated side of the child remains at a fixed offset from the same side of the form. As the form grows or shrinks, the child remains at this fixed offset. For example, if the left side of the child is attached at an offset of 10 pixels from the left side of the form, and the right side of the child is attached at an offset of 10 pixels from the right side of the form, then the child's width will always be 20 pixels less than that of the form — and will change each time the form is resized.

- `XmATTACH_OPPOSITE_FORM`. The associated side of the child is remains at a fixed offset from the opposite side of the form — *eg*, the left side of the child is attached to the right side of the form. This attachment method is often used when a fixed-size child is needed on one side of a form — such as a one-line status display at the bottom of the form. In such a case, the child should not grow or shrink when the form does; by attaching both sides of the child at a fixed offset from the same side of the form, this may be achieved.

- `XmATTACH_POSITION`. The associated side of the child is attached at a relative position based on the associated dimension of the form — top and bottom attachments are based on height, and left and right attachments are based on width. The associated side of the child remains at this relative position as the form is resized.

- `XmATTACH_WIDGET`. The associated side of the child is attached to the opposite side of another widget — top attaches to bottom, and left attaches to right. This attachment means that the position of the associated side is dependent on the position of the attached side of the attached widget.[22]

---

[22] For example, consider a form that contains two labels. The top side of the first label is attached to the top of the form, while the bottom side of the second label is attached to the bottom side of the form (both attachments are `XmATTACH_FORM`). The bottom side of the first label is attached to the top side of the second label via `XmATTACH_WIDGET`. If, for some reason, the second label should move downward (as it could if its `topAttachment`

- XmATTACH_OPPOSITE_WIDGET. The associated side of the child is attached to the same side of another widget — top attaches to top, and so on. This would typically be used in concert with XmATTACH_WIDGET in the same way that XmATTACH_OPPOSITE_FORM is used in concert with XmATTACH_FORM: to create a fixed-size widget that moves in concert with its sibling.

The attachment specification is only half of the story. Each side of the child also has resources that modify the attachment: offset, position, and widget. Depending on the form of attachment, one or more of these associated resources may be used; unused modifiers are ignored.

Offset (Form) Attachment

Offset attachment specifies the position of each child widget in terms of a fixed offset from the sides of the form. As shown by Figure 6.9, when the size of the form is changed, the children of the form change their size as needed to maintain the specified offsets.[23]

Figure 6.9. Example of offset (form) attachment

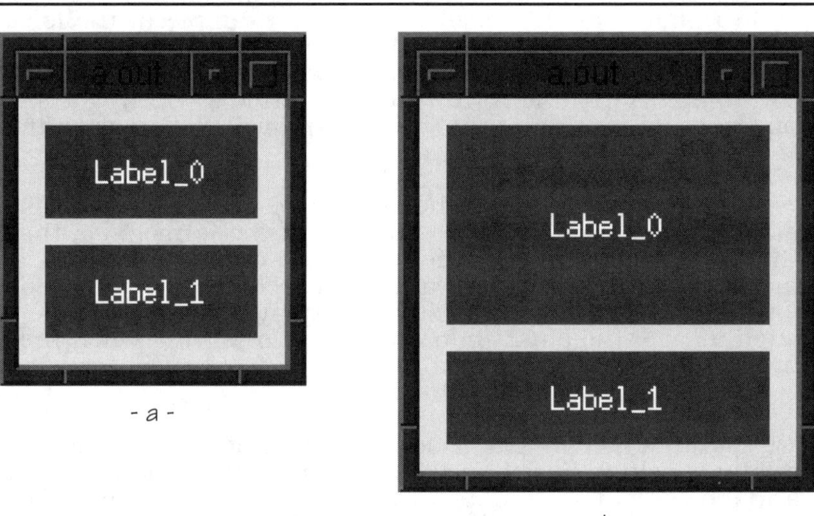

Each side of the child has an associated offset resource: topOffset, bottomOffset, leftOffset, or rightOffset. The offset value is the number of

---

resource contains XmATTACH_NONE and the form grew), the first label would grow — its bottom side would follow the top side of the second label.

[23] Label_0 has all four of its sides attached via XmATTACH_FORM, so it grows as the form grows. Label_1 has its right, left, and bottom sides attached with XmATTACH_FORM, while its top sides are attached with XmATTACH_OPPOSITE_FORM.

pixels between the side of the widget and the side of the form.[24] If the method of attachment is `XmATTACH_FORM`, this offset value is positive; if `XmATTACH_OPPOSITE_FORM`, the offset value is negative.

Starting Offset: horizontalSpacing, verticalSpacing

Although *XmForm* inherits the margin resources of *XmBulletinBoard*, it does not make use of them. Instead, it provides the resources `horizontalSpacing` and `verticalSpacing`, which contain values that are added to all child offsets — `horizontalSpacing` is added to `leftOffset` and `rightOffset`, `verticalSpacing` is added to `topOffset` and `bottomOffset`. In essence, all offsets are measured from inside the margin defined by `horizontalSpacing` and `verticalSpacing`.

It is important to note that the `horizontalSpacing` and `verticalSpacing` resources are associated with the form, whereas the attachment and offset resources are associated with the form's children. Thus, spacing need only be specified once — for the form — while offset must be specified for each child.

Position Attachment

Position attachment specifies the position of the child in terms of a ratio applied to the form's dimensions. The right and left sides are positioned in terms of the form's width, and the top and bottom are positioned in terms of the form's height. This ratio is expressed as a percentage by default, but can be changed as needed via the form's `fractionBase` resource (see below).

Use of position attachment means that, as the form's size changes, the position of the child will change in absolute terms, but will remain fixed in relative terms. This can be seen in Figure 6.10, where all four sides of both labels are attached by position. When the form grows, the labels grow also, maintaining relative size and position.

---

[24] If another `unitType` setting is in effect, pixel offsets are translated according to that setting.

Figure 6.10. Example of position attachment

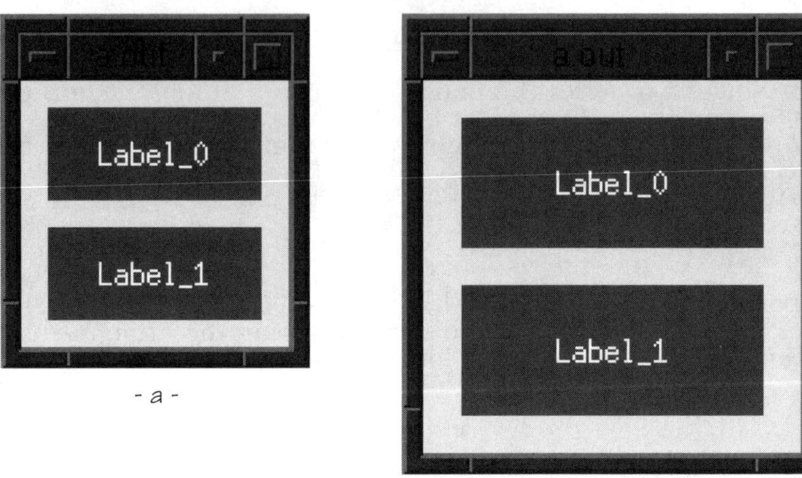

Each side of a child has an associated position resource: `leftPosition`, `rightPosition`, `topPosition`, and `bottomPosition`. When position attachment is used, the side's offset and widget resources are ignored.[25]

A position resource always contains a positive integer, ranging from 0 to the value contained in `fractionBase` (nominally 100). This number represents the numerator of the position ratio; the value in `fractionBase` is the denominator. The ratio is multiplied by the form's current width or height to determine an offset. For vertical positions, this offset is from the top of the form; for horizontal, it's from the left side.[26] Each time the form's size changes, the positions of all of its children are recalculated.

Position Denominator: fractionBase

As described above, the form's `fractionBase` resource is the denominator in the ratio used to calculate the offset of a child's side. By default, `fractionBase` contains 100, meaning that all ratios are percentages.

---

[25] This is not strictly true. While undocumented, the offset resources are available for Motif 1.0 and 1.1 and specify that the associated side is actually placed at a fixed offset from the relative position. While this technique may be useful for some programs, it is not guaranteed to work in future releases of Motif.

[26] For example, in Figure 6.10 (a & b), the left side of both labels is at position 10 (10% of width), and the right side is at position 90 (90% of width). Similarly, the top of Label_0 is at position 10 (10% of height), and the bottom of Label_1 is at position 90 (90% of height).

Why would you want to change `fractionBase`? Consider a form that is to be divided equally among nine labels, where each label must abut its neighbors. The default `fractionBase` value of 100 won't work, since 100 doesn't divide evenly by three, and positions must be specified in terms of whole numbers. Setting `fractionBase` to 90 solves the problem — now the top-left widget extends from position 0,0 to 30,30, the top-middle widget goes from 30,0 to 60,30, the top-right goes from 60,0 to 90,30, and so on.

Since `fractionBase` is associated with the form, the same value is applied to all children. As a result, you can't measure width by percentage and height by thirds. You would have to use a `fractionBase` that is divisible by both of the desired measurements — in this case, 300 — and modify the position values appropriately: 10% is represented by 30, ⅓ by 100.[27]

Widget Attachment

Widget attachment is the hardest attachment method to understand, perhaps because it is only used in concert with other attachment methods. For example, in Figure 6.11, only `Label_1` uses widget attachment — its top side is attached to the `Label_0`, and its bottom side is attached to `Label_1`. `Label_0` and `Label_1` use offset attachment. As a result, the top and bottom labels don't change size when the form does, but the middle label does.

Figure 6.11. Example of widget attachment

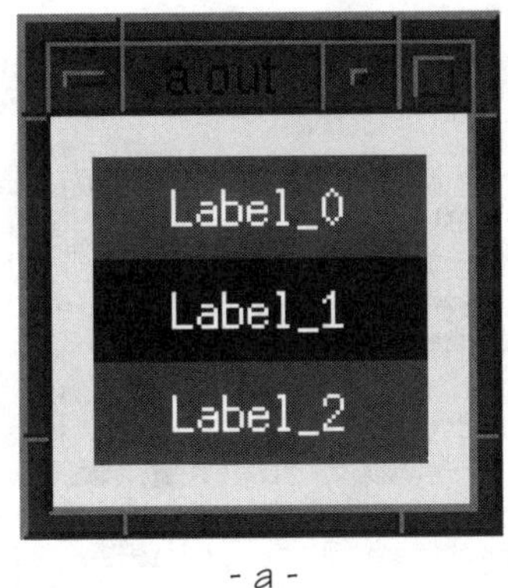

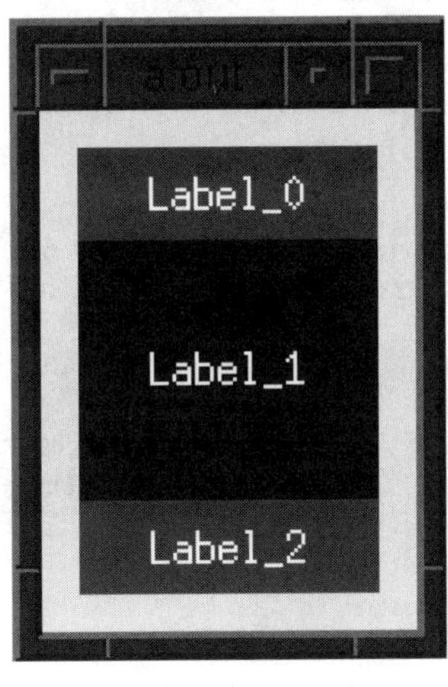

When a child's side is positioned by widget attachment, its associated offset (`leftOffset`, `rightOffset`, `topOffset`, and `bottomOffset`) and widget

---

[27] In general, `fractionBase` should contain the least common multiple of the desired measurement sizes. If this rule were applied to the above example, its value could be 150 instead of 300.

(`leftWidget`, `rightWidget`, `topWidget`, and `bottomWidget`) resources are used; the associated position offset is ignored.

The widget resource specifies the attached widget: it contains the widget ID of that widget. The offset resource specifies the distance from the attached side of the attached widget, in the same way that it specifies the distance from the side of the form for offset attachment.

Widget attachment is difficult to use for two reasons. First, there is no way to specify the attachment in a resource file — a specification such as "`Label_1.topWidget: Label_0`" will result in an error.[28] Second, and more importantly, the attached-to widget *may not exist* when the attaching widget is created. Since the order of widget creation is dependent on the program code, the attachment process is inextricably linked to that code — it must occur after the attached-to widget has been created.

Default Top-Left Attachment: rubberPositioning

Although the resource table indicates a default value of `XmATTACH_NONE` for all attachment resources, a form requires that its children establish an initial horizontal and vertical position or one will be given to them. The vertical position is dependent on the `topAttachment` and `bottomAttachment` resources — either one is sufficient to determine position. Similarly, the horizontal position is determined by the `leftAttachment` and `rightAttachment` resources.

If vertical position cannot be determined (both `topAttachment` and `bottomAttachment` contain `XmATTACH_NONE`), the form will implicitly set the `topAttachment` resource. Similarly, if horizontal position cannot be determined, the form will set the `leftAttachment` resource. The value used depends on the contents of the form's `rubberPositioning` resource.

If `rubberPositioning` contains `FALSE` (the default), the child will default to offset attachment. The value `XmATTACH_FORM` will be stored in the appropriate child resources (`topAttachment` and/or `leftAttachment`). The offset is determined from the child's initial `x` and `y` resources (which may contain zero).

If `rubberPositioning` contains `TRUE`, the child will default to position attachment. The value `XmATTACH_POSITION` will be stored in the appropriate child resources (`topAttachment` and/or `leftAttachment`), with the position determined from the child's initial `x` and `y` resources (which are converted according to the form's dimensions and `fractionBase` value).

---

[28] The specific error message is "X Toolkit Warning: No type converter registered for 'String' to 'Window' conversion". As with `unitType`, this error message indicates that the resource manager is unable to convert the ASCII widget name to its internal form — a widget ID. Additionally, you will get error messages from the form indicating that the attachment widget is `NULL`, because the resource manager was unable to perform the name-to-widget conversion.

XmForm **Examples**

Form Attachment

Figure 6.9 was produced using the program and resource file shown in Listing 6.14. As you can see, the program itself simply creates the form and labels and is largely identical to the previous sample programs. The resource file is where all the work takes place, and it is described in detail after the source listing.

Listing 6.14. Program and resource file to produce Figure 6.9

```
/**********************************************************************
**                                                                  **
**   listing_6_14.c                                                 **
**                                                                  **
**   Two labels and a Form. This program demonstrates the use of    **
**   XmForm and its applied constraints.                            **
**                                                                  **
**********************************************************************/


#include <Xm/Form.h>
#include <Xm/Label.h>


Widget  appshell,              /* Application Shell     */
        theform,               /* The Form              */
        labels[2];             /* The children          */


void main( argc, argv )
    int     argc;
    char    *argv[];
{
    appshell = XtInitialize( argv[0], "Listing_6_14", NULL, 0,
                                              &argc, argv );

    theform = XmCreateForm( appshell, "TheForm", NULL, 0 );
    XtManageChild( theform );
```

Listing 6.14. Continued.

```
    labels[0] = XmCreateLabel( theform, "Label_0", NULL, 0 );
    labels[1] = XmCreateLabel( theform, "Label_1", NULL, 0 );
    XtManageChildren( labels, 2 );

    XtRealizeWidget( appshell );
    XtMainLoop();
}
```

```
!
! Resource file used to produce Figure 6.9
!

*XmLabel.background:            red
*XmLabel.foreground:            white

*TheForm.height:                100
*TheForm.width:                 100
*Label_0.topAttachment:         ATTACH_FORM
*Label_0.topOffset:             10
*Label_0.bottomAttachment:      ATTACH_FORM
*Label_0.bottomOffset:          55
*Label_0.leftAttachment:        ATTACH_FORM
*Label_0.leftOffset:            10
*Label_0.rightAttachment:       ATTACH_FORM
*Label_0.rightOffset:           10

*Label_1.topAttachment:         ATTACH_OPPOSITE_FORM
*Label_1.topOffset:             -45
*Label_1.bottomAttachment:      ATTACH_FORM
*Label_1.bottomOffset:          10
*Label_1.leftAttachment:        ATTACH_FORM
*Label_1.leftOffset:            10
*Label_1.rightAttachment:       ATTACH_FORM
*Label_1.rightOffset:           10
```

The first point of interest is that the form's height and width resources are specified explicitly. This must be done because the form has no way of determining its size from the layout of its children — their layout is dependent on the size of the form. If you do not explicitly specify a form's size, it will attempt to determine its size from the layout of its children. Assuming that the label size was specified above, the form would be just large enough to display the largest child/offset combination (try it).

The second point of interest is that sides using `XmATTACH_OPPOSITE_FORM` specify a negative offset. This is a requirement that is often forgotten, resulting in an incorrect arrangement.

Position Attachment

To demonstrate position attachment (Figure 6.10), use the program from Listing 6.14 but substitute the resource file from Listing 6.15. The key change to this file is that the offset resources have been replaced by position resources, which contain ratios — not explicit positions.

Listing 6.15. Resource file to produce Figure 6.10

```
!
! Resource file used to produce Figure 6.10
!

*XmLabel.background:            red
*XmLabel.foreground:            white

*TheForm.height:                100
*TheForm.width:                 100

*Label_0.topAttachment:         ATTACH_POSITION
*Label_0.topPosition:           10
*Label_0.bottomAttachment:      ATTACH_POSITION
*Label_0.bottomPosition:        45
*Label_0.leftAttachment:        ATTACH_POSITION
*Label_0.leftPosition:          10
*Label_0.rightAttachment:       ATTACH_POSITION
*Label_0.rightPosition:         90

*Label_1.topAttachment:         ATTACH_POSITION
*Label_1.topPosition:           55
*Label_1.bottomAttachment:      ATTACH_POSITION
*Label_1.bottomPosition:        90
*Label_1.leftAttachment:        ATTACH_POSITION
*Label_1.leftPosition:          10
*Label_1.rightAttachment:       ATTACH_POSITION
*Label_1.rightPosition:         90
```

Widget Attachment

As indicated above, widget attachment is a complex process. To produce Figure 6.11, the program and resource file from Listing 6.16 were used. The resource specifications for Label_0 and Label_2 may be safely ignored; interest centers around Label_1.

Listing 6.16. Program and resource file to produce Figure 6.11

```
/**********************************************************************
**                                                                  **
**   listing_6_16.c                                                 **
**                                                                  **
**   Three labels and a Form. This program demonstrates the use of  **
**   XmForm's "Widget Attachment" constraint.                       **
**                                                                  **
**********************************************************************/


#include <Xm/Form.h>
#include <Xm/Label.h>


Widget   appshell,                        /* Application Shell        */
         theform,                         /* The Form                 */
         labels[3];                       /* The children             */
Arg      arglist[2];                      /* Used to set attachment   */


void main( argc, argv )
    int      argc;
    char     *argv[];
{
    appshell = XtInitialize( argv[0], "Listing_6_16", NULL, 0,
                                                &argc, argv );

    theform = XmCreateForm( appshell, "TheForm", NULL, 0 );
    XtManageChild( theform );

    labels[0] = XmCreateLabel( theform, "Label_0", NULL, 0 );
    labels[1] = XmCreateLabel( theform, "Label_1", NULL, 0 );
    labels[2] = XmCreateLabel( theform, "Label_2", NULL, 0 );
    XtManageChildren( labels, 3 );
    XtSetArg( arglist[0], XmNtopWidget,       labels[0] );
    XtSetArg( arglist[1], XmNbottomWidget,    labels[2] );
    XtSetValues( labels[1], arglist, 2 );
```

Listing 6.16. Continued.

```
    XtRealizeWidget( appshell );
    XtMainLoop();
}
```

```
!
! Resource file used to produce Figure 6.11
!

*XmLabel.background:            red
*XmLabel.foreground:            white

*TheForm.height:                95
*TheForm.width:                 100

*Label_0.topAttachment:         ATTACH_FORM
*Label_0.topOffset:             10
*Label_0.bottomAttachment:      ATTACH_OPPOSITE_FORM
*Label_0.bottomOffset:          -35
*Label_0.leftAttachment:        ATTACH_FORM
*Label_0.leftOffset:            10
*Label_0.rightAttachment:       ATTACH_FORM
*Label_0.rightOffset:           10

*Label_1.background:            Blue
*Label_1.topAttachment:         ATTACH_WIDGET
*Label_1.bottomAttachment:      ATTACH_WIDGET
*Label_1.leftAttachment:        ATTACH_FORM
*Label_1.leftOffset:            10
*Label_1.rightAttachment:       ATTACH_FORM
*Label_1.rightOffset:           10

*Label_2.topAttachment:         ATTACH_OPPOSITE_FORM
*Label_2.topOffset:             -35
*Label_2.bottomAttachment:      ATTACH_FORM
*Label_2.bottomOffset:          10
*Label_2.leftAttachment:        ATTACH_FORM
*Label_2.leftOffset:            10
*Label_2.rightAttachment:       ATTACH_FORM
*Label_2.rightOffset:           10
```

The label creation process is identical to what has gone before. However, right after the labels are created, the attachments are stored in `Label_1`. The attachment to `Label_0` could have been performed when `Label_1` was created

— a valid widget ID existed for `Label_0` at that time. However, I decided to set the attachments at one point for improved clarity.

In the resource file, the left and right attachments are to the form, which will allow the label to grow and shrink horizontally. The top and bottom attachments are set to `XmATTACH_WIDGET`; these attachments only become valid when the `topWidget` and `bottomWidget` resources are filled.[29]

---

[29] If attachment is set to widget, but the associated widget resource has not been filled (contains `NULL`), the attachment acts like `XmATTACH_FORM`, with an offset of 0.

7
Buttons

Overview

Buttons in Motif are varied in appearance and operation and are one of the primary means by which the user controls a program. Normal pushbuttons appear throughout a program, most often in dialog boxes. Cascade buttons (along with normal pushbuttons) are used to build menus. Arrow buttons are used in scrollbars, toggle buttons are used for "yes/no" choices, and drawn buttons are used when the program needs to display complex or changing graphics in a pushbutton.

All Motif buttons present a similar appearance and interaction. The button's shadow border normally causes it to appear to protrude from the screen. The user *arms* the button by moving the pointer over the screen button and pressing the its button. When armed, the screen button changes its shadow, so that it appears to be inset into the screen. If the user then releases the pointer button, the screen button is *activated* — it notifies the program that it was "pressed," and its shadow returns to normal. If the user moves the pointer away from the screen button, without releasing the pointer button, it is *disarmed* — its shadow returns to normal and nothing happens.[1] A toggle button acts in a slightly different way: clicking the pointer button while on a toggle button changes its status (and shadow) between "on" and "off" — when on, the button appears to be inset; when off, it appears to protrude.

This chapter describes three types of buttons: normal pushbuttons (the *XmPushButton* class), arrow buttons (the *XmArrowButton* class), and toggle buttons (the *XmToggleButton* class). Cascade buttons (the *XmCascadeButton* class) are described in Chapter 12; drawn buttons (the *XmDrawnButton* class) do not appear in this book.

---

[1] As you will see in the next chapter, a button actually notifies the program when it is armed, disarmed, or activated. Most programs, however, act only on button activation.

Inheritance

Buttons are primitive widgets, descended in some way from *XmPrimitive*.[2] As shown in Figure 7.1, buttons that display a label are derived from *XmLabel*; *XmArrowButton*, which does not display a label, is derived directly from *XmPrimitive*.

Figure 7.1. Motif buttons class tree

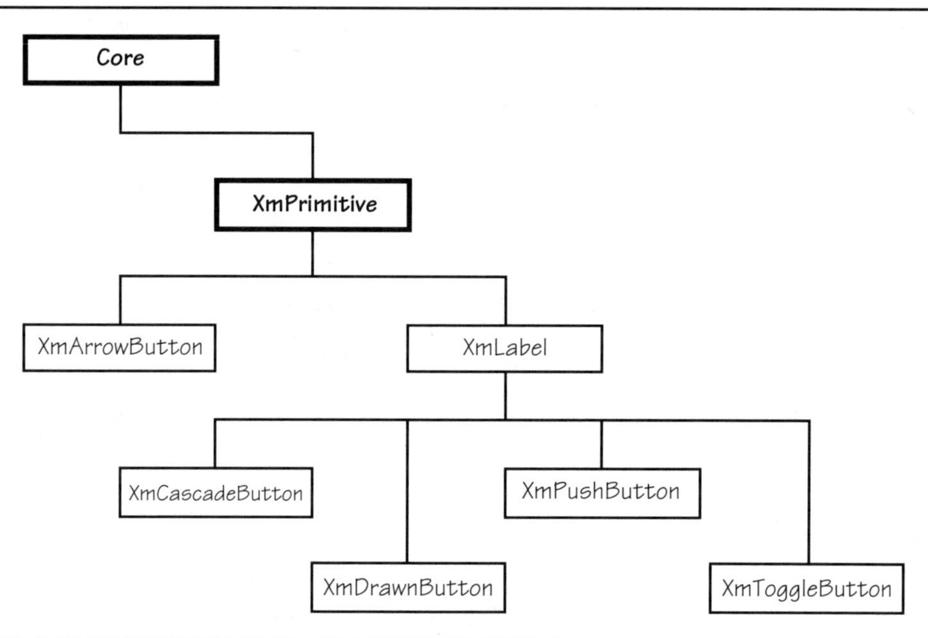

XmPushButton

Normal pushbuttons, instances of the *XmPushButton* class, are the most commonly used buttons in a Motif program. They are used extensively in menus: cascade buttons are used to "pull down" or "pop up" the menus, but normal pushbuttons are used for the menu choices. They are also used extensively in dialog boxes: all dialogs adhering to the style guide have three buttons named **OK**, **Cancel**, and **Help**. Aside from these common uses, many programs use pushbuttons in unique ways, either to control an action or simply as a means of input.

Derived from *XmLabel*, a pushbutton looks like a label with a shadow border. Figure 7.2 shows a button as it normally appears (a), and as it appears when

---

[2] As stated in Chapter 2, a "primitive" widget is one that — unlike a manager — cannot have another widget as its child.

pressed (b).[3] As you can see, the top and bottom shadows reverse when the button is pressed, giving the illusion that the button is inset rather than protruding. You might also notice that the background color of 7.2(b) is slightly darker than that of 7.2(a). When a button is pressed, its background color changes to a shade between the normal background color and the bottom shadow color, increasing the impression that the button is set into the screen.

Figure 7.2. Sample pushbuttons

Resource Table

XmPushButton's resource table is similar to that of *XmLabel* — as described above, much of a button's appearance depends on its derivation from *XmLabel*. Table 7.1 lists those resources provided by the *XmLabel* and *XmPushButton* classes. *XmLabel*'s `labelInsensitivePixmap` resource, which was not described in Chapter 5, is part of this list — it exists primarily for buttons. While most of the resources defined by *XmPrimitive* and its superclasses are not listed here, the *Core* resource `sensitive` and the *XmPrimitive* shadow resources are because they are more appropriate to pushbuttons than they are to labels. Finally, callback resources — those resources used by a pushbutton to signal the program of its status — are described in the next chapter.

---

[3] This example shows the pushbutton as the child of a bulletin board, not standing on its own. I used the bulletin board solely for its margin to better show the pushbutton's shadow.

Table 7.1. Frequently used resources: *XmPushButton*

Name	Inheritance	Type	Default Value
`armColor`	**XmPushButton**	`Pixel`	*dynamic*
`armPixmap`	**XmPushButton**	`Pixmap`	`XmUNSPECIFIED_PIXMAP`
`fillOnArm`	**XmPushButton**	`Boolean`	`TRUE`
`showAsDefault`	**XmPushButton**	`short`	`0`
`alignment`	**XmLabel**	`unsigned char`	`XmALIGNMENT_CENTER`
`fontList`	**XmLabel**	`XmFontList`	`"Fixed"`
`labelInsensitive Pixmap`	**XmLabel**	`Pixmap`	`XmUNSPECIFIED_PIXMAP`
`labelPixmap`	**XmLabel**	`Pixmap`	`XmUNSPECIFIED_PIXMAP`
`labelString`	**XmLabel**	`XmString`	*dynamic*
`labelType`	**XmLabel**	`unsigned char`	`XmSTRING`
`recomputeSize`	**XmLabel**	`Boolean`	`TRUE`
`stringDirection`	**XmLabel**	`XmString Direction`	`XmSTRING_DIRECTION_L_ TO_R`
`bottomShadow Color`	**XmPrimitive**	`Pixel`	*dynamic*
`shadow Thickness`	**XmPrimitive**	`short`	`2`
`topShadowColor`	**XmPrimitive**	`Pixel`	*dynamic*
`sensitive`	**Core**	`Boolean`	`TRUE`

Resources Derived from XmLabel

In all respects other than interaction, a pushbutton behaves like a label. Pushbuttons may be either textual (in which case `alignment`, `fontList`, `labelString`, and `stringDirection` are used) or graphic (in which case `labelPixmap` and `labelInsensitivePixmap`) are used. As with *XmLabel*, the `labelType` resource determines whether the pushbutton is textual or graphic.

Armed Appearance: armColor, armPixmap, fillOnArm

As stated above, a pushbutton is armed when the user presses the pointer button while the pointer is positioned over the pushbutton. As shown in Figure 7.2, an armed button changes both its shadow border and its background color.

The `fillOnArm` resource controls the background change: when it contains TRUE (the default), the background color changes; when it contains FALSE, the background color remains the same.

If `fillOnArm` contains TRUE, the change depends on the label's type. If the label is graphic (`labelType` contains XmPIXMAP), the contents of the `armPixmap` resource are displayed instead of `labelPixmap`. If the label is textual (`labelType` contains XmSTRING), the normal background color is replaced by `armColor`.

The `armColor` resource may be specified explicitly (for example, change the button's color from red to green when it is armed), or it may be determined dynamically. If determined dynamically, the color chosen will be a shade between the normal background color and the normal bottom shadow color. In some cases, this change in shade may be so slight as to be unnoticeable.

Default Button Indication: showAsDefault

In many cases — especially dialog boxes — a group of pushbuttons will be displayed, with one button being the default. Exactly what "default" means depends on the circumstance: for example, in a normal dialog, the user may "press" the default button by hitting the *Return* key on the keyboard. The `showAsDefault` resource specifies that the associated button is to be the default button, and it specifies the thickness of a "second shadow" that indicates that the button is a default.[4]

Sensitivity: sensitive, labelInsensitivePixmap

Sensitivity refers to whether or not a widget accepts input: it does when sensitive, it doesn't when insensitive. The ability to specify sensitivity is especially useful in a menu structure: any menus that are not applicable to the current situation may be set insensitive, prohibiting the user from making the associated menu choice.

The `sensitive` resource, defined as part of the *Core* class, determines the sensitivity of a button. When it contains TRUE (the default), the button is sensitive. When it contains FALSE, the button is insensitive. Note that all widgets have a `sensitive` resource, but it directly affects primitive widgets only.[5]

Unlike most resources, `sensitive` should not be changed using XtSetValues because sensitivity must propagate up and down the instance tree. Instead, you should use the function XtSetSensitive, prototyped in Listing 7.1. The parameters of this function are the ID of the widget to be modified (w) and the new value of its sensitive resource (value) — either TRUE or FALSE.

---

[4] In Motif Release 1.1, `showAsDefault` is used in concert with `defaultButtonShadowThickness` — a new resource. If `defaultButtonShadowThickness` is zero, then `showAsDefault` works as described above. If, however, `defaultButtonShadowThickness` is nonzero, it specifies the actual shadow thickness, and `showAsDefault` merely specifies the default button. This behavior allows the program to change the default button without concern for the proper shadow thickness (*ie*, the user can specify shadow thickness in the resource file, and the program can specify the current default simply by putting a nonzero value into `showAsDefault`).

[5] If a manager is made insensitive, its children become insensitive. The manager, however, is not affected.

Listing 7.1. Function prototype: XtSetSensitive

```
void    XtSetSensitive( w, value )
        Widget      w;
        Boolean     value;
```

The appearance of an insensitive button depends on the button's type, textual or graphic. An insensitive graphic button displays `labelInsensitivePixmap` instead of `labelPixmap`. An insensitive textual button, on the other hand, has its label "grayed out" as shown in Figure 7.3. The odd appearance of the label results from this way in which this is done: rather than changing the label's foreground color, a shadow mask is applied to its contents.

Figure 7.3. Insensitive pushbutton

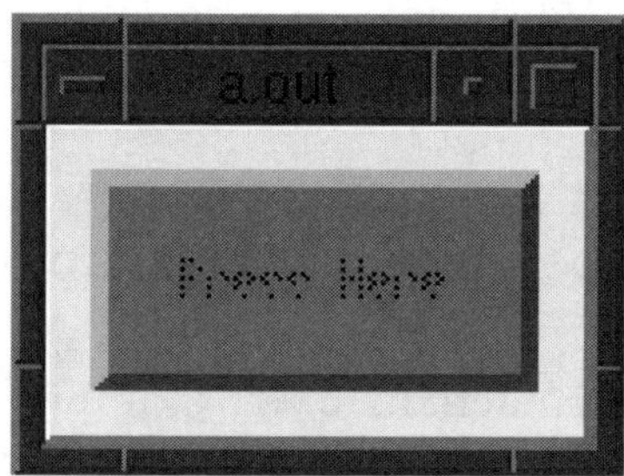

XmPushButton Example: Press Here

Figure 7.2 was produced using the program and resource file of Listing 7.2. As described above, the bulletin board exists solely to provide "dead space" to better illustrate the button's shadow border. It could be removed, resulting in a program almost identical to Listing 5.1.

Listing 7.2. Program and resource file: *XmPushButton* example

```
/***********************************************************************
**                                                                   **
**   listing_7_2.c                                                   **
**                                                                   **
**   Pushbutton and Bulletin Board. This program demonstrates the   **
**   appearance and interaction of XmPushButton.                    **
**                                                                   **
***********************************************************************/


#include <Xm/BulletinB.h>
#include <Xm/PushB.h>


Widget  appshell,                       /* Application Shell         */
        the_bb,                         /* A Bulletin Board (border) */
        the_btn;                        /* The PushButton            */


void main( argc, argv )
    int     argc;
    char    *argv[];
{
    appshell = XtInitialize( argv[0], "Listing_7_02", NULL, 0,
                                                &argc, argv );

    the_bb = XmCreateBulletinBoard( appshell, "TheBB", NULL, 0 );
    XtManageChild( the_bb );

    the_btn = XmCreatePushButton( the_bb, "TheBtn", NULL, 0 );
    XtManageChild( the_btn );

    XtRealizeWidget( appshell );
    XtMainLoop();
}
!
! Resource file used to produce Figure 7.2
!
```

Listing 7.2. Continued.

```
*TheBB.marginWidth:         10
*TheBB.marginHeight:        10

*TheBtn.height:             50
*TheBtn.width:              100
*TheBtn.foreground:         White
*TheBtn.background:         Gray50
*TheBtn.shadowThickness:    4
*TheBtn.labelString:        Press Here
```

As you can see, this sample program does not make use of any of
XmPushButton's resources. It simply treats the button like a label. As an
experiment, you should try changing the `armColor` resource; the red-to-green
change described above is interesting — the shadow colors remain based on red.
You can also change the `sensitive` resource to produce the display of Figure 7.3
and disable the button.

XmArrowButton

Arrow buttons are directional buttons, as shown in Figure 7.4. While most
people associate arrow buttons with scrollbars, where they are used to "single-
step" the slider, they are useful in any place where you want to perform a
directional increment.

Figure 7.4. Sample arrow buttons

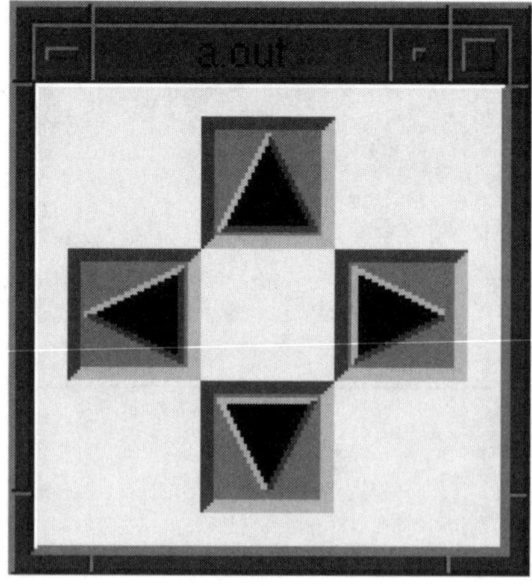

Resource Table

Table 7.2 lists the resources defined by *XmArrowButton*. This table is extremely short for three reasons. First, since *XmArrowButton* is derived from *XmPrimitive*, it supports all resources defined by *XmPrimitive* and its superclasses; these have been described previously. Second, callback resources are not described until the next chapter; they are identical to those provided by *XmPushButton*. Finally, *XmArrowButton* is a pretty simple widget, with limited functionality.

Table 7.2. Frequently used resources: *XmArrowButton*

Name	Inheritance	Type	Default Value
`arrowDirection`	**XmArrowButton**	`unsigned char`	`XmARROW_UP`

Arrow Appearance: arrowDirection

The sole resource defined by the *XmArrowButton* class describes the orientation of the arrow. The values for this resource are `XmARROW_UP` (the default), `XmARROW_DOWN`, `XmARROW_LEFT`, and `XmARROW_RIGHT`. They should be self-explanatory.

XmArrowButton **Example**

The program and resource file of Listing 7.3 were used to produce Figure 7.4. This program also uses a bulletin board to hold the buttons. In this case, it is necessary because more than one button is displayed. Note that the "up" button does not set the `arrowDirection` resource, but relies upon its default value.

Listing 7.3. Program and resource file: *XmArrowButton* example

```
/*********************************************************************
**                                                                 **
**   listing_7_3.c                                                 **
**                                                                 **
**   Arrow-Buttons and Bulletin Board. This program demonstrates the **
**   appearance and interaction of XmArrowButton.                  **
**                                                                 **
*********************************************************************/

#include <Xm/BulletinB.h>
#include <Xm/ArrowB.h>

Widget  appshell,                    /* Application Shell       */
        the_bb,                      /* A Bulletin Board        */
```

Listing 7.3. Continued.

```
        buttons[4];                        /* The Arrow Buttons        */

void main( argc, argv )
    int     argc;
    char    *argv[];
{
    appshell = XtInitialize( argv[0], "Listing_7_03", NULL, 0,
                                            &argc, argv );

    the_bb = XmCreateBulletinBoard( appshell, "TheBB", NULL, 0 );
    XtManageChild( the_bb );

    buttons[0] = XmCreateArrowButton( the_bb, "Up", NULL, 0 );
    buttons[1] = XmCreateArrowButton( the_bb, "Down", NULL, 0 );
    buttons[2] = XmCreateArrowButton( the_bb, "Left", NULL, 0 );
    buttons[3] = XmCreateArrowButton( the_bb, "Right", NULL, 0 );
    XtManageChildren( buttons, 4 );

    XtRealizeWidget( appshell );
    XtMainLoop();
}
!
```

```
! Resource file used to produce Figure 7.4
!

*XmArrowButton.width:           40
*XmArrowButton.height:          40
*XmArrowButton.foreground:      black
*XmArrowButton.background:      gray50
*XmArrowButton.shadowThickness: 4

*Up.x:              50
*Up.y:              10

*Down.arrowDirection:   ARROW_DOWN
*Down.x:                50
*Down.y:                90

*Left.arrowDirection:   ARROW_LEFT
*Left.x:                10
*Left.y:                50

*Right.arrowDirection:  ARROW_RIGHT
*Right.x:               90
*Right.y:               50
```

XmToggleButton

Most buttons are used for "one-shot" program notification: the user presses the button to initiate some action. Toggle buttons, on the other hand, maintain "on/off" information: the program is notified when the state changes, but it can access the current state at any time.

As shown in Figure 7.5, toggle buttons can have many different appearances. All of these examples use a row-column manager to hold the buttons. This is a common technique, because in most cases toggle buttons are used in groups that maintain information about related items.[6] In fact, as you saw in Chapter 6, *XmRowColumn* manager provides resources specifically for maintenance of groups of toggle buttons.

Figure 7.5(a) shows the toggle buttons in their "check-box" mode. The button's state is indicated by the box at its left side: an inset appearance means the button is "on" (set), a protruding appearance means the button is "off" (unset).[7] In a check-box layout, any number of buttons in the group may be on — buttons are not related.

Figure 7.5(b) shows the toggle buttons in their "radio-button" mode. In this mode, only one button in a group may be on at a time, similar to the tuning buttons on a radio. When the user clicks on a button that is off, that button turns itself on and notifies the row-column to turn all other buttons off. Radio-button mode is denoted by the diamond-shaped indicator, instead of the square indicator of check-box mode.

Figure 7.5(c) shows the buttons without their indicators. In this case, the entire button remains inset to indicate that it is on. There is no difference in appearance between radio-button mode and check-box mode in this state.

Figure 7.5(d) shows the buttons in a mode where the indicator disappears when the button is off. This mode is set by default when a toggle button is held in a menu; it is used to show the current state of a single item, as opposed to the state of a group of related items.[8]

---

[6] For example, a word processing application could use a group of toggle buttons to indicate the styles applied to the current text selection — bold, italic, underline, etc.

[7] "Set" and "unset" are the words commonly used to describe a toggle button's state — primarily because the name of the associated resource is `set`. To avoid confusion with the resource, this book uses the words on and off.

[8] For example, many word processors have an "outlining" mode, which is either on or off. This mode is typically set from a menu, where the outlining choice may appear among other unrelated items. In this case, you would want only to show the indicator to indicate that outline mode is in effect; when in normal mode, there is no need to display an indicator.

Figure 7.5. *XmToggleButton* examples

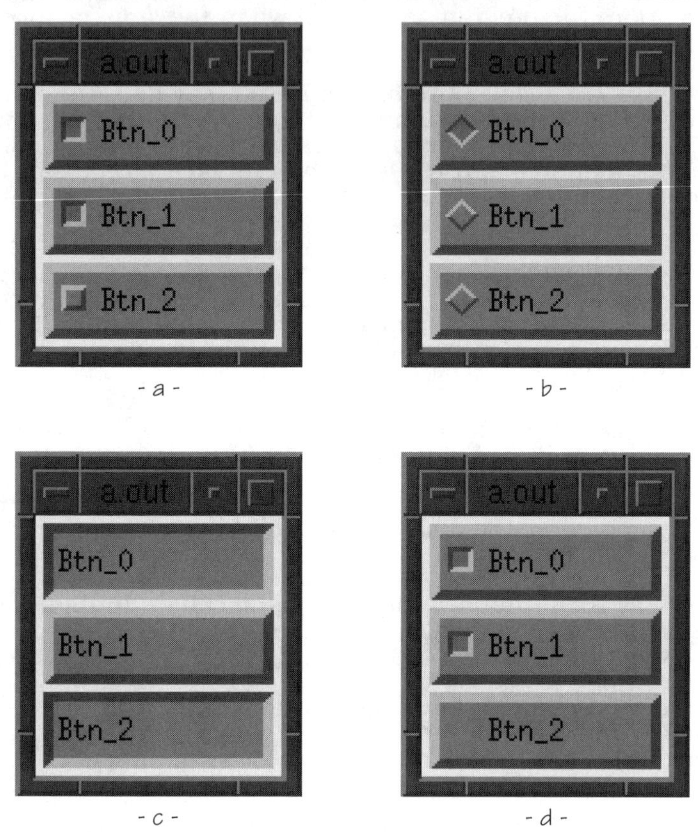

Resource Table

To support the varied modes shown in Figure 7.5, *XmToggleButton* has a fairly long list of resources, shown in Table 7.3. As it is derived from *XmLabel*, it also provides a label's resources; these are listed here, but not described. As with *XmPushButton* and *XmArrowButton*, callback resources are postponed until the next chapter.

Table 7.3. Frequently used resources: *XmToggleButton*

Name	Inheritance	Type	Default Value
fillOnSelect	XmToggleButton	Boolean	TRUE
indicatorOn	XmToggleButton	Boolean	TRUE
indicatorType	XmToggleButton	unsigned char	XmN_OF_MANY
selectColor	XmToggleButton	Pixel	*dynamic*
selectInsensitivePixmap	XmToggleButton	Pixmap	XmUNSPECIFIED_PIXMAP
selectPixmap	XmToggleButton	Pixmap	XmUNSPECIFIED_PIXMAP
set	XmToggleButton	Boolean	FALSE
spacing	XmToggleButton	short	4
visibleWhenOff	XmToggleButton	Boolean	TRUE
alignment	XmLabel	unsigned char	XmALIGNMENT_CENTER
fontList	XmLabel	XmFontList	"Fixed"
labelInsensitivePixmap	XmLabel	Pixmap	XmUNSPECIFIED_PIXMAP
labelPixmap	XmLabel	Pixmap	XmUNSPECIFIED_PIXMAP
labelString	XmLabel	XmString	*dynamic*
labelType	XmLabel	unsigned char	XmSTRING
recomputeSize	XmLabel	Boolean	TRUE
stringDirection	XmLabel	XmString Direction	XmSTRING_DIRECTION_L_TO_R
sensitive	Core	Boolean	TRUE

Resources from XmLabel

Like *XmPushButton*, *XmToggleButton* is derived from *XmLabel*, and, therefore, supports all resources defined by *XmLabel*. When the indicator is present, the toggle button places the button's label — text or pixmap — to the right of the indicator; the spacing resource specifies the distance between the indicator and label.[9]

---

[9] Note that presence of the indicator is separate from display of the indicator. Figure 7.5(c) shows toggle buttons without the indicator present; Figure 7.5(d) shows toggle buttons without the indicator displayed.

Sensitivity

Like all widgets, a toggle button may be disabled by setting its `sensitive` resource to `FALSE`. The appearance of an insensitive toggle button depends on whether it is a textual or pixmap button. For a text button, the button's label area is "grayed out" as in Figure 7.3. For a pixmap button, the pixmap changes, as described under *Pixmap Behavior*, below. In both cases, the indicator remains unaffected.

Status: set

The current status of a toggle button — whether it is on or off — is held in the resource `set`. This resource contains `TRUE` when the button is on, `FALSE` when the button is off. A program may read this resource at any time to determine the current state of the button, and it may change the button's state by installing a new value. Whenever the `set` resource is changed, the button updates its indicator.

The default value of the `set` resource is `FALSE`. Changing the value in the resource file is a good method of providing program configuration in a user-visible fashion.

Indicator Presence/Display: indicatorOn, visibleWhenOff

The `indicatorOn` resource controls the presence or absence of the button's indicator. When `indicatorOn` contains `TRUE` (the default), the button's indicator is used. When it contains `FALSE`, the button's status is shown by the appearance of the entire button, as in Figure 7.5(c).

The presence or absence of the indicator should not be confused with an indicator that simply isn't displayed, as in Figure 7.5(d). The `visibleWhenOff` resource controls the display of the indicator: when it contains `TRUE`, the indicator is displayed at all times, regardless of the button's status. When `visibleWhenOff` contains `FALSE`, the indicator is only displayed when the button is on (`set` contains `TRUE`).

The default value for `visibleWhenOff` depends on the button's parent; in most cases, the default value is `TRUE`. When the parent is a menu, however, the default value is `FALSE`. This behavior allows the program to display the condition of modal menu choices. You should be aware that a menu parent will force the value of `visibleWhenOff` to `FALSE`, even if it is explicitly set in a resource file. If you wish the value to be `TRUE`, you must programmatically set it *after* widget creation.

Indicator Appearance: indicatorType, spacing

When the toggle button is used as a check box, its indicator is a square. When used as a radio button, its indicator is a diamond.[10] The `indicatorType` resource controls this appearance: a value of `XmN_OF_MANY` (the default), specifies a square,

---

[10] The radio-button indicator is a diamond only on a color display. On a monochrome display, it is a circle.

a value of XmONE_OF_MANY specifies a diamond. If the toggle button is the child of a row-column, this value may be set automatically, as described below. Otherwise, it may be set in the resource file.

Note that this resource does not control the behavior: a toggle button by itself can use any type of indicator and will always act as a check box. Radio-button behavior is provided by the row-column parent.

The spacing resource specifies how many pixels separate the indicator from the button's label. By default, this spacing is four pixels. This resource is ignored when the indicator is not used (indicatorOn contains FALSE). It is used, however, when the indicator is simply not displayed — in that case, the label is at all times positioned as if the indicator were displayed.

Selection Behavior: fillOnSelect, selectColor

The fillOnSelect and selectColor resources of *XmToggleButton* perform the same function as the fillOnArm and armColor resources of *XmPushButton*. When the toggle button is on (set contains TRUE) and fillOnSelect contains TRUE (the default), the indicator's top and bottom shadows are swapped to give it an inset appearance, and its background color is replaced by the color in the selectColor resource.[11]

Pixmap Behavior: selectPixmap, selectInsensitivePixmap

For toggle buttons that display a pixmap, the selectPixmap and selectInsensitivePixmap resources are used. The selectPixmap resource contains a pixmap that is displayed when the button is on (set contains TRUE). The default value of this resource is the unspecified pixmap, which means that the normal pixmap (labelPixmap) is displayed, and only the indicator changes.[12]

The selectInsensitivePixmap resource is displayed when the button is on but is insensitive (the user can't change its state). This resource also defaults to the unspecified pixmap, so the default action is to display the contents of the *XmLabel* resource labelInsensitivePixmap. If neither of these resources contain a value, then the label is left completely blank — without even an indicator.

Related XmRowColumn Resources: radioBehavior, radioAlwaysOne

As described above, radio-button behavior is actually provided by the *XmRowColumn* widget class. The *XmRowColumn* resource radioBehavior controls this behavior: when it contains TRUE, all toggle-button children of the row-column act as radio buttons — only one may be on at a time. The default value of radioBehavior is FALSE, which causes toggle-button children to be treated as check boxes.

---

[11] Note that, if the indicator is not present (indicatorOn contains FALSE), the background color and shadow changes are applied to the whole button; otherwise, they just affect the indicator.

[12] The indicator changes even if selectPixmap identifies a valid pixmap.

Not only does the `radioBehavior` resource cause the row-column to manage the status of its toggle-button children, it also causes it to change their `indicatorType` resource. When the row-column is being used for radio buttons (`radioBehavior` contains `TRUE`), it will set the `indicatorType` resource of its toggle-button children to `XmONE_OF_MANY`. When `radioBehavior` contains `FALSE`, the row-column sets its children's `indicatorType` resource to `XmN_OF_MANY`.

The *XmRowColumn* resource `radioAlwaysOne` further refines the behavior of radio-button children. When `radioAlwaysOne` contains `TRUE` (the default), the row-column guarantees that the user will be unable to turn off one radio button without turning another one on. If the user tries to do so (by clicking the current "on" button), the row-column keeps the button on. If `radioAlwaysOne` contains `FALSE`, the user may turn off the current "on" button, resulting in all buttons being off (at no time, however, is more than one button permitted to be on).

You should note that `radioAlwaysOne` does not guarantee that one button will always be on, only that the user cannot cause all buttons to be off. If the program does not select an initial "on" button, none of the buttons will be on. Moreover, if the program unmanages or unmaps the current "on" button, none of the buttons will be on.[13]

XmToggleButton Examples

As with many of the figures in this book, the four configurations of Figure 7.5 were produced using a single program, shown in Listing 7.4; the resource file is responsible for the differences between the configurations. This program is the by now familiar "create a manager, create its children, and let things run." Resource files for the simple check-box and simple radio-button configurations are described below; the configurations of Figures 7.5 (c) and (d) are left as an exercise for the reader.

Listing 7.4. Program and resource file: *XmToggleButton* example

```
/***********************************************************************
**                                                                   **
**   listing_7_4.c                                                   **
**                                                                   **
**   Toggle-buttons and Row-Column. This program demonstrates the    **
**   appearance and interaction of XmToggleButton, both as a check   **
**   box and as a radio button.                                      **
**                                                                   **
```

---

[13] However, if the program attempts to programmatically turn off the currently on button, the row-column will turn it back on. In this case, programmatic control is equivalent to user control.

<hr>

Listing 7.4. Continued.

<hr>

```
************************************************************************/


#include <Xm/RowColumn.h>
#include <Xm/ToggleB.h>


Widget   appshell,                          /* Application Shell        */
         row_col,                           /* The parent               */
         buttons[3];                        /* The Toggle Buttons       */


void main( argc, argv )
    int      argc;
    char     *argv[];
{
    appshell = XtInitialize( argv[0], "Listing_7_04", NULL, 0,
                                                   &argc, argv );


    row_col = XmCreateRowColumn( appshell, "RowCol", NULL, 0 );
    XtManageChild( row_col );

    buttons[0] = XmCreateToggleButton( row_col, "Btn_0", NULL, 0 );
    buttons[1] = XmCreateToggleButton( row_col, "Btn_1", NULL, 0 );
    buttons[2] = XmCreateToggleButton( row_col, "Btn_2", NULL, 0 );
    XtManageChildren( buttons, 3 );

    XtRealizeWidget( appshell );
    XtMainLoop();
}
```

<hr>

Radio Buttons

The resource file of Listing 7.5 is responsible for Figure 7.5(a). As you can see, the row-column was left with its default settings, as were the toggle buttons (excepting appearance resources). Note again the need to explicitly set the `recomputeSize` resource; if left at its default setting, the labels shrink to their minimum necessary size.

Listing 7.5. Resource file to produce Figure 7.5(a)

```
!
! Resource file used to produce Figure 7.5a
!

*XmToggleButton.recomputeSize:      FALSE
*XmToggleButton.height:             30
*XmToggleButton.width:              90
*XmToggleButton.foreground:         black
*XmToggleButton.background:         gray50
*XmToggleButton.shadowThickness:    4
```

Check Boxes

To produce the configuration of Figure 7.5(b), the resource file of Listing 7.6 was used. The only change was to the row-column's `radioBehavior` resource. Setting this to `TRUE` changed the appearance of the toggle buttons' indicators and imposed the radio-button behavior.

Listing 7.6. Resource file to produce Figure 7.5(b)

```
!
! Resource file used to produce Figure 7.5b
!

*XmToggleButton.recomputeSize:      FALSE
*XmToggleButton.height:             30
*XmToggleButton.width:              90
*XmToggleButton.foreground:         black
*XmToggleButton.background:         gray50
*XmToggleButton.shadowThickness:    4

*RowCol.radioBehavior:              TRUE
```

8
Events and Callbacks

Overview

To this point, all of the programs in this book have been output-only. Once the `XtMainLoop` function is called, the programmer loses control of the program.

This chapter describes the *event* mechanism, by which the program is notified of changes in its environment. Each action of the user, from pointer movement to changing the size of a window, results in an event. A client may also send and receive an interclient communication event to or from another client.

Event-Driven Programming

The processing of a traditional program is linear in nature: the program is given input, performs some operations on that input, and produces output. This programming style, when applied to a user-oriented task, gives rise to decidedly user-unfriendly programs — which for decades have been the only programs available.

A user-oriented program, on the other hand, waits for user input, processes that input, then comes back for more. This results in a circular program structure, with no clear endpoint. In short, this is event-driven programming: user input is an event, the program determines what sort of processing to perform based on that event, and when it's done, it waits for another event.

In a Motif program, the programmer does not need to handle such events directly. Instead, the programmer specifies functions to be performed as a result of an event (such as the pressing of a button), and the widget is responsible for calling these functions when the event happens. The `XtMainLoop` function handles the dispatch of events to the proper widget, and the widget then passes the event to the proper piece of code — internal or programmer-written.

What Is an Event ?

An event is the notification to a client program of some change in its environment. As described above, this could result from the user moving the pointer, from the window manager resizing the program's window, or from a multitude of other actions — some initiated by the user, and some initiated by the server or another client.

Events are associated with an X window. If the user clicks the pointer button while positioned over one program's window, the associated event is sent only to the affected program; other windows on the same server do not receive the event. In a Motif program, where each widget has its own window, the event is sent to the affected widget. Thus, clicking the pointer button while the pointer is over a pushbutton activates *that* pushbutton and not any others.

How the Server Handles Events

All events are processed in some way by the display server. User-input events, such as pointer movement, are generated directly by the server — the event comes from the server's hardware. Events generated by another client, such as the window manager, also pass through the server, which acts as a "traffic cop."

When the server receives an event — from another client or its own hardware — it determines which window should receive the event. For client-generated events, this is simple: the client specifies the destination window. For pointer events (such as a button press), the server sends the event to the smallest window that contains the pointer.[1] A keyboard event is sent to the window that currently has the *input focus* (described in the next chapter).

Once the correct window is determined, the server determines whether the window actually wants to receive the event. This is done by means of an *event mask*, sent to the server by the client. Events enabled by the mask are sent to the client over the network connection. Those that are disabled are discarded by the server. Some events, as you will see below, cannot be masked and are always sent to the client — although it may choose not to process them.

Events are sent to the client in the order in which they were generated, and each event is timestamped when it is handled by the server.[2] Due to network delays, events may arrive at the client long after they were handled by the server.[3]

---

[1] This rule becomes more understandable when applied to an actual situation, such as the pushbutton-in-bulletin board of Figure 7.2. Assume that the user presses the pointer button while the pointer is inside the pushbutton's window. In this case, the pointer is also inside the bulletin board's window, and inside the shell's window, and inside the frame window (which belongs to the window manager). However, since the pushbutton's window is the smallest window of these, the button event is sent to it.

[2] This timestamp is a count of milliseconds since the server was started. It is a 32-bit unsigned value, which wraps to zero every 49.71 days.

[3] "Long" in this case is a relative term. If the client and server are running on the same machine, the delay could be less than a millisecond. If the client and server are on opposite ends of the continent, the delay could be several seconds. It is important to note, however, that there is *always* a delay. If this delay is sufficiently long, it will be noticed by the user.

How the Client Handles Events

The client's connection to the server is maintained by low-level code in Xlib. This connection is always watched: when the server sends an event to the client, that event is read and stored into the client's *event queue.*

The client's program-level code is responsible for reading the event queue on a regular basis. When an event is read, it is dispatched to the proper processing code based on its type (pointer movement, resize, etc.) and source window. In a toolkit-based program, this operation is performed by `XtMainLoop`; in an Xlib-based program, it must be performed explicitly.

Handling X Events

In a Motif program, most events are handled directly by the widget. For example, when a label widget is resized, its internal code is responsible for redrawing its contents to fit the new size. On the other hand, some programs could conceivably want to know the new size (for example, a spreadsheet might replace the label's contents with stars if it became too small to display a complete number).

A program receives events by registering an *event handler* with the widget. The type of event is specified, along with a function to be called when the event is received. The widget maintains a list of event handlers for each event type, including its internal event handlers. For any given event, a multitude of event handlers could be called — all of which must finish processing before the next event, if the user is not to notice their presence.

Types of Events

The events that may be received by a widget are listed in Table 8.1 and described below. Due to the relatively large number of events, and the fact that each has its own peculiarities, this chapter concentrates on two only: pointer motion and button presses. Appendix C describes all X events, in detail.

Table 8.1. X event types

Category	Events

Client Communication	`ClientMessage`
	`PropertyNotify`
	`SelectionClear`
	`SelectionNotify`
	`SelectionRequest`

Colormap State	`ColormapNotify`

Exposure	`Expose`
	`GraphicsExpose`
	`NoExpose`

Keyboard Focus	`FocusIn` `FocusOut`
Keyboard Input	`KeyPress` `KeyRelease`
Keymap State	`KeymapNotify`

Pointer/Button	`ButtonPress`
	`ButtonRelease`
	`EnterNotify`
	`LeaveNotify`
	`MotionNotify`

Structure Control	`CirculateRequest`
	`ConfigureRequest`
	`MapRequest`
	`ResizeRequest`

Window State	`CirculateNotify`
	`ConfigureNotify`
	`CreateNotify`
	`DestroyNotify`
	`GravityNotify`
	`MapNotify`
	`MappingNotify`
	`ReparentNotify`
	`UnmapNotify`
	`VisibilityNotify`

Client communication events allow one client to send data to another. They are
described in detail in Chapter 17.

The colormap state event, `ColormapNotify`, indicates that a window's colormap
has changed. This event is almost always left to the widget; in most cases, the

program is responsible for changing the colormap, so it does not need to be alerted to the change.[4]

Exposure events occur when a window — or portion of a window — must be redrawn. This often happens due to the stacking of windows on the server: when a window is moved, those that it previously covered must be redrawn. Although most widgets handle exposure internally, some — *XmDrawnButton* and *XmDrawingArea* — require the program to explicitly redraw their contents.[5] In some cases, a window does not need to be redrawn when exposed: if the server has *backing store*, it will maintain the contents of obscured windows.

Input focus events occur when a window gains or loses the focus. This is described in detail in the next chapter. Also described there are keyboard-input events, which are sent from the server when the user presses or releases a key.

The keymap state event, `KeymapNotify`, is sent to the program when it gains the focus. It contains an indication of which keys were pressed when the focus changed and is handled internally by those widgets that use it.

Pointer/button events notify the program of the pointer's actions. When the pointer moves, a `MotionNotify` event is generated. When a pointer button is pressed, a `ButtonPress` event is generated; its release generates a `ButtonRelease` event. Finally, when the pointer moves into or out of a window's area, `EnterNotify` and `LeaveNotify` events are generated. This chapter describes these events in detail.

Structure control and window state events are used to notify the client about changes in its windows. These events are typically handled by the widget; they are described in Appendix C.

The XEvent *Union*

Events are delivered to the client via the `XEvent` union, defined in Listing 8.1. This union contains a member for each event type; the first member, `type`, specifies the event type. Its value comes from a list of constants corresponding to the event names in Table 8.1, found in the header file `X.h`.

---

[4] Chapter 15 describes colormaps and why they would be changed.
[5] As you will see in Chapter 15, these widgets actually provide a callback for exposure, so the program does not need to handle the raw exposure event.

Listing 8.1. Type definition: *XEvent*

```
typedef union
        {
        int                     type;
        XAnyEvent               xany;
        XKeyEvent               xkey;
        XButtonEvent            xbutton;
        XMotionEvent            xmotion;
        XCrossingEvent          xcrossing;
        XFocusChangeEvent       xfocus;
        XExposeEvent            xexpose;
        XGraphicsExposeEvent    xgraphicsexpose;
        XNoExposeEvent          xnoexpose;
        XVisibilityEvent        xvisibility;
        XCreateWindowEvent      xcreatewindow;
        XDestroyWindowEvent     xdestroywindow;
        XUnmapEvent             xunmap;
        XMapEvent               xmap;
        XMapRequestEvent        xmaprequest;
        XReparentEvent          xreparent;
        XConfigureEvent         xconfigure;
        XGravityEvent           xgravity;
        XResizeRequestEvent     xresizerequest;
        XConfigureRequestEvent  xconfigurerequest;
        XCirculateEvent         xcirculate;
        XCirculateRequestEvent  xcirculaterequest;
        XPropertyEvent          xproperty;
        XSelectionClearEvent    xselectionclear;
        XSelectionRequestEvent  xselectionrequest;
        XSelectionEvent         xselection;
        XColormapEvent          xcolormap;
        XClientMessageEvent     xclient;
        XMappingEvent           xmapping;
        XErrorEvent             xerror;
        XKeymapEvent            xkeymap;
        long                    pad[24];
        }
XEvent;
```

The `xany` member bears special notice. It is a structure that contains the fields
common to all X events. It is shown in Listing 8.2 and described below.

Listing 8.2. Type definition: *XAnyEvent*

```
typedef struct
        {
        int             type;
        unsigned long   serial;
        Boolean         send_event;
        Display         *display;
        Window          window;
        }
XAnyEvent;
```

The `type` member is as in `XEvent`. Due to the way a union works, `type` is the first member of all event structures.

The `serial` member contains the serial number of the last request processed by the server for this window. This field is occasionally used for debugging under Xlib, where the order of requests is often known; it serves little purpose under Motif.

The `send_event` member is used to identify whether the event was generated by the server or another client (using the `XSendEvent` function). If it contains `TRUE`, the event came from a client; if `FALSE`, from the server.

Finally, the `display` and `window` members serve to identify the source of the event. The `display` member identifies the server connection; its contents are defined in the header file `Xlib.h`. The `window` member contains the ID of the window that first received the event; in most cases, this is the window associated with the widget where the event was registered.[6]

Registering an Event

Events are registered with a widget using the `XtAddEventHandler` function, prototyped in Listing 8.3. As described above, this function adds the specified event handler to the list of event handlers associated with the widget. It may be called multiple times for the same widget and event; if multiple event handlers are registered for the same event, they are called in an indeterminate order.

---

[6] But not always. For example, an event could be registered with a manager widget but not its children. In this case, the event handler attached to the manager would receive the notification, but the window would be that of the child. This can be useful: for example, instead of registering an event handler with all of the labels that are children of a particular manager, it could be registered once with the manager, which could find the widget ID of the child from the window ID in the event.

Listing 8.3. Function prototype: *XtAddEventHandler*

```
void     XtAddEventHandler( w, mask, nonmaskable, proc, client_data )
         Widget           w;
         EventMask        mask;
         Boolean          nonmaskable;
         XtEventHandler   proc;
         caddr_t          client_data;
```

The `w` parameter contains the ID of the widget with which the event is registered. As you will see below, this ID is passed to the event handler.

The `mask` parameter identifies those events that the handler should receive. It is a bit mask, built by "or-ing" the constants listed in Table 8.2. Since this mask is a bit mask, setting multiple bits in the mask permits multiple events to be registered by the same call — each of which is passed to the same handler. This technique is used in the example program.

The `nonmaskable` handler specifies whether nonmaskable events are to be passed to the handler. These nonmaskable events are those associated with mapping and interclient communications. If the `nonmaskable` parameter contains `TRUE`, they will be delivered to the event handler. If it contains `FALSE`, they won't. Note that the widget always receives these events; the `nonmaskable` parameter simply controls whether or not they are sent to program code. You will rarely want to receive them.

The `proc` parameter specifies the function handling the event. This is simply a function pointer; the `XtEventHandler` data type specifies a function prototype as shown in Listing 8.4.

Finally, the `client_data` parameter points to data that will be passed to the event handler on each invocation. The contents of this pointer are completely up to the programmer — it could point at any data item or function in the program, or it could contain `NULL` — it could even contain a constant value.[7] The passed value is irrevocably associated with this event registration; it cannot be changed as the program runs. However, the same event handler could be reregistered with the same (or a different) widget, with a different pointer in `client_data`.

---

[7] The `caddr_t` data type is a C type, nominally equivalent to `void *`. Many programs take advantage of the loose type-checking of common C compilers to pass constant values as `client_data` arguments; this book does not recommend the practice.

Table 8.2. Event masks

Mask Constant	Event(s) Enabled	Comments
`ButtonMotionMask`	`MotionNotify`	Notify if any mouse button pressed while pointer is moved
`Button1MotionMask`	`MotionNotify`	Notify only if mouse button #1 pressed while pointer is moved
`Button2MotionMask`	`MotionNotify`	Notify only if mouse button #2 pressed while pointer is moved
`Button3MotionMask`	`MotionNotify`	Notify only if mouse button #3 pressed while pointer is moved
`Button4MotionMask`	`MotionNotify`	Notify only if mouse button #4 pressed while pointer is moved
`Button5MotionMask`	`MotionNotify`	Notify only if mouse button #5 pressed while pointer is moved
`ButtonPressMask`	`ButtonPress`	Notify when any mouse button is pressed
`ButtonReleaseMask`	`ButtonRelease`	Notify when any mouse button is released
`ColormapChange Mask`	`ColormapNotify`	Notify when colormap changes
`EnterWindowMask`	`EnterNotify`	Notify when pointer enters window
`ExposureMask`	`Expose`	Notify when portion of window is exposed.
`FocusChangeMask`	`FocusIn` `FocusOut`	Notify when window gains or loses keyboard focus
`KeymapStateMask`	`KeymapNotify`	Describe keyboard state when focus changes
`KeyPressMask`	`KeyPress`	Notify when any key is pressed
`KeyReleaseMask`	`KeyRelease`	Notify when key is released
`LeaveWindowMask`	`LeaveNotify`	Notify when pointer leaves window
`PointerMotionHint Mask`		Modifies `PointerMotionMask`, so that the number of motion events is minimized; `PointerMotionMask` must be specified too
`PointerMotionMask`	`MotionNotify`	Notify when pointer moves
`PropertyChangeMask`	`PropertyNotify`	Notify when window property changes
`ResizeRedirectMask`	`ResizeRequest`	Capture size-change requests from children of associated window

Table 8.2. Continued.

`StructureNotify Mask`	`CirculateNotify` `ConfigureNotify` `DestroyNotify` `GravityNotify` `MapNotify` `ReparentNotify` `UnmapNotify`	Notify when window structure changes
`SubstructureNotify Mask`	`CirculateNotify` `ConfigureNotify` `CreateNotify` `DestroyNotify` `GravityNotify` `MapNotify` `ReparentNotify` `UnmapNotify`	Notify when child window structure changes
`Substructure RedirectMask`	`CirculateRequest` `ConfigureRequest` `MapRequest`	Capture structure-change requests from children of associated window
`VisibilityChange Mask`	`VisibilityNotify`	Notify when window visibility changes
gc-controlled	`GraphicsExpose` `NoExpose`	These events are selected with the `graphics_exposures` member of the graphics context; when selected, they are non-maskable.
nonmaskable	`ClientMessage` `MappingNotify` `SelectionClear` `SelectionNotify` `SelectionRequest`	These events are delivered to all windows; they may be ignored by passing `FALSE` in the `nonmaskable` parameter of `XtAddEventHandler`
special	*error event*	Protocol errors are passed from server to client using the X event mechanism; such events, however, are handled at a low level in the client code

Event Handler Prototype

All event handlers have the same function prototype, shown in Listing 8.4. The toolkit defines a type, `XtEventHandler`, for pointers to event-handler functions.

Listing 8.4. Function prototype: Event handler

```
void    funcname( w, client_data, event )
        Widget      w;
        caddr_t     client_data;
        XEvent      *event;
```

The function's name, *funcname*, is up to the programmer. The w and client_data parameters are filled from the parameters to XtAddEventHandler: the source widget is identified by w, and client_data contains a programmer-specified pointer.

The event parameter points at the received event, which is maintained by the invoking widget. The program should not change the event's contents, as it may be passed on to another event handler.[8]

Sensitivity and Events

What happens when a widget's sensitive resource contains FALSE? Does it continue to send events to registered event handlers, or does it ignore them?

The answer is "neither and both." Input events — keyboard and pointer — are ignored. They are simply discarded, and an event handler will never see them. Environment events — such as Exposure — are caught and passed on to any registered event handler.

Event-Handler Example: Mouse Tracker

This program attaches an event handler to a label widget. This function catches pointer motion and button events and prints information about the event to standard output. Example output is shown in Listing 8.5: for most events, it consists of the event type, time of occurrence, and pointer position. For button events, it adds the number of the pressed (or released) button.

---

[8] The order in which event handlers are called is indeterminate. No event handler should be written with the assumption that it will always be called before or after another event handler.

Listing 8.5. Output from *Mouse Tracker* program

```
EnterNotify
    Time     = 386214898
    x,y      = 78, 31
MotionNotify
    Time     = 386214965
    x,y      = 85, 28
MotionNotify
    Time     = 386215348
    x,y      = 85, 29

MotionNotify
    Time     = 386215381
    x,y      = 86, 33

ButtonPress
    Time     = 386215398
    x,y      = 87, 37
    Button   = 1
```

To write this program, it is necessary to understand the event structures
returned for pointer motion and button presses. These structures are
`XMotionEvent`, which holds information about pointer motion, `XCrossingEvent`,
which holds information about pointer motion into or out of a window, and
`XButtonEvent`, which holds information about button presses.

Pointer Motion Notification: XMotionEvent

A `MotionNotify` event is sent to the client whenever the pointer moves within a
client window. The data for this event is stored in the `XMotionEvent` structure,
defined in Listing 8.6, and accessed via the `xmotion` member of `XEvent`. This
event is selected using `PointerMotionMask`.

The server generates one or more pointer motion events whenever the pointer is
moved within a window.[9] The exact number of events may vary. Although the
server attempts to track the movement closely, it does not guarantee that each
pixel of movement will result in an event.

If the programmer is only interested in pointer movement while the pointer
button is down (*ie*, a drag operation), then `ButtonMotionMask` may be specified
instead of `PointerMotionMask`. To further refine this limitation, the program may
specify a particular button or group of buttons (by using `Button1MotionMask` *et al*
instead of `ButtonMotionMask`).

---

[9] "Within a window" is an important qualification. The pointer motion must start and end
   inside one window. If the motion starts in one window and ends in another,
   `EnterNotify` and `LeaveNotify` events are generated instead.

Listing 8.6. Type definition: *XMotionEvent*

```
typedef struct
        {
        int             type;
        unsigned long   serial;
        Boolean         send_event;
        Display         *display;
        Window          window;
        Window          root;
        Window          subwindow;
        Time            time;
        int             x, y;
        int             x_root, y_root;
        unsigned int    state;
        char            is_hint;
        Boolean         same_screen;
        }
XMotionEvent;
```

Like all event structures, the members `type`, `serial`, `send_event`, `display`, and `window` overlap those of the `XAnyEvent` structure. They are described above.

The `root` and `subwindow` members, in concert with the `window` member, fully identify the event source. The `root` member contains the window ID of the root window for the screen where the event occurred. The `subwindow` member is used only if the window reporting the event was not the window where the event occurred; in that case, it contains the window ID where the event occurred.[10]

The `time` member contains the event's server timestamp. This is the count of milliseconds between server startup and event occurrence.

The `x` and `y` members contain the pointer's location relative to the window reporting the event. The `x_root` and `y_root` members contain the pointer's location relative to the root window.

The `state` member contains the state of the pointer buttons and keyboard modifier keys at the time the event occurred. This state information is maintained as a set of bit flags, represented by the constants `Button1Mask`, `Button2Mask`, `Button3Mask`, `Button4Mask`, `Button5Mask`, `ShiftMask`, `LockMask`, `ControlMask`, `Mod1Mask`, `Mod2Mask`, `Mod3Mask`, `Mod4Mask`, and `Mod5Mask`. These constants are defined in the header file `X.h`; their meaning should be self-explanatory.

The `is_hint` member indicates whether the notification represents a motion hint. Motion hints are used to limit the stream of events from a single motion, and are

---

[10] Going back to the example of the manager catching events generated by its children: the `window` member contains the ID of the manager's window, and the `subwindow` member contains the ID of the child.

enabled by "or-ing" `PointerMotionHintMask` with `PointerMotionMask` in the event mask. Enabling motion hints instructs the server to send only one motion event during a movement. If this event represents a hint rather than an actual motion notification, the `is_hint` member contains the constant `NotifyHint`, otherwise it contains `NotifyNormal`.[11]

The `same_screen` member indicates whether the window where the event occurred resides on the same screen as the root window. If `same_screen` contains `TRUE`, the event window and root window are on the same screen. If `same_screen` contains `FALSE`, they aren't.

Motion Into or Out of a Window: XCrossingEvent

Movement that begins and ends entirely within one window results in a `MotionNotify` event. If the motion begins in one window and ends in another, it results in an `EnterNotify` event to the new window and a `LeaveNotify` event to the old window. Both events are reported using the `xcrossing` member of `XEvent`. This member is of type `XCrossingEvent` and is defined in Listing 8.7. The `EnterNotify` event is enabled with `EnterWindowMask`, while `LeaveNotify` is enabled with `LeaveWindowMask`.

Listing 8.7. Type definition: *XCrossingEvent*

```
typedef struct
        {
        int             type;
        unsigned long   serial;
        Boolean         send_event;
        Display         *display;
        Window          window;
        Window          root;
        Window          subwindow;
        Time            time;
        int             x, y;
        int             x_root, y_root;
        int             mode;
        int             detail;
        Boolean         same_screen;
        Boolean         focus;
        unsigned int    state;
        } XCrossingEvent;
```

---

[11] While hints minimize the number of events that a widget must process, they almost never report the correct pointer position — the program must explicitly retrieve this position with `XQueryPointer`.

Most of the members of `XCrossingEvent` are identical to members of `XMotionEvent`. The new members are as follows.

The `mode` member describes how the event was generated. A normal crossing event has a `mode` value of `NotifyNormal`. If the event was generated as a result of a "pointer grab," the `mode` member will contain either `NotifyGrab` or `NotifyUngrab`. This chapter is only concerned with normal crossing events.

The `detail` member describes how the previous and new windows are related. The contents of this member are described in detail in Appendix C. It is not important to this chapter.

The final new member, `focus`, indicates whether the window where the event occurred had the input focus at the time of event. If `focus` contains `TRUE`, the event window or one of its children had the focus. If it contains `FALSE`, another window had the focus. This member too may be ignored for the purposes of this chapter.

Pointer Button Press and Release: XButtonEvent

When the user presses or releases a pointer button, that action is reported by a `ButtonPress` or `ButtonRelease` event, enabled by the `ButtonPressMask` and `ButtonReleaseMask` constants, respectively. Both events are reported in the `xbutton` member of `XEvent`, which contains an `XButtonEvent` structure, defined in Listing 8.8.

Listing 8.8. Type definition: *XButtonEvent*

```
typedef struct
        {
        int             type;
        unsigned long   serial;
        Boolean         send_event;
        Display         *display;
        Window          window;
        Window          root;
        Window          subwindow;
        Time            time;
        int             x, y;
        int             x_root, y_root;
        unsigned int    state;
        unsigned int    button;
        Boolean         same_screen;
        } XButtonEvent;
```

Again, many of the members of XButtonEvent are identical to those of XMotionEvent. In fact, the only difference is the button member, which identifies the pressed button. The constants Button1, Button2, Button3, Button4, and Button5, defined in the header file X.h, are used to identify the button.[12]

The Program

The program of Listing 8.9 was used to produce the output of Listing 8.5. This program is identical to that of Listing 5.1, except that it includes an event handler.[13] When you run it, pointer movement and button presses will be reported on the standard output device.

Listing 8.9. Program: Mouse tracker

```
/*******************************************************************
**                                                               **
**   listing_8_9.c                                               **
**                                                               **
**   "Mouse Tracker". This program demonstrates the use of an event   **
**   handler.                                                    **
**                                                               **
*******************************************************************/

#include <Xm/Label.h>


void    EvtHandler();               /* FORWARD definition        */

Widget  appshell,                   /* The label and its shell   */
        the_label;


void main( argc, argv )
    int     argc;
    char    *argv[];
```

---

[12] These constants are generally equal to the values 1, 2, 3, 4, and 5. Since this may change depending on the server, your programs should always compare to the constants, instead of literal values.

[13] The resource file, being identical to that of Listing 5.1, is not shown here.

Listing 8.9. Continued.

```c
{
    appshell = XtInitialize( argv[0], "Listing_8_9", NULL, 0,
                                                &argc, argv );

    the_label = XmCreateLabel( appshell, "TheLabel", NULL, 0 );
    XtManageChild( the_label );

    XtAddEventHandler( the_label,
                       (PointerMotionMask | ButtonPressMask |
                       EnterWindowMask | LeaveWindowMask),
                       FALSE, EvtHandler, NULL );

    XtRealizeWidget( appshell );
    XtMainLoop();
}


void EvtHandler( w, client_data, evt_ptr )
    Widget      w;
    caddr_t     client_data;
    XEvent      *evt_ptr;
{
    switch( evt_ptr->type )
        {
        case ButtonPress:
            printf( "\nButtonPress\n" );
            printf( "    Time     = %d\n",      evt_ptr->xbutton.time );
            printf( "    x,y      = %d, %d\n", evt_ptr->xbutton.x,
                                                evt_ptr->xbutton.y );
printf( "    Button   = %d\n",      evt_ptr->xbutton.button );
            break;
        case EnterNotify:
            printf( "\nEnterNotify\n" );
            printf( "    Time     = %d\n",      evt_ptr->xcrossing.time );
            printf( "    x,y      = %d, %d\n", evt_ptr->xcrossing.x,
                                                evt_ptr->xcrossing.y );
            break;
        case LeaveNotify:
            printf( "\nLeaveNotify\n" );
```

Listing 8.9. Continued.

```
            printf( "     Time      = %d\n",      evt_ptr->xcrossing.time );
            printf( "     x,y       = %d, %d\n", evt_ptr->xcrossing.x,
                                                  evt_ptr->xcrossing.y );
        break;
    case MotionNotify:
        printf( "\nMotionNotify\n" );
        printf( "     Time      = %d\n",      evt_ptr->xmotion.time );
        printf( "     x,y       = %d, %d\n", evt_ptr->xmotion.x,
                                              evt_ptr->xmotion.y );
        break;
    default:
        break;
    }
}
```

In the main part of the program, the only difference between Listings 8.9 and 5.1 is the call to `XtAddEventHandler`. Note that a single call registers four events by specifying four masks. Note also that the nonmaskable events are ignored.

The event handler is straightforward. It is called each time a motion, crossing, or button-press event occurs, as specified by the mask at registration time. Inside the event handler, a `switch` statement determines the event type, using the `type` member of `XEvent`. Each case of the switch prints appropriate information. Although each case appears to print the same information, note that each uses a different member of the `XEvent` structure.

You might wonder why a label was chosen as the program's widget — a pushbutton would seem a more logical choice. The reason was that I wanted to illustrate the ability of *all* widgets to receive events, even those that would not normally be used for input.

Callbacks

While events are the means by which a program receives all of its input, event handling can be tedious. Consider a pushbutton: it must handle button-down and button-motion events for arming, button-up events for activation and disarming, and window-crossing events for determining whether activation is part of disarming. One of the difficulties of writing an Xlib-based client is that the program must handle all such events by itself.

X toolkits provide a higher level of program notification, the *callback*, which may be thought of as an "expected event." The widget handles low-level event processing internally and only notifies the program when it receives an event or series of events relating to its primary purpose. In the case of the pushbutton, these "expected events" are arming, disarming, and activation.[14]

The use of callbacks varies from widget class to widget class, and from program to program. Some callbacks, such as arming and disarming a pushbutton, are used by very few programs. Others, such as pushbutton activation, are used by almost all programs that use the widget.

Registering a Callback

Widget callbacks are associated with a resource. Unlike most resources, however, callbacks cannot be set in a resource file or by `XtSetValues` — and they shouldn't be read by `XtGetValues`. Instead, callback resources are modified by program code, using a registration function similar to that for an event handler.

For callbacks, the registration function is `XtAddCallback`, prototyped in Listing 8.10. As with event handlers, a particular callback could have many called procedures, or it could have none: each call to `XtAddCallback` adds a function to the named *callback list*.

Listing 8.10. Function prototype: XtAddCallback

```
void    XtAddCallback( w, callback_name, proc, client_data )
        Widget            w;
        String            callback_name;
        XtCallbackProc    proc;
        caddr_t           client_data;
```

The `w`, `proc`, and `client_data` parameters are identical to those of `XtAddEventHandler`: `w` specifies the widget, `proc` specifies the called function, and `client_data` is a pointer to program-specific data (it may be `NULL`).

The `callback_name` parameter specifies the name of the callback resource. As with any programmatically set resource, this name is prefixed by "XmN". An example, as you will see below, is *XmPushButton*'s `armCallback` resource, which is identified as `XmNarmCallback`.

Callback Function Prototype

All callback functions have the same prototype, as shown in Listing 8.11. This prototype is represented by the data type `XtCallbackProc`.

---

[14] Internally, the pushbutton processes an enormous number of events. For example, it must handle the `Expose` event in order to redraw its contents, in addition to the button and movement events described above. This is one of the reasons that Motif programs are so large: there's a lot of work going on "behind the scenes." However, since this event-handling code is in a single place (the class code), instead of multiple places as in an Xlib program, a complex program actually uses code very efficiently.

Listing 8.11. Function prototype: Callback function

```
void      funcname( w, client_data, call_data )
          Widget      w;
          caddr_t     client_data;
          caddr_t     call_data;
```

As with an event handler, the `w` parameter is passed the ID of the widget generating the callback, and the `client_data` parameter is passed the value specified when the callback was registered.[15]

The `call_data` parameter contains information specific to the callback type. This data is specific to the widget class and callback, although many callbacks use the default structure, `XmAnyCallbackStruct`, defined in Listing 8.12. The header file `Xm.h` defines data types for each callback.

Listing 8.12. Type definition: *XmAnyCallbackStruct*

```
typedef struct
        {
        int     reason;
        XEvent  *event;
        }
XmAnyCallbackStruct;
```

The `reason` member, which is the first member of all callback structures, identifies the callback using a constant from the header file `Xm.h`. This identification allows multiple callbacks to be served by a single function.

The `event` member points to the event that generated the callback. This may be used by the program to provide additional information, but must not be changed, as other functions may be registered for the same callback.[16] In some cases, the callback is not generated as the result of an event, in which case the `event` member contains `NULL`.

Removing a Callback

Most programs install a callback and leave it installed for the life of the program. In some cases, however, a callback might need to be installed for a short time, then removed. The function `XtRemoveCallback`, prototyped in Listing 8.13, performs this function.

---

[15] As with an event handler, one callback function may serve multiple widgets: the invoking widget is identified by the `w` parameter.

[16] As with event handlers, the order in which callback functions are called is indeterminate, so a program should not be designed around an expected order.

Listing 8.13. Function prototype: XtRemoveCallback

```
void    XtRemoveCallback( w, callback_name, proc, client_data )
        Widget          w;
        String          callback_name;
        XtCallbackProc  proc;
        caddr_t         client_data;
```

This function removes the callback function identified by `proc` and `client_data` from the callback list identified by `callback_name` for the widget identified by `w`. It does not affect other functions in the callback list.[17] Note that both the function address and the data pointer are used to identify the callback: the same function could be registered many times, with different data for each registration, and `XtRemoveCallback` must unlink the proper call.

Button Callbacks

Buttons — *XmPushButton*, *XmArrowButton*, and *XmToggleButton* — have callbacks to notify the program when they are armed, activated, and disarmed. Table 8.3 lists these callbacks. Unlike a normal resource table, the *Inheritance* column identifies which classes support the callback, instead of where the callback is defined.

Table 8.3. Button callbacks

Name	Inheritance	Type	Default Value
`activateCallback`	XmArrowButton XmPushButton	`XtCallbackList`	NULL
`armCallback`	XmArrowButton XmPushButton XmToggleButton	`XtCallbackList`	NULL
`disarmCallback`	XmArrowButton XmPushButton XmToggleButton	`XtCallbackList`	NULL
`valueChangedCallback`	XmToggleButton	`XtCallbackList`	NULL

---

[17] Another function, `XtRemoveAllCallbacks`, exists that removes all callbacks from a particular callback list. It should not be used, however, because Motif may add internal callbacks to a widget.

XmArrowButton *and* XmPushButton *Callbacks*

The callbacks for *XmArrowButton* and *XmPushButton* are identical. Activation is, as described before, the process of clicking the pointer button while inside the area of the screen button. Arming is the process of pressing the pointer button while inside the area of the screen button, and disarming happens when the pointer button is released. Activation is comprised of both arming and disarming, but an arm-disarm sequence can occur without activation (if the pointer is moved out of the button's window before the button is released).

Both *XmArrowButton* and *XmPushButton* pass a pointer to `XmAnyCallbackStruct`. The `reason` member contains the value `XmCR_ACTIVATE` to indicate activation, `XmCR_ARM` to indicate arming, and `XmCR_DISARM` to indicate disarming.

XmToggleButton *Callbacks*

Like the other buttons, *XmToggleButton* supports the arm and disarm callbacks, but does not support activation. Instead, it provides a callback to indicate that its value has changed. The `XmToggleButton` callbacks do not use `XmAnyCallbackStruct`, but instead use the structure defined in Listing 8.14.

Listing 8.14. Type definition: *XmToggleButtonCallbackStruct*

```
typedef struct
        {
        int     reason;
        XEvent  *event;
        Boolean set;
        }
        XmToggleButtonCallbackStruct;
```

The `reason` and `event` members identical to those of `XmAnyCallbackStruct`. Valid reasons are `XmCR_ARM` for arming, `XmCR_DISARM` for disarming, and `XmCR_VALUE_CHANGED` for toggle. The `set` member contains the new value of the button's `set` resource.

XmPushButton Callback Example: Press Here

The callback example program, shown in Listing 8.15, simply catches all of the *XmPushButton* callbacks and reports which were received, along with the types of events that generated them.[18] It is similar to the program of Listing 8.9, but substitutes a pushbutton for the label and traps callbacks instead of events. When you run this program, you will get a much better understanding of how a

---

[18] As you see, I took the easy way out and merely print the event's type. I felt that adding a `switch` statement to convert the type into a string would obscure the purpose of the program.

pushbutton works — especially the differences between arming, activation, and disarming.

Listing 8.15. Callback example: "Press Here"

```
/**********************************************************************
**                                                                  **
**   listing_8_15.c                                                 **
**                                                                  **
**   "Press Here". An example of pushbutton callbacks.              **
**                                                                  **
**********************************************************************/


#include <Xm/PushB.h>


void    ButtonCB();                         /* FORWARD Definition        */


Widget  appshell,                           /* Application Shell         */
        the_btn;                            /* The one and only label    */
void main( argc, argv )
    int     argc;
    char    *argv[];
{
    appshell = XtInitialize( argv[0], "Listing_8_15", NULL, 0,
                                            &argc, argv );

    the_btn = XmCreatePushButton( appshell, "TheBtn", NULL, 0 );
    XtManageChild( the_btn );

    XtAddCallback( the_btn, XmNarmCallback, ButtonCB, NULL );
    XtAddCallback( the_btn, XmNdisarmCallback, ButtonCB, NULL );
    XtAddCallback( the_btn, XmNactivateCallback, ButtonCB, NULL );

    XtRealizeWidget( appshell );
    XtMainLoop();
}
```

Listing 8.15. Continued.

```c
void ButtonCB( w, client_data, call_data )
    Widget                 w;
    caddr_t                client_data;
    XmAnyCallbackStruct *call_data;
{
    printf( "\nCallback Reason = %d ", call_data->reason );
    switch (call_data->reason)
        {
        case XmCR_ARM :
            printf( "(Arm)\n" );
            break;
        case XmCR_DISARM :
            printf( "(Disarm)\n" );
            break;
        case XmCR_ACTIVATE :
            printf( "(Activate)\n" );
            break;
        }
    printf( "Event Type      = %d\n", call_data->event->type );
}
```

This program highlights an interesting point, which may not have been obvious from the text. That is that, while `XtAddEventHandler` can specify any number of events (because it uses an event mask), `XtAddCallback` can only specify a single callback (because it specifies a resource name). For this reason, three calls to `XtAddCallback` were necessary.

Actions

The mouse on a typical X terminal has three buttons, but *XmPushButton* only provides a single activation callback. What do you do if you want to perform different actions depending on which button was used to activate the pushbutton? You could look at the `event` member of the callback data structure, but that means that the callback code would become more complex, and you would have to recompile if you decided to swap the actions of buttons #3 and #2.

The answer is to use an *action table* to identify the program functions and a *translation table* to link the events to the actions. An *action* is similar to a callback — both are invoked by the widget as the result of "expected events." However, an action procedure represents a "lower" level of event handling than a callback — in fact, most callbacks are invoked as part of a built-in action procedure.

Actions and translations provide a convenient means to enhance the abilities of an "off-the-shelf" widget. With appropriate action procedures, the programmer can modify a Motif widget to suit the needs of a particular program, thus foregoing the need to implement a new widget class.[19] Indeed, most existing widgets gain their functionality from action procedures; it is a rare widget that actually uses an event handler.

There are caveats to this flexibility. The first is that the *translation manager* is rather single-minded: when it matches a sequence of incoming events against a sequence in its list, it dispatches the appropriate action. If that sequence happens to be the initial part of another translation, then both are executed.[20]

A second caveat is that an action procedure receives little information when it is called: only the widget and event that caused the action to be invoked, along with constant parameters specified in the translation table. The action procedure does not receive a reason for the invocation (actions and reasons are considered identical), nor can the program specify a `client_data` pointer. All client data must be accessed via global variables.

The Action Table

An action table specifies a set of one-to-one relationships between program functions and text strings, which may then be used to identify the function in a translation table. This means that action functions are accessible to resource files — the function pointers are associated with external names. It also means that action functions are not associated with specific widgets: a given widget's translation table may specify any of a program's actions.

Action tables are physically stored as an array of `XtActionsRec` structures, defined in Listing 8.16. The `string` member points to a NUL-terminated character string; it is the external name of the action.[21] The `proc` member is a pointer to the function associated with the action; the format of such a function is described below. The `XtActionList` data type is a simple pointer to an action table; it is used in the prototype of the `XtAddActions` function.

---

[19] As Motif is a commercial product, many programmers do not have access to the source code and cannot easily implement new widget classes. This is in sharp contrast to existing "publicly accessible" widget sets, such as Athena, which may be modified at will.

[20] As an example, consider a pushbutton that is to recognize both single and double clicks. Since a single click is the initial part of the double click, both the single-click and the double-click action are executed: one after the first click, and one after the second.

[21] There is no convention for action names, even within Motif. This book uses the same conventions as for function names: words run together, with the first letter of each word capitalized.

Listing 8.16. Type definitions: *XtActionsRec, XtActionList*

```
typedef struct
        {
        char            *string;
        XtActionsProc   proc;
        }
XtActionsRec;

typedef XtActionsRec    *XtActionList;
```

Installing an Action Table

Once an action table is built — the sample program shows what one looks like —
it must be installed. The function `XtAddActions`, prototyped in Listing 8.17,
installs the action table. This function takes as parameters a pointer to the
action table (`action_list`) and the number of actions specified by the table
(`num_actions`).

Listing 8.17. Function prototype: *XtAddActions*

```
void    XtAddActions( action_list, num_actions )
        XtActionList    action_list;
        Cardinal        num_actions;
```

Action Function Prototype

An action function is similar to an event handler or callback function. Listing
8.18 contains the prototype of a generic action function.

Listing 8.18. Function prototype: Action function

```
void    funcname( w, event, params, num_params )
        Widget      w;
        XEvent      *event;
        char        *params[];
        int         *num_params;
```

The w and event parameters should by now be familiar: w is the ID of the widget invoking the action, and event is a pointer to the event that caused the action to be invoked. As with events and callbacks, an action procedure should not modify the event structure, nor should it expect to be called in a particular order relative to other action procedures or callbacks.[22]

The params and num_params parameters are used to pass character-string arguments to the action procedure. These arguments are defined in the translation table and as a result are read-only. The params and num_params parameters serve an identical purpose to argv and argc of the program's main function: params is an array of string pointers, and num_params contains the number of pointers in that array.

Due to the constant nature of such action arguments, they would not seem to be very useful. However, their use is similar to the reason member of a callback structure: a single-action procedure may be used for multiple translations, with the specific reason passed as an action argument. In addition, action arguments may be used during program debugging to provide a record of how and why an action procedure was invoked.

Translations

Action functions, and the table that identifies them, form one-half of a partnership. The other half is the translation table, which links an action to a specific set of events. Each widget instance has its own translation table, which may be changed in the resource file. Each widget class has a default translation table, used to invoke the widget's internal code; this table may be replaced or extended by the programmer.

The translations *Resource*

A widget's translation table is specified by the translations resource, defined by *Core* and shown in Table 8.4. As the translation table is defined by *Core*, all widget classes support translations. As it is a resource, each widget instance may have its own set of translations.

Table 8.4. Resource specification: *translations*

Name	Inheritance	Type	Default Value
translations	Core	XtTranslations	NULL

To the programmer, a translation table is a NUL-terminated ASCII string. Internally, it exists in a "compiled" form for quick access by the translation manager. It may be set programmatically or via a resource file. Although the resource file is the simpler approach, a quirk in the Motif resource manager means that some changes may only be performed programmatically.

---

[22] An action associated with a callback — such as the Activate action of *XmPushButton* — will, however, be called before the associated callback function.

Translation Format

As stated above, the programmer's view of a translation table is as an ASCII string. This table contains one or more translations, with newlines ('\n') to separate translations. Each translation specifies a one-to-one mapping between an event sequence and an action sequence. The format of a translation is shown in Listing 8.19.[23]

Listing 8.19. Translation syntax

```
event-sequence: action(arguments) [action(arguments)…]
```

The event-sequence is a comma-separated list of events terminated by a colon. The action is one of the names defined by the action table. Action arguments are optional; if used, they are character strings, with each argument separated by whitespace.[24] Multiple actions may be defined in a single translation; they are executed in order. If multiple actions are specified, they must be separated by whitespace.

The translation's event-sequence consists of one or more event specifications, formatted as in Listing 8.20. If multiple specifications are used, they must be separated by commas.

Listing 8.20. Event-sequence syntax

```
[modifiers]<event>[(count)][detail]
```

The *modifiers* item is equivalent to the state member of an event structure: it indicates which pointer button is down or whether the shift (or control, etc) key is pressed. Table 8.5 contains a list of supported modifier names.

The *event* item is the name of the event and must be delimited by angle brackets ("<", ">"). This name may be one of the defined X events listed in Table 8.1, or it may be one of the names listed in Table 8.6. This table includes abbreviations such as Key (which is equivalent to KeyPress) and event-modifier combinations such as Btn1Down (which is equivalent to Button1<ButtonPress>).

The *count* item represents the number of times the event occurs. This item allows repetitive events to be specified without use of a comma-separated list. If

---

[23] This specification, like others in this chapter, makes use of the following conventions: (1) Roman (upright) text is used for literal characters, (2) italics are used for "placeholders" — symbolic names that are replaced by situation-specific text, (3) italicized brackets ("[" and "]") are used to delimit optional components, and (4) an ellipsis ("...") is used to represent repetition of the preceding component(s).

[24] The translation manager decomposes the arguments string into multiple arguments based on this whitespace. There is no way to pass a multiple-word argument.

used, it must be enclosed in parentheses. A plus sign (+) may immediately follow the numerical count to indicate that any number of events greater than or equal to the specified count will be accepted. For example, if the count item contains (5+), it indicates that five or more repetitions of the event/modifier are required for a match.

The *detail* item specifies additional information about the event. For example, in a `KeyPress` event, the detail item specifies the pressed key. The header file `X11/keysymdef.h` may be referenced for key names — this is especially important for function keys, which are not represented directly by ASCII characters.

Table 8.5. Translation event modifiers

Literal Code	Description
!	Allow listed modifiers only. This code must be the first one in the modifier list. It specifies that the event will be recognized only if the specified modifiers and no others are in effect. If the exclamation point is not used, the modifiers in use must match those in the event specification, but any other modifiers may be present — they are ignored.
~	Negate next modifier. Whereas a normal modifier specifies "match this event if this modifier is present," the tilde specifies "match this event only when this modifier is not present."
:	Translate keys according to modifiers. This code applies only to `<Key>` events and must precede any other modifier (except for the exclamation point). For example: `"<Key>A"` matches any press of the "A" key, whether or not any modifiers keys are pressed — meaning that both 'A' and 'a' match the event. However `":<Key>A"` means that only the uppercase letter is accepted.
Any	Any modifier permitted. This code is optional.
None	No modifiers permitted.
Ctrl	Control key pressed during event (may be abbreviated as `c`).
Shift	Shift key pressed during event (may be abbreviated as `s`).
Lock	Shift-lock in effect during event (may be abbreviated as `l`).
Meta	Meta key pressed during event (may be abbreviated as `m`).
Hyper	Hyper key pressed during event (may be abbreviated as `h`).
Super	Super key pressed during event (may be abbreviated as `su`).
Alt	Alt key pressed during event (may be abbreviated as `a`).

Table 8.5. Continued.

`Mod1`	Modifier Key #1 pressed during event.
`Mod2`	Modifier Key #2 pressed during event.
`Mod3`	Modifier Key #3 pressed during event.
`Mod4`	Modifier Key #4 pressed during event.
`Mod5`	Modifier Key #5 pressed during event.
`Button1`	Pointer button #1 pressed during event.
`Button2`	Pointer button #2 pressed during event.
`Button3`	Pointer button #3 pressed during event.
`Button4`	Pointer button #4 pressed during event.
`Button5`	Pointer button #5 pressed during event.

Table 8.6. Translation event names

Name	Description
`Btn1Down`	Equivalent to `ButtonPress` with `Button1` modifier.
`Btn1Motion`	Equivalent to `MotionNotify` with `Button1` modifier.
`Btn1Up`	Equivalent to `ButtonRelease` with `Button1` modifier.
`Btn2Down`	Equivalent to `ButtonPress` with `Button2` modifier.

Table 8.6. Continued.

`Btn2Motion`	Equivalent to `MotionNotify` with `Button2` modifier.
`Btn2Up`	Equivalent to `ButtonRelease` with `Button2` modifier.
`Btn3Down`	Equivalent to `ButtonPress` with `Button3` modifier.
`Btn3Motion`	Equivalent to `MotionNotify` with `Button3` modifier.
`Btn3Up`	Equivalent to `ButtonRelease` with `Button3` modifier.
`Btn4Down`	Equivalent to `ButtonPress` with `Button4` modifier.
`Btn4Motion`	Equivalent to `MotionNotify` with `Button4` modifier.
`Btn4Up`	Equivalent to `ButtonRelease` with `Button4` modifier.
`Btn5Down`	Equivalent to `ButtonPress` with `Button5` modifier.
`Btn5Motion`	Equivalent to `MotionNotify` with `Button5` modifier.
`Btn5Up`	Equivalent to `ButtonRelease` with `Button5` modifier.

Table 8.6. Continued.

`BtnDown`	Equivalent to `ButtonPress`.
`BtnMotion`	Equivalent to `MotionNotify` with any button modifier (*ie*, notify of motion only while button is down).
`BtnUp`	Equivalent to `ButtonRelease`.
`Circ`	Equivalent to `CirculateNotify`.
`CircReq`	Equivalent to `CirculateRequest`.
`Clrmap`	Equivalent to `ColormapNotify`.
`Configure`	Equivalent to `ConfigureNotify`.
`ConfigureReq`	Equivalent to `ConfigureRequest`.
`Create`	Equivalent to `CreateNotify`.
`Ctrl`	Equivalent to `KeyPress` with `Ctrl` modifier.
`Destroy`	Equivalent to `DestroyNotify`.
`Enter`	Equivalent to `EnterNotify`.
`EnterWindow`	Equivalent to `EnterNotify`.
`Grav`	Equivalent to `GravityNotify`.
`GrExp`	Equivalent to `GraphicsExpose`.
`Key`	Equivalent to `KeyPress`.
`KeyDown`	Equivalent to `KeyPress`.
`Keymap`	Equivalent to `KeymapNotify`.
`KeyUp`	Equivalent to `KeyRelease`.
`Visible`	Equivalent to `VisibilityNotify`.

Translation Examples

To put the above format specifications into more concrete terms, Listing 8.21 contains example translation specifications. The first example specifies a click of pointer button #2: a press followed immediately by a release. The second example is identical, but uses modifier-event specifications instead of abbreviations. The third example specifies a "shift-click" of button #2: it uses a modifier along with abbreviated events and calls two actions as a result of the events. The third example handles keyboard input: it specifies that the action is called when a capital "Q" is pressed, and shows the use of the "detail" component. The final example handles the identical event — a capital "Q" — but specifies it in terms of a modified key.[25]

Listing 8.21. Example translations

```
<Btn2Down>,<Btn2Up>:                             ActivateTwo()
Button2<ButtonPress>, Button2<ButtonRelease>:    ActivateTwo()
Shift<Btn2Down>, Shift<Btn2Up>:                  ActivateTwo() Clear()
:<Key>Q:                                         Quit()
Shift<Key>q:                                     Quit()
```

Translation Installation: Replace, Augment, or Override

Each widget has a default set of translations defined by the widget class. In most cases, the programmer will want to change some translations, while leaving others in their default state. To this end, translations may be installed in three ways: to replace the existing translations, to augment the existing translations, and to override the existing translations.[26]

Replacement is, as its name suggests, a complete replacement of the default translations by those the programmer specifies. Augmentation is the non-destructive addition of translations to those already supported by the widget: if an event sequence in the new table matches one in the existing table, the new translation is ignored. Overriding is the destructive addition of translations: the existing translations are maintained, but if an existing event sequence matches a new event sequence, the new translation replaces the existing translation.

Installing Translations Programmatically

Programmatic installation of translations is a two-step process. First, the new translation table must be converted from a NUL-terminated string into its compiled form, then the compiled table must be installed into the widget. The function `XtParseTranslationTable`, prototyped in Listing 8.22, performs the compilation.

---

[25] Note that the key is specified by a lowercase character. This is a quirk of the translation manager: while it would accept both uppercase and lowercase for a specification of `<Key>Q`, it accepts neither for a specification of `Shift<Key>Q`.

[26] X11R5 splits a widget's translations into two parts: the base translations, defined by the widget class and accessed by the `baseTranslations` resource, and user translations, accessed by the `translations` resource.

Listing 8.22. Function prototype: XtParseTranslationTable

```
XtTranslations  XtParseTranslationTable( table )
            String  table;
```

`XtParseTranslationTable` takes a single parameter, the NUL-terminated C string containing the table. This string consists of one or more substrings, formatted as described above, with new lines separating each substring. The returned value is a pointer to the compiled table. This compiled table may be installed in multiple widgets, and cannot be freed by the program.

Once the ASCII translation table is compiled into internal form, it may be installed in a widget using either `XtAugmentTranslations` or `XtOverrideTranslations`, both of which are prototyped in Listing 8.23. The parameters to both functions are the same: the ID of the widget to receive the new translations (`w`) and the compiled translation table (`translations`).

Listing 8.23. Function prototypes: XtAugmentTranslations,
XtOverrideTranslations

```
void    XtAugmentTranslations( w, translations )
        Widget          w;
        XtTranslations  translations;


void    XtOverrideTranslations( w, translations )
        Widget          w;
        XtTranslations  translations;
```

While the above functions directly support the augment and override methods of translation installation, the replace method is supported indirectly. To completely replace a widget's default translations, you must first call `XtUninstallTranslations`, prototyped in Listing 8.24. This function removes any existing translations from the specified widget; you may then use either `XtAugmentTranslations` or `XtOverrideTranslations` to install a new translation table.

Listing 8.24. Function prototype: XtUninstallTranslations

```
void    XtUninstallTranslations( w )
        Widget          w;
```

Installing Translations via Resource File

As with most resources, installation of a translation table via resource file is simpler than programmatic installation.[27] Listing 8.25 shows the format used to specify a translation table in a resource file.

Listing 8.25. Translation table resource specification

```
widget_name.translations:    directive            \n \
                             first_translation  \n \
                             second_translation \n \
                             last_translation
```

The "directive" specifies how the translation table is to be added to the widget. The standard resource manager permits values of `#replace`, `#augment`, and `#override`, corresponding the identically named installation method. However, the Motif resource manager only supports `#replace`. As a result, the directive may be omitted from the table (and often is — see the sample program).[28]

Each line in the table, except the last, is terminated with a backslash ("\"). This indicates to the resource manager that the resource specification is continued on multiple lines.[29] Each line — again except the last — also contains a newline character ('\n'). As stated above, this is required to delimit the translations.

Translation Table Ordering

When the translation manager attempts to match an event sequence to a widget's translations, it does so by sequentially scanning the widget's translation table and using the first matching translation. This means that a sequence of translations such as that shown in Listing 8.26 will not work — the translation manager always applies the first translation, whether or not the shift key is pressed. To make these translations work, they must be reversed: in general, more specific translations should appear before their less-specific brethren.

---

[27] Unfortunately, the Motif resource manager, up through Release 1.1, does not support the augment and override installation methods. As a result, resource files cannot be used for "fine tuning" a widget's translation table — only for completely replacing that table.

[28] There is a "story behind the story" here. Motif maintains default translations in a manner that does not use the `translations` resource. If `translations` contains NULL — the default — then this other table is used. If `translations` points at a translation table, then that table is used. This is why the Motif resource manager is unable to handle the `#override` and `#augment` directives. However, the functions `XtOverrideTranslations` and `XtAugmentTranslations` do work as expected, modifying whichever table is in use.

[29] You have already seen this technique, in Listing 5.3, to specify multiple fonts for a label.

Listing 8.26. Poorly structured translations

```
<ButtonPress>:          ActionOne()
Shift<ButtonPress>:      ActionTwo()
```

Interaction of Events, Callbacks, and Translations

What happens if a widget traps events, has callbacks registered, and uses actions? The answer depends to a great deal on just how the widget is built and how you specified the translation table.

In any case, events are completely separate from translations and callbacks. You can have an *XmPushButton* widget with an event handler registered for button-press events and a callback function on the arm callback, and both will be called. A program's event handler is completely separate from that of the widget — both receive the same events.

Actions and callbacks, on the other hand, are very closely related — most callbacks are invoked as the result of actions specified by the class's default translations. As a result, if you replace the default action table, you disable normal callback invocation.

To avoid this problem, if you plan to add translations to a widget but wish to maintain its normal callbacks, you must either augment its translations (programmatically) or include the default translations in your resource file. This book specifies the default translations for *XmPushButton* and *XmText*; for other widgets, refer to the *Programmer's Reference*.

Action/Translation Example: Multibutton Pushbutton

The program and resource file of Listing 8.27 handle the case where one pushbutton is to have two actions associated with it. In this program, both action functions are identical — they print their name and arguments. The function `ActionOne` is invoked by clicking pointer button #1; `ActionTwo` invoked by clicking pointer button #2.

Listing 8.27. Program and resource file: Actions and translations example

```c
/**********************************************************************
**                                                                  **
**   listing_8_27.c                                                 **
**                                                                  **
**   Demonstration of actions and translations, using a pushbutton. **
**                                                                  **
***********************************************************************/


#include <Xm/PushB.h>


void    ActionOne();                        /* FORWARD definitions     */
void    ActionTwo();


Widget          appshell,
                the_btn;

XtActionsRec    action_tab[] = {
                                { "ActionOne", ActionOne },
                                { "ActionTwo", ActionTwo }
                                };

void main( argc, argv )
    int     argc;
    char    *argv[];
{
    appshell = XtInitialize( argv[0], "Listing_8_27", NULL, 0,
                                                &argc, argv );

    XtAddActions( action_tab, XtNumber(action_tab) );

    the_btn = XmCreatePushButton( appshell, "TheBtn", NULL, 0 );
    XtManageChild( the_btn );
    XtRealizeWidget( appshell );
```

Listing 8.27. Continued.

```c
    XtMainLoop();
}



void ActionOne( w, event, params, num_params )
    Widget      w;
    XEvent      *event;
    char        *params[];
    int         *num_params;
{
    int         i;

    printf( "\nAction 1 Invoked\n" );
    printf( "    %d Params:", *num_params );
    for (i = 0 ;  i < *num_params ;  i++)
        printf( " %s", params[i] );
    printf( "\n" );
}

void ActionTwo( w, event, params, num_params )
    Widget      w;
    XEvent      *event;
    char        *paráms[];
    int         *num_params;
{
    int         i;

    printf( "\nAction 2 Invoked\n" );
    printf( "    %d Params:", *num_params );
    for (i = 0 ;  i < *num_params ;  i++)
        printf( " %s", params[i] );
    printf( "\n" );
}
!
! Resource file for Actions/Translations demonstrator
!

*TheBtn.height:         50
*TheBtn.width:          100
*TheBtn.labelString:    Press Here

*TheBtn.translations:   \
                <Btn1Down>,<Btn1Up>:    ActionOne(Act One)  \n \
                <Btn2Down>,<Btn2Up>:    ActionTwo()
```

This program is straightforward: it defines the table of actions, then calls `XtAddActions` to install them. The `XtNumber` macro deserves note: it calculates the number of entries in an array, allowing the array to be expanded at will without changes to the `XtAddActions` call.[30]

The action procedures are as described above. They make use of the `params` and `num_params` parameters, and the translation table specifies arguments to be decomposed.

The translation table itself is the interesting thing. The button click is specified as two events, button-down and button-up. Whenever the translation manager detects these two events in the event stream without any intervening events, it calls the associated action. The table uses the combined button event names; it could use a button modifier along with `<BtnDown>` and `<BtnUp>` events (or `<ButtonPress>` and `<ButtonRelease>`).

Again, note the newline and backslash at the end of each line. The backslash by itself signals the resource manager that the resource specification is continued on the next line. The newline is converted by the resource manager, and the translation manager uses that newline to separate the transactions.

Finally, note that the table does not specify a directive — it uses the default `#replace` directive. When the directive is missing, the first translation is the first line of the resource.

XmPushButton Default Translations

XmPushButton uses the translation manager to invoke all of its callbacks. Listing 8.28 contains the translation table for a standalone pushbutton.[31] If you decide to add a new translation table to a pushbutton, including lines from this listing will enable the existing callbacks.

Listing 8.28. XmPushButton default translation table

```
<Btn1Down>:       Arm()
<Btn1Up>:         Activate() Disarm()
<Key>Return:      ArmAndActivate()
<Key>space:       ArmAndActivate()
<EnterWindow>:    Enter()
<LeaveWindow>:    Leave()
```

---

[30] The definition of this macro is `(sizeof(x) / sizeof(x[0]))`. It is also used quite often with calls to `XtManageChildren`.

[31] When a pushbutton is in a menu, it uses a different translation table. As an in-depth presentation of Motif translations is beyond the scope of this book, the reader is referred to the *OSF/Motif Programmers Reference*.

As you can see, pressing the pointer button arms the pushbutton, while releasing the pointer button (while inside the pushbutton's window) both activates and disarms the pushbutton. In addition, pressing the *Return* or *Space* keys on the keyboard (providing, of course, that the pushbutton has input focus) will also activate the button. Finally, note that the window crossing events are also trapped — leaving the window while the button is armed changes the appearance of the window.

9
Keyboard Input

Overview

While some programs do not require the use of a keyboard, most do. Programs that receive all input from button presses, pointer movement, and data files are rare; usually, the user must enter some data by typing. Even if the user does not use the keyboard to input data, it may be used in many cases to substitute for a mouse, due to traversal, accelerators, and translations.

This chapter begins with a description of how keyboard input is handled by X: how the keys are identified, how the server determines which window gets keyboard input, and how the client program handles such input. This is followed by a description of the *traversal* facility, by which the keyboard can in many cases substitute for the pointer. The rest of the chapter is devoted to the *XmText* widget class, a generic text input/edit widget that may be configured for purposes ranging from a simple input field to a text editor.

Input Focus

The list of X events may be divided into two classes: those generated by another client and those generated directly by the user. User-generated events represent interaction with the server and may be further subdivided into pointer and keyboard events.

The handling of a pointer event is simple: the pointer's location determines the window that receives the event. The keyboard, however, cannot be so directly associated with a window: one keyboard serves all windows. For this reason, the server considers one window to have the *input focus*, and all keyboard events are sent to that window.

The window manager is responsible for assigning input focus in response to user events.[1] The Motif window manager (*mwm*) has two modes of assigning input

---

[1] It is possible for a client to *grab* the focus. Except in very specific cases, however, doing so does not follow the principle of giving the user complete control of his/her environment and should be avoided.

focus: pointer and explicit.[2] In pointer mode, input focus follows the pointer: focus is changed by moving the pointer over the window that is to receive focus. In explicit mode, the user must select the window to receive focus by clicking with the pointer button anywhere in the window frame or client area. When a window has focus, *mwm* indicates that fact by changing the color of the window's frame.[3]

When the focus changes, two informational events are sent by the window manager. `FocusIn` is sent to the window receiving the focus, and `FocusOut` is sent to the window losing the focus.[4] After the focus changes, all subsequent keyboard events are delivered to the new window. A Motif client maintains its own internal focus information, allowing it to transfer the focus to a particular widget.

Keyboard Events

Each time the user presses a key, a `KeyPress` event is sent to the window that has the input focus. When the user releases the key, the server sends a `KeyRelease` event.[5] Both of these events use the same event structure, `XKeyEvent`, represented by the `xkey` member of `XEvent`.[6] This event structure identifies the window where the event occurred (the window that had the focus), the time the event occurred (in milliseconds since server startup), the state of the modifier keys and pointer buttons, the position of the pointer, and a code representing the key.

The key code returned by a `KeyPress` or `KeyRelease` event is system-dependent: it represents the server's internal key mapping. Before the key code can be used by the program, it must be converted into the system-independent form known as a *keysym*.[7] The "universe" of keysyms may be found in the header file `X11/keysymdef.h`; a given server will support some subset of this universe. Since you must use keysyms in translation tables, a printed copy of this file is helpful.

---

[2] The mode is controlled by *mwm*'s `keyboardFocusPolicy` resource setting, which can take values of `XmEXPLICIT` (the default) or `XmPOINTER`.

[3] The specific color scheme is controlled by a two sets of *mwm* resources: `activeForeground`, `activeBackground`, `activeTopShadowColor`, and `activeBottomShadowColor` for the window with the focus, and `foreground`, `background`, `topShadowColor`, and `bottomShadow` color for all other windows.

[4] These events are informational in that a window cannot prevent the focus change from occurring; the focus-change event merely notes the state change. Depending on the program, this notification may or may not be useful — for example, a word processor could catch the `FocusOut` event and repaginate the document while the user is working on something else.

[5] Not all servers send `KeyRelease` events; relying upon their presence may be dangerous. Another feature that is supported by many (but not all) servers is the ability to detect when a "modifier" key, such as *Shift*, is pressed; servers supporting this functionality send a separate event when the modifier key is pressed by itself.

[6] This structure is defined in Appendix C; this chapter does not cover direct keyboard event processing.

[7] This conversion is performed automatically inside the widget by the translation manager. If you use an event handler, you must perform this conversion explicitly. The function `XLookupString` converts a raw key code into both a keysym and its ASCII equivalent.

How the keysym is used depends on the translations of the active widget. For *XmPushButton*, the *Space* and *Return* keys activate the button (they call the `ArmAndActivate` action), the arrow and *Tab* keys initiate a traversal action (see below), and all other keys are ignored. *XmText*, on the other hand, inserts printable characters into its buffer, and performs special functions for many nonprintable key combinations (*Control-LeftArrow*, for example, moves the cursor left one word).

Traversal

Consider a data entry screen consisting of a dozen entry fields. If the pointer were the only way to move between these fields, the user would have to remove his/her hands from the keyboard for each field. Instead, Motif allows the use of the keyboard to "traverse" the fields.

Traversal is implemented as a set of actions and translations. *XmPrimitive* provides the basic traversal functionality; other widget classes may modify or extend this functionality.[8] In the standard set of functions, the arrow keys change focus between widgets in the same *tab group*, the *Tab* and *Shift-Tab* key combinations change focus between tab groups, and the *Home* key changes focus to the first widget in the current tab group.

The traversalOn *Resource*

Support for traversal is built into a widget's default translations. The `traversalOn` resource, defined by *XmPrimitive* and shown in Table 9.1, specifies whether the widget makes use of these translations. If `traversalOn` contains `FALSE` (the default), traversal is not supported by the widget; if `traversalOn` contains `TRUE`, traversal is supported.[9]

Table 9.1. The *traversalOn* resource

Name	**Inheritance**	**Type**	**Default Value**
traversalOn	XmPrimitive	Boolean	FALSE

Tab Groups

Tab groups allow the programmer to group widgets with related functions. As stated above, the *Tab* and *Shift-Tab* keys are used to move between groups, and

---

[8] For example, while the arrow keys are part of the standard traversal functionality, a multiline *XmText* widget uses them for its own purposes, and therefore, does not provide the standard functionality.

[9] The `traversalOn` resource is actually more far-reaching: it determines whether or not the widget will accept keyboard focus. For most primitive widgets, accepting focus is equivalent to enabling traversal — keyboard input is only used for traversal. For *XmText*, however, the default behavior is to accept focus; to achieve this behavior in the context of the `traversalOn` resource, *XmText* — unlike other primitive widgets — defaults `traversalOn` to `TRUE`.

the arrow keys (and *Home* key) are used to move between widgets in the same tab group. Tab groups are identified by a single widget ID — if that widget is a primitive widget, it is the sole member of the group; if it is a manager, its children are the members of the group.

Tab groups are maintained in a circular list; the function `XmAddTabGroup`, prototyped in Listing 9.1, adds groups to this list. The ordering of the groups in the list is identical to the ordering of calls to `XmAddTabGroup`; each time it is called, a new group is added to the end of the list. The list is circular, in that the last tab group is logically connected to the first: pressing *Tab* while in the last tab group shifts focus to the first group.

Also shown in Listing 9.1 is the function. This function takes a widget (manager or primitive) out of the list of tab groups; if that widget was not in the tab group list, the call is ignored. Note that, once a tab group is removed from the list, it cannot be reinserted at the same location: the list "closes up," If the widget is added again, it is placed at the end of the list.

Listing 9.1. Function prototypes: *XmAddTabGroup, XmRemoveTabGroup*

```
void    XmAddTabGroup( w )
        Widget     w;

void    XmRemoveTabGroup( w )
        Widget     w;
```

Both `XmAddTabGroup` and `XmRemoveTabGroup` take a single parameter: the ID of the widget to add or remove a tab group. As described above, if this widget is a primitive, it is the sole occupant of the group; if it is a manager, its children occupy the group.

The tab group list is "flat." Two widgets may be greatly separated in the instance tree, but if both are tab groups then they are treated identically in terms of traversal. To put this in more concrete terms: if the children of a manager form one tab group, and one of those children is also placed in its own tab group, in the context of traversal, that child is identical to its parent.

Highlighting the Active Widget

To indicate that it has the input focus, a widget may draw a highlight border around itself. This border is controlled by the resources of Table 9.2: `highlightColor` is the color used to draw the highlight border, and `highlightThickness` is the thickness of that border.[10] The default value of `highlightThickness` — zero — means that no border is drawn.

---

[10] The highlight border may also be drawn from a pixmap, using the `highlightPixmap` resource. This book only considers the "normal" case of a single-color highlight border.

Table 9.2. Highlight resources

Name	**Inheritance**	**Type**	**Default Value**
`highlightColor`	XmPrimitive	`Pixel`	`Black`
`highlightThickness`	XmPrimitive	`short`	`0`

Traversal Example: Three Tab Groups

Figure 9.1 contains an example of three tab groups, each containing one or more buttons. An *XmForm* widget holds all of the other widgets; it is used to provide positioning. The first tab group is the pushbutton at the top of the picture. The second tab group is the row-column at the bottom left, which holds three button children. Its second child has the focus, as denoted by its highlight border. The third tab group is the row-column at the lower right, with its button children.[11]

In the context of this example, it is important to note that *XmPushButton* provides a keyboard translation for its activation action. If a button has the focus, pressing either *Space* or *Return* will arm and activate the button. This means that the button may be "pressed" without the need for the user to use the mouse.

Figure 9.1. Traversal example

---

[11] As a side note, notice that the row-columns are both larger than they need to be. This is because their size is determined by the form, using attachment constraints. The size of their children, however, is determined by the `recomputeSize` — each child is only as high as it needs to be to display its label.

To produce this example, the program and resource file of Listing 9.2 were used.
The widget creation process should by now be familiar; the interesting parts of
this program are the calls to XmAddTabGroup. These calls are grouped here for
clarity; each call could have been made immediately after the associated widget
was created.[12]

Listing 9.2. Program and resource file: Traversal example

```
/*******************************************************************************
**                                                                           **
**   listing_9_02.c                                                          **
**                                                                           **
**   Demonstration of tab groups. This program uses one parent form

**   with 3 children: two row-columns (each containing 3 buttons)


**   and a pushbutton. Each of the form's children is a tab group.
**
**
**
*******************************************************************************/


#include <Xm/Form.h>
#include <Xm/RowColumn.h>
#include <Xm/PushB.h>


Widget  appshell,                           /* Application Shell        */
        the_form,                           /* The parent form          */
        rc_0, rc_1,                         /* The row-column children  */
        the_btn,                            /* The button child         */
        btns_0[3], btns_1[3];               /* Children of the rowcols  */
void main( argc, argv )
    int     argc;
    char    *argv[];
{
    appshell = XtInitialize( argv[0], "Listing_9_02", NULL, 0,
                             &argc, argv );
```

---

[12] However, such placement would make the calls hard to find. Placing all such calls in a
single group makes the tab-group layout explicit to a person reading the code.

Listing 9.2. Continued.

```c
    the_form = XmCreateForm( appshell, "TheForm", NULL, 0 );
    XtManageChild( the_form );

    the_btn = XmCreatePushButton( the_form, "TheBtn", NULL, 0 );
    XtManageChild( the_btn );

    rc_0 = XmCreateRowColumn( the_form, "RowCol0", NULL, 0 );
    XtManageChild( rc_0 );
    btns_0[0] = XmCreatePushButton( rc_0, "RC0_Btn0", NULL, 0 );
    btns_0[1] = XmCreatePushButton( rc_0, "RC0_Btn1", NULL, 0 );
    btns_0[2] = XmCreatePushButton( rc_0, "RC0_Btn2", NULL, 0 );
    XtManageChildren( btns_0, 3 );

    rc_1 = XmCreateRowColumn( the_form, "RowCol1", NULL, 0 );
    XtManageChild( rc_1 );
    btns_1[0] = XmCreatePushButton( rc_1, "RC1_Btn0", NULL, 0 );

;
    btns_1[1] = XmCreatePushButton( rc_1, "RC1_Btn1", NULL, 0 )
btns_1[2] = XmCreatePushButton( rc_1, "RC1_Btn2", NULL, 0 );
    XtManageChildren( btns_1, 3 );
    XmAddTabGroup( the_btn );
    XmAddTabGroup( rc_0 );
    XmAddTabGroup( rc_1 );

    XtRealizeWidget( appshell );
    XtMainLoop();
}
!
! Resource file used to produce Figure 9.1
!

*.traversalOn:              TRUE
*.highlightColor:           White
*.highlightThickness:       2
*TheForm.width:             200
*TheForm.height:            150
*TheForm.background:        Black
```

Listing 9.2. Continued.

```
*TheForm.*.topAttachment:          ATTACH_POSITION
*TheForm.*.bottomAttachment:       ATTACH_POSITION
*TheForm.*.leftAttachment:         ATTACH_POSITION
*TheForm.*.rightAttachment:        ATTACH_POSITION

*XmPushButton.background:          Gray25
*XmPushButton.foreground:          White

*TheBtn.topPosition:               5
*TheBtn.bottomPosition:            20
*TheBtn.leftPosition:              5
*TheBtn.rightPosition:             95

*XmRowColumn.background:           Gray50

*RowCol0.topPosition:              25
*RowCol0.bottomPosition:           95
*RowCol0.leftPosition:             5
*RowCol0.rightPosition:            45

*RowCol1.topPosition:              25
*RowCol1.bottomPosition:           95
*RowCol1.leftPosition:             55
*RowCol1.rightPosition:            95
```

The first three specifications in this resource file are the most important: traversal is enabled, highlighting is enabled (by setting `highlightThickness` to a nonzero value), and the highlight color is set.

The method of positioning the form's children is also of interest. Since all of the children are positioned by relative position, it is simpler to specify all attachment constraints at one time using a loose binding with the form name. The positioning specifications for the children are therefore minimized: only the position constraints need be specified.

XmText

XmText is Motif's general-purpose text input/output class. Depending on configuration, it may be used for purposes ranging from a simple entry field to a text editor. A text widget's contents — its text — may be modified either programmatically or via the keyboard. In addition, *XmText* supports the X selection mechanism, allowing part or all of a text widget's contents to be copied to or from another window.[13]

XmText **Resources**

XmText is a primitive widget, derived as shown by the class tree of Figure 9.2. It supports the resources defined by *Core* and *XmPrimitive*, but redefines the primitive traversal translations.

Figure 9.2. *XmText* class tree

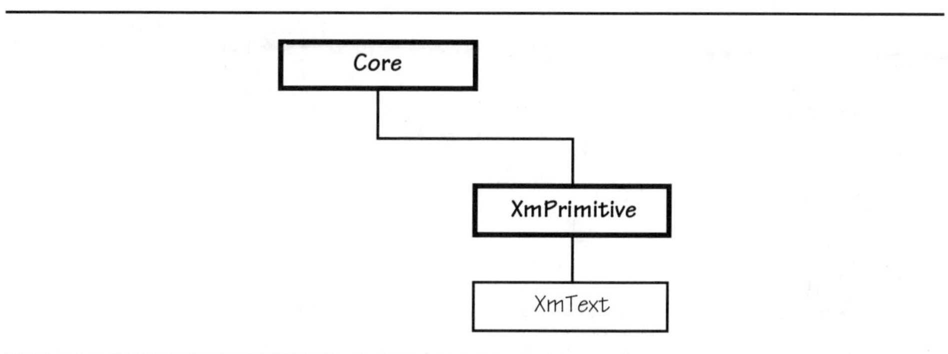

The resources defined by *XmText* are listed in Table 9.3 and described below. Resources defined by *XmPrimitive* and *Core* are not listed here, except for `traversalOn`, which has a different default value for *XmText* than for other primitive widgets.

---

[13] This window may be maintained by a different program or by a different widget in the same program. *XmText* also supports in-window cut and paste of the selection.

Table 9.3. Frequently used resources: *XmText*

Name	Inheritance	Type	Default Value
activateCallback	XmText	XtCallbackList	NULL
autoShowCursor Position	XmText	Boolean	TRUE
blinkRate	XmText	int	500
columns	XmText	short	20
cursorPosition	XmText	XmTextPosition	0
cursorPositionVisible	XmText	Boolean	TRUE
editable	XmText	Boolean	TRUE
editMode	XmText	int	XmSINGLE_LINE _EDIT
focusCallback	XmText	XtCallbackList	NULL
fontList	XmText	XmFontList	"fixed"
losingFocusCallback	XmText	XtCallbackList	NULL
marginHeight	XmText	short	3
marginWidth	XmText	short	3
maxLength	XmText	unsigned	*max_unsigned*
modifyVerifyCallback	XmText	XtCallbackList	NULL
motionVerifyCallback	XmText	XtCallbackList	NULL
pendingDelete	XmText	Boolean	TRUE
resizeHeight	XmText	Boolean	FALSE
resizeWidth	XmText	Boolean	FALSE
rows	XmText	short	1
selectionArray	XmText	Pointer	*default array*
selectThreshold	XmText	int	5
topCharacter	XmText	XmTextPosition	0
value	XmText	String	""
valueChangedCallback	XmText	XtCallbackList	NULL
wordWrap	XmText	Boolean	FALSE
traversalOn	XmPrimitive	Boolean	TRUE

Usage: editMode

An *XmText* widget may be used in either "single-line" or "multiline" mode. Single-line mode is appropriate for entry fields: the widget's contents are stored (and displayed) as a single row of text. Multiline mode is appropriate for a text editor: the widget's contents are displayed as multiple lines and stored with imbedded newlines.

Single-line mode is the default and is specified by the constant `XmSINGLE_LINE_EDIT`. The constant `XmMULTI_LINE_EDIT` configures the widget for multiline mode. Each mode has its own set of translations, as described below.

Contents: value

A text widget's contents are accessed through its `value` resource, which contains a NUL-terminated C string. If the text widget is configured for multiline mode, this string may contain embedded newlines.

Important caveats apply to programmatic access of a text widget's contents. You may use `XtGetValues` and `XtSetValues` to access the resource value, as with other resources. However, the preferred method is to use the convenience functions `XmTextGetString`, `XmTextReplace`, and `XmTextSetString`.

The reason these functions are preferred is that, while `XtSetValues` will copy the supplied string into the `value` resource, `XtGetValues` returns a pointer to the resource itself.[14] This means that, if your program frees or modifies the returned string, it damages internal widget data.[15] The convenience functions, on the other hand, work with copies of strings — the strings your program uses are separate from the strings the widget uses.

Content Controls: editable, maxLength

In some cases, you will want to prevent the user from changing the contents of a text widget — this chapter's file browser is an example. To make a text widget read-only, set its `editable` resource to `FALSE`. The default value of `TRUE` allows the widget's contents to be modified by the user. Although the widget's contents may not be changed by the user when `editable` contains `FALSE`, traversal and selection are still supported, and the program may change the widget's contents at will.

The `maxLength` resource contains the upper limit on the amount of text that may be entered by the user. This resource contains an integer value; by default it is the maximum value of an `unsigned` integer. Once the widget contains the number of characters specified in `maxLength`, text entry is disabled, as if the `editable` resource were set to `FALSE`. This can be quite useful if the program has a fixed-size buffer in which to process the widget's contents.

---

[14] This is true for Motif 1.0 only. At 1.1 and above, due to changes in the way that the widget holds its text, `XtGetValues` will retrieve a copy of the string. `XmTextGetString` is still easier to write.

[15] In addition, since the text widget reallocates its buffer space as needed, if you directly access the `value` resource, the returned pointer may not remain valid for very long.

As with `editable`, `maxLength` affects user input only. The program may change the widget's contents at will, regardless of the settings of either resource. In particular, the maximum amount of text that may be stored in an *XmText* widget is limited only by the capabilities of the computer and/or operating system.

Size: columns, resizeHeight, resizeWidth, rows

A text widget's size may be set either absolutely using its `width` and `height` resources, by parental constraint, or by the number of rows and columns in the text array. The `columns` resource specifies the width of the widget's window in terms of the average character width. The `rows` resource — which is only applicable in multiline mode — specifies the height of the widget's window in terms of the character height. Both of these measurements are relative: the absolute size is determined by the widget's font.

The `resizeHeight` and `resizeWidth` resources specify whether or not the widget attempts to resize itself to display all of its contents. If either of these resources contains `TRUE`, the widget will attempt to resize the appropriate dimension so as to display all of the text in that dimension. This means that if a line of text is 80 characters long, the widget's width is currently 60 columns, and `resizeWidth` contains `TRUE`, the widget will attempt to increase its width to display all 80 characters. Correspondingly, if the widget is sized for 10 rows and the user enters an 11th, it will attempt to increase its height.[16]

The default value of `FALSE` for both `resizeHeight` and `resizeWidth` specify that the widget is to change its size only under program or parental control. In most cases, this is the preferred operation: an entry field, for example, should not arbitrarily resize itself. In other cases, such as the memo pad program below, resizing — within limits — is a convenience.

In some cases `resizeHeight` and `resizeWidth` may have no effect. Height resizing is disabled if the text widget is the child of a scrolled window (described below). Width resizing is disabled if the widget is in multiline mode and the `wordWrap` resource contains `TRUE`; in this case, the widget simply "breaks" lines instead of increasing its width.

Content Appearance: fontList, marginHeight, marginWidth, topCharacter, wordWrap

As with *XmLabel* and its subclasses, *XmText* uses the `fontList` resource to specify the font used for its text. Like *XmLabel*, this resource defaults to the "fixed" font; unlike *XmLabel*, only one font may be used at a time.[17] An additional function of the `fontList` resource is to size the widget's window: if its size is specified via the `rows` and `columns` resources, these values must be converted according to the font used.

The `marginHeight` and `marginWidth` resources specify the distance between the sides of the widget's window and its contents: `marginHeight` specifies the top and bottom margins, and `marginWidth` specifies the right and left margins. These

---

[16] The widget "attempts" to increase its size because any such increases may be denied by its parent.

[17] This is because the *XmText* widget holds ASCII text, not a compound string.

resources are necessary because text is hard to read if it is positioned too close to another object, such as the widget"s border. The default margin size of three pixels is sufficient for most cases; large text sizes — 24 points and above — require more space.

The `topCharacter` resource specifies the position — in terms of the text buffer — of the top line of displayed text.[18] This resource is needed because a text widget may contain more text than it can display. The `topCharacter` resource specifies a character number; the row containing that character is maintained as the top line of the displayed text.[19]

The final appearance resource, `wordWrap`, specifies whether or not the text widget will insert "soft" newlines to make all lines fit in its assigned width. This capability is used only in multiline mode. If so, and if `wordWrap` contains `TRUE`, any rows that would exceed the assigned width are "broken" by "soft" newlines.

A row is "broken" by dividing it into segments, each of which is smaller than the width of the window. "Soft" newlines are the result of this process: the text appears to be split over two or more rows, but is in reality a single row: although newline characters normally separate rows, there are none between the segments of a "broken" row. *XmText* will only break rows at word spaces, defined as any whitespace that separates printable characters.

The default value of `wordWrap` is `FALSE`, meaning that rows may contain more characters than are displayed. To view hidden text (text that is outside the widget's display area) the user must "scroll" the display using the arrow keys.

Cursor Appearance: autoShowCursorPosition, blinkRate, cursorPosition, cursorPositionVisible

The general definition of "cursor" is the marker (or "sprite") that shows the current pointer position. In reference to an *XmText* widget, however, "cursor" specifies the blinking line that indicates where characters are inserted — also known as the *insertion point*.[20] The insertion point may be located at any point in the text buffer and may be moved using the pointer or the arrow keys. When a key is typed, the associated character is stored after the insertion point and the insertion point is moved to the right of the newly inserted character.

The `cursorPosition` resource specifies the position of the insertion point in terms of a character number. The insertion point is positioned *before* the character specified by `cursorPosition`: as characters are typed, they are inserted ahead of the specified character, and the value in `cursorPosition` is incremented.[21]

---

[18] Originally, this resource was named `topPosition` and was documented as such in Release 1.0 of the *Programmer's Reference*. However, due to a conflict with the form constraint of the same name, it was renamed before release.

[19] Characters in an *XmText* widget are numbered from zero; the seventh character is character number six.

[20] To avoid confusion, this book uses the term "pointer" to refer to the mouse cursor and "insertion point" to refer to the text cursor.

[21] This means that the insertion point remains positioned before the same character. Consider a text widget that contains 10 characters in its buffer. The insertion point is positioned before character number 6 (which is the seventh character in the buffer). When a new character is typed, it becomes the new character 6, the former character 6

The `autoShowCursorPosition` resource specifies whether the widget will "scroll" its display in order to keep the insertion point visible. If `autoShowCursorPosition` contains `TRUE`, the widget will scroll its display as needed to maintain visibility. If `FALSE`, the insertion point may move out of the displayed part of the buffer, meaning that the user can't see what is being typed. The default value of `autoShowCursorPosition` is `TRUE`; very few programs change it.

The physical appearance of the insertion point is a blinking vertical bar, drawn to the left of the character identified by `cursorPosition`. The appearance of this bar may be modified by the resources `blinkRate` and `cursorPositionVisible`. The `cursorPositionVisible` resource specifies whether the insertion point is displayed: if it contains `TRUE` (the default), the insertion point is displayed; if `FALSE`, it isn't displayed.

If the insertion point is visible, the `blinkRate` resource specifies the frequency of its blinking. This is expressed as a count of milliseconds, which represents "time in state" — the time that the cursor is either on or off (both times are identical). The default value of 500 means that the insertion point marker is on for half a second, then off for half a second — a cycle time of one second. If `blinkRate` contains zero, the insertion point does not blink: it remains on at all times.

Selection Control: pendingDelete, selectionArray, selectThreshold

Selection is one of the mechanisms that X provides for interclient communication. Clients are permitted to take ownership of a selection and advertise that ownership. Other clients may then request the contents of the selection, and the owning client then "delivers" the contents of the selection to the requestor. This process is described in detail in Chapter 17.

For an *XmText* widget, selection has a different — but related — definition. In this definition, selection is the process of identifying text. The user is able to select this text by a number of means, the most common of which is "dragging" the pointer, with button #1 down, over the text to be selected. Hidden to the user — and applications programmer — the widget advertises this text and will provide it to another client without program intervention.

The `selectThreshold` resource specifies the number of pixels of "drag distance" that cause a character to be entered into the selection. If the pointer is moved that many pixels into a character's area while button #1 is down, the character is added to the selection. The default value is five, meaning that the pointer must be dragged almost all the way across a character for it to be entered into the selection — an accidental drag while positioning the insertion point is unlikely to initiate a selection.

The `selectionArray` resource specifies how the widget responds to multiple clicks of the pointer button — defined as successive clicks, each within a half second of the previous. This resource is a pointer to an integer array, containing four items. In a multiple-click situation, each click increments an internal pointer, and the value at the pointed-to array item controls the action of the widget. The value of each item must be a constant from the following list:

---

becomes the new character 7, the value in `cursorPosition` is incremented to 7, and the buffer contains 11 characters.

- XmSELECT_POSITIONS. The selection is reset: the current selection is deselected, and the insertion point is set to the current pointer position. This is the single-click action.

- XmSELECT_WORD. The current word — identified by pointer position — is selected. A word is defined as a sequence of nonwhitespace characters, delimited by any number of whitespace characters (including the start or end of the text buffer).

- XmSELECT_LINE. The current line — identified by pointer position — is selected.

- XmSELECT_ALL. The entire text buffer is selected.

The default selection array contains the above four values in the order listed. A single click sets the insertion point and deselects the selection, a double click selects the current word, a triple click selects the current line, and a quad click selects the entire buffer. Since this behavior is expected by users, you should not change it without good reason.

The final selection-related resource, pendingDelete, specifies how the text widget will act when the user types while a selection is active. If pendingDelete contains TRUE (the default), the new text replaces the selection — the selection is deleted, and the insertion point is positioned between the characters that previously delimited the selection. If pendingDelete contains FALSE, the new text is inserted after the selection, and the selection remains active.

XmText Callbacks

XmText provides callbacks for activation, focus change, modification, and insertion-point movement. These callbacks are separated into two groups: notification and verification. The notification callbacks notify the program that an operation has happened; they are similar to the button callbacks described in the previous chapter. A *verification callback* notifies the program that an operation is *about to happen* and allows the program to permit or deny that operation. For *XmText*, the notification callbacks pass data in XmAnyCallbackStruct; the verification callbacks pass data in XmTextVerifyCallbackStruct, defined in Listing 9.3.

Listing 9.3. Type definition: XmTextVerifyCallbackStruct

```
typedef struct
        {
        int        reason;
        XEvent     *event;
        Boolean    doit;
        int        currInsert, newInsert;
        int        startPos, endPos;
        XmTextBlock text;
        }
XmTextVerifyCallbackStruct;
```

The `reason` and `event` members perform the same function as in all callbacks: `reason` contains a code identifying the callback, and `event` points at the event that invoked the callback.

The `doit` member is what separates a verification callback from a notification callback. Unlike other callback structures, which should never be modified by the program, the `doit` member exists for program modification: it controls whether or not the widget will perform the operation associated with the callback. Setting `doit` to `TRUE` instructs the widget to complete the operation. Setting `doit` to `FALSE` instructs the widget to ignore the operation.[22]

The `currInsert` and `newInsert` members are used for `motionVerifyCallback`. They contain the position of the insertion point before the attempted movement along with the potential position after the movement (if it is permitted). As with other text positions, characters are numbered starting from zero.

The `startPos` and `endPos` members are used for `modifyVerifyCallback`. They contain the starting and ending characters of the text buffer that are slated for replacement in terms of character positions.

The `text` member is also used for `modifyVerifyCallback`. It specifies the text to be inserted, using the `XmTextBlockRec` structure defined in Listing 9.4.

Listing 9.4. Type definition: XmTextBlockRec

```
typedef struct
        {
        char            *ptr;
        int             length;
        XmTextFormat    format;
        }
XmTextBlockRec,
*XmTextBlock;
```

The `ptr` member of `XmTextBlockRec` points at a text buffer. This buffer is not NUL-terminated; it is simply a group of bytes. The `length` member contains the number of bytes in that buffer.

The `format` member specifies the format of the buffer: whether each character uses eight or sixteen bits. Its value is either `FMT8BIT` and `FMT16BIT`, respectively, specifying eight- or sixteen-bit encoding. Programs using the ISO Latin 1 character set use 8 bit encoding; some multinational programs may use 16 bit encodings.[23]

---

[22] Even though the program is allowed — and expected — to modify `doit`, such modifications should be handled with care. The primary way to ensure such care is to use only a single callback function for each callback — multiple functions modifying the same variable can lead to unexpected results.

[23] Sixteen-bit character sets are a part of X11 Release 5 and will be supported by Motif 1.2. Until that time, all text widgets use 8-bit characters.

Activation: activateCallback

The activation callback is invoked as part of the widget's `Activate` action. This action is performed when the user types the *Return* key; it is only supported by widgets in single-line mode. This callback passes data in the `XmAnyCallbackStruct` structure; the callback reason is `XmCR_ACTIVATE`.

Focus Change: focusCallback, losingFocusCallback

An *XmText* widget signals the program when it gains focus, via `focusCallback`. This callback passes data in `XmAnyCallbackStruct`, with a callback reason of `XmCR_FOCUS`.

XmText also signals the program when focus is about to be lost via `losingFocusCallback`. This is a verification callback, with a callback reason of `XmCR_LOSING_FOCUS`. Since the callback is performed *before* the actual loss of focus, the program can deny focus loss by setting the `doit` member to `FALSE`. If the program leaves `doit` as `TRUE`, focus will be lost.[24]

Modification: modifyVerifyCallback, valueChangedCallback

Modification of an *XmText* widget's contents involves two callbacks: `modifyVerifyCallback` and `valueChangedCallback`. The first is a verification callback: it permits the program to control changes of the widget's text. The second, `valueChangedCallback`, notifies the program when the widget's contents have changed.

The `modifyVerifyCallback` call permits the program to control the text that is entered into the buffer. It is often used to impose a formatting convention on an entry field — for example, a phone number field could automatically insert the parentheses and hyphen that are normally used to segment the number. For this callback, the reason is `XmCR_MODIFYING_TEXT_VALUE`.

The `valueChangedCallback` call permits the program to access the new contents of the field. It passes data in `XmAnyCallbackStruct`, with `XmCR_VALUE_CHANGED` as the reason.

You should note that each keystroke is considered a modification. If a program spends much time in a modification callback function, it will impair the responsiveness of the widget. In addition, if both callbacks are handled, both are called for a successful modification; the verification callback is always called, and the notification callback is called if modification is permitted.

Insertion Point Motion: motionVerifyCallback

The final *XmText* callback, `motionVerifyCallback`, allows the program to control where the user places the insertion point, as well as the extent of a selection. This callback is called prior to each movement or selection; it is a verification callback, and the `reason` member contains `XmMOVING_INSERT_CURSOR`. If the cursor

---

[24] If `doit` is set to `FALSE`, the text widget grabs focus back. As stated above, this is considered a "bad habit" — no widget should arbitrarily override the user's actions.

movement or selection is acceptable, the program should leave `doit` as `TRUE`; if not acceptable, setting `doit` to `FALSE` will cancel the operation.

XmText Default Translations

Single-Line-Edit Translations

As stated above, *XmText* defines many translations for special event combinations, in some cases overriding the traversal translations provided by *XmPrimitive*. Table 9.4 lists the translations used for a text widget in single-line mode along with the actions called and a description of each action's operation.[25]

Table 9.4. *XmText* single-line-edit translations

Event Sequence	Action	Description
`<Key>Tab`	`next-tab-group`	Shift input focus to first widget in next tab group. "Wrap" from last group to first if necessary.
`Shift<Key>Tab`	`prev-tab-group`	Shift input focus to first widget in previous tab group. "Wrap" from first group to last if necessary.
`<Key>Home`	`traverse-home`	Shift input focus to first widget in current tab group.
`<Key>Up`	`traverse-prev`	Shift input focus to previous widget in current tab group. "Wrap" from first widget to last if necessary.
`<Key>Down`	`traverse-next`	Shift input focus to next widget in current tab group. "Wrap" from last widget to first if necessary.
`<Key>Left`	`backward-character`	Move insertion point one character to left.
`Ctrl<Key>Left`	`backward-word`	Move insertion point to beginning of previous word.
`Shift<Key>Left`	`key-select(left)`	Change selection state of character to left of insertion point (select if unselected, unselect if selected)). Move insertion point one character to left.
`<Key>Right`	`forward-character`	Move insertion point one character to right.
`Ctrl<Key>Right`	`forward-word`	Move insertion point to beginning of next word.

---

[25] For brevity, the parentheses associated with each action have been omitted unless a parameter is passed to the action.

Table 9.4. Continued.

`Shift<Key>Right`	`key-select(right)`	Change selection state of character to right of insertion point; move insertion point one character to right.
`<Key>Backspace`	`delete-previous-character`	Delete character to left of insertion point.
`Shift<Key>Backspace`	`delete-previous-word`	Delete word to left of insertion point.
`<Key>Delete`	`delete-next-character`	Delete character to right of insertion point. If a selection is active, *Delete* will delete the entire selection.
`Shift<Key>Delete`	`delete-next-word`	Delete word to right of insertion point.
`<Btn1Up>`	`extend-end`	Confirm current selection. This is when the widget calls `motionVerifyCallback`; if it is given the "go ahead," it then advertises the selection as described in Chapter 17.
`<Btn2Up>`	`copy-to`	Copy current selection to point specified by pointer position. If current widget does not have selection, retrieve selection data from owner. Ignore if no selection is active. If the current widget has the selection, leave selected text unchanged.
Ctrl<Btn2Up>	move-to	If current widget has selection, move selected text to current insertion point. This operation removes the text from its original position and clears the selection.
<LeaveWindow>	leave	If focus is set by pointer position (rather than explicitly), change highlighting and initiate focus change.
<FocusIn>	focusIn	Invoke callbacks in `focusCallback` list.
<FocusOut>	focusOut	Invoke `losingFocusCallback`. If given "go ahead," allow focus change to happen; if program denies focus change, grab focus back.

Multiline-Edit Translations

When the widget is used in multiline mode, some of the single-line translations are replaced by the translations of Table 9.5.

Table 9.5. *XmText* multi-line-edit translation changes

Event Sequence	Action	Description
`<Key>Tab`	`self-insert`	Insert *Tab* character into buffer at current insertion point. Move insertion point right one character (past tab).
`<Key>Home`	`beginning-of-line`	Move insertion point to start of current line.
`<Key>Up`	`previous-line`	Move insertion point to same position in previous line. If previous line is too short, move insertion point to end of line but keep track of "real" position.
`<Key>Down`	`next-line`	Move insertion point to same position in next line. If next line is too short, move insertion point to end of line but keep track of "real" position.
`<Key>Return`	`newline`	Insert *Newline* character into buffer at current position. Move insertion point past newline (*ie*, to start of new line).

Anomalies in the Default XmText *Translations*

As you look at these translation tables, you may notice several anomalies — or at least inconveniences. Most apparent is that a multiline text widget does not invoke its activation callback; instead, the *Return* key is used to start a new line. This means that the value-changed callback is the only way to notify the program that data entry has been performed.

Another multiline anomaly is that the *Tab* key inserts a tab character into the buffer instead of traversing to the next tab group. For a text editor, this is a great thing; for a data entry field, it isn't. What makes this behavior anomalous is that *Shift-Tab* maintains its default action — you can go to the previous tab group but not the next.[26]

A final anomaly of note is the use of the *Backspace* and *Delete* keys. The default action for *Delete* is to delete the character (or word, if shifted) *after* the insertion point. The *Backspace* key deletes the character (or word) before the insertion point. While this approach is fine for the IBM keyboard, where *Backspace* is part of the "normal" keyboard and *Delete* is part of the keypad, most terminals have

---

[26] This brings up another point: a multiline text widget, because it redefines the traversal translations in such a dramatic fashion, must be the sole occupant of a tab group. If it were placed in the same tab group as other widgets, there would be no way to traverse to the other widgets.

Delete as part of the normal keyboard — it's the key at the upper right, traditionally called "rubout." This means that the normal translations do not act in the way that most users feel is "correct." The only way to correct this problem is either to install a new translation table or to change the keyboard mapping (using the *xmodmap* client).[27]

Why You Can't Specify New Translations for a Multiline XmText Widget in the Resource File

If you decide to use a resource file to specify new translations for a multiline *XmText* widget — for example, if you want to correct the "tab group anomaly" — you will find that your changes are not handled as you would expect. In fact, although new translations replace the default single-line translations, a multiline widget continues to use the default multiline translations.

To understand why this happens, you must understand the process of widget initialization. When a widget is initialized, each class initializes its data in the order of the class' position in the widget's class tree. For *XmText*, this means that *Core* data is initialized first, followed by *XmPrimitive* data, followed by *XmText* data. Part of a class' initialization is the initialization of those resources defined by the class — the resource file provides initial values.

For *XmText*, this means that the `translations` resource is initialized by the *Core* superclass. If a resource specification is found, it overrides the default translations. However, the `editMode` resource is initialized by *XmText*. As part of this initialization, the additional translations are installed when `editMode` is set to `XmMULTI_LINE_EDIT`.

The result of this sequencing is that the resource-file-specified translations override the default single-line translations, meaning that the default translations are no longer available. However, the translations associated with multiline edit are installed after those from the resource file, so they override those resource-file translations that have identical event-sequences.

For this reason, if you wish to install translations in a multiline *XmText* widget that override the default multiline translations, you must do so programmatically. In addition, you must do so after the widget has been created — if you attempt to install the new translations at the time of widget creation, you are in the same situation found with a resource file.

XmText Convenience Functions

Unlike most widgets, *XmText* provides many resources that are constantly accessed by a typical program. Given the frequency of access, along with the programmer overhead involved in use of `XtSetValues` and `XtGetValues`, it was only natural that a set of functions be written to eliminate that overhead. These functions are described below.

---

[27] This is one of the problems that the "virtual keysyms" of Motif 1.1 were designed to fix.

XmTextGetString, XmTextSetString

When `XtSetValues` is used to load the `value` resource, it copies the program's string into the text widget. However, when `XtGetValues` is used to retrieve this resource, it simply returns a pointer to the text widget's internal buffer. To avoid the havoc that would result from a program that haphazardly modifies this buffer, `XmTextGetString` exists. To minimize the code involved in storing a new value, `XmTextSetString` exists. Both functions are prototyped in Listing 9.5.

Listing 9.5. Function prototypes: XmTextGetString,
XmTextSetString

```
char    *XmTextGetString( w )
        Widget      w;

void    XmTextSetString( w, value )
        Widget      w;
        char        *value
```

`XmTextGetString` takes a single parameter, the ID of the text widget. It allocates space for the widget's value and copies that value into the allocated space as a NUL-terminated string. The program is responsible for deallocating this string — with `XtFree` — when it is no longer needed.

`XmTextSetString` takes two parameters. The first is the ID of the text widget, the second is a pointer to the new value, which must be a NUL-terminated string. The contents of the passed string are copied into the widget, replacing its current value.

XmTextReplace

If you wanted to change part of a text widget's contents you could use `XmTextGetString` to get the current contents, make the changes, and use `XmTextSetString` to install the new value. Or you could use `XmTextReplace`, prototyped in Listing 9.6.

Listing 9.6. Function prototype: XmTextReplace

```
void    XmTextReplace( w, from, to, value )
        Widget      w;
        int         from;
        int         to;
        char        *value
```

Like `XmTextSetString`, the `w` parameter specifies the text widget, and the `value` parameter specifies the string to be inserted. The new value must be a NUL-terminated string. It need not be the same length as the replaced string; the widget's buffer will be expanded or contracted if necessary.

The `from` and `to` parameters specify the range of characters to be replaced, numbered from zero. The `from` parameter specifies the first character to be replaced, and the `to` parameter specifies the character *after* the last character to be replaced.[28] If both parameters contain the same value, the new string is inserted after that character position; no text is replaced.

XmTextGetEditable, XmTextSetEditable

While many applications will have text widgets that are either editable or not editable, some may need to switch the state while the program is running — for example, a text editor that offers a "read only" capability. To examine the current state, the function `XmTextGetEditable` is used. To set the state, `XmTextSetEditable` is used. Both of these functions are prototyped in Listing 9.7.

---

[28] So, to replace only the first character, `from` would passed as 0, and `to` would passed as 1.

Listing 9.7. Function prototypes: *XmTextGetEditable*, *XmTextSetEditable*

```
Boolean XmTextGetEditable( w )
        Widget       w;


void    XmTextSetEditable( w, new_state )
        Widget       w;
        Boolean      new_state;
```

For both functions, the `w` parameter specifies the text widget. `XmTextGetEditable` returns the current value of the `editable` resource; `XmTextSetEditable` stores the contents of the `new_state` parameter in `editable`.

XmTextGetMaxLength, XmTextSetMaxLength

The functions `XmTextGetMaxLength` and `XmTextSetMaxLength`, prototyped in Listing 9.8, are used to examine or change the contents of the `maxLength` resource. These functions are similar in operation to those for the `editable` resource: `XmTextGetMaxLength` takes the widget ID as its parameter and returns the value of `maxLength`, `XmTextSetMaxLength` takes the widget ID and new length as its parameters.

Listing 9.8. Function prototypes: *XmTextGetMaxLength*, *XmTextSetMaxLength*

```
int     XmTextGetMaxLength( w )
        Widget       w;


void    XmTextSetMaxLength( w, new_length )
        Widget       w;
        int          new_length;
```

XmTextGetSelection, XmTextGetSelectionPosition, XmTextSetSelection, XmTextClearSelection

These functions are used to access the widget's current selection. Unlike the other convenience functions, they do not access widget resources. Instead, they directly access the widget's internal data. All three are prototyped in Listing 9.9.

Listing 9.9. Function prototypes: *XmTextGetSelection,*
XmTextGetSelectionPoisition, XmTextSetSelection,
XmTextClearSelection

```
char    *XmTextGetSelection( w )
        Widget          w;


Boolean XmTextGetSelectionPosition( w, start, end )
        Widget          w;
        XmTextPosition  *start;
        XmTextPosition  *end;


void    XmTextSetSelection( w, start, end, time )
        Widget          w;
        XmTextPosition  start;
        XmTextPosition  end;
        Time            time;


void    XmTextClearSelection( w, time )
        Widget          w;
        Time            time;
```

`XmTextGetSelection` retrieves the current selection as a NUL-terminated character string. It takes one parameter, `w`, which is the ID of the text widget. It allocates space for the returned text; the program must use `XtFree` to deallocate this space when it has finished using it. If the widget does not have an active selection, `XmTextGetSelection` returns `NULL`.

`XmTextGetSelectionPosition` retrieves the position and length of the selection.[29] The widget is passed in `w`, and the starting and ending positions of the selection are returned in `start` and `end`, respectively.[30] The return value is `TRUE` if the widget has text selected, `FALSE` otherwise.

`XmTextSetSelection` causes the text widget to select part of its contents. As expected, this function has parameters that identify the widget (`w`) and the range to be selected (`start` and `end`). The purpose of the `time` parameter, however, is not so clear. It is a server timestamp and is required by the X selection mechanism for synchronization. The value passed should be from the event that initiated the selection.[31]

---

[29] This function is undocumented but present in Motif 1.0. It is documented for Motif 1.1 and above.

[30] `XmTextPosition` is equivalent to `long`.

[31] In almost all cases, an event *will* initiate a program-controlled selection. For example, the menu could have a "Select All" choice; the callback for this choice contains an event, which contains a timestamp. If, for some reason, your program needs to select a portion of a text widget *sans* event, you could either generate a dummy event or call the function `XtLastTimestampProcessed` (available with X11R4). Use of the constant

`XmTextClearSelection` deselects the current selection; the insertion point is unaffected. The parameters are similar to those of `XmTextSetSelection`: `w` identifies the widget, and `time` is the server timestamp from the event triggering the operation.

XmText **Example: Memo Pad**

Figure 9.3 portrays a text widget in multiline mode. Configured in this way, it serves as a simple memo pad: its contents can be modified at will while the program is running, but lost at program termination. Although the window as shown is only sufficient to hold 10 rows of 48 characters, it may be expanded as needed. In addition, the actual text may be larger than the displayed text: if the insertion point is moved outside the window border (via the arrow keys), the widget will "scroll" its contents to keep the insertion point visible.

Figure 9.3. *XmText* example: Memo pad

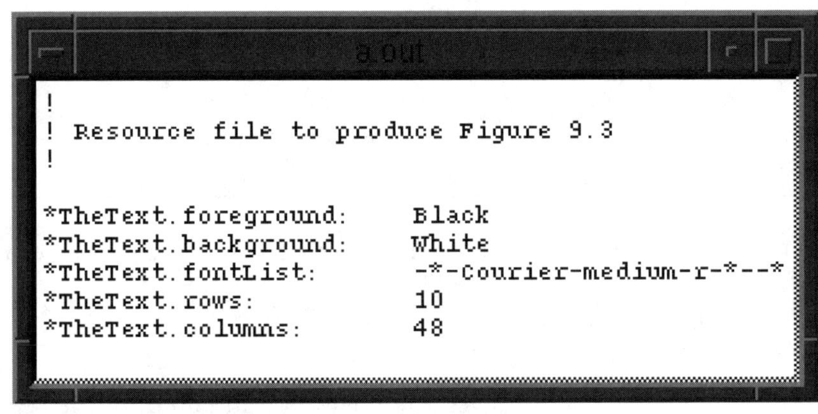

Listing 9.10 contains the program and resource file to produce the memo pad. Both are simple: the program creates and manages the text widget, and it does everything else. The resource file specifies the appearance, size, and usage of the widget.

This program truly shows the capabilities of Motif: a program the same size as "Hello World" provides a simple text editor. The addition of a few more lines of code would allow it to save and restore from a disk file.

`CurrentTime` is not acceptable, because of the possibility of a race condition — two clients vying for the selection, each with time of `CurrentTime`.

Listing 9.10. Program and resource file: Memo pad

```c
/*********************************************************************
**                                                                 **
**    listing_9_10.c                                               **
**                                                                 **
**    Memo pad using XmText.                                       **
**                                                                 **
*********************************************************************/


#include <Xm/Text.h>


Widget  appshell,                          /* Application Shell       */
        the_text;                          /* The text widget         */


void main( argc, argv )
    int     argc;
    char    *argv[];
{
    appshell = XtInitialize( argv[0], "Listing_9_10", NULL, 0,
                             &argc, argv );

    the_text = XmCreateText( appshell, "TheText", NULL, 0 );
    XtManageChild( the_text );

    XtRealizeWidget( appshell );
    XtMainLoop();
}
```

```
!
! Resource file to produce Figure 9.3
!
*TheText.foreground:    Black
*TheText.background:    White
*TheText.fontList:      -*-Courier-medium-r-*--*-100-*
*TheText.rows:          10
*TheText.columns:       48

*TheText.editMode:      MULTI_LINE_EDIT
```

XmText **Example: Entry Fields**

Figure 9.4 presents a slightly more complex example of *XmText* use. It combines three text widgets as entry fields, along with three label widgets and a bulletin board, to produce a simple data entry screen. Addition of an "OK" button — or using the "Phone" field's activation callback — would turn this sample program into the front end for an address book database.

Figure 9.4. *XmText* example: Entry fields

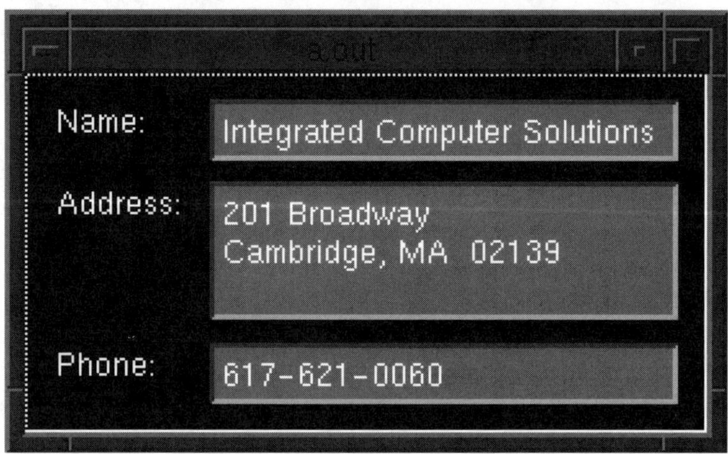

Listing 9.11 contains the program and resource file for the entry fields example. This program contains three items of interest: it makes use of the `unitType` resource, it uses tab groups, and it augments the default translations of one of the *XmText* widgets. These techniques are detailed below the listing.

Listing 9.11. Program and resource file: Entry fields

```c
/*************************************************************************
**                                                                     **
**   listing_9_11.c                                                    **
**                                                                     **
**   Demonstration of XmText as used for entry fields. Both single-    **
**   line and multi-line fields are presented, for an address card    **
**   entry form. In addition, this program demonstrates the use of     **
**   compiled-in translations.                                         **
**                                                                     **
*************************************************************************/


#include <Xm/BulletinB.h>
#include <Xm/Label.h>
#include <Xm/Text.h>


Widget          appshell,             /* Application Shell      */
                the_bb,               /* The parent            */
                labels[3],            /* Labels for the fields */
                fields[3];            /* The entry fields      */
Arg             arglist[1];           /* Used to set unitType  */
XtTranslations  ttab;                 /* Used to augment field 1 */


void main( argc, argv )
    int     argc;
    char    *argv[];
{
    appshell = XtInitialize( argv[0], "Listing_9_11", NULL, 0,
                             &argc, argv );

    XtSetArg( arglist[0], XmNunitType, Xm100TH_POINTS );

    the_bb = XmCreateBulletinBoard( appshell, "TheBB", arglist, 1 );
    XtManageChild( the_bb );

    labels[0] = XmCreateLabel( the_bb, "Name_Lbl", NULL, 0 );
    labels[1] = XmCreateLabel( the_bb, "Addr_Lbl", NULL, 0 );
```

Listing 9.11. Continued.

```c
    labels[2] = XmCreateLabel( the_bb, "Phon_Lbl", NULL, 0 );
    XtManageChildren( labels, 3 );

    fields[0] = XmCreateText( the_bb, "Name_Txt", NULL, 0 );
    fields[1] = XmCreateText( the_bb, "Addr_Txt", NULL, 0 );
    fields[2] = XmCreateText( the_bb, "Phon_Txt", NULL, 0 );
    XtManageChildren( fields, 3 );

    XmAddTabGroup( fields[0] );
    XmAddTabGroup( fields[1] );
    XmAddTabGroup( fields[2] );

    ttab = XtParseTranslationTable( "None<Key>Tab: next-tab-group()" );
    XtOverrideTranslations( fields[1], ttab );

    XtRealizeWidget( appshell );
    XtMainLoop();
}
!
! Resource file to produce Figure 9.4
!

*.background:          Black
*.foreground:          White
*.traversalOn:         TRUE
*.fontList:            -*-helvetica-medium-r-*--*-120-*

*TheBB.width:          26100
*TheBB.height:         13800

*.XmLabel.alignment:   ALIGNMENT_BEGINNING
*.XmLabel.x:           900
*.XmLabel.height:      1800
*.XmLabel.width:       5400

*Name_Lbl.labelString: Name:
*Name_Lbl.y:           900

*Addr_Lbl.labelString: Address:
```

Listing 9.11. Continued.

```
*Addr_Lbl.y:              4200

*Phon_Lbl.labelString:   Phone:
*Phon_Lbl.y:             10500

*.XmText.background:     Gray50
*.XmText.x:              7200
*.XmText.width:          18000
*.XmText.height:         2400

*Name_Txt.y:             900

*Addr_Txt.editMode:      MULTI_LINE_EDIT
*Addr_Txt.y:             4200
*Addr_Txt.height:        5400

*Phon_Txt.y:             10500
```

Measurement by Points

Expressing measurements in pixels does not make a lot of sense for this program, since it is essentially text-based and the font size is 12 points.[32] Instead, the bulletin-board's `unitType` resource is programmatically set — at time of widget creation — to `Xm100TH_POINTS`. Each child of the bulletin board then uses this value for its own `unitType` resource.

Using measurement-by-points, the height of text and label fields may be determined from the font size: 12 points for the font, 6 for top and bottom margin, 4 for shadow border, and 2 for "slop" in the points-to-pixels conversion. The result, a line height of 24 points, is actually a bit large — the top margin is bigger than the bottom margin.[32a] For a production program, you would adjust the size until it "looked right."

For other measurements, the ratio of 72 points per inch may be used. Thus, the ⅛-inch space between entry fields (as well as the space between the bulletin board and its contents) becomes 9 points, the ¾-inch-wide labels are 54 points, and the 2½-inch-wide entry fields are 180 points.

One potential drawback to measurement-by-points is that the numbers in the resource file appear awfully big: 180 points is represented by the value 18,000, because measurement is actually in terms of 100ths of a point. Although this is a drawback for most programs, which use only whole points and therefore don't

---

[32] Of course, the font height could be specified in pixels. However, this would result in a window size that varies by display — and the program would not have a consistent "look and feel."

[32a] This size difference is partly due to the space allocated in the font for "decenders," about 2 points for a 12-point font.

need the extra zeros on each value, it is useful for a precision drawing program.[33]

Use of Tab Groups

The standard Motif traversal mechanism uses the arrow keys to move between related widgets, but this program uses the *Tab* key — implemented by placing each widget in its own tab group. The reason for this is that the typical user is familiar with using either the *Tab* or *Return* key to move between entry fields — that's how most traditional programs work.

Since Motif directly supports the use of the *Tab* key, via tab groups, that is the logical way to implement the interface. The alternative — using the *Return* key — would require changing the default translations for each widget. In addition, *Return* is left in its default role of activation — allowing the user to notify the program of completed entry (should that be implemented).

Changing Multiline Translations

The problem with using tab groups is that the multiline text widget does not support the necessary translation of the *Tab* key — instead of traversing to the next tab group, it enters a *Tab* character into the text buffer. The solution is to override the default translation.

As described in the previous chapter, programmatic installation of translations is a two-step process: first the ASCII translation table must be compiled, then the compiled table must be installed into the widget. As described in this chapter, this must be done *after* the widget is created because of the way that *XmText*'s multiline translations are installed.[34]

The translation used is `"None<Key>Tab: next-tab-group()"`. The `None` modifier is needed to limit translation to the unmodified *Tab* key.[35] The `<Key>` event could be replaced by `<KeyPress>` or `<KeyDown>`; convention is to use the abbreviation. `Tab` is the name of the key, and `next-tab-group` is the action name, from Table 9.4.

---

[33] The X output model is based on the abstract entity known as a *drawable* — an entity into which a program may draw. Currently, the universe of drawables consists of windows and pixmaps. However, there is no reason why a printer interface could not be implemented as a drawable, as it is for the Macintosh, resulting in a need for the additional resolution.

[34] Although translation modification may be performed at any time after widget creation, I chose to do it just prior to widget realization, for illustrative purposes. I recommend, however, that you perform all "translation fixups" at one point in the program, and the point prior to realization is a good time. Doing so keeps compiled translation tables in plain sight, as well as allowing easier debugging when tracking translation errors.

[35] For some reason, my keyboard mapping allowed both *Tab* and *Shift-Tab* to invoke the action with the colon modifier — which was what I originally expected to use. This goes to highlight a difficulty of portable programming: everything must be specified (and tested) in great detail, and nothing may be left to the programmer's expectations.

Next Step: Change the Delete *Translations?*

Earlier in this chapter I said that the *Delete* key is usually used for deleting the previous character. This is true for keyboards from DEC, Apple, and many other vendors; it is not true for keyboards from HP and IBM. If your keyboard sends *Delete* instead of *Backspace*, you may want to change the translations on the text widget.

There are two resource-oriented ways to do this, and both present a quandary. The first is to change the default translations via the resource file. The quandary is that you will have to specify the entire list of translations from Table 9.4 or the text widgets will not behave as expected. The other method is to override the translations programmatically — you could add the additional translations to the existing `XtParseTranslationTable` call and install that compiled table in each widget. The quandary from this approach is that users of HP and IBM keyboards will not have the expected behavior — and cannot modify the behavior via the resource file.

A third method is to use the *xmodmap* client to change the key mapping and leave the widget translations along. This is a better approach, as it allows each user to set a preferred mapping, which is consistent between applications.[36]

Scrolled Text

Although a text widget may be configured to maintain insertion point visibility by scrolling the display, this ability is limited at best — expecting a user to repeatedly press the *DownArrow* key to scroll through a large text file is not a sign of good interface design. Instead, Motif provides *scrollbars*: widgets that exist to provide positional control.

A sample scrollbar — along with a border — is shown in Figure 9.5. The arrows on either end of the scrollbar allow incremental movement — equivalent to repeatedly pressing an arrow key. The black rectangle inside the scrollbar is known as the "slider." Its position shows the current position of the display, relative to the entire file; its size shows the size of the displayed area, again relative to the size of the file — the example indicates that approximately two-thirds of the file is displayed. Finally, the interior of the scrollbar is known as the "scroll region." If the pointer button is clicked while the pointer is within the scroll region, it scrolls the display by one "page" — the width of the slider. In addition, the slider may be "dragged" through the scroll region to scroll the display by a large amount.

Figure 9.5. Sample scrollbar

---

[36] The entire problem goes away with Motif 1.1.

Scrollbars, as a general topic, are presented in the next chapter. This chapter simply presents the *Scrolled Text* widget — which is not a true widget, but actually an *XmText* widget as the child of an *XmScrolledWindow* widget. This chapter will pretend, however, that *Scrolled Text* is a true widget and thus forego a complete description of *XmScrolledWindow*.

A scrolled text widget consists of an *XmText* widget, along with two optional scrollbars (and an *XmScrolledWindow* manager). The two scrollbars allow both horizontal and vertical scrolling; horizontal scrolling involves moving the current "page" left or right, while vertical scrolling involves changing the page position to another part of the file. Both scrollbars are optional; some programs use vertical scrolling, some use horizontal scrolling, and some use both (using neither is possible, but is counter to the idea of using scrolled text). By default, both scrollbars are present.

Creating a Scrolled Text "Widget"

The function `XmCreateScrolledText`, prototyped in Listing 9.12, is used to create the widgets supporting scrolled text: an *XmScrolledWindow* manager, an *XmText* child, and horizontal and vertical *XmScrollBar* children. On the surface, it appears to create a single widget, just like any other widget creation function; it takes the same parameters and returns a widget ID.

Listing 9.12. Function prototype: *XmCreateScrolledText*

```
Widget  XmCreateScrolledText( parent, name, arg_list, arg_count )
        Widget       parent;
        char         *name;
        ArgList      arg_list;
        Cardinal     arg_count;
```

The ID returned by `XmCreateScrolledText` bears closer examination. Since this function creates *several* widgets, which ID is returned? The answer is that it returns the ID of the text widget. To get the ID of the scrolled window, you must use the function `XtParent`. The text widget is created as the child of the scrolled window, and the scrolled window is created as the child of the widget specified by `parent`.

The use of the `name` parameter also requires more examination. As with most widget-creation functions, `name` specifies the name of the associated with the returned widget ID — in this case, the name of the *XmText* widget. But what is the name of the scrolled window? It is the same as the name of the text widget, but with "SW" appended — if the text widget is named `TheText`, then the scrolled window is named `TheTextSW`.

Why is the scrolled window's name important? Because the position and size of the scrolled text widget must be specified via the scrolled window — that window then divides its area between its children. As with most managers, the scrolled window will attempt to size itself based on its children's size — so it is possible to specify size in terms of the *XmText* child. However, this approach does not work when the scrolled text widget is the child of a form: applying the form's constraints to the text child does nothing; they must be applied to the scrolled window.

Scrolled Text Resources

As the scrolled text widget is actually a combination of *XmScrolledWindow*, *XmScrollBar*, and *XmText*, it provides the resources defined by all of these classes — albeit in a roundabout manner. This chapter, however, covers only those resources defined by the *XmText* class for use with scrolled text. These resources are listed in Table 9.6 and described below.

Table 9.6. Additional resources: *Scrolled Text*

Name	Inheritance	Type	Default Value
`scrollHorizontal`	XmText	`Boolean`	`TRUE`
`scrollLeftSide`	XmText	`Boolean`	`FALSE`
`scrollTopSide`	XmText	`Boolean`	`FALSE`
`scrollVertical`	XmText	`Boolean`	`TRUE`

Usage: editMode

Although you would expect *Scrolled Text* to default to multiline mode, it doesn't. This means that, for most purposes, you will need to set the `editMode` resource to `XmMULTI_LINE_EDIT`, as well as remember the interaction of multiline initialization and translations.

There are cases where a single-line scrollable text field is useful. If, for example, a program has a need for a very long text field — the variable-display component of a C++ debugger comes to mind — then use of a scroll bar may be better than the default (arrow key) method of scrolling.

Scrollbar Usage: scrollHorizontal, scrollVertical

Depending on the application, you may want both horizontal and vertical scrollbars or one but not the other. The `scrollHorizontal` resource controls the presence or absence of a vertical scrollbar: if it contains `TRUE` (the default) the scrollbar is present; if it contains `FALSE`, the scrollbar is absent. The `scrollVertical` resource performs the same function for the vertical scrollbar; its default value is also `TRUE`.

You should note that these resources may be set implicitly based on the widget's use. One such modification is the result of the `editMode` resource: if the text widget is configured for single-line mode, the `scrollVertical` resource is forced to `FALSE`. Another modification happens if the scrolled window has its `scrollingPolicy` resource (described in the next chapter) set to `XmAUTOMATIC`, in which case both `scrollHorizontal` and `scrollVertical` are forced to `FALSE`.[37]

Scrollbar Placement: scrollLeftSide, scrollTopSide

By default, scrollbars are placed on the bottom and right sides of a scrolled text widget. If your application requires different placement, the `scrollLeftSide` and `scrollTopSide` resources are used to change this behavior.[38]

The `scrollLeftSide` resource controls the position of the vertical scrollbar: when it contains `FALSE` (the default), the scrollbar is positioned to the right of the text widget; when it contains `TRUE`, the scrollbar is positioned to the left of the text. The `scrollTopSide` resource performs the same function for the horizontal scrollbar: when `FALSE` (the default), the scrollbar is placed below the text widget; when `TRUE`, the scrollbar is positioned above the text.

Scrolled Text Example: File Browser

Figure 9.6 presents a Motif replacement for the *more* file browser.[39] It is invoked using a command line of the form `"xmore filename"`, where *filename* is the name of the file to be displayed. It reads that file, then displays it in a scrolled-text widget. The user is then able to page forward or backward through the file (a decided improvement over *more*), as well as select portions of the file to copy into another window, using X's selection mechanism. There is no ability to save or modify the file; like *more*, this program is read-only.

---

[37] This behavior is not the default for a scrolled window. It is noted here, however, in expectation that you will refer to the *Scrolled Text* section first if you run into any problems with text in a scrolled window.

[38] To maintain the "Motif Look," you should give great consideration to your reasons for nonstandard scrollbar placement.

[39] This program is not yet a replacement for *more*, as it is incapable of accepting text from Standard Input. In Chapter 17, that feature is added.

Figure 9.6. File browser

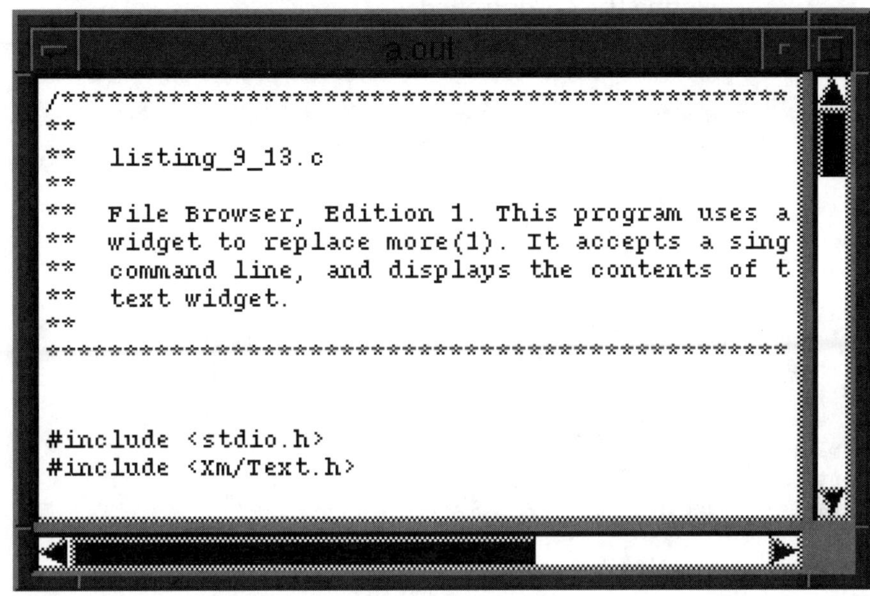

The file browser program and resource file are shown in Listing 9.13. The program is similar to the memo pad program of Listing 9.10, but adds code to read the input file. The resource file is also similar to that of Listing 9.13, but increases the height of the text widget, sets `editable` to `FALSE`, and adds a background color specification for the scrolled window manager.

The file browser was written with the assumption that it would be invoked with some number of X-specific arguments and a single filename. The X-specific arguments are removed from the command line by `XtInitialize`, leaving a single argument — the name of the input file. The function `LoadFile` opens this file, reads its contents, and calls `XmTextSetString` to store the text in the widget.

Listing 9.13. Program and resource file: File browser

```
/*************************************************************************
**                                                                     **
**    listing_9_13.c                                                   **
**                                                                     **
**    File Browser, Edition 1. This program uses a Scrolled Text       **
**    widget to replace more(1). It accepts a single file on the       **
**    command line, and displays the contents of that file in the      **
**    text widget.                                                     **
**                                                                     **
*************************************************************************/
```

Listing 9.13. Continued.

```c
#include <stdio.h>
#include <Xm/Text.h>


void    LoadFile();                      /* FORWARD Definition          */


Widget  appshell,                        /* Application Shell           */
        the_text;                        /* The text widget             */


void main( argc, argv )
    int     argc;
    char    *argv[];
{
    appshell = XtInitialize( argv[0], "Listing_9_13", NULL, 0,
                             &argc, argv );

    if (argc != 2)
        {
        fprintf( stderr, "\nbrowser: Usage:\n" );
        fprintf( stderr, "         browser FILENAME\n" );
        exit( 1 );
        }

    the_text = XmCreateScrolledText( appshell, "TheText", NULL, 0 );
    XtManageChild( the_text );

    LoadFile( argv[1] );

    XtRealizeWidget( appshell );
    XtMainLoop();
}



/**
*** LoadFile( fname )
***
*** This function opens the file and loads it into the text widget.
**/

void LoadFile( fname )
    char        *fname;
```

Listing 9.13. Continued.

```c
{
    FILE        *infile;
    long        fsize;
    char        *lclptr;

    infile = fopen( fname, "r" );
    if (infile == NULL)
        {
        perror( "browser: unable to open input file" );
        exit( 2 );
        }

    fseek( infile, 0, 2 );
    fsize = ftell( infile );
    rewind( infile );

    lclptr = (char *)XtMalloc( fsize + 1 );
    fread( lclptr, sizeof(char), fsize, infile );
    lclptr[fsize] = '\0';

    XmTextSetString( the_text, lclptr );

    XtFree( lclptr );
    fclose( infile );
}
```

```
!
! Resource file to produce Figure 9.6
!

*TheTextSW.background:  Gray50

*TheText.foreground:    Black
*TheText.background:    White
*TheText.fontList:      -*-Courier-medium-r-*--*-100-*
*TheText.rows:          15
*TheText.columns:       48

*TheText.editMode:      MULTI_LINE_EDIT
*TheText.editable:      FALSE
```

10
Scrollbars

Overview

Scrollbars, implemented by the *XmScrollBar* class, are a "position" control. They were presented in the previous chapter to control the position of text displayed by an *XmText* widget. This chapter presents scrollbars as discrete entities and as children of the *XmScrolledWindow* manager. It also presents the *XmScale* class, a "magnitude" control similar to a scrollbar.

Scrollbar Components and Terminology

The previous chapter listed the components of a scrollbar along with a description of how these components apply to a scrolled-text application. Those definitions are refined and expanded here, using Figure 10.1 as a visual aid.

Figure 10.1. Scrollbar components

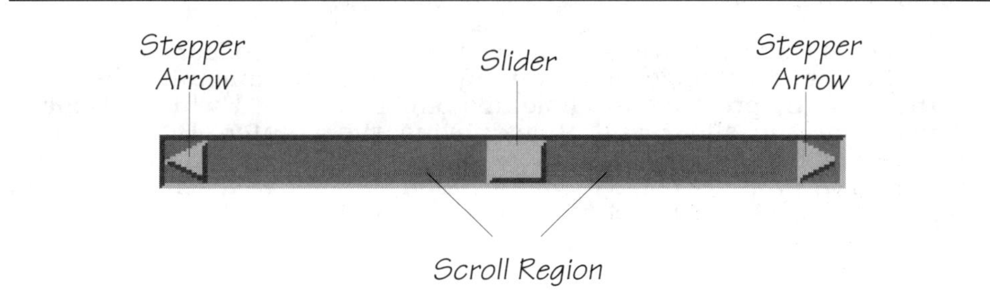

Minimum, Maximum, and Current Values

To the program, a scrollbar's scroll region represents the set of integer values between two points: the minimum and the maximum. The position of the slider represents the scrollbar's current value. The convention is to make the top or left side of the scrollbar represent the minimum value and the bottom or right side represent the maximum value but this can be changed by the program.

When the scrollbar's slider is moved — via the stepper arrows, the scroll region, or a direct drag — the scrollbar reports its new value to the program. The program then performs whatever actions are needed to make its display react to the scrollbar. A scrolled window — such as a scrolled-text widget — automatically translates scrollbar movement into display movement.

Stepper Arrows

Stepper arrows allow the user to incrementally shift the scrolled object. In terms of the scrollbar's value, each time a stepper arrow is activated it increments the current value, bounded by the maximum and minimum values.

A stepper arrow's interaction is similar to that of an arrow button. Like an arrow button, it is activated by clicking pointer button #1 while the pointer is positioned over the arrow. Also like an arrow button, it signals its activation by changing its shadow color, so that it appears to recede into the screen. Unlike an arrow button, a stepper arrow has a "repeat " capability: if the user holds the pointer button down while over the arrow, it will — after a short delay — repeatedly activate, until the user releases the pointer button. This allows a "smooth scrolling" effect: each activation changes the current value, and activations happen relatively frequently.

Slider

The *slider* provides visual feedback of the scrollbar's current value and the amount of data displayed. The left side of the slider shows the scrollbar's value; the relative size of the displayed data is shown by the slider's width (for a horizontal scrollbar) or height (for a vertical scrollbar).[1]

Not only does the slider provide visual feedback on the scrollbar's current value, it allows the user to change that value by an arbitrary amount. The user can "drag" the slider by pressing and holding pointer button #1 while the pointer is positioned over the slider and then moving the pointer. By dragging, the scrollbar's value may be set to any value — up to the maximum value minus the slider's width. A properly behaving application — such as a scrolled window — then scrolls the display to match the new slider position.

---

[1] Actually, slider width is under program control. The Motif style guide specifies that the ratio of the slider to the scroll region show the proportion of displayed data relative to the entire object, and a scrolled window enforces this behavior. However, a programmer could implement the Macintosh approach: a fixed-size slider that simply shows relative position.

Scroll Region

The *scroll region* is the "background" of the scrollbar and provides context for the feedback supplied by the slider. It also allows the user to change the current value a "page" at a time by clicking pointer button #1 while the pointer is positioned over the scroll region. This causes the slider to move toward the pointer, and like the stepper arrows, this operation is repeated for as long as the pointer button is held down.

XmScrolledWindow

XmScrolledWindow is a manager widget, derived as shown by the class tree of Figure 10.2. Unlike the manager widgets of Chapter 6, *XmScrolledWindow* does not provide management for an indefinite number of children. Instead, it has four: horizontal and vertical scrollbars, a *work window*, and a *clip window*.[2]

Figure 10.2. *XmScrolledWindow* class tree

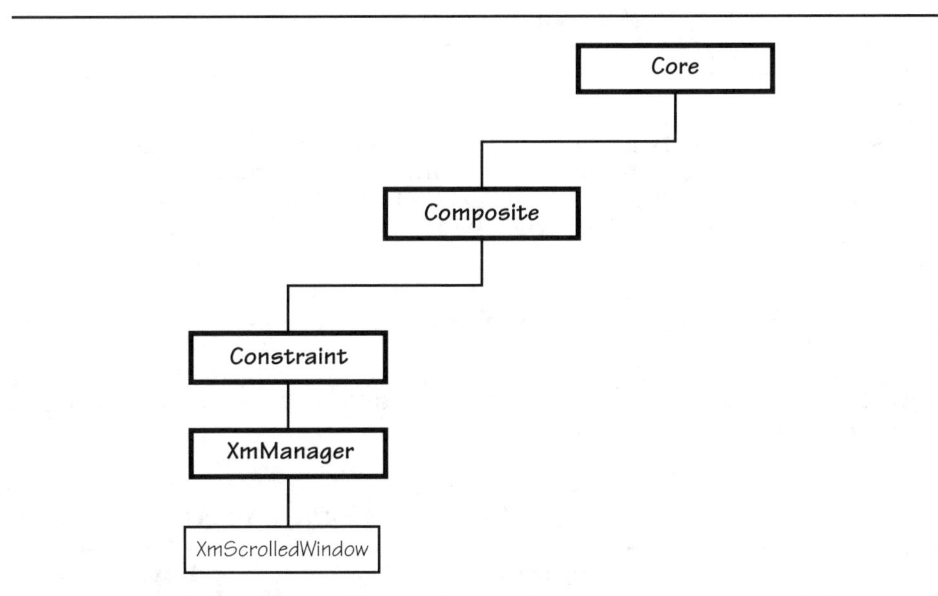

The work window is the object being scrolled. It may be any type of widget, manager or primitive. In a scrolled-text application, it is an *XmText* widget. The program is responsible for maintaining its contents; the scrolled window is simply responsible for its geometry and display. In a departure from the normal parent-child window relationship, the work window may be bigger than the scrolled window — in fact, this is the entire reason for the existence of the scrolled-window class.

---

[2] The actual term for these "children" is *sub-area*. Although in almost every program the sub-areas *are* children of the scrolled window, this is not a requirement.

The clip window represents a view into the work window as diagrammed by Figure 10.3. It is controlled by the scrolled window and is responsible for displaying the appropriate contents of the work window. The term "clip window" comes from the fact that only that part of the work window that is currently "under" the clip window is shown — in effect, the excess is "clipped off" as if by a pair of scissors.

Figure 10.3. Clip window vs. work window

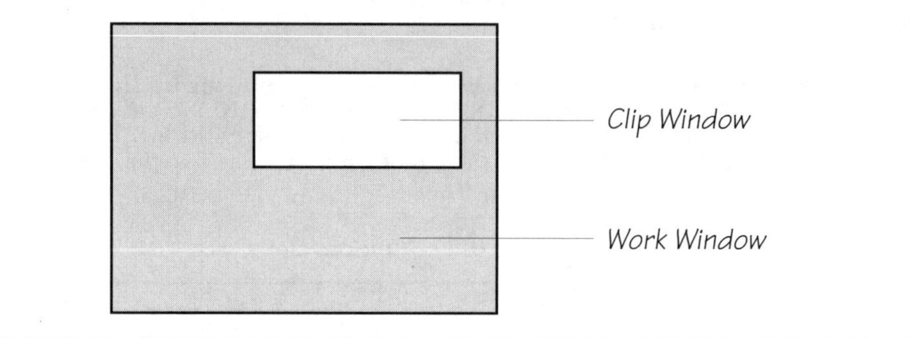

When a scrolled window is initialized, the clip window is positioned at the top-left of the work window. Its position is controlled by the scrollbars: as their values change — under either user or program control — the scrolled-window widget changes the position of the clip window.

XmScrolledWindow Resources

As it is descended from *XmManager*, *XmScrollBar* provides all resources defined by that class, as well as its superclasses. In addition, *XmScrollBar* provides the resources listed in Table 10.1 and described below.

Table 10.1. Frequently used resources: *XmScrolledWindow*

Name	Inheritance	Type	Default Value
clipWindow	XmScrolledWindow	Widget	NULL
horizontalScrollBar	XmScrolledWindow	Widget	NULL
scrollBarDisplayPolicy	XmScrolledWindow	unsigned char	XmSTATIC
scrollBarPlacement	XmScrolledWindow	unsigned char	XmBOTTOM_ RIGHT
scrolledWindowMargin Height	XmScrolledWindow	Dimension	0

Table 10.1. Continued.

scrolledWindowMargin Width	XmScrolledWindow	Dimension	0
scrollingPolicy	XmScrolledWindow	unsigned char	XmAPPLICATION_ DEFINED
spacing	XmScrolledWindow	Dimension	4
verticalScrollBar	XmScrolledWindow	Widget	NULL
visualPolicy	XmScrolledWindow	unsigned char	XmVARIABLE
workWindow	XmScrolledWindow	Widget	NULL

Appearance: scrollBarPlacement, scrolledWindowMarginHeight, scrolledWindowMarginWidth, spacing

A scrolled window supports two scrollbars: horizontal and vertical. The horizontal scrollbar may be placed on either the top or the bottom of the window; the vertical scrollbar may be placed on either the left or the right side. The scrollBarPlacement resource specifies the scrollbar placement; it can contain one of the following constants:

- XmTOP_LEFT. The horizontal scrollbar is placed at the top of the window, and the vertical scrollbar is placed on the left side.

- XmBOTTOM_LEFT. The horizontal scrollbar is placed at the bottom of the window, and the vertical scrollbar is placed on the left side.

- XmTOP_RIGHT. The horizontal scrollbar is placed at the top of the window, and the vertical scrollbar is placed on the right side.

- XmBOTTOM_RIGHT. The horizontal scrollbar is placed at the bottom of the window, and the vertical scrollbar is placed on the right side. This is the default value and is what users expect from a Motif program; it should only be changed after great consideration.

The distance between the scrollbars and the work window is specified by the spacing resource. This resource contains a count of pixels; the default of four pixels should be sufficient for most programs.

Like other managers, *XmScrolledWindow* provides an optional margin between its sides and its contents. This margin is specified by the resources scrolledWindowMarginHeight, which specifies the top and bottom margin, and scrolledWindowMarginWidth, which specifies the left and right margins. The default value for both resources is zero.

Behavior: scrollBarDisplayPolicy, visualPolicy

The `scrollBarDisplayPolicy` resource allows the scrolled window to exercise discretion over the presence or absence of its scrollbars. If it contains the value `XmAS_NEEDED` (the default), the scrolled window will only display the scrollbars when the size of the work window exceeds the size of the clip window. If it contains the value `XmSTATIC`, the scrollbars are always displayed — provided, of course, that they are not unmapped or unmanaged by the program.[3]

The `visualPolicy` resource controls whether the scrolled window attempts to grow to enclose the entire work window. If `visualPolicy` contains `XmVARIABLE` (the default), the scrolled window will attempt to grow or shrink to fit the work window, unless prevented by its parent. If `visualPolicy` contains the value `XmCONSTANT`, the scrolled window remains at its initial size — unless that size is changed by its parent — and the clip window provides a view into the work window.

The `visualPolicy` resource must be set at the time of the scrolled window's creation; it controls the way that the widget is initialized. In addition, if `visualPolicy` is `XmVARIABLE`, the `scrollBarDisplayPolicy` resource is forced to `XmSTATIC` and may not be changed to `XmAS_NEEDED`.

Interaction: scrollingPolicy

In most programs, *XmScrolledWindow* is used for its primary purpose: providing a convenient method of maintaining a "view" into a larger window. However, some applications may be too complex to take advantage of this ability — a CAD program, for example, may need to explicitly redraw its window's contents when scrolled. Even in this case, *XmScrolledWindow* may be used, as a convenient blend of a manager and automatically positioned scrollbars.

The `scrollingPolicy` resource controls whether the scrolled window or the program is responsible for scrolling. If it contains `XmAPPLICATION_DEFINED` (the default), the program is responsible for maintaining the appearance of the work window — it must directly handle the callbacks from the scrollbars. If `scrollingPolicy` contains `XmAUTOMATIC`, the scrolled window uses the clip window to provide a view into the work window.

This resource may only be set at the time of widget creation as it controls initialization of not only the scrolled window, but also of the scrollbars and clip window — these children are created along with the scrolled window if `scrollingPolicy` contains `XmAUTOMATIC`. The `scrollingPolicy` resource also controls the contents of the `scrollBarDisplayPolicy` resource: if `scrollingPolicy` is `XmAPPLICATION_DEFINED`, then `scrollBarDisplayPolicy` is forced to `XmSTATIC`.

---

[3] For example, if the scrolled window contains a text widget, and `scrollBarDisplayPolicy` contains `XmAS_NEEDED`, the scrollbars are only displayed when the contents of the text widget exceed its displayable area. In addition, only that scrollbar which is needed is displayed — if the text widget is sized for 10 rows and 48 columns and contains 5 rows of text with the longest row having 60 characters, only the horizontal scrollbar is displayed.

Sub-Areas: clipWindow, horizontalScrollBar, verticalScrollBar, workWindow

A scrolled window manages four sub-areas: horizontal and vertical scrollbars, a clip window, and a work window. Each of these areas is a widget; the resources `horizontalScrollBar`, `verticalScrollBar`, `clipWindow`, and `workWindow` hold the respective IDs of these widgets.[4]

If the `scrollingPolicy` resource is set to `XmAUTOMATIC`, the scrollbars and clip window are created along with with the scrolled window and are automatically maintained by it.[5] If `scrollingPolicy` contains `XmAPPLICATION_DEFINED`, the program must explicitly create all of the children — except the clip window, which is not used in this mode.

Creating and Initializing a Scrolled Window

A scrolled window is created using the `XmCreateScrolledWindow` convenience function, prototyped in Listing 10.1. This function creates an instance of *XmScrolledWindow* and returns the ID of that instance. Additionally, if the `scrollingPolicy` resource is specified as `XmAUTOMATIC`, `XmCreateScrolledWindow` also creates two *XmScrollBar* widgets and an *XmDrawingArea* widget (the clip window). `XmCreateScrolledWindow` *does not* create the work window; the program is responsible for its creation.

Listing 10.1. Function prototype: *XmCreateScrolledWindow*

```
Widget  XmCreateScrolledWindow( parent, name, arg_list, arg_count )
        Widget      parent;
        char        *name;
        ArgList     arg_list;
        Cardinal    arg_count;
```

If the scrolled-window's sub-areas are not created with the scrolled window — or specified as resources at the time of its creation — they may be specified at any time afterward using the `XmScrolledWindowSetAreas` function, prototyped in Listing 10.2. This function takes four parameters: the ID of the scrolled window widget (`w`), the IDs of the horizontal and vertical scrollbars (`hscroll` and `vscroll`),

---

[4] Although this book refers to these widgets as the "children" of the scrolled window, this need not be the case. In fact, each of these widgets may be at any level of the instance tree relative to the scrolled window. However, in keeping with common manager usage, this book does make scrolled-window sub-areas children of the scrolled window.

[5] When created along with the scrolled window, using the `XmCreateScrolledWindow` function, the name of the horizontal scrollbar is `hScrollBar`, the name of the vertical scrollbar is `vScrollBar`, and the name of the clip window is `scrolledWindowClipWindow`. When created with `XmCreateScrolledText`, the horizontal scrollbar is named `hbar`, the vertical scrollbar is named `vbar`, and the clipping window is not used. If you wish to change the appearance of these widgets via the resource file, you must use these names.

and the ID of the work window (`work`). Any of these parameters may be passed `NULL`; such parameters are ignored.[6] `XmScrolledWindowSetAreas` may be called multiple times; each call reconfigures the scrolled window.

Listing 10.2. Function prototype: *XmScrolledWindowSetAreas*

```
Widget  XmScrolledWindowSetAreas( w, hscroll, vscroll, work )
        Widget     w;
        Widget     hscroll;
        Widget     vscroll;
        Widget     workwidget;
```

XmScrolledWindow Example: Scrolling Row-Column

Figure 10.4 presents a row-column widget — which contains multiple label children — encased in a scrolled window. The program and resource file follow in Listing 10.3.

Figure 10.4. Row-column inside scrolled-window

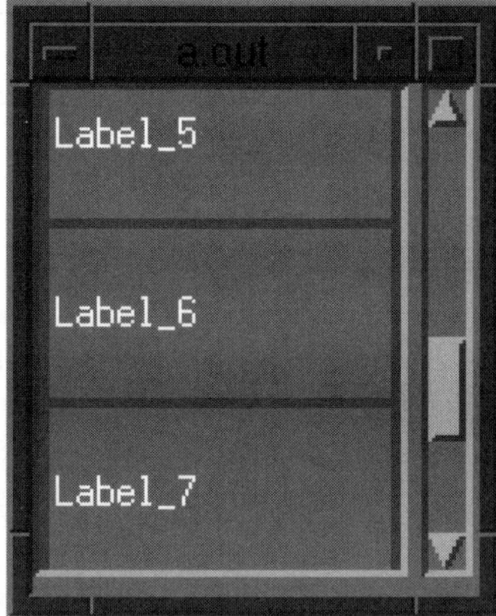

This program creates a scrolled window as the child of the application shell, creates a row-column manager as the child of the scrolled window, and creates ten labels as children of the row-column. It relies upon the

---

[6] Passing `NULL` does not disable the sub-area. To do that, you must explicitly set the associated resource to `NULL` with `XtSetValues`.

`XmCreateScrolledWindow` function to create the scrolled window's clip window and scrollbars, which are automatically installed as sub-areas. The row-column is installed as a sub-area via the `XmScrolledWindowSetAreas` function.

Of special note is the unmanagement of the horizontal scrollbar. Since it is not needed for this program — the scrolled window is sufficiently wide to display the entire row-column — its presence would be a distraction. However, by default it is created and managed. The program must therefore get its widget ID and explicitly unmanage it. An alternative — and simpler — approach would be to set the `scrollBarDisplayPolicy` resource to `XmAS_NEEDED`.[7]

Listing 10.3. Program and resource file: Row-column inside scrolled window

```c
/******************************************************************************
**                                                                          **
**   listing_10_3.c                                                         **
**                                                                          **
**   Scrolled-Window Demo. This program uses a scrolled-window to hold      **
**   a row-column, which in turn holds ten label widgets.                   **
**                                                                          **
******************************************************************************/


#include <Xm/ScrolledW.h>
#include <Xm/ScrollBar.h>
#include <Xm/RowColumn.h>
#include <Xm/Label.h>


Widget  appshell,                       /* Application Shell      */
        scroller,                       /* The scrolled-window    */
        rowcol,                         /* The row-column         */
        labels[10];                     /* The children           */

Widget  temp;                           /* Used to unmanage HScroll */
Arg     arglist[1];                     /* Ditto                  */
```

Listing 10.3. Continued.

```c
void main( argc, argv )
    int     argc;
    char    *argv[];
{
    appshell = XtInitialize( argv[0], "Listing_10_3", NULL, 0,
                             &argc, argv );

    scroller = XmCreateScrolledWindow( appshell, "Scroller", NULL, 0 );
    XtManageChild( scroller );

    rowcol = XmCreateRowColumn( scroller, "RowCol", NULL, 0 );
    XtManageChild( rowcol );

    XmScrolledWindowSetAreas( scroller, NULL, NULL, rowcol );

    XtSetArg( arglist[0], XmNhorizontalScrollBar, &temp );
    XtGetValues( scroller, arglist, 1 );
    XtUnmanageChild( temp );

    labels[0] = XmCreateLabel( rowcol, "Label_0", NULL, 0 );
    labels[1] = XmCreateLabel( rowcol, "Label_1", NULL, 0 );
    labels[2] = XmCreateLabel( rowcol, "Label_2", NULL, 0 );
    labels[3] = XmCreateLabel( rowcol, "Label_3", NULL, 0 );
    labels[4] = XmCreateLabel( rowcol, "Label_4", NULL, 0 );
    labels[5] = XmCreateLabel( rowcol, "Label_5", NULL, 0 );
    labels[6] = XmCreateLabel( rowcol, "Label_6", NULL, 0 );
    labels[7] = XmCreateLabel( rowcol, "Label_7", NULL, 0 );
    labels[8] = XmCreateLabel( rowcol, "Label_8", NULL, 0 );
    labels[9] = XmCreateLabel( rowcol, "Label_9", NULL, 0 );
    XtManageChildren( labels, 10 );

    XtRealizeWidget( appshell );
    XtMainLoop();
}
!
! Resource file to produce Figure 10.4
!

*Scroller.visualPolicy:              CONSTANT
```

Listing 10.3. Continued.

```
*Scroller.scrollingPolicy:          AUTOMATIC
*Scroller.scrollBarDisplayPolicy:   STATIC
*Scroller.height:                   150
*Scroller.width:                    129

*XmScrolledWindow.background:       Gray50
*XmScrolledWindow.foreground:       Gray75
*XmScrollBar.background:            Gray50
*XmScrollBar.foreground:            Gray75

*RowCol.background:                 Red

*XmLabel.height:                    50
*XmLabel.width:                     100
*XmLabel.background:                Gray50
*XmLabel.foreground:                White
*XmLabel.recomputeSize:             FALSE
```

The resource file seems straightforward: it essentially changes the default settings for all of the scrolled-window policy resources and sets widget colors. However, the scrolled-window `width` resource — and how I arrived at its value — deserves special note.

A scrolled window divides its assigned area among its children, with spaces between those children as specified by the `spacing` resource. Immediately inside the scrolled window is its margin, which defaults to zero pixels. In a normal scrolled window (as specified by a `scrollBarPlacement` value of `XmBOTTOM_RIGHT`), the scrollbars are on the bottom and right sides, and the work window is positioned at the top left. An undocumented fact is that the width of the vertical scrollbar (and the height of the horizontal scrollbar) is 15 pixels. Adding this width to the size of the margin and the four pixels defined by the `spacing` resource, I got a "width adder" of 19.

This "width adder" is then added to the width of the work window. This width is the sum of the maximum child width (100 pixels), the row-column's `marginWidth` resource (three pixels on each side), and the width of the row-column's shadow border (two pixels on each side). The width of the row-column is therefore 110 pixels, which when combined with the "width adder" gives a scrolled-window width of 129 pixels — give it less than this width and it doesn't display the full child, give it more, and it simply increases the size of the clip window (the work window, remember, has a fixed width determined from its children).

XmScrollBar

Scrollbars, as discrete entities, are defined by the *XmScrollBar* class. *XmScrollBar* is a primitive widget, derived as shown by the class tree in Figure

10.5. It does not provide direct support for scrolling, but notifies the program — via callbacks — of the user's interaction. The program is then expected to respond to the user's actions.

Figure 10.5. *XmScrollBar* class tree

```
            ┌──────────────┐
            │     Core     │
            └──────────────┘
                    │
                    ┌──────────────────┐
                    │   XmPrimitive    │
                    └──────────────────┘
                            │
                    ┌──────────────────┐
                    │   XmScrollBar    │
                    └──────────────────┘
```

XmScrollBar Resources

Table 10.2 lists the resources defined by the *XmScrollBar* class. *XmScrollBar* also supports all resources defined by *XmPrimitive* and *Core*; these resources are not listed or described here.

Table 10.2. Frequently used resources: *XmScrollBar*

Name	Inheritance	Type	Default Value
decrementCallback	XmScrollBar	XtCallbackList	NULL
dragCallback	XmScrollBar	XtCallbackList	NULL
increment	XmScrollBar	int	1
incrementCallback	XmScrollBar	XtCallbackList	NULL
initialDelay	XmScrollBar	int	250
maximum	XmScrollBar	int	100
minimum	XmScrollBar	int	0
orientation	XmScrollBar	unsigned char	XmVERTICAL
pageDecrementCallback	XmScrollBar	XtCallbackList	NULL

Table 10.2. Continued.

`pageIncrement`	XmScrollBar	`int`	`10`
`pageIncrementCallback`	XmScrollBar	`XtCallbackList`	`NULL`
`processingDirection`	XmScrollBar	`unsigned char`	`XmMAX_ON` `_BOTTOM`
`repeatDelay`	XmScrollBar	`int`	`50`
`showArrows`	XmScrollBar	`Boolean`	`TRUE`
`sliderSize`	XmScrollBar	`int`	`10`
`toBottomCallback`	XmScrollBar	`XtCallbackList`	`NULL`
`toTopCallback`	XmScrollBar	`XtCallbackList`	`NULL`
`value`	XmScrollBar	`int`	`0`
`valueChangedCallback`	XmScrollBar	`XtCallbackList`	`NULL`

Appearance: orientation, showArrows

Scrollbars may be oriented horizontally or vertically; this orientation is controlled by the scrollbar's `orientation` resource. When `orientation` contains the value `XmVERTICAL` (the default), the scrollbar is oriented vertically; when it contains `XmHORIZONTAL`, the scrollbar is oriented horizontally.

The `showArrows` resource controls whether or not the scrollbar contains stepper arrows. If it contains `TRUE` (the default), stepper arrows are provided. If it contains `FALSE`, stepper arrows are omitted; the user is unable to perform smooth scrolling (the slider and scroll region are the only ways to scroll in the absence of stepper arrows).[8]

Range and Current Value: minimum, maximum, value

As stated above, a scrollbar's scroll region represents the continuous set of integers between some minimum and maximum values, and the position of its slider represents a value in this set. The scrollbar's minimum value is specified by the `minimum` resource, its maximum value is specified by the `maximum` resource, and its current value is contained in the `value` resource. The default values are a minimum value of zero, a maximum value of 100, and a current value of zero.

Value-Based Appearance: processingDirection, sliderSize

The range of values represented by the scroll region may either increase or decrease from left to right (top to bottom), depending on the contents of the

---

[8] The primary reason for the existence of this resource is the *XmScale* widget, described below.

`processingDirection` resource. To specify that the scrollbar values increase from left to right (top to bottom), this resource must contain either `XmMAX_ON_RIGHT` or `XmMAX_ON_BOTTOM`.[9] To specify that values decrease from left to right, `processingDirection` must contain either `XmMAX_ON_LEFT` or `XmMAX_ON_TOP`. The default value is `XmMAX_ON_RIGHT` (`XmMAX_ON_BOTTOM`).

The `sliderSize` resource controls the displayed size of the slider, relative to the maximum and minimum values. This resource can take on values from zero, meaning that the slider is not shown, to the difference between `maximum` and `minimum`, meaning that the slider occupies the entire scroll region. To meet the Motif style criteria, the program must maintain the slider size to show the amount of data displayed. A scrolled window in "automatic" mode does this transparently.

By default, the slider size is ten pixels. If the `maximum` and/or `minimum` resource is changed from its default value, the slider size remains ten pixels or the value `maximum` - `minimum`, if that value is less than 10 pixels.

Interaction: increment, pageIncrement

As stated above, the stepper arrows exist to "smoothly" change the current value — for example, by one line of text at a time. The actual change is specified by the `increment` resource: it contains the amount added or subtracted from the current value for each click of the appropriate stepper button.

Similarly, the `pageIncrement` resource controls scrolling via the scroll region. If the pointer is positioned "below" the slider, `pageIncrement` is subtracted from `value`; if it is positioned "above" the slider, `pageIncrement` is added to `value`.[10]

Timing: initialDelay, repeatDelay

Both the stepper arrows and the scroll region will "repeat activate" if the user holds the pointer button down. The `initialDelay` resource specifies the amount of time that the pointer button must be held down for repeat to occur — the time between initial activation and first repeat. This resource contains a count of milliseconds; the default value is 250 (¼ second). The `repeatDelay` resource specifies the elapsed time between repeat activations. It also holds a count of milliseconds and has a default value of 50 (¹⁄₂₀ second).

---

[9] The values of these constants are identical, as are `XmMAX_ON_TOP` and `XmMAX_ON_LEFT`. Which constant to use depends on the scrollbar's orientation — and your desire to match constants to that orientation.

[10] "Above" and "below" depend on the scrollbar's `processingDirection` resource. In a horizontal scrollbar with `XmMAX_ON_RIGHT`, "below" means "to the left," and "above" means "to the right." If `processingDirection` contains `XmMAX_ON_LEFT`, these directions are reversed.

XmScrollBar **Callbacks**

The interaction between a scrollbar and a program is quite simple: each time the user interacts with the scrollbar, the scrollbar invokes a callback. Due to the large number of ways that the user can interact with the scrollbar, there are a large number of callbacks. All callbacks pass data in `XmScrollBarCallbackStruct`, defined in Listing 10.4.

Listing 10.4. Type definition: XmScrollBarCallbackStruct

```
typedef struct
        {
        int     reason;
        XEvent  *event;
        int     value;
        int     pixel;
        }
XmScrollBarCallbackStruct;
```

As with other callbacks, the `reason` and `event` members provide information about the call: the type of callback, and the event triggering the callback. The `value` member contains the scrollbar's new value — it is updated before the callback is called. The `pixel` member is used only for `toTopCallback` and `toBottomCallback`; it contains the position of the pointer — x for horizontal scrollbars, y for vertical scrollbars — when the user first pressed the button.[11]

Single Step: incrementCallback, decrementCallback

The `incrementCallback` and `decrementCallback` functions handle activation of the stepper arrows. The appropriate callback is called when the user first presses the arrow, as well as for each repeat activation. The scrollbar's `value` resource is changed by the contents of the `increment` resource prior to invocation of the callback.

The `reason` member contains either `XmCR_INCREMENT` or `XmCR_DECREMENT`.

Page Step: pageIncrementCallback, pageDecrementCallback

The `pageIncrementCallback` and `pageDecrementCallback` functions handle activation of the scroll region. The appropriate callback is called when the user first presses the pointer button, as well as for each repeat activation. The

---

[11] This may be used to identify whether the to-top or to-bottom movement occurred as the result of a drag (for which `pixel`'s value would refer to the middle of the scroll region) or as a result of holding the *Shift* key while clicking in one of the stepper arrows (for which `pixel`'s value would refer to and end of the scroll region). As Motif 1.0 only invokes this callback in the second case, `pixel` may be ignored.

scrollbar's `value` resource is changed by the contents of the `pageIncrement` resource prior to invocation of the callback.

The `reason` member contains either `XmCR_PAGE_INCREMENT` or `XmCR_PAGE_DECREMENT`.

Drag: dragCallback

The `dragCallback` function is invoked whenever the user changes the scrollbar's value by dragging the scrollbar slider. The scrollbar's `value` resource contains the new value, as does the `value` member of the call data structure. The callback's reason is `XmCR_DRAG`.

This callback is not invoked only when the drag completes, but at regular intervals during the drag. This allows the program to smoothly update the display in response to the drag.[12]

Begin/End: toTopCallback, toBottomCallback

These callbacks are invoked when the user performs the "to end" action: clicking on a stepper arrow while holding the *Shift* key down.[13] The callback reason is `XmCR_TO_BOTTOM` for `toBottomCallback`, `XmCR_TO_TOP` for `toTopCallback`.

Note that, if the user performs a "to end" click, the scrollbar's `value` resource is not changed, even though the callback structure contains the new value. This means that the program must explicitly change the scrollbar's `value` resource. It does, however, allow optional implementation of the "to end" action.

Generic Movement: valueChangedCallback

If a program does not need the level of detail provided by separate callbacks for each action of the user, it can instead handle `valueChangedCallback`. This callback is invoked whenever the scrollbar's value changes *and* no other callback would be called (*ie*, the appropriate callback resource contains `NULL`). It is also invoked at the completion of a slider drag.[14] The reason for this callback is `XmCR_VALUE_CHANGED`.

---

[12] Scrolled text makes use of this functionality. As the slider is dragged, the text window is continually updated to show the new position.

[13] Under Motif 1.1, these callbacks are invoked any time the slider is moved to an end of the scrollbar, whatever the reason — drag, scroll region click, normal stepper arrow click, or "to end" stepper arrow click.

[14] While the drag is occurring, `dragCallback` is continually invoked. When the drag completes — the user releases the pointer button — `valueChangedCallback` is invoked.

Getting and Setting a Scrollbar's Values Programmatically

While you can use `XtGetValues` and `XtSetValues` to access a scrollbar's value resources, Motif provides convenience functions to access the most-used of these resources. The function `XmScrollBarGetValues` retrieves a scrollbar's values, and `XmScrollBarSetValues` sets its values. Both functions are prototyped in Listing 10.5.

Listing 10.5. Function prototypes: *XmScrollBarGetValues*, *XmScrollBarSetValues*

```
void      XmScrollBarGetValues( w, value, slider_size, incr, page_incr )
          Widget      w;
          int         *value;
          int         *slider_size;
          int         *incr;
          int         *page_incr;


void      XmScrollBarSetValues( w, value, slider_size, incr, page_incr,
                              notify )
          Widget      w;
          int         value;
          int         slider_size;
          int         incr;
          int         page_incr;
          Boolean     notify;
```

For both functions, the `w` parameter identifies the scrollbar widget. The parameters of `XmScrollBarGetValues` specify pointer to variables to receive the existing values; for `XmScrollBarSetValues`, the parameters specify new values. When new values are installed into a scrollbar, the scrollbar appearance is updated to match the new values.

The `value` parameter represents the scrollbar's `value` resource. The `slider_size` parameter represents the scrollbar's `sliderSize` resource. The `incr` and `page_incr` parameters, respectively, represent the scrollbar's `increment` and `pageIncrement` resources.

The `notify` parameter, specific to `XmScrollBarSetValues`, specifies whether or not the scrollbar's `valueChangedCallback` should be invoked. If it is set to `TRUE`, the callback is invoked; otherwise it isn't.

XmScrollBar Example

As scrollbars are almost always used in concert with another widget — typically a scrolled-window widget — an example scrollbar program must be "manufactured." This sample program shown in Listing 10.6 is no exception; it simply displays a scrollbar in its own window and reports on the user's interaction with that scrollbar. Reporting is performed by attaching a callback function to all of the scrollbar's callbacks — note that the same function is used for all callbacks, with a `switch` to report the callback reason.

Listing 10.6. Program and resource file: *XmScrollBar* example

```c
/*****************************************************************************
**                                                                         **
**    listing_10_6.c                                                       **
**                                                                         **
**    Scrollbar Demo. This program simply displays a scrollbar, and        **
**    catches all of that scrollbar's callbacks.                           **
**                                                                         **
*****************************************************************************/


#include <Xm/ScrollBar.h>


void    ScrollCB();                      /* FORWARD Definition      */


Widget  appshell,                        /* Application Shell       */
        scroller;                        /* The scrollbar           */

void main( argc, argv )
    int     argc;
    char    *argv[];
{
    appshell = XtInitialize( argv[0], "Listing_10_6", NULL, 0,
                                               &argc, argv );

    scroller = XmCreateScrollBar( appshell, "Scroller", NULL, 0 );
    XtManageChild( scroller );

    XtAddCallback( scroller, XmNdecrementCallback,     ScrollCB, NULL );
    XtAddCallback( scroller, XmNdragCallback,          ScrollCB, NULL );
    XtAddCallback( scroller, XmNincrementCallback,     ScrollCB, NULL );
    XtAddCallback( scroller, XmNpageDecrementCallback, ScrollCB, NULL );
    XtAddCallback( scroller, XmNpageIncrementCallback, ScrollCB, NULL );
    XtAddCallback( scroller, XmNtoBottomCallback,      ScrollCB, NULL );
```

Listing 10.6. Continued.

```c
    XtAddCallback( scroller, XmNtoTopCallback,          ScrollCB, NULL );
    XtAddCallback( scroller, XmNvalueChangedCallback,  ScrollCB, NULL );

    XtRealizeWidget( appshell );
    XtMainLoop();
}


void ScrollCB( w, client_data, call_data )
    Widget                  w;
    caddr_t                 client_data;
    XmScrollBarCallbackStruct  *call_data;
{
    printf( "\nCallback...\n" );
    switch (call_data->reason)
        {
        case XmCR_DECREMENT :
                printf( "    Reason: Decrement\n" );
                break;
        case XmCR_DRAG :
                printf( "    Reason: Drag\n" );
                break;
        case XmCR_INCREMENT :
                printf( "    Reason: Increment\n" );
                break;
        case XmCR_PAGE_DECREMENT :
                printf( "    Reason: Page Decrement\n" );
                break;
        case XmCR_PAGE_INCREMENT :
                printf( "    Reason: Page Increment\n" );
                break;
        case XmCR_TO_BOTTOM :
                printf( "    Reason: To Bottom\n" );
                break;
        case XmCR_TO_TOP :
                printf( "    Reason: To Top\n" );
                break;
        case XmCR_VALUE_CHANGED :
                printf( "    Reason: Value Changed\n" );
```

Listing 10.6. Continued.

```
                break;
        }
    printf( "    New Value: %d\n", call_data->value );
}
```

```
!
! Resource file for scrollbar example
!

*Scroller.foreground:    Gray75
*Scroller.background:    Gray50
*Scroller.width:         200
*Scroller.height:        20
*Scroller.orientation:   HORIZONTAL
```

The resource file essentially sets the appearance resources, but it does have one specification of note: `orientation` is set to `XmHORIZONTAL`. This was done because the Motif window manager enforces a minimum width on windows — causing a vertical scrollbar to be much wider than is desirable.[15]

XmScale

A scrollbar provides the user with a "variable magnitude" control, but its appearance and interaction are targeted to control of a scrolling display — in essence, it is a "position" control. For this reason, the *XmScale* class exists; it is a general-purpose magnitude control.

Figure 10.6 presents a sample scale widget, used as a radio tuning control. The visible differences between a scale and a scrollbar are: (1) the scale does not have stepper arrows, (2) the scale's value is indicated by the center of the slider — specifically, by the line in the center of the slider, (3) the scale indicates its current value, and (4) the scale has a label. Not visible is the fact that a scale reverses the default processing direction (it's been changed for this example). Another difference is that the scale's slider remains a constant size.

---

[15] This minimum is applied to the application shell, which applies it to its child. If the scrollbar was the child of another widget (such as a bulletin board), there would be no problem.

Figure 10.6. *XmScale* example

XmScale **Resources**

Another difference between *XmScale* and *XmScrollBar* is that *XmScale* is a manager class, derived as shown by the class tree of Figure 10.7. It is a manager class in order to use code already developed for other widget classes — specifically, *XmScrollBar* and *XmLabelGadget*. A scale's scale is actually a scrollbar sans arrows (the slider differences are implemented with hidden resources); its value is displayed via a label gadget. These children are created and installed when the scale itself is created; the program can neither change these children nor add additional children to the scale.

Figure 10.7. *XmScale* class tree

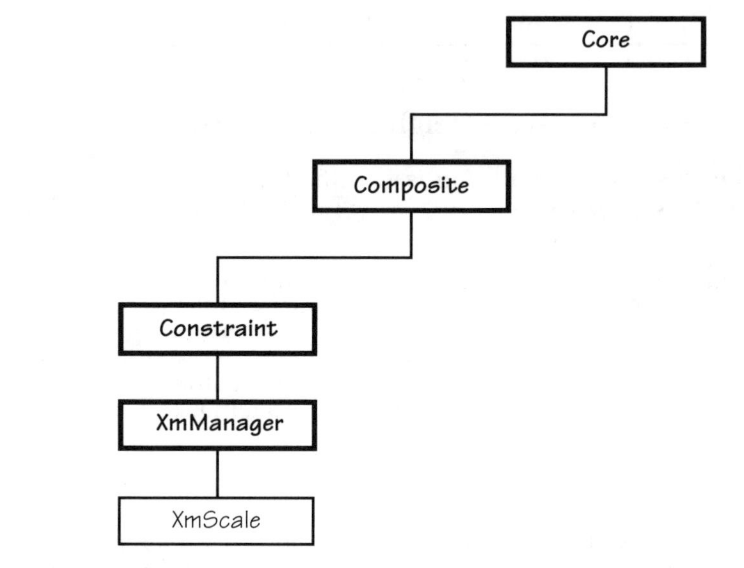

The *XmScale* class provides the resources listed in Table 10.3, as well as those defined by the *Core, Composite, Constraint,* and *XmManager* classes. As the children of a scale widget are "hidden," the programmer is unable to change their resources — or access them in any way.

Table 10.3. Frequently used resources: *XmScale*

Name	Inheritance	Type	Default Value
decimalPoints	XmScale	short	0
dragCallback	XmScale	XtCallbackList	NULL
fontList	XmScale	XmFontList	"Fixed"
highlightOnEnter	XmScale	Boolean	FALSE
highlightThickness	XmScale	short	0
maximum	XmScale	int	100
minimum	XmScale	int	0
orientation	XmScale	unsigned char	XmVERTICAL
processingDirection	XmScale	unsigned char	XmMAX_ON_TOP
scaleHeight	XmScale	Dimension	0
scaleWidth	XmScale	Dimension	0
showValue	XmScale	Boolean	FALSE
titleString	XmScale	XmString	NULL
value	XmScale	int	0
valueChangedCallback	XmScale	XtCallbackList	NULL

Appearance: orientation, scaleHeight, scaleWidth

Like *XmScrollBar*, a scale's orientation is specified by its orientation resource. Also like *XmScrollBar*, legal values are XmVERTICAL and XmHORIZONTAL, and the default value is XmVERTICAL.

Like most managers, a scale's dimensions may be determined from the dimensions of its children. However, since the scale's children are hidden to the programmer, there is no way to directly change their dimensioning resources. Instead, *XmScale* provides the scaleWidth and scaleHeight resources, which specify the dimensions of its scrollbar child. To these values, the scale adds the size of its other components and intercomponent spacing, to arrive at its overall dimensions.[16]

---

[16] A scale's dimensions may also be set by parental constraint. However, using the scale's width and height resources does not work — the scale always gives preference to its children's dimensions.

Text Appearance: fontList, titleString

As with other widgets, the `fontList` resource specifies the font used for text display. In the case of *XmScale*, this font is used for both the scale's title and its label. Like other widgets, the default value of `fontList` is the default fixed-spacing font.

An *XmScale* widget can optionally display a title at the bottom left of its window. The contents of this title are specified by the `titleString` resource; as with *XmLabel*'s title, this resource contains a compound string. Unlike *XmLabel*, the default value of `NULL` causes the scale to simply not display its title.

Interaction: processingDirection, showValue, decimalPoints

Like *XmScrollBar*, *XmScale* provides a `processingDirection` resource, which specifies which side of the scale represents its maximum value. Also like *XmScrollBar*, possible values for this resource are `XmMAX_ON_TOP`, `XmMAX_ON_BOTTOM`, `XmMAX_ON_RIGHT`, and `XmMAX_ON_LEFT`; top and left are equivalent, as are bottom and right. Unlike *XmScrollBar*, the default value is `XmMAX_ON_TOP` (`XmMAX_ON_LEFT`), which means that scales operate in a direction opposite to scrollbars.[17]

The `showValue` resource specifies whether or not the scale displays its current value. If `showValue` contains `TRUE` (the default), a label gadget is positioned above the scale's slider; this label displays the current value and is updated each time the value changes. If `showValue` contains `FALSE`, this label gadget is not maintained, and the value is not displayed.[18]

If the scale's value is displayed, the `decimalPoints` resource specifies how many digits are displayed to the right of the decimal point. This resource is needed because the scale can only hold integer values, but is often used to display decimal values — an example is Figure 10.6. The `decimalPoints` value contains an integer value, representing the number of digits (of `value`) displayed to the right of the decimal point. The default value is zero, meaning that the value is displayed as an integer value, without a displayed decimal point.

Range and Value: minimum, maximum, value

Like *XmScrollBar*, the `minimum` and `maximum` resources specify the range of values supported by the scrollbar. Also like *XmScrollBar*, the `value` resource specifies the scale's current value.

---

[17] This makes sense when comparing a vertical scrollbar with a vertical scale: the scale represents values, which naturally increase in an upward direction, whereas the scrollbar represents the scrollable area — the top of the scrollbar (`minimum`) is the top of the scrollable area. However, a horizontal scale does not make much sense — most people expect numbers to increase left-to-right, but the default scale increases right-to-left.

[18] Note that no provision is made to display the maximum or minimum values, only the current value.

XmScale Callbacks

XmScale handles the callbacks of its *XmScrollBar* child and translates them into two program-level callbacks: `dragCallback` and `valueChangedCallback`. The operation of these callbacks is different from the identically named *XmScrollBar* callbacks: `dragCallback` is called at the end of a slider drag (not during the drag), and `valueChangedCallback` is called when the user clicks in the scroll region.[19]

Both functions pass call data in the structure `XmScaleCallbackStruct`, defined in Listing 10.7. As with other callback structures, the `reason` member specifies the callback type — `XmCR_DRAG` or `XmCR_VALUE_CHANGED` — and the `event` member points at the event responsible for callback invocation. The `value` member contains the new scale value.

Listing 10.7. Type definition: XmScaleCallbackStruct

```
typedef struct
        {
        int     reason;
        XEvent  *event;
        int     value;
        }
XmScaleCallbackStruct;
```

Getting and Setting a Scale's Value Programmatically

As with *XmScrollBar*, *XmScale* has convenience functions for getting and setting its value resources. Unlike *XmScrollBar*'s convenience functions — which not only access the scrollbar's current value but also its interaction resources — *XmScale*'s convenience functions only access the scale's current value.

Both functions are prototyped in Listing 10.8. `XmScaleGetValue` returns the scale's current value; its parameters are the scale's widget ID and a pointer to the variable that receives the value. XmScaleSetValue sets the scale's current value; its parameters are the scale's widget ID and the new value.

---

[19] Unless `dragCallback` contains `NULL`, in which case `valueChangedCallback` is invoked for any change in the scale's value.

Listing 10.8. Function prototypes: *XmScaleGetValue, XmScaleSetValue*

```
void    XmScaleGetValue( w, val_ptr )
        Widget      w;
        int         *val_ptr;


void    XmScaleSetValue( w, value )
        Widget      w;
        int         value;
```

XmScale Example

Listing 10.9 presents the program and resource file responsible for Figure 10.6. The program is similar to that of Listing 10.6: it creates the scale and attaches a callback function to each of its callbacks. The callback function simply reports — by printing to standard output — the callback reason and new value.

The resource file illustrates many of the scale's resources. In particular, it changes both the default orientation and processing direction in order to present a display that is more like a real radio. The scale's range is set to the range of U.S. FM frequencies, and its default value is set to a particular frequency.

Listing 10.9. Program and resource file: Tuning scale

```
/*******************************************************************
**                                                               **
**    listing_10_9.c                                             **
**                                                               **
**    Scale Demo. This program displays a scale, and catches its **
**    callbacks.                                                  **
**                                                               **
********************************************************************/


#include <Xm/Scale.h>


void    ScaleCB();                      /* FORWARD Definition      */
```

Listing 10.9. Continued.

```c
Widget  appshell,                         /* Application Shell       */
        thescale;                         /* The scale               */


void main( argc, argv )
    int     argc;
    char    *argv[];
{
    appshell = XtInitialize( argv[0], "Listing_10_9", NULL, 0,
                                                  &argc, argv );

    thescale = XmCreateScale( appshell, "TheScale", NULL, 0 );
    XtManageChild( thescale );
    XtAddCallback( thescale, XmNdragCallback,            ScaleCB, NULL );
    XtAddCallback( thescale, XmNvalueChangedCallback, ScaleCB, NULL );

    XtRealizeWidget( appshell );
    XtMainLoop();
}


void ScaleCB( w, client_data, call_data )
    Widget                  w;
    caddr_t                 client_data;
    XmScaleCallbackStruct   *call_data;
{
    printf( "\nCallback...\n" );
    switch (call_data->reason)
        {
        case XmCR_DRAG :
                printf( "    Reason: Drag\n" );
                break;
        case XmCR_VALUE_CHANGED :
                printf( "    Reason: Value Changed\n" );
                break;
        }
    printf( "    New Value: %d\n", call_data->value );
}
```

```
!
! Resource file to produce Figure 10.6
!

*TheScale.foreground:              Gray75
```

Listing 10.9. Continued.

```
*TheScale.background:              Gray50
!*TheScale.width:                  200
!*TheScale.height:                 20

*TheScale.titleString:            Station
*TheScale.minimum:                879
*TheScale.maximum:                1079
*TheScale.value:                  1025
*TheScale.showValue:              TRUE
*TheScale.decimalPoints:          1

*TheScale.orientation:            HORIZONTAL
*TheScale.processingDirection:    MAX_ON_RIGHT
*TheScale.scaleWidth:             200
*TheScale.scaleHeight:            20
```

11
The Motif "Look"

Overview

Chapter 1 presented the idea that a Motif program was instantly recognizable — that it has a Motif "Look." Three factors contribute to this effect. First, widget appearance is defined at a low level in the class tree, by *XmPrimitive* and *XmManager*, meaning that the basic stylistic elements of a Motif program such as color scheme are present in all widgets. The second factor is that higher-level stylistic elements are consistent throughout Motif — the slider of a scrollbar, for example, has an appearance almost identical to that of a pushbutton. The third factor is that the Open Software Foundation has prescribed a standard client appearance — menu bar at the top, scrollbars (if needed) on left and bottom sides, etc — and widgets exist solely to support that standard layout.[1]

This chapter begins with a description of the components of a standard Motif client — those items that make Motif programs look alike and act alike. The *XmMainWindow* widget, which provides direct support for the standard client features, is presented next. Following *XmMainWindow* are descriptions of the *XmSeparator* and *XmFrame* widgets, which exist solely for appearance, instead of function. The chapter ends with a new program template, replacing the template of Chapter 4. The template is presented and described, then used as the foundation of a text editor application, which is further developed in subsequent chapters.

Components of a Motif Client

On an X display, a program's window has two primary parts: the *window frame* and the *client area*. The window frame is applied by the window manager, and its appearance is specific to the window manager in use. Under the Motif window manager, the window frame provides controls for moving the window, resizing the window in any direction, *maximizing* the window to the entire screen size, or

---

[1] The importance of a standard client appearance cannot be overstated. When users feel that a program will operate in an expected way, they are more willing to use the program. As simple an item as knowing how to exit a program will break down resistance to using the program.

minimizing the window to an icon. Additionally, the Motif window frame displays the name of the program's executable file and a system menu, which provides an alternative method for window-related actions such as movement.

The client area is everything inside the window frame and as such is maintained by the application shell and its children. A standard Motif application divides the client area into the five sub-areas shown in Figure 11.1.[2] The *menu bar* provides access to the program's pull-down menus; pull-downs are the primary method of entering commands to the program. The horizontal and vertical scrollbars are optional; if used, they control the display in the work area. The *command area* is also optional; if present, it is used for command-line text entry and/or message display. The *work area* is where the program interacts with the user — for a text editor, it is the editor window, for a CAD program, it is where the drawing is displayed.

Figure 11.1. Standard Motif client areas

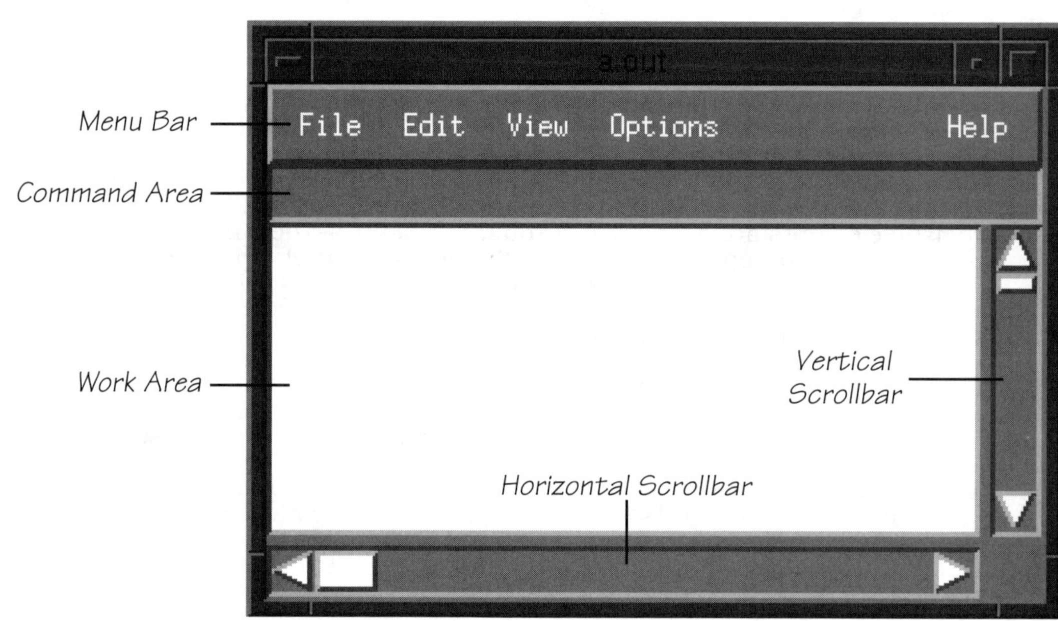

In addition to the main window, a Motif client may use *dialogs* — auxiliary windows that present information that would be distracting if displayed on the main screen (*eg*, error messages). Dialogs are often invoked by menu choices: the **File/Open** menu choice, for example, typically displays a dialog that allows the user to select a file from a list of files. They can — and should — be used in any

---

[2] This figure applies to Motif 1.0 only. For 1.1, the *command area* is positioned below the *work area*. In addition, a sixth sub-area — the *message area* — is provided below the command area.

situation where the programmer desires to focus the user on a message or control. Dialogs are described in detail in Chapter 13.

XmMainWindow

To assist the programmer in creating an application that follows the appearance standards, Motif provides the *XmMainWindow* class. *XmMainWindow* is derived from *XmScrolledWindow*, as shown by Figure 11.2. This means that support for scrollbars and a scrolling work window is "built in" and need not be replicated. In addition, *XmMainWindow* adds an additional unscrolled work window — the command area — and direct support for a menu bar. The main-window widget automatically divides its space between these sub-areas.

Figure 11.2. *XmMainWindow* class tree

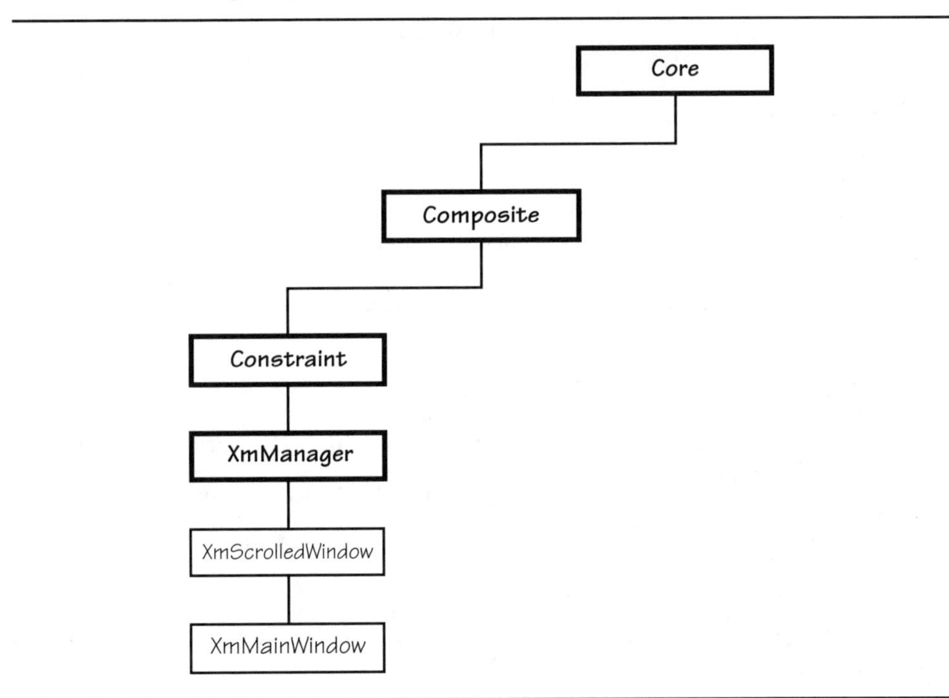

XmMainWindow **Resources**

The resources provided by *XmMainWindow* are listed in Table 11.1 and described below. In addition, Table 11.1 contains some of the resources from *XmScrolledWindow* as a reminder that these resources are often used with the main-window widget.

Table 11.1. Frequently used resources: *XmMainWindow*

Name	Inheritance	Type	Default Value
`commandWindow`	XmMainWindow	`Widget`	`NULL`
`mainWindowMarginHeight`	XmMainWindow	`Dimension`	`0`
`mainWindowMarginWidth`	XmMainWindow	`Dimension`	`0`
`menuBar`	XmMainWindow	`Widget`	`NULL`
`showSeparator`	XmMainWindow	`Boolean`	`FALSE`
`clipWindow`	XmScrolledWindow	`Widget`	`NULL`
`horizontalScrollBar`	XmScrolledWindow	`Widget`	`NULL`
`scrollBarDisplayPolicy`	XmScrolledWindow	`unsigned char`	`XmSTATIC`
`scrollBarPlacement`	XmScrolledWindow	`unsigned char`	`XmBOTTOM _RIGHT`
`scrollingPolicy`	XmScrolledWindow	`unsigned char`	`XmAPPLICATION _DEFINED`
`verticalScrollBar`	XmScrolledWindow	`Widget`	`NULL`
`workWindow`	XmScrolledWindow	`Widget`	`NULL`

Sub-Areas: commandWindow, menuBar

In addition to the sub-areas of *XmScrolledWindow* — `clipWindow`, `horizontalScrollBar`, `verticalScrollBar`, and `workWindow` — *XmMainWindow* provides a menu bar (`menuBar`) and a command window (`commandWindow`). These sub-area resources contain widget IDs and may contain `NULL`; if so, the associated sub-area is not maintained by the main window.

Appearance: mainWindowMarginHeight, mainWindowMarginWidth, showSeparator

Like *XmScrolledWindow* — and other managers — *XmMainWindow* supports an optional margin between its sides and its contents. The `mainWindowMarginHeight` resource specifies the height of the top and bottom margins; the `mainWindowMarginWidth` resource specifies the width of the right and left margins. These resources take precedence over the equivalent resources defined by *XmScrolledWindow*; if the *XmMainWindow* margin resources contain zero (the default value), then the *XmScrolledWindow* resources are used.[3]

The `showSeparator` resource specifies whether the main window displays separator widgets (described below) between the menu bar, command window,

---

[3] And since they default to zero, the default action is not to have a margin at all.

and work window.[4] If it contains TRUE, the separators are displayed; if FALSE (the default), they aren't.[5] These separators are not accessible via resources; to change their appearance, you must get the appropriate widget ID via one of the convenience functions described below.

XmMainWindow Convenience Functions

Motif provides three convenience functions associated with *XmMainWindow*. The first, XmMainWindowSetAreas, is used to reconfigure the widgets serving as the main window's sub-areas. The other two are used to access the widget IDs of the optional separator widgets.

XmMainWindowSetAreas

XmMainWindowSetAreas, prototyped in Listing 11.1, is used to reconfigure the sub-areas of a main-window widget. It is similar in operation to XmScrolledWindowSetAreas: the parameters specify widget IDs for the sub-areas, and parameters containing NULL are ignored.

Listing 11.1. Function prototype: *XmMainWindowSetAreas*

```
void    XmMainWindowSetAreas( w, menu, command, hscroll, vscroll, work )
        Widget      w;
        Widget      menu;
        Widget      command;
        Widget      hscroll;
        Widget      vscroll;
        Widget      work;
```

As with XmScrolledWindowSetAreas, the w parameter specifies the main-window widget, the hscroll and vscroll parameters, respectively, specify the horizontal and vertical scrollbars, and the work parameter specifies the work window. Additionally, the menu parameter specifies the ID of the menu bar (described in the next chapter), and the command parameter specifies the ID of the command-line widget (typically a single-line *XmText* widget).

XmMainWindowSep1, XmMainWindowSep2

If used, the main-window separators are unnamed and cannot be accessed via the resource file. If the program needs to change a resource value for one of these separators, it must get the proper widget ID and change the resource

---

[4] If any of these three sub-areas are omitted, the associated separator is not displayed.
[5] The default shadow borders around the various main window sub-areas are usually sufficient to visually separate the areas — Figure 11.1 is an example. However, separators may be useful if the color scheme eliminates such distinctions.

programmatically. The functions `XmMainWindowSep1` and `XmMainWindowSep2` are used to get the separator ID; they are prototyped identically, as shown by Listing 11.2.

Listing 11.2. Function prototypes: *XmMainWindowSep1*, *XmMainWindowSep2*

```
Widget  XmMainWindowSepn( w )
     Widget      w;
```

In the above prototype, the italicized '*n*' is either "1" or "2" — it identifies the separator. The sole parameter is the ID of the main-window widget. The return value is the ID of the specified separator — the first separator is below the menu bar, and the second separator is below the command widget.[6]

XmSeparator

Separators are widgets that exist to divide a window into visually distinct areas. Separators simply draw a line in one of the seven styles shown in Figure 11.3. This line bisects the separator's area and may be oriented horizontally or vertically. Use of separators is the choice of the programmer. They are often used in pull-down menus to separate groups of choices, and *XmMainWindow* provides optional horizontal separators between its major sub-areas.

---

[6] If either the menu bar or the command widget is omitted in a particular main-window instance, the associated separator is not maintained. The ID returned, therefore, is `NULL`.

Figure 11.3. Sample separators

XmSeparator **Resources**

XmSeparator is a primitive widget, derived as shown by the class tree of Figure 11.4. *Core* contains resources that define a separator's size and position, *XmPrimitive* defines its color scheme, and *XmSeparator* defines and implements the line styles.

Figure 11.4. *XmSeparator* class tree

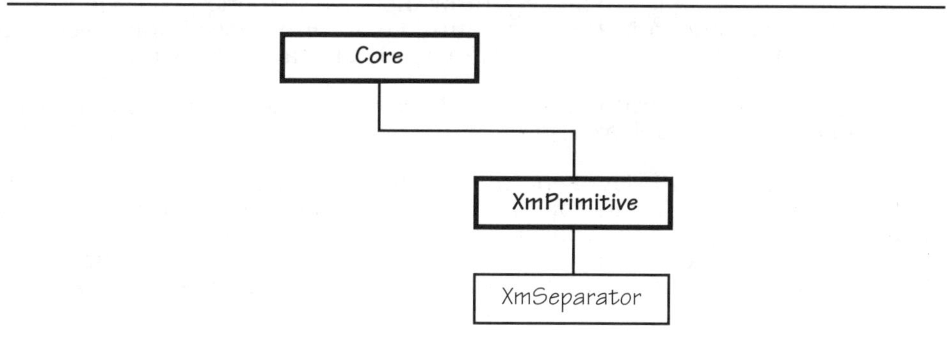

XmSeparator defines a minimal set of resources, listed in Table 11.2. It also provides resources from *Core* and *XmPrimitive*; *XmSeparator*'s use of the *Core* resources `width` and `height` deserve special note and are described below.

Table 11.2. Frequently used resources: *XmSeparator*

Name	Inheritance	Type	Default Value
`margin`	XmSeparator	`short`	0
`orientation`	XmSeparator	`unsigned char`	XmHORIZONTAL
`separatorType`	XmSeparator	`unsigned char`	XmSHADOW_ETCHED_IN
`width`	Core	`Dimension`	0
`height`	Core	`Dimension`	0

Separator Style: separatorType

The type of line displayed by a separator widget is controlled by its `separatorType` resource. The possible values for this resource — in order of the examples in Figure 11.3 — are as follows:

- `XmSINGLE_LINE`. The separator displays a single one-pixel-wide (-high) line, drawn in the foreground color.

- `XmDOUBLE_LINE`. The separator displays two one-pixel-wide (-high) lines, drawn in the foreground color and spaced one pixel apart.

- `XmSINGLE_DASHED_LINE`. The separator displays a single one-pixel-wide (-high) dashed line, drawn in the foreground color. Dashes consist of equally sized drawn and undrawn segments.

- `XmDOUBLE_DASHED_LINE`. The separator displays two one-pixel-wide (-high) dashed lines, drawn in the foreground color, and spaced one pixel apart. Dashes consist of equally sized drawn and undrawn segments.

- `XmNO_LINE`. The separator does not display any type of line. Its dimensions are filled with its background color.

- `XmSHADOW_ETCHED_IN`. The separator draws a line that appears to be inset into the screen, using its top and bottom shadow colors. The width of this line is specified by the separator's `shadowThickness` resource; half of this width is given to the top shadow color, the other half is given to the bottom shadow color. As with other widgets, the "light source" is at the top left corner of the screen. This is the default style.

- `XmSHADOW_ETCHED_OUT`. The separator draws a line that appears to be protruding from the screen, using its top and bottom shadow colors. The width of this line is specified by the separator's `shadowThickness` resource; half of this width is given to the top shadow color, and the other half is given to the bottom shadow color.

Appearance: height, width, orientation, margin

A separator's `height` and `width` resources do not bear mention because they are different from those of other widgets, but because they are the same: a separator is not simply a line, it is actually a rectangular window. This window is filled with the background color specified by its `background` resource and is bisected by the actual separation line.

This means two things. First, the appropriate dimension (height for a horizontal separator, width for a vertical separator) must be sized to contain the drawn line: one pixel for a single line, three pixels for a double line, and a variable number of pixels (*ie*, `shadowThickness`) for an etched line. Second, a separator does occupy space; this space must be considered in any calculation of window size.

Separators may be oriented either horizontally or vertically; the `orientation` resource specifies the direction. Like *XmScrollBar* and *XmScale*, `orientation` may contain either `XmHORIZONTAL` or `XmVERTICAL`. Unlike those classes, the default value is `XmHORIZONTAL`.

Finally, a separator can draw a line smaller than needed: the `margin` resource specifies the distance between the endpoints of the separator and the endpoints of its line. This is space on the right and left side of the line for a horizontal separator and on the top and bottom for a vertical separator. When drawn, a separator's line always bisects the separator; margin does not apply to space on either side of the separator line, only its endpoints.

XmSeparator Example

Figure 11.3 was produced using the sample program and resource file of Listing 11.3. The program simply creates seven separators, along with a bulletin board to hold them. The resource file then specifies the position and style of each separator.

Listing 11.3. Program and resource file: Separators example

```
/*******************************************************************
**                                                               **
**   listing_11_3.c                                              **
**                                                               **
**   Separator demo. This program displays 7 horizontal separators, **
**   each with a different style.                                **
**                                                               **
*******************************************************************/
```

Listing 11.3.Continued.

```c
#include <Xm/BulletinB.h>
#include <Xm/Separator.h>


Widget  appshell,                        /* Application Shell        */
        the_bb,                          /* The Bulletin Board       */
        separators[7];                   /* The children             */


void main( argc, argv )
    int     argc;
    char    *argv[];
{
    appshell = XtInitialize( argv[0], "Listing_11_3", NULL, 0,
                                                &argc, argv );

    the_bb = XmCreateBulletinBoard( appshell, "TheBB", NULL, 0 );
    XtManageChild( the_bb );

    separators[0] = XmCreateSeparator( the_bb, "Sep_0", NULL, 0 );
    separators[1] = XmCreateSeparator( the_bb, "Sep_1", NULL, 0 );
    separators[2] = XmCreateSeparator( the_bb, "Sep_2", NULL, 0 );
    separators[3] = XmCreateSeparator( the_bb, "Sep_3", NULL, 0 );
    separators[4] = XmCreateSeparator( the_bb, "Sep_4", NULL, 0 );
    separators[5] = XmCreateSeparator( the_bb, "Sep_5", NULL, 0 );
    separators[6] = XmCreateSeparator( the_bb, "Sep_6", NULL, 0 );
    XtManageChildren( separators, 7 );

    XtRealizeWidget( appshell );
    XtMainLoop();
}
```

```
!
! Resource file to produce Figure 11.3
!

*.background:           Gray50
*.foreground:           White
*.topShadowColor:       Gray75
*.bottomShadowColor:    Gray25
```

Listing 11.3. Continued.

```
*.shadowThickness:        4

*TheBB.background:        Black
*TheBB.shadowThickness:   0
*TheBB.marginWidth:       10
*TheBB.marginHeight:      10

*.XmSeparator.height:     10
*.XmSeparator.width:      200
*.XmSeparator.x:          10

*Sep_0.y:                 10
*Sep_0.separatorType:     SINGLE_LINE

*Sep_1.y:                 30
*Sep_1.separatorType:     DOUBLE_LINE

*Sep_2.y:                 50
*Sep_2.separatorType:     SINGLE_DASHED_LINE

*Sep_3.y:                 70
*Sep_3.separatorType:     DOUBLE_DASHED_LINE

*Sep_4.y:                 90
*Sep_4.separatorType:     NO_LINE

*Sep_5.y:                 110
*Sep_5.separatorType:     SHADOW_ETCHED_IN

*Sep_6.y:                 130
*Sep_6.separatorType:     SHADOW_ETCHED_OUT
```

XmFrame

XmFrame is a manager that is similar in purpose to *XmSeparator*: it exists to provide the Motif visual appearance in places where it would not otherwise exist. In implementation, *XmFrame* is a manager that is able to hold only a single child — it may be thought of as a limited type of bulletin board.

Figure 11.5 provides an example of *XmFrame*'s use: each of the four labels is the child of a frame. This allows the labels to have an "etched in" appearance, which is not supported by *XmPrimitive*'s shadow border. *XmFrame* could also be used in a program that blends Motif and non-Motif widgets to give the non-Motif widgets the Motif "look."[7]

Figure 11.5. *XmFrame* example

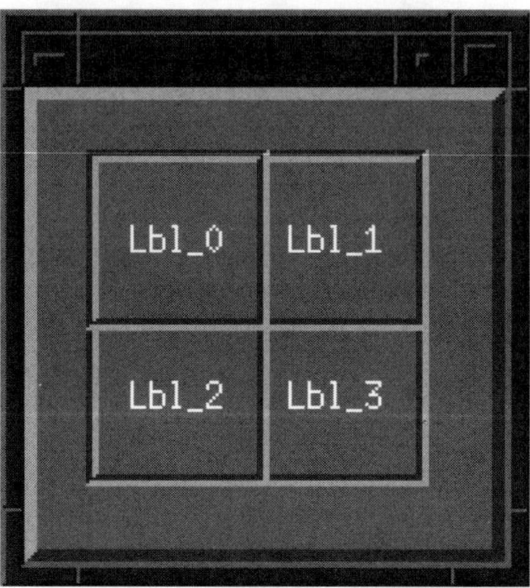

XmFrame Resources

XmFrame is derived from *XmManager*, as shown by the class tree of Figure 11.6. It mimics other managers in its implementation of a shadow border, as well as in sizing its child — its size is based on its child if possible, otherwise the child's size is based on the frame.

---

[7] Although it is possible to combine Motif with other toolkits, it is not recommended. One of the benefits of Motif is that it presents an integrated set of tools; blending Motif with another widget set destroys this integration and presents possibilities for "toolkit collision." Moreover, placing non-Motif widgets in a Motif program will almost always result in an inconsistent appearance, *XmFrame* notwithstanding.

Figure 11.6. *XmFrame* class tree

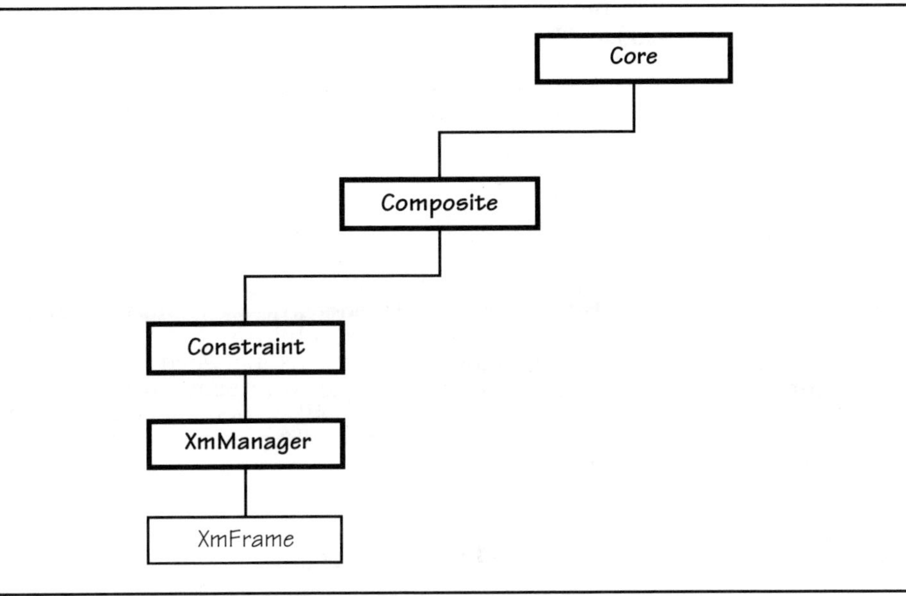

Table 11.3 presents *XmFrame's* resources; they are described below. *XmFrame* also inherits resources from *XmManager, Constraint, Composite,* and *Core.*

Table 11.3. Frequently used resources: *XmFrame*

Name	Inheritance	Type	Default Value
marginWidth	XmFrame	short	0
marginHeight	XmFrame	short	0
shadowType	XmFrame	unsigned char	XmSHADOW_ETCHED_IN

Shadow Type: shadowType

As with other managers, *XmFrame's* `shadowType` resource specifies the appearance of its shadow border.[8] Possible values are from the following list:

- `XmSHADOW_IN`. The shadow is drawn such that the frame and its contents appear inset into the screen.

---

[8] A frame's shadow border is also controlled by the *XmManager* resources `shadowThickness`, `topShadowColor`, and `bottomShadowColor`. As with all Motif shadows, the "light source" causing the shadow is positioned at the top left corner of the screen.

- XmSHADOW_OUT. The shadow is drawn such that the frame and its contents appear to protrude from the screen.

- XmSHADOW_ETCHED_IN. The shadow is drawn such that the frame and its contents appear to be on the same plane as the rest of the screen, but separated by a groove. This is the default value.

- XmSHADOW_ETCHED_OUT. The shadow is drawn such that the frame and its contents appear to be on the same plane as the rest of the screen, but separated by a ridge.

Margin: marginHeight, marginWidth

Like other managers, *XmFrame* can provide a margin between itself and its child. This margin is specified by the marginHeight and marginWidth resources: marginHeight specifies the distance between the child and the top and bottom sides of the frame, marginWidth specifies the distance between the child and the left and right sides of the frame. This margin is used in geometry computations: if the child is sized by the frame, its dimensions will be decreased by the margin; if the frame is sized by the child, its dimensions will be increased by the margin. The default margin size is zero pixels.

XmFrame **Example: Labels in Frames**

The program and resource file of Listing 11.4 were used to produce Figure 11.5. The program simply creates a bulletin board for placement, four frames as children of the bulletin board, and four labels. Note, however, that each label is the child of a different frame — although all label widget IDs are stored in the same array, they belong to different branches of the instance tree, and therefore, must be managed separately. In the resource file, note that the frames are sized by their labels, and the labels are positioned by their frames. Both sizing and positioning could be performed by the frames; like other managers, *XmFrame* can impose geometry on its children.

Listing 11.4. Program and resource file: Labels in frames

```c
/*********************************************************************
**                                                                 **
**   listing_11_4.c                                                **
**                                                                 **
**   Frame demo. This program displays four labels inside frames.  **
**                                                                 **
*********************************************************************/


#include <Xm/BulletinB.h>
#include <Xm/Frame.h>
#include <Xm/Label.h>


Widget  appshell,                       /* The Application Shell    */
        the_bb,                         /* The Bulletin Board       */
        frames[4],                      /* Frames for the Labels    */
        labels[4];                      /* The labels themselves    */


void main( argc, argv )
    int     argc;
    char    *argv[];
{
    appshell = XtInitialize( argv[0], "Listing_11_4", NULL, 0,
                                            &argc, argv );

    the_bb = XmCreateBulletinBoard( appshell, "TheBB", NULL, 0 );
    XtManageChild( the_bb );

    frames[0] = XmCreateFrame( the_bb, "Frame_0", NULL, 0 );
    frames[1] = XmCreateFrame( the_bb, "Frame_1", NULL, 0 );
    frames[2] = XmCreateFrame( the_bb, "Frame_2", NULL, 0 );
    frames[3] = XmCreateFrame( the_bb, "Frame_3", NULL, 0 );
    XtManageChildren( frames, 4 );

    labels[0] = XmCreateLabel( frames[0], "Lbl_0", NULL, 0 );
    XtManageChild( labels[0] );
    labels[1] = XmCreateLabel( frames[1], "Lbl_1", NULL, 0 );
    XtManageChild( labels[1] );
```

Listing 11.4. Continued.

```
    labels[2] = XmCreateLabel( frames[2], "Lbl_2", NULL, 0 );
    XtManageChild( labels[2] );
    labels[3] = XmCreateLabel( frames[3], "Lbl_3", NULL, 0 );
    XtManageChild( labels[3] );

    XtRealizeWidget( appshell );
    XtMainLoop();
}
```

```
!
! Resource file to produce Figure 11.5
!

*.background:           Gray50
*.foreground:           White
*.topShadowColor:       Gray75
*.bottomShadowColor:    Gray25
*.shadowThickness:      4

*.XmLabel.height:       50
*.XmLabel.width:        50

*TheBB.marginHeight:    20
*TheBB.marginWidth:     20

*Frame_0.x:             20
*Frame_0.y:             20

*Frame_1.x:             70
*Frame_1.y:             20

*Frame_2.x:             20
*Frame_2.y:             70

*Frame_3.x:             70
*Frame_3.y:             70
```

The New Standard Program Template

At this point in the book, programs are beginning to get complex. When a
program creates two or three widgets, the program template of Chapter 4 is
serviceable. However, it becomes almost unreadable for a program that creates a
dozen or more widgets — especially if those widgets have callbacks attached. For

that reason, the template of Listing 11.5 will be used for nontrivial programs in
the rest of this book.

The key benefit of this new template is that it modularizes the code associated
with each of a client's components. This code may occupy a single source file or
multiple files. The benefit to this book is that it no longer needs to present
complete program listings, instead, only those functions relevant to a topic need
be presented.

Listing 11.5. The new standard program template

```
/******************************************************************
**                                                              **
**   listing_11_5.c                                             **
**                                                              **
**   Sample program template for non-trivial programs.          **
**                                                              **
******************************************************************/


#include <Xm/MainW.h>


/******************************************************************
**                                                              **
**              F O R W A R D   D E F I N I T I O N S            **
**                                                              **
******************************************************************/

void    InitMainWindow();
void    InitMenuBar();
void    InitWorkWindow();
void    InitOther();


/******************************************************************
**                                                              **
**              G L O B A L   V A R I A B L E S                  **
**                                                              **
******************************************************************/

Widget  appshell,                    /* Application Shell    */
        mainwin,                     /* XmMainWindow         */
```

Listing 11.5. Continued.

```c
        menubar,                          /* MainWindow Menu Bar        */
        workwin,                          /* MainWindow Work Area       */
        horzscroll,                       /* MainWindow Horizontal Scrl */
        vertscroll;                       /* MainWindow Vertical Scroll */
Arg     arglist[16];                      /* For programmatic rsrc stuf */


/**************************************************************************
**                                                                     **
**   main( argc, argv )                                                **
**                                                                     **
**   Program entry point. Creates shell, calls initialization funcs,   **
**   and turns control over to event loop.                            **
**                                                                     **
**************************************************************************/


void    main( argc, argv )
    int     argc;
    char    *argv[];
{
    appshell = XtInitialize( argv[0], "ResName", NULL, 0, &argc, argv );

    InitMainWindow();
    InitMenuBar();
    InitWorkWindow();

    XmMainWindowSetAreas( mainwin, menubar, NULL,
                              horzscroll, vertscroll, workwin );

    InitOther();

    XtRealizeWidget( appshell );
    XtMainLoop();
}
```

Listing 11.5. Continued.

```
/**********************************************************************
**                                                                  **
**    InitMainWindow()                                              **
**                                                                  **
**    This function creates the main-window widget and its scrollbars.  **
**    The main-window is created as a child of the application shell.   **
**    The scrollbars are either created along with the main-window (if  **
**    its "scrollingPolicy" resource contains TRUE) or separately.      **
**                                                                  **
**    This function modifies the globals "mainwin", "horzscroll", and   **
**    "vertscroll". It accesses "appshell".                         **
**                                                                  **
**********************************************************************/


void    InitMainWindow()
{
    mainwin = XmCreateMainWindow( appshell, "MainWin", NULL, 0 );
    XtManageChild( mainwin );

/** Use this code to create scrollbars separately
    horzscroll = XmCreateScrollBar( mainwin, "HScroll", NULL,  0 );
    XtManageChild( horzscroll );
    vertscroll = XmCreateScrollBar( mainwin, "VScroll", NULL,  0 );
    XtManageChild( vertscroll );
**/

/** Use this code to access automatically-created scrollbars
    XtSetArg( arglist[0], XmNhorizontalScrollBar, &horzscroll );
    XtSetArg( arglist[1], XmNverticalScrollBar,   &vertscroll );
    XtGetValues( mainwin, arglist, 2 );
**/
}
```

Listing 11.5. Continued.

```
/**********************************************************************
**                                                                  **
**    InitMenuBar()                                                 **
**                                                                  **
**    This function creates the menu bar and all pull-down menus. The **
**    menu bar is created as the child of the main-window.          **
**                                                                  **
**    This function modifies the global "menubar", and accesses the **
**    global "mainwin".                                             **
**                                                                  **

**********************************************************************/


void    InitMenuBar()
{
    menubar = NULL;
}




/**********************************************************************
**                                                                  **
**    InitWorkWindow()                                              **
**                                                                  **
**    This function creates the work window and its children. The   **
**    work window is created as the child of the main-window.       **
**                                                                  **
**    This function modifies the global "workwin", and accesses the **
**    global "mainwin".                                             **
**                                                                  **
**********************************************************************/


void    InitWorkWindow()
{
}
```

Listing 11.5. Continued.

```
/**************************************************************
**                                                          **
**    InitOther()                                           **
**                                                          **
**    This function performs other program initialization, such as   **
**    loading any default data.                             **
**                                                          **
**************************************************************/

void    InitOther()
{
}
```

The template begins as expected, with its description and inclusion of header files. Following this is a space for forward function declarations — needed to avoid warning messages from a compiler that performs type-checking.[9] In a multifile program, this is where the program-specific header file is specified.

Next are the declarations of global variables. My philosophy is to use the minimal number of globals that allow convenient programming and debugging. To this end, the application shell, main window, and all of the main-window's sub-areas are globals. With the appropriate "private" header files, it is possible to use these variables to examine the entire instance tree. I also provide an argument array (`arglist`) as a global; this is in preference to defining one wherever the program needs to programmatically set resources.

The `main` function creates the application shell directly via `XtInitialize`. It then calls other functions to create the main window and its primary sub-areas. These functions directly modify the main-window' globals; they may also make use of local variables.

The main-window's sub-areas are installed with `XmMainWindowSetAreas`, after which any other program-specific initialization is performed (this "other" initialization may or may not involve the creation of widgets). Finally, as with the trivial program template, the application shell is realized and the program passes control to the event loop.

The function `InitMainWindow` contains the expected call to `XmCreateMainWindow`, but also contains two optional sets of code for scrollbar initialization. The first is used when the main-window's `scrollingPolicy` resource contains `XmAPPLICATION_DEFINED` (the default); it creates the scrollbars. The second is used when scrollingPolicy contains `XmAUTOMATIC`; since the scrollbars have already been created, their IDs are simply stored in the appropriate global variables.

---

[9] If you use an ANSI compiler, these declarations should be complete function prototypes. Subsequent chapters will not explicitly show this section; remember that forward declarations must be present to avoid compiler warnings.

The function `InitMenuBar` creates the menu bar and pull-down menus. It will become useful in Chapter 12, where the menu bar is presented. For now, it simply sets the global menubar variable to `NULL` so that it may be passed to `XmMainWindowSetAreas`.[10]

The function `InitWorkWindow` is responsible for creating the branch of the instance tree that becomes the main-window's work area. Depending on the application, this function may be complex or simple; for the text editor of this (and subsequent) chapters, it creates a single widget.

The `InitOther` function handles "everything else." If a program were to use a command area, it would be created here. This function might also be used for initializing libraries and variables not associated with any widgets.

The Text Editor: A Sample Application

Over the next several chapters, this book will develop a text-editor application. The core of this application is the *XmText* widget, which provides the basic text handling capability. To augment the capabilities of the text widget, the program provides a search-replace facility, runtime-selectable fonts, and — of course — the ability to load and save files.

At this point, the text editor is quite simple, as shown by Figure 11.7. In fact, it appears to be identical to the file browser of Chapter 9. In reality, it is closer to the memo pad: although it scrolls, it doesn't have the ability to load a file (the displayed text was copied from another window).

Figure 11.7. Text editor (first revision)

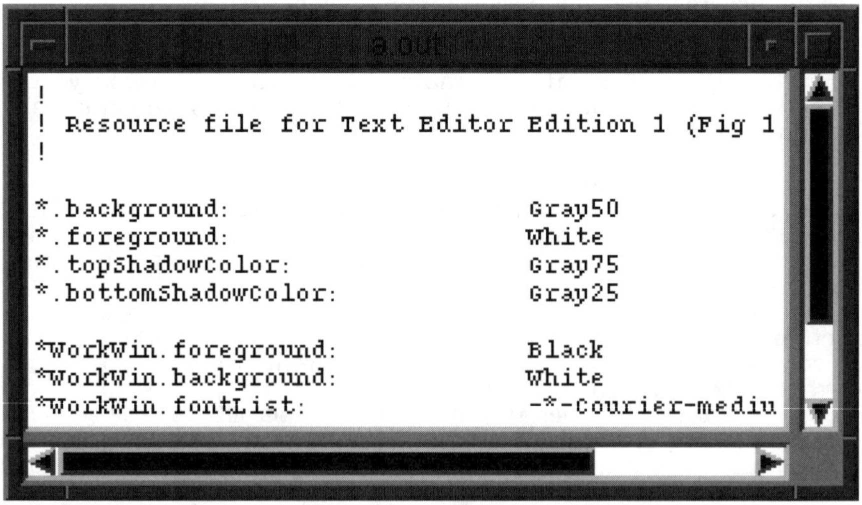

---

[10] This is an unnecessary step, since — as a global uninitialized variable — menubar contains `NULL` at program startup.

To produce this display, the program and resource file of Listing 11.6 were used.[11] The program is taken from the nontrivial program template; it differs from the template in that the main-window's scrollbars are not used. The reason for this divergence is described after the listing.

Listing 11.6. Program and resource file: Text editor (first revision)

```
/*********************************************************************
**                                                                 **
**   listing_11_6.c                                                **
**                                                                 **
**   Text Editor, Edition 1. This program will be built in Chapters **
**   11 to 14. At this point, it consists of an XmMainWindow widget, **
**   as the parent of a scrolled text "widget".                    **
**                                                                 **
*********************************************************************/


#include <Xm/MainW.h>
#include <Xm/Text.h>


/*********************************************************************
**                                                               ****
F O R W A R D    D E F I N I T I O N S            **
**                                                                 **
*********************************************************************/

void    InitMainWindow();
void    InitMenuBar();
void    InitWorkWindow();
void    InitOther();
```

---

[11] You might find, when compiling this program or one of its subsequent revisions, that your compiler runs out of symbol table space — and doesn't complete the compilation. This is a common occurrence with Motif programs due to the large number of definitions in the Motif header files. If it happens to you, you will need to increase the symbol table space, which can be done using a compiler switch. Unfortunately, the switch used depends on the origin of the compiler — and no two compilers seem to use the same switches. It is, however, documented in the *man* pages for your compiler. An alternative, of course, is to break offending files into one or more pieces, each of which is sufficiently small that it compiles without problems.

Listing 11.6. Continued.

```c
/****************************************************************************
**                                                                        **
**                 G L O B A L   V A R I A B L E S                         **
**                                                                        **
****************************************************************************/

Widget  appshell,                      /* Application Shell         */
        mainwin,                       /* XmMainWindow              */
        menubar,                       /* MainWindow Menu Bar       */
        workwin;                       /* MainWindow Work Area      */
Arg     arglist[16];                   /* For programmatic rsrc stuf */


/****************************************************************************
**                                                                        **
**   main( argc, argv )                                                    **
**                                                                        **
**   Program entry point. Creates shell, calls initialization funcs,      **
**   and turns control over to event loop.                                **
**                                                                        **
****************************************************************************/

void    main( argc, argv )
    int     argc;
    char    *argv[];
{
    appshell = XtInitialize( argv[0], "Listing_11_6", NULL, 0,
                                                &argc, argv );

    InitMainWindow();
    InitMenuBar();
    InitWorkWindow();

    XmMainWindowSetAreas( mainwin, menubar, NULL, NULL, NULL, workwin );
```

Listing 11.6. Continued.

```c
    InitOther();

    XtRealizeWidget( appshell );
    XtMainLoop();
}


/*********************************************************************
**                                                                 **
**    InitMainWindow()                                             **
**                                                                 **
**    This function creates the main-window widget. No scrollbars are  **
**    created for the main-window; they are provided by the scrolled-  **
**    window holding the text widget (ie, the work window).        **
**                                                                 **
**    This function modifies the global "mainwin", It accesses the **
**    global "appshell".                                           **
**                                                                 **
**********************************************************************/

void    InitMainWindow()
{
    mainwin = XmCreateMainWindow( appshell, "MainWin", NULL, 0 );
    XtManageChild( mainwin );
}


/*********************************************************************
**                                                                 **
**    InitMenuBar()                                                **
**                                                                 **
**    This function creates the menu bar and all pull-down menus. The  **
**    menu bar is created as the child of the main-window.         **
**                                                                 **
**    This function modifies the global "menubar", and accesses the    **
**    global "mainwin".                                            **
**                                                                 **
**********************************************************************/
```

Listing 11.6. Continued.

```c
void    InitMenuBar()
{
}




/*********************************************************************
**                                                                 **
**    InitWorkWindow()                                             **
**                                                                 **
**    This function creates the work window, which is a scrolled text  **
**    "widget."                                                    **
**                                                                 **
**    This function modifies the global "workwin", and accesses the    **
**    global "mainwin".                                            **
**                                                                 **
*********************************************************************/

void    InitWorkWindow()
{
    Widget          txtmp;

    txtmp = XmCreateScrolledText( mainwin, "WorkWin", NULL, 0 );
    XtManageChild( txtmp );

    workwin = XtParent( txtmp );
}




/*********************************************************************
**                                                                 **
**    InitOther()                                                  **
**                                                                 **
**    This function performs other program initialization, such as     **
**    loading any default data.                                    **
**                                                                 **
*********************************************************************/
```

Listing 11.6. Continued.

```
void    InitOther(){
}
```

```
!
! Resource file for Text Editor Revision 1 (Fig 11.7)
!

*.background:               Gray50
*.foreground:               White
*.topShadowColor:           Gray75
*.bottomShadowColor:        Gray25

*WorkWin.foreground:        Black
*WorkWin.background:        White
*WorkWin.fontList:          -*-Courier-medium-r-*--*-100-*
*WorkWin.editMode:          MULTI_LINE_EDIT
*WorkWin.rows:              12
*WorkWin.columns:           48
```

As you can see from `InitWorkWindow`, the text widget is actually a scrolled text widget. Why isn't it a simple *XmText*, with the main window doing the scrolling? The reason is a result of the way *XmScrolledWindow* — and therefore, *XmMainWindow* — handles automatic scrolling. In automatic mode, *XmScrolledWindow* performs its scrolling by displaying a segment of its work window in its clip window.

The result of that behavior is that the text window must be large enough to display the entire file. On the other hand, when the scrolled window and text widgets are created via `XmCreateScrolledText`, they are intimately related: the callbacks for the scrolled-window's scrollbars are tied to the text widget's internal scrolling functions. This is a much more efficient way to handle the scrolling — and it can't be performed by the main-window widget.

Given that a scrolled window is the appropriate way to handle the scrolling, the main-window's scrollbars become superfluous. So they're simply not created, and the scrolled-text window occupies the entire interior of the main window.

12
Menus

Overview

Menus provide the user of a Motif program with the ability to control the operation of that program in a "point and click" manner. They are the preferred method of program control: unobtrusive when not in use, they allow the user to quickly choose from a list of alternate actions.

Motif provides four types of menus. The *menu bar* is positioned at the top of a standard Motif program: it provides an always-accessible method of controlling the program's major functions; these functions are divided into named *topics*. Attached to the menu bar, *pull-down* menus provide a list of functions "sub-" associated each topic. *Pop-up* menus are used for context-dependent control, and are accessed by means other than the menu bar. Finally, *option menus* are used in dialog boxes and other context-dependent situations where the program needs to provide a menu that displays its current choice.

Menus are implemented using the *XmRowColumn* widget class. The menu bar is a horizontal row-column, as is an option menu; pull-down and pop-up menus are vertically oriented. The menu bar can contain only cascade-button widgets (described below); menu panes may contain any type of child, although most programs use only labels, separators, and buttons.

XmCascadeButton

The menu bar and its associated pull-down menus are made possible by the *XmCascadeButton* class. Unlike other buttons, which exist to be activated, a cascade button exists to be armed: when one is armed, it maps another widget. This allows a pull-down menu to remain hidden until the user presses the pointer button while positioned over its associated cascade button.

Cascade buttons are also unique in that they must be used in a menu. A cascade-button's parent must be a row-column, and its `rowColumnType` resource must contain `XmMENU_BAR`, `XmMENU_POPUP`, or `XmMENU_PULLDOWN`. Attempting to create a cascade button as the child of any other widget class causes an error.[1]

XmCascadeButton is derived from *XmLabel*, as shown by the class tree of Figure 12.1. In appearance, a cascade button more closely resembles a label than a pushbutton, because it does not normally display a shadow border. When armed, it does display a shadow border, but one that appears to protrude from the screen — a behavior opposite to that of an armed pushbutton.

Figure 12.1. *XmCascadeButton* class tree

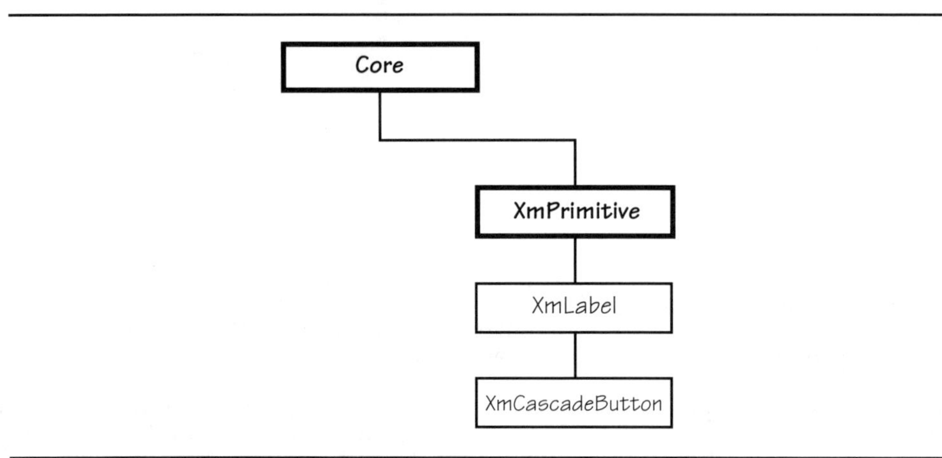

XmCascadeButton Resources

The resources defined by *XmCascadeButton* are listed in Table 12.1 and described below. *XmCascadeButton* also provides the resources defined by *XmLabel*, *XmPrimitive*, and *Core*.

Table 12.1. Frequently used resources: *XmCascadeButton*

Name	Inheritance	Type	Default Value
activateCallback	XmCascadeButton	XtCallbackList	NULL
cascadePixmap	XmCascadeButton	Pixmap	"menu-cascade"
cascadingCallback	XmCascadeButton	XtCallbackList	NULL
mappingDelay	XmCascadeButton	int	100
subMenuId	XmCascadeButton	Widget	NULL

---

[1] More correctly, it will result in an error *message*: a cascade button may be used outside of a menu, but the program will complain. Given that programs that generate error messages do not engender confidence, this practice should be avoided.

Appearance: cascadePixmap

In most applications, a cascade button resembles a label. However, if a cascade button is used in a pull-down or pop-up menu pane to invoke a *cascading menu* (described below), it indicates that fact with a pixmap positioned to the right of the label text. This pixmap is identified by the button's `cascadePixmap` resource. The default pixmap is a right-pointing arrow.

Interaction: mappingDelay

On the Macintosh, if you press the mouse button while positioned over a menu bar topic, and then move the mouse across the menu bar, the pull-down menu for each topic is displayed. This behavior is provided by Motif — it allows the user to search for the correct menu choice — but can result in a lot of communication between the program and the server.

The `mappingDelay` resource acts to minimize this excess communication: it contains a count of milliseconds between the time that the pointer enters the cascade-button and the button maps its associated menu pane. If the user quickly passes the pointer through the button's area, the menu pane is not displayed; if the pointer stays within the button's area for longer than the time specified by `mappingDelay`, the menu pane is mapped. The default value is 100, for a one-tenth second delay.

Mapped Widget: subMenuId

A cascade button exists to map a menu pane. This menu pane is a widget, and the cascade-button's `subMenuId` resource identifies this widget. The `subMenuId` resource must specify a row-column widget configured as a pull-down menu pane. As the resource manager does not provide a mechanism for widget ID specification, `subMenuId` must be set programmatically.

XmCascadeButton Callbacks

XmCascadeButton provides two callbacks: one for button arming (the pointer button is pressed while the pointer is over the screen button), and one when the button is activated (the pointer button is released while the pointer is over the screen button). Both callbacks pass call data in `XmAnyCallbackStruct`.

Arm/Cascade

When the user arms a cascade button — by moving the pointer over the button with its button pressed, it invokes the callbacks specified by `cascadingCallback`, then — after the delay specified by `mappingDelay` — maps its submenu. If the program needs to perform some action between arm and map — for example, to change the content of menu items — it should handle this callback.[2] The reason associated with this callback is `XmCR_CASCADING`.

Activation

If a cascade button is not associated with a sub-menu — its `subMenuId` resource contains `NULL` — its `activateCallback` list is invoked when the user releases the pointer button while over the cascade button. This callback is often used where a menu choice invokes a dialog box: it is needed if such a choice is in the menu bar, which must contain cascade-button children.[3]

XmRowColumn Menu Resources

XmRowColumn provides several resources designed for use with menus. These resources were not presented in Chapter 6, which described *XmRowColumn* as a general-purpose manager. They are described in this chapter, in two places: those resources associated with all types of menus are listed in Table 12.2 and described below, while those resources used only with option menus are described under *XmRowColumn* Resources Specific to Option Menus.

Table 12.2. Menu-specific *XmRowColumn* resources

Name	Inheritance	Type	Default Value
`entryCallback`	XmRowColumn	`XtCallbackList`	`NULL`
`entryClass`	XmRowColumn	`WidgetClass`	*dynamic*
`isHomogeneous`	XmRowColumn	`Boolean`	`TRUE`
`menuAccelerator`	XmRowColumn	`String`	*dynamic*
`menuHelpWidget`	XmRowColumn	`Widget`	`NULL`
`mapCallback`	XmRowColumn	`XtCallbackList`	`NULL`
`rowColumnType`	XmRowColumn	`unsigned char`	*dynamic*
`spacing`	XmRowColumn	`short`	*dynamic*
`unmapCallback`	XmRowColumn	`XtCallbackList`	`NULL`
`whichButton`	XmRowColumn	`unsigned`	*dynamic*

---

[2] For example, a program might offer a timestamp menu choice, with the current time displayed. Such a menu choice must therefore be updated each time the associated pane is mapped.

[3] The **Help** menu topic is often implemented this way — for context-sensitive help, a dialog box is often more useful than a menu.

Menu Type: rowColumnType

The `rowColumnType` resource and its possible values were presented in Chapter 6. It appears again here as a reminder that it specifies the type of menu for which a row-column instance is configured. Its default value is listed in Table 12.2 as "dynamic," instead of `XmWORK_AREA` (its default value in Table 6.2), because each type of menu has its own creation function, and this function automatically sets the value of `rowColumnType`.

Maintaining Exclusivity: entryClass, isHomogeneous

A row-column can limit the types of children that it can hold. An example is the menu bar, which may only contain cascade-button children. This limitation is controlled by the `isHomogeneous` resource: if it contains `TRUE`, all children must be of the same class; if it contains `FALSE`, children may be of any class. Like `rowColumnType`, `isHomogeneous` is set by the appropriate creation function.[4]

If `isHomogeneous` contains `TRUE`, the `entryClass` resource specifies the permitted widget class. This resource contains the widget's *class pointer*, part of its internal definition.[5] In most cases, the programmer does not need to make use of this resource: it is set automatically by the appropriate creation function.

Interaction: menuAccelerator, whichButton

Pop-up menus and the menu bar may be activated by a key sequence as described below. The `menuAccelerator` resource is used by these two types of menus and is ignored if the widget is not configured as a menu bar or pop-up menu.

The `menuAccelerator` resource contains a string that specifies a key event in the format used for translations. Only a single event may be specified, and this event must be a `KeyPress` event. Unlike a widget's translations and accelerators, the `menuAccelerator` resource is stored as a string, not a translation table.

The default value for `menuAccelerator` depends on the type of menu. For the menu bar, the default value is "<Key>F10": function key #10 activates the menu bar. For pop-up menus, the default value is "<Key>F4". If a program uses more than one pop-up menu, it must specify unique `menuAccelerator` values for each menu.

The `whichButton` resource specifies which pointer button is used to select menu items. For the menu bar and option menus, the default button is #1. For pop-up menus, the default button is #3.

---

[4] The menu bar is the only homogeneous menu; its children must be cascade buttons.

[5] Class record pointers are available to the program as opaque pointers. The names of these pointers are based on the widget's class name: the "Xm" at the beginning of the class name is replaced by "xm", and a suffix of "WidgetClass" is added. For example, the name of *XmCascadeButton*'s class pointer is `xmCascadeButtonWidgetClass`. The name of a widget's class pointer is contained in its class-specific header file, as well as in Appendix B and the *Programmer's Reference*.

Help Menu Specification: menuHelpWidget

As you will see below, while the Motif standard menu bar arranges most of its topics from left to right — as one would expect from a horizontal row-column — it has a **Help** topic on its right side, separated from the other topics. The `menuHelpWidget` resource provides this nonstandard behavior: it contains the ID of the cascade button for the **Help** menu. This resource is applicable to a row-column configured as a menu bar only; it is ignored by other menus. Its default value of `NULL` indicates that no **Help** topic is present: topics are arranged left-to-right by creation order.

XmRowColumn Callbacks

XmRowColumn provides three callbacks: `entryCallback`, `mapCallback`, and `unmapCallback`. The first is used to "redirect" the activation callbacks of a menu's children, allowing a single function — and single callback specification — to serve for all children. The second and third callbacks notify the program when a menu appears or disappears, allowing it to update any state-dependent information.

All three callbacks pass call data in the structure `XmRowColumnCallbackStruct`, defined in Listing 12.1. The `reason` and `event` members provide the same function as for other callback structures: they identify the type of callback and the event that invoked the callback. The `w`, `client_data`, and `call_data` members are used by `entryCallback` only; they contain the arguments that would have been passed to the child's activation callback function.

Listing 12.1. Structure definition:
XmRowColumnCallbackStruct

```
typedef struct
        {
        int         reason;
        XEvent      *event;
        Widget      w;
        caddr_t     client_data;
        caddr_t     call_data;
        }
XmRowColumnCallbackStruct;
```

Callback Multiplexing: entryCallback

In a complex menu system, the programmer may wish to avoid specifying callbacks for each of a menu's choices. For this reason, the `entryCallback` resource exists: it specifies a single callback function, which is invoked in place of the activation callbacks of the menu's children.[6] By default, this resource contains `NULL`, which means that the children's callbacks are invoked.

If used, `entryCallback` must be set at the time of the row-column's creation. It must be set at this time because the row-column replaces the appropriate child callbacks at the time of child creation — if and only if `entryCallback` is not `NULL`.

The `reason` value associated with this callback is `XmCR_ACTIVATE`. The `w`, `client_data`, and `call_data` members contain the arguments that would have been passed to the child's callback function.

Visibility Callbacks: mapCallback, unmapCallback

When a menu is about to be mapped, the callbacks specified by `mapCallback` are invoked, allowing the program to modify the contents of the menu with any context-dependent information.[7] The callback reason is `XmCR_MAP`; the `w`, `client_data`, and `call_data` members of the callback structure are not used.

Similarly, the functions specified by `unmapCallback` are invoked after the menu is unmapped. For this callback, the reason is `XmCR_UNMAP`, and the `w`, `client_data`, and `call_data` members are not used.

It is important to remember the order in which these callbacks are called, relative to the physical mapping and unmapping of the menu. The functions specified by `mapCallback` are called *before* the menu is mapped, allowing the program to make context-dependent changes to the menu. The functions specified by `unmapCallback` are called *after* the menu is unmapped, allowing retrieval of any state-control information, such as the current values of a menu's toggle buttons.

The Menu Bar

The menu bar is a horizontally oriented row-column, positioned at the top of a program's client window. The menu bar contains a series of cascade buttons, which specify the menu's topics — the high-level groupings of the functions provided by the menu bar.[8] Figure 12.2 shows a menu bar and its topics, along with a pull-down menu.

---

[6] Children must be buttons. For pushbuttons and cascade buttons, the `activateCallback` resource is replaced, for toggle buttons, the `valueChangedCallback` is replaced.

[7] This is especially useful with a help facility — if, for example, the user is positioned in a particular text field, the **Help** menu could contain choices leading to information about that field, text entry in general, or the current input screen. This information may be changed by the program — by changing the labels on the menu choices — just before the menu is invoked.

[8] A menu bar's topics are also referred to as the *titles* of the associated pull-down menus.

Figure 12.2. Menu bar and pull-down menu

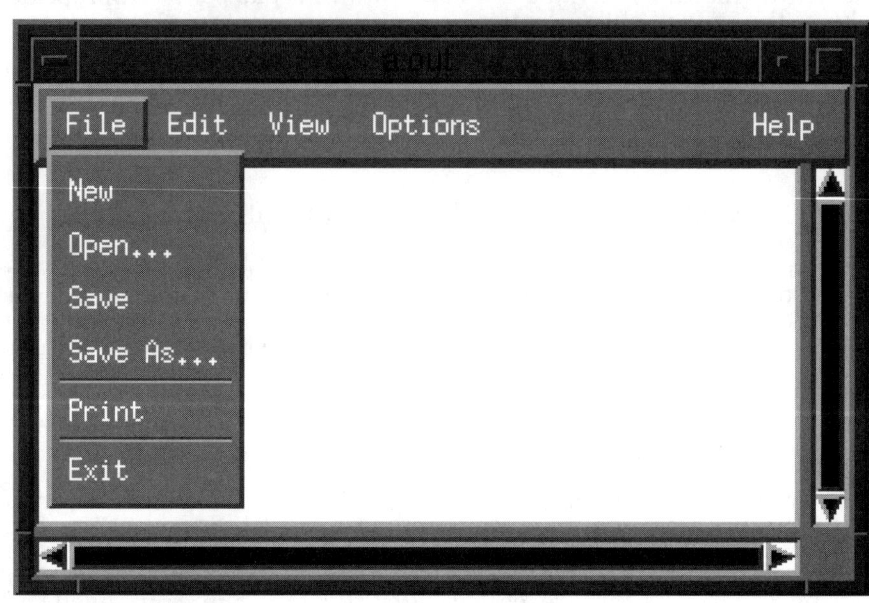

The behavior of the menu bar and its pull-down menus bears further explanation. Normally, the menu bar simply shows a list of topics, with no visual borders between the topics. When the user presses pointer button #1 while the pointer is positioned over a topic, that topic is armed: it changes its shadow border so that it appears to protrude from the screen. After a short delay, the topic button maps its menu pane. If the user then moves the pointer — with the button still down — over one of the choices in that pane, that choice is armed: it also changes its shadow border to a protruding form. If the user releases the pointer button while over a menu choice, the button representing that choice is activated — its activate callbacks are invoked — and the menu pane disappears. If, instead of selecting a menu choice in this manner, the user — with the pointer button still pressed — moves over another topic, the original menu is unmapped and the new menu is mapped.

It is important to note that, once armed, a menu topic remains armed until explicitly disarmed. Such disarming may occur by selecting a menu choice, by arming another menu, or by clicking the pointer button anywhere outside of the menu — in the same program's window, another program's window, or the root window.

In addition to pointer-based selection, menus provide a keyboard interface. The menu bar is armed by pressing the menu accelerator key: by default, *f10*. If this happens, the first topic is armed and its menu is displayed. The user can then traverse through the topics and choices: the *Left* and *Right* arrow keys move between topics, the *Up* and *Down* arrow keys move between the choices of a topic. When a menu choice is armed, pressing the *Return* key activates it. At any point, the *Escape* key disarms the current menu; it may need to be pressed multiple times to completely exit menu-selection mode.

Creating the Menu Bar: XmCreateMenuBar

Although the menu bar may be created as a row-column, with the appropriate resources set, the `XmCreateMenuBar` function is simpler. This function acts identically to the other widget-creation functions: it creates the widget (with the appropriate resource values), and returns its ID. The main-window widget should be passed as the menu-bar's parent.

Creating Menu Bar Topics: XmCreateCascadeButton

Menu bar topics must be represented by cascade buttons — the menu bar's `isHomogeneous` resource is set to `TRUE`, and its `entryClass` resource is set to `xmCascadeButtonWidgetClass`. These buttons are created using the `XmCreateCascadeButton` function, which is identical to other widget-creation functions. The menu bar widget must be specified as the parent of its cascade buttons.

The Standard Motif Menu Bar

The *Style Guide* specifies a standard configuration for the menu bar, shown in Figure 12.3(a). This standard configuration may be modified to suit the application's needs: it is strongly recommended that the **File**, **Edit**, and **Help** menus be present in every application, but the **View** and **Option** menus may not be applicable. Additional menus may be added if needed. If you do use the standard menu names, you should not change their meanings from those described below.

Figure 12.3. Standard Motif menu bar and pull-downs

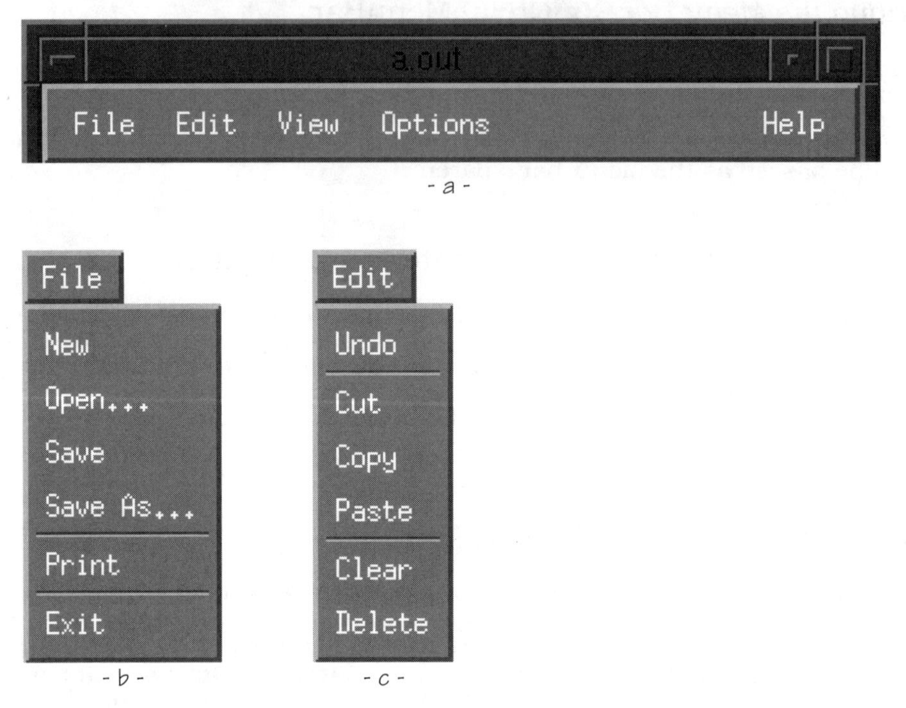

File Menu

The **File** menu contains operations that affect the entire file. The *Style Guide* divides such operations into four groups: (1) those that load a file, (2) those that save a file, (3) those that send a file to some output device, and (4) other. This menu should be present in every program and should be associated with the leftmost topic in the menu bar.

The standard **File** menu, shown in Figure 12.3(b), contains six choices, arranged into the aforementioned groups. **New** and **Open** are in the first group: **New** clears the program's workspace, and **Open** reads an existing file into the workspace. In the second group are **Save** and **Save As...**: **Save** saves the workspace in the same file from which it was loaded, while **Save As...** allows the user to save the workspace under a new filename. Group three contains a single member, **Print**, which sends the file to the system printer. Group four also contains a single member, **Exit**, which terminates the program.

Edit Menu

The **Edit** menu contains operations that modify the current workspace on a smaller scale than operations in the **File** menu. In a standard menu bar, it is the second menu from the left. Its choices are grouped into three categories: (1) undo the user's last action, (2) interface with the system clipboard, and (3) other actions.

A standard **Edit** menu, exampled by Figure 12.2(c), contains six members. **Undo** is the sole member of its category: it "undoes" the user's previous action.[9] The clipboard interface has three parts: **Cut**, which moves a selected part of the workspace to the clipboard (deleting it from the workspace), **Copy**, which copies a selected part of the workspace to the clipboard, and **Paste**, which puts the contents of the clipboard into the workspace.[10] Finally, the **Other** category provides **Clear** and **Delete** choices, both of which are optional. Both delete a part of the workspace, but **Delete** "compresses" the rest of the workspace, while **Clear** leaves blank space.[11]

View Menu

The **View** menu controls how the program displays the the workspace. Its use and contents depend on the application. For example, a spreadsheet might have **Worksheet** and **Chart** choices, while a CAD program might provide magnification and/or layer choices.

Options Menu

The **Options** menu is used to set program options. Like the **View** menu, its use and contents depend on the program. An example **Option** menu choice would be **Font**, to change the font used by a text editor. Toggle buttons are often used in option-menus, as they provide a visual representation of the current state of the program, as well as a way to change that state.

Help Menu

The **Help** menu topic always resides on the right side of the menu bar.[12] It provides the user with assistance, ranging from instructions on program use to the expected contents — and purpose — of the current input field. The contents of a help menu are application-dependent, but should be organized with the most specific help (*eg*, field-level help) at the top of the menu and least specific help (*eg*, program version number) at the bottom.

---

[9] Implementing an "undo" can be quite time-consuming — your program has to maintain "the previous state" at all times. However, the ability to correct mistakes is extremely comforting to the user.

[10] Use of the system clipboard is described in Chapter 17.

[11] Applied to an *XmText* widget, **Delete** would remove a section of the text, while **Clear** would replace that section with spaces.

[12] The menu bar's `menuHelpWidget` resource guarantees this placement.

Tailoring the Menu Bar to the Application

As indicated previously, the standard menus — or their choices — may not be applicable to all applications. The programmer should not try to force an application to fit the menu standard, but should attempt to follow it where possible. In particular, the **File** and **Edit** menus should be present in all programs and should be the two leftmost menus in the menu bar. The **Help** menu should be present and should be positioned on the right side of the menu bar. The **Exit** choice should always be the last choice on the **File** pull-down. With these "golden rules" in mind, the programmer is free to change the menu bar to suit the application.

Another "golden rule" is the grouping of items in the **File** and **Edit** menus. If new functions are added to these menus, they should be placed in the proper group — in the **Edit** menu, for example, **Find** and **Replace** would belong in the "other" group, not the "undo" group. Using separators between groups of related choices makes the grouping more apparent to the user.

A final consideration in menu design is to keep choices with devastating effects away from choices that are invoked often. In some cases, this is inevitable — the standard **File** menu, for example, has **Print** and **Exit** adjacent. If such a situation is unavoidable, you should present a warning dialog box ("Do you really want to do this?") to confirm the dangerous menu choice.

Names with an Ellipsis

Looking at the standard file menu, you see two menu choices — **Open...** and **Save As...** — that have an ellipsis as part of their name. This ellipsis indicates that the user will be presented with a dialog box upon choosing the menu item — that the program needs more information to perform the task. In the case of **Open...** and **Save As...**, this dialog box presents a list of filenames, allowing the user to choose an existing file or enter a new name from the keyboard.

Menu Bar Example: Adding a Menu Bar to the Editor

The text editor application will use the standard Motif menu bar, as shown by Figure 12.2. At this point, you have only been introduced to the menu bar and its cascade-button children, so that is the only addition to the program.

Listing 12.2 presents the changes to the program and resource file. As you can see, five new functions have been added: `InitFileMenu`, `InitEditMenu`, `InitViewMenu`, `InitOptionMenu`, and `InitHelpMenu`. Each of these functions is dedicated to a single menu topic, and at this point, merely creates the cascade button for the topic — as you will see, creating a single menu requires quite a lot of code. The `InitMenuBar` function, which was part of Listing 11.5, now creates the menu bar widget and calls the pane-initialization functions.[13]

The changes to the text editor's resource file simply set the labels used for the menu topics. In general, labels (and accelerators and mnemonics, described

---

[13] While 11.5 presented the text editor as a single source file, I have modularized it. The breakdown is essentially along the lines of the major functions: menu bar, work window, and "other."

below) are the only parts of a menu system that are specified by the resource file — the structure of the menu is part of the program code.

Listing 12.2. Text editor revision 2: Addition of menu bar

```
/**********************************************************************
**                                                                  **
**   InitMenuBar()                                                  **
**                                                                  **
**   This function creates the menu bar and all pull-down menus. The **
**   menu bar is created as the child of the main window.           **
**                                                                  **
**   This function modifies the global "menubar", and accesses the  **
**   global "mainwin".                                              **
**                                                                  **
**********************************************************************/

void    InitMenuBar()
{
    menubar = XmCreateMenuBar( mainwin, "MenuBar", NULL, 0 );
    XtManageChild( menubar );

    InitFileMenu();
    InitEditMenu();
    InitViewMenu();
    InitOptionMenu();
    InitHelpMenu();
}


/**********************************************************************
**                                                                  **
**   InitFileMenu()                                                 **
**                                                                  **
**   Creates the File menu: cascade-button, pull-down menu pane, and **
**   all menu-pane choices. Attaches callbacks to menu-pane choices. **
**                                                                  **
**********************************************************************/

void    InitFileMenu()
```

Listing 12.2. Continued.

```
**   Creates the File menu: cascade-button, pull-down menu pane, and     **
**   all menu-pane choices. Attaches callbacks to menu-pane choices.      **
**                                                                        **
*************************************************************************/

void    InitFileMenu()
{
    Widget       topic;

    topic = XmCreateCascadeButton( menubar, "FileTopic", NULL, 0 );
    XtManageChild( topic );
}


/*************************************************************************
**                                                                        **
**   InitEditMenu()                                                       **
**                                                                        **
**   Creates the Edit menu: cascade-button, pull-down menu pane, and     **
**   all menu-pane choices. Attaches callbacks to menu-pane choices.      **
**                                                                        **
*************************************************************************/

void    InitEditMenu()
{
    Widget       topic;

    topic = XmCreateCascadeButton( menubar, "EditTopic", NULL, 0 );
    XtManageChild( topic );
}

/*************************************************************************
**                                                                        **
**   InitViewMenu()                                                       **
**                                                                        **
**   Creates the View menu: cascade-button, pull-down menu pane, and     **
**   all menu-pane choices. Attaches callbacks to menu-pane choices.      **
**                                                                        **
*************************************************************************/
```

Listing 12.2. Continued.

```c
void    InitViewMenu()
{
    Widget      topic;

    topic = XmCreateCascadeButton( menubar, "ViewTopic", NULL, 0 );
    XtManageChild( topic );
}



/**********************************************************************
**                                                                  **
**    InitOptionMenu()                                              **
**                                                                  **
**    Creates the Option menu: cascade-button, pull-down menu pane, and **
**    all menu-pane choices. Attaches callbacks to menu-pane choices.   **
**                                                                  **
**********************************************************************/

void    InitOptionMenu()
{
    Widget      topic;
    topic = XmCreateCascadeButton( menubar, "OptionTopic", NULL, 0 );
    XtManageChild( topic );
}



/**********************************************************************
**                                                                  **
**    InitHelpMenu()                                                **
**                                                                  **
**    Creates the Help menu: cascade-button, pull-down menu pane, and  **
**    all menu-pane choices. Attaches callbacks to menu-pane choices.  **
**                                                                  **
**********************************************************************/

void    InitHelpMenu()
{
    Widget      topic;
```

Listing 12.2. Continued.

```
    topic = XmCreateCascadeButton( menubar, "HelpTopic", NULL, 0 );
    XtManageChild( topic );

    XtSetArg( arglist[0], XmNmenuHelpWidget, topic );
    XtSetValues( menubar, arglist, 1 );
}
```

```
*FileTopic.labelString:        File
*EditTopic.labelString:        Edit
*ViewTopic.labelString:        View
*OptionTopic.labelString:      Options
*HelpTopic.labelString:        Help
```

XmMenuShell and a Menu Pane's Instance Tree

A program's instance tree is reflected in the server's window tree, which means that — except in rare cases — a widget's window cannot be larger than its parent's window.[14] Applying this rule to the menu bar, you may wonder how a pull-down's window can be not only larger than the menu bar's window, but also completely separate from it. The answer is that a pull-down menu is not the child of the menu bar, but is actually the child of an *XmMenuShell* widget, which is the child of the menu bar.

XmMenuShell is, as its name indicates, a shell widget — an interface between the program and the server's root window. While the shell widget is a branch of the program's instance tree, it is the root of a new window subtree. This means that its size and position are independent of any other window in the instance tree.

Pull-Down Menus

Pull-down menus are vertically oriented row-column widgets, mapped under the control of a cascade button in the menu bar.[15] A pull-down menu may contain any type of child, but in practice children are limited to buttons, labels, and separators.

The relationship between the menu bar, a cascade button (topic), and its associated pull-down menu is illustrated by Figure 12.4. Both the cascade button and the menu-shell are children of the menu bar — since *XmCascadeButton* is a primitive widget, the menu shell could not be a child of

---

[14] The work area of an *XmScrolledWindow* in automatic mode is one of these exceptions.

[15] As you will see, pull-down menu panes are not always associated with the menu bar; for the present time, however, pretending this association simplifies the explanation.

the cascade-button. The pull-down menu pane is a child of the menu shell, and it's linked to the cascade-button via that widget's `subMenuId` resource.

Figure 12.4. Relationships between menu bar, cascade button, and pull-down menu

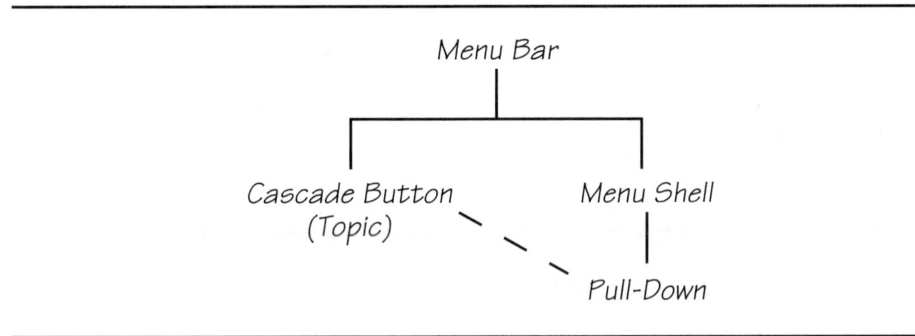

Creating a Menu Pane: XmCreatePulldownMenu

While the program could create its pull-down menus by first creating the menu shell and then creating the associated row-column, the `XmCreatePulldownMenu` convenience function does all of this in one step and returns the ID of the menu pane.[16] `XmCreatePulldownMenu` has the same parameters as other widget-creation functions: the menu bar should be specified as the `parent`, the widget's name is up to the programmer, and the `arg_list` and `arg_count` parameters specify resources for the menu pane.

Attaching a Pull-Down to the Menu Bar

Once the menu pane has been created, it must be attached to the proper cascade button by storing its widget ID in the cascade-button's `subMenuId` resource; this must be done programmatically. It may be done either at the time of cascade-button creation or afterward, depending on the order in which cascade button and pane are created.[17]

Adding Functionality

A pull-down menu — or any other type of menu — achieves its functionality from its children's callbacks. There are two ways to add such callbacks: individual callbacks on each choice or use of the pane's `entryCallback` resource.

---

[16] While menu shell is the parent of the menu pane, its presence may be ignored by the programmer: it has no resources of interest, and performs its job without program intervention.

[17] As you will see in the sample code, my preference is to create the pane first, then the cascade button — it means one less function call.

The proper approach depends on the situation: while individual callbacks take up more code, a multiplexed callback can be harder to read.[18]

In either case, callbacks should be invoked on button activation only. If callbacks are invoked on arming, the action of "dragging" the pointer down a menu will invoke each of the choices passed.

Disabling Menu Choices

In some situations, you will want to prevent the user from accessing a particular menu choice. For example, the text editor should disable its **File/Save** menu choice when there is no current filename.

While this could be done simply by removing the associated callback, the preferred method is to set its `sensitive` resource to `FALSE`, using the `XtSetSensitive` function. This method has the benefit that it provides a visual cue that the menu choice is disabled.

Pull-Down Example: Adding Pull-Down Menus to the Editor

The text editor will use the standard menu bar configuration, with sub-menus organized as shown in Table 12.3. This table also provides a description of the purpose of each menu choice. These descriptions represent the design goals of the editor — but they are not implemented in their entirety in this book.

Table 12.3. Text editor menu configuration

Topic	Choice	Description
File	New	Clears workspace and current filename.
	Open...	Displays dialog box, allowing user to select a filename from a list of existing files or enter it via the keyboard.
	Save	Saves workspace, using current filename. This choice is disabled when current filename is blank or when the workspace has not been modified.
	Save As...	Displays dialog box, allowing user to enter a new filename or select the name of an existing file. Saves file under specified name and stores specified name as the current filename.
	separator	Separates file-manipulation choices from program-exit choice.

---

[18] This book uses a single callback function for all of a menu's choices, but invokes that function with individual callbacks.

Table 12.3. Continued.

	Exit	Terminates program.
		If the contents of the workspace have been modified but not saved, this function displays a dialog box asking the user if he/she really wants to quit without saving.
Edit	Cut	Sends selected text to the system clipboard, removing it from the workspace.
	Copy	Copies selected text to the system clipboard, but does not change it in the workspace.
	Paste	Copies text from the system clipboard to the workspace, inserting it at current insertion point.
	Delete	Deletes selected text from the workspace.
	separator	Separates selection-related choices from find/replace.
Options	Font...	Presents dialog box that allows user to change font for text display.

The program segment of Listing 12.3 presents the changes to the `InitFileMenu` function and resource file to add the **File** pull-down; addition of the other menus is left as an exercise for the reader (the resource-file segment lists the additional widgets). In addition to the changes to `InitFileMenu`, Listing 12.3 also presents the `FileMenuCB` function, which handles the menu's choices. Both are described in detail below the listing.

Listing 12.3. Text editor revision 3: Addition of file menu

```
/*******************************************************************
**                                                               **
**   InitFileMenu()                                              **
**                                                               **
**   Creates the File menu: cascade-button, pull-down menu pane, and  **
**   all menu-pane choices. Attaches callbacks to menu-pane choices.  **
**                                                               **
********************************************************************/

void    InitFileMenu()
{
    Widget      topic,
                pane,
                choices[6];

    pane = XmCreatePulldownMenu( menubar, "FilePane", NULL, 0 );
```

Listing 12.3. Continued.

```c
        choices[0] = XmCreatePushButton( pane, "File_New", NULL, 0 );
        choices[1] = XmCreatePushButton( pane, "File_Open", NULL, 0 );
        choices[2] = XmCreatePushButton( pane, "File_Save", NULL, 0 );
        choices[3] = XmCreatePushButton( pane, "File_SaveAs", NULL, 0 );
        choices[4] = XmCreateSeparator(  pane, "File_Sep1", NULL, 0 );
        choices[5] = XmCreatePushButton( pane, "File_Exit", NULL, 0 );
        XtManageChildren( choices, 6 );

        XtSetArg( arglist[0], XmNsubMenuId, pane );
        topic = XmCreateCascadeButton( menubar, "FileTopic", arglist, 1 );
        XtManageChild( topic );

        XtAddCallback( choices[0], XmNactivateCallback, FileMenuCB, "New" );
        XtAddCallback( choices[1], XmNactivateCallback, FileMenuCB, "Opn" );
        XtAddCallback( choices[2], XmNactivateCallback, FileMenuCB, "Sav" );
        XtAddCallback( choices[3], XmNactivateCallback, FileMenuCB, "SAs" );
        XtAddCallback( choices[5], XmNactivateCallback, FileMenuCB, "Ext" );

        XtSetSensitive( choices[1], FALSE );
        XtSetSensitive( choices[2], FALSE );
        XtSetSensitive( choices[3], FALSE );
}


/*****************************************************************************
**                                                                         **
**    FileMenuCB( w, client_data, call_data )                              **
**                                                                         **
**    Callback procedure for the "File" pull-down. This function is        **
**    called when any of the file menu buttons are activated. The          **
**    particular operation is identified by a string accessed by the       **
**    "client_data" param.                                                 **
**                                                                         **
**    Note: This callback is only invoked on Activate, so the call         **
**          data (which describes the reason) is superfluous. It is        **
**          therefore not declared as a specific type in the func hdr.     **
**                                                                         **
*****************************************************************************/

void    FileMenuCB( w, client_data, call_data )
    Widget      w;
    char        *client_data;
    caddr_t     call_data;
{
    if (!strcmp(client_data, "New"))
```

Listing 12.3. Continued.

```
        {
        XmTextSetString( textwin, "" );
        }
    else if (!strcmp(client_data, "Opn"))
        {
        }
    else if (!strcmp(client_data, "Sav"))
        {
        }
    else if (!strcmp(client_data, "SAs"))
        {
        }
    else if (!strcmp(client_data, "Ext"))
        {
        exit( 0 );
        }
}
```

```
*FileTopic.labelString:         File
*File_New.labelString:          New
*File_Open.labelString:         Open...
*File_Save.labelString:         Save
*File_SaveAs.labelString:       Save As...
*File_Exit.labelString:         Exit

*EditTopic.labelString:         Edit
*Edit_Cut.labelString:          Cut
*Edit_Copy.labelString:         Copy
*Edit_Paste.labelString:        Paste
*Edit_Delete.labelString:       Delete
*Edit_Find.labelString:         Find...
*Edit_Repl.labelString:         Replace...

*ViewTopic.labelString:         View
*View_Top.labelString:          Top
*View_Bot.labelString:          Bottom
*View_Page.labelString:         Page...

*OptionTopic.labelString:       Options
*Option_Font.labelString:       Font...
```

The changes to `InitFileMenu` include the creation of the pull-down menu pane, the creation of the menu choices, attaching callbacks to those choices, and setting unused choices insensitive. The first part — creating the menu pane and choices — is straightforward: the pane and its shell are created with `XmCreatePulldownMenu`, and the choices are simply pushbuttons (along with one separator).

You should note that the cascade-button representing the menu topic is created *after* the menu pane. As stated above, this is done simply to minimize code: instead of setting the cascade button's `subMenuId` resource with `XtSetValues`, it is set at the time the button is created.

The callback setup also bears notice. Instead of using the `entryCallback` resource in the menu pane, I chose to use discrete calls to `XtAddCallback`. This was done so that I could pass identification data — a three-character ASCII string — in the `client_data` parameter.[19] These strings are then used in a string comparison by the `FileMenuCB` function.

The final action of `InitFileMenu` — setting unused menu choices insensitive — is done as a service for the user. As support for menu choices is added, the calls to `XtSetSensitive` are removed.

The function `FileMenuCB` handles the activation callbacks for all items in the **File** menu. At this point, it handles only two: **New** clears the contents of the text window, and **Exit** quits the program. The other choices are enabled in future chapters.

The resource file segment simply sets labels for each of the menu choices. It also presents the names I've chosen for the choices on the **Edit**, **View**, and **Options** menu.

Mnemonics

What Are Mnemonics?

In addition to pointer-based activation, a menu system should provide a keyboard interface — for those users that dislike removing their hands from the keyboard, as well as those that do not have a mouse. One way to implement keyboard input is via *mnemonics*, which allow the user to select a menu choice with a series of keystrokes.

Figure 12.5 presents the text editor menu bar and **File** menu, with mnemonics enabled. Each menu topic or choice has a single character underlined; that character is the mnemonic associated with the menu choice.

---

[19] This is my preferred method of passing identification data, since it helps identify the code used to process the menu choice. I refuse to use the common technique of passing constants as client data, although most compilers accept it.

Figure 12.5. Text editor mnemonics

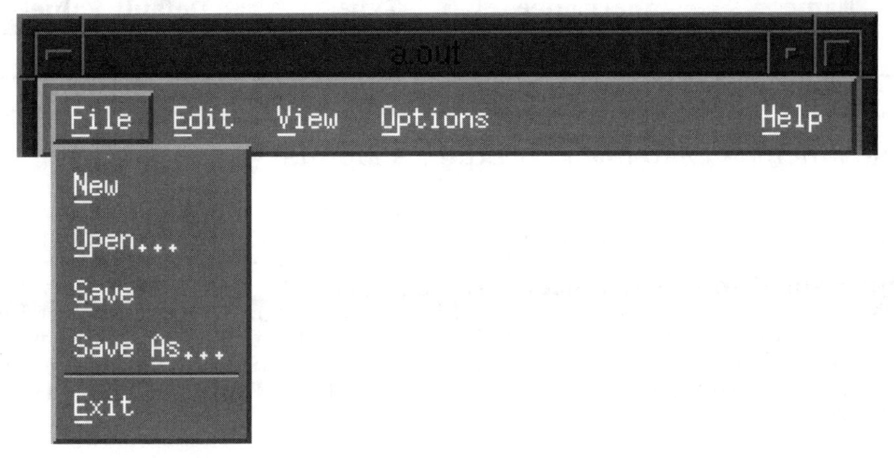

How Are Mnemonics Used?

To make use of the mnemonic associated with a menu choice, that menu must be active — it must have the keyboard focus. There are two ways to activate a menu: the first is to press the key specified by the menu bar's `menuAccelerator` resource — by default, *f10*. This activates the menu bar and allows the user to activate a menu by pressing the mnemonic associated with its topic. An alternative method of menu activation is to type the topic's mnemonic while pressing the *Meta* key.

Once a menu is activated, a choice on that menu may be activated by pressing its associated mnemonic. Mnemonics are applied only to the currently active level of a menu system — in Figure 12.5, where the **File** menu is active, pressing *E* will exit the program; it won't activate the edit menu. If a menu is active, pressing the *Escape* key deactivates it.

How Are Mnemonics Specified?

Mnemonics are specified by the `mnemonic` resource, shown in Table 12.4. This resource is defined by the *XmLabel* class, but is only applicable to the buttons derived from *XmLabel*: *XmPushButton*, *XmToggleButton*, and *XmCascadeButton*. This resource contains a single character, the mnemonic character; the default value of `'\0'` specifies that no mnemonic is present. If a mnemonic is specified, the button underlines the first occurrence of the mnemonic character in its `labelString`. If the mnemonic character is not found in `labelString`, then it is displayed to the right of the string, in parentheses.

Table 12.4. Resource specification: *mnemonic*

Name	Inheritance	Type	Default Value
mnemonic	XmLabel	char	'\0'

Adding Mnemonics to the Text Editor's Menus

Listing 12.4 is an excerpt from the text editor's resource file, showing the mnemonics for each of the menu topics and choices. While most of the mnemonics are obvious — they're the first letter of the menu choice — one in particular stands out: **Edit/Delete**. The character 'D' would seem appropriate for this mnemonic, because it isn't used by any other on that menu, but I chose 'l'.[20] The reason is that **Delete** is a destructive action, and I did not want an accidental keystroke to invoke it. Thus, the 'l' mnemonic, which is positioned away from all of the other mnemonics (except 'P' — **Paste** — which is also a destructive action).

Listing 12.4. Text editor *mnemonic* resource specifications

```
*FileTopic.mnemonic:            F
*File_New.mnemonic:             N
*File_Open.mnemonic:            O
*File_Save.mnemonic:            S
*File_SaveAs.mnemonic:          A
*File_Exit.mnemonic:            E

*EditTopic.mnemonic:            E
*Edit_Cut.mnemonic:             t
*Edit_Copy.mnemonic:            C
*Edit_Paste.mnemonic:           P
*Edit_Delete.mnemonic:          l
*Edit_Find.mnemonic:            F
*Edit_Repl.mnemonic:            R

*ViewTopic.mnemonic:            V
*View_Top.mnemonic:             T
*View_Bot.mnemonic:             B
*View_Page.mnemonic:            P
```

---

[20] I should note that the standard mnemonic for the **Delete** choice *is* D.'

Listing 12.4. Continued.

```
*OptionTopic.mnemonic:          O
*Option_Font.mnemonic:          F

*HelpTopic.mnemonic:            H
```

Menu Accelerators

What Are Menu Accelerators?

Another way to implement keyboard activation of menu items is via *menu accelerators*. Menu accelerators allow events occurring in one widget — the widget with the input focus — to invoke actions in another — a button in a menu. Where menu accelerators differ from generic accelerators is that they are more specific: menu accelerators are used only with buttons that are children of pop-up or pull-down menu panes.

The benefit of menu accelerators is that they allow instantaneous keyboard activation of a menu choice — unlike mnemonics, which require that the user first activate the proper menu, then press the key corresponding to the menu function. Instead, accelerators are handled directly by the program's translation manager, and thus bypass the focus mechanism.

Their drawback is that — unless the menu is displayed — there is no clue to their presence. As a result, accelerators are most often used by sophisticated users, who are intimately familiar with the program's operation.

How Are Menu Accelerators Used?

Figure 12.6 presents an example of menu accelerators, applied to the text editor's **File** menu. The accelerator's key sequence is displayed to the right of the choice name, providing the user with a visual indication of the accelerator's presence.

Figure 12.6. Text editor menu accelerators

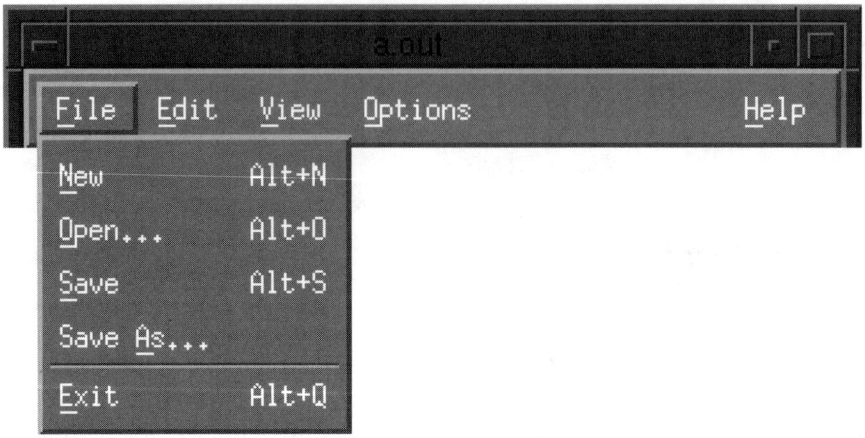

The use and naming of accelerators depends on the program.[21] The accelerators in Figure 12.6 are named according to the first letter of the associated menu choice — except for **Exit**. This change was necessary because the *Alt-E* combination — in the guise of *Meta-E* — is used as a mnemonic to activate the **Edit** menu.

How Are Menu Accelerators Specified?

Like mnemonics, menu accelerators are defined by the *XmLabel* class in order to be available to all button classes derived from *XmLabel*. Accelerators are implemented using two resources, listed in Table 12.5 and described below.[22]

Table 12.5. Resource specifications: *accelerator*, *acceleratorText*

Name	Inheritance	Type	Default Value
accelerator	XmLabel	String	NULL
acceleratorText	XmLabel	XmString	NULL

---

[21] The *Style Guide* specifies four standard accelerators, all for the **Edit** menu: *Alt-Backspace* for **Undo**, *Shift-Delete* for **Cut**, *Control-Insert* for **Copy**, and *Shift-Insert* for **Paste**.

[22] Note that, since menu accelerators are controlled by resources, their use is in reality the prerogative of the user. A knowledgeable user may completely reconfigure a program's accelerators to suit his/her tastes — or configure a program that by default does not use accelerators.

The `accelerator` resource — not to be confused with the `accelerators` resource defined by *Core* — specifies the key combination that invokes the accelerator. This key combination is specified using the same format as a translation table, with the caveat that only a single event may be specified, and that event must be a `KeyPress` event. Note that, unlike the `accelerators` resource, `accelerator` is saved as an ASCII string. The widget transparently converts and installs the appropriate translations.

The `acceleratorText` resource contains a user-friendly representation of the key combination, such as "Alt+Q". This text is displayed to the right of the button's label; like the label itself, it is a compound string. Note that the accelerator text is the responsibility of the programmer or user: the program does not automatically produce a string from the contents of `accelerator`.

Adding Menu Accelerators to the Text Editor

Listing 12.5 presents the segment of the text editor's resource file responsible for Figure 12.6. Note again that the resource file is the place where menu accelerators are specified, not the program itself. Note also the difference between the modifier key in the event specification and in the accelerator text — the event uses *Meta*, the text uses *Alt*.

Listing 12.5. Text editor *accelerator* and *acceleratorText* resource specifications

```
*File_New.accelerator:            Meta<KeyPress>n
*File_Open.accelerator:           Meta<KeyPress>o
*File_Save.accelerator:           Meta<KeyPress>s
*File_Exit.accelerator:           Meta<KeyPress>q
!
*File_New.acceleratorText:        Alt+N
*File_Open.acceleratorText:       Alt+O
*File_Save.acceleratorText:       Alt+S
*File_Exit.acceleratorText:       Alt+Q
```

Cascading Pull-Downs

A pull-down menu pane may contain any type of widget, including cascade buttons. This leads to a menu structure shown in Figure 12.7, known as a *cascading pull-down*. This structure uses a cascade button to link one menu pane with another, providing additional detail for a menu choice. It is often used instead of a dialog box to provide the user with a convenient method of performing detailed actions. If a cascade button is used in this manner, it displays the contents of its `cascadePixmap` resource — by default a right-pointing arrow — on its right side.

Figure 12.7. Cascading pull-down

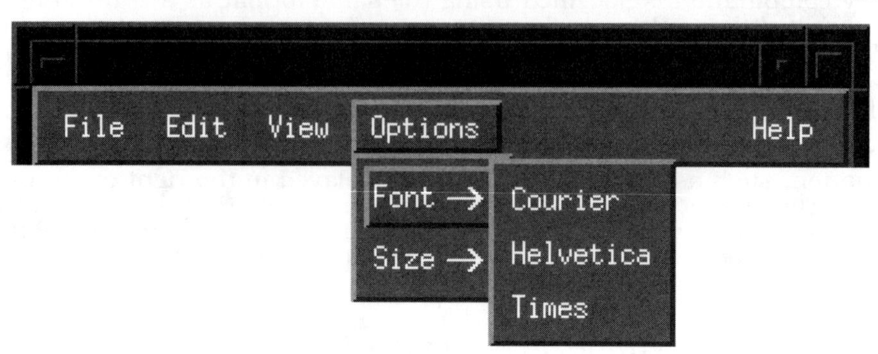

Cascading Pull-Down Example

Listing 12.6 presents the code segment responsible for Figure 12.7.[23] Both of the choices in the **Option** pane are cascading menus; the code segment contains only that code used for the **Font** choice.

Listing 12.6. Cascading pull-down code

```
void    InitOptionMenu()
{
Widget      topic, subtop1, subtop2,
            pane, subpane1, subpane2,
            choices[2], subchoice1[3], subchoice2[5];

pane = XmCreatePulldownMenu( menubar, "Option_Pane", NULL, 0 );
XtSetArg( arglist[0], XmNsubMenuId, pane );
```

---

[23] This code represents an "alternate implementation" of the text editor's `InitOptionMenu` function. It is presented for illustrative purposes only and will not remain a part of the editor program.

Listing 12.6. Continued.

```c
topic = XmCreateCascadeButton( menubar, "OptionTopic", arglist, 1 );
XtManageChild( topic );

subpanel = XmCreatePulldownMenu( pane, "Opt_Font_Fonts", NULL, 0
);
subchoice1[0] = XmCreatePushButton( subpanel, "Opt_Fnt_Cour", NULL, 0 );
subchoice1[1] = XmCreatePushButton( subpanel, "Opt_Fnt_Helv", NULL, 0 );
subchoice1[2] = XmCreatePushButton( subpanel, "Opt_Fnt_Time", NULL, 0 );
XtManageChildren( subchoice1, 3 );

XtSetArg( arglist[0], XmNsubMenuId, subpanel );
choices[0] = XmCreateCascadeButton( pane, "Option_Font", arglist, 1 );
.
.
.
XtManageChildren( choices, 2 );
}
```

In this code segment, the **Option** pane is created and attached to the cascade-button that represents the **Option** topic. Another pane is then created for the font selection submenu. This new pane is then linked to a cascade-button child of the original (**Option**) pane. The same calls are repeated to create the **Size** submenu, and then the cascade-button children of the **Option** pane are managed.

This process could be repeated, with a sub-submenu attached to the **Font** submenu. The usefulness of more than one level of cascading menus is questionable: the convenience gained by a single cascading menu is lost when the user has to navigate through multiple levels of menus (a dialog box is often more appropriate).

Pop-Up Menus

Pop-up menus are so named because they "pop up" onto the screen, unlike menus that must be "pulled down" from the menu bar. The benefit of a pop-up menu is immediacy: they are invoked either with a keyboard accelerator or the "menu button" (pointer button #3), and they appear under the pointer, ready to be used. A primary purpose of pop-up menus is to provide context-sensitive operations. For example, a data entry program could have several "defaults" menus, each associated with a particular input field. The user could then press pointer button #3 while the pointer is over a field, and the proper menu would appear, allowing rapid input of default data.

In implementation, a pop-up menu is similar to a pull-down menu. Both are vertically oriented row-columns, both must be children of an *XmMenuShell* widget, and both contain buttons that activate program functions. Pop-up menus are created with the function `XmCreatePopupMenu`, which is similar in operation to `XmCreatePulldownMenu`.

The big difference between pop-up and pull-down menus is the way that they are made visible: pull-down menus are mapped automatically by a cascade button, whereas pop-up menus must be managed explicitly by the program.[24] This is best explained by example, provided below.

Pop-up Menu Example: Color Selection Menu

In a painting program, one of the most often performed operations is changing the active color. Figure 12.8 presents a representation of such a program, along with a pop-up **Colors** menu. This menu is accessed by pressing the "menu" pointer button (button #3) while over the program's work area or by pressing the appropriate accelerator key (by default, *f4*).

Figure 12.8. Pop-up menu

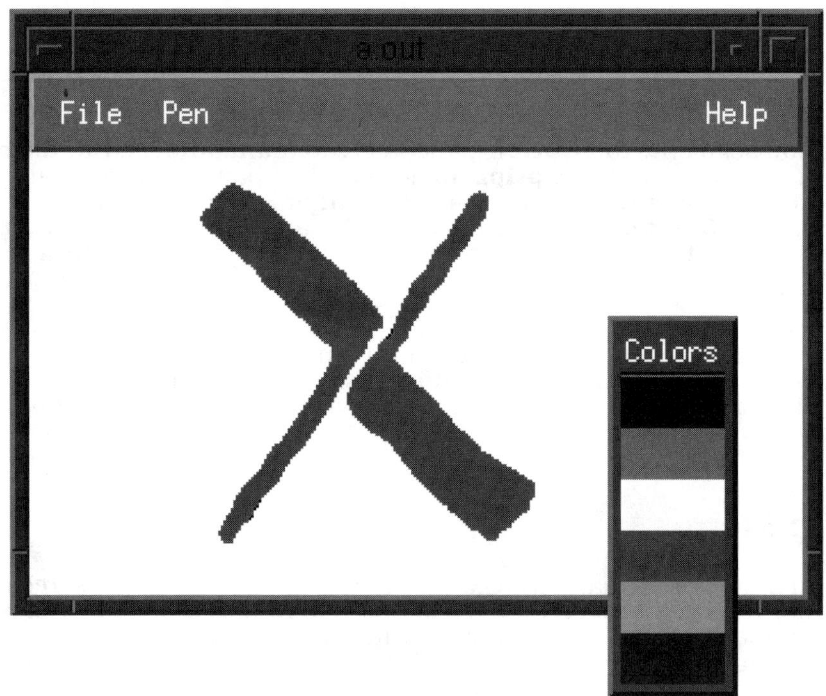

The sample code does not present an actual drawing program because such a program uses techniques described later in this book. Instead, a simple bulletin

---

[24] They may also be managed by Motif, when the user presses the key specified by the menu pane's `menuAccelerator` resource.

board simulates the work area of the drawing program, and the example is implemented with the trivial program template in Listing 12.7.

Listing 12.7. Program and resource file: Pop-up menu example

```
/*******************************************************************
**                                                               **
**   listing_12_7.c                                              **
**                                                               **
**   Demonstration of pop-up menus.                              **

    XtAddEventHandler( the_bb, ButtonPressMask, FALSE, PopPopup, NULL );

    InitPopup();
**                                                               **
*******************************************************************/


#include <Xm/BulletinB.h>
#include <Xm/RowColumn.h>
#include <Xm/Label.h>
#include <Xm/PushB.h>
#include <Xm/Separator.h>


void    InitPopup();                    /* FORWARD Definitions    */
void    PopPopup();


Widget  appshell,                       /* Application Shell      */
        the_bb,                         /* The work area    */
        popup,                          /* The pop-up menu pane   */
        pop_lbl,                        /* The pop-up's title     */
        pop_sep,                        /* Seps title from choices */
        pop_btn[6];                     /* Choices on the pop-up  */


void main( argc, argv )
    int     argc;
    char    *argv[];
```

Listing 12.7. Continued.

```c
{
    appshell = XtInitialize( argv[0], "Listing_12_7", NULL, 0,
                                              &argc, argv );

    the_bb = XmCreateBulletinBoard( appshell, "TheBB", NULL, 0 );
    XtManageChild( the_bb );
    XtRealizeWidget( appshell );
    XtMainLoop();
}


/**********************************************************************
**                                                                  **
**   InitPopup()                                                    **
**                                                                  **
**   Creates the pop-up menu pane and its children.                 **
**                                                                  **
**********************************************************************/

void    InitPopup()
{
    popup = XmCreatePopupMenu( the_bb, "Popup", NULL, 0 );

    pop_lbl = XmCreateLabel( popup, "Pop_Title", NULL, 0 );
    XtManageChild( pop_lbl );

    pop_sep = XmCreateSeparator( popup, "Pop_Sep", NULL, 0 );
    XtManageChild( pop_sep );

    pop_btn[0] = XmCreatePushButton( popup, "Pop_Black", NULL, 0 );
    pop_btn[1] = XmCreatePushButton( popup, "Pop_Gray",  NULL, 0 );
    pop_btn[2] = XmCreatePushButton( popup, "Pop_White", NULL, 0 );
    pop_btn[3] = XmCreatePushButton( popup, "Pop_Red",   NULL, 0 );
    pop_btn[4] = XmCreatePushButton( popup, "Pop_Green", NULL, 0 );
    pop_btn[5] = XmCreatePushButton( popup, "Pop_Blue",  NULL, 0 );
    XtManageChildren( pop_btn, 6 );
}
```

Listing 12.7. Continued.

```
/*****************************************************************
**                                                             **
**   PopPopup( w, client_data, event )                         **
**                                                             **
**   Button event handler. Manages popup on button #3.         **
**                                                             **
*****************************************************************/

void    PopPopup( w, client_data, event )
    Widget          w;
    caddr_t         client_data;
    XButtonEvent    *event;
{
    if (event->button != Button3)
        return;

    XmMenuPosition( popup, event );
    XtManageChild( popup );
}
```

```
!
! Resource file for Pop-up Menu Demo (Fig 12.8)
!

*.foreground:                       White
*.background:                       Gray25
*.topShadowColor:                   Gray50
*.bottomShadowColor:                Black

*TheBB.width:                       300
*TheBB.height:                      200
*TheBB.background:                  White

*Pop_Title.labelString:             Colors

*Popup.XmPushButton.width:          25
*Popup.XmPushButton.height:         20
*Popup.XmPushButton.labelString:
*Popup.XmPushButton.recomputeSize:  FALSE
```

Listing 12.7. Continued.

```
*Pop_Black.background:          Black
*Pop_Gray.background:           Gray50
*Pop_White.background:          White
*Pop_Red.background:            Red
*Pop_Green.background:          Green
*Pop_Blue.background:           Blue
```

The core of this program is comprised of two functions: `InitPopup` and `PopPopup`. `InitPopup` creates the pop-up menu and is similar to the `InitFileMenu` function of the text editor. The primary difference is that the pop-up menu pane is not linked to a cascade button.

The linking occurs in the call to `XtAddEventHandler` in the main program, which invokes the `PopPopup` function on any button press. In `PopPopup`, the button is checked, and nothing happens unless it is button #3.

If button #3 is pressed, `PopPopup` first calls the function `XmMenuPosition`. This function sets the position of the pop-up menu pane, using the pointer position as reported in the event structure.[25] Once the menu pane has been positioned, it is managed. It is important to remember that pull-down menus are mapped, but pop-ups must be managed — the menu-shell must assimilate the changes specified by the call to `XmMenuPosition`.

While this has been happening, the pointer button remains pressed. The menu appears under the pointer, and the user is able to select one of the pushbuttons contained in the menu pane. Once a choice is selected — by releasing the pointer button — its associated activation callback is invoked (none are used here), and the menu pane is automatically unmanaged.[26]

Like pull-down menus, pop-ups may contain children from any widget class. This includes cascade buttons, which may be attached to pull-down menu panes, resulting in cascading menus from a pop-up. This technique is often used when a context-sensitive menu must allow multiple sets of actions — for example, the drawing program's pop-up might have a cascading pull-down for colors and another for brush size.

Option Menus

An option menu is used in a situation where the program needs to provide a list of choices, but window space is limited, or in situations where the programmer desires to provide a visual indication of the current menu choice. In its normal state, an option menu takes up only the space needed to display its title and

---

[25] This positioning is performed by modifying the x and y resources of the menu shell. The top left corner of the shell is positioned under the pointer.

[26] Motif unmanages the pane when the pointer button is released.

current value, but when activated it displays a menu pane from which the user is able to choose a new value. To provide this functionality, an option-menu links a label (for the menu title), a cascade button (to invoke the menu pane), and a pull-down menu pane (to display the choices). The option-menu widget itself is a row-column, with its `rowColumnType` resource set to `XmMENU_OPTION`.

Figure 12.9 presents a common usage for option menus: selection of a font's family and size. In Figure 12.9(a), both option menus are in their normal state. In Figure 12.9(b), the size menu is active. One point of interest is that the option-menu's pane is positioned such that the current choice is aligned with the menu's label. Note also that the cascade button always presents its "armed" appearance, even though it isn't armed.

Figure 12.9. Option menu example

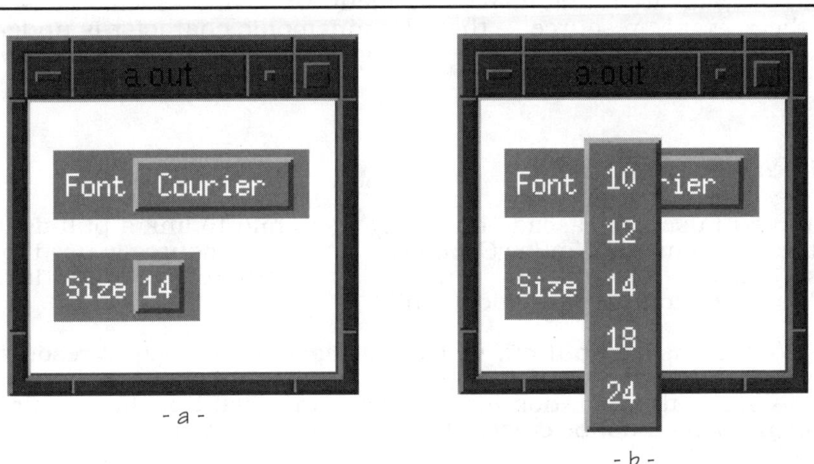

XmRowColumn Resources Specific to Option Menus

An option menu is implemented as a horizontally oriented row-column, with a label gadget and a cascade-button gadget as "hidden" children. To support this implementation, *XmRowColumn* contains resources that are used solely for option menus. These resources are listed in Table 12.6 and described below.

Table 12.6. Resource specifications: *XmRowColumn* option-menu resources

Name	Inheritance	Type	Default Value
labelString	XmRowColumn	XmString	NULL
menuHistory	XmRowColumn	Widget	NULL
mnemonic	XmRowColumn	char	'\0'
subMenuId	XmRowColumn	Widget	NULL

Menu Title: labelString

XmRowColumn's `labelString` resource exists solely for the title of an option menu. An option-menu widget uses this resource as an interface to the `labelString` resource of its hidden label gadget: the program can set and read the label's `labelString` resource via the menu's. As with any label's `labelString` resource, this resource contains a compound string, which defaults to the name of the label gadget.

Keyboard Access: mnemonic

Like pull-down menus accessed from the menu bar, an option menu supports the use of keyboard mnemonics: if the option menu is visible, pressing the mnemonic will activate it and display its menu pane. If a mnemonic is specified — using the `mnemonic` resource — then the mnemonic character is underlined in the menu's title; if the character is not found in the title string, it is displayed in parentheses to the right of the title.

Pane Linkage: subMenuId

An option menu uses its cascade-button gadget child to link a pull-down menu pane to the option menu. *XmRowColumn*'s `subMenuId` resource is used to provide this link: like the row-column `labelString` resource, `subMenuId` is a "pass through" to the option-menu's hidden child.

Unlike a normal cascade button, which can have its `subMenuId` resource set at any time, an option menu must have `subMenuId` set at the time of its creation; attempts to set it after creation are ignored. One result of this requirement is that the menu pane must be created before the option menu.

Current Choice: menuHistory

The `menuHistory` resource is not used solely for option menus: it is also used by row-columns holding radio buttons (*ie*, with the `radioBehavior` resource set to `TRUE`). In both cases, this resource holds the ID of the most recently activated child. For an option menu, this is a child of its menu pane; for a radio box, it's the last toggle button to be selected.

As used by an option menu, the `menuHistory` resource controls the position of the mapped menu pane. When the pane is mapped, `menuHistory` is queried to find the current choice. The menu pane is then positioned so that that choice is aligned with the menu title. Once a new choice is made, the ID of the button representing that choice is stored into `menuHistory`, and its label is stored in the menu's hidden cascade button.

A common use of the `menuHistory` resource is to set a default current value by storing the ID of one of the pane's buttons in `menuHistory` when the option menu is created. This technique is used in the sample program to provide a default font size of 14 points and family of Courier.

Option Menu Example: Font Family and Size

Figure 12.9 was produced with the program and resource file of Listing 12.8. This example uses a bulletin board to hold the option menus; in a practical application, they would typically be used in a dialog box. As this example exists solely to present option menus, it is based on the trivial program template.

Listing 12.8. Program and resource file: Option-menu example

```
/*************************************************************************
**                                                                     **
**   listing_12_8.c                                                    **
**                                                                     **
**   Demonstration of option-menus.                                   **
**                                                                     **
*************************************************************************/


#include <Xm/BulletinB.h>
#include <Xm/RowColumn.h>
#include <Xm/PushB.h>


void    InitFontMenu();              /* FORWARD Definitions        */
void    InitSizeMenu();

Widget  appshell,                    /* Application Shell          */
        the_bb;                      /* The work area              */
Arg     arglist[16];                 /* Used to set resources      */


void main( argc, argv )
    int     argc;
    char    *argv[];
{
    appshell = XtInitialize( argv[0], "Listing_12_8", NULL, 0,
                                        &argc, argv );

    the_bb = XmCreateBulletinBoard( appshell, "TheBB", NULL, 0 );
    XtManageChild( the_bb );

    InitFontMenu();
```

Listing 12.8. Continued.

```
    InitSizeMenu();

    XtRealizeWidget( appshell );
    XtMainLoop();
}



/*******************************************************************
**                                                               **
**    InitFontMenu()                                             **
**                                                               **
**    Creates the option-menu for font selection.               **
**                                                               **
*******************************************************************/

void    InitFontMenu()
{
    Widget       menu,
                 pane,
                 choices[3];

    pane = XmCreatePulldownMenu( the_bb, "Font_Pane", NULL, 0 );

    choices[0] = XmCreatePushButton( pane, "Font_Cour", NULL, 0 );
    choices[1] = XmCreatePushButton( pane, "Font_Helv", NULL, 0 );
    choices[2] = XmCreatePushButton( pane, "Font_Time", NULL, 0 );
    XtManageChildren( choices, 3 );

    XtSetArg( arglist[0], XmNsubMenuId, pane );
    XtSetArg( arglist[1], XmNmenuHistory, choices[0] );
    menu = XmCreateOptionMenu( the_bb, "Font_Menu", arglist, 2 );
    XtManageChild( menu );
}
```

Listing 12.8. Continued.

```
/*********************************************************************
**                                                                 **
**   InitSizeMenu()                                                **
**                                                                 **
**   Creates the option-menu for font size selection.             **
**                                                                 **
*********************************************************************/

void    InitSizeMenu()
{
    Widget      menu,
                pane,
                choices[5];

    pane = XmCreatePulldownMenu( the_bb, "Size_Pane", NULL, 0 );

    choices[0] = XmCreatePushButton( pane, "Size_10", NULL, 0 );
    choices[1] = XmCreatePushButton( pane, "Size_12", NULL, 0 );
    choices[2] = XmCreatePushButton( pane, "Size_14", NULL, 0 );
    choices[3] = XmCreatePushButton( pane, "Size_18", NULL, 0 );
    choices[4] = XmCreatePushButton( pane, "Size_24", NULL, 0 );
    XtManageChildren( choices, 5 );

    XtSetArg( arglist[0], XmNsubMenuId,   pane );
    XtSetArg( arglist[1], XmNmenuHistory, choices[2] );
    menu = XmCreateOptionMenu( the_bb, "Size_Menu", arglist, 2 );
    XtManageChild( menu );
}
```

```
!
! Resource file for Option Menu demo (Fig 12.
!

*.foreground:           White
*.background:           Gray50
*.topShadowColor:       Gray75
*.bottomShadowColor:    Gray25
```

Listing 12.8. Continued.

```
*TheBB.marginWidth:      10
*TheBB.marginHeight:     20
*TheBB.foreground:       Black
*TheBB.background:       White

*Font_Menu.x:            10
*Font_Menu.y:            20
*Font_Menu.labelString:  Font

*Font_Cour.labelString:  Courier
*Font_Helv.labelString:  Helvetica
*Font_Time.labelString:  Times

*Size_Menu.x:            10
*Size_Menu.y:            60
*Size_Menu.labelString:  Size

*Size_10.labelString:    10
*Size_12.labelString:    12
*Size_14.labelString:    14
*Size_18.labelString:    18
*Size_24.labelString:    24
```

The `InitFontMenu` and `InitSizeMenu` functions are the core of this program. As they are almost identical in content, `InitFontMenu` is described here.

The `InitFontMenu` function appears similar to the `InitFileMenu` function of the text editor. Both create a pull-down menu pane and fill it with button children. The difference is that `InitFileMenu` attaches the menu pane directly to a cascade button, and `InitFontMenu` attaches it to the option menu. Both use the appropriate widget's `subMenuId` resource to specify the linkage.

Another difference is that an option menu is managed after it is created. This is because an option menu — like the menu bar — is a part of the program's window tree, whereas pop-up and pull-down menu panes exist in separate window trees.

Finally, note that the menu panes are not children of their associated option menus. Instead, they must be children of the option-menu's parent.

Menu Summary

The following list presents a summary of the information presented in this chapter.

- Menus are implemented using the *XmRowColumn* widget class.

  The menu bar and option menus are horizontally oriented row-columns, pop-up and pull-down menus are vertically oriented row-columns. The particular type of menu is specified by the row-column's `rowColumnType` resource. *XmRowColumn* provides other resources dedicated to menu support.

  The *XmRowColumn* resources `isHomogeneous` and `entryClass` specify the type of widgets that may be children of a menu. These resources are only used for the menu bar, which is restricted to children of class *XmCascadeButton*; pop-up and pull-down menu panes may have any type of child. Although menu panes typically have only labels, separators, and buttons as children, some programs may use other types of children — for example, another row-column, to implement a set of radio buttons.

- Each type of menu has its own creation function.

  Although menus are implemented using *XmRowColumn*, creating a menu system using `XmCreateRowColumn` is inefficient, primarily because of the default resource values used by the various types of menus (not to mention the fact that pop-up and pull-down menu panes require a menu-shell parent). For this reason, Motif provides the following creation functions: `XmCreateMenuBar`, `XmCreateOptionMenu`, `XmCreatePopupMenu`, and `XmCreatePulldownMenu`. These functions set the appropriate *XmRowColumn* resources and create additional widgets where needed.

- A pop-up or pull-down menu pane must be the child of an *XmMenuShell* widget.

  Pop-up and pull-down menu panes might need to exceed the bounds of the program's window (note Figure 12.9). For this reason, they are created as the child of an *XmMenuShell* widget, which is the root of a new window subtree — completely separate from the subtree formed by the windows of the program's other widgets.

- Option menus and the menu bar are managed when created, pull-down menu panes are mapped when used, and pop-up menu panes are managed when used.

  The windows of option menus and the menu bar exist in the program's normal window subtree, meaning that they are positioned (and sized) by the menu's parents. For this reason, they must be managed when they are created.

  The window of a pull-down menu pane exists in a separate subtree, rooted by the window of the menu shell. A pull-down is managed by its creation function, and need only be mapped to be used. This mapping happens automatically as a result of the activation of a cascade button.

  The window of a pop-up menu pane also exists in a separate subtree, under control of a menu shell. However, the position of a pop-up menu may change between its uses, because it follows the pointer. For this reason, it must be managed when used, so that its parent properly adjusts its size and position. The program specifies this position before management, by calling the `XmMenuPosition` function (passing it the event responsible for the menu's appearance). Pop-up menu panes may also be managed automatically, as the result of a keyboard accelerator.

- Menus and their choices may be accessed by the keyboard, using either mnemonics and traversal or accelerators.

  XmRowColumn provides the `menuAccelerator` resource used by the menu bar and pop-up menu panes. This resource specifies a key combination — in the format used for a translation specification — which will activate the menu. The default value of this resource depends on the type of menu: `"<Key>F10"` for the menu bar, `"<Key>F4"` for a pop-up. Once activated, the arrow keys may be used for traversal: the *Up* and *Down* keys traverse between choices on a menu, and the *Right* and *Left* keys traverse between menu bar topics (and activate/deactivate the associated pull-down menu). The *Return* key activates the currently active menu choice, and the *Escape* key deactivates the menu.

  The topics on a menu bar may have a single-character mnemonic, specified by the `mnemonic` resource of *XmLabel*. Once the menu bar is activated, a pull-down menu may be activated by typing its associated mnemonic. Alternately, a pull-down may be activated without menu bar activation, by pressing the *Meta* (or *Alt*) key while typing the mnemonic.

  Single-character mnemonics are also used by the pushbuttons, toggle buttons, and cascade buttons residing in menu panes. These mnemonics are also specified by the button's `mnemonic` resource. A button may be activated by pressing the associated mnemonic key while its menu pane is active.

  Menu choices may also have accelerators, which are key sequences that activate the menu choice without the need for activating the associated menu. Menu accelerators are specified by *XmLabel*'s `accelerator` and `acceleratorText` resources; these resources are applicable only to pushbuttons, cascade buttons, and toggle buttons that reside in a menu. The `accelerator` resource should not be confused with the `accelerators` resource, defined by the *Core* class: `accelerator` provides a simpler method of implementing a keyboard accelerator than `accelerators`.

- Pull-down menus are not limited to the menu bar.

  While the term "pull-down menu" implies that the menu is pulled down from the menu bar, a Motif pull-down may be used in other circumstances as well. Cascading pull-downs are implemented by linking a pull-down menu pane to a cascade button in another menu pane; this linkage may be repeated, resulting in an infinite number of sub-[sub-...]menus. Pull-downs may also be linked with a cascade button in a pop-up menu pane. Finally, pull-downs are used to implement an option menu's list of choices.

  The one requirement for use of a pull-down menu is that it must be mapped by a cascade button — the program does not explicitly control its presence or absence.

- The parent of a pull-down menu pane depends on that menu's use.

  If a pull-down menu pane is associated with the menu bar, the menu bar is the parent of the pane. If it is associated with a pop-up or pull-down menu pane (*eg*, cascading pull-downs), then its parent is the associated menu pane. If it is associated with an option menu, its parent is the option-menu's parent.

- Each type of menu has its own purpose.

The menu bar resides at the top of every program's display, and its associated pull-downs are always accessible. A pop-up menu provides "instantaneous" context-sensitive operations. Option menus are used where space is limited, but the list of choices is long, or where the programmer desires to provide a visual indication of the menu's state.

13 Dialogs

Overview

A dialog box is a *secondary window*, managed by the program, but distinct from the program's main window. Dialog boxes exist for tasks that are tangential to the program's main purpose, to present information or allow user input. An example of this use, shown in Figure 13.1, is the text editor's **Find** dialog. While finding and selecting text is an action that is often performed by a text editor user, it is not the primary function of the editor — and should not, therefore, have a permanently dedicated space on the editor's main window.

Dialogs can serve a wide range of purposes. The **Find** dialog is an example of a task dialog: a dialog box that exists for a particular task and is present only while that task is being performed. Other dialogs are tool palettes: they provide often-used functions, and remain on screen for as long as the user requires those functions — often for as long as the program is running. Message boxes form a third class: they present a short message to the user and allow an immediate Yes/No response. Finally, input dialogs prompt the user for required input — an example is a "Open File" dialog.

Dialog Modality

One of the tenets of graphical user-interface design is that programs should be modeless: the user should be able to perform any appropriate function at any time. However, many dialog boxes are modal: they force the user to perform a specific action and do not permit any other actions until that action is complete. There are various levels of modality, each applicable to specific situations.

Modeless dialogs do not affect a user's interaction with the program; they are simply additional windows maintained by the program. Tool palettes are always modeless: they are designed to coexist with the program, not supersede it. Task dialogs are occasionally modeless: a nonmodal **Find**, for example, would allow the user to repeatedly search for an item, while editing between searches.

Figure 13.1. *Find* dialog

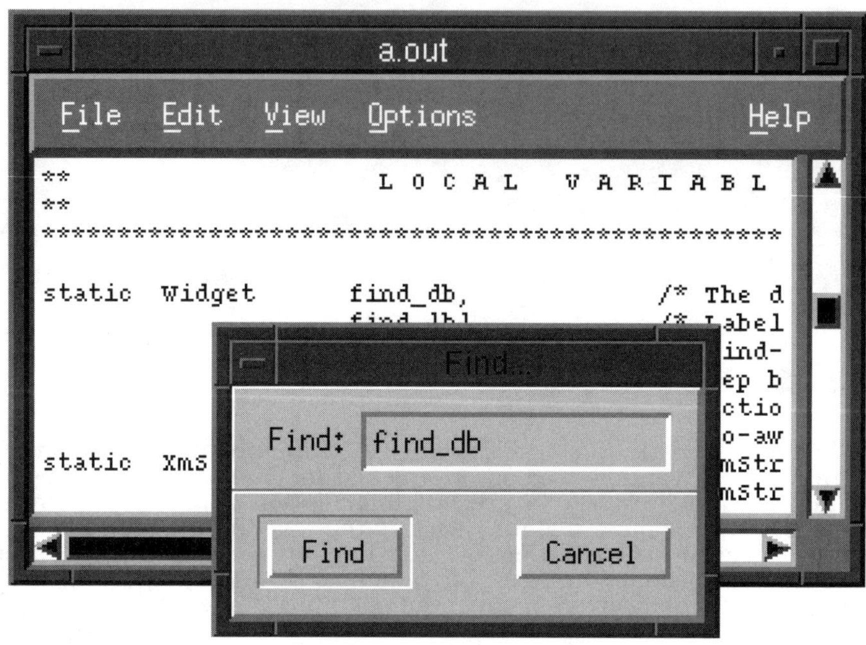

Application-modal dialogs prevent the user from performing any other actions in the same program until the dialog's purpose is fulfilled. He/she can, however, switch to another program. Message boxes are application-modal: they present information pertaining to the current situation and require a response while that situation exists. Input dialogs are often application-modal: the file-selection dialog, for example, is an integral part of the file-saving process and must not be bypassed.

System-modal dialogs prevent the user from performing any other actions in any window until the dialog's purpose is fulfilled. As such dialogs essentially take control of the system from the user, they should only be used in urgent circumstances, such as reporting a full filesystem.

Dialog Design and Components

A dialog is divided into two areas: the *presentation area* and the *confirmation area*.[1] The presentation area is at the top of the dialog box and contains the controls, tools, information, etc., presented by the dialog. In the **Find** dialog of Figure 13.1, the presentation area contains the entry field and its label ("Find:"). The confirmation area is at the bottom of the dialog and contains pushbuttons

---

[1] These terms are not "official" Motif terms.

that confirm — and act on — the content of the presentation area. In the **Find** dialog, the **Find** button confirms the text and initiates the search, while the **Cancel** button unmanages the dialog. The two areas are typically divided visually by a separator.

The pushbuttons in the confirmation area represent actions relating to the dialog. They should be organized with affirming choices on the left, negating choices on the right, and **Help** (if it is used) as the rightmost choice. Button labels should refer to specific actions: **Find** instead of **Go**. Dialog boxes should present a default operation, invoked by pressing the *Return* key. This default button is identified by a special shadow border (like the **Find** button in Figure 13.1).

XmDialogShell

As dialogs exist as separate program windows, outside of the program's normal window tree, they must have a shell between themselves and the root window. This shell is *XmDialogShell*, derived as shown by the class tree of Figure 13.2.

Figure 13.2. *XmDialogShell* class tree

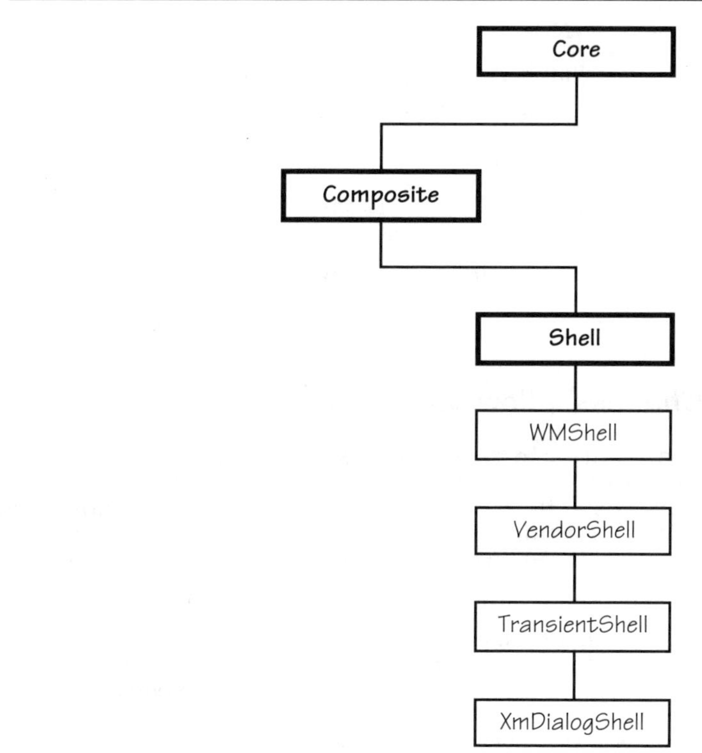

The *Shell* class is defined by Xt and provides the basic interface between the shell and the root window. *WMShell* is also defined by Xt and provides the interface between the shell and the window manager.[2] *VendorShell* is defined by Motif and provides information about the program to the Motif window manager.[3] The *TransientShell* class indicates that the shell uses a secondary window — it is an extension of the program's main window and is not iconified separately.[4]

XmDialogShell **Resources**

As a result of the many nodes in its class tree, most of the resources used with *XmDialogShell* are inherited. Table 13.1 presents a selection of these resources, with the defining class identified; they are described below.

Table 13.1. Frequently used resources: *XmDialogShell*

Name	Inheritance	Type	Default Value
allowShellResize	Shell	Boolean	FALSE
overrideRedirect	Shell	Boolean	FALSE
maxHeight	WMShell	int	-1
maxWidth	WMShell	int	-1
minHeight	WMShell	int	-1
minWidth	WMShell	int	-1
deleteResponse	VendorShell	unsigned char	XmUNMAP
keyboardFocusPolicy	VendorShell	unsigned char	XmEXPLICIT

Programmatic Size Changes: allowShellResize

One of the functions of a shell is to respond to size-change requests from its child by passing the request on to the window manager. The `allowShellResize` resource controls this process: if it contains `FALSE`, the shell ignores such requests from its child and maintains its original size. If it contains `TRUE`, the shell attempts to grow or shrink to match the desired size of its child. For a

---

[2] This interface specifies the general information about the program: its preferred size, minimum and maximum sizes, etc. Unlike resources defined by *VendorShell*, this information is the sort that would be used by any window manager; *VendorShell* provides information specific to a particular vendor's window manager.

[3] If *VendorShell* is defined by Motif, why doesn't it begin with "Xm"? The answer is that *VendorShell*, as an abstract class, is defined by Xt. Its purpose, however, is to provide an interface to window-manager-specific features, so it is implemented as part of Motif.

[4] *ApplicationShell* replaces *TransientShell* with *TopLevelShell*, so a program window may be iconified on its own.

dialog box, the default value of `allowShellResize` box is `FALSE`: the dialog maintains its initial size, unless that size is changed by the user.

Size Limits: minHeight, minWidth, maxHeight, maxWidth

When the user changes the size of a shell via the window frame resize controls, the shell must recalculate the geometry of its child — which must recalculate the geometry of its children, and so on. In some cases, the new size may be too small to display the entire dialog or too large to be useful (*eg*, a form dialog that expands its children excessively).

To limit such size changes, a shell provides specifications for minimum and maximum size. The `minHeight` and `minWidth` resources specify the desired minimum dimensions; `maxHeight` and `maxWidth` specify the desired maximum dimensions. You should note that these specifications are *desired* — the window manager has ultimate control over the size and position of a window. The default value of -1 indicates that there is no desired limit.

Window Manager Control: overrideRedirect, deleteResponse

The `overrideRedirect` resource specifies whether the window manager should actively control the shell's size and position.[5] If it contains `FALSE`, the window manager is responsible for the size and position of the shell; if it contains `TRUE`, the shell is responsible for managing its own position and dimensions. For *XmDialogShell* and *ApplicationShell*, `overrideRedirect` contains `FALSE`; for *XmMenuShell*, it contains `TRUE`.

For shells managed by the window manager, the `deleteResponse` resource controls how the shell responds to a user double-clicking in the "window menu box" (the button at the top left corner of the window frame).[6] This resource may contain one of three values: `XmDESTROY` indicates that the display connection should be closed, `XmUNMAP` indicates that the shell should be unmapped, and `XmDO_NOTHING` indicates that the action should be ignored. For *XmDialogShell*, the default is `XmUNMAP`. Dialogs that should be ever-present use `XmDO_NOTHING`; no dialog should use `XmDESTROY` because it will terminate the main program.

Focus: keyboardFocusPolicy

As stated in Chapter 9, Motif provides two methods of controlling focus: explicit, in which the user must click on the window to receive focus, and pointer, in which the window where the pointer resides has focus. This behavior is controlled at the shell level — determining which widget of the shell's descendents has the focus — by the `keyboardFocusPolicy` resource. If this resource contains `XmEXPLICIT`, subwindow focus is assigned by traversal and pointer clicks; if it contains `XmPOINTER`, subwindow focus is assigned by the pointer's position.

---

[5] The `overrideRedirect` resource should never be modified by the program. It is presented here in explanation of the difference between a menu shell and a dialog shell.

[6] Selecting **Close** from the window menu performs the same action.

Dialog Management and Unmanagement

To be used, a dialog must be present on the screen. Once the user is done with it, it should disappear. As you might guess, `XtManageChild` is used to make the dialog appear, and `XtUnmanageChild` makes it disappear. What might not be obvious is that your program manages and unmanages the dialog's *child* — not the dialog shell itself.

If you reflect on previous experience with shells, you will see that this is a common technique. The application shell isn't managed, its child — the main-window — is. Similarly, a pop-up menu's shell isn't managed, the menu-pane row-column is.

The reason for this is that a shell provides an interface to the root window: it requests a subwindow on the root, which is under the control of the window manager, not another widget. Management, however, is the process of a parent widget allocating its space between its children, initiated by a child's request for management. Thus, when you manage the child of a shell, it requests space from the shell, which requests space from the window manager.

XmBulletinBoard Dialog Resources

Most dialogs are built on bulletin board and form widgets — they are more appropriate for positioning controls, labels, and fields than managers such as XmRowColumn. For this reason, *XmBulletinBoard* defines a set of resources that are specifically designed for dialog support.[7] These resources are listed in Table 13.2 and described below.

Table 13.2. Dialog-specific resources: *XmBulletinBoard*

Name	Inheritance	Type	Default Value
autoUnmanage	XmBulletinBoard	Boolean	TRUE
cancelButton	XmBulletinBoard	Widget	NULL
defaultButton	XmBulletinBoard	Widget	NULL
defaultPosition	XmBulletinBoard	Boolean	TRUE
dialogStyle	XmBulletinBoard	unsigned char	*dynamic*
dialogTitle	XmBulletinBoard	XmString	NULL
mapCallback	XmBulletinBoard	XtCallbackList	NULL
noResize	XmBulletinBoard	Boolean	FALSE
unmapCallback	XmBulletinBoard	XtCallbackList	NULL

---

[7] As *XmForm* is derived from *XmBulletinBoard*, these resources are also present in form-based dialogs.

Usage/Modality: dialogStyle

A bulletin board may be the child of a dialog shell, or it may be used as a work area within another manager. The `dialogStyle` resource specifies this usage. In addition, if the bulletin board is the child of a dialog shell, `dialogStyle` specifies its modality. Legal values are as follows:

- `XmDIALOG_WORK_AREA`. The bulletin board is used as a child of another manager or the application shell.

- `XmDIALOG_MODELESS`. The bulletin board is used as a modeless dialog: it resides on the screen with the application's main window, but does not accept input or preempt program control unless explicitly given the focus.

- `XmDIALOG_APPLICATION_MODAL`. The bulletin board is used as an application-modal dialog: it preempts access to all other windows maintained by the same program.

- `XmDIALOG_SYSTEM_MODAL`. The bulletin board is used as a system-modal dialog: it preempts access to any other window on the server.[8]

The `dialogStyle` resource has a dynamic default value in that its default value is set by the function that creates the bulletin board. If the bulletin board is created as the child of a dialog shell, the default value is `XmDIALOG_MODELESS`. If it is created as the child of another manager, the default value is `XmDIALOG_WORK_AREA`.

Title: dialogTitle

The window manager provides a title for each framed window, which is displayed in the top portion of the window frame. *XmBulletinBoard's* `dialogTitle` resource specifies this title; it is a compound string and defaults to the bulletin board's widget name.

You should note that the contents of `dialogTitle` are not directly passed to the window manager. Instead, the bulletin board uses this resource to set the `title` resource of its shell, and the shell presents the contents of that resource to the window manager. A common error is to set `title` directly — the bulletin board overwrites it.

Size/Position Control: defaultPosition, noResize

When a dialog is managed, its desired initial size is the size of the bulletin board, which is determined from the aggregate size of the bulletin-board's children. This desired size is presented to the window manager, which may or may not grant it.[9]

---

[8] System-modal dialogs are only supported (at this time) by the Motif window manager. If you run a Motif program under another window manager, you cannot guarantee system-modality.

[9] In practice, the size request is almost always granted.

A normal client window frame includes controls that allow the user to expand or shrink the window. The presence or absence of these controls is determined by the `noResize` resource: if it contains `FALSE` (the default), the controls are present; if it contains `TRUE`, then they are absent.[10]

The initial position of the dialog is also controlled by the window manager and determined in part by the contents of the `defaultPosition` resource. If `defaultPosition` contains `TRUE` (the default), the dialog is positioned such that it is centered in its parent's window. If it contains `FALSE`, the dialog is positioned according to the window manager's positioning algorithm — the initial position is indeterminate.

Interaction: autoUnmanage, defaultButton

The normal operation of a dialog is to unmanage itself when any of its child buttons are activated. While this may be a convenience for a message box or input dialog, it is certainly an inconvenience for a tool palette. The `autoUnmanage` resource controls this behavior. When it contains `TRUE` (the default), the bulletin board adds an "unmanage me" callback to the activation callback list of each of its button children. When `autoUnmanage` contains `FALSE`, no such callback is present, and the program must explicitly unmanage the dialog when it is no longer needed.[11]

Some dialogs use a default button, which is activated when the user presses the *Return* key while the dialog is displayed. The `defaultButton` resource specifies such a button: it contains the widget ID of that button. The default value, `NULL`, indicates that there is no default button. When a default button is used, the bulletin board installs an accelerator, which redirects the the *Return* key to that button.

You should note that the `defaultButton` resource does not cause a visual indication of the button's status. To provide such an indication, you must set the button's own `showAsDefault` resource, described in Chapter 7.

---

[10] The use of this resource is not limited to dialogs. It is also effective if the bulletin-board's parent is the application shell.

[11] Note, however, that the dialog may also be unmanaged in reaction to the user, if the shell's `deleteResponse` resource contains `XmUNMAP`.

Standard Children: cancelButton

Every dialog should have a **Cancel** button — a way for the user to say "I don't want to do this." In light of this, *XmBulletinBoard* provides the `cancelButton` resource, which contains the widget ID of such a button. The bulletin board does not, however, define any special actions associated with that resource, nor does it require that the program make use of it.[12]

Callbacks: mapCallback, unmapCallback

Like the identically named *XmRowColumn* resources, `mapCallback` and `unmapCallback` allow the program to intercept the management or unmanagement of a dialog. The `mapCallback` list is invoked just before the dialog appears; its reason is `XmCR_MAP`. The `unmapCallback` list is invoked just after the dialog disappears; its reason is `XmCR_UNMAP`. Both callbacks pass call data in `XmAnyCallbackStruct`.

Building and Using a Dialog

Building and using a bulletin board or form dialog involves four steps: creating the dialog shell and manager, creating and managing the dialog's children, managing the dialog when it is needed, and unmanaging the dialog when it is no longer needed.

To create the dialog, you can create the shell and bulletin board separately or use one of the convenience functions shown in Listing 13.1: the first creates a bulletin board as the child of the dialog shell, the second creates a form. These functions take the same parameters as other widget-creation functions; the main window is a good choice for the `parent` parameter. They return the ID of the manager widget; the dialog shell is automatically created as the parent of this widget.

---

[12] The `cancelButton` resource exists primarily for subclasses of *XmBulletinBoard*, such as *XmMessageBox.*

Listing 13.1. Function prototypes:
XmCreateBulletinBoardDialog, XmCreateFormDialog

```
Widget  XmCreateBulletinBoardDialog( parent, name, arg_list, arg_cnt )
        Widget      parent;
        String      name;
        ArgList     arg_list;
        Cardinal    arg_cnt;


Widget  XmCreateFormDialog( parent, name, arg_list, arg_cnt )
        Widget      parent;
        String      name;
        ArgList     arg_list;
        Cardinal    arg_cnt;
```

The dialog's manager widget is not managed after it is created. However, the children of that manager are. The manager itself is managed when the program needs to display the dialog; it must be explicitly unmanaged when no longer useful.[13]

Bulletin-Board Dialog Example: Find

Almost every text editor offers a "find string" operation, and the one in this book is no exception. As you might have guessed, this function is implemented using a bulletin-board dialog. Figure 13.3 presents the two faces of this dialog: 13.3(a) is its initial state, and 13.3(b) is its "in process" state.

The distinction between "initial" and "in process" was first presented in the text editor's menu specification in Chapter 12. When the **Find** dialog first appears — as a result of choosing the **Find...** choice from the **Edit** menu — it presents **Find** and **Cancel** buttons. To send the dialog away without doing anything, the user presses **Cancel**. To find a string, the user types the string in the entry field and presses **Find**.

The code behind the dialog box then searches for the first occurrence of the search string in the text buffer. Assuming that it finds one, it selects that portion of the buffer and presents the dialog's second face — 13.3(b). In this second face, the dialog presents **Next** and **Done** buttons: **Next** searches for the next occurrence of the string, **Done** unmanages the dialog, leaving the current string selected.

---

[13] Unless, of course, it is unmanaged automatically as a result of the `autoUnmanage` resource or the shell's deletion response (determined by the value of its `deleteResponse` resource).

If at any point the dialog code is unable to find the search string, it simply unmanages the dialog. A more elegant solution would be to have it display a message, such as "Search string not found."

Figure 13.3. "Find" dialog: As managed and after first location

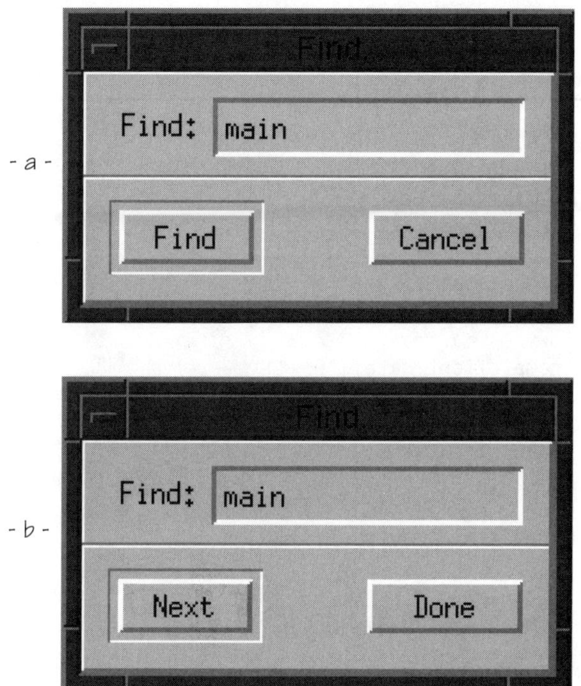

Implementing this dialog requires several changes to the text editor program, presented in Listing 13.2. The first change is to the `InitOther` function: it now calls a function to create the find dialog. The second change is to the **Edit** menu's callback function, `EditMenuCB`: it now manages the dialog box when the **Find** choice is selected. The third change is to implement the functions that support the dialog; these are described below the listing. The fourth change is to add a utility function, `StrFind`, which searches for a substring within another string: it is used to locate the search string in the text widget's buffer.[14] Finally, the resource file must be changed; this also is described below the source listing.

---

[14] This function is equivalent to the ANSI C function `strstr`; if you have an ANSI compiler, you should use `strstr` and not implement `StrFind`.

Listing 13.2. Program and resource file excerpts: Text editor revision 6 (*Find* dialog)

```
void InitOther()
{
    InitFindDB();
}
```

```
static void EditMenuCB( w, client_data, call_data )
    Widget       w;
    char         *client_data;
    caddr_t      call_data;
{
    if (!strcmp(client_data, "Cut"))
        {
        }
    else if (!strcmp(client_data, "Cpy"))
        {
        }
    else if (!strcmp(client_data, "Pst"))
        {
        }
    else if (!strcmp(client_data, "Del"))
        {
        }
    else if (!strcmp(client_data, "Fnd"))
        {
        ManageFindDB();
        }
    else if (!strcmp(client_data, "Rpl"))
        {
        }
```

```
/*********************************************************************
**                                                                 **
**            F O R W A R D   D E F I N I T I O N S                 **
**                                                                 **
*********************************************************************/

static  void    FindCB();
static  void    FindCanCB();
```

Listing 13.2. Continued.

```c
/*********************************************************************
**                                                                 **
**                  L O C A L   V A R I A B L E S                   **
**                                                                 **
*********************************************************************/

static  Widget     find_db,              /* The dialog box            */
                   find_lbl,             /* Label: "Find:"            */
                   find_txt,             /* Find-string Entry Field   */
                   find_sep,             /* Sep between pres & conf   */
                   find_btn_1,           /* Action pushbutton         */
                   find_btn_2;           /* Go-away pushbutton        */
static  XmString   find_str,             /* XmString for "Find"       */
                   can_str,              /* XmString for "Cancel"     */
                   next_str,             /* XmString for "Next"       */
                   done_str;             /* XmString for "Done"       */
static  int        finding;              /* Flag for FindCB()         */


/*********************************************************************
**                                                                 **
**   InitFindDB()                                                  **
**                                                                 **
**   Creates the "Find" dialog box, which is controlled by the     **
**   Edit/Find... pull-down menu choice.                           **
**                                                                 **
**   Modifies the global variable "find_db", and local variables   **
**   "find_txt", "find_ok_btn", and "find_nxt_btn".                **
**                                                                 **
*********************************************************************/

void InitFindDB()
{
    find_db = XmCreateBulletinBoardDialog( mainwin, "FindDB", NULL, 0 );
```

Listing 13.2. Continued.

```
        find_lbl = XmCreateLabel( find_db, "Find_Lbl", NULL, 0 );
        XtManageChild( find_lbl );
        find_txt = XmCreateText( find_db, "Find_Txt", NULL,  0 );
        XtManageChild( find_txt );

        find_sep = XmCreateSeparator( find_db, "Find_Sep", NULL, 0 );
        XtManageChild( find_sep );

        find_btn_1 = XmCreatePushButton( find_db, "Find_Btn1", NULL, 0 );
        XtManageChild( find_btn_1 );
        find_btn_2 = XmCreatePushButton( find_db, "Find_Btn2", NULL, 0 );
        XtManageChild( find_btn_2 );

        XtAddCallback( find_btn_1, XmNactivateCallback, FindCB,    NULL );
        XtAddCallback( find_btn_2, XmNactivateCallback, FindCanCB, NULL );

        XtSetArg( arglist[0], XmNdefaultButton, find_btn_1 );
        XtSetValues( find_db, arglist, 1 );

        find_str = XmStringCreate( "Find",   XmSTRING_DEFAULT_CHARSET );
        can_str  = XmStringCreate( "Cancel", XmSTRING_DEFAULT_CHARSET );
        next_str = XmStringCreate( "Next",   XmSTRING_DEFAULT_CHARSET );
        done_str = XmStringCreate( "Done",   XmSTRING_DEFAULT_CHARSET );
}




/*****************************************************************************
**                                                                         **
**   ManageFindDB()                                                        **
**                                                                         **
**   Called when the dialog box is first presented, this function          **
**   manages the DB and sets the labels of its buttons to "Find"           **
**   and "Cancel". It also sets the "finding" flag FALSE, for the          **
**   first call to FindCB.                                                  **
**                                                                         **
*****************************************************************************/
```

Listing 13.2. Continued.

```c
void ManageFindDB()
{
    XtManageChild( find_db );
    _XmGrabTheFocus( find_txt );

    XtSetArg( arglist[0], XmNlabelString, find_str );
    XtSetValues( find_btn_1, arglist, 1 );
    XtSetArg( arglist[0], XmNlabelString, can_str );
    XtSetValues( find_btn_2, arglist, 1 );
    finding = FALSE;
}



/**********************************************************************
**                                                                  **
**    FindCB( w, client_data, call_data )                           **
**                                                                  **
**    Called from the "Find" or "Next" buttons of the Find DB. This **
**    function searches for the first/next occurrence of the search **
**    string, and selects it.                                       **
**                                                                  **
**********************************************************************/

static void FindCB( w, client_data, call_data )
    Widget                w;
    char                  *client_data;
    XmAnyCallbackStruct   *call_data;
{
    static int            curpos;
    char                  *findstr,
                          *txtbuf,
                          *txtptr;
    int                   start,
                          end;

    if (!finding)
```

Listing 13.2. Continued.

```c
        {
        finding = TRUE;
        curpos  = 0;
        XtSetArg( arglist[0], XmNlabelString, next_str );
        XtSetValues( find_btn_1, arglist, 1 );
        XtSetArg( arglist[0], XmNlabelString, done_str );
        XtSetValues( find_btn_2, arglist, 1 );
        }

    findstr = XmTextGetString( find_txt );
    txtbuf  = XmTextGetString( textwin );
    txtptr  = StrFind( (txtbuf + curpos), findstr );
    if (txtptr == NULL)
        XtUnmanageChild( find_db );
    else
        {
        start = txtptr - txtbuf;
        end   = start + strlen(findstr);
        XtSetArg( arglist[0], XmNcursorPosition, end );
        XtSetValues( textwin, arglist, 1 );
        XmTextSetSelection( textwin, start, end,
                                    call_data->event->xbutton.time );

        curpos = start + 1;
        }
    XtFree( txtbuf );
    XtFree( findstr );
}


/**********************************************************************
**                                                                  **
**   FindCanCB( w, client_data, call_data )                         **
**                                                                  **
**   Called from the "Cancel" or "OK" buttons of the Find DB. This  **
**   simply unmanages the DB.                                       **
**                                                                  **
**********************************************************************/
```

Listing 13.2. Continued.

```c
static void FindCanCB( w, client_data, call_data )
    Widget              w;
    char                *client_data;
    XmAnyCallbackStruct *call_data;
{
    XtUnmanageChild( find_db );
}


/*************************************************************************
**                                                                     **
**   StrFind( s1, s2 )                                                 **
**                                                                     **
**   Returns a pointer to the first occurrence of string s2 in         **
**   string s1. Returns NULL is s2 does not occur in s1.               **
**                                                                     **
*************************************************************************/

char *StrFind( s1, s2 )
    char            *s1;
    char            *s2;
{
    char            *tmps1;
    char            *tmps2;

    for ( ; *s1 != '\0'  ; s1++)
        if (*s1 == *s2)
            {
            tmps1 = s1;
            tmps2 = s2;
            for ( ; (*s1 == *tmps2) && (*s1 != '\0') ; *s1++, *tmps2++)
                ;
            if (*tmps2 == '\0')
                return( tmps1 );
            }
    return( NULL );
}
```

Listing 13.2. Continued.

```
!###########################################################################
!
! Find Dialog Resources
!
!###########################################################################

*FindDB.width:                  180
*FindDB.autoUnmanage:           FALSE
*FindDB.dialogTitle:            Find...
*FindDB.marginWidth:            0

*FindDB.*.background:           Gray75
*FindDB.*.foreground:           Black
*FindDB.*.topShadowColor:       White
*FindDB.*.bottomShadowColor:    Gray50

*Find_Lbl.x:                    10
*Find_Lbl.y:                    12
*Find_Lbl.width:                40
*Find_Lbl.labelString:          Find:

*Find_Txt.x:                    50
*Find_Txt.y:                    10
*Find_Txt.width:                120

*Find_Sep.x:                    0
*Find_Sep.y:                    40
*Find_Sep.width:                180

*Find_Btn1.x:                   10
*Find_Btn1.y:                   50
*Find_Btn1.width:               60
*Find_Btn1.recomputeSize:       FALSE
*Find_Btn1.showAsDefault:       1

*Find_Btn2.x:                   110
*Find_Btn2.y:                   54
*Find_Btn2.width:               60
*Find_Btn2.recomputeSize:       FALSE
```

InitFindDB

The InitFindDB function initializes the dialog box and its five children: one label,
one text field, one separator, and two buttons. Widget creation is

straightforward, using the appropriate function for each child. Note again that the bulletin board is not managed after creation, but its children are.

`InitFindDB` gets interesting after all of the widgets have been created. By design, the left button performs an action — **Find** or **Next** — and the right button makes the dialog box disappear. Thus, there are two callback functions: one performs a search, the other unmanages the dialog. Since **Find/Next** is going to be the one most often used, I explicitly make it the default button, by setting the bulletin-board's `defaultButton` resource.

Finally, I create four compound strings, containing possible labels for the two buttons. Since the four tasks of this dialog box — **Find**, **Next**, **Cancel**, and **Done** — are really two tasks — **Find** and **Cancel** — I decided to use two button widgets and install the appropriate string into each button's `labelString` resource. The alternative, four pushbuttons, would mean managing the appropriate buttons for the situation. That method would result in more work for the program, as well as increased communication between the program and server. Its benefit would be that the button labels would reside in the resource file, where they could be easily changed.

ManageFindDB

The `ManageFindDB` function is called from the **Edit** menu callback function. It manages the dialog and initializes it for a new search. This initialization has two parts: setting the labels on the pushbuttons (to **Find** and **Cancel**) and setting a flag variable. This flag variable is then used to control the operations performed by the `FindCB` function.

A third part is the call to `_XmGrabTheFocus`.[15] When the dialog is managed, it becomes the topmost window and automatically receives focus. However, it has no way of determining which child is to receive focus; this must be done by the program.

FindCB

`FindCB` is the callback function attached to the dialog's left pushbutton — it is called for the **Find** and **Next** operations. The `finding` flag indicates whether or not the dialog has just been managed — whether this is a **Find** or **Next** operation. If it is a **Find**, the search position must be initialized to the first character of the text buffer.[16] In addition, the pushbutton labels must be changed to **Next** and **Done**, in preparation for future user interaction.

---

[15] This function is undocumented and specific to Motif 1.0. In Motif 1.1, it is replaced by the function `XmProcessTraversal`.

[16] Most editors "find" from the current insertion point. When I use such an editor, I almost always go to the first line before starting the search. As a result, this editor starts its searches from the beginning of the text buffer. To change this operation, merely get the contents of the text widget's `cursorPosition` resource, and use that value to initialize `curpos`.

The next step is to retrieve the search string and the contents of the editor's text buffer, both of which are *XmText* widgets.[17] You may wonder why both strings are retrieved on each call of the callback function — why not just maintain a static pointer? In the case of the text buffer, the answer is that the contents of the text buffer might change between invocations of the callback function: as implemented, this dialog is modeless, meaning that the user can edit the text between successive searches.[18] The search string is retrieved every time because maintenance of a static pointer would involve freeing the contents of the pointer when — and where — the dialog is unmanaged. In the current implementation, both strings are retrieved and then disposed of inside the function — no need to be concerned with floating pointers.

The search operation happens next. The current position — which is zero for **Find** and nonzero for **Next** — is added to the start of the text buffer to produce the unsearched substring. The `StrFind` function (or `strstr`, if you use ANSI C) searches that substring for the search string. If it returns `NULL`, the search string was not found — and the dialog is unmanaged, because it is no longer useful.

If, on the other hand, the search string was found, it must be selected. This is a two step process: first the insertion point is positioned, then the actual text is selected. The insertion point movement is required because *XmText* does not force it to follow the selection. It must be done before the selection operation, however, because movement of the insertion point clears the selection.

The selection operation itself is performed by `XmTextSetSelection`. This function requires a server timestamp, which is retrieved from the event passed in the callback structure. The bounds of the selection are found from the start position and the length of the search string.

The final operation is cleanup. If the search string was found, the search position (`curpos`) must be updated to point to the unsearched portion of the buffer. In any case, the memory allocated by `XmTextGetString` must be freed to prevent this operation from leaking memory.

FindCanCB

The `FindCanCB` function — Find Cancel Callback — simply unmanages the dialog. It is invoked by the dialog's right pushbutton (**Cancel/Done**).

Resource File Changes

Most of the resource file changes are straightforward: they establish the size and position of the dialog's elements. The color scheme changes are important, because they visually distinguish the dialog from the parent program. The explicit change to the bulletin-board's `autoUnmanage` resource is also important: if this dialog is to be truly modeless — operating in cooperation with the program, not instead of it — it must not disappear when the user presses a button.

---

[17] For illustrative purposes only, this function directly accesses the editors text buffer. In a real program, I would hide `textwin` in another source file and provide interface functions for access.

[18] So if the user changes the size of the text buffer, and the find function uses a static copy of the buffer, then the positions it determines will be inaccurate — and the user will wonder why seemingly random parts of the text are being selected.

Summary

The most important point of this example is that program actions are invoked in response to events, and the program must treat each invocation in isolation. Whereas a traditional program would treat the user's interaction — manage, make choice, act on choice, etc. — as a linear sequence of operations, which could be handled in a single function, a Motif program cannot be implemented in that way. Instead, each callback function must be implemented without assumptions on what has (or has not) been previously invoked. The use of flags and static variables provides the only means of maintaining state information.

The use of a bulletin board as the base of this dialog limits the dialog in one very important way: the bounds of its usable area are fixed. Thus, if the user desires a larger entry field, the resource file must be changed — although the dialog has resize controls, these don't expand the fields. Building the dialog from *XmForm* instead of *XmBulletinBoard* would eliminate this problem; appropriate attachments would cause the dialog components to grow or shrink with the dialog.[19]

Finally, the abnormal exit case — not finding the string when instructed to search — is handled very poorly by this program: the dialog box simply disappears, without any indication of why it did so. This shortcoming could be solved by displaying a message dialog when the search fails, leading to the next topic.

Message Boxes

The **Find** dialog would be more user-friendly if it were to display a message when unable to find the search string. The **Exit** menu choice would be more user-friendly if it displayed a warning when the user attempted to quit without saving the workspace. Both of these problems can be solved with a *message box*: a dialog that exists to alert the user to a situation and allow him or her to react to it.

Figure 13.4 presents a sample message box, in this case, designed to warn the user about quitting without saving the workspace. Like other dialogs, a message-box is split into two areas: the presentation area contains the message, and the confirmation area contains buttons that allow the user to react to the message. For this dialog, pressing the **OK** button would quit without saving the program, pressing the **Cancel** button — or the *Return* key, since it's the default button — would abort the quit, and pressing the **Help** button would provide an explanation of the message — perhaps an explanation of how to use the **Save** function.

---

[19] When a dialog's size has been changed by the user, that size change is stored by the shell. Whenever the dialog is subsequently managed, it will use the most-recently specified size values — whether set by the program or by user interaction.

Figure 13.4. Sample message box

The exclamation point on the left side of the presentation area identifies this message box as a warning message. Motif provides a set of message icons, presented in Figure 13.5. Each icon represents a particular type of message, as described below.

Figure 13.5. Message-box icons

An *error dialog* — also known as an *action dialog* — presents the icon of Figure 13.5(a). This type of dialog is used when the program has encountered an error and requires the user to correct that error. An example would be "File System Full."

An *informational dialog* presents the icon of Figure 13.5(b). This type of dialog is used to present information that does not require user action. An example would be "234 records found".

A *question dialog*, represented by the icon of Figure 13.5(c), is presented when the program needs the user to answer a simple yes/no question. A communications program could use this type of dialog to indicate a busy line and ask whether it should redial.

A *warning dialog*, presenting the exclamation point icon of Figure 13.5(d), is a more urgent version of a question dialog. It is used where the user's response may have devastating effects — as when pressing the **OK** button will allow the program to quit without saving work in progress.[20]

A *work-in-progress* dialog, which uses the icon of Figure 13.5(e), is used before and while the program is performing a time-consuming task such as a database search. It gives the user a visual reminder that the program is in fact doing something — not just "sitting there." A work-in-progress dialog should allow the user to abort the operation, although this may not always be possible after the operation commences. If the program displays work-in-progress dialogs while the operation is being performed, it should — if possible — present an indication of how much work has been done ("Searching database ... 50% complete").

A final type of message box — the generic message box — by default does not display an icon. It is used where the program has information to present that does not fall into one of the above categories.

XmMessageBox

Message boxes could be implemented as custom dialogs, using a bulletin board, two labels (one for the message, one for the icon), a separator, and three buttons. However, since they are used so often, Motif provides a prebuilt message-box class, *XmMessageBox*.

As you might expect, *XmMessageBox* is derived from *XmBulletinBoard*, as shown by the class tree of Figure 13.6. It provides the labels, buttons, and separators as "hidden" children, along with resources to access those children. In addition, it provides resources specific to message-box configuration.

---

[20] This brings up a point about default buttons. The expected response to a question dialog is **OK**, while the expected response to an error dialog is **Cancel**. The programmer should be very careful to set the appropriate default button — a warning dialog should never default to **OK**.

Figure 13.6. *XmMessageBox* class tree

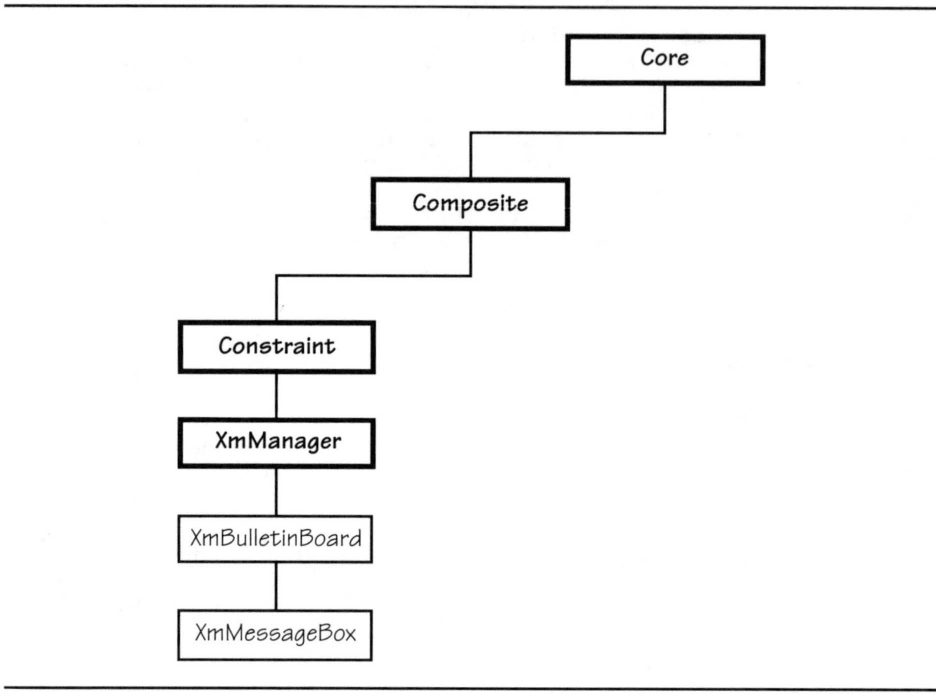

XmMessageBox **Resources**

XmMessageBox provides the resources listed in Table 13.3, along with resources defined by *XmBulletinBoard* and its superclasses. Note that Table 13.3 also includes the *XmManager* resource `helpCallback`; this resource is used only by *XmMessageBox* and other "prebuilt" dialogs.

Table 13.3. Frequently used resources: *XmMessageBox*

Name	Inheritance	Type	Default Value
`cancelCallback`	**XmMessageBox**	`XtCallbackList`	`NULL`
`cancelLabelString`	**XmMessageBox**	`XmString`	`"Cancel"`
`defaultButtonType`	**XmMessageBox**	`unsigned char`	`XmDIALOG_OK_BUTTON`
`dialogType`	**XmMessageBox**	`unsigned char`	`XmDIALOG_MESSAGE`
`helpLabelString`	**XmMessageBox**	`XmString`	`"Help"`

messageAlignment	XmMessageBox	unsigned char	XmALIGNMENT_BEGINNING
messageString	XmMessageBox	XmString	NULL
minimizeButtons	XmMessageBox	Boolean	FALSE
okCallback	XmMessageBox	XtCallbackList	NULL
okLabelString	XmMessageBox	XmString	"OK"
symbolPixmap	XmMessageBox	Pixmap	*dynamic*
helpCallback	XmManager	XtCallbackList	NULL

Use: dialogType

The dialogType resource specifies the message-box's purpose and is used by the dialog's internal code to select an appropriate icon to indicate purpose. This resource can hold one of the following constants:

- XmDIALOG_ERROR. The message box is used as an error (action) dialog.

- XmDIALOG_INFORMATION. The message box is used as an information dialog.

- XmDIALOG_MESSAGE. The message box is used as a generic message dialog (no icon).

- XmDIALOG_QUESTION. The message box is used as a question dialog.

- XmDIALOG_WARNING. The message box is used as a warning dialog.

- XmDIALOG_WORKING. The message box is used as a work-in-progress dialog.

Contents: messageString, symbolPixmap

The dialog's message string is held in the messageString resource. This resource is a "pass-through" to the message label's labelString resource. Its default value is "No Message".

The symbolPixmap resource is another pass-through, to the icon label's labelPixmap resource. The default value of this resource depends on the configuration of the message box, as specified by the dialogType resource.[21]

Appearance: messageAlignment, minimizeButtons

The message-box's messageAlignment resource is a pass-through to the message label's alignment resource. Unlike a normal label, the default value is XmALIGNMENT_BEGINNING, for a left-aligned message.

---

[21] If the symbolPixmap resource is explicitly specified, it takes precedence over the default pixmap. This allows the programmer to develop custom alerts based on a generic message box.

The `minimizeButtons` resource controls the size and position of the message-box buttons. If it contains `FALSE` (the default), all buttons are the same size — their preferred size. In essence, `minimizeButtons` is both a pass-through to the buttons' `recomputeSize` resource and a control for the message-box's button size/position code.

Behavior: defaultButtonType

A normal message box holds three buttons in the presentation area, known as the **OK**, **Cancel**, and **Help** buttons. One of these buttons may be defined as the default button, activated simply by pressing the *Return* key. The `defaultButton` `type` resource specifies which button is the default: valid constants are `XmDIALOG_OK_BUTTON`, `XmDIALOG_CANCEL_BUTTON`, and `XmDIALOG_HELP_BUTTON`. By default, the **OK** (leftmost) button is the default button.

This resource controls the content of both the `defaultButton` resource of *XmBulletinBoard* and the `showAsDefault` resource of *XmPushButton*.

Button Labels: cancelLabelString, helpLabelString, okLabelString

These resources are pass-throughs to the buttons' `labelString` resources. By default, they contain the button's name: "OK", "Cancel", or "Help". If these names are inappropriate to the dialog's purpose, they should be changed — for example, in Figure 13.4, "Quit" would be better than "OK".

Callbacks: okCallback, cancelCallback, helpCallback

These resources are pass-throughs to the `activateCallback` resources of the message-box's buttons. If your message box has actions associated with it — such as saving the workspace — you should attach the callbacks to these resources, not to the buttons themselves.[22]

XmMessageBox **Convenience Functions**

Creation

Like other dialogs, a message box consists of two parts: a dialog shell and an *XmMessageBox* widget as its child. While these widgets may be created with discrete calls — `XmCreateDialogShell` followed by `XmCreateMessageBox` — Motif provides a creation function for each type of message.

These functions — `XmCreateErrorDialog`, `XmCreateInformationDialog`, `XmCreateMessageDialog`, `XmCreateQuestionDialog`, `XmCreateWarningDialog`, and `XmCreateWorkingDialog` — are similar to `XmCreateBulletinBoardDialog` in that they create an unmanaged widget as the child of a "hidden" dialog shell and

---

[22] You should note the *XmBulletinBoard* `autoUnmanage` resource is in effect and attaches callbacks directly to the buttons.

return the ID of that widget. The message-box creation functions are more complex, however, in that they automatically set the `dialogType` resource and create the dialog's hidden children.

XmMessageBoxGetChild

While a message-box's children are normally hidden from the program, and accessed via pass-through resources, there are occasions when they must be directly accessed by the program. An example of this need is the "Can't Find" message box: the user does not need **Cancel** or **Help** buttons, so they are unmanaged as soon as the dialog is created.

To access the child of a message box, you must use the `XmMessageBoxGetChild` function, prototyped in Listing 13.3. This function returns the ID of the child widget; its parameters are the ID of the message box (`w`) and a code indicating the desired child (`child`). This code must be one of the following constants:

- `XmDIALOG_MESSAGE_LABEL`. Returns the ID of the label responsible for displaying the message.

- `XmDIALOG_SYMBOL_LABEL`. Returns the ID of the label responsible for displaying the message-box's icon.

- `XmDIALOG_SEPARATOR`. Returns the ID of the separator between the presentation and confirmation areas.

- `XmDIALOG_OK_BUTTON`. Returns the ID of the **OK** button.

- `XmDIALOG_CANCEL_BUTTON`. Returns the ID of the **Cancel** button.

- `XmDIALOG_HELP_BUTTON`. Returns the ID of the **Help** button.

- `XmDIALOG_DEFAULT_BUTTON`. Returns the ID of the default button — determined from the contents of the `defaultButtonType` resource.

Listing 13.3. Function prototype: *XmMessageBoxGetChild*

```
Widget   XmMessageBoxGetChild( w, child )
         Widget          w;
         unsigned char   child;
```

XmMessageBox Example: "Can't Find" Alert

The text editor's method of terminating a search operation — simply unmanaging the dialog box — is an example of poor user-interface design. A user familiar with the program will know what has happened, but a novice will wonder if it has somehow crashed. To fix this problem, the search operation should display a message box indicating that the search was completed. Figure

13.7 presents such a message box. In operation, the user simply clicks the **OK** button or presses the *Return* key to make the message disappear.[23]

Figure 13.7. "Search Complete" message

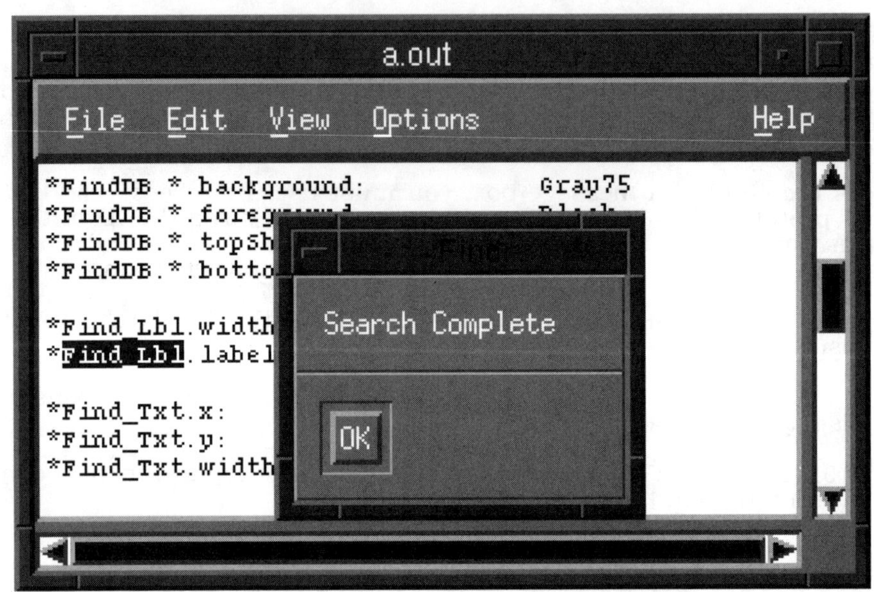

This message box was implemented using the code fragments of Listing 13.4. All changes are local to the find-dialog module. The first is at the end of the `InitFindDB` function: it is the creation of the message box. The second is in `FindCB`: it manages the message box. The third segment contains the additional resources. Not shown here is the declaration of `cantfind_db`, a variable of type `Widget`.

---

[23] This brings up another element of user-interface design: a sophisticated user will be inconvenienced by the need to explicitly send the dialog away. Optimally, the program should have a resource that controls the presence or absence of the "Search Complete" message.

Listing 13.4. Text editor revision 7: "Search Complete" dialog

```c
void InitFindDB()
{
    .
    .
    .

    cantfind_db = XmCreateMessageDialog( mainwin, "CantFind", NULL, 0 );
    temp = XmMessageBoxGetChild( cantfind_db, XmDIALOG_CANCEL_BUTTON );
    XtUnmanageChild( temp );
    temp = XmMessageBoxGetChild( cantfind_db, XmDIALOG_HELP_BUTTON );
    XtUnmanageChild( temp );
}
```

```c
static void FindCB( w, client_data, call_data )
    Widget              w;
    char                *client_data;
    XmAnyCallbackStruct *call_data;
{
    .
    .
    .
    .

    if (txtptr == NULL)
        {
        XtUnmanageChild( find_db );
        XtManageChild( cantfind_db );
        }
    .
    .
    .
}
```

```
!################################################################################
!
! "Can't Find" Alert Resources
!
!################################################################################

*CantFind.dialogTitle:          Find...
*CantFind.messageString:        Search Complete
```

The major change is to `InitFindDB`: it now creates both the find dialog and its find-complete message box.[24] Note that the **Cancel** and **Help** buttons are retrieved from the message box and then unmanaged. As they would serve no purpose to the dialog — the user's only choice is to acknowledge it — they would be a distraction.

The second change, to `FindCB`, is straightforward. You may wonder, however, why the **Find** dialog was unmanaged — shouldn't it remain on-screen until the user acknowledges the alert? The answer is that doing so would require another callback, attached to the message-box's **OK** button, that would unmanage the **Find** dialog — a result of the asynchronous nature of a Motif program.[25]

The resource file segment illustrates one of my naming conventions: the title of the message box duplicates the title of the dialog box and menu choice with which it is associated. My belief is that this presents the user with a more consistent interface.

Grabbing and Assigning Input Focus

Early in this book it was mentioned that grabbing the input focus is an impolite action, one that causes the user to distrust a program. In this chapter, however, you saw where a grab was necessary, to properly assign the focus within a dialog box.

In a normal toolkit-based program, you would use the function `XtSetKeyboardFocus` to perform a grab. However, this function should not be used in a Motif program because it interferes with the traversal mechanism — the traversal mechanism considers a particular widget to have the focus, when in reality another does.

The problem is solved with a Motif-specific function. For Motif 1.0, this is the undocumented function `_XmGrabTheFocus`, for 1.1 and above, it is `XmProcessTraversal`. Both functions are prototyped in Listing 13.5 and described below.

Listing 13.5. Function prototypes: *_XmGrabTheFocus*, *XmProcessTraversal*

```
Boolean _XmGrabTheFocus( w )
        Widget       w;


Boolean XmProcessTraversal( w, direction )
        Widget       w;
        int          direction;
```

---

[24] The creation of this message box is sufficiently trivial that I decided to create it as part of the "Find Module" initialization. In the completed editor, it is part of the "Alerts Module."

Both functions take the widget that is to receive the focus as an argument, and both return a boolean value indicating whether or not the operation was successful. `XmProcessTraversal` takes an additional parameter, which indicates the traversal operation to be performed. This operation is identified by one of the following constants:

- `XmTRAVERSE_CURRENT`. Set focus to the specified widget. If specified widget is a manager that is also a tab group, give focus to the first item in that tab group.

- `XmTRAVERSE_HOME`. In the tab group that contains the specified widget, give focus to the first widget.

- `XmTRAVERSE_NEXT`, `XmTRAVERSE_DOWN`, `XmTRAVERSE_RIGHT`. In the tab group that contains the specified widget, give focus to the widget after the specified widget.

- `XmTRAVERSE_PREV`, `XmTRAVERSE_UP`, `XmTRAVERSE_LEFT`. In the tab group that contains the specified widget, give focus to the widget before the specified widget.

- `XmTRAVERSE_NEXT_TAB_GROUP`. Set focus to the first widget in the tab group following the tab group that contains the specified widget.

- `XmTRAVERSE_PREV_TAB_GROUP`. Set focus to the first widget in the tab group preceding the tab group that contains the specified widget.

---

[25] This is also a matter of personal preference. My feeling is that once the find completes, the dialog has no reason to remain on the screen.

14
Lists

Overview

Lists are an ubiquitous element of programs built with a graphical user interface and are used for purposes ranging from file selection to command history. They are so widely used because they provide the user with an easy method of selecting one or more related items, acting as a middle ground — in terms of flexibility and immediacy of input — between menus and entry fields.

This chapter begins with the basic Motif list widget, *XmList*. It then presents the scrolled list, *XmList* as a child of *XmScrolledWindow*, and uses it to allow selection of e-mail addresses. Following this is *XmSelectionBox*, a combination of a scrolled list, text field, and buttons, used for list-based dialogs. Next is *XmFileSelectionBox*, a "pre-built" *XmSelectionBox*-based dialog, used to select files; it is used to implement the **Open...** and **Save As...** menu choices for the text editor. The chapter closes with *XmCommand*, an *XmSelectionBox*-based widget that allows textual data entry and maintains a history of previously entered strings.

XmList

Figure 14.1 presents an example of lists in use to select addresses for an e-mail program. This example contains two lists: the top list provides a catalog of e-mail addresses, and the bottom list contains selected addresses. One item in the top list is selected — the mouse button was clicked while the pointer was positioned over the item. The program then copied this item into the second list to join an existing member.

Figure 14.1. *XmList* example: E-mail address book

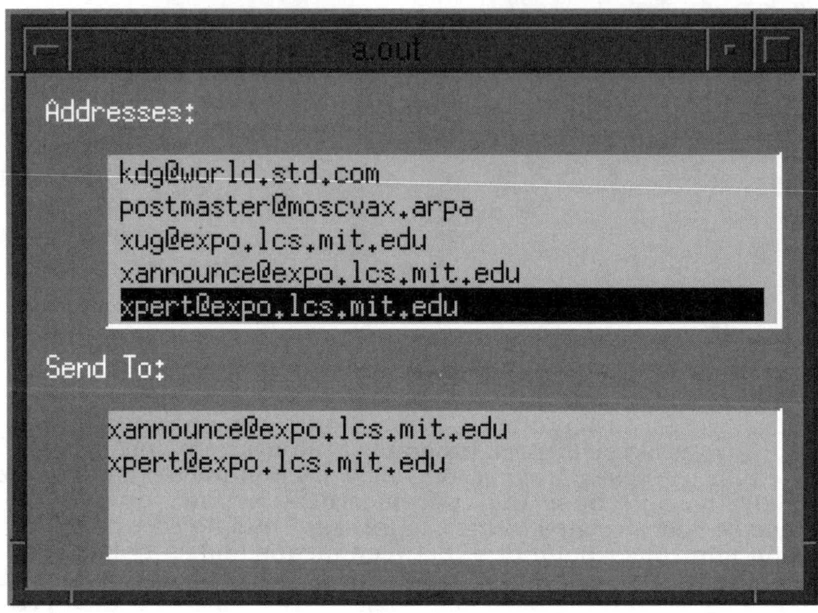

XmList is a primitive widget, derived as shown by the class tree of Figure 14.2. It is similar to the *XmText* widget in that it maintains textual data, organized in a rectangular array. Unlike *XmText*, *XmList* does not treat its contents as discrete characters, nor does it permit the user to change its contents. Instead, *XmList* maintains its contents as an array of `XmStrings`, which the program may modify.

Figure 14.2. *XmList* class tree

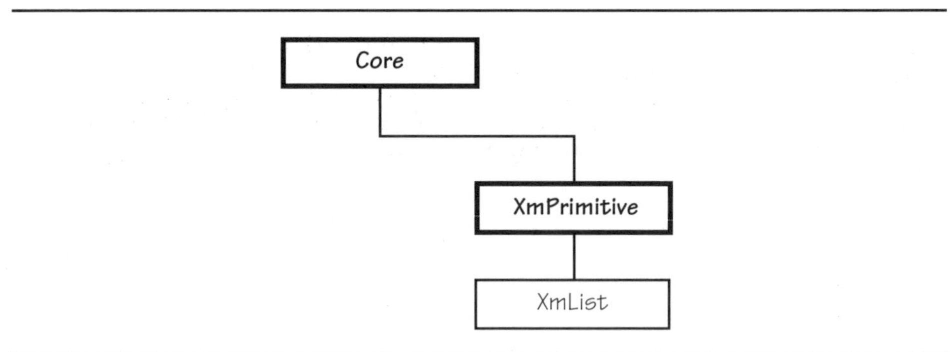

In operation, an *XmList* widget actually maintains *two* lists: the first is the list of selectable items: the widget's contents. The second is the list of selected items: those items that the user has chosen from the first list.

Selection is performed by clicking the mouse's *Select* button (button #1) while the pointer is positioned over a list item. If that item is not already selected, it becomes selected; if it is already selected, it is deselected. A selected item is indicated by "inverse video:" reversal of its foreground and background colors.

Depending on the widget's configuration, it may permit the user to select a single item or any number of items — up to the number of items in the list. In *Single Selection* mode, the user is permitted to select only one item at a time; selecting an item deselects the previously selected item (if any). *Browse Selection* mode is a refinement of single-selection mode: only one item may be selected, but the user may drag the pointer over the items in the list; each item is temporarily highlighted while the pointer is over it, and when the button is released, the item under the pointer is selected.[1] In *Multiple Selection* mode, the widget allows the user to select multiple items by clicking on each one. In *Extended Selection* mode, the widget permits the user to select multiple contiguous items, either by dragging the pointer over them or by clicking on one item, then clicking on another while the *Shift* key is pressed.[2]

A list may also be traversed and selected using the keyboard, if traversal is on. In this case, the *Up* and *Down* arrow keys move between items in the list. For extended selection, the *Shift* and *Ctrl* keys act as they do for mouse-oriented selection.[3]

XmList Resources

XmList provides the resources listed in Table 14.1 and described below. In addition, it provides those resources defined by *Core* and *XmPrimitive*.

Table 14.1. Frequently used resources: *XmList*

Name	Inheritance	Type	Default Value
automaticSelection	XmList	Boolean	FALSE
browseSelection Callback	XmList	XtCallbackList	NULL
defaultAction Callback	XmList	XtCallbackList	NULL
doubleClickInterval	XmList	int	250

---

[1] *Browse Selection* is equivalent to the way that a menu choice is highlighted when the user drags the pointer over it.

[2] Additional noncontiguous groups may be added by pressing the *Ctrl* key while starting a new selection.

[3] Because *XmList* changes the default traversal functions of the *Up* and *Down* arrow keys, a list must be the sole occupant of a tab group.

Table 14.1. Continued.

extendedSelection Callback	XmList	XtCallbackList	NULL
fontList	XmList	XmFontList	"fixed"
itemCount	XmList	int	0
items	XmList	XmStringTable	NULL
listMarginHeight	XmList	Dimension	0
listMarginWidth	XmList	Dimension	0
listSpacing	XmList	short	0
multipleSelection Callback	XmList	XtCallbackList	NULL
selectedItemCount	XmList	int	0
selectedItems	XmList	XmStringTable	NULL
selectionPolicy	XmList	unsigned char	XmBROWSE_SELECT
singleSelection Callback	XmList	XtCallbackList	NULL
stringDirection	XmList	XmString-Direction	XmSTRING_DIRECTION_L_TO_R
visibleItemCount	XmList	int	1

Appearance: fontList, listMarginHeight, listMarginWidth, listSpacing, stringDirection, visibleItemCount

Like *XmText*, *XmList* provides a margin between its borders and its contents to improve readability. For *XmList*, this margin is specified by the resources listMarginHeight and listMarginWidth: listMarginHeight specifies the margin between the contents and the top and bottom sides; listMarginWidth specifies the margin between the contents and the left and right sides. Also, for readability, *XmList* provides the listSpacing resource, which specifies the distance between items in the list. All of these resources contain pixel counts, converted according to unitType.

Also, like *XmText*, the height of an *XmList* may be determined from the number of rows it displays. *XmText* uses the rows resource for this purpose, *XmList* uses the visibleItemCount resource. This resource is used in a calculation involving the height of the widget's font, the interitem spacing, and the top and bottom margins. The default value of one guarantees that the list is visible. The height determined from the visibleItemCount resource is superseded by an explicit height specification or parental constraint.

As an *XmList* widget displays compound strings, it needs resources to control the way in which it displays such strings. Like *XmLabel*, it provides fontList and `stringDirection` resources: `fontList` specifies the font for display, while `stringDirection` specifies the default output direction for strings that do not have a direction component. Like *XmLabel,* the default values for these resources are the "fixed" font (`fontList`) and left-to-right (`stringDirection`).

Selection Model: selectionPolicy

As stated above, a list widget provides four selection models. The `selectionPolicy` resource controls this behavior; it may contain one of the following constants:

- `XmSINGLE_SELECT`. The list widget is configured for single selection mode: each click of the mouse button selects one item and deselects any previously selected item.

- `XmBROWSE_SELECT`. The list widget is configured for browse selection mode: when the pointer is dragged (with the button down) over each list item, it is highlighted; when the button is released, the currently highlighted item is selected, replacing any previous selection.

- `XmMULTIPLE_SELECT`. The list widget is configured for multiple selection mode: each click of the mouse button adds the clicked-on item to the selected-items list. If the item was previously selected, it is removed from the selected-items list.

- `XmEXTENDED_SELECT`. The list widget is configured for extended selection mode: multiple contiguous items may be added to (or removed from) the selected-items list by dragging the pointer over the items.

Behavior: automaticSelection, doubleClickInterval

As you will see below, *XmList* provides a callback for each selection mode. Normally, only the callback appropriate to the current mode is called, and it is only called when the user releases the mouse button. However, if the `automaticSelection` resource contains `TRUE`, the callback for single selection mode will be called in browse selection or extended selection mode. If these conditions are met — `selectionPolicy` contains `XmBROWSE_SELECT` or `XmEXTENDED_SELECT`, and `automaticSelection` contains `TRUE`— then the single selection callback is invoked whenever the pointer passes over an item while the button is down.

An *XmList* widget provides a "default action" callback, called when the user double-clicks on a list item. This callback is often used in a dialog box to select a single item and then invoke the callback(s) associated with the dialog's **OK** button. The `doubleClickInterval` resource controls the list's recognition of double clicks: it specifies the maximum time interval, in milliseconds, that may elapse between two successive clicks if they are to be considered a double click. The default value is 250 for a maximum elapsed time of ¼ second.

Contents: itemCount, items

The items presented by an *XmList* widget are accessed by its items resource, which contains an array of pointers to compound strings.[4] This array and the strings to which it points are maintained by the widget and are part of the widget's internal data. The array represented by the items resource contains all items maintained by the list, selected or unselected.

The itemCount resource specifies the number of items in the list. If the program installs items using the XtSetValues function, it must specify the number of items as well as the array itself. If, however, the program manages the list using the convenience functions described below, it need not explicitly change either items or itemCount: the convenience functions handle all needed changes.

Selected Items: selectedItemCount, selectedItems

An *XmList* widget actually maintains two lists: a list of items and a list of selected items. The resources selectedItems and selectedItemCount represent this second list: selectedItems is an array of XmString pointers, while selectedItemCount specifies the number of items in this array.

These resources exist for reading only. They are maintained by the widget in response to user (and program) selection operations.

XmList Callbacks

XmList provides a callback resource for each selection mode and invokes the function(s) specified by that resource whenever an item is selected. It also provides a "default action" callback, which is invoked when the user double-clicks a list item. All of these callbacks use the XmListCallbackStruct structure for their call data; it is defined in Listing 14.1 and described below.

Listing 14.1. Type definition: XmListCallbackStruct

```
typedef struct
        {
        int         reason;
        XEvent      *event;
        XmString    item;
        int         item_length;
        int         item_position;
        XmString    *selected_items;
        int         selected_item_count;
        int         selection_type;
        }
XmListCallbackStruct;
```

---

[4] The XmStringTable data type is defined as follows:
```
    typedef XmString *XmStringTable;
```
  As XmString is a pointer, this definition is equivalent to XmString array[];

As with other callback structures, the `reason` member specifies the type of callback, and the `event` member is a pointer to the event that caused the callback to be invoked. The `item` member is a pointer to the selected item, and the `item_length` member contains the number of bytes occupied by the item's compound string.[5] The `item_position` member specifies the item's position in the array represented by the `items` resource. Unlike most array indices, list position values start at one.

The `selected_items`, `selected_item_count`, and `selection_type` members are used only when the selection model allows multiple items to be selected (`selectionPolicy` contains `XmMULTIPLE_SELECT` or `XmEXTENDED_SELECT`). The `selected_items` member contains a pointer to an array of `XmString` pointers, equivalent to the `selectedItems` resource.[6] The `selected_item_count` resource contains the number of items in this array; it is equivalent to the `selectedItemCount` resource.

The `selection_type` member provides additional detail about the conditions at the time the callback was invoked. It may contain the constants `XmINITIAL`, `XmMODIFICATION`, or `XmADDITION`. `XmINITIAL` specifies that this callback contains the first item(s) selected, `XmMODIFICATION` indicates a change to the selection list, and `XmADDITION` indicates that the change is a noncontiguous addition.

Selection: browseSelectionCallback, extendedSelectionCallback, multipleSelectionCallback, singleSelectionCallback

Each of these callbacks is associated with a particular list configuration and is invoked when a list item is selected. Each presents a different callback reason: `browseSelectionCallback` uses `XmCR_BROWSE_SELECT`, `extendedSelectionCallback` uses `XmCR_EXTENDED_SELECT`, `multipleSelectionCallback` uses `XmCR_MULTIPLE_SELECT`, and `singleSelectionCallback` uses `XmCR_SINGLE_SELECT`.

Double-Click: defaultActionCallback

In some situations, such as a file-selection dialog, the user is expected to select an item from a list, then confirm the selection by performing some other action, such as pressing a button. In these cases, a sophisticated user could be better served by combining the selection and confirmation actions, which is why `defaultActionCallback` exists. It is called when the user double-clicks on a list item.

As with other list callbacks, this callback passes call data in `XmListCallbackStruct`; the valid members for this callback are `reason`, `event`, `item`, `item_length`, and `item_position`. The reason associated with this callback is `XmCR_DEFAULT_ACTION`.

---

[5] The string accessed by `item` is allocated prior to callback invocation and destroyed when the callback completes. If the program needs to preserve this string, it must make a local copy.

[6] It points at a copy of the `selectedItems` resource, which is allocated before the list of callbacks is invoked and destroyed after the callback functions are finished. If the program needs to preserve strings from this list, it must make a local copy.

XmList Convenience Functions

Programs typically perform extensive manipulation of the items in a list. To simplify these operations — and minimize direct access to the list's resources — Motif provides a set of convenience functions, prototyped in Listing 14.2 and described below.

Listing 14.2. Function prototypes: *XmList* convenience functions

```
void      XmListAddItem( w, item, position )
          Widget     w;
          XmString   item;
          int        position;


void      XmListAddItemUnselected( w, item, position )
          Widget     w;
          XmString   item;
          int        position;


void      XmListDeleteItem( w, item )
          Widget     w;
          XmString   item;


void      XmListDeletePos( w, position )
          Widget     w;
          int        position;


void      XmListDeselectAllItems( w )
          Widget     w;


void      XmListDeselectItem( w, item )
          Widget     w;
          XmString   item;


void      XmListDeselectPos( w, position )
```

Listing 14.2. Continued.

```
        Widget      w;
        int         position;


Boolean XmListItemExists( w, item )
        Widget      w;
        XmString    item;


void    XmListSelectItem( w, item, notify )
        Widget      w;
        XmString    item;
        Boolean     notify;


void    XmListSelectPos( w, position, notify )
        Widget      w;
        int         position;
        Boolean     notify;


void    XmListSetBottomItem( w, item )
        Widget      w;
        XmString    item;


void    XmListSetBottomPos( w, position )
        Widget      w;
        int         position;

void    XmListSetItem( w, item )
        Widget      w;
        XmString    item;


void    XmListSetPos( w, position )
        Widget      w;
        int         position;
```

All of the convenience functions use some combination of the parameters w, item, and position. The w parameter is the ID of the list widget and is required by all functions. The item parameter is used by those functions that identify a list item by content. Such functions operate on the first item in the list that matches the passed string. The position parameter is used by those functions that identify an item by its position. Position values start at one, with zero used to indicate the last item in the list — whatever its absolute position may be.

Adding Items: XmListAddItem, XmListAddItemUnselected

`XmListAddItem` and `XmListAddItemUnselected` both add an item to the list. Both specify the ID of the list widget, the string to add, and the position that the new item is to occupy. The difference between these functions is that `XmListAddItem` compares the new item with the list of items in the `selectedItems` resource; if the new item matches an existing selected item, it is selected when added to the list. XmListAddItemUnselected does not perform this comparison, and the new item is not selected.

Deleting Items: XmListDeleteItem, XmListDeletePos

To remove items from a list, use `XmListDeleteItem` or `XmListDeletePos`. The item is specified by content for `XmListDeleteItem`, by position for `XmListDeletePos`. When an item is deleted, it is removed from the list and the `listItems` resource is decremented. If the item is selected, it is also removed from `selectedItems`.

Selection: XmListSelectItem, XmListSelectPos, XmListDeselectItem, XmListDeselectPos, XmListDeselectAllItems

These functions select or deselect items in the list. `XmListSelectItem` selects an item by content, `XmListSelectPos` selects an item by position, `XmListDeselectItem` deselects an item by content, `XmListDeselectPos` deselects an item by position, and `XmListDeselectAllItems` deselects all items in the list. If the program attempts to select an item that is already selected, it is deselected; attempting to deselect an unselected item has no effect.

The list's selection model affects programmatic selection in the same way that it affects user-controlled selection: if the list is in single-selection or browse-selection mode, the program may not select multiple items. When the program selects an item from a list configured in either mode, any previously selected item is deselected.

The `XmListSelectItem` and `XmListSelectPos` functions have a third parameter, `notify`. This parameter controls whether or not the appropriate selection callback is invoked. If passed `TRUE`, the callback is invoked; if passed `FALSE`, the callback is not invoked. To the callback function, the only difference between invocation as a result of programmatic selection is that the `event` member of the call data structure contains `NULL`.

As a final note, remember that those functions that identify a list item by content pick the first such item in the list. Consider a list that has two items that are identical, both of which are selected. If the program calls `XmListDeselectItem`, it will always act on the first such item — the second will remain selected, no matter how many calls are made.

Query: ListItemExists

The `ListItemExists` function searches the list for an item identical to the string passed in its `item` parameter. If it finds such an item, it returns `TRUE`; if not, it returns `FALSE`. There is no way to determine *how many* items match the specification: `ListItemExists` returns when it finds the first match.

Appearance: XmListSetItem, XmListSetPos, XmListSetBottomItem, XmListSetBottomPos

Like a text widget, a list may contain more items than it can display. In such a case, the program can set the range of displayed items using these functions: `XmListSetItem` specifies the first displayed item by content, `XmListSetPos` specifies the first displayed item by position, `XmListSetBottomItem` specifies the last displayed item by content, and `XmListSetBottomPos` specifies the last displayed item by position.

Note that the physical size of the widget is the real determinant of how many items are displayed. When one of these functions is called, the displayed content of the list is redetermined, based on the specified top of bottom item.

XmList Example: E-Mail Address Selection

Figure 14.1 was produced using the program and resource file of Listing 14.3. This program only needs five widgets: a form as the parent, two labels, and two lists. For that reason, the trivial program template was chosen. Additional program notes are below the listing.

Listing 14.3. Program and resource file: E-mail address selector

```
/*********************************************************************
**                                                                 **
**   listing_14_3.c                                                **
**                                                                 **
**   List example. This program simulates address selection for an **
**   e-mail program. It presents two lists: the top list contains  **
**   all known e-mail addresses, the second contains the addresses **
**   for the current message. These lists are maintained in a form,**
**   so they may be expanded as needed.                            **
**                                                                 **
**   In a real program, this code would be in a dialog box, with the**
**   addresses read from a data file.                              **
**                                                                 **
*********************************************************************/


#include <Xm/Form.h>
```

Listing 14.3. Continued.

```c
#include <Xm/Label.h>
#include <Xm/List.h>


void    LoadAddressList();               /* FORWARD Definitions       */
void    AddressListCB();


Widget  appshell,                        /* Application Shell         */
        the_form,                        /* Child of the shell        */
        catlist,                         /* Address Catalog list
*/
cat_lbl,                     /* Address Catalog label       */
        sellist,                         /* Selected Addresses list   */
        sel_lbl;                         /* Selected Addresses label  */
Arg     arglist[16];                     /* Used to set resources     */


#define    XMS( s )     XmStringCreate( s, XmSTRING_DEFAULT_CHARSET )


void main( argc, argv )
    int     argc;
    char    *argv[];
{
    appshell = XtInitialize( argv[0], "Listing_14_3", NULL, 0,
                                        &argc, argv );

    the_form = XmCreateForm( appshell, "TheForm", NULL, 0 );
    XtManageChild( the_form );

    cat_lbl = XmCreateLabel( the_form, "CatLbl", NULL, 0 );
    XtManageChild( cat_lbl );
    catlist = XmCreateList( the_form, "CatList", NULL, 0 );
    XtManageChild( catlist );

    LoadAddressList();
    XtAddCallback( catlist, XmNbrowseSelectionCallback,
                            AddressListCB, NULL );
```

Listing 14.3. Continued.

```c
    sel_lbl = XmCreateLabel( the_form, "SelLbl", NULL, 0 );
    XtManageChild( sel_lbl );
    sellist = XmCreateList( the_form, "SelList", NULL, 0 );
    XtManageChild( sellist );

    XtRealizeWidget( appshell );
    XtMainLoop();
}


/**
*** LoadAddressList()
***
*** Fills the "items" resource of "catlist". In the real world, this
*** function would read the addresses from a data file.
**/

void LoadAddressList()
{
    XmString    addresses[9];

    addresses[0] = XMS( "kdg@world.std.com" );
    addresses[1] = XMS( "postmaster@moscvax.arpa" );
    addresses[2] = XMS( "xug@expo.lcs.mit.edu" );
    addresses[3] = XMS( "xannounce@expo.lcs.mit.edu" );
    addresses[4] = XMS( "xpert@expo.lcs.mit.edu" );
    addresses[5] = XMS( "motif@alfalfa.com" );
    addresses[6] = XMS( "info-c@research.att.com" );
    addresses[7] = XMS( "std-unix@uunet.uu.net" );
    addresses[8] = XMS( "unix-wizards@brl.arpa" );

    XtSetArg( arglist[0], XmNitems, addresses );
    XtSetArg( arglist[1], XmNitemCount, XtNumber(addresses) );
    XtSetValues( catlist, arglist, 2 );
}


/**
```

Listing 14.3. Continued.

```
*** AddressListCB()
***
*** Address List Callback. This function is called whenever an address
*** in the top list is selected. It adds that address to the bottom
*** list, if it isn't already there.
**/

void AddressListCB( w, client_data, call_data )
    Widget                  w;
    caddr_t                 client_data;
    XmListCallbackStruct    *call_data;
{
    if (!XmListItemExists(sellist, call_data->item))
        XmListAddItem( sellist, call_data->item, 0 );
}
```

```
!
! Resource file for List example (Fig 14.1)
!

*.background:                       Gray50
*.foreground:                       White
*.topShadowColor:                   Gray75
*.bottomShadowColor:                Gray25

*.XmList.background:                Gray75
*.XmList.foreground:                Black
*.XmList.topShadowColor:            White
*.XmList.bottomShadowColor:         Gray50

*.XmForm.*.topAttachment:           ATTACH_POSITION
*.XmForm.*.bottomAttachment:        ATTACH_POSITION
*.XmForm.*.leftAttachment:          ATTACH_POSITION
*.XmForm.*.rightAttachment:         ATTACH_POSITION

*TheForm.height:                    200
*TheForm.width:                     300

*CatLbl.labelString:                Addresses:
*CatLbl.alignment:                  ALIGNMENT_BEGINNING
*CatLbl.topPosition:                5
*CatLbl.bottomPosition:             10
*CatLbl.leftPosition:               2
*CatLbl.rightPosition:              98
```

Listing 14.3. Continued.

```
*CatList.listMarginWidth:        5
*CatList.topPosition:            15
*CatList.bottomPosition:         50
*CatList.leftPosition:           10
*CatList.rightPosition:          98

*SelLbl.labelString:             Send To:
*SelLbl.alignment:               ALIGNMENT_BEGINNING
*SelLbl.topPosition:             55
*SelLbl.bottomPosition:          60
*SelLbl.leftPosition:            2
*SelLbl.rightPosition:           98

*SelList.topPosition:            65
*SelList.bottomPosition:         95
*SelList.leftPosition:           10
*SelList.rightPosition:          98
```

This program presents three items of interest: the `XMS` macro, the `LoadAddressList` function, and the `AddressListCB` function. The rest of the program is straightforward: it simply creates the widgets. The resource file is also straightforward, setting the size and appearance of the widgets. I used a form in this application so that it could be resized at will — some e-mail addresses can be quite long.

The `XMS` macro exists to minimize the amount of typing required to create a compound string — in particular, to eliminate the 24 characters of `XmSTRING_DEFAULT_CHARSET`. While the programs in this book — being limited to 72-character lines — especially benefit from such a device, I find it useful in any program that makes extensive use of compound strings.

The `LoadAddressList` function exists to fill the top list with the "universe" of addresses. As noted in the comment, in the real world, the list contents would be read from a data file and added to the list with `XmListAddItem`. For this example, I wanted to illustrate the format of the `items` resource. Note that `itemCount` is explicitly specified.

The `AddressListCB` function is attached to the top list's browse-selection callback. Its purpose is to add a selected item to the bottom list, if it is not already present in that list. It accesses the selected item directly from the call data and uses `XmListItemExists` to verify uniqueness.

Scrolled List

If you compare the program of Listing 14.3 with Figure 14.1, you will note that the top list contains nine items, but only five are displayed. While it is possible

— if traversal is enabled — to use the arrow keys to select the items, there is no visible indication that the additional items exist.

To solve this problem, Motif provides the scrolled list, shown in Figure 14.3. Like scrolled ext, a scrolled list uses an *XmList* widget as the child of an *XmScrolledWindow*. Also, like scrolled-text, this configuration intimately links the scrolled window and the list — meaning that they must be created at the same time, using the `XmCreateScrolledList` function.

Figure 14.3. Scrolled list

Scrolled List Resources

As with scrolled text, the name of the list widget is passed to `XmCreateScrolledList` and is given a suffix of "SW" to produce the scrolled-window's name. The program may set the scrolled-window's resources programmatically after getting its ID with `XtParent`, or via the resource file. Table 14.2 presents the default resource values of the scrolled window, along with *XmList*'s `listSizePolicy` resource, which is described below.

Table 14.2. Frequently used resources: *XmScrolledList*

Name	Inheritance	Type	Default Value
`listSizePolicy`	XmList	`unsigned char`	`XmVARIABLE`
`scrollBarDisplayPolicy`	XmScrolledWindow	`unsigned char`	`XmAS_NEEDED`
`scrollBarPlacement`	XmScrolledWindow	`unsigned char`	`XmBOTTOM_RIGHT`
`scrollingPolicy`	XmScrolledWindow	`unsigned char`	`XmAPPLICATION _DEFINED`

Scrolled-List Behavior: listSizePolicy

The `listSizePolicy` resource controls the horizontal growth of the list. It can contain one of the following constants:

- `XmCONSTANT`. The list does not attempt to change size. If an item is wider than the list's width, a horizontal scrollbar is added to the bottom of the list.

- `XmVARIABLE`. The list attempts to grow to match the width of its widest item. If not permitted to do so, it adds a horizontal scrollbar as above.

- `XmRESIZE_IF_POSSIBLE`. The list attempts to change its width to that of its widest displayed item.[7] If not permitted to do so, it adds a horizontal scrollbar as above.

The `listSizePolicy` resource must be set at the time the list is created, as it is used for initialization of the list and scrolled window. It may not be changed at a later time.

Scrolled List Example: Scrolling E-Mail Addresses

Figure 14.3 required minimal changes to the program and resource file of Listing 14.3: the calls to `XmCreateList` were replaced by `XmCreateScrolledList`, and the lists' positions were set via their scrolled-window parents, as shown in Listing 14.4. Note that, while both lists are scrolled lists, in Figure 14.3 only the top list has scrollbars; this is due to the value of `XmAS_NEEDED` for `scrollBarDisplayPolicy`.

---

[7] In this mode, the width of an unconstrained list will change as items are scrolled into the viewing area.

Listing 14.4. Program and resource file excerpts: Scrolled list example

```
    catlist = XmCreateScrolledList( the_form, "CatList", NULL, 0 );
    XtManageChild( catlist );



    sellist = XmCreateScrolledList( the_form, "SelList", NULL, 0 );
    XtManageChild( sellist );
```

```
*CatListSW.topPosition:        15
*CatListSW.bottomPosition:     50
*CatListSW.leftPosition:       10
*CatListSW.rightPosition:      98



*SelListSW.topPosition:        65
*SelListSW.bottomPosition:     95
*SelListSW.leftPosition:       10
*SelListSW.rightPosition:      98
```

XmSelectionBox

Since a primary usage of lists is in selection of a single item — such as an e-mail address — Motif provides the *XmSelectionBox* class. *XmSelectionBox* is a manager with "prebuilt" children, designed primarily for use in a dialog box. Like *XmMessageBox*, it is derived from *XmBulletinBoard*.

XmSelectionBox has nine standard children: two labels, a scrolled list, a text field, a separator, and four buttons. Figure 14.4 presents a list containing all but one of these children: the labels identify the list and text field, the list presents the possible addresses, the text field displays the currently selected address and allows it to be modified (or allows direct entry of an unlisted address), and the buttons invoke the lists actions.

The three buttons shown perform straightforward functions: **OK** confirms the address choice, **Cancel** negates the choice (and typically closes the dialog), and

Help would provide context-sensitive help. An optional fourth button, **Apply**, is used in cases where the list could be updated: it performs the update operation.

In addition to the nine standard children, an *XmSelectionBox* may contain a tenth child: a program-created work area. If used, this child is positioned between the list and entry field. It may be any type of widget, manager or primitive.

Figure 14.4. *XmSelectionBox* example: E-mail address selection

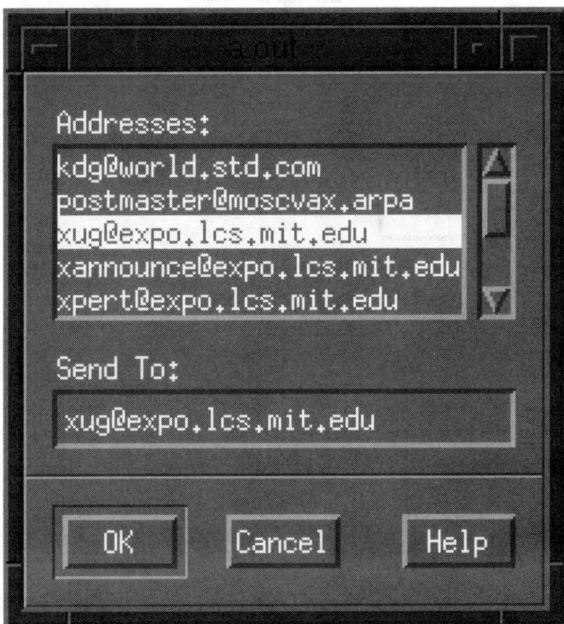

XmSelectionBox **Resources**

Like *XmMessageBox*, *XmSelectionBox* is derived from *XmBulletinBoard*, as shown by the class tree of Figure 14.5.

Figure 14.5. *XmSelectionBox* class tree

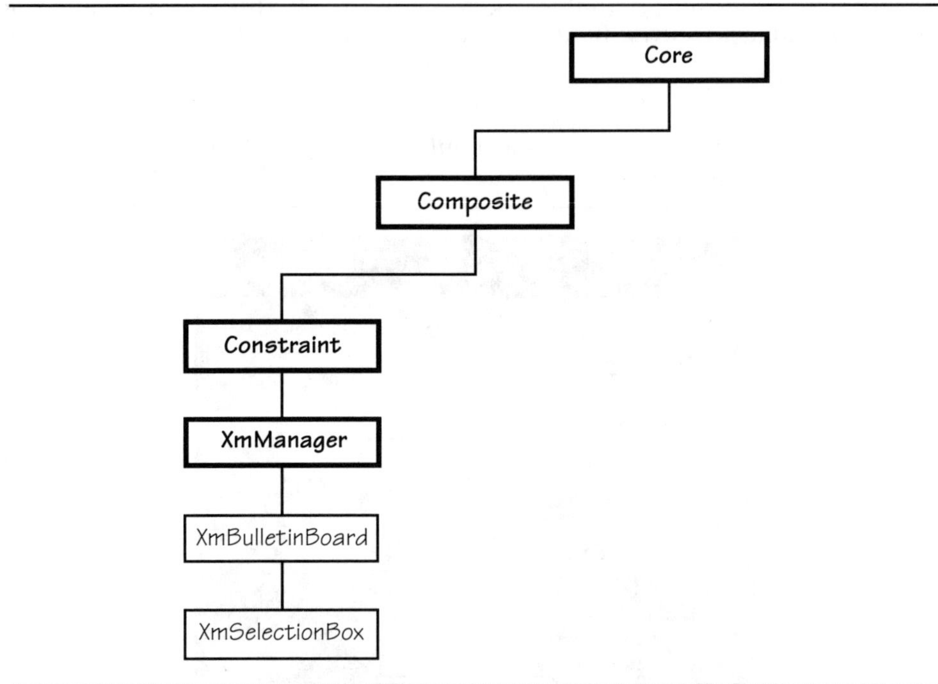

Table 14.3 lists the resources defined by *XmSelectionBox*; they are described below. Table 14.3 also lists the `helpCallback` resource, defined by *XmManager*, as a reminder that it is used with selection boxes.

Table 14.3. Frequently used resources: *XmSelectionBox*

Name	Inheritance	Type	Default Value
applyCallback	XmSelectionBox	XtCallbackList	NULL
applyLabelString	XmSelectionBox	XmString	"Apply"
cancelCallback	XmSelectionBox	XtCallbackList	NULL
cancelLabelString	XmSelectionBox	XmString	"Cancel"
dialogType	XmSelectionBox	unsigned char	*dynamic*
helpLabelString	XmSelectionBox	XmString	"Help"
listItemCount	XmSelectionBox	int	0
listItems	XmSelectionBox	XmStringTable	NULL
listLabelString	XmSelectionBox	XmString	NULL

Table 14.3. Continued.

`listVisibleItemCount`	**XmSelectionBox**	`int`	`8`
`minimizeButtons`	**XmSelectionBox**	`Boolean`	`FALSE`
`mustMatch`	**XmSelectionBox**	`Boolean`	`FALSE`
`noMatchCallback`	**XmSelectionBox**	`XtCallbackList`	`NULL`
`okCallback`	**XmSelectionBox**	`XtCallbackList`	`NULL`
`okLabelString`	**XmSelectionBox**	`XmString`	`"OK"`
`selectionLabelString`	**XmSelectionBox**	`XmString`	`"Selection"`
`textColumns`	**XmSelectionBox**	`int`	`20`
`textString`	**XmSelectionBox**	`XmString`	`" "`
`helpCallback`	**XmManager**	`XtCallbackList`	`NULL`

Use: dialogType

A selection box provides the base for several types of dialogs. A *prompt dialog* is a selection box without a list: it simply displays a message and allows the user to enter a textual reply to that message. A normal selection box is as shown in Figure 14.4: a list, a text field, and three buttons. A selection box may also be configured as a work area: a list, a text field, four buttons, and an optional additional child.

The `dialogType` resource controls a selection-box's configuration. Its value may be one of the constants from the list below. The default value depends on the selection-box's parent, as well as the function used to create the selection box.

- `XmDIALOG_PROMPT`. The selection box is used as a prompt dialog. The list and its label are not created, and the **Apply** button is created but left unmanaged. This is the default when the selection box is created by the `XmCreatePromptDialog` function.

- `XmDIALOG_SELECTION`. The selection box is used as a normal selection-box. It contains a list, a text field, their labels, and three managed buttons. The **Apply** button is created but not managed. This value is the default when the selection-box's parent is *XmDialogShell* (*ie*, when the selection box is created using `XmCreateSelectionDialog`).

- `XmDIALOG_WORK_AREA`. The selection box is used as a work area. It contains a list, an entry field, and four buttons. An additional child may be added after creation.[8] This value is the default when the selection-box is created using `XmCreateSelectionBox` but its parent *is not* a dialog shell.

The `dialogType` resource controls the initialization of the selection box. It must be set at the time of the selection-box's creation and may not be changed after creation.

Appearance: listVisibleItemCount, minimizeButtons, textColumns

A selection box determines its preferred size from the aggregate sizes of its children, modified by internally specified interchild spacing. As the children are "hidden," the only way to set their preferred sizes via a resource file is to use the resources `listVisibleItemCount`, `minimizeButtons`, and `textColumns`.

The `listVisibleItemCount` resource is a pass-through to the list child's `visibleItemCount` resource and is used to determine the height of the list. The list's `listSizePolicy` resource is set to `XmVARIABLE`, meaning that the list will grow to match its widest displayed item.

As with *XmMessageBox,* the `minimizeButtons` resource controls the size of the selection-box's buttons. It acts as both a pass-through to the buttons' `recomputeSize` resource and as a control for the selection-box's button size/position code. If `minimizeButtons` contains `TRUE`, the selection-box's buttons are sized at their minimal size, controlled by `recomputeSize`. If `minimizeButtons` contains `FALSE` (the default), the buttons are sized equally, at the preferred dimensions of the largest button.

The `textColumns` resource is a pass-through to the entry-field's `columns` resource. In practice, either the list or the entry-field controls the width of the selection box, not both. This is because both widgets are set to the same width — the width of the wider widget.

Labels: applyLabelString, cancelLabelString, helpLabelString, listLabelString, okLabelString, selectionLabelString

The selection-box's list and entry field both have associated labels, to provide the user with information regarding their use. The selection-box's `listLabelString` resource is a pass-through to the `labelString` resource for the label associated with the list, while `selectionLabelString` is a pass-through for the label associated with the entry field. While `listLabelString` does not have a default value, `selectionLabelString` defaults to "Selection".

The resources `applyLabelString`, `cancelLabelString`, `helpLabelString`, and `okLabelString` are pass-throughs to the `labelString` resource of the selection-box's buttons. Each of these strings defaults to the name of the button: "Apply", "Cancel", "Help", and "OK".

---

[8] This additional child is created and managed under program control, but is positioned under control of the selection box. Attempting to add more than one additional child results in an error.

Contents: listItemCount, listItems, textString

The `listItemCount` and `listItems` resources are pass-throughs to the `itemCount` and `items` resources of the selection-box's list. No pass-through is provided for the list's `selectedItems` resource; the selected item is automatically presented in the selection-box's entry field.

The contents of the entry field are accessed via the `textString` resource. This resource is *not* a pass-through to the `value` resource of the selection-box's text field. Instead, it contains a compound string, which is the format used by list items. The selection box converts between the compound string maintained in `textString` and the ASCII string held in the entry field.

Interaction: mustMatch

The `mustMatch` resource specifies whether the selection box verifies the contents of the entry field against the list when the user presses the **OK** or **Apply** buttons. If it contains `TRUE`, the entry-field's contents are compared against the list, using `XmListItemExists`. If a match is found, the appropriate activation callback — `applyCallback` or `okCallback` — is invoked. If the entry-field's contents do not match a list item, `noMatchCallback` is invoked. If `mustMatch` contains `FALSE`, no such check is performed, and `noMatchCallback` is never invoked.

XmSelectionBox Callbacks

Like *XmMessageBox*, *XmSelectionBox* provides callbacks linked to the activation callback list of each of the selection-box's buttons. In addition, *XmSelectionBox* provides a verification callback, which is only invoked when the user presses the **OK** or **Apply** button, the `mustMatch` resource contains `TRUE`, and the entry-field's contents do not match any of the list's items. All of these callbacks pass call data in the `XmSelectionBoxCallbackStruct` structure, defined in Listing 14.5.

Listing 14.5. Type definition: *XmSelectionBoxCallbackStruct*

```
typedef struct
        {
        int         reason;
        XEvent      *event;
        XmString    value;
        int         length;
        }
XmSelectionBoxCallbackStruct;
```

The `reason` member identifies the callback: `applyCallback` uses `XmCR_APPLY`, `cancelCallback` uses `XmCR_CANCEL`, `helpCallback` uses `XmCR_HELP`, `noMatchCallback` uses `XmCR_NO_MATCH`, and `okCallback` uses `XmCR_OK`. The `event` member points at the event that invoked the callback. The `value` member contains the contents of the entry field (textString); it isn't used by cancelCallback or helpCallback. Finally, the length member contains the number of bytes occupied by value; it is needed if the program is to copy the selected item.[9]

Creating and Using a Selection Box

The function XmCreateSelectionBox creates a stand-alone selection box, and the function XmCreateSelectionDialog creates a selection-box dialog.[10] Both functions take the same parameters as other widget-creation functions, and both return the ID of the selection box. XmCreateSelectionDialog, however, creates a dialog shell as the "hidden" parent of the selection-box.

The selection-box creation functions create and manage the children specified by the contents of the dialogType resource. If you want to add the optional work area, you must create and manage it explicitly. It will be automatically sized and positioned by the selection box.

As with other dialogs, a selection box is managed when needed and unmanaged when the user is done with it. The autoUnmanage resource defaults to TRUE, so there is often no need to attach a callback function to the **Cancel** button. The program *should* attach a callback to the **OK** and/or **Apply** buttons and retrieve the entry-field's contents from the call data.

Accessing a Selection-Box's Children

Like *XmMessageBox*, *XmSelectionBox* provides a function — XmSelectionBoxGet-Child, prototyped in Listing 14.6 — to access its "prebuilt" children. This function is the only way to directly access these children.

Listing 14.6. Function prototype: *XmSelectionBoxGetChild*

```
Widget   XmSelectionBoxGetChild( w, child )
         Widget          w;
         unsigned char   child;
```

XmSelectionBoxGetChild returns the ID of the child and takes two parameters: the ID of the selection-box (w) and a code representing the child (child). This code must be one of the constants from the following list:

- XmDIALOG_LIST. Returns the ID of the selection-box's list.

---

[9] As with the *XmList* callbacks, the value in the callback structure is allocated before the callback and deallocated afterward. If the program needs to maintain the value, it must be copied.

[10] The function XmCreatePromptDialog creates a selection-box sans list.

- `XmDIALOG_LIST_LABEL`. Returns the ID of the label associated with (and positioned above) the list.

- `XmDIALOG_TEXT`. Returns the ID of the selection-box's entry field (an *XmText* widget).

- `XmDIALOG_SELECTION_LABEL`. Returns the ID of the label associated with (and positioned above) the entry field.

- `XmDIALOG_WORK_AREA`. Returns the ID of the selection-box's additional work area widget. The creation of this widget is the responsibility of the program; if used, the widget class is program-dependent.

- `XmDIALOG_SEPARATOR`. Returns the ID of the separator between the selection-box's presentation and confirmation areas.

- `XmDIALOG_OK_BUTTON`. Returns the ID of the **OK** button.

- `XmDIALOG_APPLY_BUTTON`. Returns the ID of the **Apply** button.

- `XmDIALOG_CANCEL_BUTTON`. Returns the ID of the **Cancel** button.

- `XmDIALOG_HELP_BUTTON`. Returns the ID of the **Help** button.

- `XmDIALOG_DEFAULT_BUTTON`. Returns the ID of the default button, determined from the contents of the `defaultButton` resource.

XmSelectionBox Example: E-Mail Addresses

Listing 14.7 presents the program and resource file used to produce Figure 14.4. The selection box is displayed as the program's main window, rather than in a dialog box, allowing use of the trivial program template.

This program is almost identical in flow to that of Listing 14.3: first the widget is created, then it is filled, using the function `LoadAddressList`. The primary change is that the lists and labels of the former program are replaced by a single widget; the selection box. Even the `LoadAddressList` function is almost unchanged, except that it now installs the list via pass-through resources.

Listing 14.7. Program and resource file: E-mail address selection-box

```
/*********************************************************************
**                                                                 **
**   listing_14_7.c                                                **
**                                                                 **
**   Selection-Box Example. E-mail address selection.             **
**                                                                 **
*********************************************************************/
```

Listing 14.7. Continued.

```c
#include <Xm/SelectioB.h>


void    LoadAddressList();                  /* FORWARD Definitions        */


Widget  appshell,                           /* Application Shell          */
        the_sb;                             /* The selection-box          */
Arg     arglist[16];                        /* Used to set resources      */


#define    XMS( s )    XmStringCreate( s, XmSTRING_DEFAULT_CHARSET )


void main( argc, argv )
    int     argc;
    char    *argv[];
{
    appshell = XtInitialize( argv[0], "Listing_14_7", NULL, 0,
                                        &argc, argv );

    the_sb = XmCreateSelectionBox( appshell, "TheSB", NULL, 0 );
    XtManageChild( the_sb );

    LoadAddressList();

    XtRealizeWidget( appshell );
    XtMainLoop();
}


/**
*** LoadAddressList()
***
*** Fills the selection-box's list of addresses.
**/

void LoadAddressList()
```

Listing 14.7. Continued.

```
{
    XmString    addresses[9];

    addresses[0] = XMS( "kdg@world.std.com" );
    addresses[1] = XMS( "postmaster@moscvax.arpa" );
    addresses[2] = XMS( "xug@expo.lcs.mit.edu" );
    addresses[3] = XMS( "xannounce@expo.lcs.mit.edu" );
    addresses[4] = XMS( "xpert@expo.lcs.mit.edu" );
    addresses[5] = XMS( "motif@alfalfa.com" );
    addresses[6] = XMS( "info-c@research.att.com" );
    addresses[7] = XMS( "std-unix@uunet.uu.net" );
    addresses[8] = XMS( "unix-wizards@brl.arpa" );

    XtSetArg( arglist[0], XmNlistItems, addresses );
    XtSetArg( arglist[1], XmNlistItemCount, XtNumber(addresses) );
    XtSetValues( the_sb, arglist, 2 );
}
```

```
!
! Resource file for Selection-Box example (Fig 14.4)
!

*.background:               Gray50
*.foreground:               White
*.topShadowColor:           Gray75
*.bottomShadowColor:        Gray25

*TheSB.dialogType:          DIALOG_SELECTION
*TheSB.listVisibleItemCount: 5
*TheSB.listLabelString:     Addresses:
*TheSB.selectionLabelString: Send To:
```

XmFileSelectionBox

One common use of a selection box is selection of a file from the list of files in a
directory. Since this operation is so often used, Motif provides a dedicated widget
class: *XmFileSelectionBox*. To the "prebuilt" children of *XmSelectionBox*,
XmFileSelectionBox adds two more: another entry field and an associated label.

Figure 14.6 presents an example of a file-selection-box.[11] The additional entry field — the *file filter* — is positioned above the list. This entry field allows the user to specify a directory and filename mask for the search, using standard UNIX wildcard specification. By default, the field contains "*", specifying all files in the current directory.

The **Apply** button is managed in a file-selection-box, but is named **Filter**; it invokes the directory search. The other buttons have the same function as in other selection boxes: **OK** confirms the file selection, **Cancel** unmanages the dialog and ignores any selection, and **Help** invokes context-sensitive help if it is present.

Figure 14.6. File-selection-box example

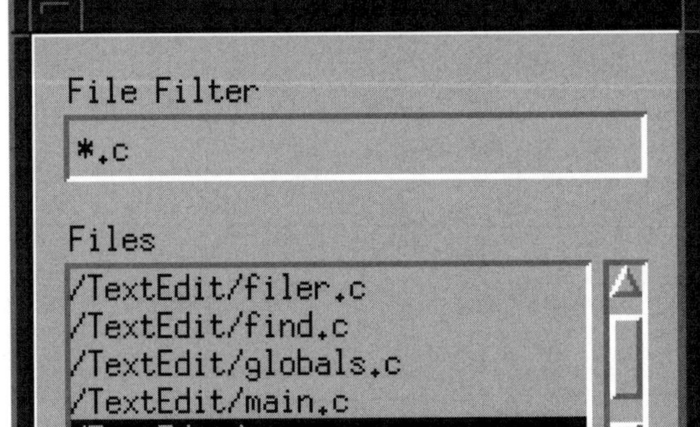

---

[11] The layout of a file-selection-box changed slightly for Motif 1.1. Instead of a single list, containing both file and directory names, there are now two lists: one for directories. In addition, whereas Motif 1.0 used fully specified names (showing all directories), Motif 1.1 lists names relative to the current directory.

XmFileSelectionBox **Resources**

To those resources defined by *XmSelectionBox*, *XmFileSelectionBox* adds the resources shown in Table 14.4 and described below. Table 14.4 also contains the `autoUnmanage` resource, which is handled differently by *XmFileSelectionBox* than by other *XmBulletinBoard*-derived classes.

Table 14.4. Frequently used resources: *XmFileSelectionBox*

Name	Inheritance	Type	Default Value
`dirMask`	XmFileSelectionBox	`XmString`	`"*"`
`dirSpec`	XmFileSelectionBox	`XmString`	`" "`
`filterLabel String`	XmFileSelectionBox	`XmString`	`"File Filter"`
`autoUnmanage`	XmBulletinBoard	`Boolean`	`FALSE`

Contents: dirMask, dirSpec

The `dirMask` resource specifies the search parameters. It may contain a complete or partial path specification. Partial specifications — those that do not begin with "/" — are rooted at the current directory. File matching is performed using UNIX's wildcard characters, meaning that the specification can be constructed to include or ignore certain files. The default value of "*" matches all files in the current directory.

The `dirSpec` resource specifies the name of the selected file. It is a pass-through to the `textString` resource and overrides the value in that resource. It maintains its value between invocations and may be used to specify a default filename. The text editor uses this capability in the **Save As...** dialog.

Behavior: autoUnmanage

Unlike the other dialogs based on *XmBulletinBoard*, *XmFileSelectionBox* sets the `autoUnmanage` resource to `FALSE` and does not permit the program to change it to `TRUE`. This is done so that the dialog will not disappear when the user presses the **Filter (Apply)** button. As a result, the program must attach callbacks to each of the other buttons — if only to unmanage the dialog.

Labels: filterLabelString

The `filterLabelString` resource is a pass-through to the `labelString` resource of the label associated with the "File Filter" entry field. By default, it contains the string "File Filter".

Creating And Using *XmFileSelectionBox*

Creation

A file-selection-box may be created using either `XmCreateFileSelectionBox` or `XmCreateFileSelectionDialog`. The former simply creates the selection box and its children, while the second creates a dialog shell as the parent of the selection box. Both functions take the same parameters as other widget-creation functions, and both return the ID of the selection box.

After the file-selection-box is created, one additional child may be created; if used, it must be managed when it is created. As with *XmSelectionBox*, this child is positioned between the list and the file-specification entry field.

Like other dialogs, a file-selection-box is created unmanaged and is managed and unmanaged as needed. Also like other dialogs, its children — "prebuilt" and additional — are managed at the time of creation.

Retrieving Child Widget IDs

Like *XmSelectionBox* and *XmMessageBox*, *XmFileSelectionBox* provides a function to retrieve the IDs of its children. This function is `XmFileSelectionBox-GetChild`, prototyped in Listing 14.8.

Listing 14.8. Function prototype: *XmFileSelectionBoxGetChild*

```
Widget  XmFileSelectionBoxGetChild( w, child )
        Widget          w;
        unsigned char   child;
```

`XmFileSelectionBoxGetChild` takes two parameters: the ID of the selection box (w) and a code representing the child (child). It returns the ID of the child. Child-selection codes are from the following list:

- `XmDIALOG_FILTER_TEXT`. Returns the ID of the filter entry field.

- `XmDIALOG_FILTER_LABEL`. Returns the ID of the label associated with (and positioned above) the filter entry field.

- `XmDIALOG_LIST`. Returns the ID of the file list.

- `XmDIALOG_LIST_LABEL`. Returns the ID of the label associated with (and positioned above) the file list.

- `XmDIALOG_TEXT`. Returns the ID of the filename entry field.

- `XmDIALOG_SELECTION_LABEL`. Returns the ID of the label associated with (and positioned above) the filename entry field.

- XmDIALOG_WORK_AREA. Returns the ID of the selection-box's additional work area child. The creation of this widget is the responsibility of the program; if used, the widget class is program-dependent.

- XmDIALOG_SEPARATOR. Returns the ID of the separator between the selection-box's presentation and confirmation areas.

- XmDIALOG_OK_BUTTON. Returns the ID of the **OK** button.

- XmDIALOG_APPLY_BUTTON. Returns the ID of the **Filter (Apply)** button.

- XmDIALOG_CANCEL_BUTTON. Returns the ID of the **Cancel** button.

- XmDIALOG_HELP_BUTTON. Returns the ID of the **Help** button.

- XmDIALOG_DEFAULT_BUTTON. Returns the ID of the default button — determined from the contents of the defaultButton resource. This is by default **Filter/Apply**.

Initiating a Search

A file-selection-box performs a directory search when any of the following actions take place: (1) the selection box is created; (2) the dirMask resource is set via XtSetValues; (3) the program calls the XmFileSelectionDoSearch function; (4) the user presses the **Filter** button; or (5) the user presses the *Return* key while the file-filter entry field has the focus. When one of these events happens, the selection box invokes the function specified by its fileSearchProc resource.

Of these initiators, the XmFileSelectionDoSearch function is most important to the program. It should be called whenever the current directory's contents have changed. In practical terms, since files can be created or deleted at random, it should be called whenever the selection box is managed.

Listing 14.9 presents the prototype of XmFileSelectionDoSearch. It takes two parameters: the ID of the selection box (w) and a search mask (mask). This mask is installed in the dirMask resource; if it is passed as NULL, the selection-box maintains its existing mask. This function does not return any value; its operation is confined to the selection-box's contents.

Listing 14.9. Function prototype: *XmFileSelectionDoSearch*

```
void    XmFileSelectionDoSearch( w, mask )
        Widget      w;
        XmString    mask;
```

Callbacks

XmFileSelectionBox provides the same callbacks as *XmSelectionBox*. However, it passes call data in `XmFileSelectionBoxCallbackStruct`, instead of `XmSelectionBoxCallbackStruct`. This structure is defined in Listing 14.10.

Listing 14.10. Type definition:
XmFileSelectionBoxCallbackStruct

```
typedef struct
        {
        int         reason;
        XEvent      *event;
        XmString    value;
        int         length;
        XmString    mask;
        int         mask_length;
        }
XmFileSelectionBoxCallbackStruct;
```

The `reason` and `event` members serve the same purpose as in other callbacks; file-selection-box callbacks use the same reasons as their selection-box counterparts. The `value` and `length` members are identical to the same members of `XmSelectionBoxCallbackStruct`: `value` contains the filename, and `length` contains the number of bytes that are occupied by that name. The `mask` and `mask_length` member are unique to the file-selection-box callback: `mask` contains the contents of the `dirMask` resource, and `mask_length` contains the number of bytes occupied by the mask.

XmFileSelectionBox Example: Open/Save As

The text editor program uses a file-selection-box to support its **Open...** and **Save As...** menu choices. The addition of this selection box is part of the implementation of the "filer" module, presented in Listing 14.11.[12] This implementation consists of five changes: calling the filer's initialization function from `InitOther`, linking the filer functions to `FileMenuCB`, implementing the filer functions, and adding new resources to the resource file. These changes are detailed after the listing.

---

[12] *XmFileSelectionBox* makes use of the regular-expression functions. If you are using a UNIX based on System V you will need to specify the *PW* library when linking. If you do not do this, the linker will report that `regcmp` and `regex` are undefined externals.

Listing 14.11. Text editor revision 8: Addition of "filer" module

```c
void InitOther()
{
    InitFiler();
    InitFindDB();
}
```

```c
static void FileMenuCB( w, client_data, call_data )
    Widget      w;
    char        *client_data;
    caddr_t     call_data;
{
    if (!strcmp(client_data, "New"))
        FileNew();
    else if (!strcmp(client_data, "Opn"))
        FileOpen();
    else if (!strcmp(client_data, "Sav"))
        FileSave();
    else if (!strcmp(client_data, "SAs"))
        FileSaveAs();
    else if (!strcmp(client_data, "Ext"))
        {
        exit( 0 );
        }
}
```

```c
/**********************************************************************
**                                                                  **
**  filer.c                                                         **
**                                                                  **
**  Text Editor -- File Open/Save Module                           **
**                                                                  **
**********************************************************************/


#include <stdio.h>
#include <string.h>

#include <Xm/FileSB.h>
```

Listing 14.11. Continued.

```c
#include <Xm/Text.h>

#include "textedit.h"


/*******************************************************************
**                                                               **
**              F O R W A R D   D E F I N I T I O N S            **
**                                                               **
*******************************************************************/

static  void InitStdFile();
static  void ManageStdFile();
static  void UnmanageStdFile();

static  void SFProc();
static  void ReadProc();
static  void WriteProc();




/*******************************************************************
**                                                               **
**              L O C A L   V A R I A B L E S                    **
**                                                               **
*******************************************************************/

char    *curfile = NULL;                /* The current filename    */
Widget  stdfile_db;                     /* The Standard File dialog */

void    (*fileproc)();                  /* The Read/Write function  */
```

Listing 14.11. Continued.

```c
/**********************************************************************
**                                                                  **
**   InitFiler()                                                     **
**                                                                  **
**   This function initializes the filer module: it clears the current **
**   filename, disables the File/Save menu choice, and creates the  **
**   Standard File dialog.                                          **
**                                                                  **
**********************************************************************/

void InitFiler()
{
    Widget        temp;

    stdfile_db = XmCreateFileSelectionDialog( mainwin, "StdFile", NULL, 0
);

    XtAddCallback( stdfile_db, XmNokCallback, SFProc, NULL );
    XtAddCallback( stdfile_db, XmNcancelCallback, UnmanageStdFile, NULL );
    XtAddCallback( stdfile_db, XmNhelpCallback, UnmanageStdFile, NULL );
}


/**********************************************************************
**                                                                  **
**   ManageStdFile( title, proc, defspec )                          **
**                                                                  **
**   This function manages the Standard File dialog. It sets the    **
**   dialog's title to the string passed as "title", installs the   **
**   function passed as "proc" in the "fileproc" variable (it gets   **
**   called by the StdFile callback handler), and stores the string **
**   passed in "defspec" in the "dirSpec" resource.                 **
**                                                                  **
**********************************************************************/

static  void ManageStdFile( title, proc, defspec )
    char            *title;
    XtCallbackProc  proc;
    char            *defspec;
```

Listing 14.11. Continued.

```
{
    XmString        temp1, temp2;

    temp1 = XmStringCreate( title,   XmSTRING_DEFAULT_CHARSET );
    if (defspec == NULL)
        temp2 = XmStringCreate( "", XmSTRING_DEFAULT_CHARSET );
    else
        temp2 = XmStringCreate( defspec, XmSTRING_DEFAULT_CHARSET );

    XtSetArg( arglist[0], XmNdialogTitle, temp1 );
    XtSetArg( arglist[1], XmNdirSpec,     temp2 );
    XtSetValues( stdfile_db, arglist, 2 );

    XmStringFree( temp1 );
    XmStringFree( temp2 );

    XmFileSelectionDoSearch( stdfile_db, NULL );

    XtManageChild( stdfile_db );

    fileproc = proc;
}


/***********************************************************************
**                                                                   **
**   UnmanageStdFile()                                               **
**                                                                   **
**                                                                   **
**   This function unmanages the Standard File dialog. It is attached **
**   to the "Cancel" and "Help" buttons, because XmFileSelectionBox  **
**   does not handle the "autoUnmanage" resource.                    **
**                                                                   **
***********************************************************************/

static  void UnmanageStdFile()
```

Listing 14.11. Continued.

```c
{
    XtUnmanageChild( stdfile_db );
}


/***********************************************************************
**                                                                   **
**   SFProc( w, client_data, call_data )                             **
**                                                                   **
**   This function is the callback procedure for the Standard File   **
**   dialog. It stores the chosen filename in "curfile", and then    **
**   calls the function pointed-to by "fileproc".                    **
**                                                                   **
***********************************************************************/

static  void SFProc(w, client_data, call_data )
    Widget                          w;
    caddr_t                         client_data;
    XmFileSelectionBoxCallbackStruct    *call_data;
{
    if (curfile != NULL)
        XtFree( curfile );
    XmStringGetLtoR( call_data->value, XmSTRING_DEFAULT_CHARSET, &curfile
);
    UnmanageStdFile();

    (*fileproc)();
}


/***********************************************************************
**                                                                   **
**   ReadProc()                                                      **
**                                                                   **
**   This function reads the file specified by "curfile" into the    **
**   editor's text buffer.                                           **
**                                                                   **
***********************************************************************/
```

Listing 14.11. Continued.

```c
static  void ReadProc()
{
    FILE    *infile = fopen( curfile, "r" );
    char    *txtbuf;
    long    size;

    if (infile == NULL)
        /* Should display error */
        return;

    fseek( infile, 0L, 2 );
    size = ftell( infile );
    rewind( infile );

    txtbuf = XtMalloc( size+1 );

    fread( txtbuf, sizeof(char), size, infile );
    XmTextSetString( textwin, txtbuf );

    XtFree( txtbuf );
}


/*********************************************************************
**                                                                 **
**   WriteProc()                                                   **
**                                                                 **
**   This function writes the editor's text buffer into a file named **
**   by "curfile".                                                 **
**                                                                 **
*********************************************************************/

static  void WriteProc()
{
    FILE    *outfile;
    char    *txtbuf;
    long    size;
```

Listing 14.11. Continued.

```c
    outfile = fopen( curfile, "w" );
    if (outfile == NULL)
        /* Should display error */
        return;

    txtbuf = XmTextGetString( textwin );
    size   = strlen(txtbuf);

    fwrite( txtbuf, sizeof(char), size, outfile );
    fclose( outfile );

    XtFree( txtbuf );
}


/***********************************************************************
**                                                                   **
**   FileNew()                                                        **
**                                                                   **
**   This function is called from the File/New menu choice. It clears **
**   the text buffer, resets the current file, and disables the File/ **
**   Save menu choice.                                               **
**                                                                   **
***********************************************************************/

void FileNew()
{
    XmTextSetString( textwin, "" );

    if (curfile != NULL)
        XtFree( curfile );
    curfile = NULL;
}
```

Listing 14.11. Continued.

```
/************************************************************************
**                                                                    **
**   FileOpen()                                                       **
**                                                                    **
**   This function is called from the File/Open menu choice. All it   **
**   does is invoke the Standard File dialog -- SFProc and ReadProc   **
**   do the real work.                                                **
**                                                                    **
************************************************************************/

void FileOpen()
{
    ManageStdFile( "Open...", ReadProc, NULL );
}


/************************************************************************
**                                                                    **
**   FileSave()                                                       **
**                                                                    **
**   This function is a link to WriteProc(), which writes the text    **
**   buffer into a file using the current filename.                   **
**                                                                    **
************************************************************************/

void FileSave()
{
    if (curfile == NULL)
        FileSaveAs();
    else
        WriteProc();
}
```

Listing 14.11. Continued.

```
/******************************************************************
**                                                              **
**   FileSaveAs()                                               **
**                                                              **
**   This function is called from the File/Save-As menu choice. It **
**   invokes the Standard File dialog, and links it to WriteProc. **
**                                                              **
******************************************************************/

void FileSaveAs()
{
    ManageStdFile( "Save As...", WriteProc, curfile );
}
!#############################################################################
!
! Standard File Dialog Resources
!
!#############################################################################

*StdFile.*.background:          Gray75
*StdFile.*.foreground:          Black
*StdFile.*.topShadowColor:      White
*StdFile.*.bottomShadowColor:   Gray50

*StdFile.listVisibleItemCount:  5
```

File-Menu Callbacks

The first change is to add functionality to the file menu by changing the
`FileMenuCB` function.[13] In keeping with the modularization scheme, menu
functionality is placed in the filer module. Thus, the only changes to `FileMenuCB`
are the addition of calls to functions in filer: `FileNew` for the **New** menu choice,
`FileOpen` for **Open...**, `FileSave` for **Save**, and `FileSaveAs` for **Save As...**.

Filer Variables and Initialization

The "filer" module contains all of the program's file input/output code. It
provides a dialog box — "Standard File" — to get a filename from the user and
functions to load that file into the text buffer and write the text buffer to the

---

[13] Note also that the menu items must be enabled by removing the calls to
`XmSetSensitive` from `InitFileMenu`.

file.[14] It also contains "glue" functions: functions called from other modules, which hide details of the filer module from those other modules.

The filer module contains three module-wide variables: `curfile`, `stdfile_db`, and `fileproc`. The `curfile` variable points to the name of the current file; when there is no current file, it is `NULL`. The `stdfile_db` variable holds the widget ID of the file-selection-box; it is the only widget ID maintained by this module — the file-selection-box maintains all of its children.

The third variable, `fileproc`, is used to allow one dialog box to serve two functions. The **Open...** and **Save As...** functions are almost identical in user interface — both present a file-selection-box to get the filename — but radically different in operation: one reads the file, the other writes it. They could be implemented with two dialog boxes, each of which calls the appropriate input/output function. However, to save code, I make both operations use the same dialog. This dialog's "OK" callback function retrieves the selected name and calls the appropriate input/output function, using `fileproc` as a pointer to that function.

This design is carried out in the `InitFiler` function. One file-selection-box is created, and the `SFProc` function is attached to its "OK" callback. The "Cancel" and "Help" callbacks do not perform any function in this program, so they are simply linked to a function that unmanages the dialog. `InitFiler` also performs other startup time operations — at this time, clearing the current filename.

ManageStdFile

The split personality of the standard-file dialog is also present in the `ManageStdFile` function. Since my convention is to have dialog titles mimic their associated menu choice, the `dialogTitle` resource must be changed for each invocation — with the appropriate title passed from the glue function.

Also passed from the glue function is the default filename. On **Open...**, the filename should be blank — the user must choose a file to open. On **Save As...**, however, the filename is the current filename, allowing the default operation of **Save As...** to be equivalent to **Save**.

Another point of interest in `ManageStdFile` is the call to `XmFileSelectionDoSearch`. In a multiuser computer system, the contents of a directory may change randomly. For this reason, the dialog's file list is updated before it is presented to the user.

SFProc

`SFProc` is the function attached to the dialog's **OK** button and is called whenever the user has selected a file. Its purpose is to retrieve the filename (passed in the call data), convert it from a compound string to a simple text string, store it as the current filename variable (`curfile`), and call the appropriate input/output function. In addition, it unmanages the dialog.

---

[14] "Standard File" is a name that comes from the Macintosh world.

ReadProc *and* WriteProc

These functions perform the actual file read/write operation. They are called from `SFProc`, using the `fileproc` pointer variable. Both get the filename from the `curfile` variable. `ReadProc` then opens the file for reading and stores its contents in the text buffer, while `WriteProc` creates the file and writes the text buffer's contents to it. As noted in the code, both functions should display a message box if any error occurs during their operation — although they don't as written.

Glue Functions: FileNew, FileOpen, FileSave, FileSaveAs

To hide filer functionality, I used these functions to "glue" the menu module to the filer module. For the most part, they simply call other filer functions; `FileNew` and `FileSave` are different, however, and deserve further note.

`FileNew` is responsible for clearing the text buffer. At the present time, it does that and also clears the current filename. For a production program, however, it should present a message box before doing any of this: the user should be notified before clearing an unsaved program.

`FileSave` is also notable in that it determines whether the filename is known. If it is, then the simple save function — `WriteProc` — is called. If not, `FileSaveAs` is invoked, to query the user for a filename. This behavior — forcing **Save As...** if the filename isn't known — is standard in many applications but is not a Motif standard.

Resources

The resource-file support for the file-selection-box is primarily concentrated on the secondary color scheme. In addition, the `listVisibleItemCount` is decreased — its default value (8) made Figure 14.6 too large.

XmCommand

Another subclass of *XmSelectionBox* is *XmCommand*, shown in Figure 14.7. *XmCommand* provides the normal selection-box interaction, allowing the user to select items from the list or directly fill the entry field. Unlike a normal-selection-box, however, a command's list is filled from its entry field — it maintains a history of the user's interaction with the widget. Each time that the user enters a command via the entry field or changes an item selected from the list, the new item is added to the end of the list, and in the future, may be selected instead of retyped.

Also, unlike a selection box, a command widget does not provide a confirmation area. One reason for this omission is that a command widget is not necessarily used in a dialog — it is often presented in a program's main window as the *command* sub-area.

Figure 14.7. *XmCommand* example

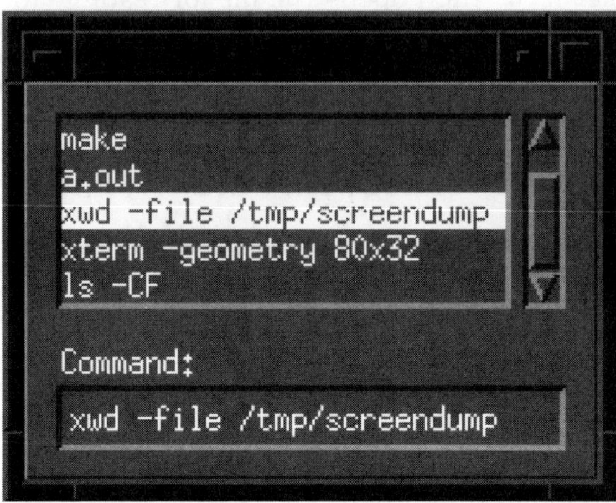

A common use for a command widget is to allow shell escapes in a program. For example, the text editor could support sorting by a shell escape: the user selects text, uses a shell escape to pass that text to the *sort* program, and the editor replaces the selection by the sorted text.[15]

XmCommand Resources

XmCommand is derived directly from *XmSelectionBox*. To the resources of *XmSelectionBox* and its superclasses, *XmCommand* adds the resources listed in Table 14.5 and described below. It also eliminates those *XmSelectionBox* resources associated with a selection-box's buttons and separator.

---

[15] While useful, this is not implemented as sample code because the mechanics of linking an X client to a normal program far overshadow the implementation of a command dialog.

Table 14.5. Frequently used resources: *XmCommand*

Name	Inheritance	Type	Default Value
`command`	**XmCommand**	`XmString`	`NULL`
`commandChangedCallback`	**XmCommand**	`XtCallbackList`	`NULL`
`commandEnteredCallback`	**XmCommand**	`XtCallbackList`	`NULL`
`historyItems`	**XmCommand**	`XmStringTable`	`NULL`
`historyItemCount`	**XmCommand**	`int`	`0`
`historyMaxItems`	**XmCommand**	`int`	`100`
`historyVisibleItemCount`	**XmCommand**	`int`	`8`
`promptString`	**XmCommand**	`XmString`	`">"`

Current Command: command

The `command` resource is a pass-through to the *XmSelectionBox* `textString` resource. It is a compound string and defaults to an empty string. The user may modify this value either by typing in the entry field or selecting an item from the history list.

Previous Commands: historyItems, historyItemCount, historyMaxItems

As the user executes each command, it is added to the end of the history list, provided it is not already in the list. This list is accessed by the `historyItems` and `historyItemCount` resources, which are pass-throughs to the *XmSelectionBox* resources `items` and `itemCount`.

If this growth of the history list was unrestricted, it could grow to an enormous length — losing much of its utility. The `historyMaxItems` resource exists to prevent this problem: when the list contains the maximum number of items, the item at the top of the list is removed when a new item is added at the bottom.

Appearance: historyVisibleItemCount, promptString

Like a selection box, the height of a command widget is dependent on the number of list items displayed. The `historyVisibleItemCount` resource controls this number; it is a pass-through to the *XmSelectionBox* resource `listVisibleItemCount`.

The `promptString` resource specifies the label displayed above the entry field. It is a pass-through to the *XmSelectionBox* resource `selectionLabelString`. The default value of this resource is ">". While that string mimics many users' shell prompt, it is not intuitive for the nonsophisticated user and should be replaced (*eg*, by "Command:").

Callbacks: commandChangedCallback, commandEnteredCallback

XmCommand provides two callbacks: `commandChangedCallback` is invoked whenever the contents of the entry field change, and `commandEnteredCallback` is invoked when the user executes a command (by pressing the *Return* key).[16] Both callbacks pass data in the same structure, `XmCommandCallbackStruct`, which is identical to `XmSelectionBoxCallbackStruct`. The reason for `commandChangedCallback` is `XmCR_COMMAND_CHANGED`, and for `commandEnteredCallback`, it is `XmCR_COMMAND_ENTERED`.

XmCommand **Convenience Functions**

Creation

Unlike *XmSelectionBox* and *XmFileSelectionBox*, *XmCommand* has only one creation function: `XmCreateCommand`. This function creates the command widget and its "prebuilt" children. The command widget is created unmanaged, its children are created managed. Unless used in a dialog, the command widget should be managed once it is created.

If you do wish to use *XmCommand* in a dialog, you must first create the dialog-shell, using the function `XmCreateDialogShell`. You can then call `XmCreateCommand`, passing the ID of the shell in the `parent` parameter. Once this is done, you can make the dialog appear by managing the command widget.

Child Access

Like *XmSelectionBox* and *XmFileSelectionBox*, *XmCommand* provides a function to access its prebuilt children. That function is `XmCommandGetChild`, prototyped in Listing 14.12. The `child` parameter is limited to three constants: `XmDIALOG_HISTORY_LIST` returns the ID of the list, `XmDIALOG_PROMPT_LABEL` returns the ID of the entry-field's label, and `XmDIALOG_COMMAND_TEXT` returns the ID of the entry field.

---

[16] The `commandChangedCallback` is linked to *XmText*'s `valueChangedCallback`, meaning that it is called on every keystroke, while `commandEnteredCallback` is linked to `activateCallback`. On activation, both callbacks are invoked — `commandChangedCallback` followed by `commandEnteredCallback`.

Listing 14.12. Function prototype: XmCommandGetChild

```
Widget  XmCommandGetChild( w, child )
        Widget        w;
        unsigned char child;
```

Value Manipulation

The functions `XmCommandSetValue` and `XmCommandAppendValue`, prototyped in Listing 14.13, may be used to fill the command widget's entry field. Both functions take as parameters the ID of the command widget (`w`) and a compound string (`string`). `XmCommandAppendValue` appends the specified string to the contents of the entry field, while `XmCommandSetValue` replaces the contents of the entry field with the string.

Listing 14.13. Function prototypes:
XmCommandAppendValue, XmCommandSetValue

```
void  XmCommandAppendValue( w, string )
      Widget    w;
      XmString  string;


void  XmCommandSetValue( w, string )
      Widget    w;
      XmString  string;
```

Error Reporting

In some applications, a program may need to display an error associated with a command widget. While this could be accomplished with a message box, *XmCommand* provides a built-in error-display capability.

This capability is provided by the function `XmCommandError` function, prototyped in Listing 14.14. This function takes two parameters: the ID of the command widget (`w`) and a compound string containing the error message (`string`). It displays this string at the bottom of the history list, separated from the rest of the list by a blank line. The message is not actually entered into the history list and is erased when the user enters the next command.

Listing 14.14. Function prototype: XmCommandError

```
void    XmCommandError( w, string )
        Widget      w;
        XmString    string;
```

XmCommand Example

Figure 14.7 was produced using the program and resource file of Listing 14.15. This program is based on the trivial program template; it simply creates and manages the command widget.

Listing 14.15. Program and resource file: XmCommand
Example

```
/*********************************************************************
**                                                                 **
**  listing_14_15.c                                                **
**                                                                 **
**  XmCommand Example.                                             **
**                                                                 **
*********************************************************************/


#include <Xm/Command.h>


Widget  appshell,                   /* Application Shell       */
        the_cb;                     /* The command box         */
Arg     arglist[16];                /* Used to set resources   */


void main( argc, argv )
    int     argc;

    char    *argv[];
```

Listing 14.15. Continued.

```c
{
    appshell = XtInitialize( argv[0], "Listing_14_15", NULL, 0,
                                            &argc, argv );

    the_cb = XmCreateCommand( appshell, "TheCmd", NULL, 0 );
    XtManageChild( the_cb );
    XtRealizeWidget( appshell );
    XtMainLoop();
}
```

```
!
! Resource file for Command example (Fig 14.7)
!

*.background:                       Gray50
*.foreground:                       White
*.topShadowColor:                   Gray75
*.bottomShadowColor:                Gray25

*TheCmd.historyVisibleItemCount:    5
*TheCmd.promptString:               Command:
*TheCmd.fontList:                   -*-Courier-medium-r-*--*-100-*
*TheCmd.width:                      200
```

15
Using Xlib With Motif

Overview

Xlib may be viewed as an "assembly language" for X. Physically, Xlib is a library of C functions, many of which translate directly into one or more protocol requests. Like a program written in assembly language, an Xlib program contains many lines of code, each of which has minimal effect. For this reason, most programmers use C instead of assembly and Motif instead of Xlib.

There are, however, times when one needs to use Xlib calls in a Motif program. While Motif provides widgets that directly support higher-order interface objects, such as menus, it does not provide functions for lower-order operations, such as drawing a line. Instead, the program must call Xlib functions to draw within the window of a Motif widget.

This chapter does not present a complete view of Xlib — that would require a book of its own. Instead, it provides a basic understanding of Xlib, including a detailed look at how the server displays images. It then presents the *XmDrawingArea* widget, a Motif widget that gives the programmer a "canvas" in which to place Xlib drawings. The chapter concludes with an example of *XmDrawingArea* in use, a "doodle" program.

The X Server

How Images Are Made

X is designed to use a *raster display* — a display that builds images out of distinct dots on the screen.[1] These dots are called *pixels*, a contraction of "picture element." On a monochrome display, pixels are either on or off — white

---

[1] This is as opposed to a "vector" display, which builds images out of lines, or vectors, caused by moving the electron beam. Older video games used vector displays, because they require less CPU power; the images, however, must be relatively simple line drawings.

or black. On a color display, pixels can take on any color. By combining enough pixels, any image can be made: a line, for example, is simply a row of identically colored pixels.

A raster display is often referred to as a "bit-mapped" display. This term indicates the way that images are stored in the display: each pixel occupies one or more bits in a memory chip. The display hardware scans the memory, one line of pixels at a time, and sends control signals to the electron beam, which paints the image on the display's screen. This scanning is repeated constantly — 70 times a second for a quality display — meaning that the image on the screen changes as the contents of the display's memory changes.

The X protocol specifies a set of commands — *graphics primitives* — which instruct the server to change the display's memory. These commands are known as "primitives" because they draw simple objects: dots, lines, arcs, rectangles, and circles. From such primitive objects, more complex objects — such as labels — may be produced.

Windows and Other Drawables

An X server does not permit a client to draw randomly on the screen. Instead, the client must perform its drawing in a *drawable*, which an abstract object maintained by the server. In practice, there are two types of drawables: *windows* and *pixmaps*.

A window represents an area of the display screen and displays what is drawn into it — if it is not obscured by another window. A pixmap is an object maintained entirely within the server's memory, which must be copied into a window for display. A program can prepare complex graphics in a pixmap, then put the finished drawing into a window.

The link between widgets and windows is intimate: each widget has an associated window, which has the position and dimensions specified by the widget's `x`, `y`, `width`, and `height` resources. The widget uses this window to display its contents, and the program can use it as the target of Xlib calls.

Exposure

At any point in its life, a window may be covered by another window. When this happens, the bits corresponding to the covered part of the bottom window are lost — they are replaced by the bits corresponding to the topmost window.

If the top window is then moved, uncovering the bottom window, those lost bits must be replaced. To do this, the server sends the window an exposure event, which specifies the part of the window that must be redrawn. The program is then expected to issue the appropriate drawing commands.

For most widgets, exposure is handled transparently by the widget's internal code. A label, for example, redraws its string. In the case of a widget that displays Xlib graphics, however, the window must be redrawn explicitly because the widget does not maintain a record of the graphics calls made to its window. The details of this procedure are described below as part of *XmDrawingArea*'s `exposeCallback` description.

Some servers provide *backing store*, a region of server memory that is used to hold the contents of obscured windows. These servers do not generate exposure events; instead, they fill exposed areas of a window from backing store. This capability represents a trade-off between server memory and network load, and its presence depends on the design goals of the server — in other words, no program should assume that its server has backing store.

Server Resources

An X server does not simply display graphics. It also maintains data items known as *server resources*, not to be confused with the program resources described previously. Server resources contain data that is held on the server but used by the program. In some cases, this data is used and maintained by the server — one example is the window structure. In others, it is data that is presented by one client for access by another — such as a text widget's selection.

Such data is held on the server for two reasons. The first is accessibility: since clients may be running on different computer systems, the only guaranteed method of interprocess communication is via the server. The other reason is efficiency: many of the structures held as server resources — such as the GC, described below — would have to be sent with each Xlib call if held by the client. Even in cases where the client and server make roughly equal use of a resource's contents, efficiency can be improved by sending only the necessary parts "over the wire."

For a particular server, a resource is identified by its *server resource ID*, a 32-bit integer value. For the program, resources must additionally be identified by their server — a single program may have connections to two or more servers.

You have already seen two examples of resource IDs in use: windows and pixmaps. Both of these objects occupy server memory, and both have associated control structures that also occupy server memory. The graphics context, described below, is another example of a server resource.

Color in a Digital World

The RGB Color Model

If you look closely at a color television, you will note that it too is a raster display. Furthermore, you can see that each pixel is comprised of three components: red, green, and blue.[2] These pixel components emit varying amounts of light, depending on the intensity of the electron beam when it shines on them. Blended together, these varying amounts of red, green, and blue light can create any visible color.

For a television, the intensity of each pixel component is specified by the video signal, which is fed to the electron beam as it shines on each pixel — and pixel

---

[2] You can see the pixels in a color TV more clearly than in a computer monitor because the monitor has higher resolution than a TV — and usually has a smaller screen. The television offers more shades per pixel, however, making it better able to represent a photographic image.

component — in turn. In the memory of a bit-mapped computer display, the intensity of each component is represented by a numerical value. In a typical system, eight bits are assigned to each color: the value 0 means the color component is off, while 255 means that it is as bright as possible. The display hardware reads these values and changes the beam intensity accordingly.

Colormaps

Although most color displays represent colors using 24 bits of information, pixels themselves are rarely stored in 24 bits of memory. If they were, a 1024x1024 pixel display would need three megabytes for its memory map. Moreover, although 24 bits of information means that the display can physically represent 16,777,216 colors, it has only 1,048,576 pixels.

For this reason, most color displays make use of a *colormap*, a table containing 24-bit color values.[3] To represent any color in the table, all that is needed is the index of the color's entry; the display hardware can then use the table to display the full 24 bits of color information. The drawback to a colormap is that the number of colors that may be *simultaneously* displayed is limited by the size of the table — most displays allow 256 entries.

There are two types of colormaps: the *hardware colormap* is used by the server to translate its screen memory into the displayed image, while each window has a *virtual colormap* that defines its own mapping. Virtual colormaps are server resources, while the hardware colormap is part of the server. When a window is topmost, its virtual colormap is copied into the hardware colormap.

Since virtual colormaps are server resources and are identified by resource ID, windows can share colormaps simply by using the same ID. This ability is used to great extent: not only do all of a client's windows use the same colormap, most clients share the same colormap, the *default colormap*.

This sharing is possible because most clients use a relatively small number of colors, and most users prefer that clients use the same color scheme. Thus, of the 256 cells available in a normal colormap, two dozen might be shared by all clients, while each client might have one or two unique colors. While sharing colormaps makes efficient use of the server's memory, it also means that the server does not need to continually swap virtual colormaps into or out of the hardware colormap.

In some cases, however, a client will need to allocate a large number of colormap cells and will not be able to use the default colormap. An example is a CAD program with three-dimensional shading. Such a program must allocate a unique virtual colormap and fill it with the necessary color cells. When it becomes the topmost window, its colormap is copied into the hardware colormap, temporarily changing the color scheme of all clients.

---

[3] Some high-end displays do in fact assign 24 bits to each pixel, allowing "photorealistic" images. Such displays are more expensive than their brethren; in most cases, they are also slower because more memory must be accessed for each operation.

The Pixel *Data Type*

Motif programmers rarely modify colormaps directly. Instead, the resource manager translates named colors into RGB values, and then allocates colormap entries for these colors.[4] The program then accesses the colors using their colormap indices, which are stored in the `Pixel` data type.

The `Pixel` type is a 32-bit unsigned integer. While most servers are limited to 8-bit colormaps, the size of `Pixel` allows it to be used even in those cases where the server supports 24-bit color — in these cases, the `Pixel` value is identical to the 24-bit RGB value.

The Color Database

The link between named colors and their RGB equivalents is provided by the color database. On a UNIX system, the file `/usr/lib/X11/rgb.txt` contains a human-readable version of this database, an excerpt from which is shown in Listing 15.1.[5]

Listing 15.1. Color database (/usr/lib/X11/rgb.txt) extract

```
112 219 147            aquamarine
50  204 153            medium aquamarine
50  204 153            MediumAquamarine
0   0   0              black
0   0   255            blue
```

The first three fields in each line contain 8-bit values for the color's red, green, and blue components. The fourth field is the color name, which may be specified in a resource file. Note that some colors — such as medium aquamarine — have multiple spellings, all of which represent the same color combination.[6]

The Standard Xlib Parameters

To send a drawing command to the server, an Xlib function needs to know three things: the display (server), the ID of the destination window, and the ID of a graphics context. The first two are associated with the widget and may be retrieved with the functions prototyped in Listing 15.2: `XtDisplay` returns a pointer to the widget's display record, and `XtWindow` returns its window ID. Both functions take the widget's ID as their sole parameter.

---

[4] Whenever possible — which is almost always — these entries are allocated from the default colormap and shared among clients.

[5] If your server is running on a UNIX system, the file `/usr/lib/X11/rgb.pag` contains a computer-readable version of the color database.

[6] Such multiply named colors exist because `rgb.txt` has been built by accretion — each vendor adds its own colors and spelling, and these changes make their way through the X community.

Listing 15.2. Function prototypes: *XtDisplay, XtWindow*

```
Display *XtDisplay( w )
        Widget      w;


Window  XtWindow( w )
        Widget      w;
```

Whereas a widget's display and window information may be retrieved from the widget itself, a graphics context is a server resource and must be allocated. The approach taken by a toolkit-based program is different from that of a native Xlib program: while the latter creates and destroys GCs as needed, the former attempts to share a GC with other clients. This is accomplished with the functions prototyped in Listing 15.3.

Listing 15.3. Function prototypes: *XtGetGC, XtReleaseGC*

```
GC        XtGetGC( w, mask, values )
          Widget      w;
          XtGCMask    mask;
          XGCValues   *values;


void      XtReleaseGC( w, gc )
          Widget      w;
          GC          gc;
```

The function `XtGetGC` attempts to find a graphics context on the server which contains the values desired; it will create one if necessary.[7] `XtReleaseGC` indicates to the server that this client is no longer using the GC. If no other client is using it, it is destroyed; otherwise, it remains in the server's memory.

The `mask` and `values` parameters of `XtGetGC` specify which members of the GC interest the client. The `mask` parameter contains a bit-mask, with each bit corresponding to one of the GC members. The `values` parameter points at an `XGCValues` structure, described below, with the desired members set to the desired values.

---

[7] This GC is *read-only*. While Xlib provides a set of functions that modify a read-write GC, such functions may not be used with a GC allocated by `XtGetGC`; instead, a new GC must be allocated.

The Graphics Context

What Is the Graphics Context?

The *graphics context* (GC) is a server resource that modifies the actions of the Xlib primitives. Its purpose is best explained by example, in this case, the drawing of a line.

Xlib provides a primitive function, `XDrawLine`, which draws a line between two points. While the operation seems to be simple, there are a host of questions that must be resolved before it can be performed. For example, what color should the line be?

The graphics context, which is passed as an argument to the `XDrawLine` function, contains the answer to that question. It also specifies whether the line is solid or dashed, the appearance of the ends of the line, and the way that the line is joined to any existing lines — as well as many other controls related and unrelated to line drawing.

Each graphics primitive requires a GC to be passed as one of its arguments. These GCs are allocated by the program as needed, using `XtGetGC`.

The Graphics Context in Detail

The graphics context is maintained by the server, and its exact contents are dependent on the server implementation — in some cases, a server may add of change fields to increase its performance. The standard GC fields, however, are represented by the structure `XGCValues`, defined in Listing 15.4 and described below.[8]

---

[8] The `XGCValues` structure is defined in the header file `X11/Xlib.h`. The constants used for various fields, as well as the mask constants for `XtGCMask`, are defined in the header file `X11/X.h`.

Listing 15.4. Type definition: XGCValues

```
typedef struct
        {
        int             function;
        unsigned long   plane_mask;
        Pixel           foreground;
        Pixel           background;
        int             line_width;
        int             line_style;
        int             cap_style;
        int             join_style;
        int             fill_style;
        int             fill_rule;
        int             arc_mode;
        Pixmap          tile;
        Pixmap          stipple;
        int             ts_x_origin;
        int             ts_y_origin;
        Font            font;
        int             subwindow_mode;
        Boolean         graphics_exposures;
        int             clip_x_origin;
        int             clip_y_origin;
        Pixmap          clip_mask;
        int             dash_offset;
        char            dashes;
        }
XGCValues;
```

Effect of the Drawing Operation: function

The function member controls the way in which a drawing function is applied to
the window. To understand this, you must remember that the action of a
drawing function is to change the contents of a window's memory map. When
the window is blank, its memory map is not blank: it is filled with bits
representing the window's background color. A drawing function changes parts
of the memory map to the bits representing the window's foreground color.
Exactly how these bits are changed depends on the contents of function. By
default, function contains the value GXcopy, which instructs the server to
overwrite the current contents of the window.

What Parts of the Memory Map Are Affected: plane_mask

The `plane_mask` member is used with servers that divide display memory into multiple planes, to specify which planes are affected by a drawing operation. On such servers, a program can draw into one set of a window's planes, while another set is displayed; when drawing is complete, the displayed set of planes may be changed. By default, `plane_mask` specifies all planes; there is rarely a need to change it.

Foreground and Background Colors: foreground, background

The `foreground` and `background` members specify colors to use when drawing into a window. The foreground color is the color used to draw lines and other objects; the background color is used when clearing parts of the window. You should note that these members are not the same as the widget's `foreground` and `background` resources: the program can use any colors for the GC's foreground and background.[9]

Line Attributes: line_width, line_style, cap_style, dashes, dash_offset

The `line_width` member simply specifies the width of any lines drawn on the screen and contains a count of pixels. Since Xlib is not part of Motif, width values specified by `line_width` are not affected by the `unitType` resource. Note that "width" is a misleading term: for a horizontal line, `line_width` actually refers to height.

The `line_style` member, in concert with the `dashes` and `dash_offset` members, allows the programmer to specify whether lines are solid or dashed. The legal values for `line_style` are as follows:

- `LineSolid` specifies that the line is drawn using the foreground color. This is the default.

- `LineOnOffDash` specifies that line segments of the foreground color alternate with equal-length undrawn segments.

- `LineDoubleDash` specifies that line segments of the foreground color alternate with equal-length segments of the background color.

For dashed lines, the `dashes` member specifies the length in pixels of each segment, and the `dash_offset` member specifies how many pixels into the cycle a line starts. This is best shown by example: Figure 15.1 shows a line drawn in `LineDoubleDash` style, with a `dashes` value of 4 and `dash_offset` of 2. For illustrative purposes, the individual pixels are shown as blocks: black for foreground, gray for background.

---

[9] The widget's internal code, however, *does* use a GC with its `foreground` and `background` members set to the values of the widget's `foreground` and `background` **resources.**

Figure 15.1. Line-style example

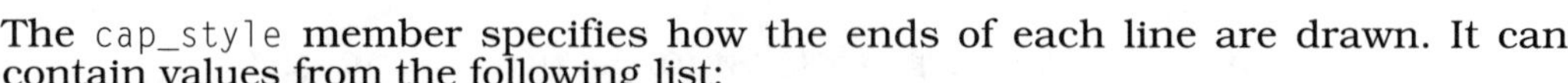

The `cap_style` member specifies how the ends of each line are drawn. It can contain values from the following list:

- `CapButt` specifies that lines are to be drawn with square ends. This is the default value.

- `CapRound` specifies that lines are to be drawn with round ends. The radius of the rounded end is equal to one-half of the line's width.

- `CapNotLast` specifies that the line is to have a square end. However, if the line width is 0 or 1, the line length is shortened by one pixel. This allows for smoother joints.

- `CapProjecting` also indicates a square end, but specifies that the line is to be extended by an amount equal to one-half of its width.

Meeting of the Lines: join_style

The `join_style` member controls how the drawing function attaches two lines — this happens when the starting point of one line is at the same location as the end point of another line. Legal values are as follows:

- `JoinRound` specifies that the meeting point is drawn as a circle — even if the line ends are square.

- `JoinMiter` (the default) specifies that the outside edges of the lines are extended, forming an acute angle at the meeting point.

- `JoinBevel` specifies that the meeting point is filled by connecting the outside edges of the lines.

The differences between these styles may not be apparent from the descriptions, so Figure 15.2 presents them graphically. Figure 15.2(a) shows `JoinRound`, 15.2(b) shows `JoinMiter`, and 15.2(c) shows `JoinBevel`. In these diagrams, the solid rectangles indicate the drawn lines, while the gray areas indicate the joints.[10]

---

[10] Note that the join style really doesn't matter when the linewidths are small — all styles appear the same. Once the lines become larger than 4 pixels or so, the different styles become apparent.

Figure 15.2. Joint styles

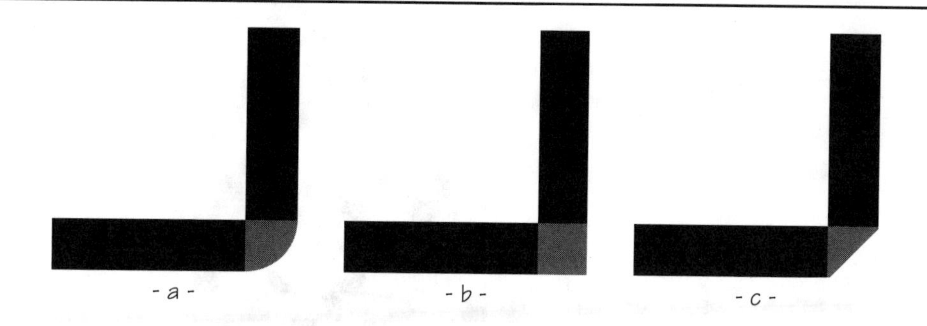

Shape Fill Controls, fill_style, tile, stipple, ts_x_origin, ts_y_origin, fill_rule

The `fill_style` member, in concert with the `tile`, `stipple`, `ts_x_origin`, and `ts_y_origin` members, specifies how filled objects are drawn. Shapes may be filled with a solid color or "tiled," by repeating the contents of a pixmap through the shape. The legal values for `fill_style` are as follows:

- `FillSolid`. The object is completely filled with the foreground color.

- `FillTiled`. The object is filled using the pixmap specified by `tile`. The first tile is placed at a position (within the window) specified by the `ts_x_origin` and `ts_y_origin` members. Subsequent tiles are placed adjacent to the first tile, until the shape is completely filled. If any tile extends beyond the boundary of the shape, that tile is trimmed to fit the shape. Figure 15.3 shows this in action.

- `FillStippled`, `FillOpaqueStippled`. The object is filled using the bitmap specified by the `stipple` member. Unlike tiling, this bitmap is drawn using the foreground and background colors of the GC (tiles contain their own colors). The difference between `FillStippled` and `FillOpaqueStippled` is that the former applies only the foreground bits to the window (so that the existing bits show through the "background" color), while the latter completely covers the window.

Figure 15.3. Tiling

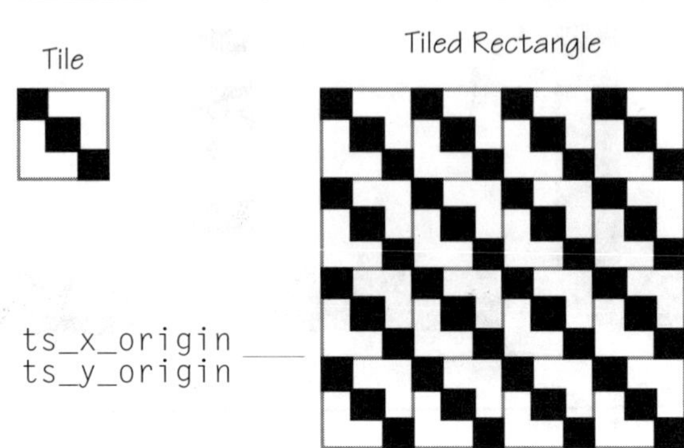

The `fill_rule` member controls how polygons are filled. For simple polygons, such as a square or hexagon, it isn't needed. However, an X polygon can be an irregular shape, with lines crossing and recrossing each other. The two fill methods are even-odd and winding and are illustrated by Figure 15.4: 15.4(a) is the polygon, 15.4(b) is the polygon filled according to the even-odd rule, and 15.4(c) is the polygon filled according to the winding rule.

The even-odd rule, enabled by the constant `EvenOddRule`, specifies that if a line drawn from a point within the polygon would cross an odd number of polygon lines on its way out of the polygon, then that point is inside the polygon. The winding rule, enabled by the constant `WindingRule`, specifies that a point is inside the polygon if a line from that point crosses an unequal number of clockwise and counter-clockwise line segments on its way out of the polygon. In this case, the "direction" of a line segment is determined by starting at an arbitrary vertex and following the lines of the polygon: a segment is clockwise if it crosses the imaginary line from left to right; counterclockwise if it crosses from right to left.

Figure 15.4. Fill rules

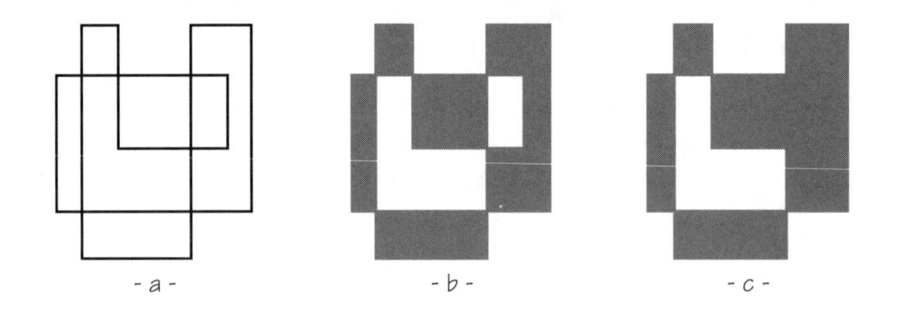

Arc Fill Control: arc_mode

The `arc_mode` member is used only when drawing filled arcs and specifies how the endpoints of the arcs are to be connected. Two values are allowed: `ArcChord` and `ArcPieSlice`. Figure 15.5 shows the result of these values: 15.5(a) uses `ArcPieSlice` (the default), while 15.5(b) uses `ArcChord`.

Figure 15.5. Arc fill modes

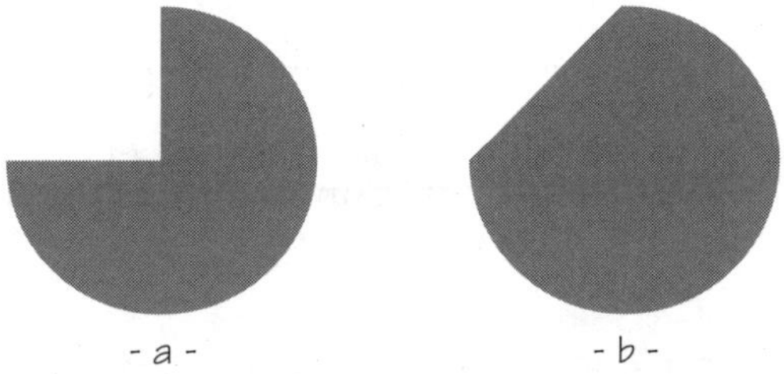

Text Drawing: font

The `font` member contains the ID of the font to use for text output.[11] It is only needed for Xlib text-drawing functions; if you use `XmStringDraw` or equivalent, the proper font is loaded as needed.

Generation of the GraphicsExpose *Event:* graphics_exposures

The `graphics_exposures` member is a flag, which comes into use only when copying data from one window to another. If `graphics_exposures` contains `TRUE` (the default), such a copy will result in either a `GraphicsExpose` or `NoExpose` event: `GraphicsExpose` indicates that the source was obscured and the destination must be drawn manually; `NoExpose` indicates that the source was not obscured and the copy completed. If `graphics_exposures` contains `FALSE`, these events are masked.

Clipping: clip_mask, clip_x_origin, clip_y_origin

It is possible, when executing a drawing function, to specify that part of the drawing is to be clipped — drawing does not take place in the clipped area. The `clip_mask` member specifies a bitmap that controls clipping: a set bit in this mask permits the function to modify the corresponding window pixel, an unset bit causes the drawing function to skip the pixel. The members `clip_x_origin` and `clip_y_origin` specify the position of the clipping mask with respect to the

---

[11] Fonts are server resources. They may be loaded into the server with the Xlib functions `XLoadFont` and `XQueryFont`.

destination window. By default, the `clip_mask` member contains the value `None`, which indicates that drawing operations are not clipped.

Most programs do not create complex clipping masks. Instead, they create a mask that exactly matches a window and use functions such as `XSetClipRectangles` to add large pieces to the mask — for example, in response to an exposure event with a nonzero count.

How Children Affect Drawing: subwindow_mode

The `subwindow_mode` member specifies how a window's children affect the operation of functions that draw into that window. If it contains `ClipByChildren` (the default), any drawing operations that would be obscured by a child window are clipped — the child window is opaque. If, however, `subwindow_mode` contains `IncludeInferiors`, the drawing operation is not clipped and writes into the screen memory occupied by the child — the child appears to be transparent.

Specifying Desired Values to XtGetGC: XtGCMask

The `XGCValues` structure contains many members that are not applicable to particular types of drawing. For example, when drawing a line, the contents of `arc_mode` may be indeterminate — they are not pertinent to the operation. For this reason, the `XtGetGC` function has the `mask` parameter, which specifies which fields are useful. The server attempts to find a GC with those fields set as desired and creates one if necessary.

Table 15.1 presents the list of constants that may be used in this mask, and the members to which they correspond. These constants are contained in the header file `X11/X.h`.

Table 15.1. *XtGCMask* constants

Constant	Corresponding Member(s)
GCFunction	function
GCPlaneMask	plane_mask
GCForeground	foreground
GCBackground	background
GCLineWidth	line_width
GCLineStyle	line_style
GCCapStyle	cap_style
GCJoinStyle	join_style
GCFillStyle	fill_style
GCFillRule	fill_rule
GCTile	tile
GCStipple	stipple
GCTileStipXOrigin	ts_x_origin
GCTileStipYOrigin	ts_y_origin
GCFont	font
GCSubwindowMode	subwindow_mode
GCGraphicsExposures	graphics_exposures
GCClipXOrigin	clip_x_origin
GCClipMask	clip_mask
GCDashList	dashes
GCArcMode	arc_mode

XmDrawingArea

All widgets are associated with windows, so a program could conceivably draw
into any widget. In practice, however, the internal exposure processing of a
widget would overwrite whatever the program had drawn into its window. For
this reason, Motif provides the *XmDrawingArea* class, which provides the
program a "canvas" in which to draw with Xlib graphics calls.

XmDrawingArea is derived from *XmManager*, as shown by the class tree of
Figure 15.6. While this derivation may seem strange — *XmPrimitive* would seem
a more appropriate superclass — it actually gives a drawing-area widget great
flexibility. One benefit is the presence of *XmManager*'s shadow border. Another is

the ability to hold a child: an *XmDrawingArea* widget could provide an ornate border around a program window.

Figure 15.6. *XmDrawingArea* class tree

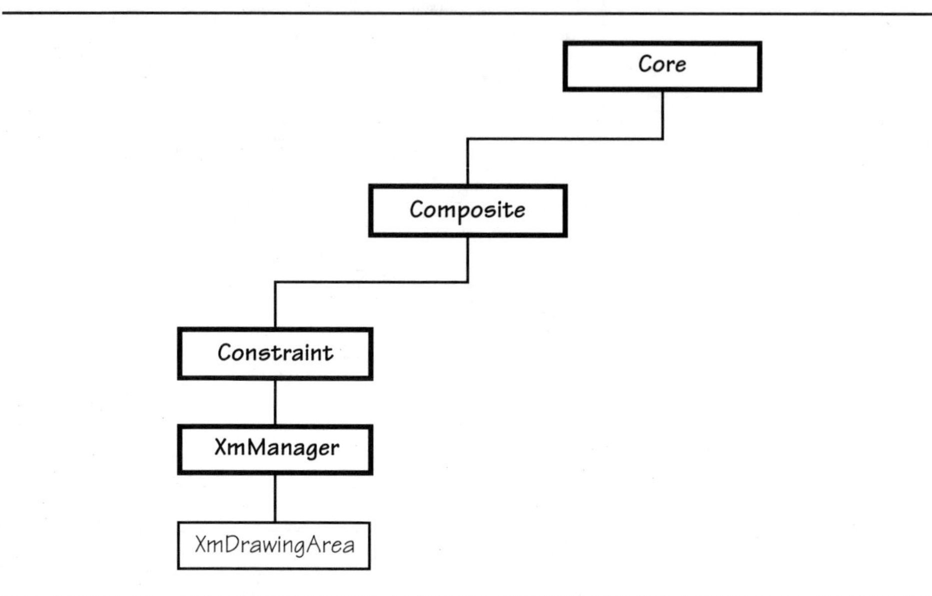

XmDrawingArea **Resources**

In addition to the resources of *XmManager* and its superclasses, *XmDrawingArea* defines the resources listed in Table 15.2. Aside from the callback lists, these resources control child management and are identical to the *XmBulletinBoard* resources with the same names.[12]

---

[12] The `marginHeight` and `marginWidth` resources specify a margin between the sides of the drawing area and its children; the `resizePolicy` resource controls how the drawing area changes size as children are added or removed.

Table 15.2. Frequently used resources: *XmDrawingArea*

Name	Inheritance	Type	Default Value
`exposeCallback`	XmDrawingArea	`XtCallbackList`	`NULL`
`inputCallback`	XmDrawingArea	`XtCallbackList`	`NULL`
`marginHeight`	XmDrawingArea	`Dimension`	`10`
`marginWidth`	XmDrawingArea	`Dimension`	`10`
`resizeCallback`	XmDrawingArea	`XtCallbackList`	`NULL`
`resizePolicy`	XmDrawingArea	`unsigned char`	`XmRESIZE_ANY`

XmDrawingArea Callbacks

XmDrawingArea invokes callbacks when it is exposed, when the user causes a key or button event to occur within its borders (user input), and when it is resized. All three callbacks pass data in the same structure, `XmDrawingArea-CallbackStruct`, defined in Listing 15.5.

Listing 15.5. Type definition: *XmDrawingAreaCallbackStruct*

```
typedef struct
        {
        int     reason;
        XEvent  *event;
        Window  window;
        }
XmDrawingAreaCallbackStruct;
```

The `reason` member of `XmDrawingAreaCallbackStruct` identifies the reason that the callback was invoked: exposure uses a reason of `XmCR_EXPOSE`, user input uses `XmCR_INPUT`, and size change uses `XmCR_RESIZE`. The `event` member points at the event that initiated the callback. Unlike most callback, the `event` member provides essential details to a drawing-area callback handler. The final member, `window`, contains the ID of the window where the event occurred; if the drawing area has children, this may be the window of a child.

Exposure: exposeCallback

When portions of a drawing-area are exposed, the server sends an `Expose` event to the widget's internal event handler. It then passes that event to the callback functions specified by the `exposeCallback` resource; they are responsible for redrawing the contents of the window. If no callbacks are registered, the drawing-area simply repaints the exposed window area with its background color.

Exposure events are contained in the `xexpose` member of the `XEvent` union. This member is of the type `XExposeEvent`, defined in Listing 15.6. As with other events, the `type` member contains the event type (`Expose`), the `serial` member contains a server sequence number, the `send_event` member indicates whether the event was server- or client-generated, and the `display` and `window` members identify the source of the event. The other members are specific to an exposure event and are described below.

Listing 15.6. Type definition: XExposeEvent

```
typedef struct
        {
        int             type;
        unsigned long   serial;
        Boolean         send_event;
        Display         *display;
        Window          window;
        int             x, y;
        int             width, height;
        int             count;
        }
XExposeEvent;
```

An exposure event indicates to the client that a rectangular portion of a window needs to be redrawn. The `x` and `y` members of `XExposeEvent` specify the position of this rectangle relative to the window; its dimensions are specified by the `width` and `height` members.

In a simple case, exposure results from a situation such as Figure 15.7(a). Window *B* covers window *A*; when it is moved, a rectangular portion of *A* becomes exposed. A more complex case is portrayed in Figure 15.7(b). In this case, two windows cover window *A*; if it is then made the topmost window ("shuffled up"), two rectangular areas of *A* become exposed — a situation that cannot be handled by the basic exposure event.

The only possible solution within the framework of `XExposeEvent` is to indicate the exposure with multiple events. Unfortunately, this can cause excessive work on the part of the program: if a line in window *A* passes through both exposed rectangles, it must be redrawn twice — one segment per event.

The `count` member provides a solution to this problem: it contains the number of events yet to be received as a result of this exposure. A value of zero means that this is the last event, and the program should redraw the window. A nonzero value indicates that the program should simply maintain a record of the exposed area, until the last event is received.[13]

---

[13] Xlib provides the ability to maintain a clipping region in a GC, composed of the rectangles that are reported in exposure events. The program can then simply redraw the entire window, and the GC will cause the server to ignore those commands that fall outside the clipping region. While this is a very elegant solution, in most cases, it is easier — and more efficient — to simply redraw the entire window on the last expose event (when `count` contains zero) and ignore all preceding events.

Figure 15.7. Two cases of exposure

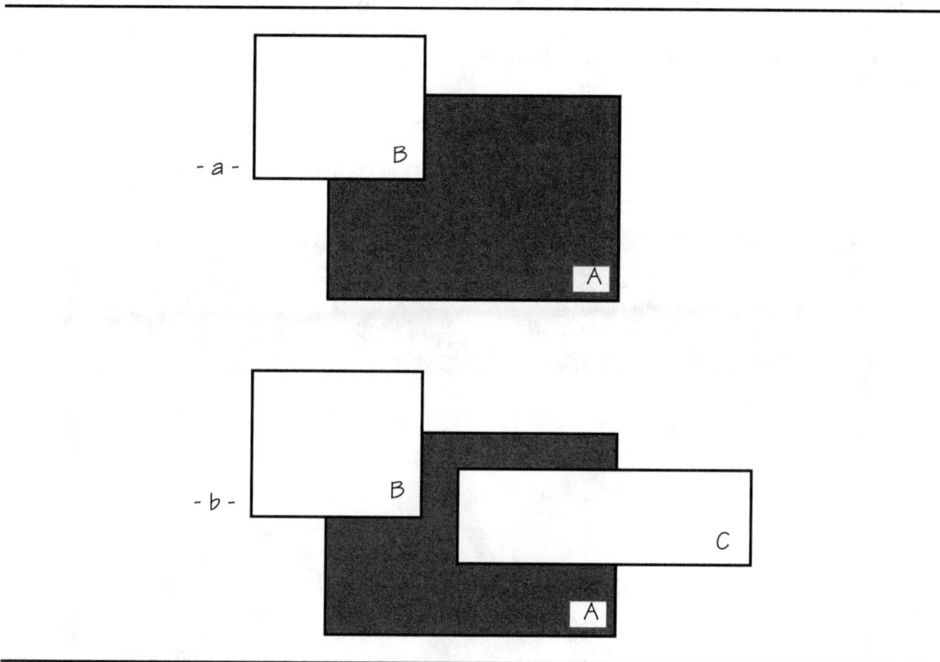

User Input: inputCallback

The functions specified by `inputCallback` are invoked whenever the user causes a button or keyboard event to occur within the window — `KeyPress`, `KeyRelease`, `ButtonPress`, or `ButtonRelease`. It is *not* invoked, however, for pointer movement. To capture movement events, the program must add an event handler.

Depending on the event type, the `event` member points at either an `XKeyEvent` or `XButtonEvent` structure. The event type may be determined using the `xany` member of `XEvent`.

Size Change: resizeCallback

The `resizeCallback` resource specifies a list of functions that are called when the drawing-area's window is resized.[14] This resize can occur for any reason — user size change, parental constraint, or programmatic size change. No event is passed for this callback; the program must get its new size from the widget's resources.

---

[14] Enlarging a window also results in exposure events.

XmDrawingArea **Example: Doodle**

Figure 15.8 presents an example of *XmDrawingArea* in use: the "Doodle" program. This program is a very simple example of a "paint" program: it allows the user to draw with the pointer in a selection of colors and pen sizes. No provision is made for saving the image or for loading an already drawn image into the program.

Figure 15.8. *XmDrawingArea* example: "Doodle"

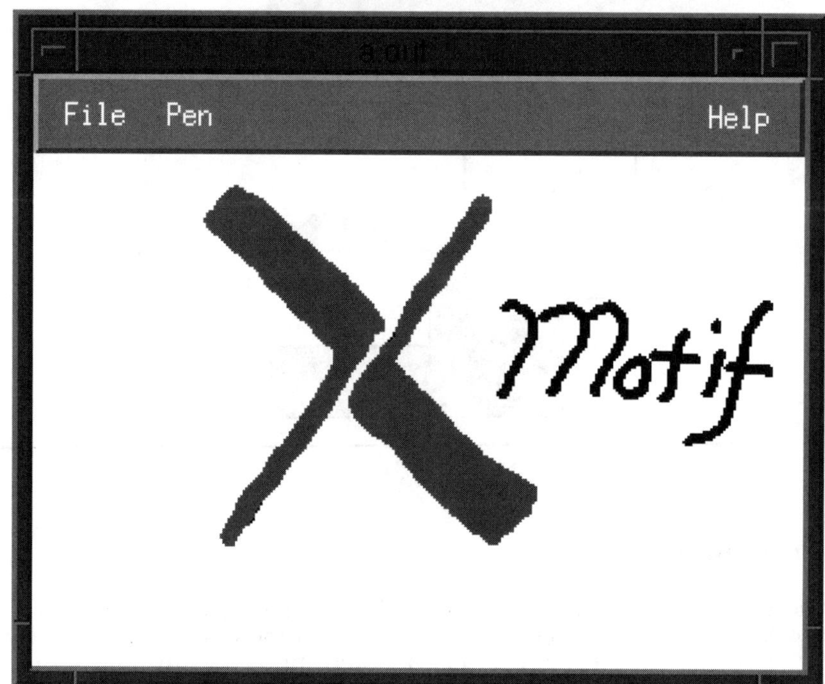

Listing 15.7 presents the program and resource file for the doodle program. It is based on the complex program template and is split into multiple modules. Tying these modules together is a program header file, `doodle.h`.

The first module, `main.c`, initializes the main window and calls the functions that initialize the rest of the program. It also contains the program's global variables and initiates the event loop.

The second module, `menu.c`, is almost identical in structure to the menu module of the text editor.[15] It presents a much smaller menu structure, however, the **File** menu contains options to clear the workspace (**New**) and terminate the program (**Exit**); the **Pen** menu allows the user to change the drawing color (**Color**) and the

---

[15] It was, in fact, copied from the text editor.

width of the lines (**Size**); the **Help** menu does nothing.[16] One interesting feature of this module is its use of cascading pull-downs for the **Pen/Color** and **Pen/Size** menu choices. Also note that the callbacks for these two menus are not in the menu module — instead, they are in the work-window module.

The third module, *workwin.c*, is where this program is unique. This module creates the work window, which is an *XmDrawingArea* widget. It also handles the various callbacks and events that affect this window. It, and the resource file, are described in more detail below the listing.

Listing 15.7. Program and resource file: Doodle

```
/*********************************************************************
**                                                                 **
**   doodle.h                                                      **
**                                                                 **
**   Doodle -- Inter-Module Header File                           **
**                                                                 **
**   Contains external declarations for all functions and interesting  **
**   variables.                                                    **
**                                                                 **
*********************************************************************/




/*********************************************************************
**                                                                 **
**       E X T E R N A L   F U N C T I O N   R E F E R E N C E S    **
**                                                                 **
*********************************************************************/

extern  void    InitMenuBar();                  /* menu.c         */

extern  void    InitWorkWindow();               /* workwin.c      */
extern  void    ClearWin();
extern  void    PenColorCB();
extern  void    PenSizeCB();
```

---

[16] Note that, aside from **File** and **Help**, this program does not follow the standard menu structure. It is an example where the standard menus do not apply to the problem being solved.

Listing 15.7. Continued.

```c
/*******************************************************************
**                                                               **
**                 G L O B A L   V A R I A B L E S               **
**                                                               **
*******************************************************************/

extern  Widget  appshell,               /* Application Shell       */
                mainwin,                 /* XmMainWindow            */
                menubar,                 /* MainWindow Menu Bar     */
                workwin;                 /* MainWindow Work Area    */
extern  Arg     arglist[16];             /* For programmatic rsrc stuf */


/*******************************************************************
**                                                               **
**   main.c                                                      **
**                                                               **
**   Doodle -- Main Module                                       **
**                                                               **
*******************************************************************/

#include <Xm/MainW.h>

#include "doodle.h"


/*******************************************************************
**                                                               **
**                 G L O B A L   V A R I A B L E S               **
**                                                               **
*******************************************************************/

Widget  appshell,                        /* Application Shell       */
        mainwin,                         /* XmMainWindow            */
        menubar,                         /* MainWindow Menu Bar     */
        workwin,                         /* MainWindow Work Area     */
        textwin;                         /* Work Window XmText widget */
Arg     arglist[16];                     /* For programmatic rsrc stuf */
```

Listing 15.7. Continued.

```c
/*********************************************************************
**                                                                 **
**                 F O R W A R D   D E F I N I T I O N S           **
**                                                                 **
*********************************************************************/

static   void    InitMainWindow();
static   void    InitOther();




/*********************************************************************
**                                                                 **
**   main( argc, argv )                                            **
**                                                                 **
**   Program entry point. Creates shell, calls initialization funcs, **
**   and turns control over to event loop.                         **
**                                                                 **
*********************************************************************/

void main( argc, argv )
    int      argc;
    char     *argv[];
{
    appshell = XtInitialize( argv[0], "Doodle", NULL, 0, &argc, argv );

    InitMainWindow();
    InitMenuBar();
    InitWorkWindow();

    XmMainWindowSetAreas( mainwin, menubar, NULL, NULL, NULL, workwin );

    InitOther();

    XtRealizeWidget( appshell );
    XtMainLoop();
}
```

Listing 15.7. Continued.

```c
/******************************************************************
**                                                              **
**   InitMainWindow()                                           **
**                                                              **
**   This function creates the main window widget and its scrollbars.  **
**   The main window is created as a child of the application shell.   **
**   .The scrollbars are either created along with the main-window (if **
**   its "scrollingPolicy" resource contains TRUE) or separately.      **
**                                                              **
**   This function modifies the global "mainwin", and accesses the     **
**   global "appshell".                                         **
**                                                              **
******************************************************************/

static void InitMainWindow()
{
    mainwin = XmCreateMainWindow( appshell, "MainWin", NULL, 0 );
    XtManageChild( mainwin );
}




/******************************************************************
**                                                              **
**   InitOther()                                                **
**                                                              **
**   This function currently does not do anything. It would be used   **
**   to initialize dialog boxes and the like.                   **
**                                                              **
******************************************************************/

static void InitOther()
{
}
```

Listing 15.7. Continued.

```
/*******************************************************************
**                                                               **
**   menu.c                                                      **
**                                                               **
**   Doodle -- Menubar Module                                    **
**                                                               **
*******************************************************************/

#include <string.h>

#include <Xm/RowColumn.h>
#include <Xm/CascadeB.h>
#include <Xm/Label.h>
#include <Xm/PushB.h>
#include <Xm/Separator.h>

#include "doodle.h"


/*******************************************************************
**                                                               **
**            F O R W A R D   D E F I N I T I O N S              **
**                                                               **
*******************************************************************/

static  void    InitFileMenu();
static  void    InitPenMenu();
static  void    InitPenColorMenu();
static  void    InitPenSizeMenu();
static  void    InitHelpMenu();

static  void    FileMenuCB();


/*******************************************************************
**                                                               **
**   InitMenuBar()                                               **
**                                                               **
**   This function creates the menu bar and all pull-down menus. The **
**   menu bar is created as the child of the main window.        **
**                                                               **
**   This function modifies the global "menubar", and accesses the **
**   global "mainwin".                                           **
**                                                               **
*******************************************************************/
```

Listing 15.7. Continued.

```c
void InitMenuBar()
{
    menubar = XmCreateMenuBar( mainwin, "MenuBar", NULL, 0 );
    XtManageChild( menubar );

    InitFileMenu();
    InitPenMenu();
    InitHelpMenu();
}




/************************************************************************
**                                                                    **
**    InitFileMenu()                                                  **
**                                                                    **
**    Creates the File menu: cascade button, pull-down menu pane, and **
**    all menu-pane choices. Attaches callbacks to menu-pane choices. **
**                                                                    **
************************************************************************/

static void InitFileMenu()
{
    Widget        topic,
                  pane,
                  choices[3];

    pane = XmCreatePulldownMenu( menubar, "FilePane", NULL, 0 );

    choices[0] = XmCreatePushButton( pane, "File_Clear", NULL, 0 );
    choices[1] = XmCreateSeparator( pane, "File_Sep", NULL, 0 );
    choices[2] = XmCreatePushButton( pane, "File_Exit", NULL, 0 );
    XtManageChildren( choices, 3 );

    XtSetArg( arglist[0], XmNsubMenuId, pane );
    topic = XmCreateCascadeButton( menubar, "FileTopic", arglist, 1 );
    XtManageChild( topic );

    XtAddCallback( choices[0], XmNactivateCallback, FileMenuCB, "New" );
    XtAddCallback( choices[2], XmNactivateCallback, FileMenuCB, "Ext" );
```

Listing 15.7. Continued.

```c
}



/**************************************************************************
**                                                                      **
**    InitPenMenu()                                                     **
**                                                                      **
**    Creates the Pen menu: cascade button, pull-down menu pane, and    **
**    all menu-pane choices. Attaches callbacks to menu-pane choices.   **
**                                                                      **
**************************************************************************/

static void InitPenMenu()
{
    Widget      topic,
                pane,
                choices[2];

    pane = XmCreatePulldownMenu( menubar, "Pen_Pane", NULL, 0 );

    choices[0] = XmCreateCascadeButton( pane, "Pen_Color", NULL, 0 );
    choices[1] = XmCreateCascadeButton( pane, "Pen_Size", NULL, 0 );
    XtManageChildren( choices, 2 );

    XtSetArg( arglist[0], XmNsubMenuId, pane );
    topic = XmCreateCascadeButton( menubar, "PenTopic", arglist, 1 );
    XtManageChild( topic );

    InitPenColorMenu( pane, choices[0] );
    InitPenSizeMenu( pane, choices[1] );
}
```

Listing 15.7. Continued.

```c
/**********************************************************************
**                                                                  **
**    InitPenColorMenu()                                            **
**                                                                  **
**    Creates the cascading pull-down for pen colors.               **
**    The attached callback is in the file "mainwin.c"              **
**                                                                  **
**********************************************************************/

static void InitPenColorMenu( parent, button )
    Widget      parent;
    Widget      button;
{
    Widget      pane,
                choices[6];

    pane = XmCreatePulldownMenu( parent, "PenColor_Pane", NULL, 0 );

    choices[0] = XmCreatePushButton( pane, "PenColor_0", NULL, 0 );
    choices[1] = XmCreatePushButton( pane, "PenColor_1", NULL, 0 );
    choices[2] = XmCreatePushButton( pane, "PenColor_2", NULL, 0 );
    choices[3] = XmCreatePushButton( pane, "PenColor_3", NULL, 0 );
    choices[4] = XmCreatePushButton( pane, "PenColor_4", NULL, 0 );
    choices[5] = XmCreatePushButton( pane, "PenColor_5", NULL, 0 );
    XtManageChildren( choices, 6 );

    XtSetArg( arglist[0], XmNsubMenuId, pane );
    XtSetValues( button, arglist, 1 );

    XtAddCallback( choices[0], XmNactivateCallback, PenColorCB, NULL );
    XtAddCallback( choices[1], XmNactivateCallback, PenColorCB, NULL );
    XtAddCallback( choices[2], XmNactivateCallback, PenColorCB, NULL );
    XtAddCallback( choices[3], XmNactivateCallback, PenColorCB, NULL );
    XtAddCallback( choices[4], XmNactivateCallback, PenColorCB, NULL );
    XtAddCallback( choices[5], XmNactivateCallback, PenColorCB, NULL );
}
```

Listing 15.7. Continued.

```c
/**********************************************************************
**                                                                  **
**    InitPenSizeMenu()                                             **
**                                                                  **
**    Creates the cascading pull-down for pen sizes.                **
**    The attached callback is in the file "mainwin.c"              **
**                                                                  **
**********************************************************************/

static void InitPenSizeMenu( parent, button )
    Widget        parent;
    Widget        button;
{
    Widget        pane,
                  choices[5];

    pane = XmCreatePulldownMenu( parent, "PenSize_Pane", NULL, 0 );

    choices[0] = XmCreatePushButton( pane, "PenSize_1", NULL, 0 );
    choices[1] = XmCreatePushButton( pane, "PenSize_2", NULL, 0 );
    choices[2] = XmCreatePushButton( pane, "PenSize_3", NULL, 0 );
    choices[3] = XmCreatePushButton( pane, "PenSize_4", NULL, 0 );
    choices[4] = XmCreatePushButton( pane, "PenSize_8", NULL, 0 );
    XtManageChildren( choices, 5 );

    XtSetArg( arglist[0], XmNsubMenuId, pane );
    XtSetValues( button, arglist, 1 );

    XtAddCallback( choices[0], XmNactivateCallback, PenSizeCB, "1" );
    XtAddCallback( choices[1], XmNactivateCallback, PenSizeCB, "2" );
    XtAddCallback( choices[2], XmNactivateCallback, PenSizeCB, "3" );
    XtAddCallback( choices[3], XmNactivateCallback, PenSizeCB, "4" );
    XtAddCallback( choices[4], XmNactivateCallback, PenSizeCB, "8" );
}
```

Listing 15.7. Continued.

```c
/***********************************************************************
**                                                                   **
**   InitHelpMenu()                                                  **
**                                                                   **
**   Creates the Help menu: cascade button, pull-down menu pane, and **
**   all menu-pane choices. Attaches callbacks to menu-pane choices. **
**                                                                   **
***********************************************************************/

static void InitHelpMenu()
{
    Widget        topic,
                  pane,
                  choices[1];

    pane = XmCreatePulldownMenu( menubar, "Help_Pane", NULL, 0 );

    choices[0] = XmCreateLabel( pane, "Help_Lbl", NULL, 0 );
    XtManageChildren( choices, 1 );

    XtSetArg( arglist[0], XmNsubMenuId, pane );
    topic = XmCreateCascadeButton( menubar, "HelpTopic", arglist, 1 );
    XtManageChild( topic );

    XtSetArg( arglist[0], XmNmenuHelpWidget, topic );
    XtSetValues( menubar, arglist, 1 );
}
```

Listing 15.7. Continued.

```c
/*********************************************************************
**                                                                 **
**   FileMenuCB( w, client_data, call_data )                       **
**                                                                 **
**   Callback procedure for the "File" pull-down. This function is **
**   called when any of the file menu buttons are activated. The   **
**   particular operation is identified by a string accessed by the**
**   "client_data" param.                                          **
**                                                                 **
**   Note: This callback is only invoked on Activate, so the call  **
**         data (which describes the reason) is superfluous. It is **
**         therefore not declared as a specific type in the func hdr. **
**                                                                 **
*********************************************************************/

static void FileMenuCB( w, client_data, call_data )
    Widget      w;
    char        *client_data;
    caddr_t     call_data;
{
    if (!strcmp(client_data, "New"))
        ClearWin();
    else if (!strcmp(client_data, "Ext"))
        exit( 0 );
}
```

```c
/*********************************************************************
**                                                                 **
**   workwin.c                                                     **
**                                                                 **
**   Doodle -- Work Window Module                                  **
**                                                                 **
*********************************************************************/
```

Listing 15.7. Continued.

```c
#include <Xm/DrawingA.h>

#include "doodle.h"


/**********************************************************************
**                                                                  **
**                 F O R W A R D   D E F I N I T I O N S            **
**                                                                  **
**********************************************************************/

static void     InitGC();
static void     DrawEvt();




/**********************************************************************
**                                                                  **
**                 L O C A L   V A R I A B L E S                    **
**                                                                  **
**********************************************************************/

static  GC          the_gc;         /* Current GC for drawing     */
static  XGCValues   gc_values;      /* Values for allocating GCs  */
static  XtGCMask    gc_mask;        /* Mask for allocating GCs    */
static  int         last_x, last_y; /* Last pointer position      */




/**********************************************************************
**                                                                  **
**   InitWorkWindow()                                               **
**                                                                  **
**   This function creates the drawing area used as the work window. **
**   It also allocates the initial (default) GC for drawing in that **
**   window, and attaches callbacks and event handlers.            **
**                                                                  **
**********************************************************************/
```

Listing 15.7. Continued.

```c
void InitWorkWindow()
{
    workwin = XmCreateDrawingArea( mainwin, "WorkWin", NULL, 0 );
    XtManageChild( workwin );

    InitGC();

    XtAddEventHandler( workwin, (ButtonPressMask | ButtonMotionMask),
                                FALSE, DrawEvt, NULL );
}




/***********************************************************************
**                                                                   **
**   InitGC()                                                        **
**                                                                   **
**   Initializes the graphics context used for drawing. This function **
**   stores default values in the variable "gc_values", which is used **
**   to tell the server about the GC we want. It also sets bits in   **
**   "gc_mask", which is used to tell the server what values we have **
**   set. Finally, it gets the work window's color scheme, sets the  **
**   line width to 1, and allocates a GC.                            **
**                                                                   **
***********************************************************************/

static void InitGC()
{
    Pixel       foreground,
                background;

    XtSetArg( arglist[0], XmNforeground, &foreground );
    XtSetArg( arglist[1], XmNbackground, &background );
    XtGetValues( workwin, arglist, 2 );

    gc_values.foreground = foreground;
    gc_values.background = background;
    gc_values.line_width = 1;
    gc_values.line_style = LineSolid;
```

Listing 15.7. Continued.

```c
        gc_values.cap_style  = CapRound;
        gc_values.join_style = JoinRound;

        gc_mask = GCForeground | GCBackground | GCLineWidth |
                  GCLineStyle  | GCCapStyle   | GCJoinStyle;

        the_gc = XtGetGC( workwin, gc_mask, &gc_values );
}




/**********************************************************************
**                                                                  **
**   DrawEvt( w, client_data, event )                               **
**                                                                  **
**   This function is attached to button-press and button-motion    **
**   events. On button press, it initializes the stored position    **
**   variables. On button-motion, it draws a line from the stored   **
**   position to the new position, then stores the new position.    **
**                                                                  **
**********************************************************************/

static void DrawEvt( w, client_data, event )
    Widget      w;
    caddr_t     client_data;
    XEvent      *event;
{
    int         new_x, new_y;

    switch (event->type)
       {
       case ButtonPress :
               last_x = event->xbutton.x;
               last_y = event->xbutton.y;
               break;
       case MotionNotify :
               new_x = event->xmotion.x;
               new_y = event->xmotion.y;
               XDrawLine( XtDisplay(w), XtWindow(w), the_gc,
```

Listing 15.7. Continued.

```
                             last_x, last_y, new_x, new_y );
                last_x = new_x;
                last_y = new_y;
                break;
        default :
                break;
        }
}




/*************************************************************************
**                                                                     **
**   ClearWin()                                                        **
**                                                                     **
**   This function clears the work window. It is attached to the       **
**   File/New menu choice.                                             **
**                                                                     **
*************************************************************************/

void ClearWin()
{
    XClearWindow( XtDisplay(workwin), XtWindow(workwin) );
}




/*************************************************************************
**                                                                     **
**   PenColorCB( w, client_data, call_data )                           **
**                                                                     **
**   This function is attached to each of the buttons in the Pen       **
**   menu's Color submenu. It takes the foreground color from the      **
**   invoking button, and allocates a GC using that color.             **
**                                                                     **
*************************************************************************/

void PenColorCB( w, client_data, call_data )
    Widget      w;
```

Listing 15.7. Continued.

```c
    caddr_t     client_data;
    caddr_t     call_data;
{
    Pixel       new_color;

    XtReleaseGC( workwin, the_gc );

    XtSetArg( arglist[0], XmNbackground, &new_color );
    XtGetValues( w, arglist, 1 );

    gc_values.foreground = new_color;
    the_gc = XtGetGC( workwin, gc_mask, &gc_values );
}




/**********************************************************************
**                                                                  **
**    PenSizeCB( w, client_data, call_data )                        **
**                                                                  **
**    This function is attached to each of the buttons in the Pen   **
**    menu's Size submenu. It is passed a string as its client data,**
**    which specifies the new pen width. It then allocates a GC     **
**    that uses that width.                                         **
**                                                                  **
**    Note: A more elegant approach to line widths would use the    **
**          button's labelString resource to specify the width.     **
**                                                                  **
**********************************************************************/

void PenSizeCB( w, client_data, call_data )
    Widget      w;
    char        *client_data;
    caddr_t     call_data;
{
    XtReleaseGC( workwin, the_gc );

    if (!strcmp(client_data, "1"))
        gc_values.line_width = 1;
```

Listing 15.7. Continued.

```c
        else if (!strcmp(client_data, "2"))
            gc_values.line_width = 2;
        else if (!strcmp(client_data, "3"))
            gc_values.line_width = 3;
        else if (!strcmp(client_data, "4"))
            gc_values.line_width = 4;
        else if (!strcmp(client_data, "8"))
            gc_values.line_width = 8;

        the_gc = XtGetGC( workwin, gc_mask, &gc_values );
}
```

```
!
! Resource file for Doodle program (Fig 15.8)
!

!##############################################################################
!
! General Resources
!
!##############################################################################

*.background:                   Gray50
*.foreground:                   White
*.topShadowColor:               Gray75
*.bottomShadowColor:            Gray25


!##############################################################################
!
! Work Window Resources
!
!##############################################################################

*WorkWin.width:                 300
*WorkWin.height:                200
*WorkWin.foreground:            Black
*WorkWin.background:            White
```

Listing 15.7. Continued.

```
!####################################################################
!
! Main Menu Resources
!
!####################################################################

*FileTopic.labelString:            File
*File_Clear.labelString:           New
*File_Exit.labelString:            Exit

*File_Exit.accelerator:            Meta<KeyPress>q
*File_Exit.acceleratorText:        Alt-Q

*PenTopic.labelString:             Pen
*Pen_Color.labelString:            Color
*Pen_Size.labelString:             Size

*PenColor_Pane.XmPushButton.width:              50
*PenColor_Pane.XmPushButton.height:             25
*PenColor_Pane.XmPushButton.recomputeSize:      FALSE
*PenColor_Pane.XmPushButton.labelString:

*PenColor_0.background:             Black
*PenColor_1.background:             White
*PenColor_2.background:             Gray50
*PenColor_3.background:             Red
*PenColor_4.background:             Green
*PenColor_5.background:             Blue

*PenSize_1.labelString:             1
*PenSize_2.labelString:             2
*PenSize_3.labelString:             3
*PenSize_4.labelString:             4
*PenSize_8.labelString:             8

*HelpTopic.labelString:            Help
*Help_Lbl.labelString:             No Help Available
```

Initializing the Work Window: InitWorkWindow, InitGC

Work window initialization involves creating the *XmDrawingArea* widget, adding
an event handler for button presses and pointer movement, and creating the
default graphics context. The first two operations are straightforward:

`XmCreateDrawingArea` creates the widget, and `XtAddEventHandler` registers the event-handling function.

Initialization of the GC is slightly more complex and takes place in the function `InitGC`. Since a GC is required for every drawing operation, the program maintains a "current" GC in the variable `the_gc`; this GC is used for every drawing operation. `InitGC` retrieves the initial GC, configured in a standard manner.

`InitGC` makes the following assumptions about the initial drawing state: the foreground and background colors will come from the widget itself, and the pen will be a single pixel wide. An additional assumption is the appearance of the lines, controlled by the `line_style`, `cap_style`, and `join_style` members. These specifications are constant and may not be changed by the user.

Using these assumptions, `InitGC` retrieves the foreground and background colors from the widget and installs them in a module-wide `XGCValues` structure.[17] It also sets the other default values in that structure, then builds a mask identifying these values. It then allocates a GC with the desired values, using `XtGetGC`. Note that this GC is allocated on the basis of its line-drawing components only, as specified by the flags passed to `XtGetGC`.

Drawing: DrawEvt

The drawing process is simple: when the pointer moves with a button pressed, the program draws a line from the current position to the previous position. The "previous position" is maintained in the variables `last_x` and `last_y`; these are set when the button is first pressed.

One important thing to note is that all pointer movement is reported in a `MotionNotify` event, whether or not the button is down. Since this program only wants button-down motion, it must specify `ButtonMotionMask` when the event handler is registered.

The drawing operation itself is performed with the Xlib function `XDrawLine`. The parameters to this function should be obvious: the display pointer and window ID, the graphics context, and the old and new positions. Note that the display pointer and window IDs are retrieved from the widget passed to the event handler. They could be retrieved using the `workwin` global, but this is a more transportable method (it works if the event handler is attached to multiple windows).

Clearing the Work Window: ClearWin

The `ClearWin` function introduces the Xlib function `XClearWindow`. It identifies the window by its display and window ID; both are retrieved from the `workwin` widget. Unlike other functions, `XClearWindow` does not require a graphics context. Instead, it fills the window with the background color established at the time of window creation.

---

[17] This extract-and-store operation could have been performed in one step, specifying the relevant `XGCValues` members in the `XtSetArg` operation. I separated the steps for illustrative purposes.

Changing Pen Color: PenColorCB

The `PenColorCB` function is attached to each of the buttons in the **Pen/Color** submenu. This function changes the graphics context by releasing the current context and allocating a new context — after changing the `foreground` member.[18] It is located in this module — instead of the menu module — precisely because it changes the graphics context.

The way in which this function changes the color is in itself interesting. Each of the labels in the **Pen/Color** submenu are blank, but have a different background color. `PenColorCB` retrieves this background color — using the passed widget ID — and installs it in the graphics context. By doing this, it eliminates the need for a search of the color database and allows the user to easily configure the set of available colors.

Changing Pen Size: PenSizeCB

The `PenSizeCB` function is attached to each of the buttons in the **Pen/Size** submenu. It too changes the GC in use by releasing the old GC and allocating a new one. It is passed a new pen width as a string in its `client_data` parameter.[19]

The Resource File

The resource file is straightforward: it assigns a default color scheme, sizes the work window, assigns a color scheme to the work window, and specifies the contents of the menu. It does contain one item of interest: the definitions for the **Pen/Color** submenu.

As described above, this submenu contains a list of blank buttons — the buttons' background color is what's important. To make such buttons, you set the `labelString` resource to a blank string. However, doing so eliminates the button's method of determining its preferred size. So, the buttons must be sized explicitly, and `recomputeSize` must be set to `FALSE` — otherwise the buttons would attempt to size themselves at minimum size.

---

[18] Note for experienced Xlib programmers: since the graphics context is allocated *read-only*, the function `XSetForeground` cannot be used.

[19] As stated in the function header, this is not a very elegant way to handle size changes. A better way would be to retrieve an ASCII representation of the size from the `labelString` resource, then convert it to a numeric value.

16
Resources Revisited

Overview

Chapter 3 presented resources and resource files: what they were and how to use them. This chapter extends that presentation, with some of the more esoteric uses of resources and their relations.

It begins with the use of program instance names, a method by which a resource file can contain two (or more) sets of specifications for a single program, with the user able to choose a set at runtime. This is followed by a description of command-line options, which are used to change resource values at runtime.

The next topic is *resource conversion*, also known as *type conversion*. This is a mechanism by which the toolkit converts data from one type to another; it is primarily used to convert the ASCII text of a resource file to the internal format of a resource. There are two parts to this description: the first is how to write and install a resource converter; the second is how to call an existing converter from within application code.

The chapter finishes with a description of *application resources*: program variables that can be set at runtime via the resource mechanism.

Program Instance Names

A user may use the same program in two or more environments and desire a unique appearance for each. For example, the appearance resources used with a color screen may not be suitable for a monochrome screen.

This customization could be performed by editing the resource file, but that process is tedious and not easy to reverse. It could also be performed by maintaining two resource files, with the `XENVIRONMENT` or `XAPPLRESDIR` variable used to select the proper one. Unfortunately, that would mean that a user must maintain duplicates of many files and be continually changing the variable's value.

a program class, while running programs are instances of that class. By identifying resources with a particular instance — by the instance's invocation name, for example — a single resource file can contain multiple sets of resources.

How the Resource Manager Finds Resource Specifications

One of the responsibilities of `XtInitialize` is the creation of a resource database. This database is compiled from several sources, ranging from program-specific resource files to system-wide defaults files. When this compilation process is complete, the resource database holds a large number of complete and partial widget-name/resource-name specifications, with associated values.

To find the specification that applies to a particular widget and resource, the resource manager builds two completely specified strings, as shown in Listing 16.1.[1] The first string is made from object names, starting with the name of the program as passed to `XtInitialize` and ending with the resource name. The second string is made from class names, starting with the program's class name as passed to `XtInitialize` and ending with the class name of the resource.

The resource manager then searches for all resource specifications that match a union of the two fully specified strings. In Listing 16.1, "*.editMode" matches, as does "*.XmText.editMode", but "*.Ix.editMode" doesn't ("Ix" may be assumed to be the name of another widget, in some other program). From this list of possible specifications, the resource manager selects the best match — the single specification that most explicitly specifies the widget. If two specifications are equally explicit, the resource manager selects the last one read.

Listing 16.1. Resource manager name templates

```
edit.MainWin.WorkWinSW.WorkWin.editMode

TextEdit.XmMainWindow.XmScrolledWindow.XmText.EditMode
```

Program Instance Names

From the above description, you can see that the `name` parameter of `XtInitialize` specifies the program name used to construct the object-name search string, while the `class` parameter is used to construct the object-class search string. You can also see that, if the program is invoked under different names, it can use different sets of resources. This is demonstrated below, where a single program's resource file contains one set of resources identified by the program class name and another identified by a particular invocation name.

One point that may not be clear, but which is vitally important, is that the default name of `a.out` can cause the resource search to fail. Listing 16.2

---

[1] This example is the text editor's main window. Note that the program name is "edit", not "a.out".

presents the problem: with the default program name, the object-name string appears to have six components, while the object-class string has five. This difference is because the resource manager has no way to distinguish between a program named "a.out" and a program named "a" that has a main-window widget named "out". In many cases, this is not a problem — the default program name has been used throughout this book without confusing the resource manager. However, in cases such as command-line options, which are implicitly prefixed by the program name, a program name of a.out will result in resource lookup failure.

Listing 16.2. Name templates, with error arising from program name *a.out*

```
a.out.MainWin.WorkWinSW.WorkWin.editMode

TextEdit.XmMainWindow.XmScrolledWindow.XmText.EditMode
```

The -name *Command-Line Option*

While the ability to invoke a program under a different name to use different resources seems useful, in practice, it isn't. This is because a user typically cannot change the name of a production program — it is stored in a read-only directory. While the user could copy the original program or simply attach a link to it (under UNIX), such operations are inelegant. Instead, the toolkit provides the -name command-line option, which changes the effective invocation name of the program. Listing 16.3 presents the format of this option, along with one of its more common uses: selecting the black-and-white resource set for the Motif window manager.

Listing 16.3. Use of the *-name* command-line option

```
progname -name instance_name

mwm -name 'mwm-bw'
```

Example: *Two Sets of Resources for One Program*

Figure 16.1 presents two examples of a label widget, with different resources specified by instance names. Notice that the window frame's title bar contains the instance name: 16.1(a) was invoked under the default name (a.out), while 16.1(b) was invoked with the name 16_04.

Figure 16.1. Two labels with different instance names

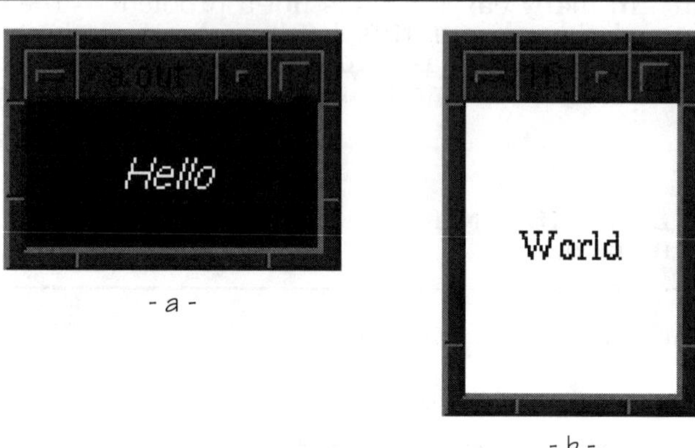

Listing 16.4 presents the program and resource file used to produce Figure 16.1: the program simply creates a label. In the resource file, one set of resources is identified by the program's class name ("Listing_16_04"), while the other is named using "16_04".[2] The first set is effective for any invocation — the resource manager will always be able to match the class name. The second set is only effective when the program is invoked with the name "16_04" — whether by use of the `-name` command-line option or by an actual executable name.

---

[2] Note also that there is no "*" at the beginning of the resource specifications — these specifications fully identify the widgets.

Listing 16.4. Program and resource file: Instance name example

```c
/**********************************************************************
**                                                                  **
**   listing_16_04.c                                                **
**                                                                  **
**   Example of program instance names. This program simply creates a  **
**   label. Its resource file, however, contains resources for both  **
**   its class name ("Listing_16_04") and an instance name ("16_04").  **
**                                                                  **
**********************************************************************/


#include <Xm/Label.h>


Widget  appshell,                      /* Application Shell      */
        the_lbl;                       /* The Label              */


void main( argc, argv )
    int     argc;
    char    *argv[];
{
    appshell = XtInitialize( argv[0], "Listing_16_04", NULL, 0,
                            &argc, argv );

    the_lbl = XmCreateLabel( appshell, "TheLbl", NULL, 0 );
    XtManageChild( the_lbl );

    XtRealizeWidget( appshell );
    XtMainLoop();
}
```

```
!
! Resource file for Instance Name example (Fig 16.1)
!

Listing_16_04.TheLbl.width:          100
Listing_16_04.TheLbl.height:         50
Listing_16_04.TheLbl.foreground:     White
Listing_16_04.TheLbl.background:     Black
Listing_16_04.TheLbl.fontList:       -*-helvetica-medium-o-*--*-140-*
Listing_16_04.TheLbl.labelString:    Hello
```

Listing 16.4. Continued.

```
16_04.TheLbl.width:              50
16_04.TheLbl.height:             100
16_04.TheLbl.foreground:         Black
16_04.TheLbl.background:         White
16_04.TheLbl.fontList:           -*-times-medium-r-*--*-140-*
16_04.TheLbl.labelString:        World
```

Command-Line Options

One of the ways that a user conveys information to a program is by the use of command-line arguments: the C compiler, for example, accepts arguments for everything from the name of the file to macro definitions. In a typical C program, these command-line arguments are accessed by the `argc` and `argv` parameters of `main`. While this mechanism is available to a Motif program, the toolkit provides another: a list of options that are recognized by `XtInitialize`.

An X program has a long list of standard options, ranging from `-display` to `-fg`. These options are recognized by `XtInitialize` and are used to initialize application or widget resources. A program may specify a list of additional options to `XtInitialize`, thus adding application-specific options to the standard set.

The usefulness of this capability depends on the program. If, for example, users are constantly changing resource values with the `-xrm` command-line option, they will almost certainly appreciate a resource-specific option (*eg,* `-fontlist`). On the other hand, it is easy to produce a long list of options that are never used.

Another Look at XtInitialize

As you will recall from Chapter 4, the prototype of `XtInitialize` is as shown in Listing 16.5. The `options` and `num_opts` parameters have not yet been used in this book and have been passed as `NULL` and zero, respectively. They exist for programs that provide additional command-line options and specify an option description array.

Listing 16.5. Function prototype: *XtInitialize*

```
Widget  XtInitialize( name, class, options, opt_count, argc, argv )
        char                *name;
        char                *class;
        XrmOptionDescRec    options[];
        Cardinal            num_opts;
        Cardinal            *argc;
        char                *argv[];
```

Option Description Array

The option description array is an array of `XrmOptionDescRec` structures, as defined in Listing 16.6. Each item in this array links an option string with a resource specification, which may identify either a program or widget resource. When the option string is encountered on the command line, the associated resource is set; the description record specifies the way that the resource is set (*ie*, does the option alone set the resource, or does it have an associated value).

Listing 16.6. Type definitions: *XrmOptionDescRec*, *XrmOptionDescList*

```
typedef struct
        {
        String          option;
        String          specifier;
        XrmOptionKind   argKind;
        caddr_t         value;
        }
XrmOptionDescRec,
*XrmOptionDescList;
```

The `option` member specifies the string used to invoke the option. This string may be any length and use any printable characters, but it should follow the UNIX convention of starting with a hyphen ("-"). `XtInitialize` will recognize any unique abbreviation of the option (*eg*, `-disp` for `-display`), but contracted names (*eg*, `-fg` for `-foreground`) must be specified explicitly. Note also that a program-specified option may not have the same name as one of the standard options; if this is attempted, the standard option takes precedence.

The `specifier` member identifies the resource changed by the option. It is identical to the widget-name/resource-name specification of a resource file and may contain wildcards or class names. The resource manager prefixes this specification with the program's instance name. If the specification begins with a star, it is applied to any matching widget; if it begins with a dot, it is applied to the application shell only.

The `argKind` member describes how the option's value is specified. It must be one of the following constants:

- `XrmoptionNoArg`. The option's value may not be specified on the command line. Instead, it is specified by the `value` member of `XrmOptionDescRec`. This mode is typically used for `Boolean` options.

- `XrmoptionIsArg`. The option string is itself the argument. This type of option is rarely used because it must serve both as identifier and value. Even the case of an option such as `-debug` may be better handled with `XrmoptionNoArg`.

- `XrmoptionStickyArg`. The option's argument is appended to the option. This method of option specification is often used by UNIX programs (for example, the C compiler's `-l` flag: `-lXm`).

- `XrmoptionSepArg`. The option's argument is the next argument on the command line. This is the most common method of specifying arguments (*eg*, `"-fg Black"`).

- `XrmoptionResArg`. The option's argument is a complete resource specification. This mode exists for the implementation of the `-xrm` option; it is rarely used elsewhere.

- `XrmoptionSkipArg`. This mode specifies that both the option and the next argument are to be ignored. It is often used in development testing: by changing a real option to a dummy "ignore" option, the program may be tested both with and without the option, without extensive changes to the command line.

- `XrmoptionSkipLine`. This mode specifies that the option and the rest of the command line is to be ignored. It is often used for the same reason as `XrmoptionSkipArg`.

The `value` member specifies a default value for the option. It is a pointer to program data, which must be of the proper type (*ie*, no conversions are performed on this value). If this member contains `NULL`, the resource value defaults to that specified by the resource file.

Example: Height and Width by Command-Line Option

Listing 16.7 presents a program that makes use of command-line options. It is simply another copy of the "Hello World" program, which allows for `-height` and `-width` options. These options store the next command-line argument in the label's `height` or `width` resource. They are defined at the beginning of the program and installed by the call to `XtInitialize`.

Listing 16.7. Program and resource file: Command-line options example

```
/*********************************************************************
**                                                                 **
**   listing_16_07.c                                               **
**                                                                 **
**   Command-line Options example. This program accepts options to **
**   change the width and height of its label.                     **
**                                                                 **
*********************************************************************/


#include <Xm/Label.h>


Widget              appshell,
                    the_label;

XrmOptionDescRec    cmd_options[] =
                    {
                        {
                        "-height",
                        "*TheLabel.height",
                        XrmoptionSepArg,
                        NULL
                        },
                        {
                        "-width",
                        "*TheLabel.width",
                        XrmoptionSepArg,
                        NULL
                        }
                    };
```

Listing 16.7. Continued.

```c
void main( argc, argv )
    int     argc;
    char    *argv[];
{
    appshell = XtInitialize( argv[0], "Listing_16_07",
                             cmd_options, XtNumber(cmd_options),
                             &argc, argv );

    the_label = XmCreateLabel( appshell, "TheLabel", NULL, 0 );
    XtManageChild( the_label );

    XtRealizeWidget( appshell );
    XtMainLoop();
}
```

Resource Converters

A `Pixel` value is a 32-bit unsigned integer, but colors are specified in the resource file by name. How, then, does the resource manager convert from string to colormap index? The answer is that it uses a resource converter, which is passed an ASCII string holding the color name. This converter searches the color database for the entry corresponding to that name, allocates a colormap cell for the color, and stores the cell index in the specified widget resource.

In most cases, the resource conversion process is transparent to the programmer and user: the resource manager comes "preloaded" with converters for most data types. In some cases, such as with the `unitType` resource, the converter exists but is not loaded into the resource manager. In this case, the programmer must explicitly load the resource converter to allow the specification of such resources in the resource file.

In still other cases, the existing converters may not be sufficient for the job. For example, the converter used to set `XmString` resources only accepts a single-line string, while compound strings can contain multiple lines. If a program uses widgets with multiline strings, the programmer must write and install an appropriate converter.[3]

Representation Types

Each resource converter converts a value of one type to a value of another type — for example, an ASCII string (`String`) to a colormap index (`Pixel`). These data

---

[3] This is true under Motif 1.0 only. Motif 1.1 has an installed converter for multiline strings.

types are identified to the resource manager by *representation types*: strings that uniquely identify a particular data type. In many cases, the representation type name identifies the data type: `XmRXmString` represents compound strings. In others, the representation type name identifies the context in which the underlying type is used: `XmREditMode` represents an `unsigned char` used with the *XmText* `editMode` resource.

Like resource names, each representation-type string is identified by a constant, prefixed by "XmR", and defined in the header file `Xm/Xm.h`.[4] Table 16.1 lists the representation-type constants from `Xm.h`, with their corresponding data types and any usage comments.[5]

Table 16.1. Representation types

Constant	Data Type	Comment
`XmRAccelerator Table`	`XtAccelerator Table`	*Core*: `accelerators` *XmSelectionBox*: `textAccelerators`
`XmRAlignment`	`unsigned char`	*XmLabel*: `alignment` *XmMessageBox*: `messageAlignment` *XmRowColumn*: `entryAlignment`
`XmRArrow Direction`	`unsigned char`	*XmArrowButton*: `arrowDirection`
`XmRBool`	`Boolean`	`Bool` is the Xlib version of `Boolean`.
`XmRBoolean`	`Boolean`	
`XmRCallback`	`XtCallbackList`	Callbacks may not be specified in a resource file; this type exists primarily for internal conversions
`XmRCallProc`	*Special*	Indicates that the associated value is a pointer to a function, which will supply the correct value when called at runtime.
`XmRChar`	`char`	
`XmRColor`	`XColor`	Contains RGB specification for a color; intermediate step in conversion of a named color to a Pixel value
`XmRCursor`	`Cursor`	Cursors are server resources; this type is a server resource ID

---

[4] For Xt-based programs, these constants are defined in `X11/Stringdefs.h` and begin with "XtR" instead of "XmR".

[5] Many of these representation types are specific to a particular widget resource (or identical resources for multiple widgets). Where this is the case, the Comment entry contains "XXX: YYY" — "XXX" is the widget class name, and "YYY" is the resource name. Some types may be used for more than one widget; each of the widget/resource pairs is listed.

Table 16.1. Continued.

`XmRDefaultButton Type`	`unsigned char`	*XmMessageBox*: `defaultButtonType`
`XmRDialogStyle`	`unsigned char`	*XmBulletinBoard*: `dialogStyle`
`XmRDialogType`	`unsigned char`	*XmSelectionBox*: `dialogType`
`XmRDimension`	`Dimension`	Equivalent to `unsigned`
`XmRDisplay`	`Display*`	Used by Xlib drawing functions
`XmREditMode`	`unsigned char`	*XmText*: `editMode`
`XmRFile`	`FILE*`	Used by C's buffered I/O library
`XmRFont`	`Font`	Xlib-level fonts, not font-lists
`XmRFontList`	`XmFontList`	
`XmRFontStruct`	`XFontStruct*`	Used for Xlib text handling
`XmRFunction`	`(*)()`	Generic function pointer, used for internal conversions
`XmRGeometry`	`String`	String representation of window geometry; used by `XGeometry` and `XParseGeometry` functions
`XmRImmediate`	*Special*	Indicates that the associated value is to be used
`XmRIndicatorType`	`unsigned char`	*XmToggleButton*: `indicatorType`
`XmRInt`	`int`	
`XmRJustify`	*Special*	Defined by Intrinsics but not used
`XmRLabelType`	`unsigned char`	*XmLabel*: `labelType`
`XmRListSize Policy`	`unsigned char`	*XmList*: `listSizePolicy`
`XmRLongBoolean`	`long`	A boolean value stored in a C long integer
`XmRMenuWidget`	`Widget`	*XmCascadeButton*: `subMenuId` *XmRowColumn*: *various*
`XmROrientation`	`unsigned char`	*XmRowColumn*: `orientation` *XmScale*: `orientation` *XmScrollBar*: `orientation` *XmSeparator*: `orientation`
`XmRPacking`	`unsigned char`	*XmRowColumn*: `packing`
`XmRPixel`	`Pixel`	Colormap index

Table 16.1. Continued.

XmRPixmap	Pixmap	Server resource ID; pixmap characteristics (*eg*, depth) depend on screen
XmRPointer	XtPointer	Generic data pointer
XmRPosition	Position	
XmRProcessing Direction	unsigned char	*XmScale*: processingDirection *XmScrollBar*: processingDirection
XmRResizePolicy	unsigned char	*XmBulletinBoard*: resizePolicy *XmCommand*: resizePolicy *XmDrawingArea*: resizePolicy
XmRRowColumn Type	unsigned char	*XmRowColumn*: rowColumnType
XmRSeparatorType	unsigned char	*XmSeparator*: separatorType
XmRShadowType	unsigned char	*XmBulletinBoard*: shadowType *XmDrawnButton*: shadowType *XmFrame*: shadowType
XmRShort	short	
XmRString	String	NUL-terminated ASCII string; the type for all conversions from a resource file
XmRString Direction	unsigned char	*XmBulletinBoard*: stringDirection *XmLabel*: stringDirection *XmList*: stringDirection
XmRStringTable	StringTable	Array of NUL-terminated ASCII strings; Don't confuse with XmStringTable
XmRTranslation Table	XtTranslations	*Core*: translations *XmBulletinBoard*: textTranslations
XmRUnitType	unsigned char	*XmManager*: unitType *XmPrimitive*: unitType
XmRUnsignedChar	unsigned char	
XmRVisualPolicy	unsigned char	*XmScrolledWindow*: visualPolicy
XmRWhichButton	unsigned int	*XmRowColumn*: whichButton
XmRWindow	Window	Server resource ID
XmRXmString	XmString	Compound string
XmRXmStringTable	XmStringTable	Array of compound strings

Preinstalled Conversions

Motif provides a set of resource converters that are installed at the time a program starts. Many of these converters are defined by the toolkit; others are specific to Motif. Table 16.2 lists these default conversions by their representation types.[6]

Table 16.2. Preinstalled conversions

From Type	To Type
XmRColor	XmRPixel
XmRInt	XmRBool
	XmRBoolean
	XmRColor
	XmRFont
	XmRPixel
	XmRPixmap
XmRPixel	XmRColor
XmRString	XmRAcceleratorTable
	XmRAlignment
	XmRArrowDirection
	XmRAttachment
	XmRBool
	XmRBoolean
	XmRChar
	XmRCursor
	XmRDefaultButtonType
	XmRDeleteResponse
	XmRDialogStyle
	XmRDialogType
	XmRDimension
	XmRDisplay
	XmREditMode
	XmRFile
	XmRFont

---

[6] There are actually more conversions than those shown: the additional conversions store values into particular widget resources and are used internally by the widgets that define them.

Table 16.2. Continued.

```
XmRFontList
XmRFontStruct
XmRIndicatorType
XmRInt
XmRKeyboardFocusPolicy
XmRLabelType
XmRListSizePolicy
XmROrientation
XmRPacking
XmRPixel
XmRPixmap
XmRPosition
XmRProcessingDirection
XmRResizePolicy
XmRRowColumnType
XmRScrollBarDisplayPolicy
XmRScrollBarPlacement
XmRScrollingPolicy
XmRSelectionPolicy
XmRSeparatorType
XmRShadowType
XmRShellUnitType
XmRShort
XmRStringDirection
XmRTranslationTable
XmRUnsignedChar
XmRVisualPolicy
XmRWhichButton
XmRXmString
XmRXmStringTable
```

Installing a Converter

While Motif provides a large number of installed converters, you may need to explicitly install a converter. One such converter is the function `XmCvtStringToUnitType`, introduced in Chapter 6. If you write your own converter, it also must be explicitly installed.

To install a converter, the program calls the function `XtAddConverter`, prototyped in Listing 16.8.[7] This function takes as parameters the representation types that the converter converts between (`from_type`, `to_type`) a pointer to the converter function (`proc`) and an optional array of arguments (`args`, with `num_args` containing the number of items in this array).

Listing 16.8. Function prototype: *XtAddConverter*

```
void    XtAddConverter( from_type, to_type, proc, args, num_args )
        String          from_type;
        String          to_type;
        XtConverter     proc;
        XtConvertArgRec args[];
        Cardinal        num_args;
```

The `args` array is used when the converter requires contextual information to perform the conversion. For example, a `String-to-Pixel` converter needs access to the widget's window to access its colormap. For such a conversion, `args` would contain references to the appropriate widget resources. For a different conversion, it might contain references to program variables.

If `args` is used, it is an array of `XtConvertArgRec` structures, defined in Listing 16.9; if not used, pass `NULL`. Each converter uses a particular set of arguments, which must be presented in an expected order. As you will see below, converters access their arguments by position only, and `XtConvertArgRec` contains no identification data.

---

[7] For X11R4, use the functions `XtSetTypeConverter` or `XtAppSetTypeConverter`.

Listing 16.9. Type definitions: *XtConvertArgRec, XtConvertArgList*

```
typedef struct
        {
        XtAddressMode     address_mode;
        caddr_t           address_id;
        Cardinal          size;
        }
XtConvertArgRec,
*XtConvertArgList;
```

The `address_id` member contains the value of the argument. It is either a pointer, an offset, or an immediate value, depending on the contents of `address_mode`. The `size` member specifies the size of the argument data, in bytes. The `address_mode` member specifies how the contents of `address_id` are used. It contains one of the following constants:

- `XtAddress`. The argument value exists in program memory, and `address_id` contains a pointer to that value. The pointed-to data must be a static variable; `address_id` must not point at something that can move while the program is running.

- `XtBaseOffset`. The argument is part of a widget's internal data, and `address_id` contains an offset from the base of a widget. This type of argument is used by widget writers only. Applications programs should instead use `XtResourceString`.

- `XtImmediate`. The `address_id` member contains the value itself. Note that such items are limited to the size of a data pointer — on most systems, four bytes.

- `XtResourceString`. The `address_id` member contains a pointer to a NUL-terminated character string, which specifies the name of a widget resource. This name is converted into an offset by the resource manager. Note that the `size` member does not specify the size of the name string, but the size of the resource.

- `XtResourceQuark`. The `address_id` member contains a quark ID that represents the name of a widget resource. As with `XtResourceString`, the resource manager converts the quark into an offset; the `size` member specifies the size of the resource.[8]

---

[8] *Quarks* are integer values associated with character strings. They exist so that string comparisons may be replaced by integer value comparisons and are described in detail below.

As an example, Listing 16.10 contains a code fragment that registers a string-to-pixel converter.[9] This conversion requires the widget's screen and colormap resources as context, and these are retrieved from the widget itself by way of conversion arguments. The code fragment sets up an argument list, then installs a converter using those arguments.

Listing 16.10. Converter installation

```
static  XtConvertArgRec string_to_pixel_args[] =
        {
            { XtResourceString, XmNscreen, sizeof(Screen*) },
            { XtResourceString, XmNcolormap, sizeof(Colormap) }
        }
    .

    .

    .

XtAddConverter( XmRString, XmRPixel, CvtStringToPixel,
                string_to_pixel_args, 2 );
```

Writing a Converter

While Motif provides a large number of prebuilt conversions — and the Xmu library provides more — there may be times when you need a conversion that does not exist. An example is the ability to specify a multiline compound string in a resource file — the converter provided with Motif 1.0 does not do this. In such a case, you must write and install your own converter.

Converter Function Prototype

Conversion functions all follow the same prototype, shown in Listing 16.11.[10] Its parameters represent the argument array passed to XtConverter (args, num_args), the source object (from), and the destination object (to). The converter reads the contents of the source object, performs the conversion, and returns a pointer to the converted value. The resource manager is responsible for setting up the source and copying the converted value into the destination.[11]

---

[9] This converter is, in fact, the preinstalled string-to-pixel converter defined by Xt. Since it is installed at program startup, there would be no need for a real program to install it explicitly.

[10] This function prototype has changed for X11R4. The new prototype takes a display pointer, as well as a pointer to space that the converter can use for the conversion. In addition, R4 conversion provides a more elegant method of memory allocation and deallocation.

[11] An important point of this process is that the resource manager does not give the converter a pointer to the destination object. This minimizes the possibility that a converter will damage the destination, and it allows an intelligent resource manager — which does not yet exist — to perform a complex conversion by invoking several converters (*eg*, the String-to-Pixel conversion could be performed as String-to-XColor, followed by XColor-to-Pixel).

Listing 16.11. Function prototype: Resource converter

```
void     funcname( args, num_args, from, to )
         XrmValuePtr     args;
         Cardinal        *num_args;
         XrmValuePtr     from;
         XrmValuePtr     to;
```

Note that the parameters args, from, and to are of type XrmValuePtr, defined with XrmValue in Listing 16.12. The XrmValue type is used because the resource manager resolves all references before calling the converter function. These resolved references may be then be accessed by their address (addr) and size (size) — there is no need for the converter function to perform address resolution itself.

Listing 16.12. Type definitions: *XrmValue, XrmValuePtr*

```
typedef struct
        {
        unsigned int    size
        caddr_t         addr;
        }
XrmValue,
*XrmValuePtr;
```

Example: Multiline XmStrings

Figure 16.2 presents a label that displays a two-line compound string. As stated above, Motif's built-in String-to-XmString conversion does not permit such a string to be specified in the resource file. To provide such functionality, a new converter is needed.

Figure 16.2. Multiline label

This new converter — and the program that uses it — is presented in Listing 16.13. A complete description follows the listing.

Listing 16.13. Program and resource file: Multiline label example

```
/**************************************************************************
**                                                                      **
**    listing_16_13.c                                                   **
**                                                                      **
**    String-to-XmString converter example. This converter allows a    **
**    program to specify multi-line XmStrings in a resource file. It    **
**    is used in the context of "Hello, World".                         **
**                                                                      **
**************************************************************************/


#include <Xm/Label.h>


void    CvtStringToXmString();          /* FORWARD Definition        */

Widget  appshell,                       /* Application Shell         */
        a_label,                        /* Dummy label               */
        the_label;                      /* The real label            */
```

Listing 16.13. Continued.

```
void main( argc, argv )
    int     argc;
    char    *argv[];
{
    appshell = XtInitialize( argv[0], "Listing_16_13", NULL, 0,
                             &argc, argv );

    a_label = XmCreateLabel( appshell, "ALabel", NULL, 0 );
    XtDestroyWidget( a_label );

    XtAddConverter( XmRString, XmRXmString, CvtStringToXmString,
                    NULL, 0 );

    the_label = XmCreateLabel( appshell, "TheLabel", NULL, 0 );
    XtManageChild( the_label );

    XtRealizeWidget( appshell );
    XtMainLoop();
}


/**
*** CvtStringToXmString( args, num_args, from, to )
***
*** Converts "String" data (NUL-terminated ASCII strings) to
*** "XmString" data (compound strings). Recognizes the sequence
*** "\n" as an embedded newline, allowing the compound string
*** to have multiple lines.
***
*** Notes:
***        - The parameters "args" and "num_args" are not used by this
***          conversion.
***        - The maximum size of the compound string is 1024 bytes. This
***          limit is imposed by the fact that the string is copied into
***          a local buffer.
**/

void CvtStringToXmString( args, num_args, from, to )
    XrmValue    *args;
```

Listing 16.13. Continued.

```
    Cardinal    *num_args;
    XrmValue    *from;
    XrmValue    *to;
{
    static char     lcl_buf[1024];
    static XmString lcl_ptr = lcl_buf;
    XmString        xms;
    String          str;
    int             siz;

    str = (String)from->addr;
    xms = XmStringCreateLtoR( str, XmSTRING_DEFAULT_CHARSET );
    siz = XmStringLength(xms);
    if (siz < 1024)
        {
        memcpy( lcl_buf, xms, siz );
        to->addr = (caddr_t)&lcl_ptr;
        to->size = sizeof(XmString);
        }
    else
        {
        to->addr = NULL;
        to->size = 0;
        }
    XmStringFree( xms );
}
```

```
!
! Resource file to produce Figure 16.2
!

*TheLabel.height:       50
*TheLabel.width:        100
*TheLabel.background:   White
*TheLabel.foreground:   Black
*TheLabel.fontList:     -*-times-medium-r-*--*-140-*

*TheLabel.labelString:  Hello\nWorld!
```

The first point of interest is the creation of a dummy label, `a_label`. This is
required because converters are installed by the initialization function of first
widget class that uses the type. In the case of `XmString`, this installation happens
in the initialization function of *XmLabel*. If the program simply installed its
converter and created `the_label`, the default converter would replace the
program's converter. By creating the dummy label first, the class is initialized

and its converter is installed. The program can then install its own converter in place of the default converter and have it available for creation of the "real" label.[12]

Once the default converter has been installed by the *XmLabel* initialization code, the program can install its own converter. Each call to `XtAddConverter` supersedes the previous call, so the program's own converter replaces the default converter. Note that no additional arguments are passed to the converter — this conversion does not require context data.

While `String-to-XmString` conversion would seem straightforward — `XmStringCreateLtoR` does the actual work — it actually manages to demonstrate many of the quirks in the X11R3 resource manager. The function `CvtStringToXmString` performs this operation, and it will be examined in detail.

The first point to note is the static buffer, `lcl_buf`. This buffer is required because the function is responsible for deallocating all memory that it allocates — if it doesn't, that memory is simply lost.[13] As a result, instead of simply returning the string produced by `XmStringCreateLtoR`, this function must copy that string into a local buffer, then explicitly deallocate it. If it is too big to fit in the local buffer, the converter fails. Note that, once the string has been copied to the static buffer, it is deallocated.

The resource converter is responsible for returning a pointer to the converted value. For a compound string, this value is an `XmString` variable, which is itself a pointer. Thus, the static variable `lcl_ptr` is used to point at the compound string data.[14]

When the converter returns, the resource manager essentially calls `XtSetValues`. The widget then makes a copy the compound-string data, using the returned pointer. Subsequent calls to the converter can therefore reuse the static buffer.

Displaying Error Messages

A conversion may fail for any number of reasons. In the example above, it will fail if the string is too long to fit in the static buffer. In the case of a symbolic constant conversion, it could fail if the user misspelled the constant. To alert the user to such errors, the toolkit provides the functions `XtWarningMsg` and `XtStringConversionWarning`, both of which are prototyped in Listing 16.14.[15] The first is a generic warning message; the second is used by converters that convert from `XmRString` to another type and produces "boilerplate" output. Both functions are simply warnings; they send text to standard error, but do not terminate execution of the program

---

[12] Most of the preinstalled converters are installed by `XtInitialize` as part of the *ApplicationShell* class initialization.

[13] One of the primary complaints about X as a whole is the fact that such memory leaks are prevalent. One of the major improvements in the X11R4 resource conversion process is the ability to register a *destructor* function, which deallocates memory allocated by the converter.

[14] Note, however, that for a `String` variable, a converter must return a pointer to the actual NUL-terminated string.

[15] X11R4 uses `XtAppWarningMsg` and `XtDisplayStringConversionWarning`.

Listing 16.14. Function prototypes: *XtWarningMsg,*
XtStringConversionWarning

```
void    XtWarningMsg( name, type, class, default, params, num_params )
        String      name;
        String      type;
        String      class;
        String      default;
        String      *params;
        Cardinal    *num_params;


void    XtStringConversionWarning( src, dst_type )
        String      src;
        String      dst_type;
```

`XtWarningMsg` provides a general error-output facility. The `name`, `type`, and `class` parameters are used to identify a message within the error database.[16] The `default` parameter specifies a default string, to be used when the error database does not contain a string. This string is output with `printf` and may contain string-output placeholders ("%s"); the `params` parameter points at an array of strings to be output in these placeholders. The number of items in the `params` array is pointed to by the `num_params` parameter.

The `XtStringConversionWarning` function is a convenience function, used only by resource converters that have a source of `XmRString`. It prints a standard error message into which is inserted the strings pointed to by the `src` and `dst_type` parameters: `src` contains the input string (`from->addr`), and `dst_type` contains the name of the destination type (*eg*, "XmString").

Listing 16.15 contains a modification to the `CvtStringToXmString` function, to produce an error message when the converted string is too long to fit into the static buffer. The first part of this listing contains the call to `XtWarningMsg`, while the second contains the message.

---

[16] On a UNIX system, this database is stored in the file `/usr/lib/X11/XtErrorDB`. It is a text file, containing error strings identified by class, name, and type (in that order). The default class for toolkit warnings is "XtToolkitError"; the name and type depend on the specific function and are listed in the document *X Toolkit Intrinsics — C Language Interface*. This file may be modified for site-specific applications; such modifications should be appended to the supplied file (note, however, that many sites *do not have* an `XtErrorDB` file).

Listing 16.15. Error-output modification to
CvtStringToXmString, with output

```
/**
*** CvtStringToXmString( args, num_args, from, to )
***
*** Converts "String" data (NUL-terminated ASCII strings) to
*** "XmString" data (compound strings). Recognizes the sequence
*** "\n" as an embedded newline, allowing the compound string
*** to have multiple lines.
***
*** Notes:
***        - The parameters "args" and "num_args" are not used by this
***          conversion.
***        - The maximum size of the compound string is 1024 bytes. This
***          limit is imposed by the fact that the string is copied into
***          a local buffer.
**/

void CvtStringToXmString( args, num_args, from, to )
    XrmValue     *args;
    Cardinal     *num_args;
    XrmValue     *from;
    XrmValue     *to;
{
    static char      lcl_buf[1024];
    static XmString lcl_ptr = lcl_buf;
    XmString         xms;
    String           str;
    int              siz;
    String           params[1];
    Cardinal         num_params;

    str = (String)from->addr;
    xms = XmStringCreateLtoR( str, XmSTRING_DEFAULT_CHARSET );
    siz = XmStringLength(xms);
    if (siz < 32)
        {
        memcpy( lcl_buf, xms, siz );
        to->addr = (caddr_t)&lcl_ptr;
        to->size = sizeof(XmString);
        }
    else
```

Listing 16.15. Continued.

```
      {
      params[0] = str;
      XtWarningMsg( "conversionError", "cvtStringToXmString",
          "ApplicationError",
          "String \"%s\" too long to convert to compound string\n",
          params, &num_params );
      to->addr = NULL;
      to->size = 0;
      }
    XmStringFree( xms );
}
```

```
X Toolkit Warning: String "Hello
World!" too long to convert to compound string
```

The primary change is the addition of a call to `XtWarningMsg`.[17] Since I wanted the warning to display the invalid string, variables (`params` and `num_params`) were defined in order to pass the string to the message. Note that the warning message is broken into two lines as a result of the newline in the original string. Note also my choices for the `name` and `type` parameters: they follow the convention used by the toolkit functions and documented by the intrinsics reference manual.

You may be wondering why I used `XtWarningMsg` instead of `XtStringConversionWarning`. The reason is that I wanted to provide more information about the error (that the string was too long), but `XtStringConversionWarning` does not allow that level of detail.[18]

Quarks

Most of the conversions performed by the resource manager involve translating an ASCII string into a constant value — for example, converting the string "ATTACH_FORM" into the constant `XmATTACH_FORM`. While this conversion may be performed using string comparisons, such comparisons tend to be inefficient — especially if all applicable strings are similar (as the form attachment constraints are). For this reason, the X resource manager provides *quarks*, integer values that represent NUL-terminated ASCII strings.

To use quarks instead of string comparisons, the program must first "quarkify" the acceptable strings and store the quark values. To make a comparison, the program converts the test string to a quark and compares that quark against the

---

[17] An additional change, required to make the warning appear with the existing resource file, was reducing the allowed string size from 1024 bytes to 32.

[18] It simply prints the message "Cannot convert string "YYY" to type XXX."

saved values. Thus, the process of comparing individual string bytes is reduced to a process of comparing integer values — along with a single lookup to "quarkify" the test string.[19]

Two functions are provided to convert between strings and quarks: `XrmStringToQuark` and `XrmQuarkToString`, both of which are prototyped in Listing 16.16. The first takes a string pointer as its parameter and returns a quark value; it is the function used most often. The second takes a quark as its parameter and returns a pointer to its associated string; it is used primarily for debugging and runtime error messages.[20]

Listing 16.16. Function prototypes: XrmStringToQuark,
XrmQuarkToString

```
XrmQuark      XrmStringToQuark( str )
              String      str;


String        XrmQuarkToString( quark )
              XrmQuark      quark;
```

Example: Unit-Type Conversion

While Motif already provides a `String-to-UnitType` conversion, such a conversion presents a good example of the use of quarks. Listing 16.17 contains such a converter; it is described in detail below the listing.

---

[19] According to Asente & Swick (*X Window System Toolkit, The Complete Programmer's Guide and Specification*, Digital Press), the process of converting a string to a quark takes approximately twice as long as a string comparison. If the initial cost of determining quark values for the legal strings is justified by the number of times the converter is called, use of quarks can result in a relatively high time savings.

[20] This string is stored in internal toolkit memory. If the program needs to modify it — or use it over a long period of time — it should make a copy.

Listing 16.17. Resource converter that uses quarks

```
/**
*** CvtStringToUnitType( args, num_args, from, to )
***
*** Converts "String" data (NUL-terminated ASCII strings) to
*** UnitType data. Recognizes five unit-type specifications:
***    PIXELS, 100TH_MILLIMETERS, 1000TH_INCHES, 100TH_POINTS,
***    and 100TH_FONT_UNITS.
*** Does not recognize any spellings other than those listed.
**/

void    CvtStringToUnitType( args, num_args, from, to )
    XrmValue    *args;
    Cardinal    *num_args;
    XrmValue    *from;
    XrmValue    *to;
{
    static unsigned char    val;
    static Boolean          inited = FALSE;
    static XrmQuark         q_pixel, q_mm, q_inch, q_pt, q_font;
    XrmQuark               q_test;

    if (!inited)
        {
        inited  = TRUE;
        q_pixel = XrmStringToQuark( "PIXELS" );
        q_mm    = XrmStringToQuark( "100TH_MILLIMETERS" );
        q_inch  = XrmStringToQuark( "1000TH_INCHES" );
        q_pt    = XrmStringToQuark( "100TH_POINTS" );
        q_font  = XrmStringToQuark( "100TH_FONT_UNITS" );
        }

    q_test = XrmStringToQuark( (char*)from->addr );
    if (q_test == q_pixel)
        val = XmPIXELS;
    else if (q_test == q_mm)
        val = Xm100TH_MILLIMETERS;
    else if (q_test == q_inch)
        val = Xm1000TH_INCHES;
    else if (q_test == q_pt)
        val = Xm100TH_POINTS;
    else if (q_test == q_font)
        val = Xm100TH_FONT_UNITS;
    else
        {
        val = XmPIXELS;
        XtStringConversionWarning( (char*)from->addr, "UnitType" );
        }
```

Listing 16.17. Continued.

```
    to->addr = (caddr_t)&val;
    to->size = sizeof(unsigned char);
}
```

While the heading of this function is similar to that of `CvtStringToXmString`, the rest is quite different, starting with the initialization code. Such code is required for any converter that uses quarks because the valid strings must be converted to quarks before use. This is done the first time that the function is called, and the quark values are stored in static variables for later use.

Following the initialization code is the heart of the function. In a fullyimplemented converter, the input string would be converted to uppercase before "quarkification" — this would give the user leeway in the actual resource specification. For simplicity, that step is ignored here, which means that only the specified spellings are permitted.

If a match is found, the appropriate constant is stored in the value. If no match is found, a warning message is displayed, and the value defaults to `XmPIXELS`. Listing 16.18 contains such a warning, resulting from improper use of case in the resource file. Notice again that the converted value is stored in a static variable, and the converter returns a pointer to that variable.

Listing 16.18. Sample output from *XtStringConversionWarning*

```
    X Toolkit Warning: Cannot convert string "1000TH_inches" to type UnitType
```

Using Converters Outside the Resource Manager

Although this book — and common usage — uses the term *resource converter*, that is not the correct term. The correct term is *type converter*, which avoids the connotation that such converters are used only within the resource manager. In fact, an installed converter may be used at any place within a program.

The benefit of converter use is in hiding the details of a data type. In some cases, such as `String-to-XmString` conversion, this hiding is not needed: Motif already provides conversion functions. In others, such as `String-to-Pixel`, the converter hides an enormous amount of detail (database lookup and colorcell allocation).

The XtConvert *Function*

To invoke a converter directly, a program calls the `XtConvert` function, prototyped in Listing 16.19.[21] The parameters to this function include a widget (`w`), the representation types of the source and destination (`from_type`, `to_type`), and pointers to `XrmValue` structures for the source and destination (`from`, `to`). The passed widget provides the resource manager with any contextual information needed for argument resolution. In most cases, the program can pass the application shell.

Listing 16.19. Function prototype: *XtConvert*

```
void    XtConvert( w, from_type, from, to_type, to )
        Widget      w;
        String      from_type;
        XrmValue    *from;
        String      to_type;
        XrmValue    *to;
```

`XtConvert` invokes the appropriate resource converter, which is responsible for performing the conversion. If conversion fails for any reason (*eg*, `XtConvert` couldn't find an appropriate converter), an error message is output and `to->addr` is set to `NULL`.

If conversion succeeds, the program must copy the value addressed by `to->addr`, if necessary using the size information in `to->size`. The program must not attempt to modify the pointed-to value; as you have seen, it is part of the converter's internal memory space.

Example: Color by Name

Listing 16.20 presents an example of direct invocation of the `String-to-Pixel` conversion. The program itself is unexceptional: it creates a pushbutton and attaches a function to its activation callback. The callback function, however, is interesting: it changes the button's background color to a named color.

This conversion process is invoked from the function `SetBackground`, which is called by the callback function. This function is responsible for preparing the arguments and calling the converter. Once the conversion has taken place, it uses `XtSetValues` to install the new color.

---

[21] X11R4 replaces `XtConvert` by `XtCallConverter`.

Listing 16.20. Conversion example: Changing a pushbutton's color in a callback

```c
/**********************************************************************
**                                                                  **
**   listing_16_20.c                                                **
**                                                                  **
**                                                                  **
Example of explicit converter calls. This program presents a        **
**   pushbutton. Each time the button is pushed, its background     **
**   color changes.                                                 **
**                                                                  **
**********************************************************************/


#include <string.h>
#include <Xm/PushB.h>


void    ButtonCB();                        /* FORWARD Definitions      */
void    SetBackground();


Widget  appshell,
        the_btn;


void main( argc, argv )
    int     argc;
    char    *argv[];
{
    appshell = XtInitialize( argv[0], "Listing_16_20", NULL, 0,
                             &argc, argv );

    the_btn = XmCreatePushButton( appshell, "TheBtn", NULL, 0 );
    XtManageChild( the_btn );

    XtAddCallback( the_btn, XmNactivateCallback, ButtonCB, NULL );

    XtRealizeWidget( appshell );
```

Listing 16.20. Continued.

```
    XtMainLoop();
}



void ButtonCB( w, client_data, call_data )
    Widget      w;
    caddr_t     client_data;
    caddr_t     call_data;
{
    static int  cnum = 0;

    switch (cnum++)
        {
        case 0 :
                SetBackground( w, "Red" );
                break;
        case 1 :
                SetBackground( w, "Green" );
                break;
        case 2 :
                SetBackground( w, "Blue" );
                break;
        case 3 :
                SetBackground( w, "Black" );
                cnum = 0;
                break;
        }
}



/**
*** SetBackground( w, cname )
***
*** Sets the "background" resource of widget "w" to the color
*** named by "cname".
**/

void SetBackground( w, cname )
    Widget      w;
    String      cname;
{
    XrmValue    from, to;
    Arg         arg;

    from.addr = cname;
```

Listing 16.20. Continued.

```
    from.size = strlen(cname);
    to.addr   = NULL;
    to.size   = 0;

    XtConvert( w, XmRString, &from, XmRPixel, &to );
    if (to.addr != NULL)
        {
        XtSetArg( arg, XmNbackground, *(Pixel*)to.addr );
        XtSetValues( w, &arg, 1 );
        }
}
```

```
!
! Resource file for Color Conversion example
!

*TheBtn.height:          50
*TheBtn.width:           100
*TheBtn.background:      Black
*TheBtn.foreground:      White
*TheBtn.fontList:        -*-times-medium-r-*--*-140-*
*TheBtn.labelString:     Press Here
```

The Conversion Cache

While many conversions are simple in nature, others require extensive processing or server communication. An example is the `String-to-Pixel` conversion: not only must it search for a name in the color database, but it must also request a colorcell allocation from the server.

To prevent the loss of efficiency that would result from repetitive conversion of the same data, the toolkit provides a *conversion cache*: a place where the conversion results are stored. When the program or resource manager requests a conversion, the cache is checked first. If the conversion has already been performed, the cached result is returned; otherwise, the appropriate converter is called, and its results are stored in the cache.

Under X11 Release 3, conversion caching was an automatic process: when a conversion was performed, the result was stored in the cache. This led to inefficient use of the cache: in most cases, the conversion would either not be repeated or was of such a simple nature that the result did not need to be cached. Moreover, items were never removed from the cache, so the cache would grow without limit.

Under Release 4, this situation was improved dramatically as part of the complete redesign of the conversion mechanism. When registering a converter under R4, the program can specify how its results are cached. Options include permanent caching, caching until the associated display connection closes, caching until the item is no longer used, and not caching the item.

Application Resources

Not only does the resource file provide an effective and easily modified method of setting the initial state of a program's widgets, it may also be used to set program variables. This is done with application resources, a technique whereby program variables are identified to the resource manager, and it attempts to initialize them.

Specifying Application Resources in the Resource File

Application resources are specified similarly to widget resources, except that they do not have an associated widget name. This results in a specification like that in Listing 16.21, which specifies a value for the `reverseVideo` resource of the program `MyProg`.[22] Note that, if the program name is not specified, it must be wildcarded.

Listing 16.21. Sample application resource specification

```
MyProg.reverseVideo:     TRUE
```

The Resource Structure

The resource manager is designed to access a widget's resources by their location within the widget's internal data structure. To allow this behavior to work with a program's variables, those variables must be contained in a data structure that mimics a widget's internal data.

While this structure may be in any scope — global, static, or automatic — it is most often global (or at least global to its source file). This is because the resource description array, described below, must be initialized with addresses derived from the resource structure.[23]

A program may have multiple application resource structures, each of which is initialized by a separate call to `XtGetApplicationResources`. In fact, even if a

---

[22] This is an application resource defined by the resource manager and used to control the default values for the `foreground` and `background` resources of all of a program's widgets.

[23] The C compiler permits such allocation only when both data structures are statically allocated, so that it can resolve offsets.

program defines only one such structure, it actually uses multiple structures: the toolkit and resource manager define their own application resources.

The Resource Description Array

Resources are declared as members of a data structure. They are identified to the resource manager an as array of `XtResource` structures, defined in Listing 16.22. Each element of this array describes a single resource: it specifies the resource's name, class, and type, its position within the resource structure, and its default value. As this array must be initialized before use, it is almost always in global scope (but may be a static global).

Listing 16.22. Type definition: XtResource, XtResourceList

```
typedef struct
        {
        String      resource_name;
        String      resource_class;
        String      resource_type;
        Cardinal    resource_size;
        Cardinal    resource_offset;
        String      default_type;
        XtPointer   default_addr;
        }
XtResource,
*XtResourceList;
```

The `resource_name` and `resource_class` fields specify the name and class of the resource. If the resource fits into one of the existing classes, you may find class specification useful; if not, the resource's class may be specified as an empty string.

The `resource_type` field is used to select an appropriate resource converter. It must contain a valid representation type — one that is associated with a registered converter. This may be one of the predefined representation types, or it may be an application-defined type (in which case the call to `XtGetApplicationResources` must occur after the converter is registered).

The `resource_size` and `resource_offset` fields are used to identify the resource, relative to its structure: `resource_offset` contains the byte offset of the member, and `resource_size` contains its size. X11 Release 3 provides the macro `XtOffset` to calculate the offset; Release 4 provides `XtOffsetOf`.[24]

The `default_type` and `default_addr` members specify a default value for the resource; this value is installed when the resource manager cannot find an

---

[24] `XtOffset` takes a type pointer, along with the member name (*eg,*, `XtOffset((struct*)`, `mbr)`); `XtOffsetOf` takes the name of the structure with the member name (*eg,* `XtOffsetOf(str, mbr)`). ANSI compilers provide the `offsetof` directive, which I prefer to either.

explicit specification. The `default_type` member specifies the representation type of the default value; if it differs from `resource_type`, the appropriate converter is invoked. The `default_addr` member contains an absolute pointer to a value of that type.

Loading the Resource Structure: XtGetApplicationResources

The program loads its application resources by calling the `XtGetApplicationResources` function, prototyped in Listing 16.23. This call must occur after the call to `XtInitialize` (which loads the resource database); it must also occur after any needed converters have been registered. It will allocate any memory needed for a resource (as for a compound string) and will install the specified default values if resources cannot be found.

Listing 16.23. Function prototype: *XtGetApplicationResources*

```
void      XtGetApplicationResources( w, base, resources, num_resources,
                                     args, num_args )
          Widget         w;
          XtPointer      base;
          XtResourceList resources;
          Cardinal       num_resources;
          ArgList        args;
          Cardinal       num_args;
```

The `w` parameter specifies a widget used to access the resource database. It is needed because the databases associated with different servers may differ due to the server's resource property. The application shell is a good widget to pass in this parameter.

The `base` parameter specifies the address of the program's resource structure. The address of its description array is passed in `resources`, and the number of items in that array is passed in `num_resources`.

Finally, `args` and `num_args` specify an argument list containing "hard-wired" values for any or all of the application's resources. As with widget resources, any values specified in this list take precedence over values in the resource file. If you use such arguments (which defeat the purpose of application resources), remember that you specify the application resource name as a string.

Example: Debugging Flag

It seems that programmers separate into two schools regarding debugging: those who rely on debugging tools such as *adb* or *xdb*, and those who insert `printf` statements into their code. Of the second school, some use conditional compilation to control this output (#`ifdef DEBUG`), while others use a runtime test (`if (debug)`). The program in Listing 16.24 uses a runtime test, controlled by the `debugOn` application resource.[25]

Listing 16.24. Program and resource file: Application resources example

```
/*****************************************************************
**                                                             **
**   listing_16_24.c                                           **
**                                                             **
**   Application Resource example. This program provides a "debugOn"  **
**   resource, which may be set to TRUE to enable runtime logging.    **
**                                                             **
*****************************************************************/


#include <Xm/Label.h>


Widget       appshell,
             the_label;

struct       ResList                      /* The application resources  */
             {
             Boolean     db_flag;         /*    "debugOn"               */
             }
             app_resources,
             def_resources = { FALSE };
XtResource   app_res_list[] =
             {
                 {
                 "debugOn",
                 "DebugOn",
                 XmRBoolean,
                 sizeof(app_resources.db_flag),
                 XtOffset(struct ResList *, db_flag),
                 XmRBoolean,
                 &def_resources.db_flag
                 }
             };
```

---

[25] My habit is to place such debugging code flush against the left margin. While this makes for an ugly source listing, it is easier to remove the calls for "production" code.

Listing 16.24. Continued.

```c
void main( argc, argv )
    int     argc;
    char    *argv[];
{
    appshell = XtInitialize( argv[0], "Listing_16_24", NULL, 0,
                             &argc, argv );

    XtGetApplicationResources( appshell, &app_resources,
                               app_res_list, XtNumber(app_res_list),
                               NULL, 0 );

    the_label = XmCreateLabel( appshell, "TheLabel", NULL, 0 );
    XtManageChild( the_label );

/* Debug */
if (app_resources.db_flag)
{
    if (the_label == NULL)
        printf( "Debug: Creation of \"TheLabel\" failed\n" );
    else
        printf( "Debug: \"TheLabel\" created, ID = %d\n", the_label );
}

    XtRealizeWidget( appshell );

/* Debug */
if (app_resources.db_flag)
    printf( "Debug: XtRealizeWidget called\n" );

    XtMainLoop();
}
!
! Resource file for Debugging Flag example
!

*TheLabel.height:       50
*TheLabel.width:        100
*TheLabel.background:   White
*TheLabel.foreground:   Black
*TheLabel.labelString:  Hello World!

*debugOn:               TRUE
!Listing_16_24.debugOn: TRUE
```

The application resources are specified in the structure `app_resources`, with default values specified in the structure `def_resources`. Both structures use a program-defined structure type, which allows the use of `XtOffset`. Declaring and initializing a default-values structure simplifies initialization of the `default_addr` member of the resource description array.

The resource description array itself is represented by `app_res_list`, initialized as part of its declaration. Things to note include the use of `XtOffset` and the name chosen for the resource's class. This name follows the convention that resource classes with one member use the name of that member, with the first letter capitalized.

The call to `XtGetApplicationResources` is straightforward; note the use of the `XtNumber` macro to specify the size of the resource description list. Note also that, as described above, this call is performed immediately after the call to `XtInitialize`.

The resource file extract shows the two methods of specifying the `debugOn` resource value. The first form wildcards the program name, while the second specifies it explicitly. I tend to prefer the first, although it will affect any widget resources that have the same name.

17
Interclient Communication

Overview

The event-driven, asynchronous nature of an X program presents challenges in interprocess communications. The traditional UNIX methods, pipes and sockets, do not fit this environment well — the file I/O functions that they use are inherently synchronous. The simplest X-specific method, sending events between client windows, is limited both in the amount of data that may be transferred and in the fact that both clients must have connections to the same server.

For the most part, these challenges have been surmounted. Since the link between client and server uses the filesystem, a program can link its own file, pipe, or socket to the client's low-level I/O code, allowing asynchronous notification of input. While events themselves may be limited in the amount of information they can carry, *window properties* allow a client to attach larger amounts of data to its window — data that may be retrieved by another client using the same server. This method is formalized in the selection mechanism. Finally, timeouts and workprocs allow a program to perform non-event-driven operations in the context of the event loop.

This chapter presents each of the above mechanisms in order from the traditional (file I/O, timeouts, and workprocs) to those specific to the X environment (interclient events, window properties, and selection). Along the way, the file browser of Chapter 9 is updated to read standard input, and the text editor is updated with clipboard cut and paste functions.

File I/O

The traditional methods of interprocess communication under UNIX are pipes and sockets, both of which are layered on the filesystem. A *pipe* is a one-way connection between processes running on the same machine: one process opens the pipe for output, another opens it for input.[1] A *socket* is similar but uses the

---

[1] The most common use of pipes is in programs run from the shell: the user pipes the
output of one program to another (*eg,* `"ls -l | more"`). In this case, the shell opens the

network mechanism, meaning that the processes may be running on different machines; additionally, a socket connection is bidirectional.

While sockets and pipes present an elegant method of interprocess communication — they are almost identical to disk files — they have one big disadvantage in the X environment: file I/O is synchronous in nature, while an X client operates asynchronously. When a program reads from a file, data may not be immediately available: it might have to be read from the disk, or in the case of a pipe or socket, it might not have been sent from the other process. In such a situation, a UNIX process *blocks*: it waits for the data to be available. This is unacceptable for an X client: while it is blocked waiting for input, many — hundreds, if not thousands — of events could accumulate in its input queue.

The solution to this problem comes from the implementation of X client-server communication — as a socket connection — and the need of a client to potentially communicate with multiple servers. This requirement must be satisfied for the X environment to function; for UNIX, it is satisfied by the `select` system call. This call allows a program to block on multiple files — it returns when one of the files has data for input.[2] By adding the program's files to the list of files monitored by Xlib, the program can be alerted when data is present.

Registering a File: XtAddInput

To register a file — either input or output — with the toolkit, use the function `XtAddInput`, prototyped in Listing 17.1.[3] This function adds the file descriptor represented by `source` to the list monitored by Xlib. When the condition represented by `condition` is present — the file is ready for reading or writing or has an exception pending — the function specified by `proc` is invoked. As with callback registration, `XtAddInput` allows the program to pass a data pointer in `client_data`. It returns an input-callback ID, which may be used to identify the callback.

Listing 17.1. Function prototype: <code>XtAddInput</code>

```
XtInputId    XtAddInput( source, condition, proc, client_data )
             int                 source;
             caddr_t             condition;
             XtInputCallbackProc proc;
             caddr_t             client_data;
```

The condition codes require further explanation. Each condition is represented by a constant: `XtInputReadMask`, `XtInputWriteMask`, or `XtInputExceptMask`. `XtInputReadMask` causes the callback to be invoked when data is available from the file. This is only useful, however, for files that represent pipes, sockets, or a

---

pipe, assigns the output side to the standard output of the first program, and the input side to the standard input of the second program; the programs themselves act as though I/O involved a terminal.

[2] It also provides a timeout capability, described below.

[3] For X11R4, use `XtAppAddInput`.

device: disk files always indicate that they have input. `XtInputWriteMask` indicates that the file may be written without blocking — again, this is primarily of use for pipes and sockets. The final condition constant, `XtInputExceptMask`, is used only with socket connections and indicates the receipt of "out-of-band" (urgent) data.

The `source` parameter also requires further explanation. The `select` call is part of the low-level file interface, which means that it uses 'file descriptors.' Most programs, on the other hand, work with the high-level, buffered interface, which makes use of 'file pointers.' To use `XtAddInput` with a high-level file, you must use `fileno` to retrieve the file descriptor from the file pointer.[4]

The Input Callback Procedure

While "input callback" is the term used to describe the linkage established by `XtAddInput`, the called function does not follow the format of other callbacks. Instead, its prototype is as shown in Listing 17.2: it receives the passed data pointer (`client_data`), a pointer to the file descriptor for which the callback was invoked (`source`), and a pointer to the callback ID (`id`). This callback does not provide a call data structure, nor does it specify a widget (since files are not associated with widgets).

Listing 17.2. Function prototype: Input callback procedure

```
void     funcname( client_data, source, id )
         caddr_t    client_data;
         int        *source;
         XtInputId  *id;
```

Removing an Input Callback

A program that accepts input from multiple file sources may need to disable the callbacks attached to one or more of these sources. To do this, it calls the function `XtRemoveInput`, prototyped in Listing 17.3. This function takes a single parameter: the callback ID returned by `XtAddInput`.

---

[4] Example:
```
         FILE    *fp;
         int     fd;

         fd = fileno(fp);
```

Listing 17.3. Function prototype: *XtRemoveInput*

```
void    XtRemoveInput( id )
        XtInputId   id;
```

Example: Adding Standard Input to the File Browser

The file browser application of Chapter 9 was meant as a replacement for the
more program. However, while it was able to read and display a named file, it
was unable to display data piped to its standard input — one of the most
common uses of *more*. Listing 17.4 presents a version of the file browser that
adds this capability: if no filename is specified on invocation, it attaches an
input callback to StdIn.

Listing 17.4. File browser, revision 2: Addition of standard-
input capability

```
/*********************************************************************
**                                                                 **
**  listing_17_04.c                                                **
**                                                                 **
**  File Browser, Edition 2. The file browser of Chapter 9, with   **
**  the capability to read StdIn if no file is specified. It uses  **
**  an input callback to provide this capability.                  **
**                                                                 **
*********************************************************************/


#include <stdio.h>
#include <Xm/Text.h>


void        LoadFile();                 /* FORWARD Definitions     */
void        UseStdIn();
void        InputCB();
```

Listing 17.4. Continued.

```c
Widget      appshell,              /* Application Shell        */
            the_text;              /* The text widget          */
long        text_cnt = 0;          /* Number of bytes in buffer */


void main( argc, argv )
    int     argc;
    char    *argv[];
{
    appshell = XtInitialize( argv[0], "Listing_17_04", NULL, 0,
                             &argc, argv );

    the_text = XmCreateScrolledText( appshell, "TheText", NULL, 0 );
    XtManageChild( the_text );

    if (argc > 2)
        {
        fprintf( stderr, "\nbrowser: Usage:\n" );
        fprintf( stderr, "        browser FILENAME\n" );
        fprintf( stderr, "        (or)\n" );
        fprintf( stderr, "        ??? | browser\n" );
        exit( 1 );
        }
    else if (argc == 2)
        LoadFile( argv[1] );
    else
        UseStdIn();

    XtRealizeWidget( appshell );
    XtMainLoop();
}



/**
*** LoadFile( fname )
***
*** Called when the text is to come from a file, this function
*** opens the file and loads it into the text widget.
**/
```

Listing 17.4. Continued.

```c
void LoadFile( fname )
    char        *fname;
{
    FILE        *infile;
    long        fsize;
    char        *lclptr;

    infile = fopen( fname, "r" );
    if (infile == NULL)
        {
        perror( "browser: unable to open input file" );
        exit( 2 );
        }

    fseek( infile, 0, 2 );
    fsize = ftell( infile );
    rewind( infile );

    lclptr = (char *)XtMalloc( fsize + 1 );
    fread( lclptr, sizeof(char), fsize, infile );
    lclptr[fsize] = '\0';

    XmTextSetString( the_text, lclptr );

    XtFree( lclptr );
    fclose( infile );
}



/**
*** UseStdIn()
***
*** This function is called when input is to come from StdIn. It
*** simply attaches an input callback.
**/

void UseStdIn()
{
    XtAddInput( fileno(stdin), XtInputReadMask, InputCB, NULL );
}
```

Listing 17.4. Continued.

```c
/**
*** InputCB( client_data, source, id )
***
*** Called whenever data is present on StdIn. This function
*** reads a single character, and appends it to the text buffer.
**/

void InputCB( client_data, source, id )
    caddr_t     client_data;
    int         *source;
    XtInputId   *id;
{
    char        lcl_buf[2];
    int         in_char;

    if ((in_char = getchar()) != EOF)
        {
        lcl_buf[0] = in_char;
        lcl_buf[1] = '\0';;
        XmTextReplace( the_text, text_cnt, text_cnt, lcl_buf );
        text_cnt++;
        }
    else
        XtRemoveInput( *id );
}
```

```
!
! Resource file for File Browser
!

*TheTextSW.foreground:   Gray25
*TheTextSW.background:   Gray50

*TheText.foreground:     Black
*TheText.background:     White
*TheText.fontList:       -*-Courier-medium-r-*--*-100-*
*TheText.rows:           15
*TheText.columns:        48

*TheText.editMode:       MULTI_LINE_EDIT
*TheText.editable:       FALSE
```

The initial part of this program is almost identical to that of Listing 9.13, except that the invocation test is performed after the text widget is created, not before. This was done because this test now does more work: it determines whether to read a file, use standard input, or display an error.

Note the presence of the `text_cnt` variable. Although Motif 1.1 provides a function to retrieve the number of characters in a text widget (`XmTextGetLastPosition`), this value must be maintained locally by a Motif 1.0 program.[5]

If the program's input comes from standard input, then the input callback must be attached; this is done in the function `UseStdIn`. The callback function, `InputCB`, is invoked whenever data is available on standard input. It reads this data in the traditional way, using the `getchar` macro. It then adds this character to the end of the text buffer, using `XmTextReplace`.

While traditional, this method is also extremely slow. The input callback must be called for each character added to the buffer. When running this program, you can watch each character being added to the buffer — at typing speed. To eliminate this problem, you can retrieve the number of available characters from the file control structure, then read that many characters in a single operation.

Finally, note that the input callback is removed once the `EOF` character is read. This is done due to the nature of UNIX pipe I/O: once the sender closes the pipe, the reader will always be able to read from it — with the read returning `EOF`. If the input callback were left in place, it would be called continually, without actually indicating the availability of data.

Timeouts

As stated above, the `select` system call allows for a timeout. The toolkit uses this capability to allow a program to perform operations at regular intervals. Timeouts are installed using the function `XtAddTimeOut`, and they invoke a timeout callback when activated.

Adding and Removing Timeouts

Timeouts are registered using the function `XtAddTimeOut`, prototyped in Listing 17.5. This function takes the timeout length (`interval`), a pointer to the timeout function (`proc`), and a pointer to program-specific data (`client_data`). The timeout interval is a count of milliseconds between the time the timeout is registered and the time the timeout procedure is invoked.[6] As with `XtAddInput`, `XtAddTimeOut` returns an ID that identifies the timeout.

---

[5] It could be determined by retrieving the widget's contents and using `strlen`, but that is extremely inefficient.

[6] While the timeout interval is specified as a count of milliseconds, it is only an approximation of the actual timeout time. Due to the way that timeout alarms are actually implemented, the true interval will be about a tenth of a second above or below the specified interval — on some systems, it can be as much as a whole second.

Listing 17.5. Function prototype: XtAddTimeOut

```
XtIntervalId    XtAddTimeOut( interval, proc, client_data )
                unsigned long         interval;
                XtTimerCallbackProc proc;
                caddr_t               client_data;
```

If the program determines that a timeout is no longer needed, it may remove the timeout with the function `XtRemoveTimeOut`, prototyped in Listing 17.6. This function takes the timeout ID as its sole parameter.

Listing 17.6. Function prototype: XtRemoveTimeOut

```
void    XtRemoveTimeOut( id )
        XtIntervalId    id;
```

The Timeout Callback

Like an input callback, a timeout callback does not use the standard callback prototype. Instead, it uses the prototype shown in Listing 17.7. The callback function is given the client data as registered with `XtAddTimeOut` (`client_data`), as well as a pointer to the ID associated with the timeout (`id`).

Listing 17.7. Function prototype: Timeout callback
function

```
void    funcname( client_data, id )
        caddr_t           client_data;
        XtIntervalId    *id;
```

You should note that the timeouts are activated only once: part of the activation process is removal of the activated timeout from the list of those installed. If a program needs a timeout to occur on a regular interval, it must explicitly reinstall the timeout each time it is activated. This also means that the ID passed to the timeout function is used only for identification: when the callback is invoked, the ID does not actually refer to a timeout.

Example: Digital Clock

One obvious use for timeouts is a clock program, as shown in Figure 17.1. Such a clock could be used in a stand-alone manner, or as part of a program such as an appointment manager.

Figure 17.1. Timeout example: Digital clock

Listing 17.8 presents the program and resource file for this clock application. The clock itself is a label widget, and the timeout callback installs the current time in its `labelString` resource. Note that the timeout is first installed immediately after the label is created and is reinstalled by the callback function. Note also the technique of passing the label widget's ID as the timeout's client data.

Listing 17.8. Program and resource file: Digital clock

```c
/**********************************************************************
**                                                                  **
**    listing_17_08.c                                               **
**                                                                  **
**    Digital clock program, implemented using a label updated by a **
**    timeout callback.                                             **
**                                                                  **
**********************************************************************/


#include <time.h>
#include <Xm/Label.h>

void    TimeoutCB();                    /* FORWARD Definitions    */
```

Listing 17.8. Continued.

```c
Widget  appshell,
        the_label;


void main( argc, argv )
    int     argc;
    char    *argv[];
{
    appshell = XtInitialize( argv[0], "Listing_17_08", NULL, 0,
                             &argc, argv );


    the_label = XmCreateLabel( appshell, "TheLabel", NULL, 0 );
    XtManageChild( the_label );

    XtAddTimeOut( 1000, TimeoutCB, the_label );

    XtRealizeWidget( appshell );
    XtMainLoop();
}




void TimeoutCB( w, id )
    Widget          w;                  /* Note implicit caddr_t cast */
    XtIntervalId    *id;                /* Ignored                    */
{
    long            clock;              /* The raw time value...      */
    struct tm       *the_time;          /* Converted to localtime...  */
    char            lcl_str[256];       /* Converted to text...       */
    XmString        xms;                /* Converted for the widget   */
    Arg             the_arg;


    XtAddTimeOut( 1000, TimeoutCB, the_label );
    clock    = time( NULL );
    the_time = localtime( &clock );
    sprintf( lcl_str, "%02d:%02d:%02d", the_time->tm_hour,
                                        the_time->tm_min,
                                        the_time->tm_sec );
```

Listing 17.8. Continued.

```
    xms = XmStringCreate( lcl_str, XmSTRING_DEFAULT_CHARSET );
    XtSetArg( the_arg, XmNlabelString, xms );
    XtSetValues( w, &the_arg, 1 );

    XmStringFree( xms );
}
```

```
!
! Resource file for Digital Clock (Fig 17.1)
!

*TheLabel.height:       50
*TheLabel.width:        100
*TheLabel.foreground:   Black
*TheLabel.background:   Gray75
*TheLabel.fontList:     -*-times-medium-r-*--*-140-*
```

Background Processing: *WorkProcs*

A *workproc* is a function that is called from `XtMainLoop`, whenever the program is waiting for an event. Workprocs provide a limited degree of background processing and are typically used in three situations.

The first situation is polling for input from a non-X, non-file source, such as shared memory. Workprocs should not be used in a time-critical polling situation, because their invocation is directly related to the number of events being received — and the time taken to process those events. However, if polling may be performed on a "catch as catch can" basis, workprocs are easier to use than timeouts — primarily because they don't need to be reinstalled on each invocation.

The second situation occurs when a function needs to be "continued" after user interaction. As an example, consider a function that manages a dialog box and must perform some processing after data is entered into that dialog. While such operations are normally performed with a dedicated callback, there are cases where that is not practical.[7] Instead, the invoking function could install a workproc that waits until dialog interaction is complete, then performs the additional processing.

The final use of workprocs is due to the non-reentrant nature of Motif and the toolbox. This is not normally a problem, because toolbox functions are invoked

---

[7] This could happen if the same dialog were to be invoked from two locations, with one performing additional processing on the results. You will see this later in the chapter, where the text editor's **Save As...** dialog is invoked during program exit.

in a linear fashion, in response to events. It becomes a problem when the program is interrupted, as with a UNIX signal.

A signal may arrive at any time and results in the invocation of a signal handler. If a signal is received while in a widget's internal code, and the signal handler attempts to access that widget, its internal state could be inconsistent. To avoid this problem, the signal handler should install a workproc to perform the widget access. Since workprocs are invoked from the event loop, the widget would be guaranteed to be in a consistent state.

Registering and Removing WorkProcs

Workprocs are installed using the function `XtAddWorkProc` and removed with the function `XtRemoveWorkProc`, both of which are prototyped in Listing 17.9. `XtAddWorkProc` takes two parameters: a pointer to the workproc function itself (`proc`), and a pointer to program-specific data (`client_data`); it returns an ID that identifies the workproc. `XtRemoveWorkProc` takes one parameter, the ID of the workproc to be removed (`id`).

Listing 17.9. Function prototypes: *XtAddWorkProc, XtRemoveWorkProc*

```
XtWorkProcId      XtAddWorkProc( proc, client_data )
                  XtWorkProc      proc;
                  caddr_t         client_data;


void              XtRemoveWorkProc( id );
                  XtWorkProcId    id;
```

Each call to `XtAddWorkProc` adds a new workproc to the list maintained by the toolkit. This list is prioritized: each time the event loop is able to call a workproc, it invokes the workproc with the highest priority, then sets that workproc's priority to the lowest value (*ie*, it will not be called again until all other workprocs have been called). New workprocs are given the highest priority; when a series of workprocs are added, each workproc has a higher priority than the one added before it (and all have higher priority than any outstanding workprocs).

The WorkProc Function

A workproc function follows the prototype of Listing 17.10. It has a single parameter in which is passed the client data pointer from `XtAddWorkProc`. When a workproc completes, it must return a `Boolean` value to the event loop: if this value contains `TRUE`, the workproc is removed from the workproc list; if it contains `FALSE`, the workproc remains in the list and is set to the lowest priority.

Listing 17.10. Function prototype: WorkProc

```
Boolean funcname( client_data );
        caddr_t client_data;
```

WorkProc Example

Listing 17.11 contains an example of a workproc used in a polling manner. Each second, the program prints the number of times the workproc was invoked in that second, and the average number of calls per second since the program started. By feeding it events — such as moving its window — you will see the capabilities and limits of a workproc.

Listing 17.11. Program and resource file: Workproc example

```
/**********************************************************************
**                                                                  **
**    listing_17_11.c                                               **
**                                                                  **
**    Workproc example. This program presents a simple label, just to  **
**    provide a window. Its real operation is a workproc, which counts  **
**    the number of times it's called each second, and prints both the  **
**    immediate count and an average.                               **
**                                                                  **
**********************************************************************/

#include <Xm/Label.h>


Boolean WorkProc();                    /* FORWARD Definitions       */


Widget  appshell,
        the_label;
```

Listing 17.11. Continued.

```c
void main( argc, argv )
    int     argc;
    char    *argv[];
{
    appshell = XtInitialize( argv[0], "Listing_17_11", NULL, 0,
                             &argc, argv );

    the_label = XmCreateLabel( appshell, "TheLabel", NULL, 0 );
    XtManageChild( the_label );

    XtAddWorkProc( WorkProc, NULL );

    XtRealizeWidget( appshell );
    XtMainLoop();
}



Boolean WorkProc( ignore )
    caddr_t     ignore;
{
    static int  tot_calls = 0,          /* Total calls            */
                tot_time  = 0,          /* Total time running     */
                calls_sec = 0,          /* Calls this second      */
                last_time = 0;          /* Time of last call      */
    int         this_time = time(NULL);
    if (last_time == 0)
        last_time = this_time;
    else if (last_time == this_time)
        {
        tot_calls++;
        calls_sec++;
        }
    else
        {
        tot_time++;

        printf( "Second %d\n", tot_time );
        printf( "    Calls    = %6d\n", calls_sec );
```

Listing 17.11. Continued.

```
        printf( "    Avg Calls = %6.1f\n", ((float)tot_calls)/tot_time );

        calls_sec = 0;
        last_time = this_time;
        }

    return( FALSE );
}
```

Sending Events Between Clients

Within the event-driven paradigm of X, the most appropriate method of communication would seem to be the event mechanism: every client, after all, must be watching for events directed to itself. This is true, with three caveats: (1) events have a limited capacity, (2) clients that use events must have windows on the same server, and (3) for one client to send an event to another, it must know the other's window ID.

The first caveat arises from the design of the X protocol: events are 32-byte datagrams. If the programs can perform communication in small pieces, they can use events directly. If not, they must use events as a means of communicating that data is available from some other source — as you will see below, the other source is often a window property.

The second caveat also arises from the X protocol design: servers are completely independent. A client may be connected to two or more servers and pass messages between them, but that operation is dependent on the client design — outside of that client, the servers themselves are not logically connected. In practical use, this is not a problem: most interclient communication occurs under the user's control, between clients on the user's server.

The third caveat requires the most consideration: communicating clients must have some way of discovering each other. One common method of learning another window's ID is from the user; this technique is used by the standard clients *xwd* and *xwininfo*.[8] An alternate method is to use the selection mechanism (described below), with an application-specific selection type. Yet another method, which could be used by programs that have other communication options available, is to exchange this information outside the X environment.[9]

---

[8] In this technique, the user is asked to position the pointer over the desired window and press a button. The original client "grabs" the button prior to this request, meaning that the button press event is sent to it. From the button press event, the client determines what window the pointer was in when its button was pressed.

[9] If another communication method is available, why use events at all? One reason is that events can be used to alert the receiver when data is available; an example would be the use of shared memory, which cannot be associated with a callback.

Sending Events: XSendEvent

When one client has the window ID of another, it can send events to that client with the XSendEvent function, prototyped in Listing 17.12. These events must be filled by the sender; the server modifies the event's send_event member only.[10] If XSendEvent can send the event to the server (the server handles sending it to the other client), it returns TRUE; if not, it returns FALSE.

Listing 17.12. Function prototype: *XSendEvent*

```
Status   XSendEvent( display, win, propagate, mask, event )
         Display     *display;
         Window      win;
         Boolean     propagate;
         EventMask    mask;
         XEvent      *event;
```

The display and win parameters identify the destination window: display specifies the destination window's server, while win is the window's server resource ID. The destination display must be a display to which the application is connected; it may be retrieved from an appropriate widget via XtDisplay. In addition to an actual window ID, two constants are allowed for the win parameter: PointerWindow specifies the window that currently contains the pointer, and InputFocus specifies the window that currently has the input focus.

The propagate parameter specifies which clients receive the event. If propagate contains FALSE, the event is sent to all clients that have attached an event handler to the destination window for one of the events specified by mask. If propagate contains FALSE, and no clients have selected an appropriate event, then the event is not sent. However, if propagate contains TRUE, and no clients have attached an event handler to the window, the event is passed up the window tree, until some client receives it.[11]

The mask parameter contains one or more event masks, as described in Chapter 8. It is used to select the clients that will receive the event. If it contains zero (no masks specified), the event is sent to the creator of the destination window; if that client no longer exists, the event is lost.[12] If mask contains one or more event masks, the event is set to those clients that have the appropriate event handler attached to the window.

The event parameter points to the actual event data. Any type of event structure is allowed. The server does not change any members of this structure, save the send_event flag. It does, however, perform "byte-swapping," so that events may

---

[10] Without the send_event member, a client-generated event would be indistinguishable from a user-generated event, meaning that a client could be "spoofed." In the case of *xterm*, for example, a user's password could be changed from events generated by another user.

[11] An exception is if the win parameter was passed as InputFocus, in which case the event is not propagated, even if propagate contains TRUE.

[12] Nonmaskable events, such as ClientMessage (see below) , are sent with a mask parameter of zero.

be sent transparently between systems that use different byte ordering (*eg*, Intel and Motorola).

The ClientMessage *Event*

While the `XSendEvent` function allows a client to send any type of event to another client, it is most often used to send a `ClientMessage` event. The `XClientMessageEvent` structure, defined in Listing 17.13, is used to hold events of this type. Other than the common (`XAnyEvent`) fields, all of the event's fields are available for the program to be used as described below.

Listing 17.13. Type definition: XClientMessageEvent

```
typedef struct
        {
        int             type;
        unsigned long   serial;
        Boolean         send_event;
        Display         *display;
        Window          window;
        Atom            message_type;
        int             format;
        union           {
                        char    b[20];
                         short   s[10];
                        long    l[5];
                        }
                        data;
        }
XClientMessageEvent;
```

The `message_type` member provides the receiver with an indication of how to treat the event data. The contents of `message_type` are left to the discretion of the programmer; the server does not make use of it. By convention, however, it contains an atom (see below) that specifies the event's contents.

The event's data area is represented by the `data` member, which is a union that can represent the data in bytes (b), short integers (s), or long integers (l). The specific data format depends on the program; any given program may use all or none of the data space. The one requirement is that the event data must be organized as bytes, short integers, or long integers, and the `format` member must contain 8, 16, or 32, respectively. This requirement allows the server to perform the byte-swapping described above.[13]

---

[13] If you do not need to worry about this architecture-dependent conversion, specify the value 8 for the `format` member; when the data is merely a collection of bytes, the server does not convert it.

Atoms

Atoms are server resource IDs that uniquely identify strings. They are thus identical in concept to quarks, but different in scope: quark associations are local to a program, while atoms are server-wide. They also differ from quarks in purpose: quarks exist to maximize the efficiency of multiple string comparisons, while atoms exist to maximize the efficiency of client-server communications.[14]

As with strings and quarks, the string-to-atom relationship is one-to-one. Once an atom is associated with a string, that association remains in effect until the server is shut down. This results in long-term consumption of server resources, so you should not create unnecessary atoms.

Converting Strings to Atoms

Atoms are associated with strings using the function `XInternAtom`, prototyped in Listing 17.14. If an atom is already associated with the string, the ID of that atom is returned; if no atom exists, one is created (subject to the `if_exists` parameter, see below).

Listing 17.14. Function prototype: XInternAtom

```
Atom      XInternAtom( display, name, if_exists )
          Display      *display;
          String       name;
          Boolean      if_exists;
```

The `display` parameter specifies the server on which the atom association is valid. The `name` parameter specifies a NUL-terminated string of arbitrary length, which is associated with the atom ID by the server.[15] The `if_exists` parameter controls whether an atom will be created if one is not already associated with the string: if it contains `FALSE`, a new atom is created; if it contains `TRUE`, the server does not create an atom. In this case, `XInternAtom` returns the constant `None`.

Motif provides the function `XmInternAtom`, prototyped identically to `XInternAtom`. It provides atom caching, meaning that it may be called multiple times but will make only one request of the server. While this would seem superfluous — most programs call `XInternAtom` only once — some Motif macros use it extensively.[16] If you decide to use `XmInternAtom` instead of `XInternAtom`, you must include the header file `X11/AtomMgr.h`.

---

[14] An atom, which occupies 32 bits, may be more efficiently communicated than an arbitrarily long string. In addition to this size savings, use of a fixed-size string identifier allows for fixed-size datagrams, eliminating the need for a length specification and its associated processing.

[15] This string is not limited to the printable ASCII character set; it may contain any eight-bit value other than '\0'. By convention, printable strings are used, with the ISO Latin 1 encoding.

[16] In particular, the macros supporting the window manager protocol interface make extensive use of `XmInternAtom`.

Converting Atoms to Strings

The conversion of an atom ID to a NUL-terminated C string is performed by `XGetAtomName`, prototyped in Listing 17.15. The `display` parameter specifies the display on which the atom exists, while the `atom` parameter specifies the atom's ID. If an atom exists with that name, its associated string is returned; this string is allocated in the program's data space and should be freed (with `XtFree`) when no longer needed. If no such association exists, `XGetAtomName` returns `NULL`.[17]

Listing 17.15. Function prototype: *XGetAtomName*

```
String  XGetAtomName( display, atom )
        Display    *display;
        Atom        atom;
```

Predefined Atoms

Some atoms are used so frequently that they have predefined IDs. Examples include the atoms representing selection types, window manager properties, and property data types, all of which are described below. The predefined IDs for these atoms represented by constants in the header file `X11/Xatom.h`; each constant has the prefix "XA_".

The X Registry and Atom Naming Conventions

One problem with program-specific atoms is that you never know whether another programmer will use the same atom name. If this happens, your program and the other program will collide — sometimes with no effect, sometimes with devastating effect.

While this is rarely a problem in programs under development, no production program should use random atom names — no matter how unique you may think they are. Instead, you should register your atoms with the *X Registry*, a service of the X consortium.[18] While registration may not guarantee that another programmer won't use your atom name, it at least guarantees that a conscientious programmer won't in production code.

Prior to registering your atom names, you will minimize the chances of collision if you follow the registry's naming conventions. These conventions are quite simple: an atom may have any name, but should be prefixed with an organization identifier. This organization identifier is an arbitrarily long string, prefixed and suffixed by underscores. For example, "_KDG_" might be such an identifier, giving rise to atom names such as "_KDG_MY_ATOM".

---

[17] Motif also provides a caching version of `XGetAtomName` called `XmGetAtomName`. The two functions are prototyped identically.

[18] Appendix E contains information on the X Registry.

Window Properties

Window properties are data buffers on the server associated with a particular window and identified by name — this name being represented by an atom. To the program, a property contains a particular data structure. To the server, a property is an arbitrarilylong data buffer, containing 8-, 16-, or 32-bit data items.

Theoretically, the size of a window property is unlimited. In practice, it is limited both by the design of the server and the amount of memory available to the server at any given time. For this reason, a programmer should give careful consideration to the question of whether a property is the best solution for a particular problem.[19] Consideration should also be given to the fact that storing data into a property involves client-server communication, which may be a problem on a network with limited available bandwidth.

Properties are used for two common purposes: (1) exchanging data with the window manager, and (2) exchanging data with another application. Properties are commonly associated with the client's application shell window, although they may be associated with any window. For window manager communication, the property must be associated with the shell window.

Property Creation and Modification

Properties are created and modified with the `XChangeProperty` function, prototyped in Listing 17.16. This function identifies the property by the atom representing its name. If the given name is on the window's list of properties, it is changed according to the function parameters. If it does not already exist, it is added.

Listing 17.16. Function prototype: *XChangeProperty*

```
int      XChangeProperty( display, win, prop, type, format, mode,
                          data, datasize )
         Display      *display;
         Window       win;
         Atom         prop;
         Atom         type;
         int          format;
         int          mode;
         caddr_t      data;
         int          n_items;
```

---

[19] Note, however, that within the X paradigm, a window property is the *only* server-based mechanism for data storage, and it is often the most convenient (given the limited size of events) for data interchange.

The property is identified by the `display`, `win`, and `prop` parameters: `display` specifies the display on which the window resides, `win` specifies the ID of the window, and `prop` is the atom representing the property name.

The `type` parameter specifies the data type of the property's contents. This value is simply stored with the property; it does not have any effect on the property's contents. The retrieving program may — or may not — use this value to convert the property data upon retrieval.

As you can see, data types are represented by atoms. Common data types, such as `int`, have predefined atoms; a program must define atoms for its own types.

The `format` parameter specifies the data type of the property's contents in the context of the server. In this context, the property contains an arbitrarily long array of 8-, 16-, or 32-bit data items, which must be converted appropriately for the clients' architectures. This data item size is stored in `format`, and legal values are 8, 16, and 32.

The `mode` parameter specifies how the passed data is to be added to an existing property. If `mode` contains `PropModeReplace`, the passed data replaces the existing contents of the property. If it contains `PropModePrepend`, the new data is stored before any existing data. `PropModeAppend` specifies that the new data is to be appended to the old. For prepend and append, the `type` and `format` values must match those already associated with the property. If not, the data is not saved, and an error is reported.

The final parameters, `data` and `n_items`, represent the data to be added to the property. The `data` parameter is a pointer to the data. while `n_items` contains the number of items in the buffer. This value depends on the `format` parameter: a 12-byte array may have 12, 6, or 3 items corresponding to `format` values of 8, 16, or 32.

Retrieving Property Contents

To retrieve the contents of a property, use the function `XGetWindowProperty`, prototyped in Listing 17.17. As with `XChangeProperty`, the property is identified by the `display`, `win`, and `prop` parameters. It is additionally identified by data type, as described below.

Listing 17.17. Function prototype: *XGetWindowProperty*

```
int      XGetWindowProperty( display, win, prop, offset, length,
                             delete, req_type, act_type, act_format,
                             n_items, bytes_after, data );
         Display     *display;
         Window      win;
         Atom        prop;
         long        offset;
         long        length;
         Boolean     delete;
         Atom        req_type;
         Atom        *act_type;
         int         *act_format;
         long        n_items;
         long        bytes_after;
         caddr_t     *data;
```

The `offset` parameter specifies an offset from the beginning of the property data and is used to select part of a property. This value is an index of 32-bit quantities, starting at zero.

The `length` parameter specifies the number of 32-bit quantities to retrieve. The retrieval length must be specified explicitly. To indicate "all of it," you must simply pass a large value.

The `delete` parameter specifies whether the property is to be deleted after the retrieval. If `delete` contains `TRUE`, and the function retrieves all of the property's data, the property will be deleted. If `delete` contains `FALSE`, or if the call did not retrieve all of the property's data (`length` was less than the actual data size), the property remains unchanged.

The `req_type` parameter is used to specify the type of data desired. This value is matched against the atom associated with the property by `XChangeProperty`; if the type requested does not match the type associated with the property, the request fails. To avoid such a comparison, use the constant `AnyPropertyType`.

The `act_type` and `act_format` parameters are used to return the actual data type and format, as specified by `XChangeProperty`. The returned type will match that passed in `req_type`, unless the latter contains `AnyPropertyType`.

The `n_items` parameter is used to return the actual number of 8-, 16-, or 32-bit items retrieved from the property. If `length` specified a value that was larger than the actual property size, the actual property size is returned in `num_items`.

The `bytes_after` parameter is used to return the number of bytes remaining in the property. This value only considers bytes physically positioned after the retrieved data; if an offset was used, those bytes skipped by the offset are not reported in `bytes_after`. One use of this field is in determining the size of a property by performing a zero-length retrieval.

Finally, the `prop` parameter is used to return a pointer to the property data. `XGetWindowProperty` allocates a buffer for the retrieved data and stores a pointer to this buffer in `prop`. This buffer must be freed by the program when it is no longer needed.

Property Destruction

When a property is no longer needed, it should be destroyed. Server memory space is not an infinite resource, and unused properties can quickly consume the available memory. To destroy a property, call the function `XDeleteProperty`, prototyped in Listing 17.18. This function uses the `display`, `win`, and `prop` parameters to identify the property. It returns zero to indicate success, and a nonzero value to indicate failure.

Listing 17.18. Function prototype: *XDeleteProperty*

```
int      XDeleteProperty( display, win, prop );
         Display    *display;
         Window     win;
         Atom       prop;
```

Discovering Available Properties

To learn what properties are associated with a window, use the function `XListProperties`, prototyped in Listing 17.19. This function identifies the window with the `display` and `win` parameters. The function returns a pointer to an array of property atoms, and it returns the number of items in this array in the `num_props` parameter. This array should be freed by the program when no longer needed.

Listing 17.19. Function prototype: *XListProperties*

```
Atom     *XListProperties( display, win, num_props );
         Display    *display;
         Window     win;
         int        *num_props;
```

Property Data Types

Window properties are identified by data type. This type is specified by `XChangeProperty` and is used by `XGetWindowProperty` to control property retrieval. A property's data type does not affect the server's treatment of the property — to it, a property is merely a collection of bytes, words, or longwords. Instead, a property's data type exists as information for the program that reads the property. It is primarily of use for the selection mechanism, where one program may need to convert another program's data into a usable format.

Property data types are predefined atoms. Table 17.1 lists the constants representing these atoms, the strings that they are associated with, and the C data type that they represent.[20] Note that programs are not limited to these predefined types: cooperating programs can define their own types (or set of types), but will not be able to use those types to exchange that data with other clients.

Table 17.1. Predefined property types

Constant	String	Description	
XA_ARC	"ARC"	XArc	(12 bytes, as six 2-byte integers)
XA_ATOM	"ATOM"	Atom	(4 byte Server ID)
XA_BITMAP	"BITMAP"	Bitmap	(4 byte Server ID)
XA_CARDINAL	"CARDINAL"	unsigned	(4 bytes)
XA_COLORMAP	"COLORMAP"	Colormap	(4 byte Server ID)
XA_CURSOR	"CURSOR"	Cursor	(4 byte Server ID)
XA_DRAWABLE	"DRAWABLE"	Drawable	(4 byte Server ID)
XA_FONT	"FONT"	Font	(4 byte Server ID)
XA_INTEGER	"INTEGER"	int	(4 bytes)
XA_PIXMAP	"PIXMAP"	Pixmap	(4 byte Server ID)
XA_POINT	"POINT"	XPoint	(4 bytes, as two 2-byte integers)
XA_RGB_COLOR_MAP	"RGB_COLOR_MAP"	Colormap	(4 byte Server ID)
XA_RECTANGLE	"RECTANGLE"	XRectangle	(8 bytes, as four 2-byte integers)

---

[20] These descriptions include the data type's size, but the actual size may differ — either due to a change in X or due to hardware considerations. A program should always use the `sizeof` operator.

Table 17.1. Continued.

`XA_STRING`	`"STRING"`	`String`	(variable length NUL-terminated ASCII string)
`XA_VISUALID`	`"VISUALID"`	`VisualID`	(4 byte Server ID)
`XA_WINDOW`	`"WINDOW"`	`Window`	(4 byte Server ID)
`XA_WM_HINTS`	`"WM_HINTS"`	`XWMHints`	(32 byte structure)
`XA_WM_SIZE` `_HINTS`	`"WM_SIZE` `_HINTS"`	`XSizeHints`	(60 byte structure)

The PropertyNotify *Event*

Whenever a property is modified, the server sends a `PropertyNotify` event to the window creator. This event is selected with `PropertyNotifyMask`; its contents are contained in the `xproperty` member of `XEvent`, defined as shown in Listing 17.20.

Listing 17.20. Type definition: *XPropertyEvent*

```
typedef struct
        {
        int             type;
        unsigned long   serial;
        Boolean         send_event;
        Display         *display;
        Window          window;
        Atom            atom;
        Time            time;
        int             state;
        }
XPropertyEvent;
```

Most of the members of `XPropertyEvent` should by now be familiar: `type` contains the event type (`PropertyEvent`), `serial` contains the number of requests processed by the server, `send_event` indicates whether the event was generated by another client, `display` and `window` identify the source of the event, and `time` contains the current server time.

The new members are `atom`, which specifies the property that was changed, and `state`, which indicates what was changed. There are two values for `state`:

NewValue indicates that the contents of the property were in some way changed, and Deleted indicates that the property was deleted.[21]

Window Manager Protocols

One use of properties is to communicate with the window manager: a program places data in specific properties on its shell window, and the window manager reads those properties on a regular basis and acts on the information. A program's title, for example, is specified with the WM_NAME property. Most such communication is handled automatically by the application shell.

Window manager protocols, however, are an area where the program is often directly involved in the communication: they are a set of conventions by which the window manager notifies the client of changes in its environment. These notifications range from requesting that the client take the input focus, to notifying the client that the user has selected **Close** from the window menu.

The WM_PROTOCOLS *Property*

Window manager protocols are controlled by the WM_PROTOCOLS property on the application shell window.[22] This property contains an array of atoms: if an atom is present, it indicates that the program supports the associated protocol. If the client does not wish to participate in *any* protocols, it signals that fact by absence of a WM_PROTOCOLS property.

At the present time, the set of protocols is limited. The ICCCM specifies three protocols and Motif adds a fourth, identified by the strings listed below. Notice that these strings are not associated with predefined atoms; the program must explicitly retrieve the associated atom value.

- WM_TAKE_FOCUS

  When a client participates in this protocol, the window manager notifies it that it has been given the focus and should assign it to a subwindow. The application shell handles this protocol automatically — setting focus to whatever widget had it last. If, however, you wish to reassign the focus to a different widget, you can trap this protocol and call _XmGrabTheFocus (or XmProcessTraversal).

- WM_SAVE_YOURSELF

  The window manager notifies those clients participating in this protocol of situations that may cause the client to be terminated. The client is then expected to save its state and update the WM_COMMAND property on its shell with a command line that will retrieve the saved state. It is not permitted to interact with the user while this is happening.

---

[21] Property changes can take several forms: creation of a new property, changing the contents of an existing property, or a zero-length append to an existing property (which does not change the property's contents, but does generate an event — and is often used to get the current server time).

[22] "WM_PROTOCOLS" is the property name; it is not associated with a predefined atom.

At the present time, `WM_SAVE_YOURSELF` is of little use since window managers have no way to restart a program. It was designed for use with *session managers*, programs that are responsible for controlling the execution of other programs.[23]

- `WM_DELETE_WINDOW`

Those clients that request participation in the `WM_DELETE_WINDOW` protocol are notified if the user terminates the display connection via the window menu — by selecting **Close** or double-clicking the menu's invocation button.

This protocol permits the client to control its demise. If it is not in effect, the window manager terminates the session by destroying the client shell's window. If in effect, the window manager notifies the client of the request, but does not directly terminate the client.

In a Motif program, this protocol is always in effect and is handled by the application shell. The shell then uses the contents of its `deleteResponse` resource to determine its action: the default value of `XmDESTROY` causes the shell to terminate the program. If the program is to handle this protocol by other means, it must set `deleteResponse` to `XmDO_NOTHING`.

- `_MOTIF_WM_MESSAGES`

This protocol is specific to Motif and allows the client to trap `f.send_msg` functions invoked from the window menu. These messages permit the use of the window menu to provide program-specific functions — such as an "on the fly" debug switch.

Protocol Callbacks

The window manager gives the client a protocol notification using a `ClientMessage` event. This event's `message_type` member contains the atom associated with the string `WM_PROTOCOLS`. Its other fields depend on the specific protocol.

While a program could perform the two-step process of adding a particular protocol atom to the `WM_PROTOCOLS` property and registering an event for the protocol, Motif provides a protocol callback, registered with the function `XmAddWMProtocolCallback`. This function is prototyped in Listing 17.21; note that to use it, you must `#include` the header file `Xm/Protocols.h`.

---

[23] The purpose and use of a session manager is still vague — at least in the X documentation. An example of its use would be in an integrated program development environment: the session manager would control execution of the various programs (editor, compiler, etc), as well as manage the exchange of data between these programs. HP's VUE environment is another example.

Listing 17.21. Function prototype:
XmAddWMProtocolCallback

```
void    XmAddWMProtocolCallback( shell, protocol, proc, client_data )
        Widget          shell;
        Atom            protocol;
        XtCallbackProc  proc;
        caddr_t         client_data;
```

`XmAddWMProtocolCallback` takes as parameters the application shell widget (`shell`), the atom representing the protocol (`protocol`), a pointer to the callback procedure (`proc`), and a client data pointer (`client_data`). It adds the protocol atom to the `WM_PROTOCOLS` property of the shell, provided it is not already there. It then associates the callback procedure with an internal event handler: the shell receives the `ClientMessage` event and invokes the callback.

To remove a program from protocol participation, three options are available. The first is `XmRemoveWMProtocolCallback`, which removes a particular callback from the list maintained by the shell for a given protocol. The protocol remains in `WM_PROTOCOLS`, however, and the shell will continue to receive protocol events. The second method is to remove the protocol atom from the `WM_PROTOCOLS` property, and this is done with the function `XmRemoveWMProtocols`. The final option is to deactivate the protocol, with the function `XmDeactivateWMProtocol`. This function simply instructs the shell to ignore protocol events; they may be reactivated at a later time with the function `XmActivateWMProtocol`. All four of these functions are prototyped in Listing 17.22; their parameters are described below.

Listing 17.22. Function prototypes:
XmRemoveWMProtocolCallback, XmRemoveWMProtocols,
XmActivateWMProtocol, XmDeactivateWMProtocol

```
void      XmRemoveWMProtocolCallback( shell, protocol, proc, client_data )
          Widget          shell;
          Atom            protocol;
          XtCallbackProc  proc;
          caddr_t         client_data;


void      XmRemoveWMProtocols( shell, protocols, num_protocols )
          Widget          shell;
          Atom            protocols[];
          Cardinal        num_protocols;


void      XmActivateWMProtocol( shell, protocol )
          Widget          shell;
          Atom            protocol;

void      XmDeactivateWMProtocol( shell, protocol )
          Widget          shell;
          Atom            protocol;
```

The parameters of `XmRemoveWMProtocolCallback` are identical to those of
`XmAddWMProtocolCallback`. The shell's protocol callback list is searched, and the
callback corresponding to the passed `protocol`, `proc`, and `client_data` values is
removed. If another callback is registered for the same protocol, it is left in place.

`XmRemoveWMProtocols` allows the program to remove one or more protocols in one
step. Its first parameter, as expected, is the ID of the application shell. Its second
parameter is an array of atoms: each atom in that array is removed from the
`WM_PROTOCOLS` property, if present. Finally, the `num_protocols` parameter specifies
the number of atoms in the passed array.

`XmActivateWMProtocol` and `XmDeactivateWMProtocol` are prototyped identically.
They act on a single protocol at a time specified by the `protocol` parameter. All
callbacks associated with that protocol are activated or deactivated, but the
protocol remains active — the shell simply ignores any associated protocol
events.

Example: Trapping WM_DELETE_WINDOW in the Text Editor

Listing 17.23 presents a text editor module that traps the `WM_DELETE_WINDOW`
protocol. It gives the user the option to terminate the program, save the
workspace and terminate the program, or ignore the close request. The save
option is implemented using existing filer code, with a workproc to sequence the

save and termination options. The program is described in detail below the source listing.

Listing 17.23. Adding a window-manager protocol interface to the text editor

```
/*********************************************************************
**                                                                 **
**   saveproto.c                                                   **
**                                                                 **
**   Text Editor -- WM_DELETE_WINDOW Protocol Interface            **
**                                                                 **
*********************************************************************/


#include <stdio.h>
#include <Xm/MessageB.h>
#include <X11/Protocols.h>

#include "textedit.h"


/*********************************************************************
**                                                                 **
**           F O R W A R D   D E F I N I T I O N S                  **
**                                                                 **
*********************************************************************/

static  void    SaveProtoCB();
static  void    InitSaveAlert();
static  void    AlertSaveCB();
static  Boolean AlertSaveWP();


/*********************************************************************
**                                                                 **
**              L O C A L   V A R I A B L E S                       **
**                                                                 **
*********************************************************************/

static  Widget  save_alert;             /* Warning Dialog          */
static  Atom    a_del_win;              /* Atom for WM_DELETE_WINDOW */
```

Listing 17.23. Continued.

```
/**********************************************************************
**                                                                  **
**    InitSaveProto()                                               **
**                                                                  **
**    This function sets up the callback for the WM_DELETE_WINDOW   **
**    protocol. To make this work, it must also modify the shell's  **
**    deleteResponse resource -- otherwise the shell kills the job. **
**                                                                  **
**********************************************************************/

void InitSaveProto()
{
    a_del_win = XInternAtom( XtDisplay(appshell),
                             "WM_DELETE_WINDOW", FALSE );
    XmAddWMProtocolCallback( appshell, a_del_win, SaveProtoCB, NULL );

    XtSetArg( arglist[0], XmNdeleteResponse, XmDO_NOTHING );
    XtSetValues( appshell, arglist, 1 );

    InitSaveAlert();
}




/**********************************************************************
**                                                                  **
**    InitSaveAlert()                                               **
**                                                                  **
**    Creates the "Quit without Saving?" message box.               **
**                                                                  **
**    Note: The "Help" button is changed to "Quit" for this dialog. **
**                                                                  **
**********************************************************************/

static void InitSaveAlert()
```

Listing 17.23. Continued.

```c
{
    Widget        temp;

    save_alert = XmCreateWarningDialog( mainwin, "SaveAlert", NULL, 0 );

    temp = XmMessageBoxGetChild( save_alert, XmDIALOG_OK_BUTTON );
    XtAddCallback( temp, XmNactivateCallback, AlertSaveCB, "Save" );
    temp = XmMessageBoxGetChild( save_alert, XmDIALOG_HELP_BUTTON );
    XtAddCallback( temp, XmNactivateCallback, AlertSaveCB, "Quit" );
}




/**********************************************************************
**                                                                  **
**    SaveProtoCB( w, client_data, call_data )                      **
**                                                                  **
**    This function handles the callback for the WM_DELETE_WINDOW   **
**    protocol. It displays a dialog, which queries whether or not  **
**    the workspace should be saved.                                **
**                                                                  **
**********************************************************************/

static void SaveProtoCB( w, client_data, call_data )
    Widget                w;
    caddr_t               client_data;
    XmAnyCallbackStruct *call_data;
{
    XtManageChild( save_alert );
}
```

Listing 17.23. Continued.

```
/***********************************************************************
**                                                                   **
**   AlertSaveCB( w, client_data, call_data )                        **
**                                                                   **
**   Callback for the "Quit without Saving?" message box.            **
**   This function either quits or saves then quits.                 **
**                                                                   **
***********************************************************************/

static void AlertSaveCB( w, client_data, call_data )
    Widget       w;
    char         *client_data;
    caddr_t      call_data;
{
    if (!strcmp(client_data, "Save"))
        {
        saved = FALSE;
        XtAddWorkProc( AlertSaveWP, NULL );
        FileSave();
        }
    else
        exit( 0 );
}




/***********************************************************************
**                                                                   **
**   AlertSaveWP( client_data )                                      **
**                                                                   **
**   Workproc to handle wait while user saves file. This function    **
**   simply waits until the global variable "saved" becomes TRUE.    **
**                                                                   **
***********************************************************************/

static Boolean AlertSaveWP( client_data )
    caddr_t      client_data;
```

Listing 17.23. Continued.

```
{
    if (saved)
        exit( 0 );
    else
        return( FALSE );
}
```

The first function, `InitSaveProto`, is called from `InitOther`. It performs two actions: adding a callback for `WM_DELETE_WINDOW` and disabling the shell's default action. Note that it must retrieve the atom associated with the string "WM_DELETE_WINDOW".

The second initialization function, `InitSaveAlert`, creates the dialog box that is presented to the user by the callback. This dialog is built from a standard warning dialog (message box), but note that the **Help** button is used to implement a **Quit** function. For this application, I wanted to give the user three choices, and a message box only has three buttons. Since the dialog presents the user with a simple choice, **Help** was not needed for its original purpose.[24]

The next function is `SaveProtoCB`, called when the shell receives the `WM_DELETE _WINDOW` event. Since the actual functionality revolves around the message box, this function simply manages that dialog.

The function `AlertSaveCB` is called from both the **Save** and **Quit** choices of the message box; the **Cancel** choice simply unmanages the dialog. The **Quit** action is simple: it terminates the program. The **Save** action, however, is more complex due to the fact that it makes use of existing filer functions.

The problem occurs because **Save** implies **Quit**. If `FileSave` operated in a linear fashion, there would be no problem: `AlertSaveCB` could simply terminate the program after `FileSave` returned. However, `FileSave` does not operate in a linear fashion: it may in turn call `FileSaveAs`, which manages a dialog box then returns — while the dialog box invokes the actual save operation. If `AlertSaveCB` were to exit immediately after calling `FileSave`, the program could terminate without saving the file.

Obviously, the program must remain alive until the file is saved, and this is the purpose of `AlertSaveWP`. This function is registered as a workproc before the call to `FileSave` and is responsible for program termination. It determines the time of termination by examining the global variable `saved`: when this variable contains `TRUE`, `SaveProc` has completed its work and the program may be terminated.[25] Note that the workproc must indicate that it hasn't finished its operation by returning `FALSE`.

---

[24] It also follows the idea of confirming buttons to the left, negating buttons to the right: **Quit** has the most negative effect, while **Save** has the most positive effect. **Cancel** is neutral.

[25] The `saved` variable is a new global variable. `AlertSaveCB` sets it to `FALSE` before initiating work, and `SaveProc` simply sets it to `TRUE` when done.

A final note about this dialog is that it is inelegant: the user is asked to save, whether or not the editor's buffer has been changed. To add this missing bit of elegance, you would add another global variable — `needs_save` — that would be set to `TRUE` by the text widget's value-changed callback and set to `FALSE` by `SaveProc`. `SaveProtoCB` would then check this variable to determine whether it needed to invoke the message box.[26]

Selection

The selection mechanism has already been presented from the user's perspective in Chapter 9. This was in the context of the text widget, where pieces of text could be selected, then copied into another widget. This type of text-based selection is provided by other programs, such as *xterm*, allowing text to be copied freely between such programs under user control.

The text widget provides data exchange using the *primary selection*.[27] The user controls the selection process: both what is selected and the clients between which it is copied. The text widget handles the user's selection operations in its internal code, and in most cases, the program is not involved — it is, however, given access to the selection via the functions `XmTextGetSelectionPosition`, `XmTextGetSelection`, `XmTextSetSelection`, and `XmTextClearSelection`.

In most programs, this is how things should be: a widget should not require the program to provide any of its functionality, including data interchange with other widgets or programs. However, the selection mechanism does provide a method of interclient communication, and for this reason, you should be familiar with its workings.[28]

The Selection Process

The selection process is performed in three steps: (1) a client acquires ownership of a selection and advertises that ownership; (2) another client determines the identity of the selection owner and requests the selection contents; and (3) the selection owner sends the selection contents to the requestor.

In the case of a text widget, step one occurs when the user or program sets the selection range. Step two occurs when the user moves the pointer over another text widget and presses pointer button #2. Step three is handled transparently by the widgets themselves, and the text is copied from the source to the destination

The *Inter-Client Communications Conventions Manual* specifies two standard selections: primary and secondary, identified by the predefined atoms

---

[26] If this were implemented, it could also be called by the **File/Exit** menu choice.

[27] X provides two standard selections: the *primary selection* and the *secondary* selection. By allowing two selections, a user can leave one selection active while transferring data using the other selection. Most users only use the primary selection, in part, because very few applications support the secondary selection (*XmText*, for example, does not at Release 1.0, but does at 1.1).

[28] Perhaps most importantly, it provides the simplest method by which clients can learn of each other. As you have seen, this knowledge is essential if clients are to communicate using X events.

XA_PRIMARY and XA_SECONDARY.[29] While these are the standard selection types, cooperating programs can define and use their own selection types, such as _KDG_PRIVATE_SELECTION. By using such a selection type, these programs can use the selection mechanism for communication, without using the standard selections (which should always be under user control).

You should note that Xlib and Xt provide functions to greatly simplify data exchange under the selection mechanism. The process described below should be considered a "behind the scenes" approach, unsuitable for actual data exchange. Unless you are writing a widget, however, you should not need to exchange data using selection — but you might need to learn of another client's existence.[30]

Acquiring and Advertising the Selection

To acquire a named selection, a program calls the function XSetSelectionOwner, prototyped in Listing 17.24.[31] This function acquires the ownership of the named selection. The selection is identified by an atom, passed in the sel_name parameter. The window is identified by the display and win parameters. The value None may be used instead of a valid window ID to cause the current owner to give up the selection — this is how XmTextClearSelection works.

The time parameter is used to arbitrate between competing requests for the same selection: the request with the latest time gets ownership. This time is a server time value and should be retrieved from the event that initiated the call to XSetSelectionOwner. You should never use the CurrentTime constant here; such usage could easily cause a race condition.

Listing 17.24. Function prototype: *XSetSelectionOwner*

```
int      XSetSelectionOwner( display, sel_name, win, time )
         Display *display;
         Atom     sel_name;
         Window   win;
         Time     time;
```

XSetSelectionOwner performs two operations: it notifies the server that the named selection is now owned by the calling client, and it sends a SelectionClear event to the previous selection owner (if any). If it fails in these actions, it returns a nonzero value to the program; otherwise, it returns zero.

---

[29] The ICCCM also specifies a standard clipboard selection. Motif, however, provides a simpler interface to the clipboard, which is described below.

[30] If you do plan to exchange data via selections, it is imperative that you read the ICCCM. There is more to the selection mechanism than the events documented here: you must also know of the standard data types and when to use them.

[31] When using a program-specific selection, you must first create an atom corresponding to the selection name.

Identifying the Selection Owner

To determine the current owner of a selection, a program calls `XGetSelection-Owner`, prototyped in Listing 17.25. The selection is identified by its display and atom, passed in the `display` and `sel_name` parameters. If the named selection has an owner, then `XGetSelectionOwner` returns the ID of the owning window; if not, it returns the value `None`.

Listing 17.25. Function prototype: *XGetSelectionOwner*

```
Window  XGetSelectionOwner( display, sel_name )
        Display *display;
        Atom     sel_name;
```

Requesting Selected Data

To request the data associated with a selection, the requestor sends a `SelectionRequest` event to the selection owner. This event is contained in the `xselectionrequest` member of `XEvent`; it uses the structure `XSelectionRequestEvent`, defined in Listing 17.26.

Listing 17.26. Type definition: *XSelectionRequestEvent*

```
typedef struct
        {
        int             type;
        unsigned long   serial;
        Boolean         send_event;
        Display         *display;
        Window          owner;
        Window          requestor;
        Atom            selection;
        Atom            target;
        Atom            property;
        Time            time;
        }
XSelectionRequestEvent;
```

The unique members of this event structure are `owner`, `requestor`, `selection`, `target`, and `property`. The `type`, `serial`, `send_event`, and `display` members are for identification, while `time` is used to check the request validity — it is described below.

The `owner` and `requestor` members identify the windows involved in the exchange: `owner` is the selection owner, while `requestor` is the event sender. While specification of the selection owner may seem superfluous, it actually allows the owner to verify the request: if the requestor is expecting to receive the selection from a different owner, there is a problem.[32]

The `selection` member identifies the requested selection — it allows the owner of multiple selection types to return the proper data.

The `target` and `property` members together identify the destination of the selection data. The selection mechanism specifies that selection data is to be stored as a property attached to the requestor's window; the `property` member identifies the desired property.[33]

The `target` member specifies the requestor's preferred data type for the selection data. If the owner is unable to provide the data in that format, it should refuse the request.

Finally, the `time` member is used as another check on the request validity. The selection owner should check each request against the time that it received selection ownership. If the request was sent prior to that time, it should be refused.

Responding to a Selection Request

When a client receives a `SelectionRequest` event, it should do two things: store the requested data as a property on the requestor's window, and send a `SelectionNotify` event to indicate this action. If unable to fulfill the request — for example, if the request had an improper `owner` member — the `SelectionNotify` event should still be sent to alert the requestor to this fact.

`SelectionNotify` events are reported in the `xselection` member of `XEvent`. The relevant structure is `XSelectionEvent`, prototyped in Listing 17.27.

---

[32] This problem can arise because of the asynchronous nature of selection ownership. If the requestor has been exchanging data with another client and the selection changes in the middle of this interchange, the request could be sent to the wrong client.

[33] Clients following an older version of the ICCCM may pass `None` in the `property` member. If this is the case, the selection owner should store the selection value in a property named from the `target` member. While this is obsolete behavior, it is possible.

Listing 17.27. Type definition: *XSelectionEvent*

```
typedef struct
        {
        int             type;
        unsigned long   serial;
        Boolean         send_event;
        Display         *display;
        Window          requestor;
        Atom            selection;
        Atom            target;
        Atom            property;
        Time            time;
        }
XSelectionEvent;
```

The `requestor` member identifies the client requesting the selection. It is filled by the selection owner and checked by the selection requester. Similarly, the `selection` and `target` members are copied from the `SelectionRequest` event and identify the desired selection and its data type.

The `property` member identifies the property where the selection contents are stored. If the selection owner is unable to fulfill the selection request, it should still send the requestor a `SelectionNotify` event, but should pass `None` in the `property` member.

The `time` member contains the server timestamp of when the selection was attached to the requestor's window. The owner may fill this member with either an existing timestamp (taken from the `SelectionRequest`) or the constant `CurrentTime`.[34]

The SelectionClear *Event*

When selection ownership changes hands, the server sends a `SelectionClear` event to the previous owner. This event is informational only; a client should not use it as a signal to take back selection ownership.[35]

A `SelectionClear` event is delivered in the `xselectionclear` member of XEvent; this member is of type `XSelectionClearEvent`, prototyped in Listing 17.28. This event contains three unique members: `window` identifies the recipient of the event (and is used for validity checking), `selection` identifies the selection type, and `time` specifies the time that the event recipient gained selection ownership — *not* the current time.

---

[34] This is one of the few cases where `CurrentTime` may be used safely.

[35] This rule applies to the primary and secondary selections, which are changed under user control. If the program is using a private selection, it may react to `SelectionClear` events in any way desired.

Listing 17.28. Type definition: *XSelectionClearEvent*

```
typedef struct
        {
        int             type;
        unsigned long   serial;
        Boolean         send_event;
        Display         *display;
        Window          window;
        Atom            selection;
        Time            time;
        }
XSelectionClearEvent;
```

Example: Exchanging Window IDs

As indicated above, the primary and secondary selections are handled automatically by widget internal code. Unless you write a widget, you will probably not need to implement the complete selection interface. However, the selection advertisement mechanism provides a simple way for clients to exchange window IDs.

As an example of this technique, the programs below exchange their window IDs under user control; Figure 17.2 presents their appearance both before and after the exchange. Both programs are built around pushbuttons. When started, they appear as shown in 17.2(a): one program advertises the selection, the other allows the user to respond. When the advertiser's button is pressed, its program acquires the ownership of a unique selection. When the responder's button is pressed, its program determines the selection owner. The responder then changes its label to the owner's window ID and sends its window ID, in a `ClientMessage` event, to that window.[36] On receipt of the message, the first program changes its label's text to the window ID of the sender. Figure 17.2(b) presents the labels after this exchange has occurred.

---

[36] Note: *not* a `SelectionRequest` event: these programs do not actually transfer data between themselves.

Figure 17.2. Communicating clients

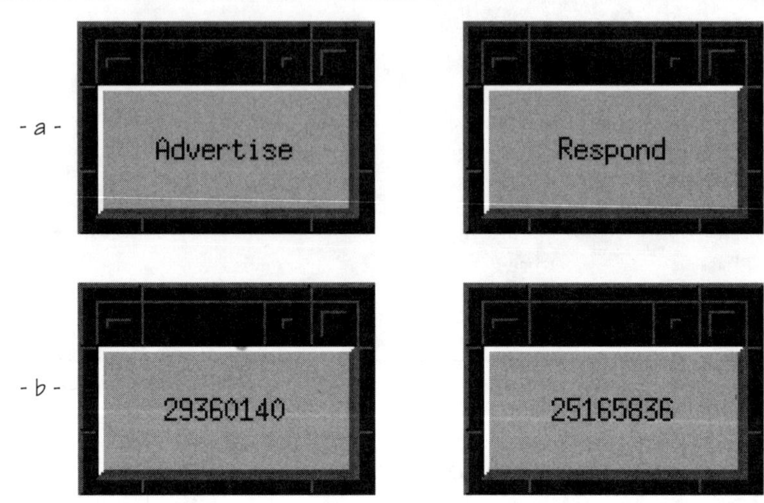

Listing 17.29 presents the programs. As stated above, both are built around pushbutton widgets to allow user control of their communication. The first program (26_A) acquires and advertises ownership of the selection _KDG_PRIVATE_SELECTION when the user presses its button. The second searches for the selection owner when its button is pressed, sends a client message to that owner, and changes its own label string.

Note in 29_A that there is no mask specified for the `ClientMessage` event. It is one of the nonmaskable events and is processed if the `nonmaskable` parameter of `XtAddEventHandler` contains `TRUE`. Note also that since there is no way to filter out unwanted nonmaskable events (such as `SelectionNotify`) before they get to the event handler, the handler itself must perform the filtering, using the event's `type` member.

Listing 17.29. Program and resource file: Communicating clients

```
/*******************************************************************
**                                                               **
**   listing_17_29_A.c                                           **
**                                                               **
**   Selection example, advertiser. This program acquires ownership  **
**   of the selection "_KDG_PRIVATE_SELECTION" when its button is    **
**   pressed. It also responds to client message events with a data  **
**   type of "WINDOW" (XA_WINDOW), by displaying the passed window ID. **
**                                                               **
*******************************************************************/


#include <Xm/PushB.h>
#include <X11/Xatom.h>


void    ButtonCB();                         /* FORWARD Definitions        */
void    ClientEvt();


Widget  appshell,
        the_btn;
Atom    a_sel_name;


void main( argc, argv )
    int     argc;
    char    *argv[];
{
    appshell = XtInitialize( argv[0], "Listing_17_29", NULL, 0,
                            &argc, argv );

    a_sel_name = XInternAtom( XtDisplay(appshell),
                            "_KDG_PRIVATE_SELECTION", FALSE );
```

Listing 17.29. Continued.

```
    the_btn = XmCreatePushButton( appshell, "TheBtn", NULL, 0 );
    XtManageChild( the_btn );

    XtAddCallback( the_btn, XmNactivateCallback, ButtonCB, NULL );
    XtAddEventHandler( the_btn, 0, TRUE, ClientEvt, NULL );

    XtRealizeWidget( appshell );
    XtMainLoop();
}



void ButtonCB( w, client_data, call_data )
    Widget              w;
    caddr_t             client_data;
    XmAnyCallbackStruct *call_data;
{
    XSetSelectionOwner( XtDisplay(w), a_sel_name, XtWindow(w),
                        call_data->event->xbutton.time );
}



void ClientEvt( w, client_data, event )
    Widget              w;
    caddr_t             client_data;
    XClientMessageEvent *event;
{
    char                lcl_str[32];
    XmString            xms;
    Arg                 the_arg;

    if ((event->type != ClientMessage) ||
        (event->message_type != XA_WINDOW))
        return;

    sprintf( lcl_str, "%d", event->data.l[0] );
    xms = XmStringCreate( lcl_str, XmSTRING_DEFAULT_CHARSET );
    XtSetArg( the_arg, XmNlabelString, xms );
    XtSetValues( w, &the_arg, 1 );
    XmStringFree( xms );
}
```

Listing 17.29. Continued.

```c
/***********************************************************************
**                                                                   **
**   listing_17_29_B.c                                               **
**                                                                   **
**   Selection example, responder. This program requests the owner of **
**   the selection "_KDG_PRIVATE_SELECTION" when its button is pushed. **
**   It displays the window ID of the selection owner, then sends its **
**   window ID in a client message.                                  **
**                                                                   **
***********************************************************************/


#include <Xm/PushB.h>
#include <X11/Xatom.h>


void    ButtonCB();                         /* FORWARD Definitions        */


Widget  appshell,
        the_btn;
Atom    a_sel_name;


void main( argc, argv )
    int     argc;
    char    *argv[];
{
    appshell = XtInitialize( argv[0], "Listing_17_29", NULL, 0,
                            &argc, argv );

    a_sel_name = XInternAtom( XtDisplay(appshell),
                            "_KDG_PRIVATE_SELECTION", FALSE );
```

Listing 17.29. Continued.

```
    the_btn = XmCreatePushButton( appshell, "TheBtn", NULL, 0 );
    XtManageChild( the_btn );

    XtAddCallback( the_btn, XmNactivateCallback, ButtonCB, NULL );

    XtRealizeWidget( appshell );
    XtMainLoop();
}



void ButtonCB( w, client_data, call_data )
    Widget              w;
    caddr_t             client_data;
    XmAnyCallbackStruct *call_data;
{
    char                lcl_str[32];
    XmString            xms;
    Arg                 the_arg;
    Window              owner;
    XClientMessageEvent evt;

    owner = XGetSelectionOwner( XtDisplay(w), a_sel_name );
    if (owner == None)
        {
        printf( "17_29_B: No owner yet\n" );
        return;
        }

    sprintf( lcl_str, "%d", owner );
    xms = XmStringCreate( lcl_str, XmSTRING_DEFAULT_CHARSET );
    XtSetArg( the_arg, XmNlabelString, xms );
    XtSetValues( w, &the_arg, 1 );
    XmStringFree( xms );

    evt.type         = ClientMessage;
    evt.display      = XtDisplay(w);
    evt.window       = owner;
    evt.message_type = XA_WINDOW;
    evt.format       = 32;
    evt.data.l[0]    = XtWindow(w);
    XSendEvent( XtDisplay(w), owner, TRUE, 0, &evt );
}
```

Listing 17.29. Continued.

```
!
! Resource file for Selection Example (Figure 17.2)
!
! Note that both files use the same resource file: the only difference
! is the buttons' labels, and these are identified by invocation name.
!

*TheBtn.foreground:       Black
*TheBtn.background:       Gray75
*TheBtn.height:           50
*TheBtn.width:            100


26_A.TheBtn.labelString:        Advertise
26_B.TheBtn.labelString:        Respond
```

The Clipboard

The selection mechanism described above allows communication of data between two clients, both of which must be active. While the selection mechanism allows a nearly infinite number of selections, each with its own name, in practice it is used with the predefined primary selection. Moreover, manipulation of the primary selection is usually handled transparently by a client's widgets — the program itself is not involved.

In addition to the primary and secondary selections, X provides another standard selection: the clipboard. The clipboard extends the user interface of the selection mechanism by providing a temporary storage location for selections. A selection may be copied into the clipboard, held in the clipboard for an arbitrarily long time, then "pasted" into another client — the original client need not be running at the time of the paste.

The clipboard is implemented as an X client and is normally executed at the same time as the window manager. This client presents a text window, which displays a "page" of its current contents. The user is able to copy text to and from this window using the standard selection mechanism, but a more sophisticated mechanism exists: clipboard copy and paste, which are performed under program control.

There is one caveat to use of the clipboard: it doesn't work under Motif 1.0. While the functions are present, they do not properly exchange data with the standard X clipboard. If you need to use the clipboard with a 1.0 program, you must transfer data using the selection mechanism; this process is described in the *Inter-Client Communications Conventions Manual.*

The xclipboard *Application*

As described above, the clipboard is an X client, *xclipboard*. It is typically started as part of session initialization and remains on the root in iconified form. When it starts, it acquires ownership of the standard selection CLIPBOARD.[37] The clipboard window — with text — is shown in Figure 17.3.

Figure 17.3. *xclipboard* program window

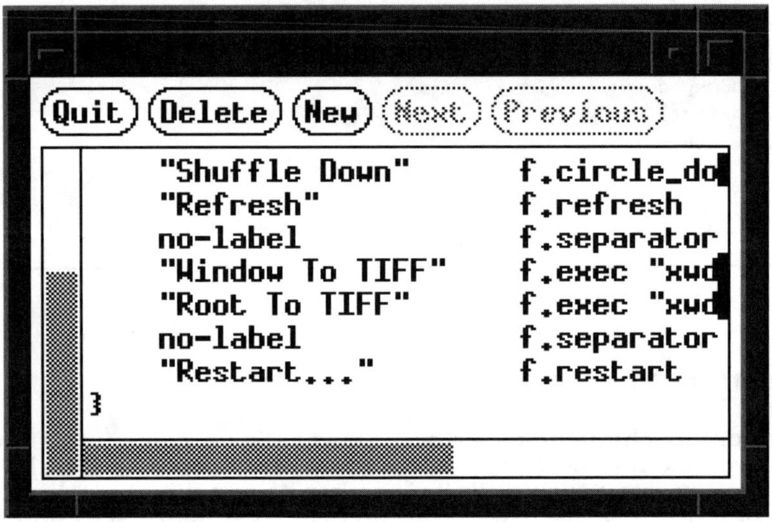

A program uses the selection mechanism, described above, to exchange data with the clipboard client. Unlike data exchange using the primary selection, which is handled transparently by the widget, clipboard data exchange is performed explicitly by the program. However, instead of using the event sequence described above, it is performed using a set of convenience functions, described below.

Clipboard Copy

Copying data to the clipboard is a three-step process. The first step is to initialize the clipboard interface; this must be done for each copy, as it sets up data structures used by Motif to handle the particular copy. The second step is to store data into these data structures. The third step is the actual communication, in which the stored data is transferred to the clipboard.

---

[37] This selection is represented by a predefined atom, XA_CLIPBOARD.

Listing 17.30. Function prototype: *XmClipboardStartCopy*

```
int     XmClipboardStartCopy( display, window, clip_label, time,
                              widget, callback, item_id )
        Display     *display;
        Window      window;
        XmString    clip_label;
        Time        time;
        Widget      widget;
        VoidProc    callback;
        long        *item_id;
```

The first step is performed by the function `XmClipboardStartCopy`, prototyped in Listing 17.30.[38] This function prepares the communications link and sets up internal buffers to handle the transfer.

The `display` and `window` parameters are used to initialize the communications interface: they specify the window used for actual communication between the client and the clipboard. Since clipboard data exchange is handled transparently, the program need not register a selection event handler for this window. More importantly, it must not register such an event handler — it would interfere with the clipboard interface.

The `clip_label` parameter contains a compound string that is associated with the data. It exists for user information, and would be displayed in association with the data by a Motif-based clipboard application. By convention, it is passed the name of the program.

The `time` parameter is passed through to the selection mechanism as described above. It is used to arbitrate competing ownership requests, as well as for validity checking.

The `widget` and `callback` parameters are used for Motif's named copy and paste. With this technique, the program simply identifies data to the clipboard — the data is transferred only if another client requests it. Since this technique is in essence normal selection and does not use the "store and forward" nature of the clipboard, it is not described here. You should pass `NULL` for both of these parameters.

The final parameter, `item_id`, is used to return an identifier for the operation's data space. It is used by all other clipboard functions to identify the particular data being transferred.

---

[38] This function and the other clipboard-related functions require the header file `Xm/CutPaste.h`.

Listing 17.31. Function prototype: *XmClipboardCopy*

```
int      XmClipboardCopy( display, window, item_id, format_name, buffer,
                              length, private_id, data_id )
         Display        *display;
         Window         window;
         long           item_id;
         char           *format_name;
         char           *buffer;
         unsigned long  length;
         int            private_id;
         int            *data_id;
```

The second step, copying data into the local storage area, is performed by
`XmClipboardCopy`, prototyped in Listing 17.31. A program may make multiple
calls to this function; each call appends data to that already in the storage area.
Note that this function does not actually copy data into the clipboard — that is
the third step.

As with `XmClipboardStartCopy`, the `display` and `window` parameters identify the
window associated with the operation. The `item_id` parameter identifies the
particular operation; its contents were returned by `XmClipboardStartCopy`.

The `format_name` parameter contains a string representing the data's format.
(Note that this parameter *is not* an atom.) This may be one of the standard
format names of Table 17.1, or it may be a program-specific name. As in other
forms of selection, this information has meaning only to the programs that
actually use the exchanged information — it is simply stored with the data.

The `buffer` parameter is a pointer to the outgoing data buffer, and the `length`
parameter contains the number of bytes in that buffer.

The `private_id` parameter is used to store a program-specific identifier for the
data segment, and the `data_id` parameter is used to return a Motif-specific
identifier for that segment. Each call to `XmClipboardCopy` stores a single data
segment in the local storage area; if a program supports copy-by-name, the
clipboard requests each segment individually, identified by their `private_id` and
`data_id` values.

Listing 17.32. Function prototype: *XmClipboardEndCopy*

```
int      XmClipboardEndCopy( display, window, item_id )
         Display        *display;
         Window         window;
         long           item_id;
```

Once all of the data has been stored in the local storage area, it must be transferred to the clipboard. This is performed by the function `XmClipboardEndCopy`, prototyped in Listing 17.32. This function uses the `display`, `window`, and `item_id` parameters to identify the local clip buffer. It performs the actual transfer without program intervention.

Aborting a Clipboard Copy

If, in the middle of a clipboard transfer, the program needs to abort the transfer, it calls the function `XmClipboardCancelCopy`. This function is prototyped in Listing 17.33 and identifies the local clip buffer by its `display`, `window`, and `item_id` parameters.

Listing 17.33. Function prototype:
XmClipboardCancelCopy

```
int      XmClipboardCancelCopy( display, window, item_id )
         Display          *display;
         Window           window;
         long             item_id;
```

Clipboard Paste

Pasting data from the clipboard to the application is a five-step process. The first step is locking the clipboard, so that another application will not interrupt the transfer.[39] Once it is locked, the program should determine whether or not appropriate data is in the clipboard, and if so, how much space it occupies. Finally, the data is retrieved from the clipboard, a three-step process similar to that of copying data to the clipboard.

---

[39] The clipboard is automatically locked by the actual retrieval operation (*StartRetrieve...EndRetrieve*), but the inquiry step requires an explicit lock. Note that no lock is needed while copying to the clipboard, because the data is stored in a local buffer then copied in one step.

Listing 17.34. Function prototypes: *XmClipboardLock*, *XmClipboardUnlock*

```
int     XmClipboardLock( display, window )
        Display         *display;
        Window          window;


int     XmClipboardUnlock( display, window, remove_all )
        Display         *display;
        Window          window;
        Boolean         remove_all;
```

The first step, locking the clipboard, is performed by `XmClipboardLock`, prototyped in Listing 17.34. The clipboard remains locked until explicitly unlocked by the program or until a copy or paste operation is completed. To explicitly unlock the clipboard, the program calls the function `XmClipboardUnlock`, also prototyped in Listing 17.34. Clipboard lock calls must be balanced by explicit unlock calls, unless the unlock call specifies that all locks are to be removed.[40]

Both `XmClipboardLock` and `XmClipboardUnlock` identify the window that is acquiring the lock, with their `display` and `window` parameters. `XmClipboardUnlock` has a third parameter, `remove_all`, which specifies whether the unlock operation removes all locks by the specified window; if it contains `TRUE`, all locks are removed, if not, only the matching lock is removed.

Once the clipboard is locked, the program determines the existence and size of the desired data with the function `XmClipboardInquireLength`, prototyped in Listing 17.35. It identifies the requesting window with the `display` and `window` parameters and the desired data type by the `format_name` parameter.[41] If a data item of the desired type is found on the clipboard, the length of that item is returned by the `length` parameter. If no such item is present in the clipboard, then `XmClipboardInquireLength` returns an error code and a length value of zero.

---

[40] If the program calls `XmClipboardLock` five times, it must call `XmClipboardUnlock` five times — or call `XmClipboardUnlock` once, with its `remove_all` parameter containing `TRUE`.

[41] Again, this parameter specifies the string name of the data type. This string should be retrieved from a predefined atom if possible.

Listing 17.35. Function prototypes:
XmClipboardInquireLength

```
int       XmClipboardInquireLength( display, window, format_name, length )
          Display         *display;
          Window          window;
          char            *format_name;
          unsigned long   *length;
```

Once the existence and length of a clipboard data item is determined, the actual item is retrieved by a three-step sequence similar to that used for copying an item into the clipboard. The first step is calling `XmClipboardStartRetrieve`, prototyped in Listing 17.36. This function initializes the local interface and locks the clipboard; its `display` and `window` parameters identify the destination window, and its `time` parameter is used for the selection mechanism.

Listing 17.36. Function prototypes:
XmClipboardStartRetrieve

```
int       XmClipboardStartRetrieve( display, window, time )
          Display    *display;
          Window     window;
          Time       time;
```

Once the local interface has been initialized, the program makes one or more calls to `XmClipboardRetrieve`, prototyped in Listing 17.37. This function identifies the destination window with its `display` and `window` parameters and the desired clipboard item with its `format_name` parameter. The `buffer` and `length` parameters identify a local buffer for the retrieval: `buffer` is a pointer to the buffer, and `length` is the size of that buffer. The actual amount of data copied is returned via the `num_bytes` parameter; in most cases, this value will equal the buffer length. Finally, the `private_id` parameter is used to retrieve the integer value associated with the clipboard buffer by `XmClipboardCopy`; if not needed, `NULL` may be passed.

Listing 17.37. Function prototypes: *XmClipboardRetrieve*

```
int      XmClipboardRetrieve( display, window, buffer, length, num_bytes,
                              private_id )
         Display         *display;
         Window          window;
         char            *format_name;
         char            *buffer;
         unsigned long   length;
         unsigned long   *num_bytes;
         int             *private_id;
```

Once the entire item has been retrieved from the clipboard — this may require multiple calls to `XmClipboardRetrieve` — the operation is finished with a call to `XmClipboardEndCopy`, prototyped in Listing 17.38. This function puts the local interface in an idle state and unlocks the clipboard. It identifies the associated window by the `display` and `window` parameters.

Listing 17.38. Function prototypes:
XmClipboardEndRetrieve

```
int      XmClipboardEndRetrieve( display, window )
         Display         *display;
         Window          window;
```

Clipboard Interface Return Values

Each of the clipboard functions described above returns an integer value. This value gives the status of the clipboard operation, and each return value has an associated constant, as below.[42]

- `ClipboardFailure` indicates that the operation could not be performed, due to an internal error. The program should do whatever it can to clean up (such as unlocking the clipboard), but it may not continue with the operation.

- `ClipboardSuccess` indicates that the operation was performed without error.

- `ClipboardLocked` indicates that the operation could not be performed because the clipboard was locked by another application. The program

---

[42] Note that these constants *do not* have an 'Xm' prefix.

can attempt to perform the operation again, but some sort of timeout should be used.[43]

- `ClipboardTruncate` is returned by `XmClipboardRetrieve`, and indicates that the passed buffer was too small to contain the entire data item. The program should continue to call `XmClipboardRetrieve` until the entire item has been retrieved.

- `ClipboardNoData` is returned by both `XmClipboardInquireLength` and `XmClipboardRetrieve`, and indicates that the clipboard does not hold data of the desired type.

Example: Adding Cut, Copy, and Paste to the Text Editor

Listing 17.39 contains the code of the "clipper" module, which supports clipboard operations for the text editor. This module allows the user to select text in the normal manner, then cut or copy that text into the clipboard, or copy the clipboard's contents into the work window, using choices from the **Edit** menu.

This code segment should be viewed as a demonstration of the clipboard interface, not as an example of code that would actually be put into a text editor. The reason for this disclaimer, as you will see below, is that Motif 1.1 contains a direct clipboard interface for *XmText* — and this code must use 1.1 in order to run.[44]

---

[43] This is a potential use for a workproc, especially when copying to the clipboard: the program would store the data in a local buffer, and the workproc would continually try to send it to the clipboard. It should, however, display a warning message if unable to do so within a few seconds, lest the user try to retrieve nonexistent data.

[44] If you are using Motif 1.0, you will be able to compile this code and it will appear to work. You will find, however, that data is not actually exchanged with the clipboard.

Listing 17.39. Text editor clipboard interface

```
/*****************************************************************************
**                                                                         **
**   clipper.c                                                             **
**                                                                         **
**   Text Editor -- Clipboard Interface Module                            **
**                                                                         **
*****************************************************************************/


#include <stdio.h>
#include <Xm/Text.h>
#include <Xm/CutPaste.h>
#include <X11/Xatom.h>

#include "textedit.h"



/*****************************************************************************
**                                                                         **
**               F O R W A R D   D E F I N I T I O N S                     **
**                                                                         **
*****************************************************************************/

static  char    *GetTextSelection();
static  void    RplTextSelection();




/*****************************************************************************
**                                                                         **
**               L O C A L   V A R I A B L E S                             **
**                                                                         **
*****************************************************************************/

static  XmString    prog_name;          /* Name of application        */
static  Display     *clip_disp;         /* Our display connection     */
static  Window      clip_win;           /* Window associated with cpy */
static  char        *data_type;         /* String for XA_STRING       */
```

Listing 17.39. Continued.

```c
/*********************************************************************
**                                                                 **
**   InitClipper()                                                 **
**                                                                 **
**   This function creates some module-static variables, which hold  **
**   identification information needed by all clipboard calls.     **
**                                                                 **
*********************************************************************/

void InitClipper()
{
    prog_name = XmStringCreate( "TextEdit", XmSTRING_DEFAULT_CHARSET );
    clip_disp = XtDisplay( appshell );
    clip_win  = None;
    data_type = XGetAtomName( clip_disp, XA_STRING );
}


/*********************************************************************
**                                                                 **
**   ClipCut( time )                                               **
**                                                                 **
**   Called from the Edit/Cut menu item, this function copies the  **
**   current work window selection to the clipboard, then deletes  **
**   it. To perform the copy, it calls ClipCopy().                 **
**                                                                 **
**   The "time" parameter comes from the invoking event, and is used  **
**   by the selection mechanism.                                   **
**                                                                 **
*********************************************************************/

void ClipCut( time )
    Time        time;
{
    ClipCopy( time );
    RplTextSelection( "" );
}
```

Listing 17.39. Continued.

```
/********************************************************************
**                                                                **
**   ClipCopy( time )                                             **
**                                                                **
**   Called from the Edit/Cut menu item, this function copies the **
**   current work window selection to the clipboard. It is also   **
**   called by the function ClipCut, to localize clipboard access.**
**                                                                **
**   The "time" parameter comes from the invoking event, and is used **
**   by the selection mechanism.                                  **
**                                                                **
********************************************************************/

void ClipCopy( time )
    Time        time;
{
    char        *txtsel;
    int         txtlen;
    int         clipstat;
    long        clip_id;
    int         tries;


    if (clip_win == None)
        clip_win = XtWindow( appshell );


    txtsel = GetTextSelection();
    txtlen = strlen( txtsel ) + 1;

    tries = 0;
    do
        clipstat = XmClipboardStartCopy( clip_disp, clip_win, prog_name,
                                         time, NULL, NULL, &clip_id );
    while ((clipstat != ClipboardSuccess) && (tries++ < 8));

    if (tries == 8)
```

Listing 17.39. Continued.

```
        {
        /* Display alert here */
        XtFree( txtsel );
        return;
        }

    XmClipboardCopy( clip_disp, clip_win, clip_id, data_type,
                    txtsel, txtlen, 0, NULL );
    clipstat = XmClipboardEndCopy( clip_disp, clip_win, clip_id );

    XtFree( txtsel );
}


/**********************************************************************
**                                                                  **
**   ClipPaste( time )                                              **
**                                                                  **
**   Called from the Edit/Paste menu item, this function copies the **
**   contents of the clipboard into the work window, at the current **
**   insertion point. If there is a current selection, it is replaced **
**   or not, depending on the contents of "pendingDelete".          **
**                                                                  **
**   The "time" parameter comes from the invoking event, and is used **
**   by the selection mechanism.                                    **
**                                                                  **
**********************************************************************/

void ClipPaste( time )
    Time        time;
{
    int         clipstat;
    long        data_len;
    long        real_len;
    char        *databuf;
    long        text_pos;
    int         tries;
```

Listing 17.39. Continued.

```
if (clip_win == None)
    clip_win = XtWindow( appshell );


tries = 0;
do
    clipstat = XmClipboardLock( clip_disp, clip_win );
while ((clipstat == ClipboardLocked) && (tries++ < 8));

if (tries == 8)
    {
    /* Display alert here */
    XmClipboardUnlock( clip_disp, clip_win, TRUE );
    return;
    }

clipstat = XmClipboardInquireLength( clip_disp, clip_win,
                                     data_type, &data_len );
if (clipstat == ClipboardNoData)
    return;

XmClipboardEndRetrieve( clip_disp, clip_win);
databuf = XtMalloc( data_len+1 );

XmClipboardStartRetrieve( clip_disp, clip_win, time );
clipstat = XmClipboardRetrieve( clip_disp, clip_win, data_type,
                                databuf, data_len, &real_len,
                                NULL );
databuf[data_len] = '\0';

RplTextSelection( databuf );
XtFree( databuf );
}
```

Listing 17.39. Continued.

```
/**********************************************************************
**                                                                  **
**   GetTextSelection()                                             **
**                                                                  **
**   This function retrieves the current text selection -- or NULL, **
**   if there is no selection.                                      **
**                                                                  **
**********************************************************************/

static char *GetTextSelection()
{
    return( XmTextGetSelection(textwin) );
}




/**********************************************************************
**                                                                  **
**   RplTextSelection( newtext )                                    **
**                                                                  **
**   This function replaces the current text selection with newtext.**
**   If there is no selection, newtext is inserted at the current   **
**   insertion point.                                               **
**                                                                  **
**********************************************************************/

static void RplTextSelection( newtext )
    char         *newtext;
{
    Boolean      stest,
                 pendel;
    int          insertion,
                 sel_start,
                 sel_end;
```

Listing 17.39. Continued.

```
    XtSetArg( arglist[0], XmNcursorPosition, &insertion );
    XtSetArg( arglist[1], XmNpendingDelete, &pendel );
    XtGetValues( textwin, arglist, 2 );

    stest = XmTextGetSelectionPosition( textwin, &sel_start, &sel_end );
    if (!stest || !pendel)
        sel_end = sel_start = insertion;

    XmTextReplace( textwin, sel_start, sel_end, newtext );
}
```

Initialization

The initialization function, `InitClipper`, is called from `InitOther` and initializes the static data items with data that must be determined at runtime. It exists primarily so that such assignments do not need to be performed inside the actual clipboard functions.

One point of note is the assignment of `None` to `clip_win`, the variable that contains the window ID used for data exchange. The actual assignment of a window ID cannot be performed at the time this function is called, because the program's widgets have not yet been realized — there are no valid window IDs. Instead, this variable is initialized by the first clipboard function that uses it; `None` is simply a flag value.

Clipboard Cut and Copy

Both the cut and copy operations are performed by the same function, `ClipCopy`. Cutting, however, is invoked from the function `ClipCut`, which performs the additional step of deleting the current selection.

The beginning of `ClipCopy` retrieves the selected text and determines its length.[45] It also sets the transfer window ID, if needed. Note that I chose the application shell. This is actually a questionable technique, because I might want to use the shell to handle other selection events; the work window would have been a better choice.

The rest of `ClipCopy` simply implements the three steps described above. It initiates the data exchange using `XmClipboardStartCopy`, which is called in a loop so that it has multiple chances to avoid a locked clipboard. If the operation is successfully initiated, `ClipCopy` then makes a single call to `XmClipboardCopy`,

---

[45] Note that the NUL-terminator is included in the length calculation. The ICCCM specifies that strings require such termination.

storing the entire selection. Finally, a call to `XmClipboardEndCopy` moves that data to the clipboard.

This function does have several failings as production code. First, the initialization loop is questionable: in all likelihood, all eight attempts will complete before the clipboard becomes unlocked — again, a workproc would be a better solution to this problem. The other main failing is that it provides error checking on initialization only: if `XmClipboardStartCopy` succeeds, this function assumes that `XmClipboardCopy` and `XmClipboardEndCopy` will succeed. This is a flawed assumption, and each call should be checked for a return of `ClipboardFailure`.

Clipboard Paste

The operation of pasting from the clipboard to the work window is performed by `ClipPaste`. As with `ClipCopy`, this function is structured according to the operations described above.

As with `XmClipboardStartCopy`, `XmClipboardLock` is enclosed in a loop, allowing the program several attempts to acquire the lock. In this case, a workproc would not be acceptable: the user expects to see data pasted immediately upon selection of the action — not several seconds afterward. If another program has the clipboard locked, the user should be alerted to this fact.

Once the clipboard is locked, `ClipCopy` determines whether data is available. If not, it returns — after unlocking the clipboard. Forgetting to perform the unlock would essentially shut down the clipboard because no client would be able to exchange data with it.

Assuming that data is available, it is retrieved with `XmClipboardStartRetrieve` and `XmClipboardRetrieve`. Note that the entire buffer is retrieved in one step — even if multiple data exchanges must be made due to limited server memory, `XmClipboardRetrieve` hides them from the program. Once the data is retrieved, it is stored in the text buffer and the space allocated for it is recovered.

Utility Functions

I decided to use utility functions to encapsulate access to the text window. There were two reasons for this decision: (1) such operations would detract from the illustration of the clipboard interface, and (2) these functions should actually be part of a "work window" module — the clipboard module should not have direct access to the text widget.

The first function, `GetTextSelection`, retrieves the current selection from the text widget. If no text is selected, it returns `NULL`. To do this, it simply calls `XmTextGetSelection`.

The second function, `RplTextSelection`, is more complex, in that it must handle both cases where the text widget has a selection range, as well as cases where it doesn't. In the latter case, `RplTextSelection` simply inserts the passed string at the current insertion point. In the former case, it either replaces the current selection or inserts the string, depending on the contents of the widget's `pendingDelete` resource.

XmText **Direct Clipboard Interface**

While the above example illustrated the use of the clipboard interface — which is not limited to text alone, it was unnecessary. The reason is that Motif 1.1 contains three functions that provide a direct clipboard interface for an *XmText* widget. These functions are prototyped in Listing 17.40 and described below.

Listing 17.40. Function prototypes: XmTextCopy,
XmTextCut, XmTextPaste

```
Boolean XmTextCopy( w, time )
        Widget       w;
        Time         time;


Boolean XmTextCut( w, time )
        Widget       w;
        Time         time;


Boolean XmTextPaste( w )
        Widget       w;
```

All three functions take the ID of the widget and return a flag indicating whether or not the operation was successful. `XmTextCopy` and `XmTextCut` take an additional parameter, `time`, used for the selection mechanism. All act identically to the functions of the "clipper" module above.

Example: Using XmText Clipboard Functions with the Text Editor

Use of these functions means that the "clipper" module is no longer necessary. Instead, these functions are called directly from the **Edit** menu callback function, as shown in Listing 17.41.

Listing 17.41. Changes to *EditMenuCB* to support *XmText* clipboard interface

```
static void EditMenuCB( w, client_data, call_data )
    Widget              w;
    char                *client_data;
    XmAnyCallbackStruct *call_data;
{
    XButtonEvent        *event = (XButtonEvent *)call_data->event;

    if (!strcmp(client_data, "Cut"))
        XmTextCut( textwin, event->time );
    else if (!strcmp(client_data, "Cpy"))
        XmTextCopy( textwin, event->time );
    else if (!strcmp(client_data, "Pst"))
        XmTextPaste( textwin );
    else if (!strcmp(client_data, "Del"))
        {
        }
    else if (!strcmp(client_data, "Fnd"))
        ManageFindDB();
    else if (!strcmp(client_data, "Rpl"))
        {
        }
```

Appendix A
ISO Latin 1 Character Set

Hex / Dec	00 / 0	01 / 1	02 / 2	03 / 3	04 / 4	05 / 5	06 / 6	07 / 7	08 / 8	09 / 9	0A / 10	0B / 11	0C / 12	0D / 13	0E / 14	0F / 15
00 / 0	NUL	SOH	STX	ETX	EOT	ENQ	ACK	BEL	BS	HT	LF	VT	FF	CR	SO	SI
10 / 16	DLE	DC1	DC2	DC3	DC4	NAK	SYN	ETB	CAN	EM	SUB	ESC	FS	GS	RS	US
20 / 32		!	"	#	$	%	&	'	(	)	*	+	,	−	.	/
30 / 48	0	1	2	3	4	5	6	7	8	9	:	;	<	=	>	?
40 / 64	@	A	B	C	D	E	F	G	H	I	J	K	L	M	N	O
50 / 80	P	Q	R	S	T	U	V	W	X	Y	Z	[	\	]	^	_
60 / 96	`	a	b	c	d	e	f	g	h	i	j	k	l	m	n	o
70 / 112	p	q	r	s	t	u	v	w	x	y	z	{	|	}	~	
80 / 128																
90 / 144																
A0 / 160		¡	¢	£	¤	¥	¦	§	¨	©	ª	«	¬		®	¯
B0 / 176	°	±	²	³	´	µ	¶	·	¸	¹	º	»	¼	½	¾	¿
C0 / 192	À	Á	Â	Ã	Ä	Å	Æ	Ç	È	É	Ê	Ë	Ì	Í	Î	Ï
D0 / 208	Ð	Ñ	Ò	Ó	Ô	Õ	Ö	×	Ø	Ù	Ú	Û	Ü	Ý	Þ	ß
E0 / 224	à	á	â	ã	ä	å	æ	ç	è	é	ê	ë	ì	í	î	ï
F0 / 240	ð	ñ	ò	ó	ô	õ	ö	÷	ø	ù	ú	û	ü	ý	þ	ÿ

Appendix B
Widget Class Summary

Overview

This appendix provides a summary of each class provided by Motif. A summary includes the class's derivation, the external name of the class pointer, and a resource table. Unlike the tables presented in the body of the book, these resource tables list all of a widget's resources. They also list the resource class and representation type constants for each resource — replacing the "Inheritance" and "Default Value" listings.

These class summaries do not provide any additional information, such as descriptions of the resources. In addition, some of the "Data Type" entries refer to types not described in this book — they come from the widget definition code.

ApplicationShell

Class Pointer: applicationShellWidgetClass

Derivation: *Core » Composite » Shell » WMShell » VendorShell » TopLevelShell » ApplicationShell*

Name	Class	Data Type	Rep Type
argc	XmCArgc	int	XmRInt
argv	XmCArgv	String *	XmRPointer

Composite

Class Pointer:	compositeWidgetClass
Derivation:	*Core » Composite*

Name	Class	Data Type	Rep Type
insertPosition	XmCInsertPosition	XtProc	XmRFunction

Constraint

Class Pointer:	constraintWidgetClass
Derivation:	*Core » Composite » Constraint*

This class does not define additional resources.

Core

Class Pointer:	widgetClass
Derivation:	*Object » RectObj » WindowObj » Core*

Name	Class	Data Type	Rep Type
accelerators	XmCAccelerators	XtTranslations	XmRAccelerator Table
ancestor Sensitive	XmCSensitive	Boolean	XmRBoolean
background	XmCBackground	Pixel	XmRPixel
background Pixmap	XmCPixmap	Pixmap	XmRPixmap
borderColor	XmCBorderColor	Pixel	XmRPixel
borderPixmap	XmCPixmap	Pixmap	XmRPixmap
borderWidth	XmCBorderWidth	Dimension	XmRDimension
colormap	XmCColormap	Colormap	XmRPointer
depth	XmCDepth	int	XmRInt
destroyCallback	XmCCallback	XtCallbackList	XmRCallback
height	XmCHeight	Dimension	XmRDimension
mappedWhen Managed	XmCMappedWhen Managed	Boolean	XmRBoolean
screen	XmCScreen	Pointer	XmRPointer
sensitive	XmCSensitive	Boolean	XmRBoolean
translations	XmCTranslations	XtTranslations	XmRTranslation Table
width	XmCWidth	Dimension	XmRDimension
x	XmCPosition	Position	XmRPosition
y	XmCPosition	Position	XmRPosition

OverrideShell

Class Pointer: overrideShellWidgetClass

Derivation: *Core » Composite » Shell » OverrideShell*

Name	Class	Data Type	Rep Type
overrideRedirect	XmCOverrideRedirect	Boolean	XmRBoolean
saveUnder	XmCSaveUnder	Boolean	XmRBoolean

Shell

Class Pointer: shellWidgetClass

Derivation: *Core » Composite » Shell*

Name	Class	Data Type	Rep Type
allowShellResize	XmCAllowShellResize	Boolean	XmRBoolean
createPopupChildProc	XmCCreatePopupChildProc	XtProc	XmRFunction
geometry	XmCGeometry	String	XmRString
overrideRedirect	XmCOverrideRedirect	Boolean	XmRBoolean
popdownCallback	XmCCallback	XtCallbackList	XmRCallback
popupCallback	XmCCallback	XtCallbackList	XmRCallback
saveUnder	XmCSaveUnder	Boolean	XmRBoolean

TopLevelShell

Class Pointer: topLevelShellWidgetClass

Derivation: *Core » Composite » Shell » WMShell » VendorShell »
TopLevelShell*

Name	Class	Data Type	Rep Type
iconic	XmCIconic	Boolean	XmRBoolean
iconName	XmCIconName	String	XmRString

TransientShell

Class Pointer: transientShellWidgetClass

Derivation: *Core » Composite » Shell » WMShell » VendorShell »
TransientShell*

Name	Class	Data Type	Rep Type
saveUnder	XmCSaveUnder	Boolean	XmRBoolean
transient	XmCTransient	Boolean	XmRBoolean

VendorShell

Class Pointer: vendorShellWidgetClass

Derivation: *Core » Composite » Shell » WMShell » VendorShell*

Name	Class	Data Type	Rep Type
deleteResponse	XmCDeleteResponse	unsigned char	XmRDeleteResponse
focusPolicy Changed	XmCCallback	XtCallback List	XmRCallback
keyboardFocus Policy	XmCKeyboardFocus Policy	unsigned char	XmRKeyboardFocus Policy
mwmDecorations	XmCMwmDecorations	int	XmRInt
mwmFunctions	XmCMwmFunctions	int	XmRInt
mwmInputMode	XmCMwmInputMode	int	XmRInt
mwmMenu	XmCMwmMenu	String	XmRString
shellUnitType	XmCShellUnitType	unsigned char	XmRShellUnitType

WMShell

Class Pointer: wmShellWidgetClass

Derivation: *Core » Composite » Shell » WMShell*

Name	Class	Data Type	Rep Type
heightInc	XmCHeightInc	int	XmRInt
iconMask	XmCIconMask	Pixmap	XmRPixmap
iconPixmap	XmCIconPixmap	Pixmap	XmRPixmap
iconWindow	XmCIconWindow	Window	XmRWindow
iconX	XmCiconX	int	XmRInt
iconY	XmCiconY	int	XmRInt
initial State	XmCInitialState	int	XmRInt
input	XmCInput	Boolean	XmRBool
maxAspectX	XmCMaxAspectX	int	XmRInt
maxAspectY	XmCMaxAspectY	int	XmRInt
maxHeight	XmCMaxHeight	int	XmRInt
maxWidth	XmCMaxWidth	int	XmRInt
minAspectX	XmCMinAspectX	int	XmRInt
minAspectY	XmCMinAspectY	int	XmRInt
minHeight	XmCMinHeight	int	XmRInt
minWidth	XmCMinWidth	int	XmRInt
title	XmCTitle	String	XmRString
transient	XmCTransient	Boolean	XmRBoolean
waitforwm	XmCWaitForWm	Boolean	XmRBoolean
widthInc	XmCWidthInc	int	XmRInt
windowGroup	XmCWindowGroup	XID	XmRWindow
wmTimeout	XmCWmTimeout	int	XmRInt

XmArrowButton

Class Pointer: xmArrowButtonWidgetClass

Derivation: *Core » XmPrimitive » XmArrowButton*

Name	Class	Data Type	Rep Type
activate Callback	XmCCallback	XtCallbackList	XmRCallback
armCallback	XmCCallback	XtCallbackList	XmRCallback
arrowDirection	XmCArrowDirection	unsigned char	XmRArrow Direction
disarmCallback	XmCCallback	XtCallbackList	XmRCallback

XmBulletinBoard

Class Pointer: xmBulletinBoardWidgetClass

Derivation: *Core » Composite » Constraint » XmManager »
XmBulletinBoard*

Name	Class	Data Type	Rep Type
allowOverlap	XmCAllowOverlap	Boolean	XmRBoolean
autoUnmanage	XmCAutoUnmanage	Boolean	XmRBoolean
buttonFontList	XmCButtonFontList	XmFontList	XmRFontList
cancelButton	XmCWidget	Widget	XmRWindow
defaultButton	XmCWidget	Widget	XmRWindow
default Position	XmCDefaultPosition	Boolean	XmRBoolean
dialogStyle	XmCDialogStyle	unsigned char	XmRDialogStyle
dialogTitle	XmCDialogTitle	XmString	XmRXmString
focusCallback	XmCCallback	XtCallbackList	XmRCallback
labelFontList	XmCLabelFontList	XmFontList	XmRFontList
mapCallback	XmCCallback	XtCallbackList	XmRCallback
marginHeight	XmCMarginHeight	short	XmRShort
marginWidth	XmCMarginWidth	short	XmRShort
noResize	XmCNoResize	Boolean	XmRBoolean
resizePolicy	XmCResizePolicy	unsigned char	XmRResize Policy
shadowType	XmCShadowType	unsigned char	XmRShadowType
string Direction	XmCStringDirection	XmString- Direction	XmRString Direction
textFontList	XmCTextFontList	XmFontList	XmRFontList
text Translations	XmCTranslations	XtTranslations	XmRTranslation Table
unmapCallback	XmCCallback	XtCallbackList	XmRCallback

XmCascadeButton

Class Pointer: xmCascadeButtonWidgetClass

Derivation: *Core » XmPrimitive » XmLabel » XmCascadeButton*

Name	Class	Data Type	Rep Type
activateCallback	XmCCallback	XtCallback List	XmRCallback
cascadePixmap	XmCPixmap	Pixmap	XmRPrimForeground Pixmap
cascading Callback	XmCCallback	XtCallback List	XmRCallback
mappingDelay	XmCMappingDelay	int	XmRInt
shadowThickness	XmCShadowThickness	short	XmRShort
subMenuId	XmCMenuWidget	Widget	XmRMenuWidget

XmCommand

Class Pointer: xmCommandWidgetClass

Derivation: *Core » Composite » Constraint » XmManager » XmBulletinBoard » XmSelectionBox » XmCommand*

Name	Class	Data Type	Rep Type
command	XmCTextString	XmString	XmRXmString
commandChanged Callback	XmCCallback	XtCallback List	XmRCallback
commandEntered Callback	XmCCallback	XtCallback List	XmRCallback
historyItemCount	XmCItemCount	int	XmRInt
historyItems	XmCItems	XmStringTable	XmRXmString Table
historyMaxItems	XmCMaxItems	int	XmRInt
historyVisible ItemCount	XmCVisibleItemCount	int	XmRInt
promptString	XmCPromptString	XmString	XmRXmString

XmDialogShell

Class Pointer: xmDialogShellWidgetClass

Derivation: *Core » Composite » Shell » WMShell » VendorShell »*
TransientShell » XmDialogShell

Name	Class	Data Type	Rep Type
deleteResponse	XmCDeleteResponse	unsigned char	XmRDeleteResponse

XmDrawingArea

Class Pointer: xmDrawingAreaWidgetClass

Derivation: *Core » Composite » Constraint » XmManager »*
XmDrawingArea

Name	Class	Data Type	Rep Type
exposeCallback	XmCCallback	XtCallbackList	XmRCallback
inputCallback	XmCCallback	XtCallbackList	XmRCallback
marginHeight	XmCMarginHeight	short	XmRShort
marginWidth	XmCMarginWidth	short	XmRShort
resizeCallback	XmCCallback	XtCallbackList	XmRCallback
resizePolicy	XmCResizePolicy	unsigned char	XmRResizePolicy

XmDrawnButton

Class Pointer: xmDrawnButtonWidgetClass

Derivation: *Core » XmPrimitive » XmLabel » XmDrawnButton*

Name	Class	Data Type	Rep Type
activateCallback	XmCCallback	XtCallbackList	XmRCallback
armCallback	XmCCallback	XtCallbackList	XmRCallback
disarmCallback	XmCCallback	XtCallbackList	XmRCallback
exposeCallback	XmCCallback	XtCallbackList	XmRCallback
pushButtonEnabled	XmCPushButton Enabled	Boolean	XmRBoolean
resizeCallback	XmCCallback	XtCallbackList	XmRCallback
shadowType	XmCShadowType	unsigned char	XmRShadowType

XmFileSelectionBox

Class Pointer: xmFileSelectionBoxWidgetClass

Derivation: *Core » Composite » Constraint » XmManager »*
XmBulletinBoard » XmSelectionBox » XmFileSelectionBox

Name	Class	Data Type	Rep Type
dirMask	XmCDirMask	XmString	XmRXmString
dirSpec	XmCDirSpec	XmString	XmRXmString
fileSearchProc	XmCFileSearchProc	XtProc	XmRProc
filterLabel String	XmCFilterLabelString	XmString	XmRXmString
listUpdated	XmCListUpdated	Boolean	XmRBoolean

XmForm

Class Pointer:	xmFormWidgetClass
Derivation:	*Core » Composite » Constraint » XmManager »* *XmBulletinBoard » XmForm*

Name	Class	Data Type	Rep Type
fractionBase	XmCMaxValue	int	XmRInt
horizontalSpacing	XmCSpacing	int	XmRInt
rubberPositioning	XmCRubberPositioning	Boolean	XmRBoolean
verticalSpacing	XmCSpacing	int	XmRInt

Name	Class	Data Type	Rep Type
bottomAttachment	XmCAttachment	unsigned char	XmRAttachment
bottomOffset	XmCOffset	int	XmRInt
bottomPosition	XmCAttachment	int	XmRInt
bottomWidget	XmCWidget	Widget	XmRWindow
leftAttachment	XmCAttachment	unsigned char	XmRAttachment
leftOffset	XmCOffset	int	XmRInt
leftPosition	XmCAttachment	int	XmRInt
leftWidget	XmCWidget	Widget	XmRWindow
resizable	XmCBoolean	Boolean	XmRBoolean
rightAttachment	XmCAttachment	unsigned char	XmRAttachment
rightOffset	XmCOffset	int	XmRInt
rightPosition	XmCAttachment	int	XmRInt
rightWidget	XmCWidget	Widget	XmRWindow
topAttachment	XmCAttachment	unsigned char	XmRAttachment
topOffset	XmCOffset	int	XmRInt
topPosition	XmCAttachment	int	XmRInt
topWidget	XmCWidget	Widget	XmRWindow

XmFrame

Class Pointer:	xmFrameWidgetClass	
Derivation:	*Core » Composite » Constraint » XmManager » XmFrame*	

Name	Class	Data Type	Rep Type
marginHeight	XmCMarginHeight	short	XmRShort
marginWidth	XmCMarginWidth	short	XmRShort
shadowType	XmCShadowType	unsigned char	XmRShadowType

XmLabel

Class Pointer:	xmLabelWidgetClass	
Derivation:	*Core » XmPrimitive » XmLabel*	

Name	Class	Data Type	Rep Type
accelerator	XmCAccelerator	String	XmRString
acceleratorText	XmCAccelerator-Text	XmString	XmRXmString
alignment	XmCAlignment	unsigned char	XmRAlignment
fontList	XmCFontList	XmFontList	XmRFontList
labelInsensitivePixmap	XmCLabelInsensitivePixmap	Pixmap	XmRPixmap
labelPixmap	XmCLabelPixmap	Pixmap	XmRPrimForegroundPixmap
labelString	XmCXmString	XmString	XmRXmString
labelType	XmCLabelType	unsigned char	XmRLabelType
marginBottom	XmCMarginBottom	short	XmRShort
marginHeight	XmCMarginHeight	short	XmRShort
marginLeft	XmCMarginLeft	short	XmRShort
marginRight	XmCMarginRight	short	XmRShort
marginTop	XmCMarginTop	short	XmRShort
marginWidth	XmCMarginWidth	short	XmRShort
mnemonic	XmCMnemonic	char	XmRChar
recomputeSize	XmCRecomputeSize	Boolean	XmRBoolean
stringDirection	XmCStringDirection	XmStringDirection	XmRStringDirection

XmList

Class Pointer:	xmListWidgetClass	
Derivation:	*Core » XmPrimitive » XmList*	

Name	Class	Data Type	Rep Type
automatic Selection	XmCAutomatic Selection	Boolean	XmRBoolean
browseSelection Callback	XmCCallback	XtCallbackList	XmRCallback
defaultAction Callback	XmCCallback	XtCallbackList	XmRCallback
doubleClick Interval	XmCDoubleClick Interval	int	XmRInt
extendedSelect ionCallback	XmCCallback	XtCallbackList	XmRCallback
fontList	XmCFontList	XmFontList	XmRFontList
itemCount	XmCItemCount	int	XmRInt
items	XmCItems	XmStringTable	XmRXmStringTable
listMargin Height	XmCListMargin Height	short	XmRShort
listMarginWidth	XmCListMarginWidth	short	XmRShort
listSizePolicy	XmCListSizePolicy	unsigned char	XmRListSizePolicy
listSpacing	XmCListSpacing	short	XmRShort
multipleSelec tionCallback	XmCCallback	XtCallbackList	XmRCallback
selectedItem Count	XmCSelectedItem Count	int	XmRInt
selectedItems	XmCSelectedItems	XmStringTable	XmRXmStringTable
selectionPolicy	XmCSelectionPolicy	unsigned char	XmRSelection Policy
singleSelection Callback	XmCCallback	XtCallbackList	XmRCallback
stringDirection	XmCStringDirection	XmString- Direction	XmRString- Direction
visibleItem Count	XmCVisibleItem Count	int	XmRInt

XmMainWindow

Class Pointer:	xmMainWindowWidgetClass
Derivation:	*Core » Composite » Constraint » XmManager » XmScrolledWindow » XmMainWindow*

Name	Class	Data Type	Rep Type
commandWindow	XmCCommandWindow	Widget	XmRWindow
mainWindowMargin Height	XmCMainWindow MarginHeight	short	XmRShort
mainWindowMarginWidth	XmCMainWindow MarginWidth	short	XmRShort
menuBar	XmCMenuBar	Widget	XmRWindow
showSeparator	XmCShowSeparator	Boolean	XmRBoolean

XmManager

Class Pointer:	xmManagerWidgetClass
Derivation:	*Core » Composite » Constraint » XmManager*

Name	Class	Data Type	Rep Type
bottomShadowColor	XmCForeground	Pixel	XmRPixel
bottomShadow- Pixmap	XmCBottomShadow Pixmap	Pixmap	XmRManBottom ShadowPixmap
foreground	XmCForeground	Pixel	XmRPixel
helpCallback	XmCCallback	XtCallback- List	XmRCallback
highlightColor	XmCForeground	Pixel	XmRPixel
highlightPixmap	XmCHighlightPixmap	Pixmap	XmRManHigh lightPixmap
shadowThickness	XmCShadowThickness	short	XmRShort
topShadowColor	XmCBackground	Pixel	XmRPixel
topShadowPixmap	XmCTopShadowPixmap	Pixmap	XmRManTop ShadowPixmap
unitType	XmCUnitType	unsigned char	XmRUnitType
userData	XmCUserData	XtPointer	XmRPointer

XmMenuShell

Class Pointer: xmMenuShellWidgetClass

Derivation: *Core » Composite » Shell » OverrideShell » XmMenuShell*

Name	Class	Data Type	Rep Type
allowShellResize	XmCAllowShellResize	Boolean	XmRBoolean
saveUnder	XmCSaveUnder	Boolean	XmRBoolean

XmMessageBox

Class Pointer: xmMessageBoxWidgetClass

Derivation: *Core » Composite » Constraint » XmManager » XmBulletinBoard » XmMessageBox*

Name	Class	Data Type	Rep Type
cancelCallback	XmCCallback	XtCallbackList	XmRCallback
cancelLabelString	XmCXmString	XmString	XmRXmString
defaultButtonType	XmCDefaultButton Type	unsigned char	XmRDefault ButtonType
dialogType	XmCDialogType	unsigned char	XmRDialogType
helpLabelString	XmCXmString	XmString	XmRXmString
messageAlignment	XmCAlignment	unsigned char	XmRAlignment
messageString	XmCXmString	XmString	XmRXmString
minimizeButtons	XmCMinimizeButtons	Boolean	XmRBoolean
okCallback	XmCCallback	XtCallbackList	XmRCallback
okLabelString	XmCXmString	XmString	XmRXmString
symbolPixmap	XmCPixmap	Pixmap	XmRManFore groundPixmap

XmPanedWindow

Class Pointer: xmPanedWindowWidgetClass

Derivation: *Core » Composite » Constraint » XmManager »*
XmPanedWindow

Name	Class	Data Type	Rep Type
marginHeight	XmCMarginHeight	short	XmRShort
marginWidth	XmCMarginWidth	short	XmRShort
refigureMode	XmCBoolean	Boolean	XmRBoolean
sashHeight	XmCSashHeight	Dimension	XmRDimension
sashIndent	XmCSashIndent	Position	XmRPosition
sashShadowThickness	XmCShadowThickness	int	XmRInt
sashWidth	XmCSashWidth	Dimension	XmRDimension
separatorOn	XmCSeparatorOn	Boolean	XmRBoolean
spacing	XmCSpacing	int	XmRInt

Name	Class	Data Type	Rep Type
allowResize	XmCBoolean	Boolean	XmRBoolean
paneMaximum	XmCPaneMaximum	int	XmRInt
paneMinimum	XmCPaneMinimum	int	XmRInt
skipAdjust	XmCBoolean	Boolean	XmRBoolean

XmPrimitive

Class Pointer: xmPrimitiveWidgetClass

Derivation: *Core » XmPrimitive*

Name	Class	Data Type	Rep Type
bottomShadowColor	XmCForeground	Pixel	XmRPixel
bottomShadow Pixmap	XmCBottomShadow Pixmap	Pixmap	XmRBottom ShadowPixmap
foreground	XmCForeground	Pixel	XmRPixel
helpCallback	XmCCallback	XtCallback List	XmRCallback
highlightColor	XmCForeground	Pixel	XmRPixel
highlightOnEnter	XmCHighlightOnEnter	Boolean	XmRBoolean
highlightPixmap	XmCHighlightPixmap	Pixmap	XmRHighlight Pixmap
highlight Thickness	XmCHighlight Thickness	short	XmRShort
shadowThickness	XmCShadowThickness	short	XmRShort
topShadowColor	XmCBackground	Pixel	XmRPixel
topShadowPixmap	XmCTopShadowPixmap	Pixmap	XmRTopShadow- Pixmap
traversalOn	XmCTraversalOn	Boolean	XmRBoolean
unitType	XmCUnitType	unsigned char	XmRUnitType
userData	XmCUserData	XtPointer	XmRPointer

XmPushButton

Class Pointer: xmPushButtonWidgetClass

Derivation: *Core » XmPrimitive » XmLabel » XmPushButton*

Name	Class	Data Type	Rep Type
activateCallback	XmCCallback	XtCallbackList	XmRCallback
armCallback	XmCCallback	XtCallbackList	XmRCallback
armColor	XmCArmColor	Pixel	XmRPixel
armPixmap	XmCArmPixmap	Pixmap	XmRPrimForeground Pixmap
disarmCallback	XmCCallback	XtCallbackList	XmRCallback
fillOnArm	XmCFillOnArm	Boolean	XmRBoolean
showAsDefault	XmCShowAsDefault	short	XmRShort

XmRowColumn

Class Pointer:	xmRowColumnWidgetClass
Derivation:	*Core » Composite » Constraint » XmManager » XmRowColumn*

Name	Class	Data Type	Rep Type
adjustLast	XmCAdjustLast	Boolean	XmRBoolean
adjustMargin	XmCAdjustMargin	Boolean	XmRBoolean
entryAlignment	XmCAlignment	unsigned char	XmRAlignment
entryBorder	XmCEntryBorder	Dimension	XmRDimension
entryCallback	XmCCallback	XtCallbackList	XmRCallback
entryClass	XmCEntryClass	WidgetClass	XmRInt
isAligned	XmCIsAligned	Boolean	XmRBoolean
isHomogeneous	XmCIsHomogeneous	Boolean	XmRBoolean
labelString	XmCString	XmString	XmRXmString
mapCallback	XmCCallback	XtCallbackList	XmRCallback
marginHeight	XmCMarginHeight	Dimension	XmRDimension
marginWidth	XmCMarginWidth	Dimension	XmRDimension
menuAccelerator	XmCAccelerators	String	XmRString
menuHelpWidget	XmCMenuWidget	Widget	XmRMenuWidget
menuHistory	XmCMenuWidget	Widget	XmRMenuWidget
mnemonic	XmCMnemonic	char	XmRChar
numColumns	XmCNumColumns	short	XmRShort
orientation	XmCOrientation	unsigned char	XmROrientation
packing	XmCPacking	unsigned char	XmRPacking
popupEnabled	XmCPopupEnabled	Boolean	XmRBoolean
radioAlwaysOne	XmCRadioAlwaysOne	Boolean	XmRBoolean
radioBehavior	XmCRadioBehavior	Boolean	XmRBoolean
resizeHeight	XmCResizeHeight	Boolean	XmRBoolean
resizeWidth	XmCResizeWidth	Boolean	XmRBoolean
rowColumnType	XmCRowColumnType	unsigned char	XmRRowColumnType
spacing	XmCSpacing	Dimension	XmRDimension
subMenuId	XmCMenuWidget	Widget	XmRMenuWidget
unmapCallback	XmCCallback	XtCallbackList	XmRCallback
whichButton	XmCWhichButton	unsigned int	XmRWhichButton

XmScale

Class Pointer: xmScaleWidgetClass

Derivation: *Core » Composite » Constraint » XmManager » XmScale*

Name	Class	Data Type	Rep Type
decimalPoints	XmCDecimalPoints	short	XmRShort
dragCallback	XmCCallback	XtCallback List	XmRCallback
fontList	XmCFontList	XmFontList	XmRFontList
highlightOnEnter	XmCHighlightOnEnter	Boolean	XmRBoolean
highlight Thickness	XmCHighlightThickness	short	XmRShort
maximum	XmCMaximum	int	XmRInt
minimum	XmCMinimum	int	XmRInt
orientation	XmCOrientation	unsigned char	XmROrientation
processing Direction	XmCProcessing Direction	unsigned char	XmRProcessing Direction
scaleHeight	XmCScaleHeight	Dimension	XmRDimension
scaleWidth	XmCScaleWidth	Dimension	XmRDimension
showValue	XmCShowValue	Boolean	XmRBoolean
titleString	XmCTitleString	XmString	XmRXmString
traversalOn	XmCTraversalOn	Boolean	XmRBoolean
value	XmCValue	int	XmRInt
valueChanged Callback	XmCCallback	XtCallback List	XmRCallback

XmScrollBar

Class Pointer: xmScrollBarWidgetClass

Derivation: *Core » XmPrimitive » XmScrollBar*

Name	Class	Data Type	Rep Type
decrementCallback	XmCCallback	XtCallbackList	XmRCallback
dragCallback	XmCCallback	XtCallbackList	XmRCallback
increment	XmCIncrement	int	XmRInt
incrementCallback	XmCCallback	XtCallbackList	XmRCallback
initialDelay	XmCInitialDelay	int	XmRInt
maximum	XmCMaximum	int	XmRInt
minimum	XmCMinimum	int	XmRInt
orientation	XmCOrientation	unsigned char	XmROrientation
pageDecrementCallback	XmCCallback	XtCallbackList	XmRCallback
pageIncrement	XmCPage Increment	int	XmRInt
pageIncrementCallback	XmCCallback	XtCallbackList	XmRCallback
processingDirection	XmCProcessing Direction	unsigned char	XmRProcessing-Direction
releaseCallback	XmCCallback	XtCallbackList	XmRCallback
repeatDelay	XmCRepeatDelay	int	XmRInt
showArrows	XmCShowArrows	Boolean	XmRBoolean
sliderSize	XmCSliderSize	int	XmRInt
toBottomCallback	XmCCallback	XtCallbackList	XmRCallback
toTopCallback	XmCCallback	XtCallbackList	XmRCallback
value	XmCValue	int	XmRInt
valueChangedCallback	XmCCallback	XtCallbackList	XmRCallback

XmScrolledWindow

Class Pointer: xmScrolledWindowWidgetClass

Derivation: *Core » Composite » Constraint » XmManager »*
XmScrolledWindow

Name	Class	Data Type	Rep Type
clipWindow	XmCClipWindow	Widget	XmRWindow
horizontalScroll Bar	XmCHorizontalScroll Bar	Widget	XmRWindow
scrollBarDisplay Policy	XmCScrollBarDisplay Policy	unsigned char	XmRScrollBar DisplayPolicy
scrollBar Placement	XmCScrollBar Placement	unsigned char	XmRScrollBar- Placement
scrolledWindow MarginHeight	XmCScrolledWindow MarginHeight	short	XmRShort
scrolledWindow MarginWidth	XmCScrolledWindow MarginWidth	short	XmRShort
scrollingPolicy	XmCScrollingPolicy	unsigned char	XmRScrolling Policy
spacing	XmCSpacing	int	XmRInt
verticalScroll Bar	XmCVerticalScrollBar	Widget	XmRWindow
visualPolicy	XmCVisualPolicy	unsigned char	XmRVisualPolicy
workWindow	XmCWorkWindow	Widget	XmRWindow

XmSelectionBox

Class Pointer: xmSelectionBoxWidgetClass

Derivation: *Core » Composite » Constraint » XmManager »*
                     XmBulletinBoard » XmSelectionBox

Name	Class	Data Type	Rep Type
applyCallback	XmCCallback	XtCallback List	XmRCallback
applyLabelString	XmCApplyLabelString	XmString	XmRXmString
cancelCallback	XmCCallback	XtCallback List	XmRCallback
cancelLabel String	XmCCancelLabelString	XmString	XmRXmString
dialogType	XmCDialogType	unsigned char	XmRDialogType
helpLabelString	XmCHelpLabelString	XmString	XmRXmString
listItemCount	XmCItemCount	int	XmRInt
listItems	XmCItems	XmStringTable	XmRXmString Table
listLabelString	XmCListLabelString	XmString	XmRXmString
listVisibleItem Count	XmCVisibleItemCount	int	XmRInt
minimizeButtons	XmCMinimizeButtons	Boolean	XmRBoolean
mustMatch	XmCMustMatch	Boolean	XmRBoolean
noMatchCallback	XmCCallback	XtCallback List	XmRCallback
okCallback	XmCCallback	XtCallback List	XmRCallback
okLabelString	XmCOkLabelString	XmString	XmRXmString
selectionLabel String	XmCSelectionLabel String	XmString	XmRXmString
textAccelerators	XmCAccelerators	Xt Translations	XmRAccelerator Table
textColumns	XmCColumns	short	XmRShort
textString	XmCTextString	XmString	XmRXmString

XmSeparator

Class Pointer:	xmSeparatorWidgetClass
Derivation:	*Core » XmPrimitive » XmSeparator*

Name	Class	Data Type	Rep Type
margin	XmCMargin	short	XmRShort
orientation	XmCOrientation	unsigned char	XmROrientation
separatorType	XmCSeparatorType	unsigned char	XmRSeparatorType

XmText

Class Pointer: xmTextWidgetClass
Derivation: *Core » XmPrimitive » XmText*

Name	Class	Data Type	Rep Type
activateCallback	XmCCallback	XtCallbackList	XmRCallback
autoShowCursor Position	XmCAutoShowCursor Position	Boolean	XmRBoolean
blinkRate	XmCBlinkRate	int	XmRInt
columns	XmCColumns	short	XmRShort
cursorPosition	XmCCursorPosition	XmTextPosition	XmRInt
cursorPosition Visible	XmCCursorPosition Visible	Boolean	XmRBoolean
editable	XmCEditable	Boolean	XmRBoolean
editMode	XmCEditMode	unsigned char	XmREditMode
focusCallback	XmCCallback	XtCallbackList	XmRCallback
fontList	XmCFontList	XmFontList	XmRFontList
losingFocusCallback	XmCCallback	XtCallbackList	XmRCallback
marginHeight	XmCMarginHeight	short	XmRShort
marginWidth	XmCMarginWidth	short	XmRShort
maxLength	XmCMaxLength	int	XmRInt
modifyVerify Callback	XmCCallback	XtCallbackList	XmRCallback
motionVerify Callback	XmCCallback	XtCallbackList	XmRCallback
pendingDelete	XmCPendingDelete	Boolean	XmRBoolean
resizeHeight	XmCResizeHeight	Boolean	XmRBoolean
resizeWidth	XmCResizeWidth	Boolean	XmRBoolean
rows	XmCRows	short	XmRShort
selectionArray	XmCSelectionArray	XtPointer	XmRPointer
selectThreshold	XmCSelectThreshold	int	XmRInt
source	XmCSource	XtPointer	XmRPointer
topCharacter	XmCTextPosition	XmTextPosition	XmRInt
value	XmCValue	String	XmRString
valueChanged Callback	XmCCallback	XtCallbackList	XmRCallback
wordWrap	XmCWordWrap	Boolean	XmRBoolean

XmToggleButton

Class Pointer: xmToggleButtonWidgetClass

Derivation: *Core » XmPrimitive » XmLabel » XmToggleButton*

Name	Class	Data Type	Rep Type
armCallback	XmCArmCallback	XtCallbackList	XmRCallback
disarmCallback	XmCDisarmCallback	XtCallbackList	XmRCallback
fillOnSelect	XmCFillOnSelect	Boolean	XmRBoolean
indicatorOn	XmCIndicatorOn	Boolean	XmRBoolean
indicatorType	XmCIndicatorType	unsigned char	XmRIndicatorType
selectColor	XmCForeground	Pixel	XmRPixel
selectInsensitivePixmap	XmCSelectInsensitivePixmap	Pixmap	XmRPixmap
selectPixmap	XmCSelectPixmap	Pixmap	XmRPrimForegroundPixmap
set	XmCSet	Boolean	XmRBoolean
spacing	XmCSpacing	short	XmRShort
valueChangedCallback	XmCValueChangedCallback	XtCallbackList	XmRCallback
visibleWhenOff	XmCVisibleWhenOff	Boolean	XmRBoolean

Appendix C
X Event Reference

Overview

This appendix details the structures comprising the XEvent union. It begins with tables, taken from Chapter 8, listing all X events and the masks used to select those events. Following these tables, each member of the XEvent union is presented individually and described in detail.

Event Types

X provides 33 distinct events, which are divided into nine categories. Table C.1, also presented as Table 8.1, lists these events in alphabetical order by category. The names in the "Events" column correspond to constants defined in the header file X11/X.h.

Table C.1. X event types

Category	Events
Client Communication	ClientMessage PropertyNotify SelectionClear SelectionNotify SelectionRequest
Colormap State	ColormapNotify
Exposure	Expose GraphicsExpose NoExpose
Keyboard Focus	FocusIn FocusOut
Keyboard Input	KeyPress KeyRelease
Keymap State	KeymapNotify
Pointer/Button	ButtonPress ButtonRelease EnterNotify LeaveNotify MotionNotify
Structure Control	CirculateRequest ConfigureRequest MapRequest ResizeRequest
Window State	CirculateNotify ConfigureNotify CreateNotify DestroyNotify GravityNotify MapNotify MappingNotify ReparentNotify UnmapNotify VisibilityNotify

Event Masks

To select an event, a program must use one of the masks in Table C.2, also presented as Table 8.2. These masks are bit masks and may be "or'd" together to select multiple events. They are defined in the header file `X11/X.h`.

Table C.2. X event masks

Mask Constant	Event(s) Enabled	Comments
`ButtonMotionMask`	`MotionNotify`	Notify if any mouse button pressed while pointer is moved
`Button1MotionMask`	`MotionNotify`	Notify only if mouse button #1 pressed while pointer is moved
`Button2MotionMask`	`MotionNotify`	Notify only if mouse button #2 pressed while pointer is moved
`Button3MotionMask`	`MotionNotify`	Notify only if mouse button #3 pressed while pointer is moved
`Button4MotionMask`	`MotionNotify`	Notify only if mouse button #4 pressed while pointer is moved
`Button5MotionMask`	`MotionNotify`	Notify only if mouse button #5 pressed while pointer is moved
`ButtonPressMask`	`ButtonPress`	Notify when any mouse button is pressed
`ButtonReleaseMask`	`ButtonRelease`	Notify when any mouse button is released
`ColormapChangeMask`	`ColormapNotify`	Notify when colormap changes
`EnterWindowMask`	`EnterNotify`	Notify when pointer enters window
`ExposureMask`	`Expose`	Notify when portion of window is exposed.
`FocusChangeMask`	`FocusIn` `FocusOut`	Notify when window gains or loses keyboard focus
`KeymapStateMask`	`KeymapNotify`	Describe keyboard state when focus changes
`KeyPressMask`	`KeyPress`	Notify when any key is pressed
`KeyReleaseMask`	`KeyRelease`	Notify when key is released
`LeaveWindowMask`	`LeaveNotify`	Notify when pointer leaves window
`PointerMotion HintMask`		Modifies `PointerMotionMask`, so that the number of motion events is minimized; `PointerMotionMask` must be specified too
`PointerMotionMask`	`MotionNotify`	Notify when pointer moves

Table C.2. Continued.

`PropertyChangeMask`	`PropertyNotify`	Notify when window property changes
`ResizeRedirectMask`	`ResizeRequest`	Capture size-change requests from children of associated window
`StructureNotify Mask`	`CirculateNotify` `ConfigureNotify` `DestroyNotify` `GravityNotify` `MapNotify` `ReparentNotify` `UnmapNotify`	Notify when window structure changes
`SubstructureNotify Mask`	`CirculateNotify` `ConfigureNotify` `CreateNotify` `DestroyNotify` `GravityNotify` `MapNotify` `ReparentNotify` `UnmapNotify`	Notify when child window structure changes
`Substructure RedirectMask`	`CirculateRequest` `ConfigureRequest` `MapRequest`	Capture structure-change requests from children of associated window
`VisibilityChange Mask`	`VisibilityNotify`	Notify when window visibility changes
gc-controlled	`GraphicsExpose` `NoExpose`	These events are selected with the `graphics_exposures` member of the graphics context; when selected, they are nonmaskable.
nonmaskable	`ClientMessage` `MappingNotify` `SelectionClear` `SelectionNotify` `SelectionRequest`	These events are delivered to all windows; they may be ignored by passing `FALSE` in the `nonmaskable` parameter of `XtAddEventHandler`
special	*error event*	Protocol errors are passed from server to client using the X event mechanism; such events, however, are handled at a low level in the client code

XEvent

The `XEvent` union provides a convenient representation of the range of events sent to an X client. Each member corresponds to one or more of the events listed in the tables above; the purpose of each is described below the listing. `XEvent` and all of its member types are defined in the header file `Xlib.h`.

Listing C.1. Type definition: *XEvent*

```
typedef union
        {
        int                     type;
        XAnyEvent               xany;
        XKeyEvent               xkey;
        XButtonEvent            xbutton;
        XMotionEvent            xmotion;
        XCrossingEvent          xcrossing;
        XFocusChangeEvent       xfocus;
        XExposeEvent            xexpose;
        XGraphicsExposeEvent    xgraphicsexpose;
        XNoExposeEvent          xnoexpose;
        XVisibilityEvent        xvisibility;
        XCreateWindowEvent      xcreatewindow;
        XDestroyWindowEvent     xdestroywindow;
        XUnmapEvent             xunmap;
        XMapEvent               xmap;
        XMapRequestEvent        xmaprequest;
        XReparentEvent          xreparent;
        XConfigureEvent         xconfigure;
        XGravityEvent           xgravity;
        XResizeRequestEvent     xresizerequest;
        XConfigureRequestEvent  xconfigurerequest;
        XCirculateEvent         xcirculate;
        XCirculateRequestEvent  xcirculaterequest;
        XPropertyEvent          xproperty;
        XSelectionClearEvent    xselectionclear;
        XSelectionRequestEvent  xselectionrequest;
        XSelectionEvent         xselection;
        XColormapEvent          xcolormap;
        XClientMessageEvent     xclient;
        XMappingEvent           xmapping;
        XErrorEvent             xerror;
        XKeymapEvent            xkeymap;
        long                    pad[24];
        }
XEvent;
```

`type`	Identification of the event type; this member contains one of the constants listed in Table C.1.
`xany`	Fields common to all events. This member is used for nonspecific event handling (*eg*, determining the source display).
`xkey`	Data for `KeyPress` and `KeyRelease` events, enabled, respectively, by `KeyPressMask` and `KeyReleaseMask`.
`xbutton`	Data for `ButtonPress` and `ButtonRelease` events, enabled, respectively, by `ButtonPressMask` and `ButtonReleaseMask`.
`xmotion`	Data for `MotionNotify` events, enabled by `PointerMotionMask`, `ButtonMotionMask` and its various "relatives," such as `Button1MotionMask`.
`xcrossing`	Data for `EnterNotify` and `LeaveNotify` events, enabled, respectively, by `EnterWindowMask` and `LeaveWindowMask`.
`xfocus`	Data for `FocusIn` and `FocusOut` events, enabled by `FocusChangeMask`.
`xexpose`	Data for `Expose` events, enabled by `ExposureMask`.
`xgraphicsexpose`	Data for `GraphicsExpose` events, enabled by the `graphics_exposures` member of the graphics context.
`xnoexpose`	Data for `NoExpose` events, enabled by the `graphics_exposures` member of the graphics context.
`xvisibility`	Data for `VisibilityNotify` events, enabled by `VisibilityChangeMask`.
`xcreatewindow`	Data for `CreateNotify`, enabled by `SubstructureNotifyMask`.
`xdestroywindow`	Data for `DestroyNotify`, enabled by `StructureNotifyMask` and `SubstructureNotifyMask`.
`xunmap`	Data for `UnmapNotify`, enabled by `StructureNotifyMask` and `SubstructureNotifyMask`.

xmap .... Data for `MapNotify`, **enabled by** `StructureNotifyMask` **and** `SubstructureNotifyMask`. **Note: this member is** *not* **used for the** `MappingNotify` **event; that event uses** `xmapping`.

xmaprequest .... Data for `MapRequest`, **enabled by** `SubstructureRedirectMask`.

xreparent .... Data for `ReparentNotify`, **enabled by** `StructureNotifyMask` **and** `SubstructureNotifyMask`.

xconfigure .... Data for `ConfigureNotify`, **enabled by** `StructureNotifyMask` **and** `SubstructureNotifyMask`.

xresizerequest .... Data for `ResizeRequest`, **enabled by** `ResizeRedirectMask`.

xconfigurerequest .... Data for `ConfigureRequest`, **enabled by** `SubstructureRedirectMask`.

xcirculate .... Data for `CirculateNotify`, **enabled by** `StructureNotifyMask` **and** `SubstructureNotifyMask`.

xcirculaterequest .... Data for `CirculateRequest`, **enabled by** `SubstructureRedirectMask`.

xproperty .... Data for `PropertyNotify`, **enabled by** `PropertyChangeMask`.

xselectionclear .... Data for `SelectionClear`, **a nonmaskable event.**

xselectionrequest .... Data for `SelectionRequest`, **a nonmaskable event.**

xselection .... Data for `SelectionNotify`, **a nonmaskable event.**

xcolormap .... Data for `ColormapNotify`, **enabled by** `ColormapChangeMask`.

xclient .... Data for `ClientMessage`, **a nonmaskable event.**

xmapping .... Data for `MappingNotify`, **a nonmaskable event.**

xerror................................. Data for protocol error events. These events are
                                        handled by the low-level interface and are not
                                        delivered to program-level code by the event
                                        mechanism.

xkeymap............................... Data for `KeymapNotify`, enabled by
                                        `KeymapStateMask`.

pad...................................... Filler data, to guarantee the size of the `XEvent`
                                        structure.

XAnyEvent

`XAnyEvent` contains fields common to all event types. It may be used for high-level event handling, such as determining whether the received event was sent from another client.

Listing C.2. Type definition: XAnyEvent

```
typedef struct
        {
        int              type;
        unsigned long    serial;
        Boolean          send_event;
        Display          *display;
        Window           window;
        }
XAnyEvent;
```

type.................................... Identification of the event type; this member
                                        contains one of the constants listed in Table C.1.

serial.................................. A count of the number of protocol requests
                                        processed by the server before this event was sent
                                        to the client.

send_event......................... A flag indicating whether another client sent the
                                        event: it is `TRUE` if the event was sent with
                                        `XSendEvent`, `FALSE` if the event was sent directly
                                        from the server.

display...................... Identification of the server that sent this event;
this is a pointer to the server's display structure.
It is primarily useful when a client has
connections open to more than one display.

window...................... The ID of the window that handled the event. In
most cases, this is the ID of the window where
the event was received. Some events, however,
are propagated up the window tree until handled.

ButtonPress, ButtonRelease

ButtonPress events are sent whenever the user presses a mouse button; a
ButtonRelease event is sent when the user releases that button. The server
determines the receiving window from the pointer position: it is the smallest
window that contains the pointer. If this window does not have an appropriate
event handler attached, the event is sent to its parent — and so on, up the tree,
until some window does handle the event (or it reaches the root window, in
which case it is discarded).

Listing C.3. Type definition: *XButtonEvent*

```
typedef struct
        {
        int             type;
        unsigned long   serial;
        Boolean         send_event;
        Display         *display;
        Window          window;
        Window          root;
        Window          subwindow;
        Time            time;
        int             x, y;
        int             x_root, y_root;
        unsigned int    state;
        unsigned int    button;
        Boolean         same_screen;
} XButtonEvent;
```

type...................... Identification of the event type: ButtonPress or
ButtonRelease.

`serial` .... A count of the number of protocol requests processed by the server before this event was sent to the client.

`send_event` .... A flag indicating whether another client sent the event: it is `TRUE` if the event was sent with `XSendEvent`, `FALSE` if the event was sent directly from the server.

`display` .... Identification of the server that sent this event; this is a pointer to the server's display structure. It is primarily useful when a client has connections open to more than one display.

`window` .... The ID of the window that handled the event. Due to propagation, this may or may not be the window where the event was first received (`subwindow`).

`root` .... The ID of the root window of the screen where the event occurred.

`subwindow` .... The ID of the window where the event actually occurred.

`time` .... The event's server timestamp — a count of milliseconds between the server start time and the time the event was sent to the client.

`x, y` .... The pointer position within the window receiving the event (`window`), measured in pixels. If the receiving window is not on the same screen as the window specified in `root` (`same_screen` contains `FALSE`), both `x` and `y` contain zero.

`x_root, y_root` .... The pointer's position relative to the root window at the time of the event. If the root window and the receiving window are not on the same screen, both `x_root` and `y_root` contain zero.

`state` .... The state of the modifier keys and pointer buttons at the time of the event. This member is a bit mask, built from one or more of the following constants:

```
Button1Mask, Button2Mask, Button3Mask,
Button4Mask, Button5Mask, ShiftMask,
ControlMask, LockMask, Mod1Mask,
Mod2Mask, Mod3Mask, Mod4Mask, Mod5Mask
```

button................................ The mouse button that invoked this event. This is
a logical button number and should be compared
against one of the following constants:

> `Button1, Button2, Button3, Button4,`
> `Button5`

same_screen..................... A flag indicating whether the receiving window
(`window`) is on the same screen as the root window
(`root`). This member will contain `FALSE` as the
result of a pointer grab; usually, it contains `TRUE`.

CirculateNotify

`CirculateNotify` events are generated when a window's position changes to the
top or bottom of the stacking order, due to a call to `XCirculateSubwindows`,
`XCirculateSubwindowsUp`, or `XCirculateSubwindowsDown`. `CirculateNotify` events
are sent to the new top and bottom windows only.

Note that a more general notification is `ConfigureNotify`; the `CirculateNotify`
event is most useful to internal widget code.

Listing C.4. Type definition: XCirculateEvent

```
typedef struct
        {
        int             type;
        unsigned long   serial;
        Boolean         send_event;
        Display         *display;
        Window          event;
        Window          window;
        int             place;
        }
XCirculateEvent;
```

type............................... Identification of the event type: `CirculateNotify`.

serial............................. A count of the number of protocol requests
processed by the server before this event was sent
to the client.

send_event .... A flag indicating whether another client sent the
event: it is `TRUE` if the event was sent with
`XSendEvent`, `FALSE` if the event was sent directly
from the server.

display .... Identification of the server that sent this event;
this is a pointer to the server's display structure.
It is primarily useful when a client has
connections open to more than one display.

event .... The ID of the window that handled the event. This
may or may not be the window being restacked.

window .... The ID of the window that is being restacked.

place .... The window's new position. The window is either
on the top of or beneath all of its siblings, as
specified by the following constants:

`PlaceOnTop, PlaceOnBottom`

CirculateRequest

`CirculateRequest` events are used primarily by the window manager to control
the   stacking   of   client   windows.   They   are   generated   when
`SubstructureRedirectMask` is in effect for a given window and a client attempts to
change the stacking order of children of that window.

When `SubstructureRedirectMask` is in effect, the circulate operation is not
performed by the original call. Instead, the event handler must perform the call
again — or, to deny the request, simply ignore the event.

Listing C.5. Type definition: *XCirculateRequestEvent*

```
typedef struct
        {
        int             type;
        unsigned long   serial;
        Boolean         send_event;
        Display         *display;
        Window          parent;
        Window          window;
        int             place;
        }
    XCirculateRequestEvent;
```

`type`	Identification of the event type: `CirculateRequest`.
`serial`	A count of the number of protocol requests processed by the server before this event was sent to the client.
`send_event`	A flag indicating whether another client sent the event: it is `TRUE` if the event was sent with `XSendEvent`, `FALSE` if the event was sent directly from the server.
`display`	Identification of the server that sent this event; this is a pointer to the server's display structure. It is primarily useful when a client has connections open to more than one display.
`parent`	The ID of the window receiving the event — the parent of the window for which the request is made. This is typically the root window.
`window`	The ID of the window that is being restacked.
`place`	The desired location for the window. Either `PlaceOnTop` or `PlaceOnBottom`.

ClientMessage

`ClientMessage` events are used for interclient communication, as described in Chapter 17. Subject to requirements described below, its contents depend solely on the sending client.

Note: All fields must be filled by the sending client. The server does not touch this event in any way, save to set the `send_event` member and byte-swap the contents (if needed).

Listing C.6. Type definition: *XClientMessageEvent*

```
typedef struct
        {
        int             type;
        unsigned long   serial;
        Boolean         send_event;
        Display         *display;
        Window          window;
        Atom            message_type;
        int             format;
        union           {
                        char    b[20];
                         short   s[10];
                        long    l[5];
                        }
                        data;
        }
    XClientMessageEvent;
```

type .... Identification of the event type: `ClientMessage`.

serial .... A count of the number of protocol requests processed by the server before this event was sent to the receiving client.

send_event .... A flag indicating whether another client sent the event; this member always contains `TRUE`.

display .... Identification of the server that sent this event; this is a pointer to the server's display structure. It is primarily useful when a client has connections open to more than one display.

window .... The ID of the window that receives the event. When sent by a client, this field must specify the window passed to `XSendEvent`; if not, the event isn't delivered.

message_type .... An atom that specifies the type of data contained in `data`. This member exists solely for the usage of the two clients; it may contain one of the predefined type atoms, an atom unique to the clients, or any 32-bit value known to both of the clients.

format .... A specification of the type of data in `data` used by the server to perform byte-swapping (if needed). This contains the value 8 if the data is a collection of bytes, 16 if it is a collection of words, and 32 if it is a collection of longwords. No other values are allowed.

data .... The event data itself. This member is a 20-byte buffer. For convenience, it is defined as a union of a 20-element character array (`b`), a 10-element short-integer array (`s`), or a 5-element long-integer array (`l`). The program may use or ignore these definitions; note, however, that the server performs byte-swapping based on the `format` member — so a data item spanning two elements may be improperly swapped.

ColormapNotify

`ColormapNotify` events are generated whenever a window's colormap is changed. In a shared-colormap environment (the X norm), colormap changes may occur whenever a program starts (and initializes its color scheme from the resource file).

Listing C.7. Type definition: *XColormapEvent*

```
typedef struct
        {
        int             type;
        unsigned long   serial;
        Boolean         send_event;
        Display         *display;
        Window          window;
        Colormap        colormap;
        Boolean         new;
        int             state;
        }
XColormapEvent;
```

type .... Identification of the event type: `ColormapNotify`.

serial .... A count of the number of protocol requests processed by the server before this event was sent to the receiving client.

send_event .... A flag indicating whether another client sent the event: it is `TRUE` if the event was sent with `XSendEvent`, `FALSE` if the event was sent directly from the server.

display .... Identification of the server that sent this event; this is a pointer to the server's display structure. It is primarily useful when a client has connections open to more than one display.

window .... The ID of the window that underwent a colormap change.

colormap .... The ID of the changed colormap. If the colormap was deleted, this member contains the value `None`.

new .... If this member contains `TRUE`, the existing colormap was changed. If it contains `FALSE`, the colormap was installed or uninstalled.

state .... If `new` contains `FALSE`, this member indicates the operation and contains one of the following constants:

```
ColormapInstalled, ColormapUninstalled
```

ConfigureNotify

`ConfigureNotify` events indicate that part of a window's configuration — its size, position, border, or stacking order — has changed. While the primary consumer of such events is a widget's internal code, some programs may use these events to alter their operation depending on available space.

Listing C.8. Type definition: *XConfigureEvent*

```
typedef struct
        {
        int             type;
        unsigned long   serial;
        Boolean         send_event;
        Display         *display;
        Window          event;
        Window          window;
        int             x, y;
        int             width, height;
        int             border_width;
        Window          above;
        Boolean         override_redirect;
        }
XConfigureEvent;
```

type........................... Identification of the event type: `ConfigureNotify`.

serial......................... A count of the number of protocol requests processed by the server before this event was sent to the receiving client.

send_event..................... A flag indicating whether another client sent the event: it is `TRUE` if the event was sent with `XSendEvent`, `FALSE` is the event was sent directly from the server.

display........................ Identification of the server that sent this event; this is a pointer to the server's display structure. It is primarily useful when a client has connections open to more than one display.

window......................... The ID of the window that underwent configuration change.

x, y........................... The new position of the top-left corner of the window border, relative to window's parent. Note that the actual window position differs from this by `border_width` pixels.

width, height.................. The new dimensions of the window, not including the border.

border_width .... The width (height), in pixels, of the border
                                surrounding the window.

above .... The ID of the [sibling] window that this window is
                                immediately above. If at the bottom of the stack,
                                this member contains the value None.

override_redirect .... The override_redirect attribute of the
                                reconfigured window. Only useful for shells, this
                                value is identical to the overrideRedirect
                                resource.

ConfigureRequest

ConfigureRequest events are used primarily by the window manager, to control
the configuration of client windows. They are generated when
SubstructureRedirectMask is in effect for a given window and a client attempts to
change the size, position, border width, or stacking order for children of that
window.

When SubstructureRedirectMask is in effect, the configuration operation is not
performed by the original call. Instead, the event handler must perform the call
again — or ignore the event, to deny the request.

Listing C.9. Type definition: XConfigureRequestEvent

```
typedef struct
        {
        int             type;
        unsigned long   serial;
        Boolean         send_event;
        Display         *display;
        Window          parent;
        Window          window;
        int             x, y;
        int             width, height;
        int             border_width;
        Window          above;
        int             detail;
        unsigned long   value_mask;
        }
    XConfigureRequestEvent;
```

type .... Identification of the event type: ConfigureRequest.

`serial`	A count of the number of protocol requests processed by the server before this event was sent to the receiving client.
`send_event`	A flag indicating whether another client sent the event: it is `TRUE` if the event was sent with `XSendEvent`, `FALSE` if the event was sent directly from the server.
`display`	Identification of the server that sent this event; this is a pointer to the server's display structure. It is primarily useful when a client has connections open to more than one display.
`parent`	The ID of the window receiving the event — the parent of the window for which the request is made.
`window`	The ID of the window for which the change is requested.
`x, y`	The desired top-left position of the window. This position actually references the window border, so the actual window position is offset by `border_width`.
`width, height`	The desired dimensions of the window, not including the border.
`border_width`	The desired width (height), in pixels, of the window border.
`above`	Used with `detail` to specify the window's position in the stacking order, relative to its siblings. Contains the ID of one of the sibling windows. May contain `None`, which modifies the usage of the `detail` member.
`detail`	Specifies the relationship of the reconfigured window, relative to that of the sibling specified by `above` or the entire window stack. May contain one of the following constants:

```
Above, Below, TopIf, BottomIf, Opposite
```

If `above` contains a valid window ID, the actions are:

`Above`: The reconfigured window should be placed just above its sibling.

`Below`: The reconfigured window should be placed just below its sibling.

`TopIf`: The reconfigured window should be placed at the top of the stack if it is obscured by the sibling.

`BottomIf`: The reconfigured window should be placed at the bottom of the stack if it obscures the sibling.

`Opposite`: A combination of `TopIf` and `BottomIf`: if the reconfigured window obscures the sibling, it is placed at the bottom of the stack; if it is obscured by the sibling, then it is placed at the top of the stack.

If `above` contains the value `None`, the actions are:

`Above`: The reconfigured window should be placed at the top of the stack.

`Below`: The reconfigured window should be placed at the bottom of the stack.

`TopIf`: The reconfigured window should be placed at the top of the stack if it would be obscured by any other window.

`BottomIf`: The reconfigured window should be placed at the bottom of the stack if it would obscure any other window.

`Opposite`: Does not make sense in this situation.

`value_mask` .... A bit mask that specifies what configuration information should be changed. The following constants represent bits in this mask:

`CWX, CWY, CWWidth, CWHeight, CWBorderWidth, CWSibling, CWStackMode`

CreateNotify

CreateNotify events are generated when a window is created and may be received by any ancestor of the newly created window. Note that — unlike the other "notify" events — this event is only enabled by SubstructureNotifyMask; for the obvious reason, a window can't receive the event indicating its own creation.

Listing C.10. Type definition: *XCreateWindowEvent*

```
typedef struct
        {
        int             type;
        unsigned long   serial;
        Boolean         send_event;
        Display         *display;
        Window          parent;
        Window          window;
        int             x, y;
        int             width, height;
        int             border_width;
        Boolean         override_redirect;
        }
XCreateWindowEvent;
```

type................................ Identification of the event type: CreateNotify.

serial............................... A count of the number of protocol requests processed by the server before this event was sent to the receiving client.

send_event.......................... A flag indicating whether another client sent the event: it is TRUE if the event was sent with XSendEvent, FALSE if the event was sent directly from the server.

display............................. Identification of the server that sent this event; this is a pointer to the server's display structure. It is primarily useful when a client has connections open to more than one display.

parent.............................. The ID of the window receiving the event.

window.............................. The ID of the newly created window.

x, y .... The position of the top-left corner of the new
                              window's border.

width, height .... The new dimensions of the window, not including
                              the border.

border_width .... The width (height), in pixels, of the border
                              surrounding the window.

override_redirect .... The `override_redirect` attribute of the
                              reconfigured window. Only useful for shells, this
                              value is identical to the `overrideRedirect`
                              resource.

DestroyNotify

`DestroyNotify` events are sent just before a window is destroyed. They may be
received either by the window itself or its parent. Note that the event handler can
not prevent destruction of the window — by the time the program receives this
event, the window is already gone.

Listing C.11. Type definition: XDestroyWindowEvent

```
typedef struct
        {
        int              type;
        unsigned long    serial;
        Boolean          send_event;
        Display          *display;
        Window           event;
        Window           window;
        }
XDestroyWindowEvent;
```

type .... Identification of the event type: `DestroyNotify`.

serial .... A count of the number of protocol requests
                              processed by the server before this event was sent
                              to the receiving client.

send_event .... A flag indicating whether another client sent the
                              event: it is `TRUE` if the event was sent with
                              `XSendEvent`, `FALSE` if the event was sent directly
                              from the server.

display.......................... Identification of the server that sent this event;
this is a pointer to the server's display structure.
It is primarily useful when a client has
connections open to more than one display.

window.......................... The ID of the window that was destroyed.

EnterNotify, LeaveNotify

`EnterNotify` events are sent to a window when the pointer enters its area;
`LeaveNotify` events are sent when the pointer leaves its area. Each time the
pointer crosses a window border, both events are sent: `LeaveNotify` to the old
window and `EnterNotify` to the new window.

Listing C.12. Type definition: *XCrossingEvent*

```
typedef struct
        {
        int             type;
        unsigned long   serial;
        Boolean         send_event;
        Display         *display;
        Window          window;
        Window          root;
        Window          subwindow;
        Time            time;
        int             x, y;
        int             x_root, y_root;
        int             mode;
        int             detail;
        Boolean         same_screen;
        Boolean         focus;
        unsigned int    state;
        } XCrossingEvent;
```

type.......................... Identification of the event type: `EnterNotify` or
`LeaveNotify`.

serial.......................... A count of the number of protocol requests
processed by the server before this event was sent
to the client.

`send_event` .... A flag indicating whether another client sent the event: it is `TRUE` if the event was sent with `XSendEvent`, `FALSE` if the event was sent directly from the server.

`display` .... Identification of the server that sent this event; this is a pointer to the server's display structure. It is primarily useful when a client has connections open to more than one display.

`window` .... The ID of the window that handled the event. Due to propagation, this may or may not be the window where the event was first received (`subwindow`).

`root` .... The ID of the root window of the screen where the event occurred.

`subwindow` .... The ID of the window where the event actually occurred.

`time` .... The event's server timestamp — a count of milliseconds between the server start time and the time the event was sent to the client.

`x, y` .... The pointer position within the window receiving the event (`window`), measured in pixels. If the receiving window is not on the same screen as the window specified in `root` (`same_screen` contains `FALSE`), both `x` and `y` contain zero.

`x_root, y_root` .... The pointer's position relative to the root window at the time of the event. If the root window and the receiving window are not on the same screen, both `x_root` and `y_root` contain zero.

`mode` .... An indication of whether the event was generated as the result of user interaction or due to a grab or ungrab operation. Values are as below:

> `NotifyNormal`: The event was generated due to user action.
>
> `NotifyGrab`: The event was generated due to a grab.
>
> `NotifyUngrab`: The event was generated due to release of a grab.

`detail` .... An indication of the relationship between the old and new windows. Values are as below:

> `NotifyAncestor`: The other window is a direct-line ancestor of the window receiving the event.

> `NotifyInferior`: The other window is a direct-line descendent of the window receiving the event.

> `NotifyVirtual`: The window receiving the event is a direct-line relative of the windows involved in the crossing (but is not directly involved the crossing).

> `NotifyNonlinear`: The windows involved in the crossing (including the event recipient) are on different branches of the window tree.

> `NotifyNonlinearVirtual`: The window receiving the event is one of the relatives of the windows involved in the crossing, and those windows are on different branches of the window tree.

`same_screen` .... A flag indicating whether the receiving window (`window`) is on the same screen as the root window (`root`). This member will contain `FALSE` as the result of a pointer grab; usually it contains `TRUE`.

`focus` .... If `TRUE`, specifies that the receiving window had the focus (or has a child that had the focus) at the time of the event.

`state` .... The state of the modifier keys and pointer buttons, at the time of the event. This member is a bit mask, containing one or more of the following constants:

> `Button1Mask, Button2Mask, Button3Mask, Button4Mask, Button5Mask, ShiftMask, ControlMask, LockMask, Mod1Mask, Mod2Mask, Mod3Mask, Mod4Mask, Mod5Mask`

Expose

Expose events are sent to a window when portions of that window are no longer
obscured by another window. They identify the rectangular window portion that
must be redrawn. A single exposure may result in one or more Expose events,
each of which identifies one portion of the exposed window.

Listing C.13. Type definition: XExposeEvent

```
typedef struct
        {
        int             type;
        unsigned long   serial;
        Boolean         send_event;
        Display         *display;
        Window          window;
        int             x, y;
        int             width, height;
        int             count;
        }
XExposeEvent;
```

type.............................. Identification of the event type: Expose.

serial........................... A count of the number of protocol requests
                                  processed by the server before this event was sent
                                  to the client.

send_event...................... A flag indicating whether another client sent the
                                  event: it is TRUE if the event was sent with
                                  XSendEvent, FALSE if the event was sent directly
                                  from the server.

display......................... Identification of the server that sent this event;
                                  this is a pointer to the server's display structure.
                                  It is primarily useful when a client has
                                  connections open to more than one display.

window.......................... The ID of the window that was exposed.

x, y............................ The top-left corner of the exposed rectangle,
                                  relative to the window.

width, height................ The dimensions of the area that must be
                            redrawn.

count......................... The number of `Expose` events yet to be received
                            for this exposure. When this member contains
                            zero, the client has received all events associated
                            with this exposure. An optimized client will
                            redraw only those areas that require redrawing
                            and will wait until `count` contains zero to do so.

FocusIn, FocusOut

Focus events are sent to a window to report gain or loss of focus: `FocusOut` is
sent to the window losing focus at that same time that `FocusIn` is sent to the
window gaining focus. Note that these events simply *report* the change — they do
not permit the program to confirm or deny it.

Listing C.14. Type definition: *XFocusChangeEvent*

```
typedef struct
        {
        int               type;
        unsigned long     serial;
        Boolean           send_event;
        Display           *display;
        Window            window;
        int               mode;
        int               detail;
        }
XFocusChangeEvent;
```

type......................... Identification of the event type: `FocusIn` or
                            `FocusOut`.

serial....................... A count of the number of protocol requests
                            processed by the server before this event was sent
                            to the client.

send_event................... A flag indicating whether another client sent the
                            event: it is `TRUE` if the event was sent with
                            `XSendEvent`, `FALSE` if the event was sent directly
                            from the server.

`display` .... Identification of the server that sent this event; this is a pointer to the server's display structure. It is primarily useful when a client has connections open to more than one display.

`window` .... The ID of the window that received the event. This may or may not be the window that gained or lost focus. If not, the `detail` member specifies the relationship of the receiving window to the windows involved in the focus change.

`mode` .... An indication of whether focus was gained/lost as the result of user interaction from a grab or ungrab operation. Values are as below:

> `NotifyNormal`: The focus change was due to user action.

> `NotifyGrab`: The focus change was due to a grab.

> `NotifyUngrab`: The focus change was due to release of a grab.

`detail`......................... An indication of the relationship between the window gaining the focus and that losing the focus. Values are as below:

> `NotifyAncestor`: The other window is a direct-line ancestor of the window receiving the event.

> `NotifyInferior`: The other window is a direct-line descendent of the window receiving the event.

> `NotifyVirtual`: The window receiving the event neither gains nor loses the focus, but is a direct-line relative of the windows involved in the focus change.

> `NotifyNonlinear`: The windows involved in the focus change (including the event recipient) are on different branches of the window tree.

> `NotifyNonlinearVirtual`: The window receiving the event neither gains nor loses the focus, but is a relative of the windows that do — and those windows are on different branches of the window tree.

> `NotifyPointer`: The receiving window neither gains nor loses the focus, but happens to contain the pointer. This value only appears due to a grab.

> `NotifyPointerRoot`: Identical to `NotifyPointer`, used when the focus changes to or from the root window.

> `NotifyNone`: The focus has been set to `None` (no window). All windows receive a `FocusOut` event.

GraphicsExpose, NoExpose

These events are generated during a call to the functions `XCopyArea` and `XCopyPlane`, and then only when the `graphics_exposures` flag (in the GC) contains `TRUE`. `GraphicsExpose` indicates that the source drawable was obscured and that the program should explicitly draw into the destination. `NoExpose` indicates that the copy was performed without a problem. As with `Expose`, one or more `GraphicsExpose` events are generated, one for each area that could not be copied. If the copy was successful, only one `NoExpose` event is sent.

Note that these events are generated *only* if `graphics_exposures` contains `TRUE`. If this is the case, they are treated as nonmaskable events: they are passed to the window's event handler if it was registered with the `nonmaskable` parameter (of `XtAddEventHandler`) set to `TRUE`.

Listing C.15. Type definitions: *XGraphicsExposeEvent*, *XNoExposeEvent*

```
typedef struct
        {
        int             type;
        unsigned long   serial;
        Boolean         send_event;
        Display         *display;
        Drawable        drawable;
        int             x, y;
        int             width, height;
        int             count;
        int             major_code;
        int             minor_code;
        }
XGraphicsExposeEvent;


typedef struct
        {
        int             type;
        unsigned long   serial;
        Boolean         send_event;
        Display         *display;
        Drawable        drawable;
        int             major_code;
        int             minor_code;
        }
XNoExposeEvent;
```

`type`	Identification of the event type: `GraphicsExpose` or `NoExpose`.
`serial`	A count of the number of protocol requests processed by the server before this event was sent to the client.
`send_event`	A flag indicating whether another client sent the event: it is `TRUE` if the event was sent with `XSendEvent`, `FALSE` if the event was sent directly from the server.
`display`	Identification of the server that sent this event; this is a pointer to the server's display structure. It is primarily useful when a client has connections open to more than one display.
`drawable`	ID of the copy destination (window or pixmap).
`x, y`	The top-left corner of the exposed rectangle, relative to the area being copied. Note that these values are not necessarily relative to the source or destination, and must be translated appropriately.
`width, height`	The dimensions of the area that must be explicitly drawn.
`count`	The number of `GraphicsExpose` events yet to be received for this exposure. When this member contains zero, the client has received all events associated with this exposure. An optimized client will draw only those areas that require it, and will wait until `count` contains zero to do so.
`major_code`	The major code for the X protocol request that resulted in the event. Unless an extension has been loaded into the server, this value will be one of the constants `CopyArea` or `CopyPlane`. An extension may generate this event for other requests, and will use another value.
`minor_code`	The minor code for the X protocol request that resulted in the event. Unless an extension has been loaded into the server, this value will be zero. An extension may generate this event for other requests and may make use of nonzero values.

GravityNotify

`GravityNotify` events are sent to windows when their parents have been resized. They report the window's new position due to gravity-induced movement. This event is primarily of use to widget writers.

Listing C.16. Type definition: XGravityEvent

```
typedef struct
        {
        int             type;
        unsigned long   serial;
        Boolean         send_event;
        Display         *display;
        Window          event;
        Window          window;
        int             x, y;
        }
XGravityEvent;
```

`type` .... Identification of the event type: `GravityNotify`.

`serial` .... A count of the number of protocol requests processed by the server before this event was sent to the client.

`send_event` .... A flag indicating whether another client sent the event: it is `TRUE` if the event was sent with `XSendEvent`, `FALSE` if the event was sent directly from the server.

`display` .... Identification of the server that sent this event; this is a pointer to the server's display structure. It is primarily useful when a client has connections open to more than one display.

`event` .... The ID of the window that received the event.

`window` .... The ID of the window that was moved.

`x, y` .... The new position of the child (`window`), relative to its parent.

KeymapNotify

KeymapNotify events are sent to a window immediately after EnterNotify and FocusIn events and contain the state of the keyboard — what keys are pressed — at the time of focus change or window crossing. This information may also be retrieved with the XQueryKeymap function.

Listing C.17. Type definition: XKeymapEvent

```
typedef struct
        {
        int              type;
        unsigned long    serial;
        Boolean          send_event;
        Display          *display;
        Window           window;
        char             key_vector[32];
        }
XKeymapEvent;
```

type .... Identification of the event type: KeymapNotify.

serial .... A count of the number of protocol requests processed by the server before this event was sent to the client. The contents of this member are identical to the preceding EnterNotify or FocusIn event.

send_event .... A flag indicating whether another client sent the event: it is TRUE if the event was sent with XSendEvent, FALSE if the event was sent directly from the server.

display .... Identification of the server that sent this event; this is a pointer to the server's display structure. It is primarily useful when a client has connections open to more than one display.

window .... The ID of the window that received the focus or now contains the pointer.

key_vector .... A bit-map of the keyboard in which each set bit indicates a pressed key; the 256 bits in this map correspond to the 256 possible key codes. Each element of the array corresponds to key codes 8*N* (where *N* is the element number) to 8*N*+7. Bits within a byte are numbered from least significant (0) to most significant (7).

As an example, key code 23 (decimal) corresponds to array element 2 and is accessed with a mask of 0x80 (1<<7).

Key codes must be translated to keysyms before use.

KeyPress, KeyRelease

KeyPress events are generated whenever a key is pressed; a KeyRelease event is generated when that key is released. Both events are always sent to the window that currently has the focus. All keys generate such events, including modifier keys such as *Shift*. Note, however, that some servers do not support KeyRelease events; programs should not rely on their presence.

Listing C.18. Type definition: *XKeyEvent*

```
typedef struct
        {
        int              type;
        unsigned long    serial;
        Boolean          send_event;
        Display          *display;
        Window           window;
        Window           root;
        Window           subwindow;
        Time             time;
        int              x, y;
        int              x_root, y_root;
        unsigned int     state;
        unsigned int     keycode;
        Boolean          same_screen;
        }
    XKeyEvent;
```

`type` — Identification of the event type: `KeyPress` or `KeyRelease`.

`serial` — A count of the number of protocol requests processed by the server before this event was sent to the client.

`send_event` — A flag indicating whether another client sent the event: it is `TRUE` if the event was sent with `XSendEvent`, `FALSE` if the event was sent directly from the server.

`display` — Identification of the server that sent this event; this is a pointer to the server's display structure. It is primarily useful when a client has connections open to more than one display.

`window` — The ID of the window that handled the event. Due to propagation, this may or may not be the window where the event was first received (`subwindow`).

`root` — The ID of the root window of the screen where the event occurred.

`subwindow` — The ID of the window where the event actually occurred — this is the window that has the input focus.

`time` — The event's server timestamp — a count of milliseconds between the server start time and the time the event was sent to the client.

`x, y` — The pointer position within the window receiving the event (`window`), measured in pixels. If the receiving window is not on the same screen as the window specified in `root` (`same_screen` contains `FALSE`), both `x` and `y` contain zero.

`x_root, y_root` — The pointer's position relative to the root window at the time of the event. If the root window and the receiving window are not on the same screen, both `x_root` and `y_root` contain zero.

state .... The state of the modifier keys and pointer
                                buttons at the time of the event. This member is a
                                bit mask containing one or more of the following
                                constants:

> `Button1Mask, Button2Mask, Button3Mask,`
> `Button4Mask, Button5Mask, ShiftMask,`
> `ControlMask, LockMask, Mod1Mask,`
> `Mod2Mask, Mod3Mask, Mod4Mask, Mod5Mask`

keycode .... The keycode of the key that was pressed
                                (released). This is a server-dependent value and
                                must be converted to a keysym before use.

same_screen .... A flag indicating whether the receiving window
                                (`window`) is on the same screen as the root window
                                (`root`). This member will contain `FALSE` as the
                                result of a pointer grab; usually it contains `TRUE`.

MapNotify, UnmapNotify

`MapNotify` events are generated when a window is mapped; `UnmapNotify` events
are generated when it is unmapped. These events are sent to the window that is
mapped/unmapped and are propagated up the window tree until handled — or
until they reach the root window, where they are discarded.

Listing C.19. Type definition: *XMapEvent*

```
typedef struct
        {
        int             type;
        unsigned long   serial;
        Boolean         send_event;
        Display         *display;
        Window          event;
        Window          window;
        Boolean         override_redirect;
        }
XMapEvent;


typedef struct
        {
        int             type;
        unsigned long   serial;
        Boolean         send_event;
        Display         *display;
        Window          event;
        Window          window;
        Boolean         from_configure;
        }
XUnmapEvent;
```

type .... Identification of the event type: `MapNotify` or `UnmapNotify`.

serial .... A count of the number of protocol requests processed by the server before this event was sent to the client.

send_event .... A flag indicating whether another client sent the event: it is `TRUE` if the event was sent with `XSendEvent`, `FALSE` if the event was sent directly from the server.

display .... Identification of the server that sent this event; this is a pointer to the server's display structure. It is primarily useful when a client has connections open to more than one display.

`event` .... The ID of the window that received the event. Due to propagation, this may or may not be the same as the window being mapped or unmapped (window).

`window` .... The ID of the window that is being mapped or unmapped.

`override_redirect` .... (`MapNotify` only) The value of the `override_redirect` attribute of the newly mapped window — only useful for shells, it is identical to the `overrideRedirect` resource.

`from_configure` .... (`UnmapNotify` only) Used to indicate whether the window was unmapped because its `win_gravity` attribute was `UnmapGravity` (and its parent was resized). If so, this member will contain `TRUE`; it usually contains `FALSE`.

MappingNotify

`MappingNotify` is sent to all windows when one of the server's internal physical-to-logical mappings (keycode to keysym, keycode to modifier, or button) is changed. Such changes occur due to calls to `XChangeKeyboardMapping`, `XSetModifierMapping`, or `XSetPointerMapping`; the *xmodmap* client is a prime generator of such calls.

Note that this event *is not* generated due to window mapping/unmapping. Note also that it is sent to all windows, is nonmaskable, but is rarely of use to program level code (it is, however, of interest to widget internal code).

Listing C.20. Type definition: XMappingEvent

```
typedef struct
        {
        int             type;
        unsigned long   serial;
        Boolean         send_event;
        Display         *display;
        Window          window;
        int             request;
        int             first_keycode;
        int             count;
        }
    XMappingEvent;
```

type................................ Identification of the event type: `MappingNotify`.

serial.............................. A count of the number of protocol requests processed by the server before this event was sent to the client.

send_event..................... A flag indicating whether another client sent the event: it is `TRUE` if the event was sent with `XSendEvent`, `FALSE` if the event was sent directly from the server.

display........................... Identification of the server that sent this event; this is a pointer to the server's display structure. It is primarily useful when a client has connections open to more than one display.

window.......................... The ID of the window receiving this event. Every window receives this event, so this member may be ignored.

request.......................... Identifies the type of remapping that generated this event. May contain one of the following constants:

    `MappingKeyboard`, `MappingModifier`,
    `MappingPointer`

first_keycode............... For keyboard and modifier mapping, this member specifies the first keycode affected by the remap. It is not used for pointer remapping.

count.............................. For keyboard and modifier mapping, this member specifies the number of keycodes — starting with `first_keycode` — affected by the remap. It is not used for pointer remapping.

MapRequest

`MapRequest` events are used primarily by the window manager to control the mapping of client windows. They are generated when `SubstructureRedirectMask` is in effect for a given window and a client attempts to map a child of that window.

When `SubstructureRedirectMask` is in effect, the map operation is not performed by the original call. Instead, the event handler must perform the call again — or ignore the event, to deny the request.

Listing C.21. Type definition: *XMapRequestEvent*

```
typedef struct
        {
        int             type;
        unsigned long   serial;
        Boolean         send_event;
        Display         *display;
        Window          parent;
        Window          window;
        }
XMapRequestEvent;
```

type........................... Identification of the event type: `MapRequest`.

serial......................... A count of the number of protocol requests processed by the server before this event was sent to the client.

send_event..................... A flag indicating whether another client sent the event: it is `TRUE` if the event was sent with `XSendEvent`, `FALSE` if the event was sent directly from the server.

display........................ Identification of the server that sent this event; this is a pointer to the server's display structure. It is primarily useful when a client has connections open to more than one display.

parent......................... The ID of the window receiving the event — the parent of the window for which the request is made.

window......................... The ID of the window requesting to be mapped.

MotionNotify

`MotionNotify` events are generated whenever the pointer moves within a window and are sent to the window in which the pointer moved. If not handled by that window, they are propagated up the window tree and discarded at the root window. `MotionNotify` events are also generated by a pointer "warp" — pointer movement resulting from a call to `XWarpPointer`.

The server attempts to closely track the motion: sending an event for each pixel moved by the pointer. If the client performs a large amount of processing for each motion event, its response time would be degraded by a long movement, which generates lots of events. To avoid this problem, it may request that movement be reported as "hints" instead of discrete motion events.

Motion hints are enabled by specifying an event mask that contains both `PointerMotionMask` and `PointerMotionHintMask`. When hints are enabled, pointer motion is reported by a single event. "Pointer motion" in this case means a series of `MotionNotify` events, without other intervening events: motion starts with the first `MotionNotify` and ends with the first nonmotion event. The motion hint is sent at the end of the motion, but will not necessarily contain the correct pointer position; the program must call `XQueryPointer` to determine the correct position.

Note that `MotionNotify` events are generated *only* when movement begins and ends within a single window. If the motion begins in one window and ends in another, `EnterNotify` and `LeaveNotify` events are generated instead.

Listing C.22. Type definition: XMotionEvent

```
typedef struct
        {
        int             type;
        unsigned long   serial;
        Boolean         send_event;
        Display         *display;
        Window          window;
        Window          root;
        Window          subwindow;
        Time            time;
        int             x, y;
        int             x_root, y_root;
        unsigned int    state;
        char            is_hint;
        Boolean         same_screen;
        }
    XMotionEvent;
```

type........................... Identification of the event type: `MotionNotify`.

serial......................... A count of the number of protocol requests processed by the server before this event was sent to the client.

`send_event` .... A flag indicating whether another client sent the event: it is `TRUE` if the event was sent with `XSendEvent`, `FALSE` if the event was sent directly from the server.

`display` .... Identification of the server that sent this event; this is a pointer to the server's display structure. It is primarily useful when a client has connections open to more than one display.

`window` .... The ID of the window that handled the event. Due to propagation, this may or may not be the window where the event was first received (`subwindow`).

`root` .... The ID of the root window of the screen where the event occurred.

`subwindow` .... The ID of the window where the event actually occurred.

`time` .... The event's server timestamp — a count of milliseconds between the server start time and the time the event was sent to the client.

`x, y` .... The pointer position within the window receiving the event (`window`), measured in pixels. Note that, if this event is a hint, the position is that at the time of the event — the program must query the server to get the actual position.

`x_root, y_root` .... The pointer's position relative to the root window.

`state` .... The state of the modifier keys and pointer buttons, at the time of the event. This member is a bit mask, containing one or more of the following constants:

> `Button1Mask, Button2Mask, Button3Mask, Button4Mask, Button5Mask, ShiftMask, ControlMask, LockMask, Mod1Mask, Mod2Mask, Mod3Mask, Mod4Mask, Mod5Mask`

`is_hint` .... A flag indicating whether this event is a hint or an actual motion event. It may be one of the following constants:

> `NotifyNormal, NotifyHint`

same_screen .... A flag indicating whether the receiving window
(window) is on the same screen as the root window
(root). This member will contain FALSE as the
result of a pointer grab; usually it contains TRUE.

PropertyNotify

PropertyNotify events are sent to a window to indicate that a property attached
to that window has been changed or deleted. If not handled by the window itself,
they are propagated up the window tree and discarded at the root window.

Note that, prior to X11R4, PropertyNotify events were often used to determine
the current server time. This was accomplished by performing a zero-length
append on a property, which would not change the property but would generate
an event. As of R4, the toolkit stores the timestamp from the most recently
received event.

Listing C.23. Type definition: *XPropertyEvent*

```
typedef struct
        {
        int             type;
        unsigned long   serial;
        Boolean         send_event;
        Display         *display;
        Window          window;
        Atom            atom;
        Time            time;
        int             state;
        }
XPropertyEvent;
```

type .... Identification of the event type: PropertyNotify.

serial .... A count of the number of protocol requests
processed by the server before this event was sent
to the client.

send_event .... A flag indicating whether another client sent the
event: it is TRUE if the event was sent with
XSendEvent, FALSE if the event was sent directly
from the server.

`display` .... Identification of the server that sent this event; this is a pointer to the server's display structure. It is primarily useful when a client has connections open to more than one display.

`window` .... The ID of the window to which the changed property belongs. Note that this may not be the window that received the event — unlike most other events, this event does not explicitly identify the receiver.

`atom` .... An atom identifying the changed property.

`time` .... The event's server timestamp — a count of milliseconds between the server start time and the time the event was sent to the client.

`state` .... Indication of the type of change. May be `NewValue`, indicating that the property was created, changed, or appended-to; or `Deleted`, indicating that the property was removed from the window.

ReparentNotify

`ReparentNotify` events are generated when a window's parent changes: when the window is moved to a new point in the window tree. This most often happens when the window manager takes a client window under its control by making it the child of a frame window.

Listing C.24. Type definition: XReparentEvent

```
typedef struct
        {
        int             type;
        unsigned long   serial;
        Boolean         send_event;
        Display         *display;
        Window          event;
        Window          window;
        Window          parent;
        int             x, y;
        Boolean         override_redirect;
        }
    XReparentEvent;
```

type.............................. Identification of the event type: `ReparentNotify`.

serial.............................. A count of the number of protocol requests processed by the server before this event was sent to the client.

send_event...................... A flag indicating whether another client sent the event: it is `TRUE` if the event was sent with `XSendEvent`, `FALSE` if the event was sent directly from the server.

display.............................. Identification of the server that sent this event; this is a pointer to the server's display structure. It is primarily useful when a client has connections open to more than one display.

window.............................. The ID of the window that was reparented

parent.............................. The ID of the new parent window.

x, y.............................. The position of the reparented window, relative to its new parent.

override_redirect.......... The `override_redirect` attribute of the reparented window. This should always contain `FALSE` — if it contains `TRUE`, the window was incorrectly reparented (it should have been left alone).

ResizeRequest

`ResizeRequest` events are used primarily by the window manager to control the size of client windows. They are generated when `SubstructureRedirectMask` is in effect for a given window and a client attempts to change the size of a child of that window.

When `SubstructureRedirectMask` is in effect, the resize operation is not performed by the original call. Instead, the event handler must perform the call again — or ignore the event to deny the request.

Listing C.25. Type definition: XResizeRequestEvent

```
typedef struct
        {
        int             type;
        unsigned long   serial;
        Boolean         send_event;
        Display         *display;
        Window          window;
        int             width, height;
        }
    XResizeRequestEvent;
```

type........................... Identification of the event type: `ResizeRequest`.

serial......................... A count of the number of protocol requests processed by the server before this event was sent to the client.

send_event..................... A flag indicating whether another client sent the event: it is `TRUE` if the event was sent with `XSendEvent`, `FALSE` if the event was sent directly from the server.

display........................ Identification of the server that sent this event; this is a pointer to the server's display structure. It is primarily useful when a client has connections open to more than one display.

window......................... The ID of the window to be resized.

width, height.................. The desired dimensions of this window.

SelectionClear

`SelectionClear` events are sent to a selection owner by the server to indicate that selection ownership has changed. They are automatically generated by calls to `XtOwnSelection` and `XSetSelectionOwner`.

Note that, although the receiving window has lost the selection, any pending transfer must be completed.

Listing C.27. Type definition: *XSelectionClearEvent*

```
typedef struct
        {
        int             type;
        unsigned long   serial;
        Boolean         send_event;
        Display         *display;
        Window          window;
        Atom            selection;
        Time            time;
        }
XSelectionClearEvent;
```

type............................ Identification of the event type: `SelectionClear`.

serial.......................... A count of the number of protocol requests processed by the server before this event was sent to the client.

send_event...................... A flag indicating whether another client sent the event: it is `TRUE` if the event was sent with `XSendEvent`, `FALSE` if the event was sent directly from the server.

display......................... Identification of the server that sent this event; this is a pointer to the server's display structure. It is primarily useful when a client has connections open to more than one display.

window.......................... The ID of the window that is losing the selection (the receiver of this event).

selection....................... An atom identifying the selection type.

time............................ The server time when the receiver lost the selection.

SelectionNotify

`SelectionNotify` events indicate that a selection has been delivered to a requestor. They are always sent from one client to another, never from the server to a client. This event is nonmaskable and is always delivered to the window requesting a selection.

This event is always sent as part of a selection transfer, and certain members are filled from the `SelectionRequest` event that initiated the transfer. Specifically: `selection`, `target`, and `property`.

Note that this event is sent *after* the data has been successfully stored. To confirm storage, the sender should accept `PropertyNotify` events on the destination window. This rule is modified for the incremental transfer protocol, specified by the ICCCM to avoid large data exchanges.

Listing C.26. Type definition: XSelectionEvent

```
typedef struct
        {
        int             type;
        unsigned long   serial;
        Boolean         send_event;
        Display         *display;
        Window          requestor;
        Atom            selection;
        Atom            target;
        Atom            property;
        Time            time;
        }
XSelectionEvent;
```

type .... Identification of the event type: `SelectionNotify`.

serial .... A count of the number of protocol requests processed by the server before this event was sent to the client.

send_event .... A flag indicating whether another client sent the event. It always contains `TRUE`.

display .... Identification of the server through which this event was sent; this is a pointer to the server's display structure. It is primarily useful when a client has connections open to more than one display.

requestor .... The ID of the window that requested the selection. This should be the ID of the event receiver.

selection .... An atom identifying the selection type.

`target`	An atom identifying the data type of the stored selection.
`property`	An atom identifying the property in which the selection data was stored.

While this member is usually filled from the corresponding `SelectionRequest` event, there are several cases where it may contain `None`. The first is if the selection owner could not provide the selection data as the desired type (as specified by `target`). The second is if the selection owner was unable to store the property, due to a server error (such as lack of memory). The third is that the requestor sent its request to an invalid owner (*ie*, the request time was outside the range in which the owner owned the selection).

Note that the receiver is responsible for deleting the data when it is no longer needed. Once the data is delivered, the selection owner no longer touches it.

`time`	The time that the selection was stored in the destination. This is often sent as `CurrentTime` — it is one of the few places where use of `CurrentTime` is acceptable.

SelectionRequest

`SelectionRequest` events are sent from one client to another to request the contents of a named selection. They are nonmaskable, and are typically sent from the `XConvertSelection` function.

Listing C.28. Type definition: XSelectionRequestEvent

```
typedef struct
        {
        int             type;
        unsigned long   serial;
        Boolean         send_event;
        Display         *display;
        Window          owner;
        Window          requestor;
        Atom            selection;
        Atom            target;
        Atom            property;
        Time            time;
        }
XSelectionRequestEvent;
```

`type` .... Identification of the event type: `SelectionRequest`.

`serial` .... A count of the number of protocol requests processed by the server before this event was sent to the client.

`send_event` .... A flag indicating whether another client sent the event: it is always `TRUE` for this event.

`display` .... Identification of the server through which this event was sent; this is a pointer to the server's display structure. It is primarily useful when a client has connections open to more than one display.

`owner` .... The ID of the window that owns the selection. This must be set by the sender or the event will not be delivered; it is set automatically by `XConvertSelection`.

`requestor` .... The ID of the window requesting the selection.

`selection` .... An atom identifying the selection type.

target   An atom identifying the desired data type for the
                          selection data. This is used by the owner to
                          convert from its internal format to a format that
                          the requestor can use. If unable to perform this
                          conversion, the sender may refuse to send the
                          selection data.

property   An atom identifying the property in which the
                          selection data should be stored.

                          An obsolete convention is to use target to
                          identify the property, and to pass None in
                          property. Clients are encouraged to support this
                          convention, but such support is not required.

time   The time that the requestor sent this event. This
                          is a server timestamp and should be used by the
                          selection owner to verify that the requestor sent
                          the request to the correct owner (*ie*, it should
                          check the send time against the time that it
                          received the selection).

VisibilityNotify

VisibilityNotify events are sent to a window whenever its visibility status
changes. Such changes happen because the window is obscured (or was
obscured) by another window, *not* because the window was mapped or
unmapped.

Listing C.30. Type definition: XVisibilityEvent

```
typedef struct
        {
        int               type;
        unsigned long     serial;
        Boolean           send_event;
        Display           *display;
        Window            window;
        int               state;
        }
XVisibilityEvent;
```

type   Identification of the event type: VisibilityNotify.

serial .... A count of the number of protocol requests processed by the server before this event was sent to the client.

send_event .... A flag indicating whether another client sent the event: it is TRUE if the event was sent with XSendEvent, FALSE if the event was sent directly from the server.

display .... Identification of the server that sent this event; this is a pointer to the server's display structure. It is primarily useful when a client has connections open to more than one display.

window .... ID of the window that underwent a visibility change.

state .... The current visibility state. Values as below:

> VisibilityUnobscured: The window was partially or completely obscured; now it is unobscured.
>
> VisibilityPartiallyObscured: The window is now partially obscured, due to movement of another window. It may have been unobscured, partially obscured, or completely obscured prior to this movement.
>
> VisibilityFullyObscured: The window is completely obscured. It may have been unobscured, partially obscured, or completely obscured previously by a window other than the one that completely obscures it now.

Appendix D
Changes In X And Motif

Overview

While this book was written for X11 Release 3 and Motif 1.0, the fact remains that these versions are obsolete. This appendix, therefore, provides a selection of the improvements that were added for X11 Releases 4 and 5, and Motif 1.1 — the versions that were current as this book went into production.

From Motif 1.0 to 1.1

Lots of Bug Fixes

While this topic may seem to be in questionable taste, it is important to recognize. While Motif 1.0 did not have an inordinate amount of bugs for a software project of its size, Motif 1.1 has significantly fewer. For this reason alone, you should upgrade to 1.1 if possible.

If not, be aware that "memory leaks" are especially prevalent in 1.0 — some the fault of Motif, some the fault of X. Note also that not all functions act as advertised — the clipboard interface is a prime example.

New Widget Class: XmTextField

The *XmTextField* class is a single-line text widget designed for entry fields. It contains much of the *XmText* single-line functionality, without the overhead needed to support multiline editing and scrollbars.

Changes to Existing Widget Classes

Many existing widget classes have been changed — some slightly, others drastically. Most of these changes have been to appearance (*eg,*

XmFileSelectionBox) or to default resource values. A few of the changes have been the addition or deletion of resources (*eg*, addition of the *XmPushButton* resource `defaultButtonShadowThickness`).

In general, this book is not affected by such changes. In some cases, however, it may not describe the best possible technique due to concerns of backward compatibility.

New Library Functions

The Motif 1.0 *Programmer's Reference* contains 930 pages, while the 1.1 edition contains 1,212 pages. While some of these pages represent revised documentation and some are dedicated to the *XmTextField* widget class, the majority are devoted to new library functions.

Many of the new functions are convenience functions for existing widgets: *XmList* provided 15 convenience functions for 1.0 but 25 in 1.1, while *XmText* went from 10 to 31. It should be noted that some of these functions — particularly those associated with *XmText* — were present in 1.0, but simply not documented.

Another area of increase is functions dedicated to menu creation. The functions `XmCreateSimpleMenuBar`, `XmCreateSimplePulldownMenu`, `XmCreateSimplePopupMenu`, `XmCreateSimpleOptionMenu`, and their varargs counterparts allow the programmer to create a complete menu structure — buttons and all — with a few function calls.

Virtual Event Bindings

If you are working with 1.1, you might have been confused in Chapters 8 and 9, where the default translations for *XmPushButton* and *XmText* were presented — this book bears no relationship to the 1.1 *Programmer's Reference*. Instead of event sequences like `<Btn1Up>`, the *Programmer's Reference* uses sequences like `BSelect Press`.

The latter is a virtual binding and provides an additional level of indirection between a widget's actions and the events that invoke those actions. The Motif translation manager automatically translates virtual bindings into physical event bindings at runtime.

Motif is configured with bindings appropriate to each vendor's equipment, but these bindings may be overridden in one of two ways. The first is with the file `.motifbind`, which contains mappings between virtual and physical events. If used, this file must be present in the user's home directory; it is read whenever a Motif client starts.

The second method is with the application resource `defaultVirtualBindings`. This resource, if used, contains a set of virtual-to-physical mappings exampled by Listing D.1. Note that, like the `translations` resource, each mapping occupies its own line, and lines are separated by newline characters.

Listing D.1. Example settings for *defaultVirtualBindings* resource

```
*defaultVirtualBindings:                                              \
            KBackTab      : Shift<Key>Tab                      \n\
            KTab          : <Key>Tab
```

Program-Controlled Traversal

As described in Chapter 13, under *Grabbing and Assigning the Input Focus*, Motif 1.0 had a limited mechanism for assigning input focus: `_XmGrabTheFocus`. With 1.1, a program has complete access to the traversal mechanism via `XmProcessTraversal`. This technique is described in Chapter 13.

Conversion Between Compound Strings and Compound Text

The Motif compound string is a method of encapsulating character-set information along with the text to which it applies. The ICCCM makes use of a similar compound-text format, defined in the document *Compound Text Encoding*. The primary use of this format is interclient data exchange: for maximum portability, each client should be able to convert between compound text and its internal text format.

The X miscellaneous utilities library provides functions to convert between normal strings and compound text, and Motif provides functions to convert between Motif compound strings and compound text. These functions are prototyped in Listing D.2: `XmCvtCTToXmString` converts compound-text data to a compound string, and `XmCvtXmStringToCT` converts a compound string to compound text. In both cases, the compound-text data is accessed with a normal character pointer.

Listing D.2. Function prototypes: *XmCvtCTToXmString, XmCvtXmStringToCT*

```
XmString     XmCvtCTToXmString( ctext )
             char          *ctext;


char         *XmCvtXmStringToCT( xms )
             XmString     xms;
```

From X11 Release 3 to Release 4

Derivation of Core from Object, RectObj, and WindowObj

Core is the root of the R3 intrinsics class tree. Motif, with its use of gadgets, breaks *Core* into three parts: *Object*, *RectObj*, and *WindowObj*. Widgets are derived from all three components, while gadgets are derived from *Object* and *RectObj* only.

R4 incorporates this new derivation of *Core*, providing direct support for "nonwidget objects" — but doesn't itself define any such objects. The result is that Motif will now peacefully coexist with other widget sets: it uses the same Xt library, and programs can mix Motif widgets with non-Motif widgets.

Interclient Communications Conventions

As of R3, the ICCCM was a proposed standard. While many clients honored its conventions, they were not required to do so. For R4, not only is the ICCCM a true standard, it has been revised and expanded, with more thought given to areas such as client/window-manager communication.

Shared Libraries

Release 4 marked the use of shared libraries, by which multiple applications can share a single copy of a library function. This reduces the size of programs both on-disk and in-memory: instead of actual library code, programs using a shared library simply contain references to that library.

There are two drawbacks to the use of shared libraries. The first is that the library must be installed for a program to run — it's no longer self-contained. This problem is often discovered at a large installation, typically when new machines are purchased.

The second problem with a shared library occurs if a shared function uses static data. Some shared library implementations share this static data, meaning that each program attempts to use — and modify — a single data item. This is especially a problem with the toolkit for the reason described below.

Use of Application Context Now Required

The *application context* is a data structure internal to the intrinsics, which contains program-level information. This information includes a list of the open display connections, program-level callback lists (*eg*, timeouts), program-specific resource converters, pointers to the various error handlers, and other information used by the intrinsics to maintain a program.

The application context structure has been a part of the intrinsics since Release 3, but was largely ignored by R3 programs. This happened primarily because the

Xt library contains a default application context structure, which is all that was needed by most programs.[1] This book follows that habit.

With Release 4 and shared libraries, however, this default application context structure could no longer be used: the default structure is a static data item, which would be used and modified by all programs using the library. For those installations that do not use shared libraries, portability concerns still make the use of a program-specific application context a high priority.

Many programs require only two changes: replacement of `XtInitialize` by `XtAppInitialize` and replacement of `XtMainLoop` by `XtAppMainLoop`. Both of these functions are prototyped below in Listing D.3.

The primary change to the initialization function is the replacement of the program name by a pointer to an `XtAppContext` variable. `XtAppInitialize` creates a unique application context and stores a pointer to this context in the referenced variable. It retrieves the program name from the argument list, so it does not need to be passed explicitly.

Listing D.3. Function prototype: *XtAppInitialize*
XtAppMainLoop

```
Widget   XtAppInitialize( context, class, options, num_opts, argc, argv )
         XtAppContext         *context;
         char                 *class;
         XrmOptionDescRec     options[];
         Cardinal             num_opts;
         Cardinal             *argc;
         char                 *argv[];


void     XtAppMainLoop( context )
         XtAppContext         context;
```

As stated above, these functions are the only two that must be changed in a typical program. All widgets are associated with an application context at time of creation, so widget-related functions can determine the application context — default or unique — from the widget's internal data.[2]

Since the application context is used for most toolkit operations, those functions that do not work with widgets must have their context explicitly specified. Such functions include those to register timeouts and workprocs, as well as resource converters. In this book, such functions have used the default application context. As with `XtInitialize`, however, each such function has a version —

---

[1] A disincentive to use of a program-specific application context was that a program couldn't use `XtInitialize`. Instead, it had to perform the job of `XtInitialize` and explicitly call the various initialization functions. For R4, `XtAppInitialize` is present.

[2] When a widget is created, it is associated with the same application context as its parent. The application shell is associated with an application context by `XtAppInitialize`, meaning that that context is used for all widgets in the instance tree.

identified by "App" in its name — that makes use of an explicit application context.

Table D.1 lists the explicit-application-context functions identified by their "default" versions; due to space constraints, it does not provide detail information. Note also that some of these functions were not covered in this book (*eg*, `XtError`/`XtAppError`), and some are called by other functions, not by program code (*eg*, `XtCreateShell`/`XtAppCreateShell`, which is called by `XtInitialize`/`XtAppInitialize`).

Table D.1. List of functions that require application context

"Default" Function	App-Context Function
XtAddActions	XtAppAddActions
XtAddConverter	XtAppAddConverter
XtAddInput	XtAppAddInput
XtAddTimeOut	XtAppAddTimeOut
XtAddWorkProc	XtAppAddWorkProc
XtCreateShell	XtAppCreateShell
XtError	XtAppError
XtErrorMsg	XtAppErrorMsg
XtGetErrorDatabase	XtAppGetErrorDatabase
XtGetErrorDatabaseText	XtAppGetErrorDatabaseText
XtGetSelectionTimeout	XtAppGetSelectionTimeout
XtMainLoop	XtAppMainLoop
XtNextEvent	XtAppNextEvent
XtPeekEvent	XtAppPeekEvent
XtPending	XtAppPending
XtProcessEvent	XtAppProcessEvent
XtSetErrorHandler	XtAppSetErrorHandler
XtSetErrorMsgHandler	XtAppSetErrorMsgHandler
XtSetSelectionTimeout	XtAppSetSelectionTimeout
XtSetWarningHandler	XtAppSetWarningHandler
XtSetWarningMsgHandler	XtAppSetWarningMsgHandler
XtWarning	XtAppWarning
XtWarningMsg	XtAppWarningMsg

Resource Conversion Mechanism

The Release 4 resource conversion mechanism represents a giant leap forward from Release 3. As indicated in Chapter 16, its most obvious new features are a new cache mechanism and the ability to allocate memory inside a converter — and have that memory properly deallocated by the resource manager.

Items not noted in Chapter 16 include the fact that resource converters now return a `Boolean` result to indicate whether or not the conversion could be performed. Also, converters now take a `Display` pointer as their first parameter; it is used to retrieve the appropriate application context. Finally, the method of direct invocation has changed: `XtConvert` has been replaced by `XtCallConverter`.

Fallback Resource Values

An additional step has been added to the task of building a resource database: loading fallback resources from program code. Unlike "hard-wired" resources, fallback resources are defaults used only when no other specification is applicable. In essence, they are equivalent to a program-specific defaults file that is encoded into the program. Fallback resources may be specified in the call to `XtAppInitialize` or with the function `XtAppSetFallbackResources`.

Variable-Argument Functions

ANSI C codifies a technique long used by C hackers: using the addressing capabilities of C to allow a function to have a variable argument list. An example of such a function is `printf`, which can accept an unlimited number of arguments; the format string specifies the number and type of each argument.

The Release 4 toolkit uses this 'varargs' capability to allow specification of resource values in a function call, replacing the argument arrays used by this book. Such functions are identified by a name that starts with "XtVa", rather than "Xt". They are best explained by example: Listing D.4 shows the use of `XtVaSetValues`, a replacement for `XtSetValues`.

Listing D.4. Use of *XtVaSetValues*

```
Widget      w;                          /* XmText widget           */
    .

    .

    .
XtVaSetValues( w, XmNheight, 50, XmNwidth, 100, NULL );
```

As you can see, this function specifies resources as a list of name/value pairs terminated by `NULL`. Any varargs function needs to determine the end of its list; `printf` uses its format string, while the toolkit functions use `NULL`. If you omit the `NULL` entry, the function will continue to access "arguments" from essentially random memory locations — stopping when it by chance finds a memory location that contains `NULL`.

You should note that varargs interfaces are not fully supported by Motif. While the Intrinsics provide a varargs widget creation function (`XtVaCreateWidget`), Motif does not provide such functions (*ie*, there is no `XmVaCreateText`). Motif does, however, make use of varargs functions for one-step menu creation, with `XmVaCreateSimpleMenuBar` and its relatives.

New Function: XtLastTimestampProcessed

While many operations — such as acquiring selection ownership — require a server timestamp, versions of X prior to Release 4 had no simple way to retrieve such a timestamp. If a callback happened to contain a timestamped event, you were in luck. If not, you would have to find some way to retrieve one: a classic method was performing a zero-length property append, and trapping the resulting `PropertyNotify` event.

Release 4 provides the function `XtLastTimestampProcessed`, prototyped in Listing D.5. When a timestamped event — such as a button or movement event — is received, its timestamp is stored. It is retrieved with `XtLastTimestampProcessed`, which uses a display pointer to identify the timestamp source.[3] You should note that there is no guarantee that the returned timestamp will be up to date: if the program has not received a timestamp-bearing event in three seconds, the returned timestamp value is three seconds old.

Listing D.5. Function prototype: *XtLastTimestampProcessed*

```
Time    XtLastTimestampProcessed( display )
        Display    *display;
```

From X11 Release 4 to Release 5

Internationalization

Release 5 includes features to simplify the internationalization of programs, allowing them to be configured for different countries with minimal effort. The primary effect on the programmer is that characters may now occupy 16 bits, rather than 8. This was described in Chapter 9, in reference to the *XmText* callback structures. This feature is not yet implemented in Motif.

---

[3] Different displays will have different timestamps for the same point in time, due to different start times.

Addition of Font Server and Font Scaling

These items are of primary interest to users and administrators; neither affect the programmer directly. The addition of a font server means that physical font data need not be stored permanently on a display server: it will retrieve fonts from the font server as needed. Font scaling is a method for describing a font mathematically, allowing the server to produce any size "on the fly." It means that a user is not limited in the selection of font sizes to those bitmaps supported by the server.

Changes to Resource Search Path

While Motif has supported an internationalized resource search path — using the `LANG` environment variable — for some time, this path is now part of the intrinsics. In addition, the user is now allowed greater flexibility in specifying a unique search path via the `XFILESEARCHPATH` and `XUSERFILESEARCHPATH` environment variables.

A final — somewhat esoteric — change is that the resource manager now associates resources with a particular screen of a display, allowing separate resource specifications on a per-screen basis. This feature is most useful with software such as Apple's Mac-X, which uses screen numbers to control window attributes: one screen is for monochrome windows, one is for color. In this environment, program that makes extensive changes to the resource database (a topic not covered in this book) must explicitly identify the screen. Again, for most programs, this is handled automatically by `XtAppInitialize`.

New Resource Component: '?'

In most resource files, a loose binding is used to wildcard the program's class name. However, since a loose binding substitutes for zero or more components in a resource specification, if two widgets have the same name, it will have greater effect than desired — the same specification is applied to both.

For Release 5, the resource manager recognizes a question mark as substituting for a single component in the resource specification. This is illustrated by Listing D.6, in which it is used to represent the program class name (with a loose binding for comparison).

Listing D.6. Example use of '?' resource component

```
?.TheLabel.background:   White
*.TheLabel.background:   Black
```

Use of #include *in Resource Files*

Resource files may now incorporate other named files, using the #include notation shown in Listing D.7. Unlike the #include directive of the C preprocessor, there is no default search path for the resource manager: the included file's name must be completely specified, or it is assumed to be located relative to the current directory. If the resource manager finds the file, its contents replace the line containing the #include specification.

Listing D.7. Example use of '?' resource component

```
! Get the test resources
#include    testresources.TextEdit
```

Other notes about the #include specification are that whitespace may appear between "#" and "include", that "#" must be the first character on the line, and that "include" must be specified in lowercase. The first two notes are interesting in that they indicate that "#" may become a general directive specification — providing an additional incentive not to use it for a comment.

New Resource: baseTranslations

To add flexibility to widget translation modification, the baseTranslations psuedo-resource has been added. This resource takes precedence over the widget's class translations, but is subordinate to an explicit specification for the translations resource. It is designed for use in system-wide application defaults files, leaving translations available for a user's changes.

Appendix E
Where To Go For More Information

Overview

While this book has tried to present most of what you need to know to write a Motif program, there's always more to learn. The X book market is growing daily, and while my editor will not permit me to mention competitors' books, some of them are quite good — after you've bought and read this book. In addition to "how to" books, both the Open Software Foundation and the X Consortium have manuals that are indispensable to a full-time X programmer. Finally, there are various support groups, filled with people who will console you when things don't go right — and then help you to make them go right.

Documentation

X Documentation

There is an enormous amount of documentation that comes as part of the X window system. At the risk of offending those who have spent the last several years working on it, I must say that it varies from very good to not-so-good. However, it is filled with valuable information and is, in my opinion, an indispensable reference.

The following documents are a selection of those available. As stated above, they are part of the X source distribution and are present as both *troff* source files and PostScript output. If your vendor did not provide you with X source, you might have to retrieve them as described below.

- *Inter-Client Communications Conventions Manual*

  This document describes the mechanisms by which X clients are expected to interact. Most of its contents are of interest to widget writers, but some topics are of interest to all programmers. It is certainly not a book to read in one sitting, and most topics require some meditation before use.

- *Xlib — C Language X Interface*

  As you might expect, this document describes the Xlib programming interface. It is targeted at those who are writing applications in Xlib, but also contains information (such as event processing) useful to all programmers. If you plan to use Xlib with Motif, it is a good reference, although you might have to look in several places for information. It has been rewritten for Release 5, with the goal of logical presentation.[1]

- *X Toolkit Intrinsics — C Language Interface*

  This document describes the X toolkit and the internal structure of widgets. It is more useful to a widget writer than an application programmer, but does describe those toolkit functions used by client programs.

- *X Logical Font Description Conventions*

  This document describes the font naming conventions. Chapter 5 of this book presented these conventions from an application programmer's perspective; the XLFD is more of a rigorous specification.

- Manual Pages

  The X manual pages essentially provide an extract of information from the above documents. They do have the benefit of gathering information that may be distributed in the source volume. Unfortunately, they are not distributed in PostScript form; you will have to run *troff* to produce printed output.

Motif Documentation

The Open Software Foundation has published several books about Motif. Of these, I consider the following two to be indispensable.

- *OSF/Motif Programmer's Reference*

  This is the authoritative book on the Motif programming environment. It describes each widget class, its resources, default translations, callbacks, and any related convenience functions. While it is occasionally inaccurate, it is certainly the most definitive reference available.

- *OSF/Motif Style Guide*

  This book specifies how a Motif client should appear and describes the techniques used to achieve that appearance. Be certain that you buy the 1.1 edition (or later): it is significantly improved from the 1.0 version.

---

[1] As I am still working with Release 4, I have not spent much time with the new book. From its table of contents, however, I believe that it is indeed organized in a more logical fashion than the R4 version.

Mailing Lists/NetNews

A network mailing list is like a large user group that communicates via e-mail, containing members from all over the world. Mailing-list members range from novices to the people responsible for writing the software — people from OSF and the X Consortium are regular contributors to the X mailing lists.

As denoted by the heading, the general topic of mailing lists has two faces: actual mailing lists and NetNews. True mailing lists are implemented with mail "repeaters": central mailboxes that rebroadcast all received messages to the people on the list. This method is costly in both disk space and network bandwidth because a copy of each message is sent to each recipient. NetNews is a refinement of the mailing list: messages are stored on a site-wide basis and are read from that central repository by interested people.

There are three "newsgroups" that will be of interest to readers of this book: *comp.windows.x*, *comp.windows.x.motif* and *comp.windows.x.announce*. The first two are general discussion groups: *comp.windows.x* is concerned with all areas of X, while *comp.windows.x.motif* is limited to discussion of Motif-specific items. Both groups have a high message traffic: 100+ messages per day for *comp.windows.x.motif* and over 250 per day for *comp.windows.x*. The final newsgroup, *comp.windows.x.announce*, is used solely by the X Consortium to announce important information about the X software — such as the date of a new release.

While most midsize and larger sites have a NetNews "feed," smaller sites may have to rely on mailing lists. If this is the case with your site, you should ask your system administrator to set up local redistribution. Assuming that you're not the only interested reader, this will minimize the number of messages sent from the central mailbox to your site.[2]

The newsgroups listed above are "gatewayed" to mailing lists: each message posted to the newsgroup is passed on to the list, and vice versa. The *comp.windows.x* newsgroup is associated with the *xpert* mailing list, the *comp.windows.x.motif* newsgroup is associated with the *motif* mailing list, and *comp.windows.x.announce* is associated with *xannounce*. Other lists are available for topics ranging from X and the Amiga to Open Look.

Each of these lists handles subscription requests in the same way: you send a mail message to a subscription mailbox, and you are added to the list. The subject line of this message contains the list name in capital letters, followed by "addition request". The body of the message must contain the mailbox address of your local distribution node. The mailing list and subscription addresses are shown in Table E.1. Note that you *do not* send subscription requests to the mailing list address. Note also that the *xannounce* list does not permit individual recipients; you must provide a local distribution address.

---

[2] You might also learn that a local distribution facility is already in place.

Table E.1. Mailing lists, with subscription addresses

List	List Address	Subscription Address
xpert	`xpert@expo.lcs.mit.edu`	`xpert-request@expo.lcs.mit.edu`
motif	`motif@alfalfa.com`	`motif-request@alfalfa.com`
xannounce	`xannounce@expo.lcs.mit.edu`	`xannounce-request@expo.lcs.mit.edu`

The FAQs

"FAQ" stands for "Frequently Asked Questions," and The FAQs are monthly publications in the *comp.windows.x* and *comp.windows.x.motif* newsgroups. These publications contain a collection of questions, ranging from simple to complex, along with suggested answers from experienced users. They are designed to both minimize the repetition of such questions and to provide a communal reference.

Both publications are released on or about the first of each month; each month they are updated with material collected during that month. Since the volume of newsgroup traffic is so high, they are typically removed from a site's news directory within a week. If you have Internet FTP access, you can retrieve copies of both from `export.lcs.mit.edu`.[3] Both are found in the `/contrib` directory; the Motif FAQ is named `Motif-FAQ`, while the general X FAQ is simply named `FAQ` (`FAQ.Z` is compressed and is one-half the size of the uncompressed version).

Getting X and Motif Software

The X software is copyrighted but publicly available. Motif, on the other hand, is commercial software. Most UNIX computer systems come with a binary version of X, and systems from OSF members usually come with a binary version of Motif.

X Sources

If you desire the X sources, you have several options. The first and easiest is to copy them from someone you know. The second, available if you have network access, is to download them from an archive server. These servers store the distribution in compressed TAR files, occupying about 45 megabytes while compressed, and 130 uncompressed.[4] Two of the better-known archive servers are `export.lcs.mit.edu` (18.24.0.12) and `ftp.uu.net` (137.39.1.9).

---

[3] Note: *not* `expo.lcs.mit.edu`.

[4] These numbers are for R4, and include both the core distribution and contributed programs. The R5 core distribution alone occupies 32 megabytes compressed.

The final option for X distribution software is to contact the X Consortium directly, at the address below. Distribution is available in a limited selection formats — primarily 9-track magnetic tape.

Bob Scheifler
MIT X Consortium
Laboratory for Computer Science
545 Technology Square
Cambridge, MA 02139

Motif

Motif is a commercial product, but OSF members typically provide binary licenses with their equipment. If your computer maker is not a member of OSF — or doesn't provide you with a copy of Motif — you may be able to get a version from Integrated Computer Solutions, at the address listed below. As of this writing, they offer Motif for Apple Macintosh, Sun 3 and 4, DECStation/RISC, Sony NEWS, and Silicon Graphics Iris.

Integrated Computer Solutions
201 Broadway
Cambridge, MA 02139

E-mail: *info@ics.com*

If, on the other hand, you desire Motif source, you will have to contact the Open Software Foundation directly, at the address below.

Open Software Foundation
11 Cambridge Center
Cambridge, MA 02142

Getting this Book's Sample Programs

If you don't like to type and have a network connection, you can retrieve this book's sample programs from the following sources. They examples are stored in a compressed TAR file, which occupies about 100k in compressed and 300k in uncompressed form.

From *export.lcs.mit.edu*: In the `/contrib` directory, under the name `pwm-xmpl.tar.Z`.

From *uunet.uu.net*: In the `/published` directory, under the name `pwm-examples.tar.Z`.

Glossary

<table>
<tr><td>accelerator</td><td>An event that is received by one widget but processed by another. In the common usage, menu choices are associated with accelerator keys; when the appropriate key sequence is entered, the menu choice is invoked.

Note that the X toolkit provides one accelerator mechanism, while Motif provides another. The X mechanism is more general, allowing any event to be piped from one widget to another, but requires these pipes to be specified by program code. The Motif method applies to menu choices only and is limited to key events, but may be specified in a resource file.</td></tr>
<tr><td>action</td><td>A program function that is identified by name and may be linked to an event sequence in a translation table. Actions may be viewed as an extension of the callback mechanism, although in practice callbacks are often invoked by actions.</td></tr>
<tr><td>action dialog</td><td>A type of message box that notifies the user that intervention is needed by the program. This is also known as an error dialog.</td></tr>
<tr><td>action table</td><td>An array that associates a program's functions with action names. This table is installed with the function <code>XtAddActions</code>.</td></tr>
<tr><td>activation</td><td>The act "pressing" a Motif button — clicking the pointer button while positioned over the screen button.</td></tr>
<tr><td>application context</td><td>A data structure that contains program-level context information, such as a list of open display connections. The intrinsics provides a default application context, but this should only be used by programs running under X11R3 (because it could be improperly shared by the libraries of R4).</td></tr>
</table>

application modal   A condition in which the application limits the user to a limited set of prescribed actions, specifically those associated with a *dialog box*. The user is, however, able to work with a different application.

application resource   A program variable that is set via the resource file. Application resources are specified in the program code, and loaded using the mechanism provided for widget resources.

application shell   The root of a program's *instance tree*. It is a *top-level shell* and is responsible for negotiating with the *window manager* to determine the size of the program's *client area*.

arm   The act of "pressing and holding" a Motif button — pressing but not releasing the pointer button while positioned over the screen button.

Arming is the first half of *activation*, but the button may be *disarmed* without activating the button.

atom   A server resource ID that represents a text string.

Atoms provide the basis for interclient communication via the server: when a client registers a character string with the server, that string is permanently associated with an atom ID; any other client that registers the same string will be given the same ID.

One of the primary benefits of atoms is that they reduce the client-server communication load by replacing an arbitrarily long text string with a 32-bit resource ID.

attachment   The method used to position the child of an *XmForm* widget.

Each side of the child has an associated attachment constraint. That constraint may specify that the child's side is to be attached to the same or opposite side of the parent, to the same or opposite side of another widget, at a relative position based on the form's size, to a fixed position, or not at all (no attachment).

backing store

A region of server memory that is used to store obscured portions of windows.

When the windows are exposed, their contents are filled from the backing store; the program does not receive `Expose` events. While the use of backing store reduces client-server communication (and client processing time), it is not supported by all servers and is a finite resource when supported. For this reason, no client should be written with the assumption that exposure processing will be obviated by backing store.

bitmap

A rectangular array of monochrome pixels. Since each pixel is either on or off, it may be represented by a single bit.

Bitmaps may be contained in files created using the *xbitmap* client, or as an array defined in the program. Data in a bitmap is stored in row-major order: the first byte of the bitmap corresponds to the leftmost eight pixels of the top row of the image. Bits are represented in a byte from most significant to least significant: the high-order bit of the first byte of the bitmap corresponds to the top-left pixel in the image.

blocking

The condition in which an I/O function (such as `read`) waits for I/O to commence. For reading, this is the wait for a buffer to fill; for writing, the wait for previous buffers to be physically written. When a program blocks, its execution is suspended until it can perform the operation — an X client in this state does not process events.

browse selection

See *list selection modes*.

callback

A program function invoked by a widget — a "call back into program code." Also refers to the situation responsible for invocation of this function (*eg*, "activation callback").

Callbacks may be viewed as "expected events," representing the primary functions of a widget. A pushbutton, for example, has callbacks for *arming*, *disarming*, and *activation*. It does not have callbacks for other events, such as button motion, because these events are not part of the pushbutton's function.

callback list   The list of functions maintained by a widget for a particular callback.

A widget provides a resource for each for its callbacks. This resource holds a list of functions, all of which are called whenever the callback action occurs. Functions are added to this list with `XtAddCallback` and removed with `XtRemoveCallback` or `XtRemoveAllCallbacks`.

cascading menu   A pull-down menu that is invoked from another pull-down menu, providing additional detail.

check box   A toggle button used to indicate on/off data. Connotes a group of toggle buttons, representing related but individual data items; any number of buttons in group may be on, as contrasted to *radio buttons*.

child   Applies to a widget in an instance tree: that widget's children are the widgets that are immediately connected but at a lower level in the tree (farther from the root).

class   The definition of an object, as opposed to its *instance*. *Class* connotes general appearance and action, whereas *instance* connotes specifics.

In a typical object-oriented language, an object's class consists of its data definition and methods. Widgets follow this definition: a widget class defines the capabilities of the widget, along with the internal data structures that support those capabilities.

Programs are also classed (see *program class name*). A program's class indicates its executable file; an instance of the program is the code and data as they appear in memory while running.

Finally, *class* may be used to group things with similar data and use, as with resources. Although resources are not objects, classing is a way to distinguish between an abstract resource type (*eg,* "pixmap") and the specific uses of that type of resource (`backgroundPixmap` and `topShadowPixmap`).

class pointer

The pointer to a widget's *class record*.

This pointer is used to identify a widget's class. It is used in places such as the *XmRowColumn* resource `isHomogeneous`, which limits the children of a row-column to a particular class.

Each widget class has a predefined class-pointer variable, declared by its class-specific header file. This name of this variable is typically formed by changing the initial "X" of the widget's class name to "x" and adding the suffix "WidgetClass" (*eg*, the name of the class pointer for *XmPushButton* is `xmPushButtonWidgetClass`).

class record

An internal widget data structure that contains information common to all instances of a class. This information consists of a widget's resource descriptions, as well as pointers to its internal functions.

class tree

A representation of the derivation of a group of objects. The root of the tree is the most basic object class. Each class represents either a branch or a leaf in the tree: if the class is *subclassed*, it is a branch, otherwise it is a leaf.

The *RectObj* and *Object* widget classes together form the root of the Motif class tree. The *Core* class is the trunk, with the *XmGadget* class a branch that diverges at the roots. Classes such as *XmPrimitive* and *XmManager* form the branches, with the leaves being classes such as *XmArrowButton*.

client

A program that uses the X Protocol for communication with a *server*.

client area

That part of a client's top-level window that is maintained by the client. It is surrounded by the *window frame*, which is maintained by the window manager.

clip window

Part of a scrolled window (*XmScrolledWindow*). The clip window holds the currently displayed part of the *work window*.

clipboard

A standard X client (*xclipboard*) that holds data for use by other clients.

The clipboard is an extension to the *selection* mechanism. Normally, two clients exchange the contents of a selection in real time. The clipboard is a third client: the first client sends data to the clipboard, then the second client reads that data from the clipboard. This allows the data to be held over a long period of time and means that the first client does not need to be running for the data to be retrieved by the second client.

Whereas widgets typically handle the *primary* and *secondary* selections transparently, the program must explicitly interact with the clipboard.

colormap

An array containing RGB values used to minimize the amount of space consumed by a display's memory map.

Instead of specifying each pixel by its 24-bit RGB value, a colormap-based system identifies colors by their colormap index — in most cases, this is an 8-bit value. The colormap trade-off is reduced memory usage *vs* limited color selection (256 colors for an 8-bit colormap).

Colormaps are stored on the server and accessed by server resource ID. In most cases, widget-based programs do not need to handle colormaps directly: such operations are performed by the widget's internal code.

column-major

A method of accessing a rectangular array in which a linear list of items is placed into the array by columns: the first item is in the top left position, the second item is below the first, and so on.

In Motif, "column-major" is typically used to describe a vertically oriented *XmRowColumn* widget.

command area

That part of a Motif client's top-level window that is used for direct command input. It is supported by the *XmMainWindow* widget, but many programs do not use it.

command line

The command entered by a user to execute a program, which specifies the program's name and its arguments. Under C, the command line is referenced via the `main` function's `argc` and `argv` parameters.

compound string   Motif's implementation of character strings, represented by the `XmString` data type.

Compound strings consist of segments that specify text, character set, and directional information. A single string may have many such segments, or it may have only two (text and character set).

confirmation area   The part of a dialog that allows the user to confirm his/her actions, usually by pressing a button. See also *presentation area*.

constraint   Any rule that a manager widget uses to impose resource values on its children.

Explicit Geometry Constraints are resources defined by the manager but accessed as if defined by the child. Such resources directly affect the contents of the child's `x`, `y`, `width`, and `height` resources. An example is the `topAttachment` resource of *XmForm*.

Implicit Geometry Constraints are resources defined by the manager that indirectly affect the size and position of the child. An example is the `marginHeight` resource of *XmBulletinBoard* — only those children that would overlap the margin are affected by the constraint.

Nongeometry Constraints are resources defined by the manager that affect the values of child resources other than `x`, `y`, `width`, and `height`. An example is the `labelFontList` resource of *XmBulletinBoard*, which imposes a value on the `fontList` resource of any children derived from *XmLabel*.

Note that *dynamic* resources, such as `background`, are not considered constraints. In the case of dynamic resources, the child retrieves the value stored in the parent's identical resource; the parent does not impose a value on the child.

control   A widget, such as a pushbutton, that allows a user to invoke a program action via a physical action (in the case of the pushbutton, by clicking).

conversion cache   A cache maintained by the *resource manager* to hold converted resource values.

Use of this cache improves the speed both of conversions that must be performed many times, as well as conversions that are performed few times but require a long time to perform (such as those that require communication with the server).

default colormap   A *colormap* that is by default given to windows created on a particular screen. If all clients use the default colormap, then the appearance of the screen need not change when a client becomes topmost — something that does happen when clients use individual colormaps.

defaults file   Another name for *resource file.* The term "defaults file" connotes that the resources specified by the file are default values and may be overridden by command-line specifications or other resource files.

derivation   The process of creating one class from another class. The created class incorporates all data and code of the existing class, treating such as its own. Also known as *subclassing.*

destructor   A function that is responsible for deallocating memory associated with an object.

The *resource manager* of X11R4 allows *resource converters* to have associated destructors, meaning that they may freely allocate memory for the conversion. The destructor is called when the associated widget is destroyed to destroy the memory allocated by the converter.

dialog   An auxiliary window, which allows a program to present information that is not appropriate in its main window.

An example of such information is a warning message, which could be "lost" if presented in the program's main window. Another would be a special-purpose operation, such as a text editor's "find" command, which would not be in constant use.

dialog modality   A way of referring to the impact that a dialog has on the user. It may be *modeless,* indicating that it coexists with the other windows on the screen; *application modal,* indicating that it prevents interaction with other windows associated with its client; or *system modal,* which indicates that it takes control of the user's display and prevents interaction with any other screen windows.

dialog shell   A shell widget used to provide a link between a program dialog and the root window. Dialog shells are similar to *application shells* in their interaction with the window manager.

disarm

Applies to Motif buttons. The act of releasing the pointer button after the screen button has been *armed*. If the pointer is within the area of the screen button when the pointer button is released, the screen button is both disarmed and *activated*. If the pointer is outside the area of the screen button, the button is disarmed without activation.

drawable

An object to which the program may direct Xlib drawing commands. A drawable is an abstract object; at present, the only real drawables are *windows* and *pixmaps*.

encapsulation

The technique of "hiding" an object's internal data and code. Access to this hidden data and code is provided by the object's *methods* — its external interface.

Applied to Motif, a widget encapsulates the code and data used to maintain its appearance and interaction, with access provided by the widget's resources.

error dialog

A *message box* used to inform the user of a program error. Also known as an *action dialog*.

event

The method by which an X client receives input.

The server sends each client a steady stream of events, generated either by the user or by another client. The client is expected to respond to each type of event in an appropriate manner: an `Expose` event prompts the client to redraw its window, while a `KeyPress` event provides the client with typed input.

event handler

A program function that is tasked to receive and process a particular set of events.

event mask

A bit-mask that selects the event types processed by a particular *event handler*.

event queue

The set of events that have been sent from the server to the client but have not yet been processed by the client. Each client has its own event queue, which may contain few or many events (depending on how often it is read and how many events are being sent). Each event is delivered to the client in the order in which it occurs.

explicit geometry constraint

See *constraint*.

extended selection

See *list selection modes*.

file filter

A partial path specification, which defines the search parameters for a *file selection box*.

focus   See *input focus.*

font family   A set of character designs based on common characteristics. Also known as a *typeface.*

                          For example: *Times* is a font family, *Times Roman* and *Times Italic* are fonts from that family.

grab   The act of redirecting the pointer or focus from one client to another.

                          In some cases, this may be very useful: *xwd*, for example, grabs the pointer so that it receives input when the user clicks on another window. In most cases, however, grabs are not expected by the user and should be avoided.

graphical user   A user interface implemented using graphics, as
interface   opposed to a user interface implemented using characters (textual user interface).

                          The primary advantage of a *GUI* is that it looks better than a *TUI.* This advantage exists because the interface designer is able to focus the user's attention using graphical techniques. For example: a word processor is able to visually separate its menu bar from its input area by making the menu appear as a series of buttons. In a textual user interface, even with different colors to differentiate the menu bar from the text area, the uniform size of the characters tends to leave the user's eye without direction.

                          Second, a graphical user interface usually provides a "what you see is what you get" (*WYSIWYG*) appearance. Again using a word processor as an example: the user's productivity is increased (and the number of test pages is decreased) if the text appears on screen in its final form.

                          Finally, a graphical user interface is typically designed to make the user interact with the program. Users have a "pointing device," such as a mouse, and most programs require usage of the mouse for program input (such as selecting a menu item).

graphics context   A data structure used by the server to control the operation of Xlib *graphics primitives.* It contains information common to many primitives, such as the foreground color, minimizing the parameters that must be passed to a specific primitive.

graphics primitive

A command used to draw a "low-level" graphical figure, such as a line or an arc. These commands are known as "primitives" because all complex objects may be drawn with a combination of these commands (for example, a decagon is simply a set of ten lines).

GUI

See *graphical user interface.*

hardware colormap

The *colormap* used by the actual display hardware, to convert `Pixel` values into RGB tuples. In many cases, its contents are identical to the *default colormap.*

implicit geometry constraint

See *constraint.*

information dialog

A *message box* used to provide the user with information of a noncritical nature. Unlike an *action dialog* or a *question* dialog, it does not normally provide the user with the ability to control program flow (*ie*, its buttons do not invoke actions other than to close the dialog).

inheritance

A description of the *derivation* of a class.

input focus

The method used by the server to direct keyboard events to a single window. The server keeps track of which window has the focus and sends all key events to that window. Clients may be assigned the focus as the result of user interaction, or they may explicitly *grab* the focus.

insertion point

For an *XmText* widget, the blinking line that indicates where characters are to be inserted.

instance

An example of a *class*. A class consists of data definitions and code. An instance of that class is the in-memory data associated with those definitions. A class may have multiple instances, and each instance may contain different data.

instance tree

A representation of the parent-child relationships between a program's widgets. The application shell is the root of the tree, managers with children are the branches, and primitive widgets (and managers without children) are the leaves. Also known as the *management tree.*

instantiation

The process of creating an instance of a class.

In Motif, instantiation of a widget class is performed by calling the class' creation function (*eg*, `XmCreateLabel`).

intrinsics

See *X intrinsics.*

ISO Latin 1   A character set defined by the International Standards Organization (ISO), containing the characters in use in the United States. It is a superset of the ASCII character set.

See Appendix A.

keysym   A symbolic representation of a keyboard key. Keysyms are required because each server identifies physical keys by different methods. By referring to keys by symbolic names, the program is not tied to a particular vendor's keyboard.

list selection modes   The method in which items may be selected from an *XmList* widget.

Single selection specifies that only one item may be selected at any time. When an item is selected, any previous item is deselected.

Browse selection is a refinement of *single selection* that allows the user to "drag" over several items in the list. Each item is highlighted when the pointer passes over it; the item highlighted when the button is released is selected. Like single-selection mode, only one item may be selected at a time; dragging, however, does not deselect the currently selected item.

Multiple selection allows the user to select multiple items, by clicking on each in turn. Items must be explicitly deselected.

Extended selection is a refinement of multiple selection, and allows the user to select contiguous items by dragging the pointer. Additionally, it allows the selection of noncontiguous blocks, by holding the *Shift* key down while making a selection.

loose binding   A method of wildcarding widget or class names in resource files. A loose binding, represented in the resource file by a star (*) separating two parts of a widget's name, indicates an ancestor-descendent relationship with any number (zero to infinite) of relatives in the middle.

major dimension   The dimension in which a row-column widget "prefers" to grow.

This "preference" is a result of the row-column's orientation: a vertical row-column prefers to grow vertically, whereas a horizontal row-column prefers to grow horizontally.

management   The process by which a child's geometry is brought under control of its parent.

management tree   See *instance tree*.

manager   A widget capable of having children and managing the geometry of those children. In general, managers are subclasses of *Composite*; in the Motif environment, they are also subclasses of *XmManager*.

mapping   The process by which a widget is made visible.

maximize   The process of increasing a window to the full size of the screen. The Motif window frame contains a button that allows the user to do this (it is also a choice on the window menu). See also *minimize*.

menu   A user-interface construct that permits the user to select a single choice from several provided, typically using the pointer.

The Motif environment supports four types of menus, all of which use buttons to select actions. The menu bar is a horizontal row of buttons at the top of the screen; arming one of these buttons causes a "pull down" menu to appear. A pull-down menu is a vertical column of menu choices, attached physically and logically to one of the choices in the menu bar. A pop up menu is a vertical or horizontal set of buttons, which is invoked by another widget and which appears at the current pointer position. An option menu presents a label, a current value, and a vertical selection of pushbuttons that appear when the user presses the pointer button while the pointer is positioned over the current value.

menu accelerator   A key sequence that invokes a menu item from anywhere in the program. This key sequence is specified by a resource of that menu item, and is automatically handled by the Motif resource manager.

The menu accelerator mechanism is both easier to use and more specific in operation than the standard X *accelerator* mechanism.

menu bar   A horizontally oriented set of buttons, located at the top of a client's *client area*. Each button, when pressed, activates a pull-down menu pane.

The primary benefit of a menu bar is that it is always available to the user — choices may be selected from the menu bar in a *modeless* manner.

menu shell   A type of *shell* that provides an interface between a pull-down or pop-up menu pane and the root window.

message The method by which an object's *methods* are invoked.

message box A dialog box used to display a message, which allows for a yes/no reply to that message. Such dialogs are built with the *XmMessageBox* class.

method The code that manipulates an object's data. Methods are internal to the object, are defined as part of the object's *class*, and are invoked by *messages*.

minimize To iconify a client's window. Minimization, like *maximization*, is invoked by the user via either a button on the *window frame* or a choice in the *window menu*.

minor dimension The dimension in which a row-column widget does not "prefer" to grow.

This "preference" is a result of the row-column's orientation: a vertical row-column prefers to grow vertically, whereas a horizontal row-column prefers to grow horizontally. However, if the row-column is prevented from growing in its preferred direction (*major dimension*), it must grow in its nonpreferred direction: a vertical row-column adds another column, a horizontal row-column adds another row.

mnemonic A one-character code used to activate a menu choice. A mnemonic is only active when the associated menu choice is visible, unlike a *menu accelerator*.

modeless In general, "modelessness" is a condition in which the user may perform one of many relevant actions. It is the antonym of *modal*, the condition in which the user must perform a specific action. One of the design goals of a good user interface is that it be modeless.

See also *dialog modality*.

multiple selection See *list selection modes*.

nongeometry constraint See *constraint*.

object An abstract programming entity consisting of both data and code.

An object's *class* defines the structure of the object's data, as well as the program code that manages that data. An *instance* of the object is an actual embodiment of the object data in the program's memory space. The object's code, being part of the class definition, is shared among all instances of the class.

object-oriented programming

A programming paradigm in which data structures combine data and functions (*methods*). These functions are invoked by *messages*, and the object's interface is represented by the set of messages that it is designed to interpret. Normal program code is not permitted direct access to an object's internal data.

One tenet of object-oriented is the separation of *class* and *instance*: a class is the object's data definition and associated code, while an instance of the class is a particular set of data. Another is *inheritance*, or *derivation*, by which new objects are built from existing objects.

OOP

See *object-oriented programming*.

Open Software Foundation

A consortium of vendors dedicated to producing a standard version of the UNIX Operating System, named OSF/1. Motif is the graphical user interface for this operating system.

option menu

A menu used to set a single data item. An option menu consists of a label identifying the data item, a cascade-button that both invokes the menu's pull-down pane and displays the current value of the item, and a pull-down pane that allows the user to set the item's value.

OSF

See *Open Software Foundation*.

parent

Applies to a widget in an instance tree: that widget's parent is the widget that is immediately connected but at a higher level in the tree (closer to the root).

pipe

A unidirectional method of interprocess communication, in which the file interface is used to connect two processes running on the same system. Data written at one end of the pipe is read from the other.

pixel

The unit subdivision of a display screen or image. All screen images are comprised of one or more pixels. On a black-and-white monitor, pixels are either "on" or "off"; on a color monitor, pixels are a set color. The size of a pixel depends on the resolution of the screen; common sizes provide resolution of 75 dots-per-inch and 100 dots-per-inch.

Pixels are addressed by their position on the screen; the top-left pixel is assigned a position of 0,0.

pixmap

An object maintained by the server that can accept drawing commands, but that does not display its contents. A pixmap may be thought of as a hidden window that does not generate events.

point size A method of measurement, traditionally applied to text. One *point* is roughly equal to $\frac{1}{72}$ inch.

pointer The X term for a mouse or any similar pointing device. The pointer provides a client with position-specific information; it also provides up to five buttons, used to trigger program actions.

Note that the pointer is both a physical device and an abstract user-interface object.

pop-up menu A menu that appears under the pointer, allowing immediate access. It is typically (when supported) invoked by pressing pointer button #3.

presentation area That part of a dialog that presents information and allows for user input. See also *confirmation area*.

primary selection One of the standard X *selections*. Used by the *XmText* widget for exchange of textual data with other clients/widgets.

primitive *Widgets*: A widget that acts on its own and cannot contain children — any widget derived from *XmPrimitive*. *XmLabel*, *XmPushButton*, and *XmText* are all examples of primitive widgets.

Graphics operations: A simple graphics call, such as that to draw a line. Complex graphics tasks — such as drawing a box — may be built from primitives.

program class name A name used to identify the resources belonging to a particular client. This name is used to identify program-specific *resource files* as well as in the selection of a widget's resource specifications.

prompt dialog A limited *selection box*, which provides the user with a message, a place in which to enter a textual reply to that message, and buttons with which to select an action associated with the reply.

propagate A description of the method used to handle events received by a window that does not have a registered event handler.

If an event (such as a button press) occurs in a window that does not have an appropriate event handler, it is passed (propagated) to the window's parent. It makes its way up the window tree in this fashion, until it is either handled by a window or passes to the root window (where it is discarded).

property See *window property*.

pull-down menu A type of menu that is invoked in response to the user's interaction with a cascade button. Pull-down menus are used in conjunction with the menu bar, as well as with option menus. They may also be invoked from other pull-down and pop-up menus, a technique known as *cascading pull-downs*.

quad width The width of the widest character in a font. This is also known as the *em-width*, since the widest character in a standard font is the capital 'M'.

quark A 32-bit integer that uniquely identifies a character string, within the context of a particular client. Quarks are used primarily by the resource manager to minimize the time spent in comparing resource (and widget) name strings.

See also *atom*.

question dialog A type of *message box*, used to present the user with a simple yes/no question and accept his/her reply.

radio buttons A group of buttons, related such that only one may be "on" at any given time. The *XmRowColumn* and *XmToggleButton* classes together provide support for radio buttons.

raster display A display technology that forms images out of discrete *pixels*.

realization The process of creating a window for a widget. Before realization, the widget exists solely within the client; after realization, it has both client and server components.

representation type A name associated with a data type, used by the resource manager to identify the source and destination types for conversion.

Representation type names are represented by constants defined in the header file `Xm/Xm.h`. Each of these constants begins with the prefix "XmN". While most data types have a one-to-one relationship with a representation type name, some (such as `unsigned char`) may have multiple associated representation types — each providing context for a particular conversion.

resource

A widget data value that is accessible to the program and is used to control the appearance and/or operation of its widget.

Resources are defined by the widget *class*, but are associated with a particular *instance*. They may be set at the time of widget creation using a *resource file*, or changed/examined at any time during a program's operation, using the functions `XtGetValues` and `XtSetValues`.

resource class

A method of grouping individual widget resources so that related resources may be set using a single reference.

resource converter

A function that converts data from one type to another (also known as a *type converter*). Used by the resource manager, primarily to convert the ASCII text of a resource file into a resource's internal data type.

resource database

The collection of resource specifications that apply to a particular program. This database is built from multiple resource files, ranging in scope from those that affect all clients to those particular to a client. It is used to set the initial value of a widget's resources.

resource file

An ASCII file that contains resource specifications, which are loaded into the *resource database* at the time of program startup.

The use of resource files allows a program to be customized easily, by means of changes to the appropriate file — there is no need for recompilation.

root window

The root of a server's *window tree*, owned by the *window manager*.

row-major

A method of accessing a rectangular array in which a linear list of items is placed into the array by rows: the first item is in the top left position, the second item is to the right of the first, and so on.

In Motif, "row-major" is typically used to describe a horizontally oriented *XmRowColumn* widget.

sash

A control used to adjust the pane size of a paned window. A sash is a square control, similar to a pushbutton; one is placed between every two children of the paned window.

scroll region

The "background" of a scrollbar. The scroll region is the area in which the slider moves, and represents the total scrollable area of the viewed data.

scrollbar

A control used to provide "position" interaction. Used primarily in cases where all of a program's output will not fit in the allocated window; scrollbars allow the user to move pieces of the data into or out of the window.

secondary selection

One of the X standard *selections*.

secondary window

A window that contains information that is auxiliary to that presented in a program's main window. Secondary windows are under control of the *window manager*: they have *window frames* and may be moved and resized (by the user) independently of the program's main window. They are built using a *dialog shell*.

selection

Selection mechanism: A method of interclient communication, whereby one client advertises the availability of data, and another requests that data by sending the first a request. Such transfers are typically initiated by the user.

Named selection: A particular communications path within the selection mechanism. When a client advertises the availability of a selection, it names that data; other clients can discover the advertiser of a particular name. X specifies three "standard" names: *primary*, *secondary*, and *clipboard*, which must be used according to a fixed set of rules. Cooperating clients, however, may select any name for a "private" selection.

Applied to XmText: A text widget allows the user to select text, by dragging the pointer over the desired text (with button #1 down). It highlights this text and also advertises it as the *primary selection*.

selection box

A dialog that presents the user with a list of items, a text field that displays an item selected from that list (and which allows entry of a new item), and buttons that act on the selected item.

sensitivity

The way in which a widget handles input events (keyboard and pointer). An *insensitive* widget discards such events, a *sensitive* widget processes them.

A widget's sensitivity state is most often used to "turn off" buttons, especially in menus, when they are not applicable to the current program context.

separator

A widget that exists to provide visual separation between areas of a window. They are often used in pull-down menus to visually group related menu choices.

server

The user's workstation; a computer/terminal that provides the user with a bit-mapped display and input devices (keyboard and pointer), and communicates with client programs using the X protocol.

server resource

A generic name for objects maintained by the server, such as windows, pixmaps, fonts, etc. Server resources are identified by *server resource IDs*.

server resource ID

A 32-bit unsigned integer value that identifies a server resource. Resource IDs are unique for a particular resource type and server.

shell

An interface between the program and the root window; the root of a window subtree.

Two types of shells exist: *Transient shells* are not registered with the window manager; they simply provide a new window subtree, which is separate from — and may obscure parts of — the other windows maintained by a program. A *top-level shell*, on the other hand, provides the program with a base for a *secondary window* — it has a *window frame* and may be moved or resized by the user.

siblings

Widgets that are *children* of the same *parent*. Siblings compete with each other for shares of the parent's available space; *management* is the process of allocating this space between them.

single selection

See *list selection modes*.

slider

That part of a *scrollbar* that both indicates the size and position of the currently visible data (relative to the total amount of data) and allows the user to quickly change that position.

socket

A bidirectional method of interprocess communication that uses the file mechanism. Sockets typically represent network connections, and the communicating processes may reside on different machines.

standard error

One of the files that are provided to every program: standard error is used to report error messages. It is accessed by the `stderr` variable and is by default attached to the user's terminal.

standard input

One of the files that are provided to every program: standard input is used to provide the program with input; It is accessed by the `stdin` variable and is by default attached to the user's keyboard.

standard output   One of the files that are provided to every program: standard output is used for general program output. It is accessed by the `stdout` variable and is by default attached to the user's terminal.

stepper arrow   That part of a *scrollbar* that allows the user to incrementally change the position of the *slider*. Stepper arrows are provided to both increase and decrease the position of the slider, relative to the *scroll region*.

sub-area   Another name for the children of certain widgets (*eg*, *XmMainWindow*). The term "sub-area" connotes that such children occupy predefined areas of the parent's window.

subclass   A class that is built (*derived*) from another class (the *superclass*).

superclass   A class that provides the base upon which another class (the *subclass*) is built (*derived*).

supporting superclass   A *superclass* that exists *solely* to provide the base for another class and is not in itself *instantiated*.

Applied to Motif, *Core* is a supporting superclass: it is used to provide all widget classes with basic window-manipulation functions, but is not itself used by a program.

system-modal   A state in which an application allows the user to perform only a limited set of actions and does not permit the user to perform any actions outside of that set — in any application.

tab group   A grouping of widgets that allows *traversal* between group members by use of the arrow keys. Traversal between tab groups is provided by use of the *Tab* and *Shift-Tab* key combinations.

Tab groups may contain a single primitive widget or they may contain all children of a single manager widget. A single tab group may not contain widgets from different parts of the instance tree.

tight binding   A method of specifying widget and class names in resource files. A tight binding, represented in the resource file by a dot (.) separating two parts of a widget's name, indicates an explicit parent-child relationship.

top-level shell   A *shell* that is actively managed by the *window manager*, with a *window frame* that allows the user to change its size and position.

Examples are *application shell* and *dialog shell*.

transient shell   A *shell* that is not actively managed by the window manager. It exists to provide a root for a temporary window subtree, which may overlap parts of a client's other subtrees.

An example is a *menu shell*.

translation   A linkage between an event sequence and a program *action*.

translation manager   Part of a client's event processing code. The translation manager matches each event received against the *translation table* for the receiving widget. When the event-sequence of a recognized *translation* is detected, the action associated with that translation is invoked.

translation table   The list of *translations* associated with a particular widget.

traversal   The ability to change focus from one widget to another by use of the keyboard — via the arrow keys and *Tab* key.

This ability is particular to Motif; it is not provided by the standard toolkit. As a result, standard methods for changing focus do not work reliably under Motif.

type conversion   See *resource conversion*.

unmanage   The process of removing a widget's geometry from the control of its parent. At this time, it is also *unmapped*.

unmap   The process of making a widget invisible — hiding its window. Unless it is simultaneously *unmanaged*, however, the space it occupies is not redivided among its siblings.

verification callback   A type of callback specific to the *XmText* widget, which allows the program to confirm or deny a proposed action.

virtual binding   A Motif-specific method of defining event sequences for translation tables. Virtual bindings provide a level of indirection between event sequences and the translation that uses those sequences.

As an example, a widget might use the virtual binding `KBackSpace` to delete the previously entered character. The actual event sequence represented by this virtual binding may be changed, using the file `$HOME/.motifbind`, without changing the widget's translations. In addition, changing the binding in this way affects all widgets, whereas a translation table change would affect a single widget only.

virtual colormap

The *colormap* associated with a window. This colormap is "virtual" because it is not necessarily the same as the *hardware colormap* — when a window is brought to the front of the display, its virtual colormap is installed as the hardware colormap.

warning dialog

A type of *message box* that exists to warn the user of a problem and accept a yes/no response to that warning. It is of more import than an *information dialog*, but less than an *error dialog* or *action dialog*.

widget

The basic user-interface element of a Motif-based program: a widget is responsible for the content and interaction of an X window.

widget ID

A value that represents a widget and is passed-to or returned-from functions that manipulate widgets.

window

Client window: The client's area on the screen. This may actually contain many *X windows*.

X window: A rectangular area of the screen that can display output and accept input.

window frame

A frame placed around a client window by the *window manager*. This frame contains the client's name, controls for moving and sizing the client window, and a window menu providing other operations.

window manager

A client that controls the position and size of other clients' windows. Only one window manager runs at a time, and it controls the *root window*.

window property

Data that is stored on the server and associated with a window. Properties are the primary means of interclient communication involving large amounts of data.

window tree

The tree formed by the parent-child relationships of all windows on a particular server. The *root window* is the root of this tree, and *shells* are the roots of subtrees, which belong to clients. Note that each widget is associated with a window, and a program's *instance tree* reflects — with slight differences due to menus and dialogs — that client's window tree.

work area

That part of a standard Motif client where most of the interaction with the user occurs. The work area usually occupies almost all of the *client area*; it is bordered by the *menu bar* on the top and *scrollbars* on the right and bottom.

work window

For scrolled windows and main windows, the *sub-area* where actual work takes place, differentiated from control sub-areas such as scrollbars. In a main-window, the *work window* is identical to the client's *work area*.

work-in-progress dialog

A type of *message box* that alerts the user to the onset or status of a time-consuming operation. This message box may optionally provide buttons to confirm or deny (terminate) the operation.

workproc

A function that is called while the client is waiting for events.

The workproc facility provides for a limited amount of "background" client processing. It is often used in conjunction with signals to guarantee that operations invoked by a signal do not interrupt a widget's internal code (which is not reentrant).

X Intrinsics

The name of the Xt library, which provides the basic code for widget manipulation and the supporting superclasses used by all widget sets.

X Protocol

The specification for communication between client and server.

Xlib

A set of functions that provide low-level access to the *X Protocol* for a C program. The functions provided by Xlib include those to open and maintain a display connection and maintain and interact with a window via that connection.

Xt

See *X Intrinsics*. This name comes from "X Toolkit."

Index